The University of Law
incorporating The College of Law

The University of Law, 133 Great Hampton Street, Birmingham B18 6AQ
Telephone: 01483 216041   Email: library-birmingham@law.ac.uk

Birmingham I Bristol I Chester I Guildford I London I Manchester I York

PEARSON

At Pearson, we believe in learning – all kinds of learning for all kinds of people. Whether it's at home, in the classroom or in the workplace, learning is the key to improving our life chances.

That's why we're working with leading authors to bring you the latest thinking and best practices, so you can get better at the things that are important to you. You can learn on the page or on the move, and with content that's always crafted to help you understand quickly and apply what you've learned.

If you want to upgrade your personal skills or accelerate your career, become a more effective leader or more powerful communicator, discover new opportunities or simply find more inspiration, we can help you make progress in your work and life.

Pearson is the world's leading learning company. Our portfolio includes the Financial Times and our education business, Pearson International.

Every day our work helps learning flourish, and wherever learning flourishes, so do people.

To learn more, please visit us at **www.pearson.com/uk**

The Financial Times

With a worldwide network of highly respected journalists, *The Financial Times* provides global business news, insightful opinion and expert analysis of business, finance and politics. With over 500 journalists reporting from 50 countries worldwide, our in-depth coverage of international news is objectively reported and analysed from an independent, global perspective.

To find out more, visit **www.ft.com/pearsonoffer/**

The Financial Times Guide to Investing

The definitive companion to investment and the financial markets

Third edition

Glen Arnold

Harlow, England • London • New York • Boston • San Francisco • Toronto • Sydney • Auckland • Singapore • Hong Kong
Tokyo • Seoul • Taipei • New Delhi • Cape Town • São Paulo • Mexico City • Madrid • Amsterdam • Munich • Paris • Milan

PEARSON EDUCATION LIMITED

Edinburgh Gate
Harlow CM20 2JE
United Kingdom
Tel: +44 (0)1279 623623
Web: www.pearson.com/uk

First published 2004 (print)
Second edition published 2010 (print)
Third edition published 2014 (print and electronic)

© Glen Arnold 2004, 2010 (print)
© Glen Arnold 2014 (print and electronic)

The right of Glen Arnold to be identified as author of this work has been asserted by him in accordance with the Copyright, Designs and Patents Act 1988.

Pearson Education is not responsible for the content of third-party internet sites.

ISBN: 978–1–292–00507–2 (print)
         978–1–292–00517–1 (PDF)
         978–1–292–00516–4 (ePub)
         978–1–292–00515–7 (eText)

British Library Cataloguing-in-Publication Data
A catalogue record for the print edition is available from the British Library

Library of Congress Cataloging-in-Publication Data
Arnold, Glen.
   The Financial times guide to investing : the definitive companion to investment and the financial markets / Glen Arnold. -- Third edition.
      pages cm. -- (Financial times guides)
ISBN 978-1-292-00507-2 (pbk.)
1. Investments. I. Financial times (London, England) II. Title. III. Title: Guide to investing.
HG4515.A76 2014
332.6--dc23

                    2014017035

10 9 8 7 6 5 4 3 2 1
18 17 16 15 14

Front cover image © Getty Images

Print edition typeset in 9/13pt StoneSerITC by 3
Print edition printed and bound in Great Britain by Ashford Colour Press Ltd, Gosport, Hampshire.

NOTE THAT ANY PAGE CROSS REFERENCES REFER TO THE PRINT EDITION

To two inspiring teachers of what is really valuable, Chris and Brenda Arnold, my parents

Contents

About the author

Glen C. Arnold, PhD, has held positions of Professor of Investment and Professor of Corporate Finance, but came to the conclusion that academic life was not nearly as much fun as making money in the financial markets. As a wealthy investor in his early 50s, Glen now spends most of his time running his own equity portfolio (www.glen-arnold-investments.co.uk) and a property development company from his office in the heart of rural Leicestershire.

Glen is happy to share his ideas with fellow enthusiasts in the City of London through seminar sessions. He also leads investing seminar days for private investors; see www.glen-arnold-investments.co.uk

Glen is the author of the investing classics *The Financial Times Guide to Value Investing, The Great Investors* and *Get Started in Shares.*

He wrote the market-leading university textbooks, *Corporate Financial Management, Modern Financial Markets and Institutions* and *Essentials of Corporate Financial Management.* He is also the author of three definitive books on finance: *The Financial Times Guide to Banking, The Financial Times Handbook of Corporate Finance* and *The Financial Times Guide to the Financial Markets.* All these books are available from Financial Times Publishing.

Acknowledgements

This book draws on the talents, knowledge and contributions of a great many people. I would especially like to thank the following.

Warren Buffett who kindly assisted the illustration of key points by allowing the use of his elegant, insightful and witty prose.

My personal assistant, Susan Henton, for her hard work, professionalism and enthusiastic support.

Riccardo Landucci of stockbrokers Charles Stanley who took time to read Chapter 4 and made valuable suggestions for improvement.

The team at Pearson Education (FT Publishing) who, at various stages, contributed to the production of the book: Chris Cudmore, Kat Habershon, Anna Campling, Lucy Carter, Linda Dhondy and Melanie Carter.

Publisher's acknowledgements

We are grateful to the following for permission to reproduce copyright material:

Figures

Figure 3.3 from London Stock Exchange; Figures 4.1, 4.2, 4.3, 4.4, 4.5, 4.6, 4.7, 4.8, 4.9, 4.10, 4.11, 4.12, 4.13, 4.14, 4.15, 4.16 from www.advfn.com; Figure 4.17 from www.directorsholdings.com; Figure 5.1 from www.morningstar.co.uk; Figure 5.2 courtesy of Schroders plc; Figure 8.7 courtesy of Intercontinental Exchange, Inc.; Figure 14.1 reprinted with permission of The Free Press, a division of Simon & Schuster, Inc. from *Competitive Strategy: Techniques for Analyzing Industries and Competitors* by Michael E. Porter. Copyright © 1980, 1998 by The Free Press. All rights reserved. Figure in Box 20.3 reprinted with permission from Yahoo. © 2014 Yahoo.

Articles

Articles 3.1, 3.2, 3.3, 3.4, 3.5, 3.6, 3.7, 4.1, 4.2, 5.1, 5.2, 5.3, 5.4, 5.5, 5.6, 5.7, 5.9, 6.1, 10.1, 13.1, 13.2, 13.3, 13.4, 13.5, 13.6, 16.1, 16.2, 16.3, 17.1, 19.1, 19.2, 19.3 © The Financial Times Limited. All Rights Reserved; Article 5.8 from Warren Buffett's letter to shareholders accompanying the 2005 Annual Report of Berkshire Hathaway, Inc., reproduced with kind permission of the author. Copyright remains with Warren Buffett; Article 8.1 courtesy of Neil Collins.

Text

Text on pages 439–40 from Warren Buffett's letter to shareholders accompanying the 1993 Annual Report of Berkshire Hathaway, Inc., reproduced with kind permission of the author. Copyright remains with Warren Buffett.

In some instances we have been unable to trace the owners of copyright material, and we would appreciate any information that would enable us to do so.

What's new in the third edition

The financial markets have always been dynamic places, but the last few years have witnessed a particularly fast rate of change. Not only have we had to cope with the aftermath of the financial crisis – during which we all came to appreciate the importance of effective markets – but we have seen stock markets merge and change methods of operation, new financial instruments rise in popularity and new accounting/tax rules. Clearly, this new book is long overdue. Here are *some* of the ways it improves on the old one:

- **Don't be ripped off**. Updated guide posts to avoid the loss of your nest egg to idiots and knaves.

- **Which website for what topic?** Websites are important sources of information, but we need guidance on what each website is useful for. Where a website will help you keep up to date, find data or provide a useful tool, it is referenced in the relevant chapter (over 140 websites are listed).

- **Unit trust and other collective investing is explained in more detail** – with even more warnings against overpaying.

- **Tax, etc**. Updating of tax avoidance moves you can make, tax rates, changes in cash/share ISAs, changes to capital gains tax and various ways of saving tax.

- **New section on dividend payments and what to watch out for.**

- **Jargon-busting**. The extensive glossary has been enlarged even more, so you can look up a range of words, phrases and concepts.

- **Tapping into the *Financial Times***. Extensive use of recent *Financial Times* articles and FT tables to illustrate and expand upon the material in the chapters.

- **Up-to-date statistics**. A very wide array of statistics ranging from investor returns on shares and bonds to amounts raised by companies on the stock market.

Introduction

There are some myths about investment, many of which are perpetuated by finance industry insiders. Myth one is that financial assets and markets are hideously complicated and confusing. Myth two is that you have to pay large sums to 'experts' who will then make far greater returns on your money than you could achieve on your own.

In truth the most important things you need to know about investing are simple. They are based on common sense and can be understood by anyone with a modicum of intelligence. It is just that the jargon and the detail obscure the view of outsiders peering through trying to see what it is all about. This book, in a step-by-step way, first explains the simple essence of investment and the functioning of the financial markets. It allows you to focus on what is really valuable, discarding grand-sounding but unimportant layers of mumbo-jumbo. It then goes on to explain the practicalities of investing, such as where to find a broker and how to go about buying shares. It explains the variety of financial securities you can place money into, from bonds and unit trusts to traded options and exchange-traded funds. It also has a key section providing tools allowing you to analyse companies.

As for the argument that you *need* to employ an 'expert' to run your investments – well, this is complete nonsense. For a start, the majority of professional fund managers underperform the stock market. This has been observed year after year. You haven't heard about this? Well, of course you haven't. It is not the sort of thing that fund managers publicise. Some researchers even asked various fund managers to pit their wits against an ape in the selection of share portfolios. The subsequent portfolio performance was noted most carefully. You've guessed who won! Even on a random basis we should find that 50 per cent of professional fund managers beat the market and 50 per cent do worse, but they don't even manage that.

Don't misunderstand me: some professionals, in some circumstances, have their uses. But to imagine that the private investor is generally at a disadvantage to the professional and should always defer to their superior insight is just plain wrong. Sure, you need some basic knowledge (which this book will help with), and you need some dedication to the task, but please don't be browbeaten into believing that the pinstriped suits have a competitive advantage over you, with your down-to-earth focus on what really matters and some sound investment tools. Share investment is about businesses – when you buy a share you buy a portion of the ownership of a business. Let me emphasise that a share is not a gambling counter in a short-term random game of chance; it represents ownership of something that will probably outlive you, and its value depends on what will happen to that company years from now. It is not too difficult for you to become more knowledgeable about that business than a fund manager stuck in London who has a portfolio of shares in 200 different companies.

Once you have a grounding in the principles of investment you will free yourself from the assumption that the professionals know best and that you could not achieve a good return without them. You will be aware of a range of alternatives to simply handing your money to, say, an ISA manager. Sometimes the financial service house can do things better and cheaper than you could on your own. But, quite often, you end up paying huge fees for atrocious performance. This book will help you decide when to manage your money yourself and when to employ others.

A third myth is that only wealthy people can afford shares and other financial assets. In reality people of relatively modest means invest in the stock market. It is possible to start with only £20 per month. In Chapter 2 there is an example of a woman who stretched herself to put £100 per month into shares over a 20-year period. The sacrifice was worth it: by the time she retired the fund had grown to be worth many millions of pounds – all for £100 per month. And this was achieved by gaining the same annual returns as the UK stock market as a whole – it wasn't that she bought all the best shares on the market and with perfect foresight ignored what turned out to be the worst ones.

Read on: investing can be profitable and fun!

Investment basics

1

What is investment?

To appreciate fully what it means to be an investor, I ask you to imagine that you do not live in the twenty-first century, with its vast range of financial instruments. You live in a simpler time. You are a member of the Victorian middle class, and life has been good to you. A substantial nest-egg has been built up over the years, but you are dissatisfied with the 2 per cent annual return you are getting on it in the local bank.

A couple of acquaintances, Mr Stephenson and Mr Brunel, are enthusiasts for a revolutionary technology that will improve the lives of the British people tremendously: the railways. Although the social benefits are wonderful, and it gives Stephenson and Brunel a warm feeling to think that they might contribute to people's well-being, this is not their primary motivation. No, they like the idea of becoming very wealthy. The way in which they expect to become rich is to build and operate a railway.

There is one thing stopping them from building their railway: it costs £2 million to build the line and pay for carriages, provide working capital for day-to-day needs, etc. They have only £100,000 between them. What a frustrating situation. They know that the railway will generate profits that dwarf the £2 million initial cost, and yet they can't persuade a bank to put up the £1.9 million needed.

Partnerships

An alternative approach of funding has been tried – indeed they suggested it to you as well as a couple of dozen other investors. This is to form a **partnership**. Each partner puts in, say, £50,000 and the rest is borrowed from a bank. Then, when the profits start to roll in (after paying the bank interest) the partners get an equal share. Of course, in addition Stephenson and Brunel would take a salary to compensate them for giving up time to manage the railway. You and most of the other investors who were approached rejected this offer for two very simple reasons. First, under partnership law each partner is **liable** for all the debts of the business. So if the business failed to produce a profit and the assets became worthless, and yet there are large bank debts, the bank would first of all try to get its money back from the business. Its next move would be to claim the money it is owed from each of the partners. Business partners have been known to lose their houses, furniture, everything, in order to pay off a business's creditors. You have seen too many landed gentry made homeless to want to invest in a business under a partnership, thus you decided to keep your money safe and not to risk it in industry of any kind.

The second problem with partnership arises if one of the partners wishes to leave (or dies). The leaving partner is generally entitled to a fair share of the value of the partnership. This can be terribly disruptive to a business, as assets may have to be sold to pay the partner off. Indeed, partnerships tend to be dissolved if one member wishes to leave and then a new partnership is created to carry on the business thereafter. It is certainly no way to run a railway.

So the two issues Stephenson and Brunel have to deal with are: the **unlimited liability** of the investors; and the **continuity** of business in the case of investors wishing (or forced) to disinvest.

Limited liability

Fortunately there is a form of business structure that addresses these two difficulties that lead to a restricted flow of funds from the **savers** in society to productive investment in real business assets: a company or corporation is set up as a 'separate person' under the law. It is the company that enters legal agreements such as bank loan contracts, not the owners of the company shares. The company can have a **perpetual life**. So, if an investor wishes to cash in his chips he does not have the right to insist that the company liquidate its assets and pay him his share. The company continues but the investor sells his share in the company to another investor. This is great – it gives managers the opportunity to plan ahead, knowing the resources of the business will not be withdrawn; it gives other shareholders the reassurance that the company can achieve its goals without disruption.

One of the most important breakthroughs in the development of UK capitalism and economic progress was the introduction of **limited liability** in 1855. There were strong voices heard against the change in the law. It was argued that it was only fair that **creditors** to a business could call on the shareholders in that business to bear the responsibility of failure. However, a stronger argument triumphed. This is that it is better for society as a whole if we encourage individuals to place their savings at the disposal of entrepreneurial managers for use in a business enterprise. Thus factories, ships, shops, houses and even railways will be built and society will have more goods and services.

Insisting on *un*limited liability for investors made them hesitant to invest and thus reduced overall wealth. Limited liability companies are what (for the most part) we have today, and we should be very grateful for it. Creditors quickly adjusted to the new reality of lending without a guarantee other than from the company. They became more expert and thorough in assessing the risk of the loan going bad (**credit risk**) and they called for more information; legislators helped by insisting that companies publish key information.

So, back to your nineteenth-century dilemma over whether to invest in Stephenson and Brunel's brilliant idea. What they intend to do is to create a company with limited liability for the shareholders. The company will issue 1.5 million shares. Each share will have a **par value** of £1. Sometimes companies sell shares at the par value and sometimes they sell them at greater than the par value. The par value (also called the nominal or face value) is merely a nominal figure, useful for record keeping, but unrelated to the market value of a share. In the case of Stephenson and Brunel Ltd, the shares are to be offered to investors at par. The company also borrows £500,000 from a bank.

Ordinary shares and extraordinary returns

The vast majority of shares issued by companies are **ordinary shares**. When you buy one of these you are buying a set of legal rights. Significantly, one of the rights you do not receive is a guarantee of any return on the money you hand over to buy the ordinary shares. The company, run by its managers, has no obligation either to give you a **dividend** (a payout of profit) or to hand your capital back. The managers may promise to do their best with the financial resources entrusted to them, but they cannot be legally forced to give a return. This contrasts sharply with the deal the company agrees to with bank lenders. Here the company is legally responsible to provide regular interest payments and pay off the capital at the end of the loan term.

It does not sound like such a good deal for the ordinary shareholders. They put money in, they cannot take it out again (the best they can hope for is to sell the holding to another investor), and the company has no obligation to pay them anything. It gets worse. If the company is **wound up**, then the assets are sold and the shareholders will be entitled to receive a share of the money raised from the sale. Ah yes, but not until all other interested parties have had their guaranteed amounts first. So if taxes are owed Her Majesty's Revenue and Customs (HMRC) gets its money, and then it's the turn of the various lenders and **trade creditors** (suppliers of goods and services not yet paid). If the company issued preference shares (see Chapter 7) then these holders are entitled to receive a payment. It is only in the (unlikely) event that there is any money left after so many snouts in the trough that the ordinary shareholders get anything.

Given these disadvantages of shares, there must be something attractive to entice investors. There is. Shareholders own all the value that is created by a business after lenders and others have received the amounts they are owed. If the business does well then it is perfectly possible for a £1,000 investment in ordinary shares to become worth over £1 million. It has happened time and again. There are millionaires today who put relatively small amounts into companies destined to become market leaders – Vodafone, Glaxo, Amazon, Intel and Berkshire Hathaway are just a few examples.

Shareholder rights

Shareholders own the business and have ultimate control over any surplus it generates now and into the future. To try and protect their wealth, ordinary shareholders have rights under the law. For example, they each have votes in proportion to their shareholding. They can vote on important matters such as the composition of the team of directors. If the directors appear to be steering the company in the wrong direction or merely feathering their own nest, then they can be voted off the board in an **annual general meeting** (AGM) or an **extraordinary general meeting** (EGM) called by the shareholders. Shareholders vote on whether more shares should be issued, and whether the company should merge with another company. Shareholders are also entitled to receive regular financial information. Every year the company must produce accounts which must be sent to all shareholders. Shareholders must also have notice of important events affecting the business, such as a major downturn in business, loss of a key contract, or the sale of a division.

Let us imagine that Stephenson Brunel Ltd has sold all 1.5 million ordinary shares at £1 each. You have agreed to buy 50,000 of these shares. You are legally committed to deliver £50,000 to the company. That is the maximum amount that can be claimed from you. In transferring this money from your bank account you accept that you are taking on significantly more risk than if it was steadily accumulating at 2 per cent per year. **Risk** merely means that there is a range of possible outcomes rather than certainty over what will happen. While there wasn't complete certainty over the bank account investment (the bank might have gone bankrupt), the dispersion of possible outcomes was likely to be in a narrow range with the probability of complete loss very low. The return on the Stephenson Brunel Ltd shares, however, has a very wide dispersion of possible outcomes with fairly high probabilities of an extremely good outcome or of an extremely poor outcome (loss of all money).

You hold 50,000 of the 1,500,000 shares and therefore your votes account for 3.33 per cent of the total – the vast majority of ordinary shares have the right to one vote each. (This is not always the case. Companies can issue shares that have, say, 10 votes while issuing other shares with only one vote each. Alternatively, they can issue some shares with no votes at all, alongside others with votes.) You use your votes at the EGM to help select directors. So, the company is up and running, ready to lay track.

A money-making machine

Over the next two years the line is constructed, trains are bought, stations built and the first paying passengers are delighted. The company now has total assets of £2.3 million. It also has bills it has not yet paid (**trade creditors** or **payables**) of £400,000 and bank debt of £500,000. The £1.4 million of **net assets** (i.e. after deduction of liabilities, £2,300,000–£400,000–£500,000) are owned by the ordinary shareholders. This will be shown in the year-end **balance sheet (statement of financial position)** as **shareholders' funds**. Because Stephenson Brunel Ltd has 1.5 million ordinary shares outstanding, each share has a claim of 93.33 pence of net assets (£1,400,000 divided by 1,500,000 shares). A holder of 50,000 shares would be entitled to £46,667 if the company were liquidated (assuming the assets could be sold at balance sheet values). A holder of 100,000 shares would be entitled to £93,333, and so on. So you can see why ordinary shares are often referred to as **equities** – each share represents an equal stake in the business, not just for dividends but also for assets.

You might now be thinking you've made a big mistake in buying these shares: you put in £50,000 and the assets of the firm have declined by 6.67 pence per share. But you must not be hasty in reaching a judgement. Very few shares are valued on the basis of their **asset backing**. In buying a share you are entitled to receive a portion of the *future* value generated by the business, and a business is a lot more than the assets shown on the balance sheet. What creates value is the physical assets *combined with* a number of intangible elements such as the strong strategic position of the firm, the reservoir of experience of the managerial team, or the special relationship the company forms with customers, government, suppliers, etc.

Stephenson Brunel Ltd didn't just build a railway, it created an **economic franchise** (see the discussion in Chapter 15). That is, it put itself in a position that gives it **pricing power**, whereby it can charge customers a price far above the cost of providing the service. It has an almost impregnable monopoly in providing rail transport in the part of the country where it operates. Would-be competitors simply can't challenge the company for its customers (termed **'strong barriers to entry'**). As a result of its economic franchise it is able to generate exceptional long-run rates of return on the capital put into the business.

Dividends and retained earnings

The power of that franchise starts to become apparent in the third year. The company makes a profit (earnings), after paying interest and taxes, of £750,000. The directors now have a choice to present to the equity holders (ordinary shareholders). The company could retain all of its earnings to invest in extending the network (**retained earnings**) or it could pay out some (or all) of it to shareholders in the form of dividends. Note that, whichever course of action is taken, the money belongs to shareholders – earnings retained in a business are there because shareholders consent to their money being left there.

Suppose that the directors (with the agreement of the shareholders) decide on a 50 per cent **payout ratio**, that is, half of the earnings after tax are paid out in dividends. The shareholders will receive a dividend of 25p per share (£375,000 divided by 1,500,000 shares).

The retained earnings of £375,000 increases shareholders' funds from £1,400,000 to £1,775,000. So, shareholders have not only received a 25p dividend for each share they hold, but the retained earnings have increased the asset value of each share in the company from 93.33 pence to 118.33 pence (£1,775,000 divided by 1,500,000 shares).

It is crucial to note that 118.33p does not represent the value of one share should you wish to sell. There will be plenty of people willing to pay a lot more than this to buy the right to receive all the future dividends from a company with such a strong market position. There is every reason to believe that the earnings and dividends per share will rise by large percentages over the next decade or two. Perhaps someone will pay £10 per share, or maybe even £100, for a fast-growing company of this kind. Not bad, considering that you paid only £1.

What if I want to sell?

This leads us neatly on to another piece of the jigsaw that is the modern financial system. If you did want to sell your shares, where would you go? And how do you know you are getting a reasonable amount for your shares?

Well, you could advertise in the local newspaper, but you are unlikely to attract a great deal of interest. Or, perhaps, you could ask friends if they want to buy from you – but this could be a social gaffe.

Fortunately, long before the Victorian era, systems had been set up to assist investors wanting to sell (and buy) company shares. Way back, in the sixteenth and seventeenth centuries, companies had been formed for sea voyages and trading with distant places around the world. If an investor wanted to sell his share of the future profits he could do so by going through the market in shares in the coffee houses around Threadneedle Street in the City of London. In 1773 the New Jonathan's coffee house had become known as Britain's leading **'stock exchange'**. In 1802, the **London Stock Exchange** was formally constituted. By the 1840s there were hundreds of companies' shares listed. Investors could buy or sell shares through members of the stock exchange.

Primary and secondary markets

The London Stock Exchange performs two vital roles to encourage investors to invest in industry. The first is the operation of a **primary market**. This is where companies sell shares to investors and then use the proceeds in their businesses. Stock markets also provide a **secondary market** where shares are traded between investors. An efficient and trustworthy secondary market is needed to encourage investors to buy shares in the primary market. Investors like to know that there is a place they can go to sell shares quickly, cheaply and without having to reduce the price, that is, to sell at the going rate. In other words, investors need a **liquid** market. A liquid market is one where there are numerous competing buyers and sellers allowing the outcomes of many buy and sell orders to set the market price. It is one where there is so much activity that the sale of 50,000 shares in a day would not cause the price to fall: the market would quickly absorb the shares.

The market also needs to be a **fair game** (or a level playing field) and not a place where some investors, brokers, fund raisers or financiers are in a position to profit unfairly at the expense of other participants. This means, for instance, that **insider dealing** is prohibited, that is, company officers or others with private knowledge are forbidden to use that knowledge to trade in the company's shares.

Brokers who act for shareholders are well regulated so that they act in the interest of investors. **Market makers**, who stand ready to buy and sell shares from investors on their own behalf in the stock exchange, follow strict codes of behaviour. It is a market that is well regulated to avoid abuses, negligence and fraud in order to reassure investors who put their savings at risk. Furthermore, investors need information on companies and share price activity so stock exchanges insist on minimum standards of information flow from companies and help disseminate company announcements. They also publish prices at which trading occurred and other **share trading data** (e.g. volume of trades).

A good secondary market allows the separation of long-term investment in **real assets** by firms and short-term investment by shareholders in **financial assets** called ordinary shares. The English language is often inadequate, and here is a case in point. The word 'investment' is used for two purposes. Companies invest in real assets that range from buildings and machinery to intangibles such as patents, brands and copyrights. This is productive investment that adds to the output of an economy. However, investment in the form of buying shares in the secondary market, from another investor, is not necessarily going to put more money into wealth-creating assets. It is simply the transfer of cash from one investor, and the ownership of the shares from the other. Then again, without a good secondary market, people will invest less in the primary market and less productive real investment will take place.

Bonds

If you wish to invest in a business but are unable to bring yourself to take the risk associated with shares, a good alternative is to purchase a **corporate bond**. A bond is a long-term contract in which bondholders lend money to a company. In return the company promises to pay the bond owners a series (usually a series) of interest payments known as **coupons**, until the bond matures. At *maturity* the bondholder receives a specified principal sum called the **par**, **face** or **nominal value** of the bond. This is usually £100 or £1,000 in the UK. The time to maturity is generally between 7 and 30 years. Bonds are a form of debt finance and are not ownership capital. The holders are not entitled to vote at the company meetings (AGMs or EGMs). A lower **rate of return** is offered on bonds than could be expected on shares because bond investors have a number of safeguards that equity investors do not. The interest on bonds is paid out before ordinary share dividends are paid, so there is a greater certainty of receiving a return than there is for equity holders. Also, if the firm goes into liquidation, the bondholders are paid back before shareholders receive anything. Furthermore, bondholders often insist on taking **collateral** for the loan (assets that may be seized by the lender if the borrower reneges), and may restrict managerial action so they don't make the firm too risky. Offsetting these plus points for bonds is the fact that lenders do not, generally, share in the value created by an extraordinarily successful business. They receive only the contracted amount of interest.

Some bonds are traded in the secondary market of the stock exchange, but more often through specialist bond dealers. So despite companies obtaining long-term finance for years ahead, the investor who provides that money can sell the bond to another investor to liquidate his holding.

Capital structure

The shareholders in a company such as Stephenson Brunel Ltd may be more than happy for the company to borrow some funds either from a bank or a bond issue due to the **leverage** (or **gearing**) effect. To understand this, imagine that the firm is now five years old and has long since paid off all its bank borrowings. It has proposed a major new investment in branch lines that will require £5 million. It could go to its shareholders, selling them additional shares through a **rights issue** (more about this later) to obtain all the extra £5 million from them. But consider this: the investment is expected to produce a return of 20 per cent per year on the money invested: £1 million per year on the £5 million raised from the shareholders. This is good, but the shareholders could be made even better off by an alternative **capital structure** (the proportion of debt to equity making up the total finance supplied to the company). If the company obtained £1 million from equity holders and £4 million from bondholders it could generate much higher returns for its shareholders. If we assume that bondholders require a return of 6 per cent per year, then the benefit of financial leverage to shareholders can be seen. The company creates £1 million of extra pre-interest income per year. Of that £240,000 (6 per cent of £4 million) has to go to pay the interest on bonds. That leaves £760,000 per year for the equity holders, who only put up an extra £1 million – a 76 per cent return per year!

Not bad. But there is a downside to **financial leverage**. A company can have too much debt, too many regular interest payment commitments, so that it cannot survive a decline in its underlying business. By borrowing more it adds to its **fixed costs** (the extra interest each year), and a couple of years of losses can wipe out the net assets and force liquidation. However, in the case of Stephenson Brunel Ltd there is little need to worry. Balance sheet net assets after five years of operating now stand at £10 million and revenues are still growing. Debt of £4 million and annual interest of £240,000 should not be too much of a problem.

Stocks and shares

The terms **'stocks' and 'shares'** are used interchangeably and confusingly in the financial press, particularly when referring to the US markets. In the UK we define shares as equity in companies; the **'risk capital'** as described above. Stocks are financial instruments that pay interest, such as bonds. However, in the USA shares are also called **'common stocks'** and the shareholders are sometimes referred to as *'stockholders'*. So when some people use the term 'stocks' they could be referring to either bonds or shares.

Rights issues

Now imagine that the railway company has been operating for 10 years. It has paid out large dividends over the decade and still has shareholders' funds of £12 million on its balance sheet. Unfortunately, borrowings are also quite large at £15 million, and interest rates in the economy generally are high and on an upward trend. The directors, still led by Mr Stephenson and Mr Brunel, would like to spend £10 million building an extension to the current lines. This plan makes good economic sense and should be funded, but the company would be taking on too much risk if it borrowed the additional £10 million – the annual fixed cost of the interest bill could cripple the company. So it decides to sell more shares, which have the advantage over debt capital of not carrying the right to receive an annual payout. Equity capital has the benefit that it acts as a 'shock absorber' to business crises because a company can choose not to pay a dividend when times are bad.

Under UK law it is generally not possible for the company to sell the new shares to raise the £10 million to outside investors without first offering them to existing shareholders (called a **pre-emption right**). The owners of the company are entitled to subscribe for the new shares in proportion to their existing holding. This will enable them to maintain their existing percentage ownership – so, if a shareholder currently owns 10 per cent of the shares he/she is entitled to purchase 10 per cent of any new shares issued. While those shareholders who take up their rights will have the same proportion of the company cake as they had before, each slice of the cake becomes bigger because the company has more financial resources under its control. Rights issues are a popular method of raising new funds – they are relatively easy and cheap for companies. (There is a lot more on rights issues in Chapter 16.)

Financial institutions

So we have now covered the absolute core issues in investment. It is about buying legal rights (shares, bonds, etc.) from a company. The company then uses the money raised from investors to create wealth (hopefully!), which is then shared between the investors. If a company's shares and bonds are traded on a stock exchange they can easily be sold on to other investors in the secondary market.

Having dealt with the basics we need to explain the role of financial intermediaries in assisting the working of the system.

Investment banks

The directors and managers of a railway company, or a manufacturing or service firm, are not generally expert in the workings of the financial markets. They tend to buy such expertise from the **investment banks**. These organisations will, for a fee, advise a company considering **floating** its shares on the stock exchange. Companies coming to the market for the first time to raise fresh equity capital (or merely to allow a secondary market in the company's shares) have to go through a number of procedures to reassure the market regulators, and, through them, the investing public, that they are sound companies run by trustworthy people. The investment bank can act as a **sponsor** to a company. It will investigate the company thoroughly before attaching its good name to the stock market newcomer. Agreeing to be a sponsor sends a signal to investors that the company is well run and has good prospects. If the sponsor suspects that the senior managerial team is too dependent on one individual or is lacking in vital expertise and balance it will suggest (insist on) the appointment of some new directors before flotation can take place. If the company is judged to be worthy of joining the stock market then the sponsor will coordinate the activities of all the other organisations involved: **brokers** assist with pricing and selling the shares; **underwriters** agree to buy any shares not bought by the investing public; accountants draw up detailed figures on performance and financial strength; solicitors deal with all the legal procedures. The sponsor also helps to create the **prospectus**, which provides vital information on the company needed for potential investors to make a buy decision. (New issues are covered in Chapter 16.)

Other areas in which investment bankers help companies include the process, tactics and regulatory issues of merger with other companies (mergers are discussed in Chapter 18). They might also assist with raising new funds for the firm after its shares have been quoted on the stock exchange for a while. This could be by selling new equity (e.g. rights issue), or by selling bonds, or selling some other financial instrument (e.g. convertibles).

Initial public offerings (companies floating on the stock market), **seasoned equity offerings** of shares of companies already on the exchange (e.g. through rights issues) and mergers can be big money-spinners for the investment banks. The fees earned can run into tens of millions of pounds and an individual banker with a good reputation can earn millions of pounds a year in bonuses from completing these deals.

Investment banks also act as brokers for the buying and selling of securities on the financial markets. Some may have market-making arms that assist the operation of secondary markets. Another branch of the bank may assist companies with export finance.

A major field for many investment banks is assisting investors rather than companies. They offer portfolio management services to rich individuals who lack the time or expertise to devise their own investment strategies. They also manage collective investment vehicles such as unit trusts (see Chapter 5) as well as the portfolios of some pension funds and insurance companies. (See my book *The Financial Times Guide to Banking* (2014) for more on investment bankers.)

The asset transformers

So, investment banks are completely different from retail high street banks (although many are owned by **conglomerate** or **universal banks** that have both investment banking and retail banking arms). The primary role of the **retail banks** is to take in numerous small deposits lent to the banks for short periods of time (i.e. you can get at the money in your current account instantly) by offering low-risk investment to millions of savers (not many of us have to worry about the risk of failure of banks to pay out what we have in our bank accounts). They then lend this money to companies needing large sums for long periods of time, and that money is put at considerable risk. The retail banks act as **asset transformers**. They transform small deposits into large loans for firms by aggregating the savers' money. They transform risk, offering depositors (investors in bank accounts) low risk but lending the money out at high risk. And they transform maturity: taking in short-term money and lending it long-term. They can do this very valuable trick because of the economies of scale they enjoy: efficiencies in gathering information on the risk of lending to a particular firm; the ability to spread risk by lending to a large number of companies; the systems they have developed to reduce transaction costs associated with setting up a lending agreement or monitoring a loan.

Investment banks have virtually abandoned the activity of taking in deposits and lending to borrowers; although some activity of this kind does go on, it tends to be for large sums, at least £250,000. They much prefer to charge fees to companies and investors for carrying out specialist tasks and to trade on their own account in various markets, such as foreign exchange, derivatives and equity markets, to try and make a profit – this is called **proprietary trading**.

Pension funds

Most of us pay into **pension funds** during our working lives to build up a pot of money that we can draw from on retirement. The pension fund **trustees** have to decide what to do with this money over the decades between payment in and withdrawal in the form of a pension. They place some or all of the money with specialist investment managers. Large sums have built up in UK pension funds over the last 50 years – over £2,000,000 million (£2 trillion). A large proportion of pension fund money is used to buy UK company shares. UK pension funds put even more money into overseas equities, while many foreign funds invest in UK shares. Thus, when selling shares, companies regard the pension fund managers as gatekeepers to a key source of funds. It is also interesting to note that even though only 9 million or so UK individuals are capitalist owners of industry by owning shares directly, almost all the rest of the adult population has a substantial proportion of their wealth tied up in equities via their pension schemes. So almost all of us have an interest in the stock market and the performance of company shares.

Insurance companies

Insurance companies also own a portion of UK shares (about 6 per cent). As well as **general insurance** against contingencies such as fire, theft and accident, insurance companies build up large funds by persuading savers to buy products such as life assurance, endowment policies and personal pensions (more on this in Chapters 5 and 17). This money is invested mostly in shares but also in bonds and property. Over £1.5 trillion is invested in this way.

The risk spreaders

Investors with only a few thousand pounds to invest know that they should diversify, but if they buy 10 different companies' shares the transaction costs would swallow a large proportion of the fund. Also investors often wish to invest in specialist areas, say Japanese shares or US hi-tech shares, but are wary of doing so because they lack the expertise. This is where the **pooled funds** (also known as collective funds) come in. They assist the flow of money from savers to productive investment by gathering together lots of small amounts that are then invested in dozens or hundreds of company shares, bonds or other securities.

Unit trusts, investment trusts and open-ended investment companies (OEICs) offer investors a way of spreading risks. They even present the possibility of the investor putting just a few dozen pounds a month into the markets. There are over 2,000 different UK unit trusts, investment trusts and OEICs, with over £800,000 million invested.

Be proud to be a capitalist!

We have seen that the modern financial system encourages savers to plough their money into real assets to produce wealth. It is this wealth that all the social services (health care, education, etc.) rely on for resources. There simply would not be this wealth without the revolution in social technology over the last two hundred years. We need to mobilise the savings of millions of people. We do that by permitting limited liability, by developing well-regulated primary and secondary markets, by having strong property rights defendable in the courts, and by having financial institutions that assist firms or investors to find one another, to form contracts, to provide specialist knowledge and to monitor the progress of companies. In this way the financial system is the vital lubricant of the economy. Investors, even though they act in their own self-interest – they want to become rich – in doing so bring about the creation of vast quantities of real assets, leading to greater social well-being. This is not an original thought. Even before the formal creation of the Stock Exchange, Adam Smith in 1776 pointed out the value to society of individuals acting for profit.

> The businessman by directing ... industry in such a manner as
> its produce may be of the greatest value, intends only his own
> gain, and he is in this, as in many other cases, led by an invisible
> hand to promote an end which was no part of his intention. Nor
> is it always the worse for the society that it was no part of it.
> By pursuing his own interest he frequently promotes that of the
> society more effectually than when he really intends to promote it.
> *(The Wealth of Nations, 1776)*

So, be proud to be a capitalist. Your saving results in wealth creation. Hold the banner high: I invest to make myself rich, but I also allocate resources to firms that I think can use them best to produce goods and services people need and/or want. In a world without equity and bond investors looking purely for profit the railways would not have been built, the drugs industry would be a lot smaller and Silicon Valley would still be producing fruit.

A note of warning – investment and speculation

Benjamin Graham is regarded as the greatest thinker on investment who has ever lived. He was a young man working on Wall Street in the 1920s and got caught up in the euphoria of the time. It was described as a 'new era' because of all the new technology driving industry forward. Share prices rose, and experienced market participants and newcomers bought vast quantities of shares without investigating the companies underlying the shares. They would buy on a rumour, or a tip, or because the share price had risen a lot the week before. They had seen other people succeed by buying anything fashionable, so they figured they could also join the bandwagon. (Similar buying attitudes prevailed towards companies with '-tech' at the end of their names in the 1960s or with '.com' in the 1990s or with social networking in 2011–14.)

Benjamin Graham lost a fortune in the Crash. He gave a lot of thought in the Great Depression to differences between investment and mere speculation. The conclusion of his ruminations led him to reject the common idea that the difference lies in the *type* of investment purchased. He also dismissed the *length of time a security* is held. He saw that the distinction lies in the *mind* of the person making the buying and selling decisions. It is the attitude of the individual that is key. The speculator's primary concern is with anticipating and profiting from market fluctuations. In contrast, 'an investment operation is one which, upon thorough analysis, promises safety of principal and a satisfactory return. Operations not meeting these requirements are speculative.'[1]

We return to the railway-building story. If you were an investor rather than a speculator you would have thoroughly considered the business plan of Stephenson and Brunel and satisfied yourself that your capital was not being exposed to unreasonable risk. You would have judged the competence and integrity of the managerial team and you would not have expected to make short-term profits by quickly trading the shares. You would also have ensured that the shares were not being offered to you at a high price.

Many of the early investors in the nineteenth-century railway companies achieved terrific returns, rather like the returns that early buyers of Internet and telecom shares achieved in the late 1990s. Then speculative fever took over. People just threw money at anyone who proposed the setting up of a railway. Share prices skyrocketed and eventually the bubble burst, leaving many with massive losses and a lifelong aversion to the stock market. This book will hopefully help you to

---

[1] B. Graham and D. Dodd, *Security Analysis* (McGraw-Hill, 1934), p. 54.

be an informed investor and not a speculator in shares. You will not develop an aversion to shares, but rather respect shares as portions of a business, and enjoy the thrill of finding good companies to invest in at reasonable prices.

2

The rewards of investment

Becoming a millionaire

At the age of 20, Sally Kelk decided to put £100 per month into an investment fund that invested in a broad range of shares on the London Stock Exchange. She did this for the last 20 years of the twentieth century. The return that she achieved during this period amounted to 19 per cent per annum (the actual average annual return for UK shares between 1980 and 1999). At the age of 40, in the first week of the new millennium, she sold all of her shares. She banked £215,245. Not bad for the sacrifice of £100 per month, or a total of £24,000. She feels the sacrifice was not too onerous as she spread the pain of saving over 20 years.

It gets even better. Sally has a chance of being a millionaire! She concluded in 2000 that she did not need to use any of the £215,245 and decided to invest it in the stock market again and leave it there for the next 25 years when she expects to retire. Will she retire comfortably? You bet she will. If average annual returns over the first 25 years of the twenty-first century are the same as those over the last 20 years of the twentieth century, so that the fund grows by 19 per cent per year, Sally will have over £16.6 million by her 65th birthday. That is the power of compounding the return! **Compounding** is ploughing back the income received and then getting a return on the accumulated ploughed-back money as well as the original capital.

Of course, we have made some crude assumptions in this analysis. First, the annual rate of return of 19 per cent is what is called a **nominal return**. That is, it does not take into account the fact that much of the return is compensation for inflation, which was high in the 1980s. If we remove the inflation element and concentrate on the returns in constant purchasing power terms (that is, the **real** rate of return) the annual rate of return falls to 13.1 per cent. This is still good, but does not lead to such an impressive sum at the end of Sally's 25-year investment, in 2025: she would have to scrape by in her retirement with a mere £4.7 million.

Second, the last two decades of the twentieth century produced unusually high returns on shares. The second half of this chapter contains some more precise returns figures, but suffice it to say that over the twentieth century as a whole equities gave a real return (after taking off inflation) of 5.7 per cent per year on average, not the 13.1 per cent which was achieved in the last two decades. If we were to project forward from the year 2000 to Sally's retirement date the growth of £215,245 at a rate of 5.7 per cent the total amounts to £860,613. This is less impressive, perhaps, but it is expressed in year 2000 purchasing power. In other words, Sally can buy four times as many goods and services at the end as at the beginning.

If we allow for a little inflation, then we can make an estimate of the size of the pot of money in nominal terms (in year 2025 money): £215,245 compounded at a rate of return of 9 per cent for 25 years amounts to £1.86 million. So, Sally has every chance of being a millionaire in 2025 regardless of other incomes, assets, etc. Good luck to her. She had the foresight and the discipline to leave her money in shares, and it has paid off handsomely.[1]

Simple and compound interest

Figure 2.1 demonstrates the power of compounding. It shows the difference in the size of a pot of money at various points in the future when the pot is allowed to grow at simple interest (i.e. interest on the initial capital only) and compound interest (each year interest is added to the pot and future interest is paid on both the initial capital and the interest that has accumulated from previous years). The figures are based on an initial investment of £100 with annual interest of 10 per cent. At simple interest a £100 fund becomes worth only £600 after 50 years. However, if interest is received on accumulated interest (compound interest) the £100 is turned into £11,739.[2] Einstein has been (wrongly, apparently) quoted

---

[1] There is a third factor we have ignored – taxation. Sally might (probably will) have to pay income tax on dividends and capital gains tax on the sale of shares – we consider this in Chapter 17.

[2] Compounding calculations are explained in the appendix to Chapter 2 of G. Arnold, *Corporate Financial Management* (Financial Times Prentice Hall, 2012) and in Chapter 5 of G. Arnold, *Modern Financial Markets and Institutions* (Financial Times Prentice Hall, 2012).

as saying that compound interest is the eighth wonder of the world. Charlie Munger, a billionaire investor, says never interrupt it unnecessarily.

Long-term investment is like planting trees. At first you can only find enough money to buy a few saplings. They look small and pathetic. Then you add to your collection month by month. For the first few years your wood looks unimpressive and hardly worth the effort. Still, you nurture and keep adding to it. Perhaps later you stop buying more saplings and decide to devote merely the minimal effort. Perhaps you turn away to other interests for a few years. Then, when you do look again, you are amazed to find that what was scrubland has been transformed into a magnificent arboretum with fine strong specimens. Time has worked its magic. What seem like small annual rates of growth can, with compounding, produce a great mass from small beginnings.

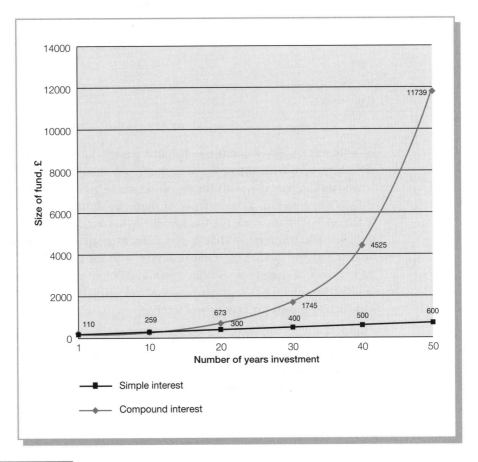

Figure 2.1   **The magic of compounding**

How well have investors fared in the past?

An interesting question to ask is: what would be the value today of an investment made at various points in history? The size of the return depends very much on the type of financial securities purchased (Table 2.1). For instance, £100 placed in government bonds in January 1900 (lending to the UK government by buying bonds from it is one of the safest forms of investment) would, with income reinvested, be worth £30,591 by the beginning of 2014. This is a nominal return (no adjustment for inflation) of 5.2 per cent per year. Even with the effects of inflation removed the real size of the investment grows from £100 to £392 (an annual real return of 1.2 per cent).

Table 2.1   **What a £100 investment in 1900 would be worth at the beginning of 2014, with all income reinvested**

	If invested in UK equities (shares)	If invested in UK government bonds (gilts)
Money (nominal) return	£2,214,856	£30,591
Real return	£28,386	£392

Source: Data sourced from *Equity Gilt Study 2014* (Barclays Capital).

Investing in UK government bonds (gilts) has produced a return that has more than kept pace with inflation, so perhaps you should be impressed. However, when you compare this with the return on shares you might change your mind. If £100 was placed in a broad range of shares in January 1900, by January 2014, with dividends reinvested, the fund would be worth £2,214,856 in nominal terms or £28,386 in real terms – that is, 284 times as many goods and services can be bought with the fund at the end of 114 years as at the beginning. This remarkable performance of shares comes from a seemingly small extra average annual return (a difference of 3.9 per cent: whereas equities earned 5.1 per cent per year, gilts earned 1.2 per cent per year in real terms).

Perhaps 114 years is a little too long as a time frame for even the most dedicated long-term investor, so let's look at the returns over shorter periods. Table 2.2 shows that placing money in a building society account, the preferred choice of many savers, generally produces very poor returns compared with equities, or even gilts.

| Table 2.2 | Real returns on UK financial securities (per cent per annum) and the value of an initial investment of £100 at the end of the period (income reinvested before any tax deduction) |

	114 years (1900– 1.1.2014)	50 years (1964– 1.1.2014)	20 years (1994– 1.1.2014)	10 years (2004– 1.1.2014)	1 year (2013– 1.1.2014)
Equities	5.1%	5.5%	4.1%	5.0%	17.4%
Gilts	1.2%	2.5%	3.5%	2.5%	−9.6%
Building society accounts		0.8%	0.1%	−1.3%	−2.4%
Inflation	3.9%	5.9%	2.8%	3.3%	2.7%

Source: Data sourced from *Equity Gilt Study 2014* (Barclays Capital)

Table 2.3 breaks the returns down by decade. Only one decade of the past 110 years has shown negative equity returns (after including dividend income), the 1913–1923 period, and in most decades equities have outperformed gilts.

| Table 2.3 | Real rates of return (% p.a.) for UK securities |

	Equities	Gilts
1903–1913	3.3	−0.2
1913–1923	−1.3	−3.1
1923–1933	9.6	9.6
1933–1943	3.2	0.5
1943–1953	2.7	−2.4
1953–1963	12.1	−1.7
1963–1973	1.5	−3.7
1973–1983	5.2	1.9
1983–1993	12.9	7.6
1993–2003	3.2	4.6
2003–2013	5.0	2.5

Source: Data sourced from *Equity Gilt Study 2014* (Barclays Capital).

The importance of income

The total return that an equity investor receives consists of two elements:

- **Dividends**. These are generally paid every six months from the after-tax profits of the company. Directors decide the proportion of earnings to be paid to shareholders, subject to shareholder approval. Note, however, that a company may not pay dividends. The reasons for this include that the company is currently unprofitable, or that it is fast-growing and needs to use all cash generated to invest in productive assets.

- **Capital gain**. The share price rises over time due to an increase in the underlying value of the business (or to temporary enthusiasm for the shares by investors, which may or may not be rational).

So, where do the terrific returns on shares come from: is it predominantly from dividends or capital gains? Well, over a single year the returns on equities are largely due to share price movement; dividend income contributes a relatively small amount. However, long-term returns are overwhelmingly due to dividends. For example, if a UK equity investor had chosen to spend dividends received on a £100 investment made in 1900 as each year passed, rather than reinvest, by January 2014 capital gains alone take the fund to only £14,915[3] (nominal return). On the other hand, another investor who reinvested dividends over the 114 years would have had a fund worth £2,214,856 (nominal return).

More on dividends

The first dividend each year is called an **interim dividend** or **interim payment** and is sent shortly after the end of the first six months of the company's financial year (this is not the same as the calendar year because companies can choose the date for their year-end). The amount you receive depends on the number of shares you hold because all dividends are on a per-share basis; announced as pence or euro cents per share.

The second payment is called the **final dividend**[4] which will arrive a few months after the end of the financial year. First, the **preliminary results** (profits, etc.) for the year are published a few weeks after the year-end and the dividend amount is proposed by the directors within these. These accounts are a first draft and are not the official version.

---

[3] Barclays Capital *Equity Gilt Study 2014*. The real value of the fund in 1900s pounds is £191.

[4] It may be called the *second interim dividend*.

When the final report and accounts are published a month or so later the shareholders are invited to attend the annual general meeting (AGM) where they are able to vote to approve or reject the dividend proposed in the report by the board of directors (they rarely reject). If they cannot attend they can send in their vote by post. The final dividend then arrives a few days after the AGM. If you add the interim and the final dividend together you have the **total dividend** for the year.

Some companies pay only a final dividend and no interim (due to lower administration costs), others pay no dividend at all for many years. This is often because they need the cash to invest in exciting projects: for example, Apple did not pay a dividend for many years when it was developing the iPhone and the iPad. A few UK and European companies pay dividends every quarter. These are mostly companies with large scale operations in America and with a high proportion of US shareholders (e.g. BP). Most US companies pay **quarterly dividends**.

How much is paid?

Companies can choose the level of the dividends they pay. They can pay more than the total of the year's profits after tax if they want, so long as they have accumulated profits from previous years still within the company.[5] Most companies however settle in a band of dividend payments which are around 40–60 per cent of that year's annual profits after tax.

Generally, directors bend over backwards to avoid sudden changes in dividends. There are two main reasons for this. Firstly, some investors like to have a predictable income stream from their shares; there are 'clients' for steady dividend payers. The problem is that profits in many industries can be quite volatile. If the company stuck rigidly to say a 50 per cent payout of after-tax profits, the dividend too would jump about from one year to the next, upsetting many owners.

The second reason is that dividend changes are taken as a signal by investors of the level of confidence directors have in the rising prosperity of the firm. A steadily rising dividend from one year to the next signals that the

---

[5] They can only pay dividends out of **revenue reserves** which is the stock of previous years' profits that have not yet been paid out plus the gains made when non-current assets ('fixed asset' in old parlance) are sold. This is after deduction of tax on these and netting out any losses made on disposal of non-current assets.

company is on an improving trend. When it is hit by temporary bad weather the directors do not cut the dividend unless they really have to (e.g. they are over-indebted). Likewise, when they have an unusually good year they do not raise the dividend to match the improvement in short-term profits for fear that they might have to cut it again the following year.

When do I get paid?

Companies have a financial calendar, usually available to view on their websites, which sets out when dividends will be paid. This will help you find out when you need to be an owner of a share in order to receive a dividend. We will use the case of Sainsbury to illustrate – see Table 2.4.

Sainsbury's year-end is 16 March 2014. So the profits for the previous 12 months are added up and a balance sheet (statement of financial position) is drawn up for that date. This takes time to do and so the company does not announce its preliminary results until 7 May. This is remarkably fast; most companies take at least two months. In this announcement there will be a figure proposed as the dividend amount (the final for the year).

The company does not pay the dividend on this **announcement day** (also called the **declaration day**). Rather it states something like it 'will be paid on 11 July to shareholders on the Register of Members at the close of business on 16 May'. That may seem like a long time to wait, but there are sound reasons for the delay.

Table 2.4	Sainsbury's financial calendar
11 Jul 2014	Final dividend: paid
09 Jul 2014	2014 Annual General Meeting
16 May 2014	Final dividend: record date
14 May 2014	Final dividend: ex-dividend
07 May 2014	Preliminary results
03 Jan 2014	Interim dividend: paid
22 Nov 2013	Interim dividend: record date
20 Nov 2013	Interim dividend: ex-dividend
13 Nov 2013	Interim results

Source: Data sourced from www.j-sainsbury.co.uk/investor-centre/financial-calendar/

First, the directors need to figure out who is actually a shareholder and so entitled to receive the dividends. Every working day some holders of shares sell them to new investors and so the list of registered shareholders changes frequently. It is thought best to set a date sometime in the future which is the day when the share register will be looked at to see who is on it. Those on the list will get dividends. In the case of Sainsbury this date was 16 May 2014.

However, this is not the end of the story: remember, the final dividend for the year is merely 'proposed' by the directors. It has to be approved by the shareholders at the Annual General Meeting. So the payout cannot take place until after the meeting – this is just in case the shareholders decide something different (very unlikely, but it could happen). So the date of actual payment via direct electronic bank transfer to your account or by receiving a cheque is made a few days after the AGM.

So, you now ask why are there two dates for dividend eligibility in Table 2.4, one called **'ex-dividend date'** and the other the **'record date'**? The two are necessary because of the delay in registering you as a new shareholder when you buy a share. If you went to your broker and instructed her to buy a share today, she would **execute** the trade today ('execution day') but it usually takes three days to settle the deal (becoming two days after October 2014). This is when the trade is finished and your name is put on the shareholder register. This is the date you actually pay for the shares and become the owner.

If Sainsbury is intent on looking at the share register on 16 May to check who is eligible for the dividend then it needs to warn potential new buyers of shares that there will be a date two days earlier, before which they have to execute the deal to buy the shares to get the dividend. Thus if you buy on the day before it goes ex-dividend you will be registered as the shareholder on 16 May. If, however, you purchase on the ex-dividend day, 14 May, you will not be registered until 17 May, which is too late to receive the dividend. The records will show the old shareholder as the owner and the dividend will flow to him.

The ex-dividend (XD or xd) day is the key date for an investor because buying shares on or after it excludes the possibility of receiving the dividend. Prior to trading ex-dividend the shares will have been labelled **cum-dividend** following the announcement that a dividend will be paid.

Don't worry about sharp share moves on ex-div day

Novice investors can get caught out by the apparent weird movements in share prices on ex-dividend days – they seem to plummet. But that is just the logical consequence of any new buyer losing the right to receive dividend income a few weeks hence.

Downloading data on dividends for a company

One source of information on a company's dividends is to visit its website and examine the reports and accounts going back many years. An alternative is to visit one of the free financial websites where the dividend history is available. Chapter 4 has more on financial websites.

International comparison

To test if the returns on UK equities and gilts are unusual, Table 2.5 shows the real returns on shares and government bonds for 21 countries for 114 years. Clearly there is similarity in the returns across countries and in the size of the gap between equity returns and government bond returns. However, it is important to note that the small differences in annual percentage returns shown can compound to large differences in the wealth available to investors at the end of a long period. For example, over 114 years the investment of one unit of local currency in the Belgian equity market in 1900 would have grown by a factor of 19 in real terms, whereas a corresponding investment in Australia would have grown 3,423-fold.

Equities versus gilts

Another interesting question: how many times over a five-year period has equity provided a real return greater than gilts? The answer is provided in Table 2.6, which shows that of the 110 (overlapping) five-year periods between 1900 and 2013 in 81 cases equities have performed better than gilts. Similar results are obtained from periods of 2, 3, 4, 10 and 18 years. Shares generally perform best, but there can be quite long periods where equities perform badly – equities underperformed gilts for a decade or more on 22 occasions.

| Table 2.5 | Real returns on equities and government bonds: an international comparison, 1900–2013 (% p.a.) |

	Equities	Bonds
Australia	7.4	1.5
Austria	0.7	−4.1
Belgium	2.6	0.2
Canada	5.7	2.1
Denmark	5.2	3.1
Finland	5.3	0.0
France	3.2	0.0
Germany	3.2	−1.6
Ireland	4.1	1.4
Italy	1.9	−1.5
Japan	4.1	−1.0
Netherlands	4.9	1.5
New Zealand	6.0	2.0
Norway	4.3	1.8
Portugal	3.7	0.6
South Africa	7.4	1.8
Spain	3.6	1.4
Sweden	5.8	2.6
Switzerland	4.4	2.2
UK	5.3	1.4
USA	6.5	1.9
World	5.2	1.8

Source: Data sourced from Elroy Dimson, Paul Marsh, Mike Staunton and Michael Mauboussin, *Credit Suisse Global Investment Returns Yearbook 2014.*

| Table 2.6 | Performance of UK equities relative to gilts 1900–2013 |

	Length of holding period in years					
	2	3	4	5	10	18
Equities outperform gilts, number of periods	77	83	84	81	83	85
Equities underperform gilts, number of periods	36	29	27	29	22	12
Total number of periods	113	112	111	110	105	97
Equity outperformance proportion of periods	68%	74%	76%	74%	79%	88%

Source: Data sourced from *Equity Gilt Study 2014* (Barclays Capital).

What about risk?

So shares have generally been a good form of investment, but there is a downside. We have already seen that shares can produce negative real returns for periods as long as a decade. Between 2000 and 2003 UK shares halved in price, as did Japanese shares. German shares fell by two-thirds. They rallied until, in late 2007, they fell again in dramatic fashion. In the 2008 collapse the world index of shares fell by 55 per cent.

It does not take long when looking at statistics like these to form the impression that shares are risky. This is confirmed by Figure 2.2, which shows the real annual returns on shares for each year going back to 1900. Over the 114-year period shares produced negative returns in over a third of the years. Some of these losses are very large. For example, imagine you are an investor holding a portfolio of shares worth £100,000 at the start of 1973. By the end of that year your portfolio would be valued at only £65,000. Perhaps at that point you would swallow the line that equities always bounce back (as the equity analysts and press are so fond of telling us) and decide to hold on to your shares for another year.

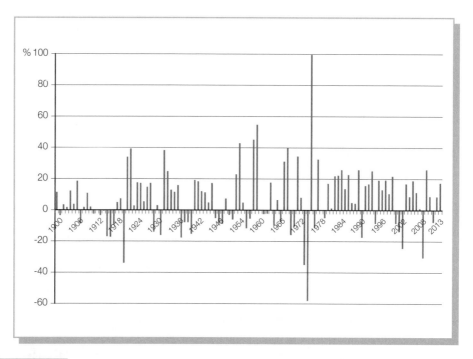

Figure 2.2 **Annual real equity returns, 1900–2013 (%)**

Source: Data sourced from *Equity Gilt Study 2014* (Barclays Capital)

Calamity! By the end of 1974 your holding would be worth a mere £27,235. Now you are, along with many investors, feeling very fed up with shares and everything to do with the stock market. Perhaps you decide to take what little you have left and put it somewhere safer. But the capricious and restless market tricks you again. If you held on to the shares the value would have risen by 99.6 per cent during 1975. However, it would take until 1983 for your £100,000 to be restored to you (in real terms).

Share investors must be able to accept that equity markets can fall by very large percentages during a day and that individual holdings can become worthless overnight as companies go into liquidation. If you are unable to accept this degree of volatility perhaps you should be investing somewhere else. Building society and bank accounts beckon.

Year to year real returns on gilts can also be volatile. As Figure 2.3 shows, there have been many years when gilt investors have lost more than 10 per cent of their investment.

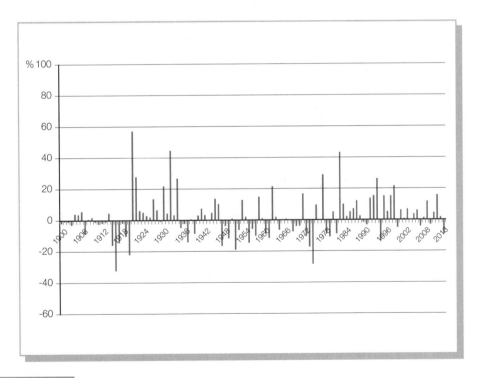

| Figure 2.3 | **Annual real gilt returns, 1900–2013 (%)** |

Source: Data sourced from *Equity Gilt Study 2014* (Barclays Capital)

Closing comment

While it is important to acknowledge the possibility of negative share return performance, even over periods as long as 10 years, we must not become too pessimistic. Shares on average gave investors very good returns during the last century. I am convinced that they will do so again, just as long as investors avoid buying when the market is being 'irrationally exuberant' and blowing up a bubble. Shares should be viewed as long-term investments and not short-term gambling counters.[6] Good returns are available for equity investors who are prepared to bide their time. Note that even if you had bought shares at the peak of the market at the beginning of 1973 and you had experienced a fall in market value to a mere 27 per cent of initial investment over the first two years, if you had held these shares for a further 28 years your average annual real return would have been 7 per cent. Your initial investment of £100,000 would be worth £664,884 in 1973 money or over £5 million in year 2000 money. Clearly patience and resilience in the face of market volatility can pay off.

There are good reasons for the superior returns in equity investment. Shares represent the risk capital of businesses. This money is put at high risk. Companies go into liquidation and markets turn down violently. Bond investors settle for a trade-off between lower risk and lower returns (although even they can get overpriced, thereby becoming poor investments).

Despite the risk of individual shares and the risk of the entire share market at certain times, broadly based portfolios held for substantial periods have given handsome returns.

Further reading

Credit Suisse Global Investment Returns Yearbook. This is an annual publication produced by London Business School experts Elroy Dimson, Paul Marsh and Mike Staunton. It can be downloaded from Credit Suisse's website.

Dimson, E., Marsh, P. and Staunton, M. (2002) *Triumph of the Optimists: 101 Years of Global Investment Returns* (Princeton University Press). Some valuable statistics for returns on various investments around the world with an equally useful discussion.

---

[6] If you would like to learn more about the nature of share 'investing' as opposed to 'speculation' you would be welcome on one of our seminar days – see www.glen-arnold-investments.co.uk – which take things up a notch from this book.

Barclays Capital *Equity Gilt Study*. This is an annual publication (usually in February) providing very useful statistics and insightful discussion (it costs £100).

3

Stock markets

The world has changed dramatically in the last 30 years. The strong ideological opposition to capitalism has been replaced with stock markets in Moscow, Warsaw and Ho Chi Minh City. China, of all places, has two thriving stock exchanges, in Shanghai and Shenzhen, with over 2,400 companies listed. There are tens of millions of Chinese investors – more than in the UK – who can only be properly described as 'capitalists' given that they put at risk their savings on the expectations of a reward on their capital.

Over 140 countries now have stock markets. There must be something of great value offered by stock markets to pull so many societies towards them. Jiang Zemin, China's former president, spoke with the fervour of a recent convert in declaring that robust stock markets are a vital component of a modern economy – they can bring great benefits to investors, companies and society, according to this new enthusiast. This chapter will concentrate on describing UK markets, but the principal features tend to be found in all stock exchanges.[1]

What is a stock market?

Stock markets are where government and industry can raise long-term capital and investors can buy and sell securities.[2] Markets, whether they are for shares,

---

[1] Stock exchange and stock market will be used interchangeably. *Bourse* is an alternative word used particularly in Continental Europe.

[2] These are the principal and historical functions of stock markets. However, major markets, such as the London Stock Exchange, now also trade a variety of securities, some of which are short term.

bonds, cattle or fruit and vegetables, are simply mechanisms to allow the possibility of trade between individuals or organisations. Some markets (e.g. for sheep) are physical: there is a place at which the buyers and sellers meet. Other markets (e.g. for foreign currency), are merely a network, based on communication via telephone and computer, with no physical meeting place.

A few stock exchanges around the world still have a place where buyers and sellers (or at least their representatives) meet to trade. For example, the New York Stock Exchange (NYSE) continues to make use of a large **trading floor** with thousands of face-to-face deals taking place every working day (**open outcry trading**). This is the traditional image of a stock market, and if television reporters have a story about what is going on in the world's security markets, they often show an image of traders rushing around, talking quickly amid a flurry of small slips of paper on the NYSE trading floor.

Such a television reporter in London has more difficulty finding an image to represent security dealing. The London Stock Exchange (LSE), like many in the world today, has no trading floor. In the 1980s it decided to switch to a computer system to link the buyers and sellers. This allows for a more efficient market than the old system and allows traders to be located anywhere; so long as they can link up to the LSE central computer, they can trade. Television journalists usually resort to reporting from one of the many dealing rooms owned by the financial groups. There they find rows of desks with hundreds of computer screens. The people in front of the screens may be **brokers** acting on behalf of investors buying or selling shares/bonds into the market. One of the screens on a desk will display the information on the LSE central computer, showing latest trading prices, for example. Other screens may show information about companies, news, or perhaps provide analytical tools. Even though these *agents* of the buyers and sellers of shares don't physically meet their counterparts in other security house dealing rooms to complete a deal, there are times when good TV camera shots of frazzled and exhausted dealers can be obtained to show on the evening news – usually when the market has fallen a lot in one day.

Brokers and market makers

It is perfectly legal for investors to deal directly with each other **off the exchange**. (There are special forms that record the transfer of shares from one name to another – see Chapter 4.) However, the majority of share deals are conducted through brokers who act as agents for buyers and sellers. One broker will not contact another broker to complete the deal but will instead often go to a **market maker**. These middlemen stand ready to buy or sell shares on their own account.

They quote two prices: the price at which they are willing to buy and the price they offer shares for sale (called **'making a book'**). During the day they anticipate that they will make numerous deals buying shares and a roughly equal number selling shares in a company. The small *margin* between the buying and selling prices delivers a profit to the market maker. There are usually many market makers trading in a particular company's shares. A high degree of competition between them ensures that the market makers' spread between the *bid* (buying) and *offer* (selling) prices does not get too wide, putting investors at a disadvantage. (For more details on share trading, see Chapter 4.) Note that there are two alternative systems also operated by the LSE which do not require market makers, but market makers are nevertheless encouraged to participate.

Pricing – good old supply and demand

How are the prices of shares and other securities set? They are determined in much the same way as the prices for other goods and assets bought and sold in market places: by the forces of supply and demand.

Imagine a share is currently priced by market makers at 149p–150p. This means that the (say) four different market makers trading in this share stand ready to buy at 149p and sell at 150p. (It is unusual that all the market makers offer exactly the same prices, but please bear with the simplification for now.) Let us further assume that the current market price is in **equilibrium** – that is, the forces of supply and demand are evenly balanced. The market makers will experience this equilibrium by a steady flow of buy and sell orders roughly matched in terms of volume. So we start with stability and the market makers feel no pressure to alter the price.

Now suppose that a negative item of news is released about the company. Investors become more pessimistic about the prospects for the firm's future profits. Many of those who would have been buyers at 150p now decide not to pick up the telephone to ask their brokers to buy, thus demand falls. At the same time an increased number of sellers contact their brokers with instructions to sell. The price of 149p seems excellent to them given the poorer prospects.

The market makers stand in the middle receiving an unbalanced set of orders: there are now many more sell orders than buy orders. At 149p–150p the shares are no longer in equilibrium. Market makers need to balance their books, that is, they need to find a roughly equal number of buyers and sellers. In the situation described they are faced with a deluge of sell orders and a **buyers' strike**. Something has to give. Most of the market makers are quick to change the prices they offer. In fact many changed prices when they saw the news about the company on one of their computer screens. That is, they *marked down* the bid–offer spread. Some tried 148p–149p, but found that this was still not low enough to balance supply and demand. Certainly some investors were attracted to buy at 149p but nothing like enough to create equilibrium. At prices of 145p–146p the number of sell orders (at 145p) slows dramatically, while the number of buy orders (at 146p) increases. Finally the market reaches a new equilibrium at 144p–145p. At least it does until the next piece of news or sentiment hits shares generally, or this company specifically.

What about those market makers who kept their price at 149p–150p? They would have found a massive number of investors offering to sell shares at 149p. The rule is that market makers are obliged to buy at the price they advertise on the LSE computer system (for deals up to a set maximum quantity of shares). They do not hold high levels of inventory in the shares in which they deal because they don't have the enormous sums of money this would require (they deal in hundreds of different companies' shares). They must quickly sell the shares they purchase. Unfortunately they find that the highest price available from other market makers has fallen to 144p. They lose 5p on every share they purchase. It is clear that all market makers have to respond to shifting market forces and cannot stand still.

The system described above is based on market makers to illustrate how supply and demand interact to alter prices. Since 1997 alongside the market maker system the London Stock Exchange has developed an **'order-driven' system** of trading, in which it is possible for buyers and sellers to transact with each other (usually via brokers) leaving out the market makers. The same forces of supply and demand are at work. (The order-driven system is described in Chapter 4.)

A short history of the London Stock Exchange

Businesses need capital to begin and to grow. **'Capital'** simply means stored wealth and resources. Stock markets assist the flow of capital from savers to businesses seeking funds. They do this through two main types of capital markets: the equity markets for trading of company shares; and the bond markets for trading the debt of companies and governments.

Capital markets go back a long time. In the late Middle Ages in the Italian city states securities very much like modern shares were issued and traded, as were government bonds. The demand from investors in British companies to be able to buy and sell shares led to the creation of a market in London. At first this was very informal; holders of financial securities (e.g. shares) would meet at known places, especially coffee-houses in the ancient part of London: **the City** (the **'Square Mile'** that the Romans built a wall around, just to the north-west of the Tower of London). Early in the nineteenth century the Stock Exchange developed a set of rules and procedures designed to enable investors to buy and sell shares with ease and to minimise the risk of fraud or unfairness.

The rapid economic expansion of the nineteenth century fuelled the demand for share issuance and the trading of shares between investors. Eventually there were 20 stock exchanges in cities up and down the UK. These have now been amalgamated with London.

'Big Bang'

Because of the LSE's origin it tended to be a very clubby place. Members of the club (brokers, etc.) ran things with a bias toward their own interests. There was little competition and commission rates were kept high. It became clear in the 1970s and 1980s that the LSE was losing trade to overseas stock markets. The large financial institutions, such as pension funds and insurance companies, were naturally in favour of a shift from fixed commission rates being paid to brokers to negotiated commissions. Further pressure was applied by the competition watchdogs to break up the cosy cartel.

The gentlemanly way of doing business ended in 1986 with the **'Big Bang'**. This is the term used for a collection of reforms implemented at the same time: fixed broker commissions disappeared; foreign competitors were allowed to own member firms (market makers or brokers); and the screen-based computer system of trading replaced floor-based trading.

The market makers and brokers quickly passed into the hands of large financial conglomerates. Commission fell sharply for large orders (from 0.4 per cent to around 0.2 per cent of the value traded). However, **private clients** (investors buying small quantities of shares on their own account) saw an initial slight rise in commission because it had previously been subsidised by the fees charged to the institutions. Brokers started to specialise. Some would offer the traditional service of advice and dealing, whereas others would offer a no-frills dealing-only service. (This **execution-only** service is now very cheap – see Chapter 4.)

The new financial conglomerates, offering a wide range of services, such as retail banking, market making, broking, investment management and insurance, were now able to compete with the big players in New York, Tokyo, Frankfurt and Geneva. To prevent conflicts of interest within the financial service firms damaging the position of clients, **'Chinese walls'** were established. These were designed as barriers to prevent sensitive information being passed on to another branch of the organisation. For example, if an investor holding 10 per cent of the shares of a company asks the broker department to sell his shares, he does not want, say, the fund (asset) management department to hear about it before he has off-loaded his shares at a good price – the fund managers may sell first, depressing the price. Likewise, the **corporate finance department** assisting a company trying to acquire a competitor should be prevented from passing on this information to other members of the financial conglomerate as they may be tempted to buy shares in the target company prior to the bid, in the expectation of making a large return on the announcement (a form of **insider dealing**).

Chinese walls have worked reasonably well, but they are not as strong as the public relations department of these financial organisations would have you believe.

Recent moves

After centuries of being an organisation owned and run by its members, in 2001 the LSE became a public limited company with its shares traded on a secondary market – the shares are quoted on its own Main Market (Official List) and anyone is now free to purchase these shares. It has come a long way from its clubby days. It remains one of the biggest stock markets in the world – see Table 3.1 (note the position of China's exchanges having leap-frogged most western markets recently).

Table 3.1   Capitalisation (market value of shares) of non-foreign companies

Exchange	USD billion, end 2013
NYSE Euronext (US)	17,950
NASDAQ OMX (US)	6,085
Japan Exchange Group	4,543
London Stock Exchange Group	4,429
NYSE Euronext (Europe)	3,584
Hong Kong Exchanges	3,101
Shanghai SE	2,497
TMX Group	2,114
Deutsche Börse	1,936
SIX Swiss Exchange	1,541

Source: World Federation of Exchanges, *2013 WFE Market Highlights* (www.world-exchanges.org), 2014.

In 2004 the Stock Exchange moved from its historic site in Old Broad Street to Paternoster Square near St Paul's Cathedral. The exchange toyed with the idea of moving out of the City but decided that its identity is tied too closely to the Square Mile to move outside.

The international scene

More change is in the air. Stock exchanges all over Europe have been busy merging. The French, Dutch, Belgian and Portuguese *bourses* merged around the turn of the millennium to form **Euronext** which, in turn, merged with the New York Stock Exchange in 2007 and the **American Stock Exchange** in 2008 to create **NYSE Euronext**. To make an even larger collection of exchanges NYSE Euronext was bought in 2013 by **IntercontinentalExchange (ICE)** a group of derivative exchanges, but there are plans to separate off the European stock markets from the rest of the group. The London Stock Exchange has merged with its Italian counterpart and **NASDAQ**, the US giant, has merged with **OMX Nordic** (comprising the Baltic and Scandinavian exchanges) to form **NASDAQ OMX**. The **Deutsche Börse**, which tried to get hitched to other exchanges several times is still something of a loner.

The European Union has encouraged greater competition for share trades through '**MiFID**' legislation. This is the **Markets in Financial Instruments Directive** (first launched in 2007). Brokers must now demonstrate that they are achieving the keenest price and using the most efficient, cost-effective systems. New exchanges (cross-border outfits such as BATS, Chi-X and Turquoise) sprang up to compete with the traditional exchanges. These **multi-lateral trading facilities** (MTFs) have taken a significant share of trading in large companies' shares.[3]

Variety of securities traded

The LSE creates a market place for many other types of financial securities besides shares – see Figure 3.1.

There are five types of fixed-interest securities traded in London: gilts, local authority bonds, foreign government bonds, sterling corporate bonds and Eurobonds. The UK government bond (or gilt) market (lending to the UK government) is big. In 2013, for example, over £160 billion of gilts were sold to add

---

[3] There is more on new trading facilities in my book *Modern Financial Markets and Institutions* (Financial Times Prentice Hall, 2012).

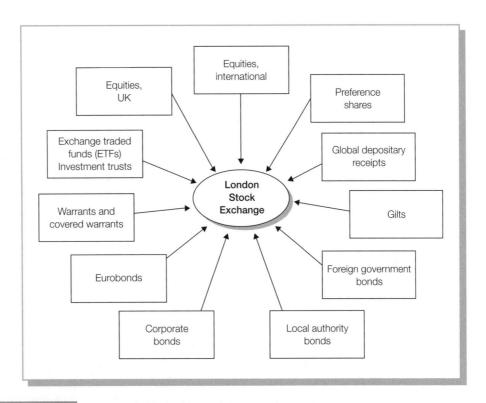

Figure 3.1   Types of financial security sold on the London Stock Exchange

to the £1,270 billion or so already in issue. In addition, foreign governments sold over £2 billion of bonds through the LSE. **Sterling bonds** issued by companies (**corporate bonds** where the interest and the final redemption payment are in pounds sterling) comprise a much smaller market than government bonds. During 2013, UK companies sold 1,379 new **Eurobonds** in London worth a total of £78.7 billion, making this the biggest fixed-income market (bonds are described in Chapter 6).

Specialist securities, such as warrants and covered warrants, are normally bought and traded by a few investors who are particularly knowledgeable in investment matters (warrants are a type of derivative security and are discussed in Chapter 10).

In addition to trading shares of overseas companies (international equities), there is a market in **depositary receipts, DRs**. These are certificates that can be bought and sold, and represent evidence of ownership of a company's shares held by a depository. Thus, an Indian company's shares could be packaged in, say, groups of five by a depository (usually a bank) which then sells a certificate representing a bundle of shares. The depositary receipt can be denominated in a currency other than the corporation's domestic currency and dividends can be received in the currency of the depositary receipt (say, pounds) rather than the currency of the original shares (say, rupees). These are attractive securities for sophisticated international investors because they may be more liquid and more easily traded than the underlying shares.

Exchange traded funds (ETFs) and **Exchange traded commodities (ETCs)** are low-cost companies that invest money raised (by selling shares) into a range of shares or other securities to track a particular stock market index (e.g. the FTSE 100 index) or other sectors (e.g. commodity prices). See Chapter 5.

LSE's primary market

Through its control of the primary market in listed securities, the LSE has succeeded in encouraging large sums of money to flow annually to firms wanting to invest and grow (Table 3.2). In 2014 there are over 900 UK companies on the Main Market (Official List). The vast majority of these raised funds by selling shares, bonds or other financial instruments through the LSE either when they first floated or in subsequent years (e.g. through a rights issue). Over 1,000 companies are on the Exchange's market for smaller and younger companies, the **Alternative Investment Market (AIM)**, which started in 1995. These companies, too, have raised precious funds to allow growth.

In 2013 alone UK-listed firms on the LSE raised new capital amounting to £98 billion by selling equity and fixed interest securities. This is the equivalent of £1,581 per man, woman and child in the UK. Of course, in the same year companies would also have been transferring money the other way by, for example, redeeming bonds, paying interest on debt or dividends on shares. Nevertheless, it is clear that large sums are raised for companies through the primary market.

Each year there is great interest and excitement inside dozens of companies as they prepare for flotation. The year 2013 was a watershed year for 33 UK and 12 foreign companies that joined the Main Market, and 99 that joined the AIM.

Given the high costs associated with gaining a place on the Main Market or AIM in the first place (£500,000 or more for MM) it may be a surprise to find that the **market capitalisation** (share price × number of shares in issue) of the majority of quoted companies is less than £100 million – see Figure 3.2 (techMARK is explained later in this chapter).

Table 3.2 Money raised by UK companies on the Main Market and money raised on the Alternative Investment Market (including international companies on AIM), 2004–13 (in £m)

Year	New companies on Main Market		Other Main Market issues*		Eurobonds		AIM	AIM	AIM
	Number of companies	Equity money raised (£bn)	Number of issues	Money raised (£bn)	Number of issues	Money raised (£bn) AIM	Number of UK companies joining	Number of international companies joining AIM	Total money raised on AIM (£bn)
2004	55	3.4	680	8.0	1,170	127.5	294	61	4.7
2005	84	6.0	765	7.6	1,099	148.3	399	120	8.9
2006	77	8.4	655	12.9	1,500	216.5	338	124	15.7
2007	73	7.6	465	8.8	2,025	165.9	197	87	16.2
2008	52	3.1	404	51.7	2,101	432.4	87	27	4.3
2009	17	0.4	379	73.6	1,858	254.6	30	6	5.6
2010	58	7.1	390	12.2	2,096	184.5	76	26	7.0
2011	41	9.2	580	2.5	2,317	196.4	67	23	4.3
2012	26	1.9	469	3.8	2,167	139.5	47	24	3.1
2013	33	7.9	406	11.6	1,379	78.7	77	22	3.9

*'Other issues' are for companies that have been on the Stock Exchange for many years raising more equity funds through, say, a rights issue.

Source: Data sourced from London Stock Exchange (www.londonstockexchange.com). Factsheets and Main Market and AIM Statistics files are located in the statistics section.

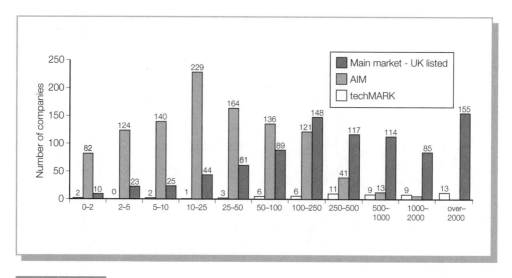

Figure 3.2   **Distribution of companies by equity market value, December 2013**

Source: Data sourced from London Stock Exchange, www.londonstockexchange.com/statistics/historic/main-market/dec-13.pdf

The secondary market

The amount of shareholder-to-shareholder trade is very large. On a typical day over 600,000 bargains (trades between buyers and sellers) are struck between investors in shares on the LSE, worth over £4 billion. The size of bargains varies enormously, from £500 trades by private investors to hundreds of millions by the major funds, but the average is around £6,000.

The secondary market turnover exceeds the primary market sales. Indeed, the amount raised in the primary equity market in a *year* is about the same as the value of shares that trade hands *daily* in the secondary market. This high level of activity ensures a liquid market enabling shares to change ownership speedily, at low cost and without large movements in price – one of the main objectives of a well-run exchange. You are able to buy or sell shares during the 'trading hours', which are between 08.00 and 16.30 Monday to Friday.

The Main Market (The Official List)

Companies wishing to be listed have to sign a **listing agreement** that commits directors to certain standards of behaviour and levels of reporting to shareholders. To **'go public'** and become a **listed company** is a major step for a firm, and the substantial sums of money involved can lead to a new, accelerated phase of business growth. Obtaining a quotation as a listed company is not a step to be taken lightly; the legal implications are enormous. The **United Kingdom Listing Authority (UKLA)**, part of the Financial Conduct Authority (FCA), rigorously enforces a set of demanding rules, and the directors will be put under the strain of new and greater responsibilities both at the time of flotation and in subsequent years.

Joining the Main Market of the LSE involves two stages. The securities (usually shares) have to be: (a) admitted to the Official List by the UKLA; and also, (b) admitted by the Exchange for trading.

Many firms consider the stresses and the costs worth it because listing brings numerous advantages. For example, there are large benefits to shareholders. The LSE's Main Market is one of the world's most dynamic, transparent and liquid markets for trading shares and other securities. Shareholders benefit from the availability of a speedy, cheap secondary market if they wish to sell. Not only do shareholders like to know that they can sell shares when they want to, they may simply want to know the market value of their holdings even if they have no intention of selling at present. By contrast, an unquoted firm's shareholders often find it very difficult to assess the market value of their holding.

Also, the floated companies gain access to a large pool of investment capital allowing firms to grow. Because investors in financial securities with a stock market quotation are assured that they are generally able to sell their shares quickly, cheaply and with a reasonable degree of certainty about the price, they are willing to pay a higher price than they would if selling was slow, or expensive, or the sale price was subject to much uncertainty caused by illiquidity.

The status and visibility of a company can be enhanced by being included on the prestigious Official List. Banks and other financial institutions generally have more confidence in a quoted firm and therefore are more likely to provide funds at lower cost. Their confidence is raised because the company's activities are now subject to detailed scrutiny. Furthermore, the publicity surrounding the process of gaining a quotation may have a positive impact on the image of the firm in the eyes of customers, suppliers and employees, and so may lead to a beneficial effect on day-to-day business.

In order to create a stable market and encourage investors to place their money with companies, the UKLA tries to reduce the risk of investing by ensuring that the firms obtaining a quotation abide by high standards and conform to strict rules. For example, the directors are required to prepare a detailed **prospectus** ('**listing particulars**') to inform potential investors about the company. (More on this in Chapter 16.)

Companies obtaining a listing must ensure that at least 25 per cent of their share capital is in public hands, to ensure that the shares are capable of being traded actively on the market.[4] 'Public' means people or organisations not associated with the directors or major shareholders. If a reasonably active secondary market is not established, trading may become stultified and the shares may become illiquid. Also, many crucial shareholder votes require a 75 per cent majority and so allowing dominant owners more than 75 per cent puts too much power in their hands.

The UKLA tries to ensure that the 'quality' of the company is sufficiently high to appeal to the investment community. The management team must have the necessary range and depth, and there must be a high degree of continuity and stability of management over recent years. Investors do not like to be over-reliant on the talents of one individual and so will expect a team of able directors, including some non-executives, and an appropriately qualified finance director.

The UKLA usually insists that a company has a track record (in the form of accounting figures) stretching back at least three years. This applies to companies that have a **premium listing**, the vast majority of listed companies. Recently, a **standard listing** regime has been introduced which does not require three years of figures and is far less tough on a number of other quality indicators and ongoing restraints, such as requiring shareholder approval for significant transactions. Given that few firms have gone for standard listing we will concentrate on describing premium listing in the rest of the text.[5] It would seem that companies recognise the advantages of being under a regime of tight rules because of the extra reassurance for shareholders, and so are generally sticking with premium listings.

The company floating on the Main Market via a premium listing hires a **sponsor** (**issuing house**) to advise on the process and provide reassurance to the UKLA

---

[4] If there is plenty of liquidity the UKLA may, at its discretion, reduce the minimum free float – usually to around 20 per cent.

[5] In 2013 the LSE went even further and introduced 'Admission via the High Growth Segment'. This requires only 10 per cent of the shares in a free float (minimum £30 million). It is even more lightly regulated. Again, few, if any, companies are queuing at the door for this.

and the investment community about the quality of the company and compliance with the listing rules. The sponsor (approved by the UKLA) may be a bank, stockbroker or other professional adviser. Even though the sponsor's fee is paid by the company floating, the sponsor is an organisation with a high reputation to preserve and will not hesitate to drop a bad company or suggest changes to a mediocre one. Clearly, Merlin Entertainments (Alton Towers, Legoland, etc.) made the grade – see Article 3.1.

Article 3.1

Merlin launches long-awaited share sale

By Anousha Sakoui

Merlin Entertainment, the owner of Madame Tussauds waxworks and Legoland, launched its long-awaited initial public offering of shares on Wednesday, detailing plans to raise up to £800m in a sale that will value the private equity owned theme park operator at up to £3.34bn.

The fun park operator set out expectations to price each share at between 280p and 330p, raising £200m to pay down debt and a further £600m that will allow its existing investors to cash out.

The offer comes amid a revival of the London IPO market and following the privatisation of postal operator Royal Mail whose shares soared in the days following its market debut. The UK's 59 IPOs so far this year have raised a total of $12.6bn according to Dealogic.

The revival is a global one, with bankers in the US already working on share sales for some of the world's biggest brands, such as social media group Twitter and hotel group Hilton. Twitter was meeting investors this week as part of a much anticipated $1.6bn stock market debut.

Merlin plans to float between 20 to 30 per cent of its shares on the London stock market. The group is also attempting to lure its own customers into the share sale, offering members of the public spending at least £1,000 each on shares a 30 per cent discount for one year on theme park annual passes.

"We believe that Merlin Entertainments has bright prospects for the future and the listing will provide us with the platform for our next stage of development," said Nick Varney, Merlin's chief executive.

Company directors have to jump through hoops to obtain a listing in the first place. But even after flotation they are unable to relax. The UKLA insists on **'continuing obligations'** designed to protect or enlighten shareholders. All **price-sensitive information** has to be given to the market as soon as possible and there must be 'full and accurate disclosure'. Information is price-sensitive if it might influence the share price or the trading in the shares. Investors need to be sure that they are not disadvantaged by market distortions caused by some participants having the benefit of superior information. Public announcements will be required in a number of instances, for example: the development of major new products; the signing of significant contracts; details of acquisitions; a sale of large assets; a change in directors; or a decision to pay a dividend. Barclays got into trouble for not informing the market about an important transaction – see First citation of Article 3.2.

Article 3.2

Barclays contests £50m fine for breach of listing rules

By Daniel Schäfer, Patrick Jenkins and Caroline Binham

Barclays' legal woes resurfaced when the bank said it was contesting a regulator's £50m fine for acting "recklessly" by failing to disclose £322m in fees paid to Qatari investors during its emergency cash call five years ago.

The regulator's conclusions that Barclays will have to pay a fine for breaching listing rules was revealed in the lender's prospectus for a £5.8bn rights issue on Monday. But it added that it continued "to contest the findings".

The Financial Conduct Authority's verdict, in warning notices from last week, relate to its investigations over alleged improper payments to Qatar during Barclays' two 2008 fundraisings.

According to Barclays, the FCA said two agreements to pay a total of £322m over five years had been struck primarily for Qatar's participation in the cash calls and not to obtain advisory services, as had been argued by the bank.

Qatar Holding and Challenger, an investment vehicle of Sheikh Hamad bin Jassim bin Jaber al-Thani, the former prime minister of Qatar, injected £6.1bn into Barclays in 2008, allowing the bank to escape a government bailout.

The warning notices also said Barclays had been in breach of a requirement to act with integrity towards holders and potential holders of shares, and had therefore acted "recklessly".

There are strict rules concerning the buying and selling of the company's shares by its own directors once it is on the stock exchange. Directors are prevented from dealing for a minimum period (normally two months) prior to an announcement of regularly recurring information such as annual results. They are also forbidden to deal before the announcement of matter of an exceptional nature involving unpublished information that is potentially price-sensitive. These rules apply to any employee in possession of such information. All dealings in the company's shares by directors have to be reported to the market

Most (free) financial websites (e.g. www.advfn.com or www.iii.co.uk) show all major announcements made by companies going back many years, including director purchases and sales.

The Alternative Investment Market

There is a long-recognised need for small young companies to be able to raise equity capital. However, many of these are excluded from the Main Market because of the cost of obtaining and maintaining a listing. London, like many developed stock exchanges, has an alternative equity market that sets less stringent rules and regulations for joining or remaining quoted (often called **second-tier markets**).

Lightly regulated or unregulated markets have a continuing dilemma. If the regulation is too lax, scandals of fraud or incompetence will arise, damaging the image and credibility of the market, and thus reducing the flow of investor funds to companies. The German small companies market, Neuer Markt, was forced to close down in 2002 because of the loss of confidence among investors: there were some blatant frauds as well as over-hyped expectations, and share prices fell an average of 95 per cent. On the other hand, if the market is too tightly regulated, with more company investigations, more information disclosure and a requirement for longer trading track records prior to flotation, the associated costs and inconvenience will deter many companies from seeking a quotation.

The driving philosophy behind the AIM is to offer young and developing companies access to new sources of finance, while providing investors with the opportunity to buy and sell shares in a trading environment run, regulated and marketed by the LSE. Efforts were made to keep the costs down and make the rules as simple as possible. In contrast to the Main Market, there is no requirement for AIM companies to have been in business for a minimum three-year period or for a set proportion of their shares to be in public hands – if they wish to sell only 1 per cent or 5 per cent of the shares to outsiders then that is OK. However, investors have some degree of reassurance about the quality of companies coming to the market. These firms have to appoint, and retain at all times, a **nominated adviser** and **nominated broker**. The nominated adviser (**'nomad'**) is selected by the corporation from a Stock Exchange approved register. These advisers have demonstrated to the Exchange that they have sufficient experience and qualifications to act as a 'quality controller', confirming to the LSE that the company has complied with the rules. Unlike with Main Market companies there is no pre-vetting of admission documents by the UKLA or the Exchange, as a lot of weight is placed on the nomad's investigations and informed opinion about the company.

Nominated brokers have an important role to play in bringing buyers and sellers of shares together. Investors in the company are reassured that at least one broker is ready to help shareholders to trade. They also represent the company to investors (a kind of PR role). The adviser and broker are to be retained throughout the company's life on the AIM. They have high reputations and it is regarded as a very bad sign if either of them abruptly refuses further association with a firm.

AIM companies are also expected to comply with strict rules regarding the publication of price-sensitive information and the quality of annual and interim reports (there is more on accounts in Chapter 11). Upon flotation, an AIM admission document is required. This is similar to a prospectus required for companies floating on the Main Market, but is less detailed and therefore cheaper. But even this goes so far as to state the directors' unspent convictions and all bankruptcies of companies where they were directors. The LSE charges companies a few thousand pounds per year to maintain a quotation on the AIM. If to this amount is added the cost of financial advisers and of management time spent communicating with institutions and investors, the annual cost of being quoted on the AIM runs into tens or hundreds of thousands of pounds. This can be a deterrent for many companies. AIM companies are not bound by the Listing Rules administered by the UKLA but instead are subject to the AIM rules, written and administered by the LSE.

The annual expense of managing a quotation on the AIM is less. For example, AIM companies do not have to disclose as much information as companies on the Official List. Price-sensitive information will have to be published, but normally this will require only an electronic message from the adviser to the Exchange rather than a circular to shareholders.

Article 3.3 shows a company, Servelec, that chose the Main Market because it wants 'bigger cheques from institutional investors' to help buy other technology companies. Article 3.4, on the other hand, shows an even larger company, Asos, content with being on the AIM.

Servelec IPO lifts Sheffield tech profile

By Sally Davies

Performing as strippers was the job of last resort for Sheffield's former metalworkers in the hit British film *The Full Monty*. Today, they might find more luck as programmers.

Servelec, a software and services company with roots in the city's once-proud steel mills, is set to float 68.3m shares on London's main stock exchange today with an expected valuation of £122m.

Servelec had revenues of £39.4m last year, with a profit before tax of £10.9m. "Investors' appetite for risk has increased – we see what's going on the other side of the pond and the successes there," says Adam Lawson, analyst at Panmure Gordon, referring to the big valuations for tech companies listing in the US.

"There's an increasing understanding that there are some very disruptive technologies being developed and growth opportunities arising out of a desire to replace legacy systems with newer and more advanced technologies."

Servelec's automation arm provides software and control systems to major UK utilities, broadcasters, lighthouses and North Sea oil rigs.

Servelec, which was advised by Investec, joined the main market rather than the more flexible Aim in order to attract bigger cheques from institutional investors, says Mr Stubbs [Chief Executive].

The company comes to the London market with no debt and £5m in cash – which Mr Stubbs indicates will be used for acquisitions. "What Servelec is good at is improving efficiency," says Mr Stubbs. "We want to buy smaller companies with good technology that are looking to become part of a larger company to accelerate their growth."

Asos board could size up blue-chip weight

By Kate Burgess

If you saw an elephant perched on a termite mound, you would ask why. So why are shares in Asos, the online retailer of cut-price designer labels and looky-likey glamour rags, still pretending it is a tiddler whose natural habitat is Aim?

In an alternative world, Asos' market capitalisation of £4bn would rank it alongside the UK's biggest 100 companies on the London stock market.

Asos is by far the biggest stock on Aim and more than twice the size of its nearest neighbours,

Article 3.4   Continued

Indus Gas and Gulf Keystone Petroleum. GKP, whose market capitalisation is less than £2bn, says it is too big for the junior market. It heads a queue of Aim companies hoping that a full London Stock Exchange listing will bring investors flocking to their doors.

But while GKP is busy buffing up its governance to suit the LSE's premium listing requirements, Asos says it is content to stay where it is. Apparently it has the big-name institutional investors it wants – including Standard Life, Fidelity, Capital and Baillie Gifford – and needs no others.

Not that the Aim team at the LSE is complaining. Asos shines like a beacon on the junior market. Asos' governance and record of disclosure would not need much spit and polish for it to slip easily into the main market, unlike some of its Aim peers.

For the LSE's Aim team, Asos also validates its determined stance on sizeism. Aim won't filter out companies that fall below a set market capitalisation on the basis that some tiddlers really do grow from termite eggs to elephants.

When Asos' shares were floated at 20p on the junior market 12 years ago, it raised £2.3m, valuing the company at £12m. All that the founders offered investors was an idea of selling a film star look via a website – "As Seen On Screen". In the beginning the company was too small to stock clothes bigger than a size 12.

On Thursday the company said sales rose in the year to August by 40 per cent to £537m. The shares, which are up 158 per cent over the year, rose another 14 per cent last week to £57. It is curious that the exchange's main market team cannot persuade Asos of the potential benefits and comforts associated with being an LSE blue chip.

Asos maintains it has no reason to abandon its nursery for the bigger market. Mr Robertson says: "Aim serves us really well".

But perhaps the board should reconsider and look ahead to the moment when sales and profits fail to meet the heady expectations of bulls. Then Asos might be glad of the weightier investor base that supports the shares of FTSE 100 big beasts.

techMARK and techMARK mediscience

In 1999, at the height of the high technology fever, the LSE launched a 'market within a market' called techMARK. This is part of the Main Market and is therefore not really a separate market. It is a grouping of technology companies on the Official List. One of the reasons for its creation was that many companies failing to fulfil the requirement of a three-year account history necessary to join the Official List had relatively high market values and desired the advantages of being on a prestigious market. The LSE relaxed its rule and permitted a listing if only one year's accounts are available for techMARK companies. This allowed investors to invest through a well-regulated exchange in companies at an early stage of development, such as Freeserve and lastminute.com. The LSE does insist that all companies joining techMARK have at least 25 per cent of their shares in a free float.

TechMARK mediscience is a separate grouping of Main Market health care companies.

ICAP Securities & Derivatives Exchange (ISDX)

Companies that do not want to pay the costs of a flotation on one of the markets run by the LSE (this can range from £100,000 to £1 million just for getting on the market in the first place) and the ongoing annual costs, could go for a quotation on London based **ISDX** (formerly **PLUS Stock Exchange**). By having their shares quoted on ISDX, companies provide a service to their shareholders, allowing them to buy and sell shares. It also allows the company to gain access to capital, for example, by selling more shares in a rights issue, without submitting to the rigour and expense of a quotation on the LSE. The downside for investors is that trading in ISDX-quoted shares can be illiquid (not many buyers and sellers), with high dealing costs. Bid-offer spreads are frequently 30–50 per cent despite there often being a number of competing market makers making a market in a company's shares.

Joining fees range from a minimum of £15,000 to a maximum of £50,000 (for the largest companies). There is an annual fee of £6,500. When companies join the market there are 'corporate adviser's' fees of around £20,000. If new capital is raised fees can climb above £100,000. Companies also pay an annual retainer fee to their corporate advisers. Companies are now required to have one-tenth of their shares in public hands, in a 'free float'.

ISDX companies are generally very small and often brand new, but there are also some long-established and well-known firms, such as Quercus Publishing and Adnams, the brewers.

Note that the criteria for companies gaining admission for a quote on ISDX Growth Market do not include compliance with the UKLA rules, so investors have far fewer quality assurances about these companies. However, ISDX companies have to adhere to its code of conduct, for example, insider trading by directors is prohibited; they must have a corporate adviser (e.g. an investment bank, accountant or lawyer) at all times; an 'admission document' (prospectus) must be produced for companies listing; and the market must be properly informed of any developments or any information that may have an impact on the financial status of the company. The corporate adviser will insist that good accounting systems are in place with annual audited accounts and semi-annual accounts. They also ensure that the company has at least one non-executive director, and adequate working capital. Articles 3.5 and 3.6 show the stress that ISDX puts on raising the standards of corporate governance, financial strength and reporting.

Article 3.5

ICAP rebrands Plus exchange business

By Vanessa Kortekaas

ICAP has relaunched a trading venue for small and medium sized companies. The world's largest interdealer broker unveiled the ICAP Securities & Derivatives Exchange (ISDX) – a rebranded version of the Plus exchange business.

ICAP said its priority was raising the quality of companies traded on the exchange, to make it a competitor to the AIM. The group is developing a points system to assess companies hoping to come to the market, as well as those whose shares are already quoted on the exchange.

"We will be raising the bar for the companies we have on the exchange as well," explained Seth Johnson, chief executive of ISDX. "They will have time to pull their socks up if they currently need to."

Mr Johnson said his objective was to make the relaunched exchange – where shares in Arsenal Football Club and Shepherd Neame are currently traded – "better value" than alternative exchanges for SMEs.

He said the points system ICAP is developing would be based on measures of a company's financial strength and would reassure investors by bringing more clarity to the listing process.

There are 133 companies quoted on the ISDX with an average market cap of £10m.

ICAP said it was focusing on raising the quality of companies on the exchange rather than aiming to attract a specific number of new listers next year.

Article 3.6

ISDX penalises Colombian Mineral Resources following rules breach

By Brooke Masters

An Ireland-registered coal mining company has been fined £100,000 for lying about its funding in the first disciplinary action taken by the ICAP Securities & Derivatives Exchange since taking over the Plus market last year.

According to the disciplinary notice, Colombian Mineral Resources told investors and the exchange at the time of its March 2012 admission to trading that it had received €11.6m from a placing, but the money was never paid. The company revealed the shortfall six months later and said its plans to explore mining concessions in Colombia had been delayed by the funding problems.

Article 3.6	Continued

The £100,000 fine is the largest sanction available to the ISDX. The move is intended to reassure investors that the small-cap exchange's new owner takes its rules seriously.

CMR "committed serious and flagrant breaches [of ISDX] rules. . . and has threatened market integrity – notably by creating a false market and undermining market confidence," said James Godwin, the exchange's director of regulation.

The company's shares were withdrawn from trading on the ISDX Growth Market in February of this year.

There are over 90 companies with a combined market capitalisation of around £2 billion paying for the ISDX Growth Market quote dealing facility. In addition ISDX provides an alternative trading facility for dozens of securities that have been admitted to trading on other EU markets.

ISDX is often seen as a nursery market for companies that eventually grow big enough for AIM or the Main Market – see Article 3.7 for an example. Despite this many companies are happy to remain on ISDX for several years and have no desire to increase their costs by moving up to the LSE markets.

Article 3.7

New recruits raise hopes for Aim

By Jonathan Moules

One of the main reasons it is claimed that the UK has yet to produce a world-beating technology company on the scale of Facebook, Apple or Google is that the public markets in London are not well suited to such ambitious businesses. While the London Stock Exchange and its junior version, the Alternative Investment Market, could certainly learn a thing or two from their peers across the pond, several fast-growing homegrown technology companies do continue to show faith in these markets.

The question is whether this trickle can ever build into a torrent big enough to make Aim the market of choice for the UK's most exciting new digital companies.

One of the latest arrivals is One Media, a digital music and video rights owner, whose catalogue of more than 170,000 music tracks and 5,000 hours of video ranges from the songs of 1970s punk pioneers the New York Dolls to the British children's television shows of the cute glove puppet bear Sooty.

One Media, which is profitable and debt free, makes money from its vast database of content by repackaging it for sale through more than

Article 3.7   Continued

200 digital music and video stores, including iTunes, Amazon, Spotify and YouTube.

It announced in a regulatory filing that it will move from ICAP Securities & Derivatives Exchange to Aim because the latter is a more liquid market. It is also an opportunity to attract new investors.

Michael Infante, chief executive and chairman, said: "The choice was, do we privatise or move up? It was a decision that we can grow."

Aim is valuable for a company such as One Media because it has sufficient scale, Mr Infante notes. Acquisitions have been critical and One Media has made 85 of these since 2006, ranging from a couple of thousand pounds in price to six-figure sums. "There is an opportunity to ramp that up to two to three million [dollars], but I cannot see us raising money like that on a smaller market, like Plus [ISDX]."

Another technology company to make the decision to join Aim is Starcom, a fast-growing and profitable developer of wireless security gadgets, such as smart locks. Eitan Yanuv, Starcom's finance director, said Aim was the obvious choice for a company with a global outlook because it attracts investors from around the world with an international outlook. However, he also likes the way that companies on Aim can return to the market for future funding rounds as their operations grow without the hassle of organising an initial public offering on a main market such as the LSE. "It works very well with young growing companies like ours," he says, noting that Starcom raised £2.7m when it listed in February. "We can raise what we need to get to the next stage, then, when we reach that next stage, you have the support of the market."

Who owns UK shares?

There has been a transformation in the pattern of share ownership in Britain over the last five decades (see Table 3.3). The tax-favoured status of pension funds made them a very attractive vehicle for savings, resulting in billions of pounds being put into them each year. A large proportion of this money used to be invested in equities, making pension funds the most influential investing group on the stock market in the 1980s. However, in the last two decades pension funds have been taking money out of UK quoted shares and placing it into other investments such as overseas shares, bonds and venture capital. Insurance companies similarly rose in significance, increasing their share of quoted equities from 10 per cent to about one-quarter by the 1990s. However, they too have fallen in significance as they switched funds to alternative investments such as overseas shares, property, bonds and hedge funds.

The group which decade after decade decreased in importance is ordinary individuals holding shares directly. They used to dominate the market, with

54 per cent of quoted shares in 1963 but this figure has now gone as low as 10.7 per cent. Investors have tended to switch from direct investment to collective investment vehicles. They gain benefits of diversification and skilled management by putting their savings into unit and investment trusts or into endowment and other savings schemes offered by the insurance companies and pension funds.

The most remarkable trend has been the increasing share of equities held by overseas investors: only 7 per cent in 1963, but 53 per cent in 2012. This increase partly reflects international mergers where the new company is listed in the UK. Also foreign companies sometimes float their UK subsidiaries but hold on to a large shareholding. It also reflects an increasing tendency of investors to buy shares in overseas markets, as markets have liberalised and welcomed foreigners. Of the UK shares held by overseas investors one-half are held by North Americans and one-quarter by Europeans. In addition, large **sovereign wealth funds** (run by governments on behalf of their people for the long term) are investing, say oil money, in shares around the world: for example, the biggest, Norwegian fund, with £600 billion, holds shares in just about every large company in Europe.

In the 'Other' category note that hedge funds have become increasingly important equity buyers. Also, the UK government bought vast numbers of shares in Royal Bank of Scotland and Lloyds in 2008–09.

Table 3.3   Ownership of UK-quoted shares, distribution by sector (%)

Sector	1963	1975	1989	1997	2006	2012
Individuals	54	38	21	17	13	11
Pension funds	6	17	31	22	13	5
Insurance cos.	10	16	19	24	15	6
Rest of the world	7	6	13	28	40	53
Unit trusts, investment trusts	–	–	8	6	4	11
Others (banks, public sector, other financial institutions (e.g. hedge funds) charities, plus unit and investment trusts prior to 1989)	23	24	8	3	16	14

Source: Data sourced from *Office for National Statistics*. Ownership of UK Quoted Shares 2012 and previous reports. *The Office for National Statistics*, www.ons.gov.uk

Although the mode of investment has changed from direct to indirect, Britain remains a society with a deep interest in the stock market. Very few people are immune from the performance of the Exchange. The vast majority have a pension plan or endowment savings scheme, an individual savings account (ISA) or a unit trust investment. Some have all four. The *equity culture*, or trend toward 'equitisation', is even stronger in some other countries. In the USA, for instance, almost one-half of all households now own shares (either directly or through mutual funds and self-select pension funds).

The role of stock exchanges

Traditionally, exchanges perform the following tasks to play their valuable role in a modern society:

- Supervision of trading to ensure fairness and efficiency.

- The authorisation and regulation of market participants such as brokers and market makers.

- Creation of an environment in which prices are formed efficiently and without distortion (**price discovery** or **price formation**). This requires not only regulation of a high order and low transaction costs but also a liquid market in which there are many buyers and sellers, permitting investors to enter or exit quickly without moving the price.

- Organisation of the clearing and **settlement** of transactions (after the deal has been struck the buyer must pay for the shares and the shares must be transferred to the new owners – see Chapter 4).

- The regulation of the admission of companies to the exchange and the regulation of companies on the exchange.

- The dissemination of information (trading data, prices and company announcements). Investors are more willing to trade if prompt and complete information about trades and prices is available.

In recent years there has been a questioning of the need for stock exchanges to carry out all these activities. In the case of the LSE the settlement of transactions was long ago handed over to an organisation called **CREST** (discussed in Chapter 4). The responsibility for authorising the listing of companies has been transferred to the UKLA arm of the Financial Conduct Authority. The LSE's **Regulatory News Service,** which distributes important company announcements and other price-sensitive financial news, now has to compete with other distribution platforms outside the LSE's control as listed companies are now able to choose between providers for news dissemination platforms. Despite all this upheaval, the LSE still retains an important role in the supervision of trading and the distribution of trading and pricing information.

Useful websites

www.advfn.com	ADVFN
www.batstrading.co.uk	BATS Chi-X Europe
www.deutsche-boerse.com	Deutsche Börse
https://europeanequities.nyx.com	Euronext
www.fese.eu	Federation of European Securities Exchanges
www.fca.org.uk	The Financial Conduct Authority
www.ft.com	The Financial Times
www.ftse.com	FTSE indices
www.iii.co.uk	Interactive Investor
www.isdx.com	ICAP Securities and Derivatives Exchange
www.londonstockexchange.com	London Stock Exchange
www.nasdaqomx.com	NASDAQ OMX
https://nyse.nyx.com	New York Stock Exchange and Euronext
www.ons.gov.uk	Office for National Statistics
www.fca.org.uk/firms/markets/ukla	The United Kingdom Listing Authority
www.world-exchanges.org	World Federation of Exchanges

4

Buying and selling shares

There is absolutely no reason to be in awe of stockbrokers, nor of the process of buying or selling shares. Stockbrokers need you more than you need them. It is a highly competitive business, with dozens of brokers offering to help you make a transaction – so much so that you can now deal for less than £10. These people are very keen on offering you a service. So regard yourself as being in charge and shop around.

This chapter will allow you to find the service that suits you best. You will, after reading it, be more informed about the different levels of service that you can ask for. For example, do you want to choose shares yourself without advice? In which case you will be looking for a cheap and efficient **'execution-only'** service. On the other hand, you may welcome advice from a broker. This service will cost more, but not as much as when you ask a broker to manage your portfolio at their discretion.

This chapter also considers what to look for when choosing a broker, and describes what happens behind the scenes after you have instructed your broker to act. Stockbroking has moved so far away from the days of long lunches and high charges that a large proportion of dealing is now done without the need to speak to a broker – via the Internet. Again online dealing is a highly competitive market and you just need a modicum of knowledge to get the most appropriate service for you.

Stockbroker services[1]

If you wish to buy or sell shares (or other securities) on the London Stock Exchange you have to do it through a stockbroker. There are two types of broker: **retail** (also called **private-client** for the **private investor**) **brokers** act for investors; **corporate brokers** act on behalf of companies (e.g. providing advice on market conditions or representing the company to the market).

Before being able to deal you will have to *register* with a private-client broker – this simply involves providing a few details about yourself. The broker will check your creditworthiness (e.g. banker's reference). Anti-money-laundering requirements mean some extra hassle. To prove you are who you say you are hard copy documents are required, such as a passport or driving licence and utility bills. The whole process may take two weeks or so. Many brokers then set up an account so that you can deposit money into it. This will reassure the broker that you will have money to pay for a trade in a timely fashion (rather than having to wait for a cheque in the post). There are three main types of service provided by retail brokers (hereafter referred to simply as 'brokers'): execution-only, advisory and discretionary. Which of these is most suitable for you depends on your circumstances.

Execution-only (or dealing-only) service

Here the broker carries out your purchase or sale order as instructed without offering any investment advice. It is the cheapest way to buy and sell shares. A typical minimum **commission** is around £10–£20, but can be as little as £6. You need to be trading 20 times each month for this! These figures would apply if you were buying, say, £1,000 of shares. Charges normally rise as the size of order increases. So for a £5,000 bargain £20–£30 is more typical. However, brokers have become so keen to gain business that it is sometimes possible to deal for £10 or so, even for orders of £25,000.

The figures given so far are for online dealing. If you use phone and postal dealing then the typical ranges of fees are somewhat higher: minimum commission of around £15 to £35; for £5,000 bargains, £25 to £80; for £25,000 bargains, £50 to £200. Some brokers charge even when you are not dealing, through monthly or quarterly account fees which can be as much as £10 per month. The justification is that the fee covers the cost of distributing dividends and issuing statements. Shop around! There are over 50 dealing-only brokers in

[1] I am very grateful to Riccardo Landucci, a stockbroker at Charles Stanley, who kindly read this chapter and made valuable suggestions for improvement.

the UK to choose from. Also, once you are registered with a particular broker, it is important to keep an eye on the fee levels charged, as they may change for the worse – see Article 4.1.

Article 4.1

Brokers push out small investors

By Josephine Cumbo

Private investors say they are being forced out of the UK's largest execution-only stockbrokers by a sudden jump in fees charged to "small" investors.

Brokers admit that they are losing clients who trade thousands of pounds following the introduction of new charges that penalise low volume traders.

In recent weeks, hundreds of investors have closed their accounts after being hit with new or higher charges and trading inactivity fees.

"If a new charging structure is being introduced, an investor will need to work out what it means for them and then carefully consider how the new charges stack up with that of those offered by different providers," said Billy Mackay, head of marketing with AJ Bell, the stockbroking services provider.

There are regular savings schemes for investing in shares which offer low brokerage charges. Thus you might commit, say £20 or £50 per month. When you want to buy, your order is grouped with those of other investors and then executed together several times each month. The buying fees can then be as low as £1.50 (sale fees can be around £10–£20). The disadvantage of these schemes is the inability to trade at a time you think best, but they are a cost-effective way of starting a portfolio.

Execution-only dealing is very popular, with over 90 per cent of investors now in the habit of using an execution-only broker – see Article 4.2. It is particularly appropriate if you have the time and inclination to make investment decisions on your own. If you have greater confidence in your own research and judgement than the broker's, then execution-only is the service for you. The downside is that you will not be able to discuss your ideas with a broker. It is also said that you will miss out on hot tips – but then, selecting on the basis of hot tips is not investing but speculating, and is generally unprofitable (according to the academic evidence).

British investors choose the DIY option

By Vanessa Kortekaas

Britain is increasingly becoming a nation of do-it-yourself investors, with assets managed by execution-only stockbrokers jumping by a fifth in the past nine months alone.

Funds under administration by execution-only brokers, which do not provide financial advice to clients, increased from £92bn at the end of last year to £110bn on September 30, according to research firm ComPeer.

"It's not just small clients, it's clients who have a lot of money and [are] choosing to manage their own affairs," Tim May, chief executive of the Wealth Management Association, said.

Mr May said that part of the increase in DIY investing was a result of regulations to encourage transparency in fees charged by investment managers.

ComPeer said that a survey in October of 1,000 UK-based investors showed that half of the people polled said that they would probably invest without taking financial advice.

James Hamilton, an analyst at Numis Securities, said. "A lot of people have said, 'OK I think I can [invest] myself and I'll save myself the fee.'"

Advisory dealing service

Under this arrangement the broker will give you investment advice, but the decision on whether to buy or sell rests with you. The broker will not take any investment decisions without your authority. Roughly one-quarter of UK investors have opened these 'dealing with advice' accounts. This is the more traditional stockbroking service in which the broker knows the client sufficiently well for meaningful discussion of ideas and strategies. It allows the investor to test ideas with someone who is in touch with the market full-time. Also, broker reports on companies or sectors, newsletters or market reviews may be sent to clients. Tax advice and portfolio valuation may also be forthcoming. The advisory service costs more than execution-only. The broker earns money through charging commission on each deal rather than by charging for advice directly. A typical minimum transaction charge would be between £20 and £50. This rises to £40–£100 for £5,000 deals and £200–£300 for £25,000 transactions. Alternatively, transaction charges can be kept low, with the broker charging an annual fee, say 0.85 per cent of the value of the portfolio. The cost varies tremendously from broker to broker, as does the quality of the service. Some advisory brokers go further for their clients than others. While many will wait for a call from an investor before offering advice, others are more willing to initiate the contact.

Taking the initiative one stage further, some brokers now differentiate between their advisory dealing service and their **advisory portfolio management** (or just **advisory managed**) service. The advisory dealing service is taken to be a reactive one in which the broker gives advice after being asked for it on specific shares, whereas under the advisory portfolio management service the client is contacted once or twice per month with advice on their portfolio and its constituent shares – this is usually when there is a good reason, such as news on a particular company, sectors, etc. With the advisory portfolio management approach the broker is knowledgeable about the client's overall financial profile and can advise appropriately. One drawback with this type of arrangement is that the investor might be encouraged to deal frequently – good for brokers but, more often than not, very bad for the wealth of investors. Fees mostly based on the size of the portfolio of assets rather than on transaction fees removes some of the incentive for the stockbroker to **churn** your portfolio (make unnecessary trades to generate fees – nowadays churn is less of a concern given the pressure applied by the regulator, the Financial Conduct Authority, to ensure that stockbrokers' compliance offices are monitoring accounts to prevent churn – they ask their managers to justify the level of trading on an account). It also gives an incentive to increase the size of the pot. Thus the broker may recommend going into cash rather than sticking with shares at times of market exuberance, so that total asset size is preserved.

Discretionary service

Under this type of service the broker is paid to manage the investor's portfolio at the broker's discretion. Thus the broker takes decisions on which shares to buy and sell without consulting the investor on each deal. The client is informed after the event. Giving the broker authorisation to act before getting the investor's approval allows the snatching of good opportunities as they arise in fast-moving markets (one of the common complaints of advisory brokers is that their clients are not always available – oddly enough, they like to live a life beyond their portfolio – and so fleeting chances are missed as permission to buy is not given quickly). Furthermore, many clients simply do not want to spend time managing their portfolios. They don't want to devote effort to developing investment skills. They therefore place their money in the hands of professionals. Prior to running your portfolio the broker will meet you to gain an understanding of your particular circumstances, your investment aims and any restrictions you would like to place on the portfolio (e.g. no investment in tobacco or arms).

Only around 5 per cent of UK investors have discretionary portfolio management accounts with brokers. One of the reasons for the low take-up is that brokers generally insist on a minimum portfolio size of £50,000 (although a few go as low as £25,000). Some set the minimum at £100,000 or even higher. The average discretionary portfolio is around a quarter of a million. Another reason is the cost of the service. Not only are investors usually charged commission (at about the same level as advisory clients) on each transaction but they are also charged an *annual fee* related to the total value of the portfolio. This is generally between 0.5 and 1 per cent. Some brokers have high dealing charges (1.25 per cent or more) and low annual fees, whereas others charge a mere £20 or so for each transaction but load the costs on to the annual fee, while a few now offer a fee-only service. The amount you pay generally depends on the frequency of trading – the discretion over which you have granted to the broker. Be on your guard against churning. It is disturbing that very few brokers offer to charge on the basis of the returns they achieve.

Choosing a stockbroker

There are many ways of finding a stockbroker. The London Stock Exchange (www.londonstockexchange.com) publishes a complete list of its members. The Wealth Management Association (WMA) provides lots of information on their website www.thewma.co.uk (or telephone 020 7448 7100), including stockbrokers' contact names, addresses, telephone numbers and an outline of the kinds of services offered. Investors are regularly surveyed for their opinions on broker performance and costs in investment magazines such as *Investors Chronicle*. Investors also find brokers through personal recommendation.

Choosing a broker means selecting the right combination of cost and services. The following selection criteria may help you draw up a shortlist of brokers and make a final selection:

■ **Charges**. Of course, the lower the commissions for trading the better, but you should allow for the possibility of improved service at extra cost. An important aspect of improved service is the effort put into **'price improvement'** which is taking action to obtain better prices than the current bid and offer prices shown on the screens, through, say, haggling with a market maker. The charging structure will make a big difference to your choice of broker. For example, an investor who does not want to pay for advice and trades many times each month with bargain sizes of around £5,000 will prefer a broker who charges a low fixed rate regardless of bargain size, say £20 each time. Another trader, who buys and sells £1,000 of shares, may prefer a broker who charges a percentage of the amount of the trade, say, 1.0 per cent. If you are a **buy-and-hold investor**, with few transactions, commission costs will not be a great concern. But if you are very active the charges mount up dramatically. Then you may opt for the cheapest mode of transacting – usually online, though some telephone brokers can also be cheap.

■ **Location**. The possibility of being able to talk to a broker face-to-face may lead investors to favour a local broker. This can be particularly valuable for discretionary and advisory portfolio management, where the broker needs to know the investor's circumstances and investing objectives. Local brokers may also be knowledgeable about companies in the region.

■ **Contact**. In surveys investors usually place the ability to contact brokers at the top of their worry list. There are many complaints about telephone lines being busy when a client wishes to deal. People can be put on hold for 20 minutes or more. This can seem like an eternity when you are trying to sell and the market is falling like a stone. Brokers are also criticised for not calling back when they promised to do so. Online orders are often executed very slowly at busy times, as the IT systems suffer from overload. Unfortunately, this is one of those factors that you do not really find out about until you experience it. However, it might be worth asking other clients of your shortlisted brokers if they have any complaints. It could be useful to be able to switch to telephone dealing if the online system is down, and vice versa. So consider a broker that gives you this flexibility.

■ **Administration**. The second factor most complained about is the quality of the administration. Record keeping is sometimes poor, as is the administration of dividends and taxation matters. The paperwork may reach the investor weeks after the event. You do not have to put up with this: other brokers are highly praised for the speed and efficiency of their administration.

■ **Expertise**. You need a broker who is well resourced, has access to high-quality external data and attracts talented managers. This is especially important if you are asking for portfolio management services. You do not want your nest egg managed by a graduate trainee trying to learn on the job. Ask what experience the firm has in managing portfolios of the type and size you have in mind.

■ **Performance**. Unfortunately independently constructed league tables of portfolio managers' performance are not available and so comparison is all but impossible. Brokers do provide statistics, but you must view them with caution.[2] Recommendation may be your main hope.

---

[2] There is a problem in compiling and comparing statistics on performance because what the service brokers provide is specific to the particular needs of the clients. For example, is the client risk averse? How diverse is their general portfolio, i.e. how much investment do they have outside of shares?

■ **Interest**. Brokers hold money in cash accounts on behalf of investors. Some of these accounts offer miserly rates of interest. If you are likely to deposit substantial sums with a broker you need to ask what rate of interest you will receive prior to the purchase of shares. Also, if you need temporary **credit**, what limit will the broker allow you to go up to?

Here are some other questions you might ask:

■ Is the firm authorised by the Financial Conduct Authority? Your assets may have little protection if it is not. Try www.fca.org.uk, or telephone the FCA consumer help line (0800 111 6768).

■ What insurance does the brokerage have in place against fraud or negligence?

■ What can you expect in terms of newsletters, company analysis, sector analysis, or regular portfolio valuation?

■ Does the broker offer a dealing service for securities other than UK listed shares, such as overseas shares, traded options and bonds?

■ If you are trading online, what Internet security features are in place?

About half of UK investors open accounts with more than one broker – it does not cost anything to open two or three accounts. One reason for multiple accounts is to avoid the frustration of not being able to contact a broker – if one is not picking up the phone another might. Investors may also require specific services that their main broker either does not provide or supplies at a higher price.

Finding prices and other information

So, you've chosen your broker and you're getting ready to invest, but where can you find share prices and other information about a company? One source is the daily newspaper coming through your letterbox. The only problem with this is that the information is quite old – at least 12 hours. The Internet has been a great boon for investors looking to gather information and it is very handy for trading shares. In the past 15 years there has been a revolution in the way investors discover key data about a company and select shares. Prior to the online delivery of information traders had to write to or phone a company to get a copy of the annual report; charts of share prices were only for those in the City with a Reuters screen and it took an age for company announcements to trickle through. Today a quick online search delivers company reports going back 10 years (or more) as well as an astounding array of stock market statistics and views on companies:

from when directors bought shares in their own companies to share price histories to bulletin board discussions about the company's latest product.

The company's website

The place to start is the website of the company you are interested in. There are two aspects to this. First how does it present itself on the Internet and what can you glean about the underlying business strengths in terms of customer appeal, etc. Second, the financials: i.e. how has it been performing with regard to making profits for shareholders? And how strong is the financial structure (e.g. does it have too much debt and is therefore too risky)?

You can gain a feel for the quality of the company's communication efforts at this point as well as gain some insight into its competitive position benchmarked against other players in the industry. Of course, you are reading a cleaned-up PR version, and so a reasonable amount of scepticism is required, but by combining this information with material from other sources you can start to build a picture.

A good antidote to corporate PR is to search the company name or its brand products and adding the word 'reviews' to see what customers thought of it; if a lot are upset with the company you may decide to pass on this investment.

Those companies with a high consumer focus (e.g. Vodafone and Marks and Spencer) have websites mostly concerned with selling products or an image of the firm to the public. Simply searching using the company name you may find it difficult to discover the material directed at investors. To get there more directly I usually search on 'investor relations'.

Newspaper websites

Many broadsheet newspapers supply articles free to anyone who visits their websites and you will be able to search for articles going back many years. The most sought-after financial papers, the *Financial Times* and *The Wall Street Journal,* allow you access to many parts of their sites for free but restrict your ability to search their archive of articles to only a limited number of articles in any given period. If you want more you will have to subscribe.

Financial websites

Specialist financial websites offer much more than share prices. You can learn a tremendous amount about a company by visiting the sites. Furthermore, you do not have to limit yourself to using just one. By registering with half a dozen (taking two or three minutes for each) you can access an even wider range of information. The only downside is they will send you junk mail – frequently. Here are some of the players in the business – consult their websites for current services:

www.advfn.com	ADVFN
www.digitallook.com	Digital Look
www.iii.co.uk	Interactive Investor
www.londonstockexchange.com	London Stock Exchange
www.moneyam.com	MoneyAM
www.morningstar.co.uk	Morningstar
www.fool.co.uk	Motley Fool
www.proquote.net	Proquote
www.tddirectinvesting.co.uk	T.D. Direct Investing
https://uk.finance.yahoo.com	Yahoo! Finance

Getting the most out of financial websites

Figure 4.1 shows the home page of ADVFN. Other websites have similar features, with some better than others on particular aspects. I'm not promoting ADVFN; I just need to make use of one of the major suppliers to illustrate the amazing variety of information available.

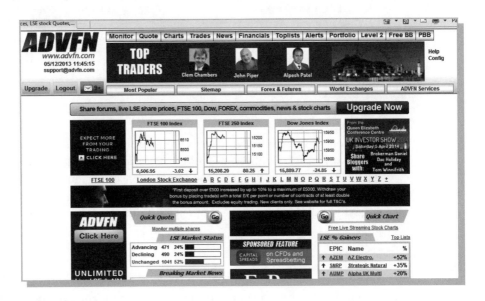

Figure 4.1   The home screen for ADVFN

Source: www.advfn.com

After logging in you may want to look up the price of a particular share. Click on the 'Quote' button (top left of screen), shown in Figure 4.2.

Figure 4.2   Home screen with a focus on the 'navigation bar' showing the quote button

Source: www.advfn.com

The page that this takes you allows you to search for a particular company – see Figure 4.3.

Figure 4.3   The quote page

Source: www.advfn.com

Operators in the markets (brokers, etc.) reduce the names of companies down to very short **'stock symbols'** or **'codes'**. They are also called **tickers** and **EPIC** or **TIDM** codes. So, for example, Marks and Spencer is reduced to MKS. Most of us do not know the codes that we need, but we can look them up. So, on the quote page if you click on 'Shares A–Z' a screen similar to that in Figure 4.4 will appear.

Prices

Let's search for Marks and Spencer. Make sure that the correct market is being searched – on this screen the default setting is for the London Stock Exchange (you can look at shares on dozens of markets around the world). Also check that the type of security is the one you want – in this case 'Stocks & Indices' is correct.

The buttons on the right permit us to search an alphabetical list. Where it says zero we put in 'M', and in the next box 'A', and then click on 'Filter'. When we have found Marks and Spencer in the list we click on 'MKS'.

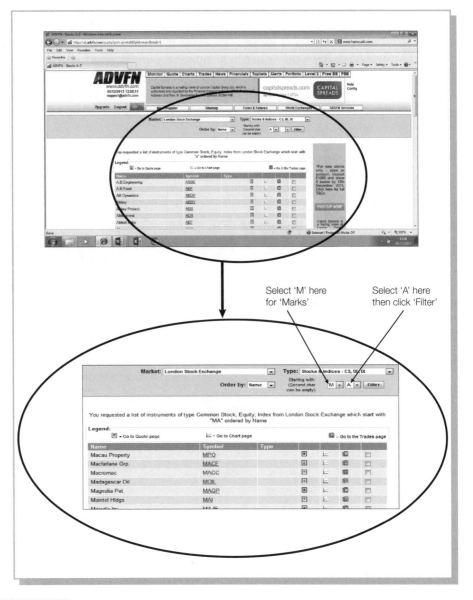

Figure 4.5 shows some of the data displayed on the quote page for MKS. There is the latest traded price 'Cur' (meaning current) at 468.8p. The current offer price if you want to buy is 469.1p, whereas if you are interested in selling the bid price is 468.9p (but a good broker might be able to improve on these prices). Also displayed are the highest and lowest prices so far today. Between the stock market opening at 8 a.m. until 12.37 p.m., when the screenshot was taken, 704,787 shares were traded. You are also presented with some financial data: the last 12 months of sales at MKS (£10,026.8 million); annual profit; earnings per shares (EPS); price–earnings ratio (see Chapter 12 for a description of EPS and PE ratio); and the current market value of all MKS's ordinary shares, that is a 'market capitalisation' of £7,572 million. The final line shows the most recent trade to go through: 1,000 shares at a price of 469.055p.

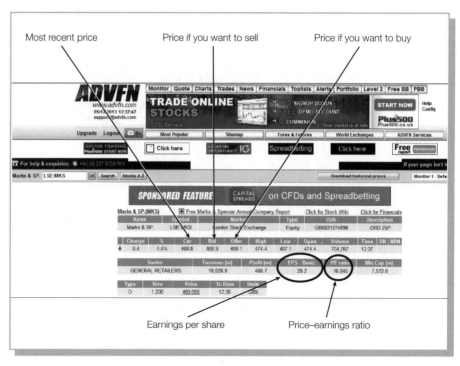

Figure 4.5   Quote page for Marks and Spencer

Source: www.advfn.com

News

Scrolling down that page you will come across the 'Recent News' section. All the financial websites supply company announcements and other news. The news for MKS on ADVFN is displayed in Figure 4.6.

Recent News			
Date	Time	Source	Headline
02/12/2013	14:27	UKREG	Marks & Spencer Group PLC Total Voting Rights
22/11/2013	11:11	UKREG	Marks & Spencer Group PLC Director/PDMR Shareholding
05/11/2013	18:12	DJFR	INDICES: Le FTSE 100 a clôturé en retrait de 0,3% avant la réunion de la BoE
05/11/2013	17:39	DJN	LONDON MARKETS: ABF, Banks Drag FTSE 100 Lower Despite Strong Data
05/11/2013	17:18	DJN	EUROPE MARKETS: European Stocks Retreat From Five-year High
05/11/2013	17:15	DJN	EUROPE MARKETS: European Stocks Retreat From Five-year High
05/11/2013	09:26	CERFI	Marks & Spencer: bien orienté après ses semestriels.
Set a News Alert for MKS			More MKS News

Figure 4.6   Obtaining news on the company – an ADVFN screen

Source: www.advfn.com

Clicking on the headline will bring up the full news story. The system carries news and announcements going back many years. So, for example, if you wanted to find out if periodic director statements on the progress of the company proved to be accurate or generally over-optimistic you can read both the statements going back 10 or more years and the subsequent reported results.

Bulletin boards

By scrolling down the quote screen for Marks and Spencer you can see the message/discussion board or 'bulletin board' – see Figure 4.7. This can be an important source of information. The entries are written by anyone registered with the website. Through these it is possible to correspond with like-minded investors – which helps to make the game of investing less lonely as well as exposing you to alternative views.

People that post on these 'threads' usually adopt nicknames. Some are well informed and can add to your knowledge of the company; but beware, others know little, are trying to ramp up or push down a share, or are there just for a rant. Be particularly wary of those who claim they know a takeover bid is coming or the directors are about to sell a large chunk of shares or they have some other inside information. They are trying to get a share price movement so that they can make money for themselves. If they really had this inside knowledge do you really think they would share it with you? And anyway insider dealing is illegal.

Tip: it is worth looking at a number of website discussion boards to help build up background knowledge.

Some websites have both free bulletin boards and a premium service that you have to pay to join. ADVFN offer the 'premium' version (the button to click on is at the top of each page: 'PBB'). These tend to attract more serious investors.

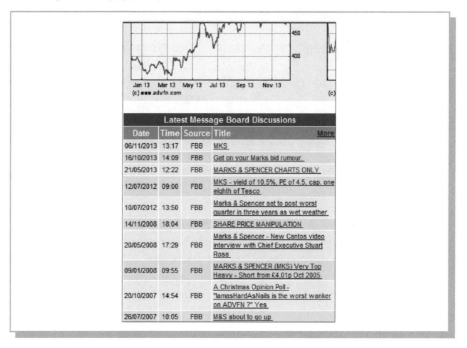

Figure 4.7   **A discussion board**

Source: www.advfn.com

The most active bulletin boards are:

- ADVFN: www.advfn.com

- Interactive Investor: www.iii.co.uk

- MoneyAM: www.moneyam.com

- Motley Fool: www.fool.co.uk

- Yahoo! Finance: www.uk.finance.yahoo.com.

Financial data

At the top right of the home page for M&S there is 'Click for Financials' – see Figure 4.8.

Figure 4.8   Obtaining financial data on the firm

Source: www.advfn.com

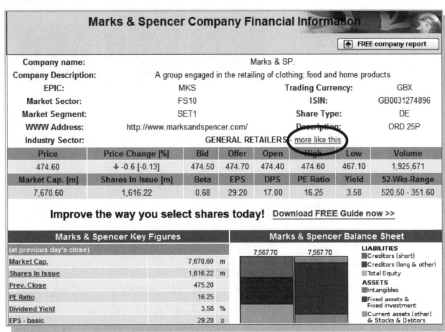

Figure 4.9   Company financial information presented on ADVFN

Source: www.advfn.com

By clicking through to this page you have access to a very long list of key financial numbers including a wide range of financial ratios, profit numbers and balance sheet numbers going back four years, share price performance over various periods, a share chart and dividend history – see Figures 4.9 and 4.10.

A useful feature on this page (see Figure 4.9) is the 'more like this' button which will take you to a list of companies in the same industry on the LSE. It is always important for an investor to be aware of the relative strengths of competitor firms. By following the links you can discover a wide range of information about *some* of the companies that compete. However, you may need to take a more international perspective because the company's main competitors may not be quoted on the LSE. For example, Rolls-Royce aero engines compete against rival products from US General Electric and Pratt & Whitney.

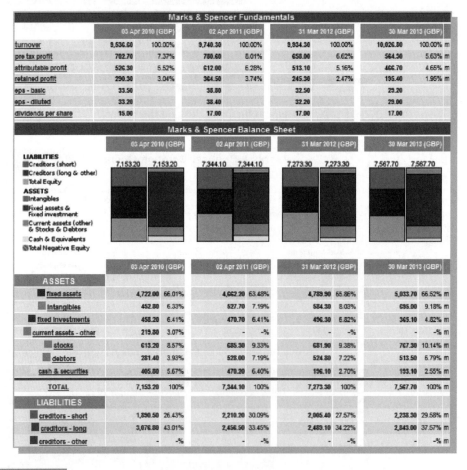

Figure 4.10   Some of the accounting data on ADVFN

Source: www.advfn.com

We do not have space in this chapter to discuss all the different financial ratios and measures displayed on a page like this (as in Figure 4.10), but these are explained in Chapters 11, 12 and 13.

Monitoring

Going back to the home screen for ADVFN (Figure 4.1 earlier) you can see a string of buttons going across the top – see Figure 4.11.

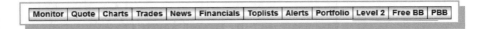

Figure 4.11   **The main buttons to click**

Source: www.advfn.com

The 'Monitor' button allows you to track a number of companies and indices – see Figure 4.12.

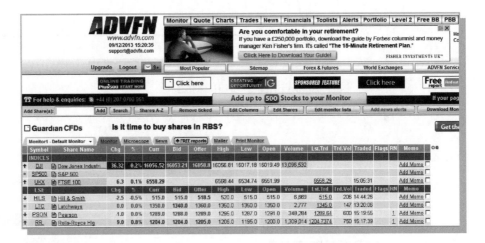

Figure 4.12   **Monitoring a selected group**

Source: www.advfn.com

Once a company is on your monitor list you merely click on the company name to obtain more detail, without having to look-up its code. You can also see if there is any recent news about the companies on the list. To add companies to the list just find the relevant code.

Share price charts

The 'Charts' button at the top of the home page allows you to draw share price charts – see Figure 4.13.

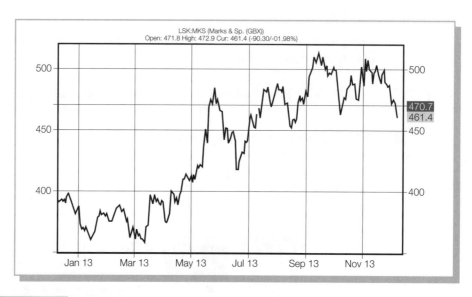

Figure 4.13 Share price chart for M&S

Source: www.advfn.com

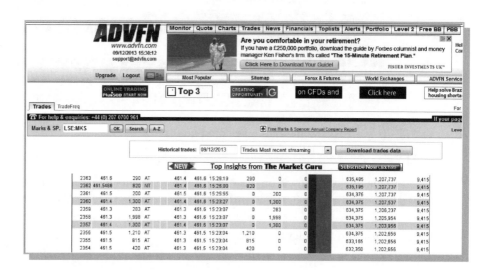

Figure 4.14 A history of trades in M&S's shares

Source: www.advfn.com

A history of trades

The next button, 'Trades' (in Figure 4.11 earlier), allows you to see the actual deals that have been made in the market. As you can see in Figure 4.14 there is a trade in M&S every few seconds (in the 7th second after 3.23 p.m. there were three trades at 461.3p or 461.4p). Other (much smaller) companies may go days without a single trade. It is possible to see the trades of days past as well as the current day.

News

The 'News' button (see Figure 4.11 earlier) brings you to a page displaying the major news stories of the day (e.g. a merger bid). By inputting the code for the company in which you have an interest you can see all the past announcements, etc. An alternative use for the news button is to get a continuous stream of news as it is released from all companies on the market – this is updated as you look at it.

Toplists

The 'Toplists' button (see Figure 4.11 earlier) is a great way of selecting, from all the shares on the market, a shortlist of companies based on key criteria, e.g. those that have produced the best or the worst five-year returns. You can then filter out those that, say, were unprofitable last year, or those with a market capitalisation greater than, say, £100 million, and so on. Figure 4.15 shows only a few of the factors that can be used to rank and separate companies.

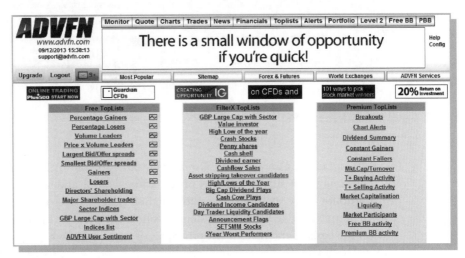

Figure 4.15 Filtering and ranking companies on the markets

Source: www.advfn.com

Alerts

The 'Alerts' button (see Figure 4.11 earlier) permits you to program the system to tell you if a particular threshold is reached, e.g. the share price of M&S falls below £4.00, or an event occurs. There are three types of alerts: share price alerts, news alerts and bulletin board alerts. In each case, you can ask the financial website to send you an e-mail message when something happens.

Creating real and virtual portfolios

The 'Portfolio' button (see Figure 4.11 earlier) allows you to set up a number of hypothetical or real portfolios and then follow the shares through time. Figure 4.16 shows that the portfolio gains and losses are totalled automatically. You can click through from the company names in the portfolio list to more detailed information on the company.

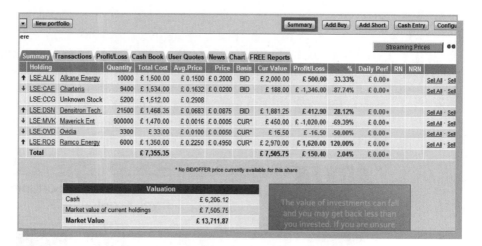

Figure 4.16   A portfolio screenshot

Source: www.advfn.com

You can create as many portfolios as you want. So you might want to follow the performance of shares with low price–earnings ratios and set up a series of such portfolios every six months and follow their progress over the subsequent years. Or you might like to set the system to follow the progress of companies selected on the basis of the investment principles of Warren Buffett.

When checking your portfolio, beware of the psychological problem we humans have when it comes to what behaviouralists call 'narrow framing'. In this context we lose sight of the bigger investment picture and feel pain as a result. On any one day or month there is a roughly 50:50 chance that your portfolio will be up or down. It turns out that we humans feel a loss much more keenly than a gain.

So if we are continually looking to see whether we have made money in the past few hours or lost it we will suffer the pain of loss regularly and this will outweigh the pleasure we feel on up-days. This can lead to some bad decisions as we go on a desperate search for short-term fixes to feel the pleasure of a gain.

Do not narrow frame – see the bigger picture, which is that shares generally give a satisfactory return over a number of years, but there will be many bumps along the way. Do not be distracted and depressed by the bumps.

Be a long-term investor in good companies. Consider whether it makes sense to look at your portfolio returns every day. Yes, look at company performance and other data relevant to that performance (e.g. technological change in the industry), but not at stock market ups and downs. This is one of the key lessons from the great investors Benjamin Graham and Warren Buffett.[3]

Level 2

Brokers and many financial websites offer **Level 2** (or **Level II**) prices. Level 2 allows you to see on your computer the orders for shares that other traders are putting into the LSE's system, with prices they are willing to pay or sell for, and the quantity they are willing to trade. We saw in Figure 4.5 (earlier) Level 1 data: simply bid and offer prices, price of last trade executed, current day's high and low, percentage change from the previous close of trading, the volume traded, etc.

Having Level 2 permits a greater understanding of the current supply and demand conditions because it allows the private investor to see the current unfilled buy and sell orders, which can change in front of their eyes as the system continuously streams updates. This provides a better understanding of how the share price is derived and helps in timing the placing of an order. A screenshot of Level 2 prices is shown later in the chapter (in Figure 4.20), where the trading mechanisms are discussed.

Level 2 is useful if you are a regular trader, but for many long-term buy-and-hold investors who trade infrequently it seems quite expensive at £24 or more per month. (If you trade a lot through one broker, say 30 trades per month, they may

---

[3] If you would like to know more on sound investment philosophies you might like to read my books *Great Investors* (Financial Times Prentice Hall, 2011) or *The Financial Times Guide to Value Investing* (Financial Times Prentice Hall, 2009) or consult www.glen-arnold-investments.co.uk

set you up with Level 2 for nothing, but you'll be paying them a lot every month in dealing charges.)

Directors' dealings

Another piece of the information jigsaw you might find useful is whether the directors of the company have been buying or selling its shares. Many investors take a purchase as an indicator of a positive opinion of the firm's prospects by someone with superior access to information – if they are spending their own money on the shares perhaps there is reason to think they might be undervalued. On the other hand, a sale may not be as negative as it first appears – school fees might need to be paid, or rational diversification is taking place: much depends on context. A good website for directors' dealings is Directors Holdings which displays what directors bought/sold – see Figure 4.17.

MARKS & SPENCER GROUP PLC

Directors Holdings | Deals | Chart

All Deals

Dec. Date	Deal. Date	Type	Director	Pos	No. of shares	Price	Value	Current price
28/08/2013	27/08/2013	BUY	Bousquet-Chavanne, Patrick	ED	2,000	483.68 p	£9,674	460.35 p
28/08/2013	27/08/2013	BUY	Bousquet-Chavanne, Patrick	ED	2,000	483.68 p	£9,674	460.35 p
12/06/2013	11/06/2013	EXR	Sharp, Steven	ED	267,291	0.00 p	£0	460.35 p
12/06/2013	11/06/2013	SEXR	Sharp, Steven	ED	126,070	443.36 p	£558,944	460.35 p
12/06/2013	11/06/2013	EXR	Dixon, John	ED	258,138	0.00 p	£0	460.35 p
12/06/2013	11/06/2013	SEXR	Dixon, John	ED	131,701	442.15 p	£582,316	460.35 p
12/06/2013	11/06/2013	SELL	Dixon, John	ED	6,445	443.74 p	£28,599	460.35 p
12/06/2013	11/06/2013	EXR	Wade-Gery, Laura	ED	119,751	0.00 p	£0	460.35 p
12/06/2013	11/06/2013	SEXR	Wade-Gery, Laura	ED	56,482	445.24 p	£251,480	460.35 p
12/06/2013	11/06/2013	EXR	Rowe, Steve	ED	76,934	0.00 p	£0	460.35 p
12/06/2013	11/06/2013	SEXR	Rowe, Steve	ED	36,288	442.15 p	£160,447	460.35 p
22/02/2013	22/02/2013	BUY	Halford, Andy	NED	3,000	377.30 p	£11,319	460.35 p
16/01/2013	11/01/2013	DRIP	Sharp, Steven	ED	854	367.40 p	£3,138	460.35 p
16/01/2013	11/01/2013	DRIP	Dixon, John	ED	38	367.40 p	£140	460.35 p

Figure 4.17   Directors' dealings

Source: www.directorsholdings.com

What happens when I buy or sell shares?

Now you've reached the exciting moment of actually buying (or selling) a share. There are many ways you can do this, the most common being via the telephone or the Internet. When you telephone your broker you will be asked your name (and possibly your account number). Then you will tell the broker that you want to trade in the shares of a particular company and ask for the current price. The broker will give you not one price, but two. The first is the price at which you can sell the shares, the other is the price at which you can buy.

To start with, we are going to look at the quote-driven method of trading with market makers at the centre of the process. Many UK shares are now traded in alternative ways; these are discussed later. What happens with quote-driven trading is this: when you mention the company name the broker immediately punches into his computer the company code. The computer is linked to the London Stock Exchange Automated Quotations (**SEAQ**™, pronounced 'see-ack') system. This is a computerised system for distributing the prices offered by market makers. So within milliseconds of your mentioning your interest in the company the broker has on his screen all the prices that different market makers are willing to pay as well as all the prices they are willing to sell the shares for.[4] A typical SEAQ screen is shown for a company in Figure 4.18.

There are about 36 equity market makers but not all of them choose to make a market in the company displayed in Figure 4.18. This screen shows that nine market makers are offering prices. The fact that there are a relatively large number of competing organisations willing to quote prices indicates that this is a large company with a liquid secondary market in its shares. Small companies may have only two or three market makers willing to display prices on SEAQ. The minimum number of market makers quoting prices for a share to remain on SEAQ is two. (If fewer than two are willing to offer prices then the share is transferred to SETSqx – see later.) The **'bid' price** is the price at which the market maker is willing to buy. So, in the case of the market maker NUMS the bid price is 34p (bottom left of Figure 4.18). The **'offer' price** is the price at which the market makers are willing to sell – NUMS offers these shares at 36p. The spread between the two prices represents a hoped-for return to the market maker.

It can be confusing and time-consuming for the broker to look at all the prices to find the best current rates. Fortunately they do not have to do this as SEAQ displays a **'yellow strip'** above the market makers' prices, which provides the identity of the market makers offering the best bid and offer prices (these are called **'touch' prices**). It is the price in the yellow strip that the broker will immediately report to you over the telephone. In this case you will be told 35–36. So, if you were happy with 36p you would then instruct your broker to buy, say, 5,000 shares.

The market makers prices are quoted as **'firm' prices**. That is, the LSE insists that the market maker trade at these prices if a broker (investor) has been attracted to do a deal based on the posted prices. They cannot change them when they are

---

[4] If you are dealing online instead of speaking to a broker, you will call up the broker's website using your user ID and password. You will then input the name of the company or its code and view the prices (a simple summary of current prices if you are on a Level 1 system, or a display of a range of dealers prices if you are on Level 2).

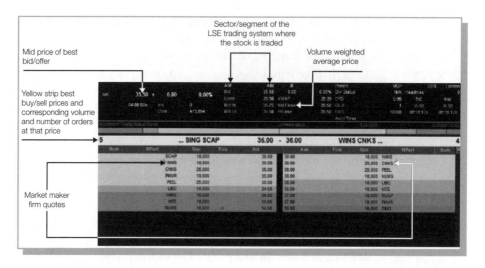

Figure 4.18   A typical SEAQ screen

contacted by the broker if the transaction is below the **exchange market size** or
EMS (also called **normal market size** or **NMS**). (This is set at approximately 2.5
per cent of the average daily customer turnover.) It is displayed at the top of the
screen. For deals larger than the EMS the market maker is allowed to change prices
and will give the broker a price when he calls. Of course prices can be changed
at any time on the SEAQ system so the market maker can adjust in response to
the weight of buying and selling pressure, and in response to what other market
makers are offering. In this case the EMS is 10,000, so your 5,000 share order does
not require a special price quote and you will be able to trade at the prices shown
(or better).

Next, the broker (or the website) asks what type of order you would like to make.
You have several options:

- You could ask your broker to execute your order **at best**. This means that the
trade is completed immediately at the best price available. If the broker is
unable to obtain the shares at the price he quoted to you (because, say the
market makers' quotes change in the few seconds or minutes between you
saying you would like to buy and the market makers' being contacted), you
may end up paying more than you thought (or less). Also, many brokers try
to obtain prices 'inside the price quotes', i.e. they 'price improve'.

- If the uncertainty of dealing at best is too much, you can place a **limit
order**. Here you specify the maximum price at which you are willing to buy
or the minimum price at which you are willing to sell. The order can stay on

the system until it is fulfilled (up to 90 days) or until cancelled (**good-till-cancelled** order) or until a fixed expiry date is reached regardless of whether it has been completed.

■ An **execute and eliminate** order means that the transaction is completed in part or in full immediately. A price limit is set by the investor. If not completed immediately the order expires on the spot. If only some of an order is fulfilled the remainder expires.

■ With a **fill or kill** order a maximum (minimum) price is stated. If the deal cannot be executed in its entirety at this price or better, the entire order expires.

■ With a **stop-loss order** your broker is instructed to sell shares you hold if they fall below a stated price. The idea is to protect your portfolio against a dramatic and sudden downward move, thus protecting the bulk of your funds. Personally, I do not see the point in them. If you are 'investing' rather than 'speculating on market moves' then you will have thoroughly analysed the company and judged it a good one to hold at that price. If it falls then it is an even better buy! If the fundamental strengths of the company have deteriorated then this may induce a sell, but not a fall in share price *per se.*

Now the broker has all the information needed to enter the market place and buy shares. A good broker will read back your order to you: 'Buy 5,000 shares in ABC on an execute or eliminate basis with a maximum price of 36p.' He will then ask you to confirm that you would like him to go ahead (telephone calls are recorded). At this point you are making a legal commitment to enter the transaction with the broker. This is your last chance to back out.

When your broker hears that you wish to go ahead you can either stay on the line to await confirmation that the order has been completed or ask the broker to call you back. Next, the broker telephones the market maker offering the keenest price and a deal is struck verbally.[5] All trades are reported to the central computer at the heart of SEAQ and disseminated to market participants within three minutes.[6] This gives a great deal of transparency to the system, allowing everyone to see a range of recent prices – see Figure 4.19.

While the traditional way of trading is for brokers to telephone market makers, today the majority of private investor trades are made through **retail service**

---

[5] The stockbroker is allowed to complete the deal 'in-house' by taking on the deal himself if he can match the best prices offered by the market makers.

[6] Market makers are permitted to delay reporting very large orders for a few hours, or even days, to allow them to unwind very large positions.

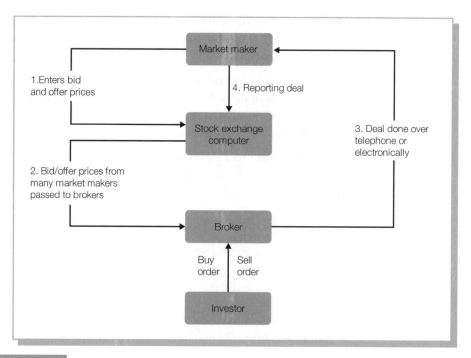

Figure 4.19   The SEAQ quote-driven system for trading shares

providers (**RSP**s). Telephone and Internet-based execution-only stockbrokers charge a very low price for each trade. One of the ways in which they keep costs down is to put small trades (usually those under the exchange market size) through a RSP network. Brokers may have 5–10 RSP relationships. The RSPs relieve the burden for market makers and brokers of having to pick up the telephone to strike a deal for orders of merely a few hundred shares. An electronic system polls the market makers that are acting as RSPs (and the electronic order-books of LSE, such as the Stock Exchange Electronic Trading System (SETS) – discussed later) for their bid and offer quotes. The investor is then told the most competitive RSP quote via the computer screen (if dealing online) or via the telephone. Typically the two-way quote is valid for up to 15 seconds. For an online investor, if the deal is acceptable a click on the relevant screen button will secure the deal. The RSP network then automatically and instantaneously executes the order electronically, saving time and money. Furthermore, the RSP network may allow for a slight improvement in the quoted price displayed on financial websites, i.e. better than the price shown in the yellow strip (price improvement service). For orders larger than the NMS it is usually preferable for the investor to get the broker to talk directly to the market maker.

The next day you should receive a **contract note** in the post (or by email). This will state the price, the time of the deal, the number of shares, the broker's commission and the charge of 0.5 per cent of the value of your purchase in **stamp duty** for Main Market shares (this is a form of taxation that applies to purchase only, but not to AIM shares since 2014). Check the details to make sure they match your expectations and file the note so you have a record (it will be useful when it comes to filling out tax returns).

If you have a broking account, then the broker will debit (credit) the account two business days after the transaction.

If you have opted to receive **share certificates** (see below) then these will be sent to you by the registrar of the firm in which you now hold shares.

An alternative mechanism

Note that the SEAQ system is now only used for 580 or so AIM shares; those that have two or more market makers. We now turn to an alternative approach that is especially useful for heavily-traded shares on the Main Market and on AIM.

There has been some criticism of trading systems based on market makers quoting bid and offer prices. Investors comment that with the **quote-driven** systems the middle man's (the market maker's) cut comes from them. Wouldn't it save them money if buyers could trade with sellers at a single price so as to eliminate the loss of the bid–offer spread? Well, many stock exchanges in the world do operate this type of **'order-driven' trading system**. These markets allow buy and sell orders to be entered on a central computer, and investors are automatically matched (they are sometimes called **matched-bargain systems** or **order book** trading). In 1997 the LSE introduced an order-driven service known as **SETS (Stock Exchange Electronic Trading System)**. This now operates for about 900 particularly liquid, frequently traded shares, including the largest 600 or so on the Main Market (those in the FTSE All-Share Index) and the most liquid AIM and Irish securities.

SETS is a computerised system in which dealers (via brokers) enter the prices at which they are willing to buy or sell. They can then wait for the market to move to the price they set as their limit. Alternatively, they can instruct brokers to transact immediately at the best price currently available on the order book system. The LSE SETS computer does not simply act as a price-information system – as the SEAQ does – it executes the trades.

SETS derives market prices as follows: buyers and sellers enter a price limit at which they are willing to deal as well as the quantity of shares they want to trade. These prices are displayed anonymously to the entire market. An example of prices and quantities is shown in the lower half of Figure 4.20 – a reproduced SETS screen as seen by brokers.

The buy orders are shown on the left and the sell orders on the right. So, we can observe for this company that trader 'PMUR' (a market maker in this case) has entered that they are willing to buy 15,000 shares at a maximum price of 142.25p (bottom line on the buy side of the screen). Someone else (more than one, actually) has entered that they would like to sell 15,000 shares at a minimum price of 157.75p – see sell side of the screen on the right (towards the bottom we have prices of 157.75p, which are reasonable and then below that we have silly sell limits entered of 222p, etc., nowhere near the trading price). Clearly the computer cannot match these two orders and neither of these two investors will be able to

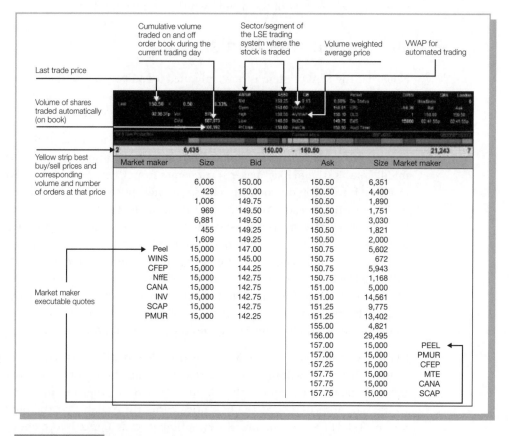

Figure 4.20   A typical SETS screen

trade. They will either have to adjust their limit prices or to wait until the market moves in their favour.

As we travel up the screen we observe a closing of the gap between the prices buyers are willing to pay and the offering price of sellers. Just below the 'yellow strip' we see that a buyer wants 6,006 shares at 150p whereas a seller is prepared to accept 150.50p for 6,351 shares. Now we are getting much closer to a match. Indeed if we look above the yellow strip we can see the price where buyers and sellers were last matched – the 'last traded price' is 150.50p. These screens are available to market participants (or, at least, their brokers) at all times and so they are able to judge where to pitch their price limits. For example if I was a buyer of 5,000 shares entering the market I would not be inclined to offer more than 150.50p given the current state of supply and demand. On the other hand if I was a seller of 5,000 shares I would recognise that the price offered would not have to fall below 150p to attract buyers.

If however I was a buyer of 30,000 shares rather than just 5,000 I have two options: I could set a maximum price of 150.50p in which case I would transact for 21,243 immediately (all the 150.50p sale entries added up) but would leave the other 8,757 unfilled order in the market hoping for a general market price decline; alternatively, I could set my limit at 150.75p in which case I could transact with those investors prepared to sell at 150.50p and 150.75p. The unfilled orders of the sellers at 150.75p are carried forward on SETS.

Supporters of the older quote-driven system say that a major problem with the order-driven system is that there may be few or no shares offered at prices close to a market clearing rate and so little trade can take place. In other words the market can be very illiquid. There may indeed be times when no sellers are posting sensible prices and other times when buyers are scarce. This is when the quote-driven system may be more liquid because market makers who make a book in a company's shares must continuously offer prices and are obliged to trade at the price shown. By way of counter-criticism, it is alleged there have been times when it has been difficult to contact market makers to trade at their displayed prices, even though in theory they are obliged to make themselves available to quote and trade at bid and offer prices throughout the trading day.

To improve trading liquidity on SETS in 2007 the system was modified so that market makers can now post prices on it. Thus it offers a continuous order book with automatic execution (via computer rather than market maker systems), but also has market makers providing continuous bid and offer prices for many shares (but these trades are executed through the automatic system). It is thought that by having the two systems combined there will be tighter bid–offer spreads, greater transparency of trades and improved liquidity.

A third trading system – SETSqx

The underlying logic of the quote-driven system is that through the competitive actions of numerous market makers, investors are able to buy or sell at any time at the best price. A problem arises for some very small or infrequently traded firms. Market makers are reluctant to commit capital to holding shares in such firms, and so for some there may be only one market maker's quote, for others there may be none. The LSE introduced **SETSqx** (Stock Exchange Electronic Trading Service – quotes and crosses) as a trading platform for less liquid shares.

On SETSqx a single market maker's quote can be displayed if a market maker is interested in quoting price. An investor wanting to trade with a market maker can do so in the normal way (as described under the SEAQ system). In addition, throughout the day there are auctions in which investors make bids and the system matches up buyers and sellers at a single price. These auctions take place at 8 a.m., 11 a.m., 3 p.m. and 4.35 p.m. In the five minutes of the auction traders (you and me, via our brokers) can put in limit prices for buys and sells. They can keep withdrawing and modifying them during this period because the system is suspended from matching trades. They can see other people's bids however and this helps to decide the price level for their limit. After the 5 minutes are up the computer moves to a new phase where it does set a price at which trades will be automatically completed, informed by the most recent bids; a price that permits the maximum number of trades.

Currently all Main Market securities not on SETS (over 700 shares) are on SETSsq, as are all AIM securities with less than two market makers (over 300 shares).

What happens after dealing?

When a trade has been completed and reported to the exchange it is necessary to **clear** the trade. That is, the exchange ensures that all reports of the trade are reconciled to make sure all parties are in agreement as to the number of shares traded and the price. The exchange also checks that the buyer and seller have the cash and securities to do the deal. Also the company registrar is notified of the change in ownership. Later the transfer of ownership from seller to buyer has to take place; this is called **settlement**. These days clearing frequently does not just mean checking that the buyer and the seller agree on the terms of the deal; the clearing house also acts as a **'central counterparty'** which acts as a buyer to every seller and a seller to every buyer. This reduces the risk of failure to complete a deal by guaranteeing that shares will be delivered against payment and vice versa. Shares on SETS and SETSqx go through those central counterparty organisations approved by the LSE.

In October 2014 the Exchange moved to a **'two-day rolling settlement'** (trading day +2, or **T+2**), which means that investors normally pay for shares two working days after the transaction date. Before 1996 the transfer of shares involved a tedious paperchase between investors, brokers, company registrars, market makers and the Exchange. The 'new' system, called **CREST**, provides an electronic means of settlement and registration. This 'paperless' system is cheaper and quicker – ownership is transferred with a few strokes of a keyboard.

Under the CREST system (www.euroclear.com) shares are often held in the name of a **nominee company** rather than in the name of the *beneficial owner* (i.e. the individual or organisation that actually bought them). Brokers and investment managers run these nominee accounts. So your broker would hold your shares electronically in his nominee account and would arrange settlement through his membership of the CREST system. There might be dozens of investors with shares held by a particular nominee company. The nominee company appears as the *registered owner* of the shares as far as the company (say, BP or BT) is concerned. Despite this, the beneficial owners will receive all dividends and the proceeds from the sale of the shares via the nominee company. One reason for this extra layer of complexity in the ownership and dealing of shares is that because nominee holdings are recorded in electronic form rather than in the form of a piece of paper (**'dematerialisation'**) when a purchase or sale takes place all that is needed is a quick and cheap adjustment to the electronic record. Investors have no need to bother with share certificates.[7]

Placing shares in a nominee account can remove a lot of administrative work for investors. For example, if you wish to sell shares held in certificated form (i.e. a piece of paper) it is necessary to sign a stock transfer form and send it with the share certificate to your broker, who will then check the form and pass it on to the company registrar. Postal dealing and settlement is clearly impossible within the T+2 settlement time, as well as being more fiddly for brokers. Many brokers allow you to delay settling a deal beyond two days. They may permit T+5, T+10, or even T+20.[8] This is subject to special arrangement, and there will be additional administrative costs to pay. So those clients who use the nominee system will be settled at T+2 while for private investors, who prefer to receive certificates, settlement is more likely to be T+10.

Many investors oppose the advance of CREST nominee accounts because under

---

[7] The nominee company is ring-fenced, so that if the broker goes bust the shares in the nominee are unaffected. In the event of fraud, investors are guaranteed compensation of up to £50,000 under the Investor Compensation Scheme if they are dealing through a broker authorised by the FCA (see Chapter 19).

[8] To deal beyond T+2 you may have to pay additional sums to market makers.

such a system they do not automatically receive annual reports and other documentation, such as an invitation to the AGM.[9] They also potentially lose the vote (after all, the company does not know who the beneficial owners are). Shareholders can also miss out on **perks**, such as a 20 per cent discount voucher to use in Moss Bros (see www.hl.co.uk for a list of perks). Those investors who take their ownership of a part of a company seriously can insist on remaining outside CREST. In this way they receive share certificates and are treated as the real owners of the business. This is more expensive when share dealing, but that is not a great concern for investors who trade infrequently. Another advantage of being outside the nominee system is that you are not tied to a single broker for all your deals. (The cost of transferring 20 shares in a nominee account to another broker can be over £400.) Around 7 million UK shareholders still hold their shares in certificated form.

There is a compromise position: **personal membership of CREST** (also called **sponsored membership**). The investor is then both the legal owner via CREST and the beneficial owner of the shares, and also benefits from rapid (and cheap) electronic share settlement.[10] The owner will be sent all company communications and retain voting rights. However, this can be more expensive than the nominee CREST accounts run by brokers. Personal CREST account costs vary from broker to broker. Some do not charge, while others ask for £200 per year. Some brokers make an extra charge (say £10) for each trade through a personal CREST. Many brokers do not offer CREST personal accounts.

If you are thinking of opting for a nominee service you might like to ask the following:

- What charges will be levied for what services?
- How will the investments be protected while in the nominee account?
- Will I receive annual reports and accounts, the right to vote, invitations to AGMs and EGMs, and perks?

---

[9] With the standard nominee service offered by brokers, investors can request that reports and accounts, perks and invitations to company meetings be passed on. Brokers may also communicate votes on company matters to AGMs. They may be charged extra for these services.

[10] The broker still acts as sponsor, even though the accounts are held in the shareholder's name.

Ways of paying for your shares

■ Open a deposit account with the broker or bank. Your broker is able to draw money from the account on your behalf at any time to settle deals.

■ Send a cheque in the post. Your broker may not be willing to buy for you until the cheque is cleared, especially if you have a two-day deadline for settlement.

■ Visit a high street broker and pay there and then, for example by credit card.

■ Pay by debit card over the telephone.

Internet dealing

The majority of execution-only share trades are conducted online. Internet dealing has many advantages: it can be very cheap and quick to deal; and you can trade wherever you like, without having to communicate with a broker in normal office hours. Furthermore, your PC/tablet/mobile can be used to download vast amounts of information, including real-time price quotes, market news and commentary, charts of share prices and volume of trades, detailed company information, brokers reports and forecasts.

In a typical Internet-based transaction, when you have viewed the prices on screen and placed an order, you are given 15 seconds to accept or reject the deal. If you click 'accept' the transaction is completed immediately and a contract note is emailed.

While online trading is low cost, there are still some problems:

■ Some systems are crash-prone. Computer failure can be very frustrating, so always have a back-up method of trading. It might be worth opening accounts at two or more brokers.

■ The security of information in cyberspace is a worry for many people, although encryption technology is helping the situation.

■ Internet dealing usually requires the use of a nominee account to allow for speedy and cheap settlement, eliminating the possibility of receiving certificates with most brokers, although some do offer this service (for an additional charge).

■ The simplicity and speed of trading may lead investors to trade too frequently or to make reckless trades – many day traders lose a fortune in transaction costs.

■ Watch out for silly mistakes resulting in purchase of the wrong number of shares by punching on the wrong key.

Direct market access

Direct market access (DMA) systems allow private investors to trade directly in the stock market, placing buy and sell orders into the LSE's electronic order books alongside the professionals. To do this you need to download the necessary software from a DMA provider – a service offered by some stockbrokers. Despite the direct link into the market you will still be trading via a broker when using DMA.

To use DMA you will subscribe for a Level 2 package (see earlier) so that you can see the buy and sell orders placed by other investors, and then be able to watch your order flash up on the SETS or SETSqx screen.

With ordinary online dealing your broker's system seeks out the best price from several RSPs. However, this may not be the best price possible – there are several advantages in inputting your own buy and sell prices:

■ **Better prices and a greater chance of execution**. Say you want to sell shares in a company and observe a quoted spread of 200p–202p (the lowest price sellers are willing to accept is 202p and the highest price a buyer is willing to pay is 200p). A non-DMA trader could expect to get 200p, but a DMA trader might place a limit order of say 201.5p to entice a deal. Being able to see everyone else's buy and sell orders including the amounts on offer allows you to get a feel of the balance of supply and demand, which helps in selecting where to pitch your price.

■ **Speed**. Your order goes into the system in a fraction of a second after you press your keyboard button and may be completed immediately. Also you can trade on breaking news. For example, other traders may have left sell orders on the SETS system. When positive news is announced for a company (e.g. a big contract win) these other investors may be slow in changing their prices. If you have DMA and spot the news early enough you might bag a bargain.

■ **Testing and adjusting prices**. You will be able to see where your order lies on the LSE's order book and how close you are to getting it filled. This allows you to adjust the price if you wish to find a counterparty and trade immediately.

The cost of a DMA service varies tremendously. Furthermore the sector is evolving, as brokers supplying the software and access arrangements compete vigorously with each other. For infrequent traders the software and Level 2 data can cost hundreds of pounds per year, but if you trade, say, 15 times or more in a month these costs might be waived. Much depends on the special offers available at brokers. DMA is really only suitable for frequent traders (at least five times per week) who have the time to watch markets for hours on end.

Another problem with DMA is the danger of hitting the wrong button – **'fat-finger trades'**. Investors have been known to buy instead of sell (or vice versa); or to trade 10 times the amount they meant to; or to accidentally put in a silly price, e.g. selling a share at a fraction of its true value.

DMA traders can also become frustrated if they lose access to the markets at a vital moment. A lost Internet connection or software failure could result in serious loss. Ask your broker if they can accept telephone orders if the DMA system fails.

Not everyone is able to obtain DMA because brokers vet clients to ensure they have sufficient knowledge to trade in this way.

Transferring shares without brokers

It is possible to complete an **off-market transfer** without the use of a broker if the transfer is between people you know, such as friends or spouses. You need to complete a **stock transfer form**, which is available free from the company registrar, or from brokers, banks or on the Internet[11] (legal stationers will charge you for the form). The transfer form on the back of share certificates is for use when you are trading in the stock market, so is not suitable for DIY share selling or gifting. You need to have a share certificate to complete a transaction without a broker. If the shares are held in a broker's CREST nominee account the broker will charge for the transfer. Stamp duty does not apply to transfers between spouses or gift transfers. For other Main Market company transfers the completed form is sent to the Her Majesty's Revenue and Customs Stamp Office with a cheque for stamp duty of 0.5 per cent. The stamp office will return the form (after stamping it) for you to send to the registrar of the company who will issue a new certificate.

---

[11] Make sure you download the UK version.

Useful websites

www.advfn.com	ADVFN
www.fca.org.uk	Financial Conduct Authority
www.londonstockexchange.com	London Stock Exchange
www.euroclear.com	CREST
www.thewma.co.uk	Wealth Management Association

The investment spectrum

5

Pooled investments

Instead of buying shares individually, investors can pool their money and buy shares (and other assets) collectively. There are some significant advantages of **pooled** (**collective**) investment. First, a more diversified portfolio can be created. Investors with a relatively small sum to invest, say £3,000, would find it difficult to obtain a broad spread of investments without incurring high transaction costs. If, however, 10,000 people each put £3,000 into a fund there would be £30 million available to invest in a wide range of securities. A large fund like this can buy in large quantities, say £100,000 at a time, reducing dealing and administrative costs per pound invested. Thus risk is reduced by diversification and costs are reduced by economies of scale in share dealing and administration (e.g. time spent managing the portfolio).

Second, even very small investors can take part in the stock market. If you have only £50 a month to invest it is possible to gain exposure to the equity market by investing through pooled funds. Unit trusts, for example, are often willing to sign you up for a drip feed approach to investing in the markets.

Third, you can take advantage of professional management. You can avoid the demanding tasks of analysing and selecting shares, bonds, etc., going into the market place to buy, collecting dividends and so on by handing the whole process over to professional fund managers. Finally, you can enter exotic markets that would otherwise be beyond your reach. Perhaps you wish to invest in South American companies, US hi-tech or some other category of far-flung financial securities, but consider the risk and the complexities of buying shares direct too great. Collective funds run by managers familiar with the relevant country or sector can be a good alternative to going it alone.

These advantages are considerable but they can often be outweighed by the disadvantages of pooled funds, including high costs of fund management and underperformance compared with the market index. You will also lose any rights that accompany direct share investment, including the right to attend the company's AGM or receive shareholder perks. And you lose the fun of selecting your own shares with its emotional highs and lows, triumphs and lessons in humility.

Unit trusts

With unit trusts the securities purchased by the investor are called *'units'*. The value of these units is determined by the market valuation of the securities owned by the fund. So, if, for example, the fund collected together £1 million from hundreds of small investors and issued 1 million units in return, each unit would be worth £1. If the fund managers over the next year invest the pooled fund in shares which rise in value to £1.5 million the value of each unit rises to £1.50.

Unit trusts are **'open-ended'** funds, which means that the size of the fund and the number of units depend on the amount investors wish to put into the fund. If a fund of 1 million units suddenly doubled in size because of an inflow of investor funds (not because the underlying investments rise in value), it would become a fund of 2 million units through the creation and sale of more units.

If the example trust with 1 million units attracts a lot of interest because of its great first year performance (say the underlying shares have risen 50 per cent) it might then sell an additional million units at £1.50 each to become a fund with total assets of £3 million.

Unit holders sell units back to the managers of the unit trust if they want to liquidate their holding (turn it into cash). The manager would then either sell the units to other investors or, if that is not possible because of low demand, sell some of the underlying investments to raise cash to redeem the units. Thus the number of units can change daily, or at least every few days.

Pricing

The pricing of unit trusts is not quite as simple as described above. In fact, the units generally have two prices. The total value of the investments underlying the fund is usually calculated once a day using a method prescribed by the Financial Conduct Authority (FCA). From this value the price a new investor has to pay to buy – the **offer price** – is calculated. The offer price is the price the trust would have to pay to purchase the investments currently held plus dealing costs, administration expenses and other charges. The total sum is divided by the number of units in issue.

The **bid price** (the price you can get if you want to sell) is usually set at 3–6 per cent below the offer price (for funds invested in shares). The **spread** between the bid and offer prices pays for two things. Firstly, fund administration, management, and marketing. Secondly, the market makers' spreads, stamp duty and brokers' commissions payable by the fund when it buys and sells shares (bonds, etc.).[1]

Most unit trusts are priced on a **forward basis**, which means that the price paid by a buyer of units will be fixed at a particular time of the day (often 12.00 noon) that is yet to come – so when you make out an order to buy you do not know what price you will pay, which is determined by what happens to the prices of the securities in the fund between now and the fixing price. Some funds still charge the *historic* price, taking the value from the last valuation.[2]

When judging the performance of a unit trust you must bear in mind the influence of the spread. For example, if the quoted prices for a unit move up from 200p–210p to 250p–262.5p the return (the difference between buying and selling price) is 250p–210p, which is merely 19 per cent, not 25 per cent. Clearly the bid–offer spread means that your fund has to work hard to produce good returns in the short term. One way of looking at this is: if you sign a cheque for £10,000 and the spread is 5 per cent, only £9,500 is left in the fund for you to draw out after one day.

Until 2013 quite a high proportion of the initial charge in the bid–offer spread (maybe 4–5 per cent) could be commission payable to financial advisers selling the units to investors. Usually the financial adviser (or discount broker or fund supermarket/platform) waived most of this commission because they wanted to encourage purchase through them. They benefitted from the 0.5–0.75 per cent annual commission of the value of your unit holding (called **'trail commission'**). This has now changed – see later in this chapter.

Who looks after the unit holders' interests?

There are four levels of protection for the unit holder:

1 *The trustee and auditor.* The trustee, usually a bank or insurance company, keeps an eye on the fund manager(s) to make sure they abide by the terms

---

[1] Unit trusts have been given the option of single pricing, with charges shown separately. Most still have a bid–offer spread.

[2] Some use a mix of historic and forward pricing.

of the **trust deed** – for example, sticking to the stated investment objectives (e.g. investing in Japanese equities). Importantly, the trustee holds all the assets of the fund in their name on the unit holder's behalf, so if anything untoward happens to the fund manager the funds are safeguarded. The trustee also oversees the unit price calculation and ensures the Financial Conduct Authority regulations are observed. The auditor checks that the accounts have been drawn up properly.

2 *The Financial Conduct Authority.* The FCA authorises both the manager and the trustee to hold those roles. Only funds authorised by the FCA are allowed to advertise in the UK – these are **AUTs, Authorised Unit Trusts.** Unauthorised unit trusts, most of which are established offshore (outside the jurisdiction of the FCA) are available, but you should be aware that they carry more risk by virtue of their unregulated status.

3 *The Ombudsman.* Complaints that have not been satisfactorily settled by the management company can be referred to the Financial Ombudsman Service – see Chapter 19 – which can force compensation.

4 *The Financial Services Compensation Scheme.* Up to £50,000 is available for a valid claim – for example, when an FCA *authorised* fund becomes insolvent or suffers from poor investment management – see Chapter 19.

Charging

There are many charges:

- *Initial charge* (**'sales'** or **'front-end' charge**). This is included in the spread between the bid and offer prices. So if the fund has a spread of 6 per cent it might allocate 5 per cent as an initial charge. Some unit trusts have dropped initial charges to zero – particularly those investing in interest-bearing securities (bonds, etc.) and tracker funds (see later).

- *The Annual Management Charge, AMC.* Until 2014 this was typically 1.00–1.80 per cent (for actively managed funds rather than trackers), but now that the adviser's/platform fees have been separated a typical actively managed fund charges between 0.65 per cent and 1 per cent. But the platform may charge up to 0.45 per cent on top to hold your investments – see later. If an independent financial adviser is organising the purchase for you, rather than a platform, you might have to pay a few hundred pounds in advice fees upfront. The AMC is deducted from the fund on a daily basis, so you may not notice it being taken as the fund's price is subtly adjusted downwards. Over time the annual fees have a larger effect in reducing the value of your investment than the initial charge.

■ *Ongoing charges*. Further costs on top of the AMC are taken from the fund annually. When these are added to the AMC we arrive at the ongoing charges. The additional items include: fees to the trustee, custodians (who hold the underlying securities), investment adviser (fund managers often get unit holders to pay for research on top of the AMC. Yes, 'experts' hiring others to analyse, but not paying for it out of their pocket!), fund valuers, marketers, accountants and auditors, regulators, insurers, lawyers, professional advisers and VAT on these charges. A charge of about 0.15–0.5 per cent per year generally covers these legal, audit and other administration costs. This is also deducted automatically by the fund manager on a daily basis. It was not until 2012 that fund managers, regulators and commentators started the switch to the term 'ongoing charge' which was previously called the **'Total Expense Ratio', TER.** Ongoing charges/total expense ratios can be obtained from www.funds.ft.com and www.bestinvest.co.uk.

■ *Various other deductions not included in the published ongoing charges*: e.g. transaction costs associated with buying and selling securities such as brokers fees, bid/offer spreads on shares or bonds and transaction taxes such as stamp duty (0.5 per cent) in the UK. Don't forget that you would incur these costs anyway if you were buying the shares directly – and without the economies of scale of the fund. However, a fund with a high turnover in its portfolio (selling shares and replacing them with others) can pay out over 1 per cent per annum in additional costs – a more typical figure is less than this for active funds (probably around 0.4 per cent) and can be as low as 0.1 per cent for trackers. Many commentators think that high-turnover funds are poor value – see Article 5.1. Some investment managers spread trading costs across all investors. However, many recognise that many of the transactions are forced on the fund because investors are coming into or leaving it. Where this happens, the transaction costs may be charged to those investors. Another cost might be **performance fees** if the manager does well relative to the market segment (around 5 per cent have performance fees). It may seem odd when your fund is down 10 per cent that a performance fee is paid, but this can happen if the market index is say down 15 per cent in the same period.

■ *Exit charges*. Some funds make an exit charge instead of an initial charge if you cash in within, say, the first five years.

Article 5.1

The hidden costs of portfolio turnover

By Alice Ross

Investors should be wary of fund managers who turn over their portfolios too much, advisers warn – as they can incur large additional costs that are not stated in their annual management charges.

Fund managers who buy and sell shares too often can rack up extra costs for investors in the shape of stamp duty, commission to stockbrokers and the difference between the buying and selling price for shares – the "bid/offer" spread. Some funds have an annual turnover rate of more than 500 per cent.

"When someone turns over a portfolio more than 100 per cent in a year, you could legitimately ask: what are you doing?" says Robert Reid, an adviser at Syndaxi. "I think the method of getting information to the average individual is so poor that they're making their decisions on advertisements as opposed to reality."

Alan Miller, founder of SCM Private, points out that the average UK All Companies fund has an annual turnover rate of 89 per cent. Each trade, he calculates, costs 1.04 per cent – comprising 0.5 per cent stamp duty, 0.3 per cent commission paid to stockbrokers (0.15 per cent on both purchase and sale) and 0.24 per cent (0.12 per cent each year) on the bid-offer spread. This adds 0.9 per cent to the stated average total expense ratio (TER) of about 1.6 per cent.

However, none of these costs appears in a fund's TER. Investors can check a fund's annual statement for details of extra costs incurred in dealing, such as 0.5 per cent stamp duty and commission to stockbrokers – but bid/offer spread costs are not included at all.

"If the end investor knew how much his turnover was costing him, he'd have a fair picture of how much his fund cost and he'd probably make a different decision," says Miller.

Finding this out will be even harder when new rules known as Ucits IV will waive the requirement for an annual statement to include portfolio turnover figures.

Miller argues that funds with lower turnover actually perform better. The 20 funds with the highest turnover last year in the IMA's All Companies sector returned just 4.7 per cent to investors in the three years to the end of February. The 20 funds with the lowest turnover had an average performance of 16.8 per cent over the same period.

But how often fund managers buy and sell shares in a mutual fund is only part of the problem. Investors can also incur dealing costs in their own portfolios by ditching poor performers too readily.

Nick Blake, head of sales at Vanguard, the low-cost fund manager, says that part of the blame for this falls on financial advisers, who prefer to be seen taking action rather than doing nothing.

The True and Fair Campaign (www.trueandfaircampaign.com) argues that British investors have been misled by the fund industry with hidden charges and lack of clarity, and call for transparency on where investors' money is invested, the underlying costs of

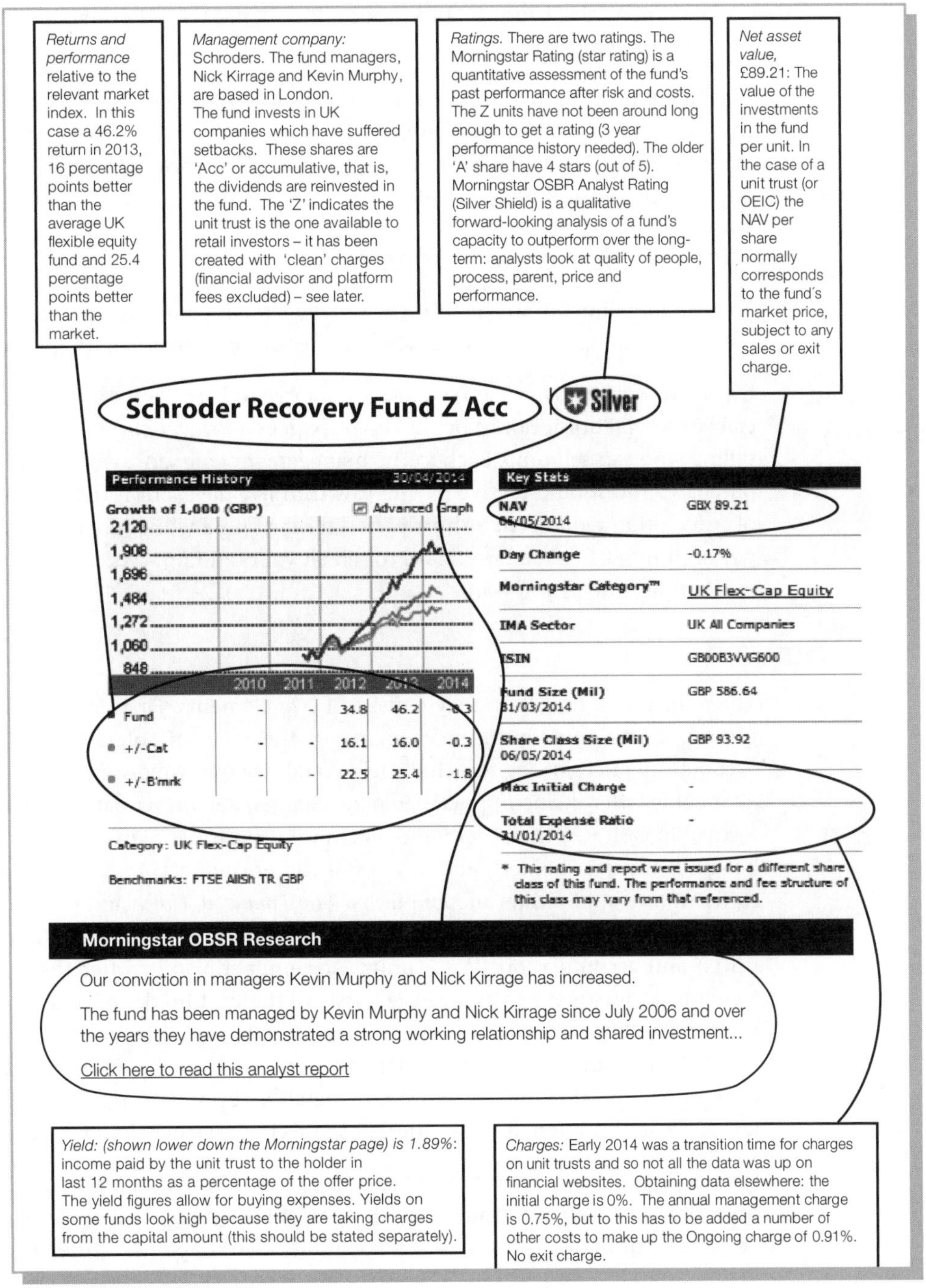

Returns and performance relative to the relevant market index. In this case a 46.2% return in 2013, 16 percentage points better than the average UK flexible equity fund and 25.4 percentage points better than the market.

Management company: Schroders. The fund managers, Nick Kirrage and Kevin Murphy, are based in London. The fund invests in UK companies which have suffered setbacks. These shares are 'Acc' or accumulative, that is, the dividends are reinvested in the fund. The 'Z' indicates the unit trust is the one available to retail investors – it has been created with 'clean' charges (financial advisor and platform fees excluded) – see later.

Ratings. There are two ratings. The Morningstar Rating (star rating) is a quantitative assessment of the fund's past performance after risk and costs. The Z units have not been around long enough to get a rating (3 year performance history needed). The older 'A' share have 4 stars (out of 5). Morningstar OSBR Analyst Rating (Silver Shield) is a qualitative forward-looking analysis of a fund's capacity to outperform over the long-term: analysts look at quality of people, process, parent, price and performance.

Net asset value, £89.21: The value of the investments in the fund per unit. In the case of a unit trust (or OEIC) the NAV per share normally corresponds to the fund's market price, subject to any sales or exit charge.

Schroder Recovery Fund Z Acc   **✪ Silver**

Performance History   30/04/2014

Growth of 1,000 (GBP)   ☑ Advanced Graph

	2010	2011	2012	2013	2014
Fund	-	-	34.8	46.2	-6.3
+/-Cat	-	-	16.1	16.0	-0.3
+/-B'mrk	-	-	22.5	25.4	-1.8

Category: UK Flex-Cap Equity

Benchmarks: FTSE AllSh TR GBP

Key Stats

NAV 06/05/2014	GBX 89.21
Day Change	-0.17%
Morningstar Category™	UK Flex-Cap Equity
IMA Sector	UK All Companies
ISIN	GB00B3VVG600
Fund Size (Mil) 31/03/2014	GBP 586.64
Share Class Size (Mil) 06/05/2014	GBP 93.92
Max Initial Charge	-
Total Expense Ratio 31/01/2014	-

* This rating and report were issued for a different share class of this fund. The performance and fee structure of this class may vary from that referenced.

Morningstar OBSR Research

Our conviction in managers Kevin Murphy and Nick Kirrage has increased.

The fund has been managed by Kevin Murphy and Nick Kirrage since July 2006 and over the years they have demonstrated a strong working relationship and shared investment...

Click here to read this analyst report

Yield: (shown lower down the Morningstar page) is 1.89%: income paid by the unit trust to the holder in last 12 months as a percentage of the offer price. The yield figures allow for buying expenses. Yields on some funds look high because they are taking charges from the capital amount (this should be stated separately).

Charges: Early 2014 was a transition time for charges on unit trusts and so not all the data was up on financial websites. Obtaining data elsewhere: the initial charge is 0%. The annual management charge is 0.75%, but to this has to be added a number of other costs to make up the Ongoing charge of 0.91%. No exit charge.

Figure 5.1   **Details for a unit trust displayed on Morningstar's website**

Source: www.morningstar.co.uk

investment and product information that is presented consistently and understandably.

The *Financial Times* publishes unit trust bid and offer prices every day; some in the newspaper but a more complete list is on the website, www.ft.com. Many other websites show unit trust prices. An example is shown in Figure 5.1, reproduced from Morningstar's website.

How do you buy or sell units?

You can buy direct from the unit trust management company. Alternatively, you could buy through a financial adviser, broker or fund supermarket (platform).

If you are worried by prices being set on a forward basis, you can tell your financial adviser/platform not to buy if the price goes above a *limit*. When it comes to selling, you can sell units back to the management company, which is obliged to purchase. You should receive payment within five days, but if the fund has a lot of redemption requests in a short period it may take a while to sell securities and pay off unit sellers. You don't have to sell all your holding – you can dispose of as much or as little as you want.

Returns

The return on a unit trust may consist of two elements. First, income is usually gained on the underlying investments in the form of interest or dividends. Second, the prices of the securities held could rise over time. Some units pay out all income, after deducting management charges, etc. on set dates (usually twice a year)[3] in cash. On the other hand, **accumulation units** reinvest the income on behalf of the unit holders, and as a result the price of accumulation units tends to rise more rapidly than income units. The *Financial Times* and other financial websites show listings for prices of **income** ('Inc') units (also called **distribution units**) and accumulation ('Acc') units. Accumulation units offer the benefit of avoiding reinvestment costs and the hassle to the unit holder of purchasing new units. As well as a trust issuing accumulation units and distribution units it may issue different units to institutional investors (with much lower management charges because they buy in bulk) than retail investors. Confusingly, these different classes are referred to as different share classes rather than unit classes.

Dividends paid by unit trusts and OEICs are treated in the same way as dividends from ordinary company shares in UK companies for tax, that is 10 per cent is deducted, but higher rate tax payers pay more – see chapter 17.[4] Interest distribu-

---

[3] Some trusts pay out quarterly or monthly.
[4] No UK tax on dividends from investments in foreign securities.

tions paid by UK unit trusts and OEICs are treated in exactly the same way as interest on bank, building society and local authority savings – see Chapter 17. With accumulation units the income is reinvested net of basic rate tax on the dividends received from the companies, e.g. 10 per cent of the gross dividend is deducted. However higher rate tax payers have to declare the increase in accumulation units due to dividends and interest received, even though not sent to them, and pay extra tax – see Chapter 17. But these payments on annual income are deductible from any capital gains tax calculation after selling your units.

Types of trust available

There are around 180 fund management groups offering over 2,000 unit trusts or their cousins, the OEICs (see below). UK All Companies funds invest at least 80 per cent of their assets in UK shares. To this classic type of unit trust have been added a very wide range of trusts with amazingly diverse objectives. Some funds focus investment in shares paying high dividends (e.g. UK Equity Income), others split the funds between equity and bonds (e.g. UK Equity and Bond Income), while some invest mostly in gilts or corporate bonds. Some place most of their money in smaller companies, some in Far East shares. A few trusts invest in property. The possibilities are endless – see www.investinginfunds.org for a definition of dozens of classes of funds. The main categories are:

■ **Income funds**. Aim to produce a regular income from the underlying investments, which may be paid out to the investor or invested back into the fund.

■ **Growth funds**. Aim to grow the capital over the long term, thus many investments may have low or no current dividends but have high capital gain potential. The funds that produce income as part of their total return usually reinvest it back into the fund.

■ **Specialist funds**. Includes property funds and funds with a specialised and narrow investment focus, such as technology or gold. The specialist **absolute return** funds rather than trying to beat a benchmark index such as an index of European shares aim to obtain a positive return even when particular share and/or bond markets are going down by switching to those sectors thought likely to rise. Thus the manager has to be free to transfer money from one set of equity/bond markets to others quickly.

■ **Capital protection funds**. Funds that aim to protect your capital. There is some potential for investment return, but the main emphasis is on safety. Underlying assets might be short-term lending to highly reputable governments and companies.

Schroder Recovery Fund

an Authorised Unit Trust of Schroder Unit Trusts Limited
Class Z Accumulation (GB00B3VVG600)

This fund is managed by Schroder Unit Trusts Limited, which is a member of the Schroders Group.

Objectives and Investment Policy

Objectives

The fund aims to provide capital growth.

Investment Policy

At least 80% of the fund will be invested in shares of UK companies. The fund has no bias to any particular industry or size of company.

The fund invests in companies that have suffered a major profit or share price setback, but which appear to have good long-term prospects and the potential for significant share price gains. These could simply be companies whose share prices appear low relative to their long-term profit potential, or firms that are currently underperforming in profit terms, but have a clear and credible route for turning this around.

The fund may also invest in other financial instruments and hold cash on deposit. Derivatives may be used to achieve the investment objective and to reduce risk or manage the fund more efficiently.

Benchmark

The fund is not managed with reference to a financial index.

Dealing Frequency

You may redeem your investment upon demand. This fund deals daily.

Distribution Policy

This unit class accumulates income received from the fund's investments, meaning it is kept in the fund and its value is reflected in the price of the unit class.

Risk and Reward Profile

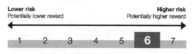

Lower risk — Potentially lower reward   Higher risk — Potentially higher reward

1   2   3   4   5   **6**   7

The risk and reward indicator

The risk category was calculated using historical performance data and may not be a reliable indicator of the fund's future risk profile.

The fund's risk category is not guaranteed to remain fixed and may change over time.

A fund in the lowest category does not mean a risk-free investment.

The fund is in this category because it can take higher risks in search of higher rewards and its price may rise and fall accordingly.

Other particular risks

Liquidity risk / small cap liquidity risk: Investments in small companies can be difficult to sell quickly which may affect the value of the fund and, in extreme market conditions, its ability to meet redemption requests upon demand.

Operational risk / third parties: The fund's operations depend on third parties and it may suffer disruption or loss in the event of their failure.

Charges

One-off charges taken before or after you invest	
Entry charge	None
Exit charge	None

This is the maximum that might be taken out of your money before it is invested.

Charges taken from the fund over a year	
Ongoing Charge	0.91%
Charges taken from the fund under certain specific conditions	
Performance fee	None

The charges you pay are used to pay the costs of running the fund, including the costs of marketing and distributing it. These charges reduce the potential growth of your investment.

The entry and exit charges shown are maximum figures and in some cases you might pay less. You can find out the actual entry and exit charges from your financial advisor.

The ongoing charges figure is based on the last year's expenses for the year ending December 2012 and may vary from year to year.

Please see the prospectus for more details about the charges.

Past Performance

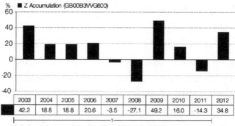

	2003	2004	2005	2006	2007	2008	2009	2010	2011	2012
	42.2	18.8	18.8	20.6	-3.5	-27.1	49.2	16.0	-14.3	34.8

1 Performance shown during this period predates the launch of this share class and has been simulated using the history of a similar share class within the fund.

Past performance is not a guide to future performance and may not be repeated. The value of investments may go down as well as up and you may not get back the amount you originally invested.

The chart shows performance in British pound after the ongoing charges and the portfolio transaction costs have been paid. Entry and exit charges are excluded from calculations of past performance.

The fund was launched on 5 May 1970.

Figure 5.2   Schroder's UK Recovery Fund KIID, Class 'Z' Accumulation units

Source: Schroders plc

Minimum investment

Some trusts ask for an initial minimum investment of only £250 or so, whereas others insist on at least £1,500. Thereafter you are often entitled, under a **savings plan**, to put in as little as £50. It is often possible to use shares instead of cash as payment for units through a share exchange scheme.

Key Investor Information Document (KIID)

The KIID, produced by the fund, provides the most important facts in a standardised, jargon-free way, allowing comparison between funds helping you to assess if a fund will meet your needs at a reasonable cost. It covers:

■ Fund objective and investment policy (e.g. shares/bonds, geographical focus, business sector, say green energy firms only).

■ Risk and reward. An estimate of the likelihood of the fund losing money on a scale of 1 to 7. Of course, risk and return are usually inversely related.

■ Charges.

■ Past performance over a number of years and degree of volatility.

■ Other elements, e.g. how to obtain the prospectus, annual and half-yearly reports.

■ Name of trustee.

Figure 5.2 shows the main elements of the KIID for Schroder's UK Recovery fund.

Following your units' progress

A **manager's report** will be sent to you every six months detailing the performance of the fund over the half year and the events in the market(s) in which the fund invests, and explaining the manager's investment strategy. It will also comment on future prospects, list the securities held by the fund and display the fund's financial accounts.

At least once a year you will receive a *statement* showing the number of units you hold and latest prices. The statement will also give a run-down of any additional investment, reinvestment or encashments you have made since the last statement.

Between receiving reports and statements you can contact the management company over the telephone. They *may* be prepared to discuss the investment performance of the fund and current outlook. They will certainly be willing to deal with general administration queries and, of course, give information on other products they might sell you.

One place to track your units is in newspapers such as the *Financial Times. Money Management* magazine tracks fund performance over periods of one, two, three and five years. Many websites, such as fund supermarket websites (see later), carry details of units. You could visit the fund manager's website, or go to a general site such as:

www.citywire.co.uk	Citywire
http://funds.ft.com/uk	Financial Times
www.iii.co.uk	Interactive Investor
www.investinginfunds.org	Investment Management Association
www.lipperweb.com	Lipper (Reuters)
www.morningstar.co.uk	Morningstar UK
www.standardandpoors.com	Standard & Poor's funds
www.moneyextra.com	Moneyextra
www.trustnet.com	Trustnet

Switching funds

Many fund management companies allow you to switch from one trust within its stable to another for a charge much lower than the usual initial charge. So, if you think US hi-tech has reached its peak you might ask the manager to transfer your holding to, say, a UK smaller company fund.

Active versus passive?

It costs more to run a fund in which the manager is spending time and effort carefully selecting shares (an **'actively managed'** fund) than one where the manager simply buys and holds a broad range of shares matching a market index (e.g. FTSE 100), called a **tracker** (or **passive** or **indexed**) fund. Study after study concludes actively managed funds fail to outperform the market (on average). Some active managers will outperform, but how much of that is due to random chance and how much is due to superior ability is very much moot. After all, put 100 idiots at a roulette wheel and some will walk home wealthy; evidence of fat wallets (or their backers' wallets) does not make them smart. The fund management industry is not populated by idiots. There are some very smart fund managers, using sound investment principles. And, over many years it is possible to observe some extraordinary returns. However, it is difficult to identify real investing skill before the event and many out-performers over three or four year spans are simply lucky.

Trackers will also underperform the benchmark index, but at least the ongoing costs of the fund are significantly less than most actively managed funds. Typically trackers' ongoing costs are between 0.2 per cent and 1 per cent, while actively managed funds are around 1.5 – 1.8 per cent if you include the adviser's/platform's charge for holding your investments. You need to be convinced of superior security picking skills of your chosen manager to sacrifice, say 1.8 per cent, of your annual return. This small sounding sum could amount to 25 per cent or more of your fund over a decade or so.

If you invested £20,000 in a fund with no charges, and it grew by 6 per cent annually for 20 years, you would get £64,143 – just over £44,000 growth. If you invested in an active fund with the industry average ongoing charge of 1.67 per cent, your fund would be reduced to £46,689 – meaning £17,454 of your growth goes on charges. If the TER was 2.5 per cent, about £24,000 would be paid out in charges. That is not even factoring other costs, such as transaction costs of security dealing.

John Authers, a commentator on investment matters at the *Financial Times*, leaves us in no doubt concerning his view that active funds are generally too costly for the service they provide – see Article 5.2. Bear in mind that the high charges are often levied to cover the fiddly business of dealing with investors putting in only a few thousand pounds. Larger investors (e.g. pension funds buying unit trusts) benefit from much lower charges. In another article he points out that charges for investors in US funds have fallen under the pressure of investors' insistence, in the light of the evidence of low costs being vital to overall returns, to an average of 0.64 per cent for equity funds (compared with 0.93 per cent a decade ago). American investors seek out cheap funds more than Europeans. Consider this though: there is a major problem with too much passive investing; without a large body of investors/managers actively looking for underpriced securities the market would drift to inefficient prices, so there is a limit to the proportion of shareholdings that should be held passively without thought to the value of the underlying shares.

Article 5.2

Beware the costs of actively managed funds

By John Authers

Why defend the indefensible? Traditional actively managed mutual funds [e.g. unit trusts] are obsolete. They have nothing left to recommend them. And yet attempts to point out the blatant superiority of newer passive investment products provoke furious defences from brokers.

Their arguments are so threadbare that they can only be motivated by a desire to keep the commissions coming. But they are a formidable obstacle to needed change.

Let us be clear about the model that must be replaced; managers try to beat market

Article 5.2   Continued

indices with a portfolio of about 100 stocks. Such diversification makes it hard to beat the market. But the risk of being caught in a crash is undimmed. And while many managers are smart enough to beat the market, they cannot do so and still pay themselves decently.

A recent survey by the London investment consultancy Style Research of how 425 global equity funds benchmarked against the MSCI World index performed last year makes this clear. Measuring the performance of the funds' holdings, without including costs, 59 per cent of them beat the index. Once costs to investors were included, only 31 per cent beat the index. So 28 per cent of the funds had index-beating managers who charged too much in fees to allow their clients to beat the index.

Looking at European equity mutual funds, Karl-Heinz Thielmann of Long-Term Investing Research in Karlsruhe found their total average costs (including bid-offer spread, market impact [buy/sell orders move share prices on the market adversely for the trader], and costs caused by managing in- and outflows of money from clients) were about 4 percentage points (3 percentage points in the US). Their outperformance, before costs, was about 2 percentage points.

How, then, to reduce costs? The best answer yet devised is to offer index funds, which merely replicate the index. This can be done cheaply with computers. But index funds tend not to pay much commission. This spurs brokers' ire.

First, they argue that active managers can take evasive action in a market dive, while index funds blindly fall with the market. This is specious on several levels. Active managers underperform consistently, throughout bull and bear markets. Over the past five years, according to Morningstar, 61 per cent of balanced funds and 67 per cent of US equity funds failed to match their index.

Moreover, they are paid to pick stocks, not to time the market. It is not an equity fund manager's job to make a big switch into bonds or cash. And the argument for index funds is not that they are lower risk, but that due to their lower costs their returns for any level of risk are likely to be higher than for equivalent active funds.

A second argument is that index funds are guaranteed to lose to the index, thanks to their costs. This is true, but specious. The odds are that they will perform better than an active fund. And they enjoy economies of scale. For example, the SPDR, which tracks the S&P 500, had a 2012 return just 0.01 percentage point less than that of the S&P, according to Bloomberg.

A third argument is that choosing index funds entails ignoring active managers who consistently outperform. But this small band of managers may be exactly the ones to avoid. History shows that persistent outperformance attracts inflows, which increases costs for the fund, and makes it harder to outperform. Eventually performance comes crashing back to earth.

Indexing's critics have one decent argument. Index funds are dumb. They buy at whatever valuation the market offers. If everyone invested through index funds, markets would cease to function; nobody would be seeking out inefficiencies.

How to deal with this? One way is to find low-cost ways to manage funds without accepting market valuations. For example, funds can buy only stocks that appear cheap by a specific metric. Another option is to abandon diversification and really try to beat the market. This is risky. But according to Morningstar, most sector fund managers, investing only in a small universe of stocks, do beat their benchmarks. When combined with index funds inside pension funds, such funds make great sense.

The industry has far to go before future retirees get the deal they deserve. But its current *modus operandi* burdens investors with too many costs. This must change. When brokers brandish the rosy five-year returns of active mutual funds, they will be defending the indefensible.

While many active managers pretend to be actively sifting companies to select only the most underpriced, in reality they create portfolios that are very similar to a broad cross section of the market – **'index huggers'** or **'closet trackers'** or **'closet indexers'** – see Article 5.3 – and yet they charge the high fees of proper active managers.

Pull closet indexing out of the closet

By John Authers

In the UK, people are trying to pull closet indexing out of the closet. It is a fight that could have global implications.

This is one issue on which there is no need to sit on the fence. The debate between active managers, who try to beat their benchmark, and passive managers, who merely track it, will go on and on. But everyone can agree that there is no case for closet indexing – the practice of running an "active" fund, charging active management fees but, in practice, offering an investment that merely hugs the index.

This is, in effect, a tax on millions of investors, for no economic benefit and helps pump up asset bubbles. It impedes capitalism and the efficient allocation of capital.

A report published last month by SCM Private, a London-based investment adviser, described closet indexation as "a UK epidemic". After analysing £120bn in UK funds, it alleged that investors could have saved £1.86bn in fees if they had switched from underperforming UK equity funds to alternative cheaper index funds.

SCM Private emotively accused the UK fund industry of "systematic abuse of the public" and alleged that it had failed to behave with integrity. This is strong language, so let us look at the charges in detail.

Closet indexing has been well explored in academia. It is measured by "active share", a concept invented by the Yale academics Antti Petajisto and Martijn Cremers. For US funds

benchmarked to the S&P 500, it measures the fraction of a fund's holdings that differ from the S&P. For example, if a fund's holdings are identical to the index, except that it holds no shares in Apple (worth 5 per cent of the index) and has invested that money elsewhere, it will have an active share of 5 per cent.

A passive index tracker has no active share. A fund that invests only in obscure stocks not in the benchmark has an active share of 100 per cent. Once active share drops below 60 per cent, the academics said, a fund is a possible "closet indexer".

SCM Private found that only 24 per cent of 127 UK funds benchmarked to the FTSE-All Share index had an active share above 70 per cent. This compares with 65 per cent of a sample of US funds that had an active share this high.

Overall, the UK funds had an active share of 60 per cent, compared with 75 per cent in the US.

The chances are tiny that a few tweaks to the index would do well enough to overcome the extra fees that active managers charge, which are on average three times the fees charged by trackers. And indeed 88 per cent of funds with an active share under 50 per cent did not match their index.

Why does this happen? The problem derives from the incentives for fund managers who are paid not to beat the market but to accumulate assets. This is because they charge a percentage fee on assets under management and are judged by comparison to their benchmark index and

Article 5.3   Continued

to their peers. To hold on to assets, therefore, it is vital not to underperform their peers. Make a big contrarian bet and you may be separated from the herd. So everyone herds into the same stocks.

As passive investing through index trackers has taken hold, active managers have grown more conscious of their benchmark index. This is clear from the language they use. Two decades ago, a portfolio manager would say he "owned" a stock. Now he is more likely to say he is "overweight" it, always implicitly comparing with the index.

This phenomenon helps create investment bubbles, as overvaluations naturally occur when everyone invests in the same thing.

It also creates opportunities for those who have the courage to search for them. SCM Private found that 72 per cent of the UK funds with a high active share succeeded in beating their index. This is in line with international research. The Cremers and Petajisto research found that in the US, funds with the highest active share beat the index by more than 1 per cent per year, even after taking their fees into account.

The UK is not alone. Research led by Mr Cremers looked at 21,684 funds in 30 countries, managing some $10tn as of December 2007. Closet indexing was dominant in some countries, accounting for 40 per cent of equity funds in Canada, and 81 per cent in Poland.

It also found that countries with the most explicit indexing were also likely to have less closet indexing, while active funds there would charge lower fees. Passive trackers provided stiff discipline for the rest of the sector. It also found that most active funds fail to beat their benchmark – but that the more genuinely "active" a fund, the more likely it was to outperform.

Fixing the problem needs a radical overhaul of the way fund managers are paid. For now, funds must be forced to publish their active share. Before being flushed down the toilet, closet indexing must be pulled out of the closet.

Clean funds

Under the pre-2014 regime an annual fund management charge of say 1.5 per cent would typically be split three ways: a financial adviser generally received 0.5 per cent trail commission per year for selling the units to the investor and supposedly continuing to advise; a discount broker or platform (see later) would get say 0.25 per cent per year while the units (or OEICs) are held; leaving 0.75 per cent for the fund manager. In many situations the adviser was by-passed and the platform received 0.75 per cent each year. Often some of the adviser and/or platform commissions were reimbursed to the investor.

Nowadays the fees to the adviser and platform are removed from the AMC and are paid for separately and explicitly for the investor to see. This leaves the **'clean'** (**unbundled**) fund charge – in theory this should be 0.75 per cent (typically), but many fund managers in switching to clean funds are charging more.[5] On the other hand, some fund managers have been pressurised by the platforms to lower the AMC to around 0.6 per cent when sold through their platform, but they then charge the investor annual platform fees of 0.35 per cent or 0.45 per cent.[6]

Points to bear in mind when choosing a unit trust

■ Unit trusts should be viewed as medium- to long-term investments, given that the upfront charges are so high. It is no good flitting in and out.

■ Advertisements showing a fund manager's performance should be taken with a large pinch of salt. They will be very selective about the starting date (choosing a low point) in order to impress you. Furthermore, there is a mass of evidence to show that past performance is a very poor guide to how well a fund will perform in the future. It is very unusual for a fund to outperform consistently over the medium and longer term. Surprisingly often top performing funds over one- or five-year periods end up falling to the bottom of the league tables in the next period. Novice investors are often lured into buying recent top performers, only to find that the sector where the fund focuses turns out to be in a bubble, and future returns are disappointing. Even if you find a fund that has shown a sustained high performance you may then discover that what made the fund work well in one economic period serves less well in the next. Also, outperformance may be due to taking more risk.

■ A dilemma arises for investors when a fund manager leaves a management company. Should you stick with the trust or move with the manager? This is a serious issue given that less than two-thirds of managers have run their funds for as long as three years. Following a 'star' fund manager to a new company is not always possible, and besides the costs of doing so can be high. Some funds have one star player, while others have a talented team. Going for a team may leave you less vulnerable to the departure of particular

---

[5] Those currently paying trail commission on unit trust, with-profits policies or pension funds to financial advisers or an intermediary (e.g. discount brokers and platforms) for an investment product purchased before 31 December 2012 and who no longer need advice can get out of it by selling the investment and buying it back through a discount broker or platform that does not charge trail commission. An annual fee might be charged but this may be significantly less than trail commission. Watch out for exit fees though. Trail commission on these pre-2013 sales will end in April 2016 anyway.

[6] Some charge a flat fee rather than a percentage of your investments which can be better value.

managers. Citywire (www.citywire.co.uk) tracks the performances of individual fund managers rather than funds.

- It is possible for your money to be trapped within a unit trust. In 2008, when property prices were plunging and it became difficult to sell property, a number of property unit trusts announced that unit holders could not redeem units without giving months of notice for fear that the managers would become forced sellers of assets at distressed prices.

- Some funds can grow too big. For example a fund focused on small French companies that has €1 billion under management may not be able to limit itself to the true bargains, or even to small companies, given that the manager has to invest somewhere.

- Some funds can be too small. Many of the costs of running a fund are fixed such as the manager's research time, thus average costs per unit can rise if there is only a few million to invest. The fund management house may bear the extra costs for a time, but, if there is no improvement, eventually it will close.

- Few fund managers invest a substantial proportion of their own wealth in their funds – see Article 5.4.

Article 5.4

Impetus for managers to invest in own funds

By Ruth Sullivan

Fund managers who put their own money into the funds they run are less likely to take undue risks and expose investors to big losses. That is the theory anyway, and there is growing interest in the practice.

"Having skin in the game is gaining traction but is more prevalent in the US and the UK than in continental Europe," says Amin Rajan, chief executive of Create Research, a consultancy. However, the increase has been slow. According to a survey of global managers by Citi and Create Research, just 8 per cent put their bonuses into the funds they manage, while a further 13 per cent plan to in the next 12 months.

Some asset managers require their fund managers to defer as much as half of their bonus by investing it into their own funds over a three to four-year period, which can be "a big incentive for managers", says Pars Purewal, at PwC. This requirement is increasing in the UK because of the need to align interests between fund managers and clients and "prevent managers taking unnecessary risks", he adds.

Much depends on the culture of the asset manager. Some believe it is an essential part of the business ethos, making investors feel more confident.

Henderson Global Investors, a UK-based investment house, is one of these. "Most fund

Article 5.4   **Continued**

managers invest a meaningful amount in their funds [here]. It shows their interests are aligned with investors," says Jamie Legg, at Henderson.

"It is a genuine conviction in the stocks they run. Why wouldn't they?" says Mr Legg.

Vanguard Group, a US asset manager, takes it a step further and has "a client pledge to invest our own money alongside our investors", says Tom Rampulla of Vanguard Investments UK.

The asset manager requires all employees to invest in house funds and fund managers can invest in their own or other Vanguard funds.

Senior managers and executives have "most or all their personal financial assets in Vanguard funds", adds Mr Rampulla.

However, not all investment houses believe it is necessary for long-only managers to invest in their own funds. Most funds are designed to track and beat indices and most of the returns will be driven by what the benchmark does.

In the US, where disclosure of how much managers invest in their own funds has been obligatory since 2006, there is evidence of a growing trend to co-invest.

A couple of technical terms

- **Undertaking for Collective Investment in Transferable Securities (UCITS)** are open-ended funds regulated under European law and that can be marketed freely across EU member states.

- **Non-UCITS Retail Schemes (NURS)** are funds authorised to be sold to the public in the UK that are not governed by the European regulation of funds under the 'UCITS Directive', because they invest in assets (e.g. gold funds) that this Directive does not permit or comply with different concentration limits. They are required instead to meet standards set by the UK financial services regulator.

Open-ended investment companies (OEICs)

OEICs (pronounced 'oiks') have been around since the late 1990s, and many unit trusts have turned themselves into OEICs. OEICs are very similar to unit trusts, so much of what has already been said applies to them. A crucial difference is that an OEIC is a company that issues shares rather than a trust that issues units. One similarity is that it is 'open-ended' in that it can expand or contract the number of shares in issue in response to demand. Also OEICs are regulated by the FCA in a similar way to unit trusts, so investor protection is much the same. Investment in OEICs may also be made on a regular basis, say £50 per month, or as a lump sum.

An OEIC has an **Authorised Corporate Director** managing the fund. It also has a **Depositary** (usually a large bank) which, similar to the trustee for a unit trust, ensures safekeeping of the assets (custody), collecting of income, the delivery and receipt of underlying securities and the payment of tax. The oversight of the duty of care element is undertaken by the OEIC board of directors. The ACDs remit is to invest shareholder's funds in accordance with the OEIC's objectives under the oversight of the board of directors. Compared with unit trusts, OEICs have a simpler pricing system because there is one price for both buyers and sellers. Charges and dealing commissions are shown separately (which makes them more transparent than unit trusts). When OEICs are bought or sold the price is directly related to the value of the underlying assets and not based on the supply and demand for its shares (as with investment trusts – see later). The price is calculated daily, usually 12 noon in London. Some OEICs charge an exit fee.

The OEIC (and unit trust) may be a stand-alone fund or created under an **'umbrella' structure**, which means that there are a number of sub-funds each with a different investment objective (one sub-fund may focus on US shares, another on UK shares, etc.). Each sub-fund could have different investors and asset pools. The advantage to the investor of the umbrella structure is that reallocating money within one fund management group to different investment categories is made easier and cheaper.

When there are a large number of new purchasers (or sellers) of OEIC shares the fund may incur high costs to buy (sell) underlying securities, e.g. broker fees. This damages the interests of older holders of OEIC shares. To balance the interests of the old and new holders the new members may be charged a **dilution levy** (typically 0.5–2 per cent), the proceeds of which are held in the fund rather than being extracted by the manager. An alternative is to apply a **swinging single price** which adjusts the buy/sell price to include the transaction costs for the shareholder doing the transaction.

Exchange traded funds (ETFs)

Exchange traded funds (ETFs) take the idea of tracking a stock market index or sector a stage further. ETFs are set up as companies issuing shares. The money raised is used to buy a range of securities such as a collection of shares in a particular stock market index or sector, such as the FTSE 100 or pharmaceutical shares. They are open-ended funds – the ETF shares are created and cancelled as demand rises or falls. However, they differ from unit trusts and OEICs in that the pricing of ETF shares is left up to the market place. ETFs are quoted companies and you can buy and sell their shares at prices subject to change throughout the day (unlike unit trusts and OEICs, where prices are set by formula once a day).

Despite an ETF's price being set by trading in the stock market they tend to trade at, or near to, the underlying net asset value (NAV) – the value of the shares in the FTSE 100, for instance. This is different from investment trusts, which frequently trade significantly below or above net asset value.

Newly created ETF shares are delivered to market makers (or other **'authorised participants'**) in exchange for an entire portfolio of shares matching the index (not for cash). The underlying shares are held by the ETF fund manager, while the new ETF shares are traded by the market maker in the secondary market. To redeem ETF shares, the ETF manager delivers underlying shares/securities to the market maker in exchange for ETF shares. ETF managers only create new ETF shares for market makers with at least £1 million to invest, so private investors are excluded at this level. However, private investors can trade in existing ETF shares in the secondary market.

If the price of an ETF share rises above the value of the underlying shares, there will be an **arbitrage** opportunity for the market maker. Arbitrage means the possibility of simultaneously buying and selling the same or similar securities in two markets and making a risk-free gain, for example buying bananas for £1 in one market and selling them for £1.05 in another. In this case the ETF share representing, say, the top 100 UK shares is trading above the price of the 100 shares when sold separately. Market makers, spotting this opportunity, will swap the underlying basket of shares for a creation unit of ETF shares, thus realising a profit by then selling the ETF shares into the market. Then the new supply of ETF shares will satisfy the excess demand and ETF prices should fall until they are in line with the underlying NAV.

If the ETF share price falls below the underlying shares' value the market maker will exploit this by having the ETF shares redeemed by the ETF manager. The market maker ends up with the more valuable underlying shares and the supply of ETFs in the market place has fallen, bringing the price back up to the NAV.[7]

While the essence of the process creating ETFs and the relationships between market makers and ETF managers is as described above, it is a little more complicated than this. If you would like to know the technicalities read Box 5.1.

---

[7] Of course, there will also be trading actions in the market place by ordinary investors that bring the ETF price towards the value of the underlying shares, e.g. if the ETF is high relative to the underlying then investors will be tempted to sell it, to bring down its price.

Box 5.1   Creation of ETFs

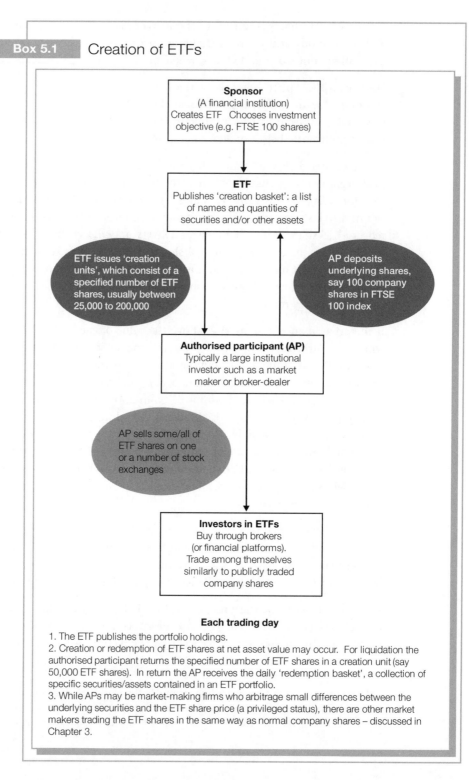

Sponsor
(A financial institution)
Creates ETF   Chooses investment
objective (e.g. FTSE 100 shares)

ETF
Publishes 'creation basket': a list
of names and quantities of
securities and/or other assets

ETF issues 'creation units', which consist of a specified number of ETF shares, usually between 25,000 to 200,000

AP deposits underlying shares, say 100 company shares in FTSE 100 index

Authorised participant (AP)
Typically a large institutional
investor such as a market
maker or broker-dealer

AP sells some/all of ETF shares on one or a number of stock exchanges

Investors in ETFs
Buy through brokers
(or financial platforms).
Trade among themselves
similarly to publicly traded
company shares

Each trading day

1. The ETF publishes the portfolio holdings.
2. Creation or redemption of ETF shares at net asset value may occur. For liquidation the authorised participant returns the specified number of ETF shares in a creation unit (say 50,000 ETF shares). In return the AP receives the daily 'redemption basket', a collection of specific securities/assets contained in an ETF portfolio.
3. While APs may be market-making firms who arbitrage small differences between the underlying securities and the ETF share price (a privileged status), there are other market makers trading the ETF shares in the same way as normal company shares – discussed in Chapter 3.

An advantage arising from market makers and ETF managers not handing over cash, but instead swapping ETF shares and underlying shares, is that there are no brokerage costs for buying and selling shares. This makes transactions cheap.

Spreads for investors – the difference between the buying and selling prices of ETFs on stock markets – are generally around 0.1–0.3 per cent (although spreads can widen to 10 per cent or more at times of extreme volatility, for example, after 11 September 2001). While there is no initial charge with ETFs, annual management charges plus other costs (the total expense ratio) range between 0.09 and 0.75 per cent but are typically between 0.3 and 0.5 per cent – these are deducted from dividends. ETFs are sometimes a more expensive way of tracking an index than some particularly cheap unit trust and OEIC passive funds because they incur additional costs in ensuring trading ability through the day and in paying a stock market listing fee. But overall the low-charging providers of ETFs, unit trusts, OEICs and investment trusts have comparable fees, but note the need to look for the low charging ones! A typical ETF, if there is such a thing, has a lower ongoing change than a comparable unit trust or OEIC. In addition to the ongoing change there may be fees to make use of an index (the FTSE might charge, for example), to service an account and to pay custodians to look after the assets.

Private investors purchasing ETFs from brokers will be charged a minimum of £10 to £40 per trade. No stamp duty is payable on purchase, nor does the ETF pay stamp duty when it purchases underlying shares, etc. Prices and other information are available at www.funds.ft.com – see Box 5.2 for an example. This particular ETF, tracking the FTSE All-Share index, charges investors 0.3 per cent annually.

There are hundreds of equity ETFs, from those that track the US market (e.g. S&P 500 index) or European shares (e.g. EURO STOXX 50), to more specialised funds such as information technology companies across the globe. There are also hundreds of ETFs with bonds as the underlying securities. In all, over £1,000 billion is invested in ETFs worldwide.

ETFs pay dividends in line with the underlying constituent shares or other income such as interest on bonds, quarterly or semi-annually. This is reflected in the 'yield' quoted on financial websites such as iShares (www.uk.ishares.com), Deutsche (www.etf.db.com) and Trustnet (www.trustnet.com/ETFHome). Make sure the yield you see quoted is the sum of the historic 12-month distribution payments made by the ETF divided by the ETF price after deduction of account charges, to compare across providers. Some 'yields' are what the underlying holdings pay out rather than what the ETF pays – Morningstar (www.morningstar.co.uk/uk/etfs) corrects for this when comparing ETFs.

Box 5.2   An example of an ETF

Source: www.funds.ft.com

Innovation

We have moved a long way from the simple traditional equity ETFs developed in the 1990s and described above. Nowadays the ETF may not purchase all the shares in the index but merely a sample. This is useful for ETFs invested in, say, Chinese or Vietnamese shares where government restrictions may prevent purchasing all the shares in the index. Also, the exchange-traded concept has been extended beyond equities and bonds to foreign exchange rates, property, commodities and commodity indices (**exchange traded commodities, ETCs**)[8]. Instead of the provider holding the underlying instrument or commodity the investment is in swaps or other derivative instruments (holding a ton of actual pork belly for lengthy periods may be a wasting asset). Derivatives are also used for hundreds of equity and bond ETFs.[9]

The problem with derivative-based ETFs is that there is a risk that the counterparties providing the derivatives may not be able to meet their obligations and then the ETF holder may not have anything tangible backing up the ETF shares. Also if the ETF does not buy the underlying securities but instead relies on derivatives, and then goes bust, it could be more complicated for the investor to retrieve their investment. That said, many markets cannot be accessed through the traditional route and derivative value movement is the only option to track a market. Also swap-based deals can be cheaper than buying say 100 companies' shares. The use of derivatives for many EFTs – **'synthetic replication'** of an index – has stimulated debate in the ETF world as to whether ETFs consisting solely of derivatives are truly ETFs at all. But, regardless of some misgivings it looks as though the volume of synthetic ETFs will overtake that of the traditional **physical ETFs ('physical-replication')**.

Another 'innovation' in the field is the creation of **actively managed ETFs**. This really does confuse the picture. Instead of passively tracking an index the managers of these instruments try to outperform it by picking winners. Of course,

---

[8] Unlike ETFs, ETCs may or may not have UCITs safeguards

[9] Swaps allow you to exchange a series of future cash payment obligations. For example, an ETF agrees to receive the percentage return on a share market index such as the FTSE 100 from a counterparty (usually an investment bank). In return the ETF pays the swap dealer the return on another underlying, e.g. a collection of bonds. The money previously raised by the ETF when it sold shares in itself is invested in these bonds and so the ETF gets the bond return. This can then be passed on to the swap counterparty; so what it receives from bonds, it passes on, making this side of the deal neutral. Thus it has a net exposure to the returns on the FTSE 100 in each period (i.e. every trading day). Of course, if the FTSE 100 return for a period is less than the bond return then the ETF makes a net payment to the counterparty and the value of each ETF share falls.

they need compensation for the intellectual effort, which means that fees are higher, negating the most important selling point of ETFs.

A further move is for ETFs to 'short' the market, so that they rise in value when the market falls (through derivatives). Going even further, you can get double the effect of the market fall. Not only are these types of ETFs more expensive to hold, but the other side of the coin from gaining double if you guess right is that you lose double if you guess wrong. As well as these **'inverse ETFs'** there are other 'leveraged' ETFs that *rise* a multiple of an underlying market's *rise.*

Pros and cons of ETFs

Among the advantages of ETFs are the following:

- They are listed companies on stock exchanges with active secondary markets. Being open-ended, there is no danger of over-supply of shares as ETF managers always stand ready to buy.

- They trade at, or very near to, net asset value and track the index closely (although some are closer than others), i.e. a smaller **'tracking difference'.**

- They can be traded at real-time prices throughout the day.

- They incur low management and other costs, which are transparent.

- No stamp duty payable.

- Many can be held in an ISA or self-invested personal pension to save tax. Non-UK registered ETFs may not have these tax benefits – check before buying.

- They can be bought to gain exposure to foreign markets cheaply.

- ETFs offer a much wider choice of markets to track than unit trusts trackers, ranging from Brazilian shares to commercial property and hedge funds.

- Transparency on what your money is invested in with physical ETFs.

There are, however, disadvantages:

- Stockbrokers' fees can eat into profits of frequent traders.

- If the ETF provider does not buy the underlying securities, but instead relies on derivatives, additional risks are introduced.

- If you want to drip-feed money into your fund each month this is likely to be more expensive with an ETF than a unit trust or OEIC because of the charges associated with buying and selling.

■ Physical ETFs may lend out the shares, etc. in the portfolio to other financial institutions for a fee (who may, for example, sell them expecting to buy them back later at a profit). If they do not return them, investors in the ETF are exposed to the risk of loss (despite the holding of some collateral from the borrowers). The risk of such a failure is very small, but not unimaginable. Check to see if your ETF provider lends its securities, and whether the fees received are split with you.

■ There is no Financial Services Compensation Scheme protection (see Chapter 19) if the fund goes bust.

Investment trusts (investment companies)

Investment trusts (companies) place the money they raise in assets such as shares, gilts, corporate bonds and property. Unlike unit trusts, they are set up as companies (they are not trusts at all!) and are subject to company law.[10] If you wish to place your money with an investment trust you do so by buying its shares. Investment trusts are floated on the London Stock Exchange where there is an active secondary market. They are described as **closed-end funds** because they do not create or redeem their shares on a daily basis in response to increases or decreases in demand (in contrast to unit trust, OEICs and ETFs). The number of shares is fixed for a long period of time, as with any other company that issues shares.

The trust will have a constitution[11] that specifies that its purpose is to invest in specific types of assets. It cannot deviate from this. So it may have been set up to invest in Japanese large company shares, US biotechnology shares, or whatever, and it is forbidden from switching to a different category of investment. This reassures the investor that money placed with a particular trust to invest in, say, UK large companies won't end up in, say, Russian oil shares. Of course, if you want to take the risk (and possible reward) of investing in Russian oil shares you can probably find an investment trust that specialises in these – there are, after all, about 300 investment trusts quoted in London, with total assets of over £100 billion, to choose from.

As a company an investment trust will have a **board of directors** answerable to shareholders for the trust's actions and performance. With investment trusts being closed-end funds the amount of money under the directors' control is fixed,

---

[10] There are 'investment trusts', which are UK registered and managed in the UK, alongside 'offshore investment companies' which are free of some of the UK restrictions.
[11] Comprising its memorandum, articles of association and the prospectus on flotation.

which enables them to plan ahead with confidence unconcerned that tomorrow investors may want to withdraw money from the fund. Investors cannot oblige the trust to buy the shares should they want to sell (in contrast to unit trusts and OEICs). They have to sell to another investor at a price determined by the forces of supply and demand in the secondary market. Purchases and sales are made through stockbrokers in the same way as for any other company share.

The selection of investments for the trust and the general management of the fund may be undertaken by an in-house team of investment managers who are employees of the trust (a *'self-managed'* **trust**) or the investment management task may be handed over to external managers. Most are externally managed. In addition to the 300 or so investment trusts, around 100 investment companies are venture capital trusts (VCTs) which are given tax breaks by the UK government to encourage investment in small businesses not listed on a stock market. See Chapter 17 for more on VCTs.

Discounts and premiums

There are two factors that influence the share price of an investment trust. Firstly, the value of the underlying assets owned by the trust. This is expressed as a **net asset value** per share. In theory the trust's share price should be pretty close to the value of the assets held. But in practice they frequently sell at a large **discount** to NAV – only a few sell at a **premium** to NAV. Discounts of 10–20 per cent are not uncommon; they have even reached 68 per cent. The main factor that drags the price below NAV is the lack of demand for the shares. Here is a typical scenario.

Example

In year X there is great interest in, say, eastern European smaller companies so an investment trust is set up and offers its shares (say, 50 million) for sale at £1 each. With the money raised, £50 million of eastern European company shares are bought by the trust. For the next year the underlying assets (all those shares in Polish companies, etc.) do no more than maintain their value of £1 per investment trust share, and so NAV is constant. Nothing in the fundamentals has changed. However, enthusiasm for investing in these up-and-coming nations grows among the UK investing public. The investment trust shareholders who want to sell find that they can do so in the LSE secondary market at above NAV. New buyers are willing to pay £1.08 per share – an 8 per cent premium to the NAV.

However, in the following year a worldwide recession strikes and investors head for safe havens; they pile into bonds and familiar shares at home. The NAV of the trust's shares falls to 60p as prices plummet on the eastern European stock exchanges. What is worse for the investment trust shareholders is that sentiment has become so pessimistic about eastern European companies that they can only sell their shares for 50p. They trade at a discount of 16.67 per cent to NAV (10p/60p).

Discounts may seem to present an excellent opportunity: you can buy assets worth 60p for 50p. However, they can be bad if the discount increases during the time you hold the shares. As you can see from the last column in Box 5.3, the discounts can be quite substantial. The *Financial Times* publishes the share prices and NAVs of investment trusts (companies) daily on the 'Share Services' pages. Additional information about individual investment trusts is at www.ft.com.

While much of the discount on a typical investment trust is due to negative sentiment there are some rational reasons for shares selling below NAV:

■ Investors may think trust managers are incompetent and likely to lose more value in the future.

■ NAV is calculated after deducting the nominal (stated book) value of the debt and preference shares. In reality, the trust may have to pay back more on the debt and preference shares than this.

■ Liquidating the fund incurs costs (e.g. contract cancellations, advisers' fees, stock brokers' fees) so NAV is not achieved.

While most investment trusts invest in stock market quoted companies there are **private equity investment trusts** which invest in companies not quoted on a stock exchange, either directly buying their shares or by placing the money with other fund organisations that invest in private firms.

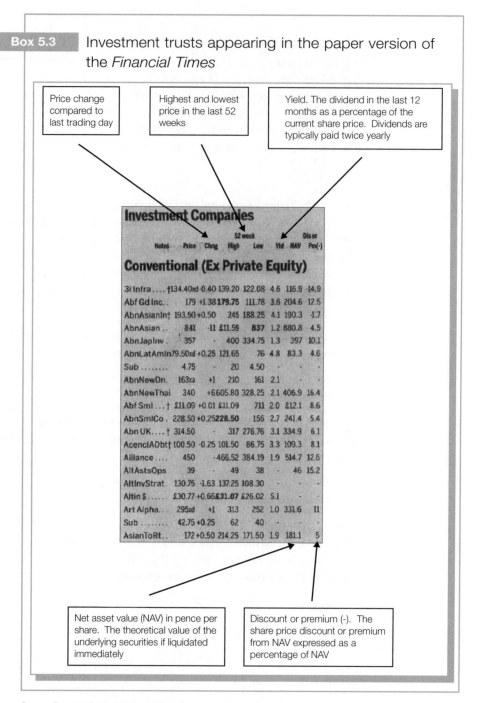

Box 5.3   Investment trusts appearing in the paper version of the *Financial Times*

Price change compared to last trading day

Highest and lowest price in the last 52 weeks

Yield. The dividend in the last 12 months as a percentage of the current share price. Dividends are typically paid twice yearly

Investment Companies

Notes	Price	Chng	52 week High	Low	Yld	NAV	Dis or Pm(-)

Conventional (Ex Private Equity)

3i Infra....	†134.40xd	-0.40	139.20	122.08	4.6	116.9	-14.9
Abf Gd Inc..	179	+1.38	**179.75**	111.78	3.6	204.6	12.5
AbnAsianIn†	193.50	+0.50	245	188.25	4.1	190.3	-1.7
AbnAsian ..	841	-11	£11.59	**837**	1.2	880.8	4.5
AbnJapInv .	357	-	400	334.75	1.3	397	10.1
AbnLatAmIn	79.50xd	+0.25	121.65	76	4.8	83.3	4.6
Sub	4.75	-	20	4.50	-	-	-
AbnNewDn.	163xa	+1	210	161	2.1	-	-
AbnNewThai	340	+6	605.80	328.25	2.1	406.9	16.4
Abf Sml ...†	£11.09	+0.01	£11.09	711	2.0	£12.1	8.6
AbnSmlCo .	228.50	+0.25	**228.50**	156	2.7	241.4	5.4
Abn UK....†	314.50	-	317	276.76	3.1	334.9	6.1
AcenciADbt†	100.50	-0.25	101.50	86.75	3.3	109.3	8.1
Alliance	450	-	466.52	384.19	1.9	514.7	12.6
AltAstsOps	39	-	49	38	-	46	15.2
AltInvStrat	130.75	-1.63	137.25	108.30	-	-	-
Altin $......	£30.77	+0.66	£31.07	£26.02	5.1	-	-
Art Alpha...	295xd	+1	313	252	1.0	331.6	11
Sub	42.75	+0.25	62	40	-	-	-
AsianToRt..	172	+0.50	214.25	171.50	1.9	181.1	5

Net asset value (NAV) in pence per share. The theoretical value of the underlying securities if liquidated immediately

Discount or premium (-). The share price discount or premium from NAV expressed as a percentage of NAV

Source: Financial Times, 7 January 2014.

Costs for the investor

When buying (or selling) investment trust shares commission will be payable to your stockbroker[12] as usual when buying shares (see Chapter 4). There will also be the market marker's spread between the buying and selling price. This is generally 1–2 per cent, but for less frequently traded trusts it can be 5–10 per cent.

The fund managers' costs for managing the investments and for administration are charged to the fund, either against annual income or against capital. A typical ongoing charge (or TER), including the costs of investment management and administration, directors' fees, audit fees and share registration expenses, is between 1.3 and 1.8 per cent,[13] but this excludes performance fees that managers sometimes take. Ongoing charges on some particularly low-cost equity-invested funds can be as low as 0.44 per cent, but most property focused investment trusts and private equity investment trusts tend to cost north of 2.5 per cent. See www.theaic.co.uk for ongoing charge rates and performance fee rates. Article 5.5 provides more detail on fees and Article 5.6 looks at the decreasing use of performance fees.

Article 5.5

New fund fees muddy the waters

By Elaine Moore

Managers of investment trusts have been accused of confusing investors by announcing a change to the way they disclose their charges.

From June, investment trusts will no longer publish a total expense ratio (TER) in the literature they provide to investors.

Instead, trusts will show an "ongoing charge", which will include management fees, registration fees and other administrative costs – but not performance fees.

Campaigners said the new ongoing charges measure will show investors just a fraction of the amount that is taken from their funds.

Some are continuing to lobby the industry for the adoption of a "total cost of ownership" figure – capturing every expense, including entry or exit fees, performance fees, trading costs and fund platform charges. The Association of Investment Companies (AIC) said performance fees would be published alongside the new ongoing charge.

➡

---

[12] Investment trusts are also sold through financial advisers and platforms/supermarkets. The trust may also have a savings scheme allowing the investor to buy a few shares each month (starting from as little as £20 per month) or make a lump sum purchase from £250 – see their websites.

[13] The 'annual management charge', often highlighted by fund managers and shown to be significantly below these percentages, excludes a lot of the costs.

Article 5.5   Continued

"The ongoing charges figure is not supposed to show the total cost, it is an element of it," explained Ian Sayers, director-general at the AIC. "I think the process of providing a total cost will be done in stages." Philippa Gee, managing director of Philippa Gee Wealth Management, said: "It is hard to find a solution that will cover every charge faced by an investor, but it's something that needs to be changed. TERs didn't include all charges, neither do ongoing charges. We aren't there yet."

What's included in 'ongoing charges'?	What's excluded from 'ongoing charges' and the 'total expense ratio' (TER)?
Annual management charge	Entry and exit charges
Directors' fees and expenses	
Audit and tax compliance fees	Trading costs
Custody/depositary	Interest costs
Fund administration	Share buybacks/issue costs
Fund accounting	
Company secretarial	Soft [extra] commission to [brokers] and other similar arrangements [often in return for services such as research sent to fund manager]
Irrecoverable VAT	Restructuring costs
Registrar	Tax charge
Marketing	
Insurance	Currency profit/loss on revenue bank account
Registration fees, regulatory fees and similar charges	Brokerage
	Stamp duty

What's *not included* in 'ongoing charges' but included in the 'total expense ratio' (TER)?

Performance fees

Source: Association of Investment Companies

Trust performance fees axed

By Jonathan Eley

City of London Investment Trust, one of the oldest and largest generalist investment trusts, said this week it would remove its performance fee and charge only a management fee, prompting analysts to predict that more would follow.

Henderson, which manages the trust, said it hoped the move would make it "more attractive to a wider audience of retail investors." The annual management fee will henceforth be 0.365 per cent and the ongoing charges in respect for this year should be around 0.45 per cent – less than some tracker funds.

Performance fees tend to be more common among investment trusts than among open-ended funds. They are meant to align the interests of managers with those of investors,

but critics say they are too complicated and reward managers for doing what they should be doing anyway.

Julian Bartlett, chairman of the investment management group at Grant Thornton, said that a long period of meagre returns meant that many performance fees were not delivering for managers. "If you're an investment trust board looking to keep your trust competitive, removing a performance fee that's never been activated, or is underwater, is an obvious place to start."

City of London is the sixth investment trust to abolish a performance fee so far this year. The majority of trusts (62 per cent) still have some kind of performance fee, according to the AIC.

Borrowing

Investment trusts have the freedom to borrow (unlike unit trusts or OEICs). Borrowing to buy assets is fine if the return on assets over time exceeds the interest charged. However, it is a two-edged sword. The risk associated with gearing up returns becomes all too apparent when asset values fall. Take the case of our trust investing in eastern Europe. If it had sold 50 million shares at £1 each and also borrowed £50 million to buy £100 million of eastern European shares the NAV would still start at £1 per share (£100 million of assets minus £50 million debt owed, for 50 million shares). If underlying asset values fall by 40 per cent because of the fall in the Warsaw Stock Exchange, the *net* asset value per share falls dramatically from £1 to 20p – an 80 per cent fall – because the assets fall to £60 million, but the debt remains at £50 million:

Value of eastern European shares   £60m

Less debt   £50m
                                                      ———
                                                       £10m

Net asset value per share: £10m/50m = 20p

You can see why trusts that borrow a lot can be very volatile.

Tax

Capital gains tax is not payable by a trust on gains made within the trust. The income received by the trust is taxed, but then shareholders receive a tax credit to reflect the fact that tax has already been paid. Shareholders pay capital gains tax on the sale of their IT shares in the normal way – see Chapter 17. ISAs or a personal pension can be used to hold trust shares. Stamp duty of 0.5 per cent is payable when buying IT shares.

Split-capital investment trusts ('dual capital' trusts)

Around the turn of the millennium many perplexed trust shareholders lost a lot of money on split-capital investment trusts largely as a result of not under-standing the nature of the financial instruments they had bought. In the late 1990s they were often told that 'split' shares were some of the safest you could buy. The reality was that many of these shares were highly risk-loaded.

Split-capital trusts simultaneously issue different types of shares – the shares are 'split' into different forms. Generally they offer **income shares** that entitle the holder to receive all (or most) of the income from the investment portfolio (e.g. dividends from underlying shares), and **capital shares** that entitle the owner to receive all (or most) of the rise in the capital value of the portfolio over the life of the IT, but not to receive dividends. Splits have a specified number of years (usually fewer than 10) of existence so that the capital shareholder knows when these shares will pay out (and the income shareholder knows when payments will cease).

Income shares offer a relatively high income to compensate for the low prede-termined sum that will be paid at the end of the trust's life when the shares are redeemed (some pay the initial amount back, some may only pay 1p at the end). The high yields on these shares seem very attractive to some people (e.g. the retired); but these investors must also weigh up the potential loss on capital value of the shares. For example, a £1 share that offers an income of 15 pence per year may seem good value, but not if the capital value is declining at 12 per cent per year. Also the income is not guaranteed and is likely to fluctuate from year to year.

Capital shares attract investors wanting high exposure to rises in stock markets. The drawback is they are last in the queue for payouts after all the other classes of shareholders have received their entitlements. So if the trust goes into liquidation they are unlikely to get anything back.

While splits started with these two categories of shares it wasn't long before other types appeared. For example, some trusts issued income, capital shares and a third type of share called **zero dividend preference shares**. 'Zeros' pay no income during the life of the trust but they do offer a predetermined return at the end. They are therefore less risky than income or capital shares.

The problem that arose in the period 2000–2002 was that many split-capital investment trusts borrowed significant sums of money. Debt interest and the capital repayment on debt take precedence over the payout to zero or to capital and income shares on an annual basis or in liquidation. When the stock market declined the effect of this gearing was to exaggerate the fall in trusts' underlying share values. What really messed things up for shareholders of splits was that many trusts surreptitiously invested large proportions of their funds in other highly borrowed splits (over 70 per cent of the fund was invested in other splits in some cases). They were later accused of artificially keeping other splits alive as a form of mutual back-scratching between trust managers. Panic ensued as investors realised the danger to which they were exposed, especially for those in the technology sector. Some lost 90 per cent or more of value on their shares. Zeros were supposed to be very safe because of the guaranteed payout at the end and the superiority over other shares for any payout. However, the gearing and the cross-shareholding in a declining market meant that in many cases they failed to pay out the promised amounts – some became worthless.

There are two lessons from this story: keep an eye on the borrowing; and keep an eye on cross-shareholdings in other trusts. The FCA has now tackled the latter problem by removing the scope for cross-shareholdings. Note, however, that investment trusts have a lower level of protection for investors than unit trusts or OEICs. They are regulated by company law and the FCA's listing rules, but people who buy shares in investment trusts other than through advisers are not covered under the Financial Services Ombudsman Scheme. Note however that the person appointed as fund manager must be authorised by the FCA as competent.

Dividends and yields

Investments trusts have an advantage over unit trusts in being able to pay out dividends even if the underlying shares, etc. in the fund are cutting their dividends/interest. They can make these payments out of 'revenue reserves' (income received in the past but not paid out to shareholders). The use of this power means there might be a difference between the advertised yield, based on the dividend paid by the IT, and the yield based on the income that it receives.

Financial advisers and investment trusts

The size of the investment trust sector relative to open-ended funds was held back due to the pre-2013 commission paid by the latter to financial advisers to sell them. There was no incentive for advisors to draw investors' attention to investment trusts when they could sell them open-ended funds. Now that funds cannot pay commission to professionals advising investors (following the introduction of the Retail Distribution Review) we expect to see more investment trusts being sold.

Websites for investment trusts

www.theaic.co.uk	Association of Investment Companies
www.uk.advfn.com	ADVFN
www.bestinvest.co.uk	Bestinvest
www.citywire.co.uk	Citywire
www.iii.co.uk	Interactive Investor
www.investegate.co.uk	Investegate
www.morningstar.co.uk/uk/etfs	Morningstar
www.theitlist.co.uk	Theitlist
www.trustnet.com/ETFHome.aspx	Trustnet
www.whichinvestmenttrust.com	Whichinvestmentrust.com

Investment platforms/supermarkets

Investment platforms (also called fund platforms or investment supermarkets), available online or offline, allow you to invest in a range of unit trusts, investment trusts, ETFs, OEICs, shares, corporate bonds, and gilts. You can pick one, two or a dozen funds and other investments from one or many different management companies. Furthermore, you can hold the funds within an Individual Saving Account, ISA or a Self-invested Personal Pension, SIPP (see Chapter 17) to obtain tax benefits.

Additional services include two investment reports each year showing a valuation and performance record of all your different funds and other investments brought together, and the ability to switch to alternatives funds within a portfolio, ISA or SIPP for a low (or no) charge. Also, a consolidated annual tax report and tax certificate will be sent to you (usually in May) which will detail all the income received into your account in the tax year to 5 April, making your tax return easier to complete. The platforms often employ experts providing analytical reports of funds and shares available to clients, usually on the website.

You can open an online account with a debit card (or send a cheque) and start buying funds with only a £500 lump sum or by adding £50 per month to your account with a regular savings plan. While you are deciding where to invest or just want to sit out of the market, you can simply hold cash within your cash account at the platform receiving a modest interest. When buying shares or bonds platforms often offer cheap share dealing – as little as £5 per deal for frequent traders (normally around £10–£15 for infrequent traders).

Investment supermarkets have helped reduce the demand for independent financial advisers (IFAs) because investors can select from a wide range of investments without needing to pay advice fees. Platforms stress that they do not give advice or recommendations, but do provide information and guidance to try to make investors aware of the various alternative investment options and type of account open to them. Some do this through an online questionnaire, which elicits responses to draw your attention to issues such as your risk tolerance given your family's financial position. In short, platforms are only for those comfortable making their own investment decisions. Before bypassing IFAs you might like to consider the following:

▪ You may need more tailored advice, especially given the bewildering choice (there are at least 4,000 funds). You will be required to pay for this advice separate to any investments.

▪ Some are not true supermarkets allowing you to choose from a very wide range, but merely act as portals for selling specific funds they have selected. Others have thousands of funds etc., from all sorts of fund management companies

Holding investments via a platform should be relatively safe given that they are regulated by the Financial Conduct Authority (FCA). Your investments will be held in a 'nominee' account, which means you're not the legal owner but are entitled to receive what you're owed. If a platform goes bust or runs off with your money you'll only be covered by the Financial Services Compensation Scheme (FSCS) for up to £50,000 – see Chapter 19.

So, how are platforms rewarded for the service they provide?

They have an income from the brokerage fees charged for buying and selling shares, investment trusts, ETFs, gilts and bonds for you and from running your ISA or SIPPs (say 0.5 per cent per year of the value held). They also place the cash you deposit with them elsewhere (usually with banks) to gain a higher return than you receive. Furthermore the platform might charge you for reinvesting dividends received and for transferring your investments to another platform/broker ('exit fees'). With regard to unit trusts and OEICs, until 2014 they benefitted from a share of the commission these funds paid each year (say 0.25 percentage points of the annual management charge of 1.5 per cent). However the regulators now forbid this commission. Some platforms have switched to charging a flat fee rather than a percentage of the value of your fund portfolio – say £20 per quarter. Others charge a percentage of the funds' value in your portfolio, say 0.35 or 0.45 per cent per year as a **'platform fee'**. Under this new charging regime they will refund to you any trail commissions paid by funds to the platform (this will only be until April 2016 when all trail commission ceases, even on old funds).

Pressure is coming from platforms for fund managers to reduce charges for investors – see Article 5.7. Hargreaves Lansdown got the average fund management charge down to 0.65 per cent per year for those on its select list. Within that, the top 27 funds averaged 0.54 per cent. But most investing clients pay a platform charge of 0.45 per cent (which falls to 0.25 per cent if your portfolio is between £250,000 and £1 million). Rival Fidelity claimed it had forced AMCs down to an average of 0.64 per cent for funds on its select list. Its annual service charge for investors is 0.35 per cent. Other rivals charge a fixed amount. So shop around.

Article 5.7

Fund groups told to slash fees or lose business

By Chris Flood

Hargreaves Lansdown, the online supermarket for funds and shares, is playing hardball on pricing with asset managers that want their products included on its influential buy list.

Hargreaves, the third-largest UK fund platform, with assets of £37bn, is demanding asset managers cut their fees for products that might feature in an updated version of its widely followed Wealth 150 list.

"We heard that one leading fund manager was told that it would have to drop its pricing by 30 per cent even to be considered for inclusion," said an executive at a rival platform.

Article 5.7 Continued

Danny Cox, head of financial planning at Hargreaves Lansdown, said: "Yes, we are playing hardball with regard to pricing. Every basis point of savings will be passed on to the investor."

The tough stance threatens fund managers' profits, with rival platform operators also seeking price cuts.

Fund platforms are an increasingly important part of the chain between asset managers and investors in the UK, accounting for almost half of all sales to retail clients so far this year.

One unhappy fund manager said: "How is an investor to know if these funds are any good or just cheap if Hargreaves is only prepared to market those funds on which it has been given a deal."

But some are understood to have agreed to so-called "superclean" fees of 50 basis points [0.5%] for equity funds and less for bond funds with Hargreaves.

Source: Flood, C. (2013) Fund groups told to slash fees or lose business, *Financial Times*, 24 November 2013. © The Financial Times Limited 2013. All Rights Reserved.

Some websites for fund supermarkets

www.alliancetrustsavings.co.uk	Alliance Trust Savings
www.barclaysstockbrokers.co.uk	Barclays Stockbrokers
www.bestinvest.co.uk	Bestinvest
www.charles-stanley-direct.co.uk	Charles Stanley
www.cofunds.co.uk	Cofunds
www.comparefundplatforms.co.uk	Compare Fund Platforms
www.fundsdirect.co.uk	Fundsdirect
www.fidelity.co.uk	FundsNetwork (Fidelity)
www.hl.co.uk	Hargreaves Lansdown
www.iii.co.uk	Interactive Investor
www.selftrade.co.uk	Selftrade
www.tddirectinvesting.co.uk	TD Direct Investing
www.share.com	The Share Centre
www.cavendishonline.co.uk	Cavendish Online
www.rplan.co.uk	rplan

With-profits policies

Hardly anyone buys with-profit policies these days. After reading the disadvantages you will appreciate why. Because millions of UK citizens still have hundreds of billions of pounds saved in old with-profits funds I'll describe the nature of these 'investments' here.

With-profits policies could be in the form of an **endowment** policy (often linked to a mortgage), a **personal pension** or a long-term investment in **with-profits bonds**. Many company pension schemes are also invested in with-profits funds. Technically and contractually, a with-profits policy is a form of life insurance (i.e. there is a payment on death). In reality, the majority of policies are essentially savings products with a nominal insurance content.

With-profits policies generally work as follows. Life insurance companies set up a fund and invite people to place their savings in the fund either as a lump sum or through a regular savings plan (say, £20 per month). The fund then invests in a range of international and UK shares, bonds, property etc. The life insurer guarantees a minimum return to be paid out at the end of the policy life, which can be 5, 10 or even 25 years away. This is called the **basic sum assured**. Suppose, for the sake of argument, that this is £10,000 in 10 years' time. When the underlying investments in the fund produce returns the policyholders are given 'bonuses' – a share of the profits the insurance company has achieved on the invested money. Policyholders receive a **reversionary bonus** (also called a **regular** or **annual** or **interim** bonus) annually. This is added to the policy's guaranteed sum.

However, if the year's returns have been particularly good – say, the stock market rocketed – the policyholders will not receive a reversionary bonus of the same magnitude, because insurance companies attempt to smooth reversionary bonus rates over time, avoiding sharp changes from one year to the next. They hold back profits in good years so that they can maintain a reasonably good reversionary bonus in years of poor investment performance. This is called **smoothing**.

Once the reversionary bonus is added to the fund it cannot be taken away. So, if the basic sum assured starts at £10,000 and at the end of the first year the insurance company announces a reversionary bonus of 4 per cent the new guaranteed sum becomes £10,400. The guaranteed amount is payable on death or at maturity of the policy.

Thus as profits are made on underlying investments the insurance company locks in a return for the policyholder that cannot be taken away. So even if, in future years, shares, bond and property markets crumble, the investor is guaranteed a minimum amount (this is assuming the life assurance company manages to avoid liquidation in such dire circumstances – this is not always a safe assumption). As well as the reversionary bonuses the insurer pays a **terminal** (final) bonus at the end of the policy (or on death if this is earlier).

A variation on the theme is **unitised with-profits funds**. Here the premiums paid by individuals buy units of a fund in a similar way to investing in unit trusts. Unlike the conventional with-profits funds there is no basic sum assured but the bonuses are smoothed.

Treat these schemes with great caution

Criticism has been heaped on with-profits policies:

1 Insurance companies have far too much discretion over bonuses. With-profits policyholders cannot be entirely sure that they are getting the full benefit from the returns generated using their money. There is a lack of transparency in four areas:

  – the underlying investment return;

  – the smoothing of the return;

  – the charging of costs;

  – the connection between the with-profits fund and the insurance firm's other businesses.

2 The wide discretion of insurance companies has been used to build up **orphan assets** (**inherited estates**). These are reserves that an insurance company holds back from policyholders to act as a buffer should the market decline. There were many years when returns on funds were much greater than the bonuses granted on policies. It would seem that the insurance companies have been far too cautious. In other words, policyholders have been underpaid.

3 A massive penalty imposed for cashing-in early. Only about one-third of 25-year policies are held to maturity. In many cases holders receive less than the money they put in (and less than the guaranteed value) especially if they surrender the policy within the first three to five years.

4 With-profits policies are marketed as a low-risk product, but this is not always true. For example, Equitable Life was forced to severely cut the bonuses to some policyholders because it had promised high returns to other savers, and was forced by the courts to pay out on the guaranteed annuities, leaving a shrunken pot of money for everyone else. The lack of transparency at Equitable Life meant that policyholders were unable to discern the risk to their savings until it was too late.

5 Insurance companies have also been accused of being too optimistic at times. For example, many people were sold endowment policies related to house mortgages. The monthly payments into the policies were set at a level thought to be enough to pay off the mortgage in, say, 25 years. When markets turned sour many shocked policyholders received a letter stating that they were unlikely to have enough saved in the policy to be able to pay off the mortgage at the end of the term – unless, of course, they handed over more money to the insurance company to increase the size of the pot.

6   There appears to be no correlation between the levels of charges and the performance of the funds.

Insurance company bonds

With insurance company investment bonds you invest a lump sum (usually £5,000 or more) with an insurance company for a fixed period, say five years, in return for a fixed rate of interest and a small element of life insurance. **Guaranteed income bonds** (**GIBs**) invest money raised in a portfolio of low-risk bonds (e.g. gilts) and then pay to the holder a regular income net of basic rate income tax once a year (or monthly). With growth bonds the interest accumulates until the maturity date. Insurance company bonds are relatively safe investments if held to maturity, but returns are low. If you don't hold to maturity and choose to cash in early (if the insurance company allows this) you will probably suffer a penalty. **With-profits bonds** provide a guaranteed bonus, which cannot be withdrawn, plus a terminal bonus which is not guaranteed. You need to read the small print with some guaranteed income bonds. It could be that the guaranteed income (say, a spectacular 10 per cent per year) comes at the price of a loss in the capital value – £10,000 at the beginning of five years is only, say £8,000 at the end.

Distribution bonds (also sold by insurance companies) invest in a mixture of equity, fixed income securities (e.g. gilts, corporate bonds) and property, but will be biased toward interest paying instruments. Unlike with-profits funds they do not smooth out income from one year to the next or offer the protection of reversionary bonuses, so the payout fluctuates. Exit penalties for cashing in during the first five years can be high. They are more straightforward than with-profits policies because returns are not clouded by smoothing.

Stock-market-linked bonds

Offered by insurance companies, banks, building societies and other investment firms, stock-market-linked bonds provide a return that goes up with a stock market index. Products with similar characteristics are called by a variety of names, for example: **structured investment products**, **defined-return bonds**, **guaranteed equity bonds** and **protected bonds**. As an investor you commit a lump sum for, say, five years. Typically, the provider offers your capital back at the end, plus all of the increase in, say, the FTSE 100 index over the five years up to a maximum of, say, 65 per cent – if the index doubles you will not benefit beyond the 65 per cent limit. The provider does not actually buy shares but instead uses the money to buy a mixture of interest-bearing securities (or zero coupon bonds) and derivatives which rise in value if the FTSE 100 rises. So, it could be that £8,500 of your £10,000 investment buys bonds which, after five years, give a return of £10,000. Another £1,000 is used to buy call options on the stock market index which gains in value if the market rises (see Chapter 8), and the remaining £500 is a fee for the financial institution.

With the guarantee that you will at least get back your original lump sum these instruments provide an underpinned way of benefiting should the stock market index rise significantly (assuming the financial institution does not go bust during the five years). However, bear in mind that your return is only *linked* to the stock market index. This is not the same as receiving the returns by holding, say, the top 100 shares. First, you are missing out on an important element of return, the dividend income. Second, you usually only receive a proportion of the capital gain over the five years, not the full gain. Furthermore, there are stock-market-linked bonds that don't provide complete protection on the downside. If the index falls by more than a stated percentage the guaranteed amount will fall below the initial capital. Some providers offer the investor choices, such as a 100 per cent money-back guarantee plus 55 per cent of the rise in the FTSE 100 index, or a 95 per cent guarantee and 110 per cent of the rise in the FTSE 100.

Many financial product providers came under attack for misselling what became known as **precipice bonds** to investors who thought they were buying a safe investment. Precipice bonds offer the return of the original capital, but only in specific circumstances. If the market index falls below a predetermined level the guarantee no longer applies. So, a typical precipice bond may offer 7 per cent annual income over the next three years. It also offers a return of the initial capital at the end of three years if the market index does not fall by more than, say, 20 per cent from its start level. However – and this is where the danger lies – after the 20 per cent barrier has been breached, for every 1 per cent fall in the FTSE 100 the investor loses 2 per cent of the capital value. Hence the nickname precipice bonds – the value of your savings can fall steeply. Look out for names such as 'high income' or 'extra income' bonds or 'plans'. Only invest in these products if you understand and can withstand the downside risk.

Kick-out plans offer investors the return of their original capital plus a coupon, say 10 per cent after 12 months only if say the FTSE 100 index is equal to, or higher than, its level at the start. If the index is lower the plan does not pay out, but continues for another 12 months and then another, and so on, until the original index level is passed. When an anniversary is reached where the FTSE

100 index has climbed back to the beginning level the accumulated coupons are paid. If the coupon is 10 per cent and the trigger occurs on the third anniversary, the investor receives the capital plus 30 per cent. With some of these plans if the index falls more than 50 per cent the investor loses 1 per cent for every 1 per cent fall in the index below its starting level. Beware of counterparty risk: Lehman Brothers made some of these guarantees – just before going bust.

Two final points on stock market-linked bonds:

- The complicated payout conditions on all these bonds mean that investors need to be disciplined enough to read the small print.

- Enquire into the payout if you cash in early – is this guaranteed or dependent on market values?

Money markets

Private investors can place money into money market funds. The money markets are wholesale financial markets (i.e. those dealing with large amounts) in which lending and borrowing on a short-term basis takes place (less than one year) between institutions. While the minimum amount needed to buy instruments or deposit money in this market is around £500,000 the private investor can access it through **money market** funds, which gather together small amounts from hundreds or thousands of investors and then invest in a range of short-term securities. Some of these money market funds require the investor to deposit as little as £1,000, others demand a minimum of £25,000.

The advantage of pooling money when buying wholesale securities means that better rates of return can be achieved by the collective fund. Also, because the fund is well diversified across borrowing companies, governments and other institutions the money market fund manager can offer relatively safe returns to private investors.

Typically, a money market fund will have no initial charge. When all the annual costs are included the total expense ratio (TER) can typically range from around 0.15 to 0.5 per cent.

The following are some typical instruments held by a money market fund:[14]

- Treasury bills (lending short-term to the government);

---

[14] For more on money markets consult G. Arnold (2012) *The Financial Times Guide to Financial Markets* or G. Arnold (forthcoming) *The Financial Times Guide to Bond and Money Markets*, both Financial Times Prentice Hall.

■ commercial paper (lending for a few days to companies and other organisations);

■ certificate of deposits (lending to a bank).

Money market accounts are often offered by high street banks, the interest rates on which vary with the rates paid on the money markets. Thus the rate fluctuates frequently, sometimes every day. These accounts may be instant access or you may have to give, say, one month's notice to access your money. The risks with investing in money market funds are low, but there are some:

■ The bank/institution running the fund may go bust.

■ The managers may bias the investments held toward the riskier end while staying within the definition of money market, e.g. securities issued by poorly managed companies. Investigate where the manager actually invests.

■ When short-term interest rates are very low these funds may offer virtually no return.

Hedge funds

Hedge funds are collective investment vehicles that admit only a small number of wealthy individuals or institutions. They are free from many types of regulation designed to protect investors, being created either offshore (e.g. Cayman Islands) and/or onshore as private investment partnerships. To place your money with a hedge fund you are generally expected to have a net worth (excluding main residence) of at least £600,000 and to be prepared to commit hundreds of thousands of pounds to the fund.

Originally, the word 'hedge' made some sense when applied to these funds. They would, through a combination of investments, including derivatives, try to hedge risk while seeking a high absolute return (rather than a return relative to an index). Today the word 'hedge' is misapplied to most of these funds because they generally take aggressive bets on the movement of currencies, equities, stock markets, interest rates, bonds, etc. around the world. They frequently add to the risk by borrowing a multiple of the amount put in by the wealthy individuals or institutions, or use derivatives to lever up return and risk.

The freedom from regulation is a major selling point for hedge funds as it means that they are not confined to investing in particular classes of security, or to particular investment methods. For example, they are free to go *short* (selling shares they don't own in the expectation of buying them back at a lower price later) which they wouldn't be able to do in many regulated environments. They can borrow over 10 times the size of the fund to take a punt on small movements in currency rates. Some are active in the derivatives and a range of other highly specialised markets that traditional domestic investment funds are much more cautious about entering.

Conventional fund managers too often pat themselves on the back if they produce a negative return of 15 per cent while the market fell by 16 per cent. Hedge funds are seen as different in that they are not content with negative performance. Another supposed attraction is that the investments and markets they enter are supposed to have a negative correlation[15] with domestic equities – an attractive proposition in a declining equity environment market. But the evidence shows that hedge fund returns frequently decline alongside equity market decline.

If the hedge fund does well the managers receive exceptional rewards. A typical fee structure might be 1–2 per cent of the fund value regardless of performance; on top of this 20 per cent of any generated profits are taken by the managers.

It is impossible to state where hedge funds as a whole sit in the risk–reward spectrum. Some are managed to be relatively safe, while others are dedicated to extreme actions in obscure corners of the financial world. Some have outper-formed the FTSE 100 index while many have failed completely (only a fraction of those in business five years ago are still operating). Performance statistics are sketchy at best, and often downright misleading. One of the major risks investors have largely ignored is the lack of transparency about where their money is being used, which makes it difficult to assess how the fund would survive extreme and unpredictable markets. There is also a greater vulnerability to fraud due to the opacity of funds and absence of regulations. Moreover, there are now thousands of hedge funds to choose from and there is a fear that there simply aren't enough talented (and honest!) managers to go round.

Bringing home the significance of high fees

When a fund manager or financial adviser tells an investor that the annual fees/deductions payable are 1.5 or 2 per cent of the amount invested it is easy to miss the significance of the figure for the future well-being of the investor. It seems to be such a trifling amount and the mind can quickly dismiss it.

To explore how the deductions can impact on the amount accumulated within an investor's saving fund Table 5.1 displays some theoretical, but realistic, invest-

---

[15] Negative correlation means that returns go the opposite way: when domestic equities are down the hedge fund instruments are up, and vice versa.

ment returns over a 10-year period, following a lump-sum £20,000 investment at the outset.

In the first case we have the end value available following self-investment in a broad range of shares that give an average of 8 per cent return per year. In this case (as with all the others) we assume away the bid–offer spread costs associated with buying and selling shares in the markets. Rational investors (as opposed to short-term speculators) keep these costs to a minimum, by trading infrequently. After 10 years the savings amount to £39,147, thus the investment fund has almost doubled.

Not all investors have the time, inclination or self-confidence to invest in a broad range of shares and achieve reduced risk through diversification. To lift the burden of investing in the equity market they may approach a professional fund manager. Another good reason to invest through a collective fund is that the investor is faced with prohibitively high transaction costs when placing a small amount of money in a portfolio of shares. Furthermore, there is the hassle of managing a personal portfolio, e.g. dealing with dividends, rights issues, takeover bids.

Thus investing via a pooled investment fund makes a lot of sense for many people. What is often overlooked is that paying high fees usually results in poorer returns to the ultimate investor rather than excellence. Some high-quality managers do exist and achieve such high pre-fee returns they can justify the enhanced bonuses of the manager – the problem is in identifying these professionals in advance. For most of us the safer option is to look for a low-cost option to achieve a broad spread.

A unit trust, with 5 per cent initial fee/adviser's fee and 1.5 per cent annual charge split between the fund manager and the platform (Case 2 in Table 5.1), shows a large reduction in investor wealth after 10 years compared with the self-invest approach: the fund drops from £39,147 to only £31,973. To hand over more than £7,000 to fund managers to achieve returns equal to the market return (which would put them in the category of one of the better performers) seems a little excessive. By shopping around for a low-cost fund more is available at the end – Case 3 produces £34,873.

If you are sceptical about finding an active fund manager who can outperform the market sufficiently well to justify the high fees then perhaps you would select to put your money into an exchange traded fund which bought all the shares in a broad market index (or cheap market tracking unit trust, OEIC or investment trust) with a cost of a mere 0.3 per cent per year (Case 4). Such an approach will produce £37,988. This is over £6,000 more than the standard actively managed unit trust!

Table 5.1 Investment returns on self-investment and fund investment under various fees deduction scenarios

Time (years)	Return %	Case 1 Self-investment		Case 2 Unit trust (no fees) from provider (initial charge 5%; annual charge 1.5%)		Case 3 Unit trust with reduced initial and annual charge (initial charge 1.5%; annual charge 1%)		Case 4 Exchange Traded Fund (initial charge 0; annual charge: 0.3%)		Case 5 Hedge fund (initial charge 0; annual charge 2% plus 20% of any positive return on the fund)	
		Fees (£)	Capital	Fees (£)	Capital	Fees (£)	Capital	Fees (£)	Capital	Fees (£)	Capital
Start		0	20,000	1,000	19,000	300	19,700		20,000		20,000
1	8	0	21,600	285	20,212	197	21,063	60	21,535	720	20,880
2	16	0	25,056	303	23,094	211	24,189	65	24,906	1,086	23,135
3	0	0	25,056	346	22,748	242	23,947	75	24,831	463	22,672
4	−24	0	19,043	341	17,029	239	18,018	74	18,815	453	16,778
5	16	0	22,089	255	19,458	180	20,692	56	21,760	873	18,589
6	8	0	23,857	292	20,699	207	22,124	65	23,430	669	19,407
7	16	0	27,674	310	23,651	221	25,407	70	27,098	1,009	25,201
8	24	0	34,315	355	28,887	254	31,189	81	33,500	1,462	25,201
9	−8	0	31,570	433	26,177	312	28,407	101	30,728	504	22,681
10	24	0	39,147	393	31,973	284	34,873	92	37,988	1,542	26,582

Hedge funds sell themselves on the claim that they can do well in any market, whether the financial markets are booming or collapsing. We discovered in 2008 that hedge funds went down with the rest – with a few exceptions – and that many equity-focused funds were closet market trackers. Again, if you are smart enough to analyse/guess which will outperform perhaps their fees of 2 per cent plus 20 per cent of any positive return are justified. However, as Case 5 shows, if the fund merely performs in line with the market, the hedge fund manager takes away so much of the return in the good performing years that the investor is left with only a little more than what they started with. Admittedly, some managers charge less than these percentages. Some also have 'high water-marks' which means that they must make good previous years' negative returns (or, perhaps, a minimum positive return) before charging the performance bonus. This will mitigate this problem, but you still have the difficulty of being *really* certain that the manager will outperform spectacularly to justify paying a high set annual fee plus bonuses.

Warren Buffett brilliantly describes how fund managers and others in the financial industry have benefitted from the ignorance of ordinary investors in the story of the Gotrocks and the Helpers (see Article 5.8).

Article 5.8

Gotrocks and Helpers

By Warren Buffett

Shareholders, through a series of self-inflicted wounds, are in a major way cutting the returns they will realize from their investments. The explanation of how this is happening begins with a fundamental truth: With unimportant exceptions, such as bankruptcies in which some of a company's losses are borne by creditors, *the most that owners in aggregate can earn between now and Judgement Day is what their businesses in aggregate earn*. True, by buying and selling what is clever or lucky, investor A may take more than his share of the pie at the expense of investor B. And, yes, all investors *feel* richer when stocks soar. But an owner can exit only by having someone take his place. If one investor sells high, another must buy high. For owners as a whole, there is simply no magic – no shower of money from outer space – that will enable them to extract wealth from their companies beyond that created by the companies themselves.

Indeed, owners must earn less than their businesses earn because of 'frictional' costs. And that's my point: These costs are now being incurred in amounts that will cause shareholders to earn *far* less than they historically have.

To understand how this toll has ballooned, imagine for a moment that all American corporations are, and always will be, owned by a single family. We'll call them the Gotrocks. After paying taxes on dividends, this family – generation after generation – becomes richer by the aggregate amount earned by its companies. Today that amount is about $700 billion annually. Naturally, the family spends some of these dollars. But the portion it saves steadily compounds for its benefit. In the Gotrocks household everyone grows wealthier at the same pace, and all is harmonious.

But let's now assume that a few fast-talking Helpers approach the family and persuade each of its members to try to outsmart his relatives by buying certain of their holdings and selling them certain others. The Helpers – for a fee, of course – obligingly agree to handle these transactions. The Gotrocks still own all of corporate America; the trades just rearrange who owns what. So the family's annual gain in wealth diminishes, equaling the earnings of American business *minus* commissions paid. The more that family members trade, the smaller their share of the pie and the larger the slice received by the Helpers. This fact is not lost upon these broker-Helpers: Activity is their friend and, in a wide variety of ways, they urge it on.

After a while, most of the family members realize that they are not doing so well at this new 'beat-my-brother' game. Enter another set of Helpers. These newcomers explain to each member of the Gotrocks clan that by himself he'll never outsmart the rest of the family. The suggested cure: 'Hire a manager – yes, us – and get the job done professionally.' These manager-Helpers continue to use the broker-Helpers to execute trades; the managers may even increase their activity so as to permit the brokers to prosper still more. Overall, a bigger slice of the pie now goes to the two classes of Helpers.

The family's disappointment grows. Each of its members is now employing professionals. Yet overall, the group's finances have taken a turn for the worse. The solution? More help, of course.

It arrives in the form of financial planners and institutional consultants, who weigh in to advise the Gotrocks on selecting manager-Helpers. The befuddled family welcomes this assistance. By now its members know they can pick neither the

right stocks nor the right stock-pickers. Why, one might ask, should they expect success in picking the right consultant? But this question does not occur to the Gotrocks, and the consultant-Helpers certainly don't suggest it to them.

The Gotrocks, now supporting three classes of expensive Helpers, find that their results get worse, and they sink into despair. But just as hope seems lost, a fourth group – we'll call them the hyper-Helpers – appears. These friendly folk explain to the Gotrocks that their unsatisfactory results are occurring because the existing Helpers – brokers, managers, consultants – are not sufficiently motivated and are simply going through the motions. 'What,' the new Helpers ask, 'can you expect from such a bunch of zombies?'

The new arrivals offer a breathtakingly simple solution: *pay more money.* Brimming with self-confidence, the hyper-Helpers assert that huge contingent payments – in addition to stiff fixed fees – are what each family member must fork over in order to *really* outmaneuver his relatives.

The more observant members of the family see that some of the hyper-Helpers are really just manager-Helpers wearing new uniforms, bearing sewn-on sexy names like HEDGE FUND or PRIVATE EQUITY. The new Helpers, however, assure the Gotrocks that this change of clothing is all-important, bestowing on its wearers magical powers similar to those acquired by mild-mannered Clark Kent when he changed into his Superman costume. Calmed by this explanation, the family decides to pay up.

And that's where we are today: A record portion of the earnings that would go in their entirety to owners – if they all just stayed in their rocking chairs – is now going to a swelling army of Helpers. Particularly expensive is the recent pandemic of profit arrangements under which Helpers receive large portions of the winnings when they are smart or lucky, and leave family members with all of the losses – and large fixed

| Article 5.8 | Continued |

fees to boot – when the Helpers are dumb or unlucky (or occasionally crooked).

A sufficient number of arrangements like this – heads, the Helper takes much of the winnings; tails, the Gotrocks lose and pay dearly for the privilege of doing so – may make it more accurate to call the family the Hadrocks. Today, in fact, the family's frictional costs of all sorts may well amount to 20% of the earnings of American business. In other words, the burden of paying Helpers may cause American equity investors, overall, to earn only 80% or so of what they would earn if they just sat still and listened to no one.

Long ago, Sir Isaac Newton gave us three laws of motion, which were the work of genius. But Sir Isaac's talents didn't extend to investing: He lost a bundle in the South Sea Bubble, explaining later, "I can calculate the movement of the stars, but not the madness of men." If he had not been traumatized by this loss, Sir Isaac might well have gone on to discover the Fourth Law of Motion: *For investors as a whole, returns decrease as motion increases.*

Source: Warren Buffett, Chairman's Letter to Shareholders accompanying the 2005 Annual Report of Berkshire Hathaway. Reproduced with kind permission of the author. Copyright remains with Warren Buffett.

Article 5.9 presents the views of a respected economist on the dangers of paying high fees.

| Article 5.9 |

The charges laid against us
INVESTING

By John Kay

Over the 42 years that Warren Buffett has been in charge of Berkshire Hathaway, the company has earned an average compound rate of return of 20 per cent per year. For himself. But also for his investors. The lucky people who have been his fellow shareholders through all that time have enjoyed just the same rate of return as he has. The fortune he has accumulated is the result of the rise in the value of his share of the collective fund.

But suppose that Buffett had deducted from the returns on his own investment – his own, not that of his fellow shareholders – a notional investment management fee, based on the standard 2 per cent annual charge and 20 per cent of gains formula of the hedge fund and private equity business. There would then be two pots: one created by reinvestment of the fees Buffett was charging himself; and one created by the growth in the value of Buffett's own original investment. Call the first pot the wealth of Buffett Investment Management, the second pot the wealth of the Buffett Foundation.

How much of Buffett's $62bn would be the property of Buffett Investment Management

Article 5.9   Continued

and how much the property of the Buffett Foundation? The completely astonishing answer is that Buffett Investment Management would have $57bn and the Buffett Foundation $5bn. The cumulative effect of "two and twenty" over 42 years is so large that the earnings of the investment manager completely overshadow the earnings of the investor. That sum tells you why it was the giants of the financial services industry, not the customers, who owned the yachts.

So the least risky way to increase returns from investments is to minimise agency costs – to ensure that the return on the underlying investments goes into your pocket rather than someone else's.

The effect of these costs on returns depends on the frequency with which you deal. Online trading is so inexpensive and easy that you may be tempted to trade often. But only one thing eats up investment returns faster than fees and commissions, and that is frequent trading. Do not succumb. Do not accept the invitation to subscribe to level two platforms or direct market access. The total costs of running your own portfolio should be less than 1 per cent per year.

Investing in actively-managed funds will cost you more. The choice of funds, both open and closed-end, is unbelievably wide. There are more funds investing in shares than there are shares to invest in. This situation doesn't make sense, and is both cause and effect of the high charges. Costs need to be high to recover the expenses of running so many different, mainly small, funds that all do much the same thing. At the same time, the high level of charges encourages financial services companies to set up even more funds....

... This plethora of choice would be less confusing if all funds, managers and advisers were excellent, but most are not.

The underlying problem is one of information asymmetry. The marketing of financial services emphasises quality, not price, and for good reasons. It would be worth paying more – a lot more – to get a good fund manager. But since it is hard to identify a good fund manager, good and bad managers all charge high fees, with the consequences described above....

... The most attractive equity-based funds for small investors are generally indexed funds, exchange traded funds, and investment trusts (closed-end funds) with low charges and significant discounts to underlying assets. These funds provide more than sufficient choice for normal purposes. All of them can be accessed through your online execution-only share-dealing account.

6

Bonds

Bonds can be good investments for private investors to hold. They offer a higher income than a building society deposit account, with the possibility of some capital growth. They generally offer lower risk than shares, but offsetting this is the fact that they offer a lower return.

A bond is a long-term contract in which the bondholder lends money to a company, government or some other organisation. In return, typically, the company or government promises to pay predetermined regular interest and a capital sum at the end of the bond's life. Basically, bonds may be regarded as merely IOUs with pages of legal clauses expressing the promises made. They are the most significant financial instruments in the world today, with tens of trillions of pounds, dollars, etc. in issue. They come in all shapes and sizes, from UK government bonds to Chinese company bonds.

The advantage of placing your money with an organisation via a bond is that you are *promised* a return. Bond investors are exposed to less risk than share investors because the promise is backed up with a series of legal rights, among them the right to receive the annual interest before the equity holders receive any dividend. So in a bad year (with, say, no profits) the bond investors are far more likely to receive a payout than the shareholders. This is usually bolstered with rights to seize company assets if the company reneges on its promise. There is a greater chance of saving some of your investment if things go very badly for the firm if you are holding its bonds rather than its shares, because on liquidation the proceeds raised by selling off the assets are used to pay the holders of debt-type financial securities first, before shareholders receive anything.

Offsetting these plus points are the facts that bondholders do not (usually) share in the value created by an extraordinarily successful business, and there is an absence of any voting power over the management of the company.

Confusingly, many investment products are described as 'bonds' but are not true bonds in the sense of being loans. For example, guaranteed equity bonds, with-profits bonds, distribution bonds and single-premium bonds issued by insurance companies (see Chapter 5), and 'bonds' issued by building societies. The only bonds we will deal with in this chapter are long-term *loan* contracts.

Bonds are often referred to collectively as **fixed-interest securities**. While this is an accurate description for many bonds, others do not offer *regular* interest payments that are *fixed* amounts. Nevertheless they are all lumped together as fixed-interest to contrast these types of loan instrument with equities that do not carry the promise of a return.

Gilts

In most years the British government does not raise enough in taxes to cover its expenditure. It makes up a large part of the difference by selling bonds. These are called 'gilts' because in the old days you would receive a very attractive certificate with gold-leaf edges (**gilt-edged securities**). Buying UK government bonds is among the safest form of lending in the world. The risk of the UK government failing to pay is infinitesimally small.[1]

While the risk of non-receipt of interest and capital is minute if you buy and hold gilts to the maturity date, you can lose money buying and selling gilts from year to year (or month to month) in the secondary market before they mature (this was shown in Chapter 2). There have been many occasions when, if you purchased at the start of the year and sold to another investor in the secondary market at the end of the year, even after receiving interest, you would have lost 5 per cent or more. On the other hand, there were many years when you would have made large gains.

The government issues gilts via the UK **Debt Management Office (DMO)** (www.dmo.gov.uk). The gilts are sold with a **nominal (face** or **par)** value of £100. This is not necessarily what you would pay. The nominal value signifies what the government will pay *you* at the end of, say, 5, 10 or 25 years. This is how much the gilt will be redeemed for on the **redemption** date. You might pay £100 or £99

---

[1] Bonds issued by governments are known as **sovereign bonds**.

or £100.50, or some other sum for it, depending on the coupon offered and the general level of interest rates in the markets.

The **coupon** (sometimes called the dividend) is the stated annual rate of return on the nominal value of the bond. It is a percentage figure shown immediately after the name of each gilt. So, for example, a Treasury 4pc '22 pays out £4 each year for every £100 nominal. Then in the year 2022 the nominal value of £100 is paid when the gilt is redeemed. The coupons are paid twice yearly in two equal instalments.

The names assigned to gilts (also called **stocks**), such as Exchequer, Treasury or Funding, are useful for distinguishing one from another but have no particular significance beyond that. What is more important is whether they are dated, undated or conversion. **Dated gilts** have a fixed date(s) at which they are redeemed.[2] A few **undated gilts** exist, such as War Loan 3½ pc, which can only be redeemed at the government's discretion. The government can go on paying £3.50 per year for ever. **Conversion gilts** allow the investor to choose whether to convert a gilt to another more attractive one.

Gilts are classified according to the current life left as from now (not from when they were first issued). **Shorts** are those that will be redeemed within five years (or seven years, depending on who you talk to).[3] Those with 5–15 years to run are **medium-dated**. If maturity is at least 15 years (or 12 years) away the gilt is **long-dated**. And, of course, there are undated gilts.

Prices and returns

The coupons showing on different gilts can have a wide range, from 2.5 per cent to 8.75 per cent. These were (roughly) the rates of interest that the government had to offer at the time of issue – some were issued 80 or more years ago. However, things have moved on since issue and these percentages are not the rates of return offered on the gilt to a buyer in the secondary market today.

So, if we take an undated gilt offering a coupon of 2.5 per cent on the nominal value we may find that investors are buying and selling a bond that offers £2.50 per year at a price of £50, not at its nominal value of £100. This gilt offers an investor today a yield of 5 per cent:

---

[2] In the past, the government has issued double-dated gilts with a band of maturity dates. Only one of these bonds remains in issue, 12% Exchequer Stock 2013–2017. The government can choose to redeem these gilts in whole, or in part, on any day between the first and final maturity dates. Until it is redeemed £12 will be paid each year in coupons on a £100 nominal amount.

[3] **'Ultra-shorts'** may be up to three years to redemption.

$$\frac{£2.50}{£50} \times 100 = 5\%$$

Thus we see some bonds trading above and, as in this case, below the nominal value of £100 in the secondary market. By means of variation in the price of the bond, investors are able to receive the current going rate of return for that type of investment.

Yield

There are, in fact, two types of yields on dated gilts, and on other bonds with fixed redemption dates. The case of a Treasury 10 pc with five years to maturity currently selling in the secondary market at £120 will serve to illustrate the two. From the name of the gilt we glean that it pays £10 per year (10 per cent of the nominal value of £100). For £120 investors can buy this gilt from other investors on the secondary market to receive an **interest yield** (also known as the **current yield, flat yield, income yield, simple yield** and **running yield**) of 8.33 per cent:

Interest yield = Gross (before tax) interest coupon/Market price × 100

$$= \frac{£10}{£120} \times 100 = 8.33\%$$

This is not the true rate of return available to the investor because we have failed to take into account the capital loss over the next five years. The investor pays £120 but receives only the nominal value of £100 at the end. If this £20 loss is apportioned over the five years it works out at £4 per year. The capital loss as a percentage of what the investor pays (£120) is £4/£120 × 100 = 3.33 per cent per year. This loss to redemption has to be subtracted from the annual interest yield to give an approximation to the **redemption yield** (also called **yield to maturity, YTM**): 8.33 per cent – 3.33 per cent = 5 per cent. This is sometimes called **gross redemption yield** because it does not allow for tax levied on the income received from it. While this example tries to convey the essence of redemption yield calculations, it oversimplifies in that a compound interest-type calculation is required to obtain a precise figure.[4]

---

[4] For more details, see Chapter 11 of G. Arnold, *Corporate Financial Management* (Financial Times Publishing, 2012) or G. Arnold *The Financial Times Guide to Bond and Money Markets* (Financial Times Publishing, forthcoming).

The general rules are as follows:

■ If a dated gilt (or other bond) is trading at less than £100 the purchaser will receive a capital gain between purchase and redemption and so the redemption yield is greater than the interest yield.

■ If a dated gilt is selling at more than £100 a capital loss will be made if held to maturity and so the redemption yield is below the interest yield.

Of course, these capital gains and losses are based on the assumption that the investor buys the gilt and then holds to maturity. In reality many investors sell a few days or months after purchase, in which case they may make capital gains or losses dependent not on what the government pays on maturity but on what another investor is prepared to pay. This, in turn, depends on general economic conditions – in particular, projected general inflation over the life of the gilt: investors will not buy a gilt offering a 5 per cent redemption yield over five years if future inflation is expected to be 7 per cent per year for that period. Interest rates (particularly for longer-term gilts) are thus strongly influenced by market perceptions of future inflation, which can shift significantly over a year or so, hence the high annual gains or losses in the secondary gilt market (shown in Chapter 2).

Bond prices and redemption yields move in opposite directions. Take the case of our five-year gilt offering a coupon of 10 per cent with a redemption yield of 5 per cent. If general interest rates rise to 6 per cent because of an increase in inflation expectations, investors will no longer be interested in buying this gilt for £120, because at this price it yields only 5 per cent. Demand will fall, resulting in a price reduction until the bond yields 6 per cent. A rise in yield goes hand in hand with a fall in price.

Redemption yields for gilts are quoted daily online by the Debt Management Office at www.dmo.gov.uk as well as at www.ft.com and many other financial websites, e.g. www.bloomberg.com, www.fixedincomeinvestor.co.uk, www.hl.co. uk, www.londonstockexchange.com, www.selftrade.co.uk, www.iii.co.uk and www.fitchratings.com.

Quotes

The gilts market is focused around **gilt-edged market makers (GEMMs)** who are prepared to buy from or sell to investors. They quote two prices: the **bid price** is the price at which they will buy, and the **offer price** is their selling price. The UK gilts table shown daily in the *Financial Times* shows the middle price, half way between the bid and offer price – see Box 6.1.

Note that the redemption yield shown in the *Financial Times* is relevant if you are an investor on that particular day paying the price shown. However, if you bought your gilt years ago and expect to hold to maturity you will receive the yield that was obtainable at the time of purchase.

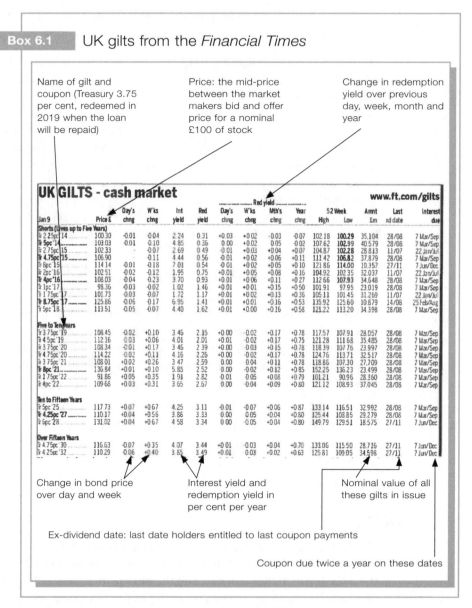

Box 6.1   UK gilts from the *Financial Times*

Name of gilt and coupon (Treasury 3.75 per cent, redeemed in 2019 when the loan will be repaid)

Price: the mid-price between the market makers bid and offer price for a nominal £100 of stock

Change in redemption yield over previous day, week, month and year

Change in bond price over day and week

Interest yield and redemption yield in per cent per year

Nominal value of all these gilts in issue

Ex-dividend date: last date holders entitled to last coupon payments

Coupon due twice a year on these dates

Source: www.markets.ft.com/research/Markets/Bonds, 9 January 2014.

Buying and selling gilts

You can buy or sell gilts through brokers or investment platforms in the same fashion as with shares (see Chapter 4 and 5). Telephone or online dealing is offered by many brokers. You would state the nominal value of the gilts you want to deal and whether you want to trade 'at best' (the best price currently in the market) or with a limit on the price you are prepared to pay (or sell for).

High street banks, some building societies, independent financial advisers and even some solicitors and accountants will buy or sell gilts for you.

You can buy and sell gilts in the primary and secondary market via the DMO's Gilt Purchase and Sales Service using Computershare (www-uk.computershare. com). You will have to fill in forms to become an 'Approved Group of Investors' member. You post a completed form with a cheque – see www.dmo.gov.uk. You are not able to specify the price or a maximum/minimum price at which your purchase/sale of gilts are to be made.

Unlike the purchase of shares you do not have to pay 0.5 per cent stamp duty.

Another way of gaining exposure to the gilt (and/or corporate bond) market is to buy units in a unit trust or investment trust that specialises in the type of bonds you are interested in. You gain professional management and diversification but you will pay fees (sometimes over 1 per cent per year, which is a lot as a proportion of the annual interest on gilts of say 3 or 4 per cent). Exchange traded funds (see Chapter 5) are another alternative.

Cum-dividend and ex-dividend

Gilts usually pay coupons twice a year. Between payments the interest accrues on a daily basis. If you buy a gilt you are entitled to the accrued interest since the last coupon. You will receive this when the next coupon is paid. That is, you buy the gilt **cum-dividend**. Gilts (and other bonds) are quoted at **clean prices** – that is, without taking account of the accrued interest. However, the buyer will pay the clean price plus the accrued interest value (called the **dirty price** or **full price** or **invoice price**) and receives all of the next coupon. So, if you buy a gilt four months before the next coupon due you would pay the clean price, say, £98 plus 60 days' accrued interest.

If you bought just before the coupon is to be paid the situation is different. There would not be enough time to change the register to make sure that the coupon goes to the new owner. To allow for this problem a gilt switches from being quoted cum-dividend to being **ex-dividend** seven days before an interest payment. If you buy during the ex-dividend period the person you bought from would receive the accrued interest from the issuer – this would be reflected in the price you pay.

Index-linked gilts

There is a hidden danger with conventional gilts – **inflation risk**. Suppose that you, along with the rest of the gilt-buying community, figure that inflation over the next 10 years will average 2.5 per cent. As a result you buy 10-year gilts that have a redemption yield of 4.8 per cent giving a comfortable real income over and above cost-of-living rises. However, two years later inflation starts to take off (oil prices quadruple, or the government goes on a spending spree). Now investors reckon that inflation will average 6 per cent over the following eight years. As a result your gilt yield will fail to maintain your capital in real terms.

The government introduced a type of bond that ensures you receive a return above the inflation rate throughout the entire life of the bond. These are called **index-linked stocks (gilts)**, where the coupon amount and the nominal value are adjusted or uplifted according to the Retail price index (RPI). The gilt initially offers to pay £100 at the end of its term, say 10 years away. It also offers to pay a low coupon, say 2 per cent. The key thing about index-linked bonds is that neither the capital sum on maturity nor the coupon stays at these levels unless inflation is zero over the next 10 years.

Suppose inflation is 4 per cent over the first year of the bond's life. The payout on maturity rises to £104. This inflation-linked uplift happens every year. So, if over the 10 years the inflation measure has risen by 60 per cent, the payout on the bond is £160. This means that you can buy just as many goods and services at the end with the capital sum as at the beginning of the bond's life (if you paid £100). Furthermore, the coupon rate also rises through the years if there is inflation. So, after the first year the coupons go up by 4%, that is, £2 × 1.04 = £2.08. (The situation is slightly more complicated than this in that the inflation figures used are those for three[5] months preceding the relevant coupon dates, but this example illustrates the principle.)

Because most investors hold them to maturity secondary trading is thin and dealing spreads wider than for conventional gilts.

While these are virtually risk-free investments if held to maturity the price of the bonds in the secondary market fluctuates on a daily basis. Thus you could buy at, say 130 and end up selling a year later at 110 resulting in a negative return. A viable alternative is index-linked national savings certificates available at post offices (www.nsandi.com).

---

[5] For bonds issued prior to July 2005 the lag is eight months.

Corporate bonds

Corporate bonds offer a higher rate of return than gilts but, as you might expect, this comes with a greater degree of risk. It has been known for companies to be unable to pay interest and principal on the bonds they issue, and for bond-holders to end up with nothing following liquidation. This downside should not be overemphasised because the vast majority of corporate bonds pay out the full promised amount. They are certainly much safer than investing in shares.

Corporate bonds are generally **negotiable** (that is, tradable in a secondary market). They come in a variety of forms. The most common is the type with regular (usually annual or semi-annual) fixed coupons and a specified redemption date. These are known as **straight**, **vanilla** or **bullet bonds**. Other bonds are a variation on this. Some pay coupons every three months, some do not pay a fixed coupon but one which varies depending on the level of short-term interest rates (**floating-rate** or **variable-rate bonds**), some have interest rates linked to the rate of inflation. In fact, the potential for variety and innovation is almost infinite. Bonds issued in the last few years have linked the interest rates paid or the principal payments to a wide variety of economic events, such as a rise in the price of silver, exchange-rate movements, stock market indices, the price of oil, gold or copper – even to the occurrence of an earthquake. These bonds were generally designed to let companies adjust their interest payments to manageable levels in the event of the firm being adversely affected by some economic variable changing. For example, a copper miner pays lower interest on its finance if the copper price falls. Sampdoria, the Italian football club, issued a €3.5 million bond that paid a higher rate of return if the club won promotion to the 'Serie A' division. If the club rose to the top four in Serie A the coupon would rise to 14 per cent.

Debentures and loan stocks

In the UK and a few other countries the most secure type of bond is called a **debenture**. They are usually secured by either a fixed or a floating charge against the firm's assets. A **fixed charge** means that specific assets are used as security, which, in the event of default, can be sold at the insistence of the debenture bondholders and the proceeds used to repay them. Debentures secured on property may be referred to as **mortgage debentures**. A **floating charge** means that the loan is secured by a general charge on all the assets of the corporation. In this case the company has a high degree of freedom to use its assets as it wishes, such as sell them or rent them out, until it commits a default which 'crystallises' the floating charge. If this happens a receiver will be appointed with powers to dispose of assets and to distribute the proceeds to the creditors. Even though floating-charge debenture holders can force a liquidation, fixed-charge debenture holders rank above floating-charge debenture holders in the payout after insolvency.

The terms 'bond', 'debenture' and **'loan stock'** are often used interchangeably and the dividing line between debentures and loan stock is a fuzzy one. As a general rule, debentures are secured (have the backing of collateral) and loan stock is unsecured, but there are examples that do not fit this classification. If liquidation occurs the unsecured loan stockholders rank beneath the debenture holders and some other categories of creditors such as the tax authorities.[6]

Trust deeds and covenants

Bond investors are willing to lower the interest they demand if they can be reassured that their money will not be exposed to a high risk. This reassurance is conveyed by placing risk-reducing restrictions on the firm. A **trust deed** (or bond indenture) sets out the terms of the contract between bondholders and the company. A trustee (if one is appointed) acting for the bond holders ensures compliance with the contract throughout the life of the bond and has the power to appoint a receiver (to liquidate the firm's assets). If a trustee is not appointed, the usual practice is to give each holder an independently exercisable right to take legal action against a delinquent borrower. The loan agreement will contain a number of **affirmative covenants**. These usually include the requirements to supply regular financial statements, interest and principal payments. The deed may also state the fees due to the lenders and details of what procedures are to be followed in the event of a default, such as non-payment of interest.

In addition to these basic covenants are the **negative (restrictive) covenants**. These restrict the actions and the rights of the borrower until the debt has been repaid in full. Some examples are:

- **Limits on further debt issuance**. If lenders provide finance to a firm they do so on certain assumptions concerning the riskiness of the capital structure. They will want to ensure that the loan does not become riskier due to the firm taking on a much greater debt burden relative to its equity base, so they limit the amount and type of further debt issues – particularly debt which is higher (**senior debt**) ranking for interest payments and for a

---

[6] In the US and other markets a debenture is an unsecured bond and so the holders become general creditors who can only claim assets not otherwise pledged to creditors. The secured form of bond is referred to as the mortgage bond and unsecured shorter-dated (less than 10 years) issues are called notes.

liquidation payment. **Subordinated debt (junior debt)** – with low ranking on liquidation – is more likely to be acceptable.

■ **Dividend level.** Lenders are opposed to money being taken into the firm by borrowing at one end, while being taken away by shareholders at the other. An excessive withdrawal of shareholders' funds may unbalance the financial structure and weaken future cash flows.

■ **Limits on the disposal of assets.** The retention of certain assets, such as property and land, may be essential to reduce the lenders' risk.

■ **Financial ratios.** A typical covenant here concerns the interest cover, for example: The annual profit will remain four times as great as the overall annual interest charge (see Chapter 12 for more on interest cover under 'income gearing'). Other restrictions might be placed on working capital ratio levels and the debt to net assets ratio.

While negative covenants cannot ensure completely risk-free lending, they can influence the behaviour of the managerial team so as to reduce the risk of default. The lenders' risk can be further reduced by obtaining guarantees from third parties (e.g. guaranteed loan stock). The guarantor is typically the parent company of the issuer.

Repayments

The principal on many bonds is paid entirely at maturity. However, there are bonds which can be repaid before the final redemption date. A common approach is for the company to issue bonds with a range of dates for redemption; so a bond dated 2020–2024 would allow a company the flexibility to repay a part of the principal in each of four years. Another way of redeeming bonds is for the issuing firm to buy the outstanding bonds by offering the holder a sum higher than or equal to the amount originally paid. A firm is also able to purchase bonds on the open market.

Some bonds are described as 'irredeemable' (perpetual) as they have no fixed redemption date. From the investor's viewpoint they may be irredeemable, but the firm has the option of repurchase and can effectively redeem the bonds.

Bond variations

Bonds which are sold at well below the par value are called **deep discounted bonds,** the most extreme form of which is the zero coupon bond. These are sold at a large discount to the nominal value. The investor makes a capital gain by holding the bond instead of receiving coupons. For example, a company may issue a bond at a price of £60 which is redeemable at £100 in eight years. These bonds are particularly useful for firms with low cash flows in the near term – for example, firms engaged in a major property development that will not mature for many years.

Floating rate notes (FRNs) (also called **'variable-rate notes'**) are instruments that pay an interest that is linked to a benchmark rate – such as the **London Inter-Bank Offered Rate (LIBOR)**. LIBOR is the rate that banks charge each other for borrowed funds. The issuer will pay, say, 70 basis points (0.7 percentage points) over LIBOR. The coupon is set for, say, the first 6 months at the time of issue, after which it is adjusted every 6 months; so if LIBOR was 4 per cent, the floating rate note would pay 4.7 per cent for that particular period of six months.[7]

Trading in the corporate bond market

The gilts secondary market is very liquid, with a single government bond issue raising billions and with thousands of investors trading in the market. By contrast, corporate bond market activity can be very low. Companies may raise merely tens or hundreds of millions of pounds in an issue, and most investors buy and hold to maturity. Some companies issue bonds on a regular basis, every few months or years, each with its own coupons and terms, thus there might be a dozen bonds for one company, and thousands of different corporate issues in the secondary market place. The wide range reduces the market depth for any one issue. Some corporate bonds are sufficiently liquid to trade on the London Stock Exchange, but the vast majority of trading occurs in the **over-the-counter (OTC)** market directly between an investor and a bond dealer. **Bond dealers** stand ready to quote a bid and an offer price depending on whether you want to buy or sell. Your broker will have to contact a number of these dealers by telephone to get quote prices. The bid–offer spreads are generally higher than for equities – even large company bonds can have a spread of 15 per cent, but most are less than this.

Because most corporate bond market trading is a private matter between the dealer and its customer in the OTC market it is difficult to obtain prices of recent trades. They are not shown in the *Financial Times*, for example. Some websites provide prices and other details on a few dozen corporate bonds, e.g. www.fixedincomeinvestor. co.uk, www.hl.co.uk, www.stockcube.investorschronicle.co.uk, www.selftrade.co.uk, www.markets.ft.com/research/Markets/Bonds. In a range of bonds can be achieved by purchasing specialised exchange traded funds, unit trusts, or investment trusts.

Corporate bonds have generally been the province of of investing institutions, such as pension and insurance funds. Private investors tend not to hold them,

---

[7] If you want to research corporate bonds a good place to start is the issuing company's website. If you know the year of issue you can download the relevant annual report telling you about the issue. You can also read the bond prospectus on the company's website.

mainly due to the large amounts of cash involved – occasionally £1,000 minimum, more often £50,000. The par value on one bond at, say, £50,000, €50,000 or $50,000 is said to have a minimum 'lot' or 'piece'. However, in 2010, the London Stock Exchange opened a secondary market trading facility for small investors, where lots are just £100 or £1,000, and the costs of trading are relatively low. Its Order Book for Retail Bonds, ORB (www.londonstockexchange.com) offer retail investors the opportunity to trade a number of gilts, corporate bonds and international bonds (see later).

There is another class of bonds targeted at retail investors, but these do not have a secondary market and cannot be held in ISAs. They have been dubbed mini-bonds and are issued in very small amounts by small companies such as the £2.5 million issue by bed maker Warren Evans, with a coupon of 7.5 per cent. With these bonds you are lending for the full term (usually 3–5 years), to a small, usually unquoted firm with less open accounting than quoted firms. The marketing and information material has not been vetted by the Financial Conduct Authority, unlike ORB bonds. Mini-bonds share with ORB bonds the exclusion from the Financial Services Compensation Scheme (see Chapter 19).

Credit rating

Firms often pay to have their bonds rated by specialist **credit-rating** organisations. Investors are advised to pay close attention to the outcome of these rating exercises. The *debt rating* depends on the likelihood of payments of interest and/or capital not being made (that is, **default**) and on the extent to which the lender is protected in the event of a default by the loan contract (the *recoverability* of debt).[8] UK government gilts have an insignificant risk of default whereas unsecured subordinated corporate loan stock has a much higher risk. We would expect that firms in stable industries with conservative accounting and financing policies and a risk-averse business strategy would have a low risk of default and therefore a high credit rating. Companies with a high total debt burden, a poor cash flow position, in a worsening market environment causing lower and more volatile earnings, will have a high default risk and a low credit rating. The leading organisations providing credit ratings are Moody's, Standard

---

[8] The rating agencies say that they do not in the strictest sense give an opinion on the likelihood of default, but merely evaluate relative creditworthiness or relative likelihood of default, and because rating scales are relative, default rates fluctuate over time. Thus, a group of middle-rated bonds are expected to be consistent in having a lower rate of default than a group of lower-rated bonds, but they will not, year-after-year, have a default rate of say 2.5%.

and Poor's (S&P) and Fitch. The highest rating is AAA (S&P), Aaa (Moody's) or AAA (Fitch), pronounced 'triple-A'. Such a rating indicates very high quality, with an extremely strong capacity to repay interest and principal. Single A indicates a strong capacity to pay interest and capital, but some degree of susceptibility to impairment as economic events unfold. BBB indicates adequate debt service capacity but vulnerability to adverse economic conditions or changing circumstances. Debt rated B or C has predominantly speculative characteristics. The lowest is D, which indicates the firm is in default. Ratings of BBB– (S&P and Fitch) or Baa3 (Moody's) or above are regarded as **'investment-grade debt'** – this is important because many institutional investors are permitted to invest in investment-grade bonds only (see Figure 6.1). Bonds rated below this are called **high-yield (or junk) bonds**.

Bond credit ratings are available at www.standardandpoors.com, www.moodys. com and www.fitchratings.com.

Note that the specific loan is rated, rather than the borrower. If the loan does not have a rating it could be that the borrower has not paid for one, rather than implying anything sinister.

High-yield (junk) bonds

High-yield or junk bonds are debt instruments offering a high return with a high risk. They may be either unsecured, or secured but ranking behind senior loans. This type of debt generally offers interest rates 2–9 percentage points higher than that on senior debt and frequently gives the lenders some right to a share in equity values should the firm perform well. It is a kind of hybrid finance ranking for payment below straight debt but above equity – it is thus described alternatively as **subordinated**, **intermediate** or **low-grade**. One of the major attractions of this form of finance for the investor is that it often comes with equity warrants or share options attached (see Chapters 8 and 10) which can be used to obtain shares in the firm – this is known as an **'equity kicker'**. These may be triggered by an event taking place, such as the firm joining the stock market.

High-yield bond finance tends to be used when bank borrowing limits are reached and the firm cannot or will not issue more equity. The finance it provides is cheaper (in terms of required return) than would be available on the equity market, and it allows the owners of a business to raise large sums of money without sacrificing control. It is a form of finance that permits the firm to move beyond what are normally considered acceptable debt–equity ratios (gearing or leverage levels).

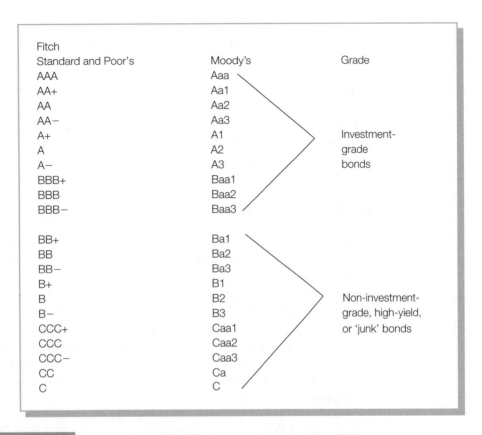

Figure 6.1 　　Moody's, Standard & Poor's and Fitch's rating scales

Bonds with high-risk and high-return characteristics may have started as apparently safe investments but have now become riskier ('fallen angels'), or they may be bonds issued specifically to provide higher risk financial instruments for investors.

Be aware of **'fallen angel risk'**. Bond fund managers, pension funds, etc. are reluctant (or forbidden) to hold anything below investment grade so a downgrade to junk status can lower the price of the bond considerably as major investors exit.

Investment-grade bond prices and returns tend to move in line with gilt interest rates influenced by perceptions of future inflation rather than the risk of default (although risk of default has a role to play). Junk bond prices (and their yields), on the other hand, are much more related to the prospects for the company's fundamentals because the company needs to thrive if it is to cope with high debt levels and raised interest, and cause the equity kicker to have some value. Many of the factors that affect equity valuation (see Part 3) also have an impact on junk bond valuations. As a result high-yield bonds tend to be more volatile than investment-grade bonds, going up and down depending on expectations concerning the company's survival, strength and profitability.

Private investors are unlikely to be investing directly in the high-yield bond market as this is a market for professionals, but may invest via corporate bond funds (e.g. unit trusts). These offer economies of scale in research and in dealing, as well as the advantage of diversification. However, there is a price to pay: management charges can be heavy (see Chapter 5).

Convertible bonds

Convertible bonds (or convertible loan stock) carry a rate of interest in the same way as ordinary bonds, but they also give the holder the right to *exchange* the bonds at some stage in the future into ordinary shares according to some prearranged formula.[9] The owner of these bonds is not obliged to exercise this right of conversion, and so the bond may continue until redemption as an interest-bearing instrument. Usually the **conversion price** is 10–30 per cent greater than the existing share price. So, if a £100 bond offered the right to convert to 40 ordinary shares the conversion price would be £2.50 (that is, £100/40) which, given the market price of the shares of, say, £2.20, would be a **conversion premium** of:

$$\frac{2.50 - 2.20}{2.20} \times 100 = 13.6\%$$

The right to convert may state a specific date or several specific dates over, say, a four-year period, or any time between two dates. In a rising stock market it is reasonable to suppose that most convertible bonds issued with a small conversion premium will be converted to shares. However, this is not always the case.

In a rising stock market it is reasonable to suppose that most convertible bonds issued with a small conversion premium will be converted to shares. However, this is not always the case, and many have not been converted leaving only an interest return. The value of a convertible bond (a type of 'equity-linked bond') rises as the value of ordinary shares increases, but at a lower percentage rate. The value could be analysed as a 'debt portion', which depends on the discounted value of the

---

[9] Alternatively they may be convertible into preference shares, or into shares lacking votes.

coupons, and an 'equity portion', where the right to convert is an equity option (see chapter 8). If the share price rises above the conversion price the investor may choose to exercise the option to convert if he/she anticipates that the share price will at least be maintained and the dividend yield is higher than the convertible bond yield. If the share price rise is seen to be temporary the investor may wish to hold on to the bond. If the share price remains below the conversion price, the value of the convertible will be the same as a straight bond at maturity.

Convertibles with large conversion premiums trade much like ordinary bonds because the option to convert is not a strong feature in their pricing. They offer higher yields, and prices are not volatile. Those trading with a small conversion premium have lower yields and the prices are more volatile as they are more closely linked with the share price.

The advantages of convertible bonds to investors are:

■ They are able to wait and see how the share price moves before investing in equity.

■ In the near term there is greater security for their principal compared with equity investment, and the annual coupon is usually higher than the dividend yield.

The bonds sold may not give the right to conversion into shares of the issuing company, but shares of another company held by the issuer. The term **'exchangeable bond'** is probably more appropriate in these cases.

Foreign bonds

A foreign bond is a bond denominated in the currency of the country where it is issued when the issuer is a non-resident.[10] For example, in Japan bonds issued by non-Japanese companies denominated in yen are foreign bonds. (The interest and capital payments will be in yen.) Foreign bonds in Tokyo are known as Samurai bonds; foreign bonds issued in New York and London are called Yankees and Bulldogs, respectively. In the Netherlands you will find Rembrandts and in Spain Matador bonds.

Foreign bonds are regulated by the authority where the bond is issued. These rules can be demanding and an encumbrance to companies needing to act quickly and

---

[10] A bond denominated in the issuer's local currency and offered to local residents is a 'domestic bond'.

at low cost. The regulatory authorities have also been criticised for stifling innovation in the financial markets. The growth of the less restricted Eurobond market has put the once dominant foreign bond market in the shade.

Eurobonds

Let's get one misunderstanding out of the way: Eurobonds are unconnected with the currency of the Eurozone countries! They were in existence decades before Europe thought of creating the euro. The term 'euro' in Eurobond does not even mean European. So what are they, then?

Eurobonds are bonds sold outside the jurisdiction of the country of the currency in which the bond is denominated. So, for example, the UK financial regulators have little influence over the Eurobonds denominated in sterling issued in Luxembourg, even though the transactions (e.g. interest and capital payments) are in pounds. Bonds issued in US dollars in Paris are outside the jurisdiction of the US authorities.

Eurobonds are medium- to long-term instruments (three or more years) not subject to the rules and regulations which are imposed on foreign bonds, such as the requirement to issue a detailed prospectus.[11] More importantly, they are not subject to an **interest-withholding tax**. In the UK most domestic bonds are subject to a withholding tax by which income tax is deducted before the investor receives interest. Interest on Eurobonds is paid gross without any tax deducted – which has attractions to investors keen on delaying, avoiding or evading tax. Moreover, Eurobonds are normally **bearer bonds**, which means that the holders do not have to disclose their identity – all that is required to receive interest and capital is for the holder to have possession of the bond. In contrast, UK domestic bonds are registered, which means that companies and governments are able to identify the owners.

Despite the absence of official regulation, the International Capital Market Association (ICMA), a self-regulatory body, imposes some restrictions, rules and standardised procedures on Eurobond issue and trading.

The *Financial Times* publishes a table showing a selection of secondary market prices of international and emerging market bonds. This gives the reader some idea of current market conditions and rates of return demanded for bonds of different maturities, currencies and riskiness – see Box 6.2.

---

[11] Although EU rules mean that a prospectus is required if the bond is marketed at retail (non-professional) investors.

Box 6.2   International bond prices in *The Financial Times*

BONDS - GLOBAL INVESTMENT GRADE

Jan 10	Red date	Coupon	S*	Ratings M*	F*	Bid price	Bid yield	Day's chge yield	Mth's chge yield	Spread vs Govts
US$										
Hutchison 03/33	01/14	6.25	A-	A3	A-	99.68	-	-	-3.02	-
Misc Capital	07/14	6.13	BBB	Baa2	-	102.18	1.36	-0.07	0.03	1.30
BHP Paribas	06/15	4.80	A-	Baa3	A	104.86	1.38	-0.02	0.17	1.26
GE Capital	01/16	5.00	AA+	A1	-	108.15	0.84	-0.04	-0.06	0.46
Erste Euro Lux	02/16	5.00	A+	-	-	102.95	3.51	0.04	-0.38	3.09
Credit Suisse USA	03/16	5.38	A	A1	A	109.01	1.08	-0.02	0.09	0.35
SPI E&G Aust	09/16	5.75	A-	A3	A-	109.01	2.25	0.08	0.21	1.45
Abu Dhabi Nt En	10/17	6.17	A-	A3	-	113.90	2.30	-0.14	-0.14	1.12
Swire Pacific	04/18	6.25	A-	A3	A	113.97	2.75	0.00	0.07	1.11
ASNA	11/18	6.95	A-	Baa2	A	119.57	2.58	-0.14	-0.17	0.96
Codelco	01/19	7.50	AA-	A1	A+	119.65	3.21	0.05	0.04	1.57
Bell South	10/31	6.88	A-	WR	A	112.88	5.71	-0.11	-0.22	2.85
GE Capital	01/39	6.88	AA+	A1	-	128.35	4.90	-0.11	-0.19	1.07
Goldman Sachs	02/33	6.13	A-	Baa1	A	113.73	5.00	-0.12	-0.21	2.14
Euro										
SNS Bank	02/14	4.63	BBB	Baa3	BBB+	100.25	1.91	0.04	0.15	1.80
JPMorgan Chase	01/15	5.25	A	A3	A+	104.63	0.58	-0.01	-0.10	0.47
Hutchison Fin 06	09/16	4.63	A-	A3	A-	109.27	1.10	-0.14	-0.14	0.77
Hypo Alpe Bk	10/16	4.25	-	A1	-	98.31	4.91	-0.04	-2.20	4.66
GE Cap Euro Fdg	01/18	5.38	AA+	A1	-	114.83	1.53	-0.07	-0.04	0.96
Unicredit	01/20	4.38	BBB	Baa2	BBB+	109.06	2.73	-0.08	-0.29	1.65
ENEL	05/24	5.25	BBB	Baa2	BBB+	112.30	3.79	-0.04	-0.11	1.94
Yen										
Deutsche Bahn Fin	12/14	1.65	AA	Aa1	AA	101.02	0.49	0.02	0.03	0.42
Nomura SecS 3	03/18	2.28	-	-	-	104.32	1.20	-0.01	-0.39	1.05
£ Sterling										
Sbugh Estates	09/15	6.25	-	-	A-	106.84	2.11	-0.05	0.00	1.57
ASIF III	12/18	5.00	A+	A2	A	110.90	2.59	-0.10	0.04	0.84

US $ denominated bonds NY close; all other London close. S* - Standard & Poor's, M* - Moody's, F* - Fitch.
Source: ThomsonReuters

Labels to the left of the figure:

Issuer

Redemption date

Coupon as a % of par value

Credit ratings

Current bond price, with par set at 100

Gross (before deduction of tax) yield to maturity (redemption yield)

Spread to the government bond interest rate in that denomination. The extent to which the redemption yield (bid yield) is greater than that on a government bond of the same length of time to maturity

BONDS - HIGH YIELD & EMERGING MARKET

Jan 10	Red date	Coupon	S*	M*	F*	Bid price	Bid yield	Day's chge yield	Mth's chge yield	Spread vs US
High Yield US$										
Kazkommerts Int	04/14	7.88	B	Caa1	B	99.25	-	-	-8.72	-
Bertin	10/16	10.25	BB	Ba3	-	111.40	5.67	0.20	-0.45	4.94
High Yield Euro										
Royal Carib Crs	01/14	5.63	BB	Ba1	-	99.84	-	-	-1.54	-
Kazkommerts Int	02/17	6.88	B	Caa1	B	98.00	7.62	0.00	0.03	7.29
Emerging US$										
Bulgaria	01/15	8.25	BBB	Baa2	BBB-	107.35	0.85	-0.04	-0.23	0.73
Peru	02/15	9.88	BBB+	Baa2	BBB+	108.96	1.32	-0.05	0.26	1.20
Brazil	03/15	7.88	BBB	Baa2	BBB	107.18	1.52	-0.18	-0.21	1.41
Mexico	09/16	11.38	BBB+	Baa1	BBB+	127.15	1.03	0.09	0.00	0.23
Philippines	01/19	9.88	BBB-	Baa3	BBB-	132.13	2.92	-0.08	-0.07	1.18
Brazil	01/20	12.75	BBB	Baa2	BBB	146.90	3.91	-0.12	-0.02	1.61
Colombia	02/20	11.75	BBB	Baa3	BBB	142.60	3.86	-0.04	0.14	1.56
Russia	03/30	7.50	BBB	Baa1	BBB	116.65	4.14	0.06	0.00	2.51
Mexico	08/31	8.30	BBB+	Baa1	BBB+	135.03	5.23	0.01	-0.07	2.34
Indonesia	02/37	6.63	BB+	Baa3	BBB-	99.00	6.71	0.02	0.11	2.83
Emerging Euro										
Brazil	02/15	7.38	BBB	Baa2	BBB	106.75	0.90	-0.18	-0.25	0.73
Poland	02/16	3.63	A-	A2	A-	106.19	0.57	-0.12	-0.12	0.38
Turkey	03/16	5.00	NR	Baa3	BBB-	106.04	2.06	-0.01	0.09	1.87
Mexico	02/20	5.50	BBB+	Baa1	BBB+	117.07	2.45	-0.01	-0.13	1.38

US $ denominated bonds NY close; all other London close. *S - Standard & Poor's, M - Moody's, F - Fitch.
Source: ThomsonReuters

The change in the redemption yield over past day/month

Source: *Financial Times*, 10 January 2014.

7

Unusual share investments

Buying shares in companies quoted on the London Stock Exchange's Main Market or the AIM remains the main investment route for most people. However, there are ways of spicing up your investment portfolio by stepping outside the conventional. You could, for example, invest in companies just starting up, or those that are young and looking for expansion capital. These companies will be years away from obtaining a secondary market quotation for their shares and so, in becoming a **'business angel'** investor, you are accepting that it may be difficult to dispose of your shares even if the company is progressing nicely. You are also accepting a relatively high degree of risk of complete failure. But the upside, if all goes well, can be tremendous. Investors putting just a few thousand pounds in a small company have become very wealthy following the firm's flotation, or when it is sold to another company. For example, Body Shop investor Ian McGlinn was a garage owner who put £4,000 into Body Shop in 1976. His 23 per cent stake was later sold to L'Oréal for nearly £150 million.

Venture capital investing and other **private equity** investing is usually on a larger scale than business angel investing and is generally conducted through funds, such as 3i or Electra, which are able to gather together money from numerous investors to channel it to unquoted companies needing millions of pounds to set up or grow. Investing in these funds has the advantage of diversified exposure to many fast-growing dynamic companies as well as benefiting from the experience of professional venture capital managers able to sort the wheat from the chaff.

A third possibility is investment in overseas shares. There is a certain logic to not having all your eggs in one economic basket (the UK economy) and spreading your portfolio across a number of countries. Many emerging economies offer the prospect of rapid development and high share returns. On the other hand, there are dangers in operating in poorly regulated and unfamiliar territory.

Finally, **preference shares** offer a route to investment with less risk than ordinary shares but with higher returns than on bonds.

Business angels (informal venture capitalists)

Business angels are wealthy individuals, generally with substantial business and entrepreneurial experience, who usually invest between £10,000 and £250,000 primarily in start-up, early stage or expanding firms. About three-quarters of business angel investments are for sums of less than £100,000, with the average investment around £25,000–£30,000. The majority of investments are in the form of equity finance but angels do purchase debt instruments and preference shares. They usually do not have a controlling shareholding and they are willing to invest at an earlier stage than most formal venture capitalists. (They often dislike the term 'business angel', preferring the title **'informal venture capitalist'**.)

Business angels are generally looking for entrepreneurial companies with high aspirations and potential for growth. A typical business angel makes one or two investments in a three-year period, often in an investment syndicate led by an **'archangel'**, an experienced investor coordinating the group. They generally invest in companies within a reasonable travelling distance from their homes because most like to be 'hands-on investors', playing a significant role in strategy and management – on average, angels allocate 10 hours a week to their investments. Most angels take a seat on the board.[1] Business angels are patient investors willing to hold their investment for at least five years.

The main way in which firms and angels find each other is through friends and business associates, although there are a number of formal networks. Useful contacts include the following:

www.advantagebusinessangels.com	Advantage Business Angels
www.angelsden.com	Angels Den
www.angelinvestmentnetwork.co.uk	Angel Investment Network
ww2.angelbourse.com	Angelbourse
www.beerandpartners.com	Beer & Partners
www.dcxworld.com	Development Capital Exchange

---

[1] Having said this, many business angels (generally those with investments of £10,000–£20,000) have infrequent contact with the company.

www.gov.uk/government/ organisations/department-for-business-innovation-skills	Department for Business, Innovation and Skills
www.entrust.co.uk	Entrust
www.fisma.org	FISMA
www.lbangels.co.uk	London Business Angels
http://www.nwbusinessangels.co.uk	Northwest Business Angels
www.ukbusinessangelsassociation.org.uk	UK Business Angels Association
http://www.yaba.org.uk	Yorkshire Association of Business Angels

Angel network events are organised where entrepreneurs can make a pitch to potential investors, who, if they like what they hear in response to their questions, may put in tens of thousands of pounds. Prior to the event the network organisers (or a member) will generally screen the business opportunities to avoid time wasting by the no-hopers. To be a member of a network investors are expected to either earn at least £100,000 per year or have a net worth of at least £250,000 (excluding main residence). If you have a specialist skill to offer (e.g. you are an experienced company director or chartered accountant), you may be permitted membership despite a lower income or net worth.

Returns to business angel investments are often negative. However, they can be spectacular; the angels who together put €2 million into Skype multiplied their money by 350 times when the company was sold to eBay for €2.1 billion.

Many business angel deals are structured to take advantage of tax breaks such as those through enterprise investment schemes (EISs) which offer income tax relief and capital gains tax deferral. For more on tax, see Chapter 17.

Crowdfunding

There are many websites which connect entrepreneurial firms seeking equity or debt capital with investors in the **crowdfunding** (also known as **crowd financing** or **crowd sourced capital**) sector. You can look at a range of companies pitching to raise a few hundred thousand or millions from hundreds of investors putting in amounts ranging upwards from just a few hundred pounds. Examples include:

www.crowdcube.com	Crowdcube
www.crowdfunduk.org	Crowdfunduk
www.fundingcircle.com	Funding Circle
www.kickstarter.com	Kickstarter
www.nesta.org.uk/project/crowdfunding	Nesta
www.seedrs.com	Seedrs

The online platforms usually vet the applications from companies. Investors can often participate in strategic decision making and have voting rights

Venture capital and other private equity

The distinction between venture capital (VC) and private equity is blurry. Some use **private equity** to define all unquoted company equity investment, others confine 'private equity' to management buy-outs and the like of companies already well-established, leaving **'venture capital'** for investment in companies at an early stage of development with high growth potential. Both types are medium- to long-term investment and can consist of a package of debt and equity finance. Venture capitalists take high risks by investing in the equity of young companies often with a limited (or no) track record. Many of their investments are into little more than a management team with a good idea – which may not have started selling a product or even developed a prototype. It is believed, as a rule of thumb in the VC industry, that out of 10 investments two will fail completely, two will perform excellently and the remaining six will range from poor to very good.

High risk goes with high return. Venture capitalists expect to get a return of between five and 10 times their initial equity investment in about five to seven years. This means that the firms receiving equity finance are expected to produce annual returns for investors of at least 26 per cent. Alongside the usual drawbacks of equity capital from the investors' viewpoint (last in the queue for income and on liquidation, etc.), investors in small unquoted companies also suffer from a lack of liquidity because the shares are not quoted on a public exchange. There are a number of different types of venture funding (these days the last five will often be separated from VC and grouped under the title private equity).

- **Seedcorn**. This is financing to allow the development of a business concept. Development may also involve expenditure on the production of prototypes and additional research. Usually financed by business angels rather than venture funds.

- **Start-up**. A product or idea is further developed, and/or initial marketing is carried out. These companies are very young and have not yet sold their product commercially. Usually financed by business angels rather than venture funds.

- **Other early-stage**. Funds for initial commercial manufacturing and sales. Many companies at this stage will remain unprofitable.

- **Expansion (development or growth)**. Companies at this stage are on a fast-growth track and need capital to fund increased production capacity, working capital and further development of the product or market.

▨ **Management buy-outs (MBOs)**. Here a team of managers make an offer to their employers to buy a whole business, a subsidiary or a section so that they own and run it for themselves. Large companies are often willing to sell to these teams, particularly if the business is underperforming and does not fit with the strategic core business. Usually the management team have limited funds of their own and so call on venture capitalists to provide the bulk of the finance.

▨ **Management buy-ins (MBIs)**. A new team of managers from outside an existing business buy a stake, usually backed by a VC fund. A combination of an MBO and an MBI is called a 'BIMBO' – buy-in management buy-out – where a new group of managers joins forces with an existing team to acquire a business.

▨ **Leveraged buy-out (LBO)**. The buy-out of an existing company or division, with 60–90 per cent of the money coming from debt. Private equity groups usually supply much of the debt as well as equity, the rest of the debt comes from banks or the financial markets.

▨ **Secondary purchase**. A private equity-backed company is sold to another private equity fund.

▨ **Public-to-private (PTP)**. The management of a company currently quoted on a stock exchange may return it to unquoted status with the assistance of VC finance being used to buy the shares.

Private equity firms are less keen on financing seedcorn, start-ups and other early-stage companies than expansions, MBOs, MBIs, LBOs and PTPs. This is largely due to the very high risk associated with early-stage ventures and the disproportionate time and costs of financing smaller deals. To make it worthwhile for a private equity or VC organisation to consider a company the investment must be at least £250,000 – the average investment is about £5 million – and it is difficult to find venture capitalists willing to invest less than £2 million.

Because of the greater risks associated with the youngest companies, the VC funds may require returns of the order of 50–80 per cent per annum. For well-established companies with a proven product and battle-hardened and respected management the returns required may drop to the high 20s. These returns may seem exorbitant, especially to the managers set the task of achieving them, but they have to be viewed in the light of the fact that many VC investments will turn out to be failures and so the overall performance of the VC funds is significantly less than these figures suggest. In fact the British Private Equity and Venture Capital Association reports that returns on funds are not excessively high. Taken as a whole, the return to investors net of costs and fees was 13.1 per cent per annum to the end of 2012 for funds raised between 1996 and 2008. This compares well with average annual returns of around 8.8 per cent on UK quoted shares in the 10 years to the end of 2012. However, as Table 7.1 shows, within the overall figure the real winners have been those backing MBOs; venture capital investors achieved returns of under 1 per cent per year.

Table 7.1	Returns on UK private equity funds Internal rates of return (IRR) to investors since inception of the fund from 1996 to December 2012, net of costs and fees. Only funds raising money 1996–2008[2]	
		Per cent per annum
Venture capital funds		0.4
Small management buy-outs		16.0
Mid management buy-outs		13.3
Large management buy-outs		14.7
Total		13.1
Comparators' returns over 10 years to December 2012		
UK listed shares (FT All-Share)		8.8
Overseas equity		9.3
UK bonds		6.3
Overseas bonds		7.3
Property		5.7

Source: Data sourced from *Performance Measurement Survey 2012*, BVCA, PricewaterhouseCoopers and Capital Dynamics, www.bvca.co.uk.

Private equity categories

As you have gathered by now, as share investment outside stock markets has grown it has become differentiated. The main categories are shown in Figure 7.1, with private equity as the umbrella term covering the various activities. In this more differentiated setting the term venture capital is generally confined to describing the building of companies from the ground floor, or at least from a very low base.

---

[2] Funds raised from 2009 onwards are not included in the calculation of since-inception returns as these funds are still at the early stage of their life cycle, and their investment return during this period does not provide a meaningful indication of their performance at liquidation.

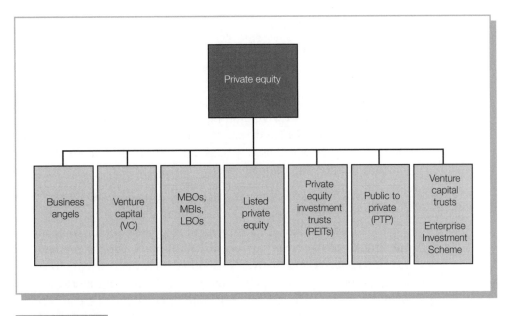

Figure 7.1 Categories of private equity

Management buy-outs and buy-ins of established businesses (already off the ground floor) have become a specialist task, with a number of dedicated funds. Many of these funds are formed as private partnerships by wealthy individuals and a high proportion are American owned.

Small investors can buy shares in **Listed Private Equity (LPEQ)** funds which are companies investing in unquoted companies but which have their own shares quoted on a stock exchange. There are about 80 investable listed private equity companies in Europe, with a total market capitalisation of €45 billion, of which €12 billion are London-listed companies (see www.lpeq.com). They come in two varieties; firstly, those that are straightforward listed companies, and those that are listed as investment trusts, called **private equity investment trusts (PEITs)**. They are stock market quoted investment trusts with a focus on investing their shareholders' money in more risky, unquoted, developing companies.[3] The disadvantage of listed private equity companies is the absence of special tax concessions compared with venture capital trusts and enterprise investment schemes – see Chapter 17. However investors are able to exit their investments easily by dealing on the stock market.

---

[3] However, some PEITs invest in private equity funds ('fund of funds').

Leverage and exits

For the larger investments, particularly MBOs and MBIs, the private equity fund may provide only a fraction of the total amount required. Thus, in a £50 million buy-out the private equity firm might supply (individually or in a syndicate with other funds), say, £15 million in the form of share capital (ordinary and prefer-ence shares). Another £20 million may come from a group of banks in the form of debt finance. The remainder may be supplied as **mezzanine debt** – high-return and high-risk debt which usually has some rights to share in the spoils should the company perform exceptionally well.

Private equity managers generally like to have a clear target set as the eventual **'exit'** (or **'take-out'**) date. This is the point at which the private equity investors reap their rewards. Many exits are achieved by the sale of the company to another firm (**trade sale** or **corporate acquisition**), but a popular method is flotation on a stock market. Alternative exit routes are for the company to repurchase its shares or for the private equity fund to sell the holding to an institution such as an investment trust or another private equity group (a **secondary buy-out** or **secondary sale**).

Managerial control

Private equity funds are rarely looking for a controlling shareholding in a company and are often content with a 20–30 per cent share.[4] They may also supply funds through the purchase of convertible preference shares which give them rights to convert to ordinary shares – which will boost their equity holding and increase the return if the firm performs well. In an initial investment agreement they may insist on some widespread powers. For instance, the company may need to gain the private equity firm's approval for the issue of further securities, and they may hold a veto over acquisition of other companies. Even though their equity holding is generally less than 50 per cent, the private equity funds frequently have special rights to appoint a number of directors. If specific negative events happen, such as a poor performance, they may have the right to appoint most of the board of directors and therefore take effective control. More than once the founding entrepreneur has been aggrieved to be removed from power. (Despite the loss of power, he or she often has a large shareholding in what has grown to be a multi-million-pound company.)

The private equity firm can help a company with more than money. It usually

---

[4] However, MBO and MBI funds usually take most of the shares of a company because the investee company is so large the management team can only afford a small proportion of the shares.

has a wealth of experience and talented people able to assist the budding entrepreneur. Many of the UK's most noteworthy companies were helped by the VC industry – for example, Cambridge Silicon Radio, Waterstone's bookshops, Oxford Instruments (and in America: Google, Apple, Sun Microsystems and most of Silicon Valley).

Points for investors concerning angels and private equity

▓ The tax breaks for investors in this area are great – see Chapter 17.

▓ This is high-risk investing. Because you have to be able to withstand the occasional disaster, you should not put a large proportion of your funds in investments of this type.

▓ Management charges can be high with private equity funds. They could consist of an initial charge of 5 per cent, followed by annual charges of 2.5 per cent plus performance fees (usually 20 per cent of returns).

▓ These investments can be illiquid in the early years.

▓ Have you the time and experience to be a business angel in the 'hands-on' sense?

▓ This area of investment has its fair share of sharks and charlatans, so be careful – it also helps to be part of a network of investors.

Overseas shares

UK shares account for about 8 per cent of the value of equities quoted on stock exchanges around the world. Why limit yourself to British companies when there are so many opportunities elsewhere? In the past the answer to this question from many investors was that trading foreign shares involved more cost, more risk and generally more hassle. Matters have improved dramatically as the Internet has made the obtaining of information about overseas companies much easier, as well as allowing online trading. The intense competition between brokers invading each other's geographic territory has pushed down costs and increased the quality of services. The shift to electronic trading and settlement of share transactions in the majority of developed overseas markets has simplified administration processes enormously. Less paper passing through fewer hands and more electronic keyboard strokes has resulted in lower costs and fewer mistakes. Encouraged by this modernisation, over one-fifth of UK investors have taken the plunge and bought non-UK shares.

Many UK brokers offer access to international markets. Competition in this area is hotting up, particularly for online execution-only trading. In some cases commissions have fallen to the same level as for dealing in UK shares, but more typically you might pay 1.5–2 times as much. Charges for overseas broking are often raised because of the cost of paying **custodian** fees, that is, paying a broker in the other country to act as a nominee, holding the shares, handling dividends and other administrative activities. Orders placed with your broker are executed directly through the overseas exchange. You can set price limits or instruct your broker to trade at best (see Chapter 4).

Your broker is likely to ask you to sign a **Risk Warning Notice** acknowledging that you are aware of additional risks of overseas investment. There is also a form (W-8BEN) stating your non-US status so that US dividends can be paid without the full tax amount deducted from that income. In most developed markets settlement is two or three days after the trade, so brokers need access to your money quickly. Therefore they generally insist on the setting up of a **broking account** (a broker cash management account) and nominee account (see Chapter 4). For regular overseas traders it is usually wise to operate with semi-permanent foreign currency accounts in, say, dollars or euros as this will reduce the costs of regular currency conversions.

It is possible to open a foreign currency account and trade through an **overseas broker**. The initial deposit is fairly high at around $10,000, but the Internet makes communicating cheap, quick and simple.

UK taxation is payable on income and capital gains from overseas equities in the normal way. However, if withholding tax has already been charged overseas the UK investor can claim a tax credit to avoid being charged twice. Her Majesty's Revenue and Customs allows any share quoted on a recognised investment exchange to be held in an ISA or self-invested personal pension. Most countries do not impose stamp duty on share purchases.

Points to consider about investing abroad

- Many brokers will only deal in the leading companies in the leading stock markets.

- Shareholder rights are not as well protected in many countries as in the UK. Even some European countries have poor reputations for matters such as protecting small shareholders, openness to takeover, amount of information released and concentration of boardroom power in a clique (families often rule the roost from behind the scenes). Large international businesses tend to be better and follow best international practice.

■ Keeping track of medium-sized and small companies can be difficult. Information may not be supplied in English, either by the company or brokers. Newspapers such as the *Financial Times* cover the large firms, but obviously cannot bring to your attention details about every foreign company. Try www.adr.com from J.P. Morgan, www.advfn.com and national Yahoo! Finance sites.

■ You could be exposed to currency shifts. However, if you have investments in a number of currencies you can take a sanguine swings-and-roundabouts attitude to this.

■ On the whole, it is still more expensive to buy abroad than at home.

■ In the developing world, trading systems may be inefficient: settlement systems often rely on paper, which can be carelessly handled, even lost. Share certificates have been known to arrive months after the transaction. Insider trading and corruption can mean that the outsider is at a considerable disadvantage.

■ Political risks – meaning negative consequences as a result of government action, e.g. nationalisation without compensation – are a serious worry in some parts of the world, despite a general shift to international openness and respectability.

■ You may have to file a tax return in the relevant country.

Alternatives to investing directly in overseas shares include the purchase of **depositary receipts** (see Chapter 3 for a description). Many foreign companies have depositary receipts traded on the London Stock Exchange (also, many have their shares listed through LSE's International Order Book). **American depositary receipts** are available in the USA. If you simply want to invest in an overseas stock market generally, rather than picking individual shares, then open-ended funds, investment trusts and exchange-traded funds are possible routes to go – but watch out for high fees (see Chapter 5). A further approach, which is more short-term investing, is to buy contracts for difference or spread-betting positions that benefit if the shares in the main index in another country go up (see Chapter 10). Your bet is in sterling and your winnings (or losses) are in sterling with spread betting.

Also many UK companies (e.g. Shell and Vodafone) derive a large part of their profits from overseas, and so you could gain international exposure by buying UK shares in a UK regulatory environment.

Emerging and frontier

Emerging stock markets are those in countries with relatively low/middle incomes but with rapid economic growth, for example China, Indonesia and India, or countries that have reached a fairly high level of income per head but which have small underdeveloped stock markets and limited internationalisation of financial markets (e.g. many eastern European countries, Turkey and Chile).

The place where the line is drawn between advanced and emerging economies and stock markets is highly subjective. Different researchers use different factors to classify countries, so there are many alternative lists of emerging markets but the core countries are the BRIC countries: Brazil, Russia, India and China.

Frontier markets are places that have stock markets where you can invest but they tend to be very small with few companies listed. Turnover of shares is generally low and there might be government restrictions placed on your ability to buy into their companies. They are often poor countries such as Kenya, Vietnam and Tanzania. They are a subset of emerging markets with such low market capitalisations and turnover that they are not included in the larger emerging market indexes (for that they need a minimum number of quoted companies of a certain size and free float – the proportion of shares available for ordinary shareholders to buy – plus an openness to foreign ownership). They can be exciting places for you to pick up high-growth companies in high-growth economies at a time when most investors are steering clear. But beware of the extra risk associated with a lower quality legal environment, capricious governments and suspect corporate governance.

Unfortunately, not many UK brokers will buy frontier market shares for you. They simply do not have the systems and overseas contacts in place. As a result most investors gain exposure to frontier markets by investing through a collective fund such as a unit trust or investment trust.

Some useful websites for investors in overseas shares

Stock exchanges such as the New York Stock Exchange (www.nyse.com), have very good websites providing information and links. As well as these you might like to try the following:

www.bloomberg.com	Bloomberg
www.schwab.com	Charles Schwab
www.money.cnn.com	CNNMoney
www.corporateinformation.com	Corporate Information
www.digitallook.com	Digital Look
www.edgr.com	Edgar Online

www.euroland.com	Euroland
www.ft.com	Financial Times
www.hoovers.com	Hoovers
www.idealing.com	iDealing.com
www.reuters.com	Reuters
www.wsj.com	The Wall Street Journal
www.tdwaterhouse.co.uk	T. D. Waterhouse
https://uk.finance.yahoo.com	Yahoo!Finance

Brokers' websites can provide you with details about their services and supply research tools.

Preference shares

Preference shares (prefs) appeal to investors seeking regular stable income as they offer their owners a fixed rate of dividend each year. However, if the firm has insufficient profits the amount paid will be reduced, sometimes to zero. Thus, there is no guarantee that an annual income will be received, unlike with debt capital. The dividend on preference shares is paid before anything is paid out to ordinary shareholders – indeed, after the preference dividend obligation has been met there may be nothing left for ordinary shareholders. Preference shares are attractive to some investors because they offer a regular income at a higher rate of return than that available on fixed-interest securities (e.g. bonds). However, this higher return also comes with higher risk, as the preference dividend ranks after bond interest, and upon liquidation preference holders are further back in the queue as recipients of the proceeds of asset sell-offs.

Preference shareholders are not usually able to benefit from any extraordinarily good performance of the firm – any profits above expectations go to the ordinary shareholders. Also preference shares usually carry no voting rights, unless the dividend is in arrears or in the case of a liquidation.

One of the reasons why companies issue preference shares is that the dividends can be omitted for one or more years. This can give the directors more flexibility and a greater chance of surviving a downturn in trading. Contrast this with debt capital, which carries an obligation to pay interest regardless of the firm's difficulties. Although there may be no legal obligation to pay a dividend every year the financial community is likely to take a dim view of a firm that missed a dividend – this may have a deleterious effect on the price of the ordinary shares as investors become nervous and sell. Also preference shares are an additional source of capital, which, because it does not (usually) confer voting rights, does not dilute the influence of the ordinary shareholders on the firm's direction.

While it is possible to make capital gains by trading in and out of preference shares they tend to be much less volatile than ordinary shares and generally behave more like bonds responding to interest rate changes.

There are a number of variations on the theme of preference share. Here are some features that can be added:

- **Cumulative**. If dividends are missed in any year the right to eventually receive a dividend is carried forward. These prior-year dividends have to be paid before any payout to ordinary shareholders.

- **Participating**. As well as the fixed payment, the dividend may be increased if the company has high profits (the additional payment is usually a proportion of any ordinary dividend declared).

- **Redeemable**. These have a finite life, at the end of which the initial capital investment will be repaid. The more common **irredeemables** have no fixed redemption date from the holder's point of view, but the issuer may have reserved fixed dates when they can choose to redeem.

- **Convertibles**. These can be converted into ordinary shares at specific dates and on preset terms (e.g. one ordinary share for every two preference shares). These shares often carry a lower yield (dividend as a proportion of share price) since there is the attraction of a potentially large capital gain.

- **Variable rate**. A variable dividend is paid. The rate may be linked to general interest rates or to some other variable factor.

Stamp duty of 0.5 per cent is payable on purchase of prefs, and the capital and income tax treatment is the same as for ordinary shares. The prices and dividend yields of preference shares are quoted in the *Financial Times*, alongside prices of ordinary shares. Note that many have very few trades in the secondary market and so it may be difficult to buy or sell in volume.

8

Options

Derivatives – options, futures, warrants, etc. – are the subject of this chapter and the next two. Derivative instruments have become increasingly important for professional investors over the last 30 years. However, they are not just the province of professionals. Private investors can also exploit these powerful tools to either reduce risk or to go in search of high returns. Naturally, exceptionally high returns come with exceptionally high risk. So traders using derivatives for this purpose need to understand the risk they are exposed to. Many people (and giant companies) have lost fortunes by allowing themselves to be mesmerised by the potential for riches while failing to take the time to fully understand the instruments they were buying. They jumped in, unaware of or ignoring the potential for enormous loss.

Here (and in the following two chapters) we describe the main types of derivatives and show how they can be used for controlling risk (hedging) and for revving-up returns (speculation). We also try to convey the downside so that investors can go into these markets with their eyes open.

What is a derivative?

A derivative instrument is an asset whose performance is based on (derived from) the behaviour of the value of an **underlying** asset (usually referred to simply as the 'underlying'). The most common underlyings are commodities (e.g. tea or pork bellies), shares, bonds, share indices, currencies and interest rates. Derivatives are contracts which give the right, and sometimes the obligation, to buy or sell a quantity of the underlying, or benefit in another way from a rise or fall in the value of the underlying. It is the legal *right* that becomes an asset, with its own value, and it is the right that is purchased or sold.

Derivatives instruments have been employed for more than two thousand years. Olive growers in ancient Greece, unwilling to accept the risk of a low price for their crop when harvested months later, would enter into **forward agreements** whereby a price was agreed for delivery at a specific time. This reduced uncertainty for both the grower and the purchaser of the olives. In the Middle Ages forward contracts were traded in a kind of secondary market, particularly for wheat in Europe. A futures market was established in Osaka's rice market in Japan in the seventeenth century. Tulip bulb **options** were traded in seventeenth-century Amsterdam.

Commodity futures trading really began to take off in the nineteenth century with the Chicago Board of Trade regulating the trading of grains and other futures and options, and the London Metal Exchange dominating metal trading.

So derivatives are not new. What is different today is the size and importance of the derivatives markets. We have witnessed an explosive growth in volumes of trade, the variety of derivatives products, and the number and range of users and uses.

What is an option?

An option is a contract giving one party the right, but not the obligation, to buy or sell a financial instrument, commodity or some other underlying asset at a given price, at or before a specified date. The purchaser of the option can either exercise the right or let it lapse – the choice is theirs.

A very simple option would be where a firm pays the owner of a piece of land a non-returnable **premium** (say, £10,000) for an option to buy the land at an agreed price (say, £1 million) because the firm is considering the development of a retail park within the next five years. The property developer may pay a number of option premiums to owners of land in different parts of the country. If planning permission is eventually granted on a particular plot the option to purchase may be **exercised**. In other words, the developer pays the price agreed at the time that the option contract was arranged, to purchase the land. Options on other plots will be allowed to lapse and will have no value. By using an option the property developer has 'kept the options open' with regard to which site to buy and develop and, indeed, whether to enter the retail park business at all.

Options can also be **traded**. Perhaps the option to buy could be sold to another company keener to develop a particular site than the original option purchaser.

It may be sold for much more than the original £10,000 option premium, even before planning permission has been granted.

Once planning permission has been granted the site may be worth £1.5 million. If there is an option to buy at £1 million the option right has an **intrinsic value** of £500,000, representing a 4,900 per cent return on £10,000. From this we can see the gearing effect of options: very large sums can be gained in a short period of time for a small initial cash outlay.

Share options

Share options have been traded for centuries but their use expanded significantly with the creation of traded option markets in Chicago, Amsterdam and, in 1978, the London Traded Options Market. In 1992 this became part of the London International Financial Futures and Options Exchange (LIFFE – pronounced 'life'). Euronext bought LIFFE in 2002 and it is now called NYSE Liffe.

A share **call option** gives the purchaser a right, but not the obligation, to *buy* a fixed number of shares at a specified price at some time in the future. In the case of traded options on LIFFE, one option contract generally relates to a quantity of 1,000 shares. The seller of the option, who receives the **premium**, is referred to as the **writer**. The writer of a call option is obliged to sell the agreed quantity of shares at the agreed price sometime in the future. **American-style options** can be exercised by the buyer at any time up to the expiry date, whereas **European-style options** can only be exercised on a predetermined future date. Just to confuse everybody, the distinction has nothing to do with geography: most options traded in Europe are American-style options.

Call option holders (call option buyers)

Now let us examine the call options available on an underlying share, Tesco on 14 January 2014. There are a number of different options available for this share, many of which are not reported in the table presented at www.ft.com, part of which is reproduced as Figure 8.1.

So, what do the figures mean? If you wished on 14 January to obtain the right to buy 1,000 shares on or before late February 2014[1] at an **exercise price** of 340p, you would pay a premium of £47.50 (1,000 × 4.75p). If you wished to keep your option to purchase open for another month you could select the March call. But

---

[1] Expiry of options is on the third Friday of the expiry month.

			Call option prices (premiums) in pence
Expiry month	January	February	March
Exercise price			
330p	4.5	9	10.75
340p	1	4.75	6.5
Share price on 14 January 2014 = 331.2p			

Figure 8.1   **Call options on Tesco shares, 14 January 2014**

Source: Data sourced from *Financial Times*, www.advfn.com and https://globalderivatives.nyx.com *provide a wider range of option prices (more companies and more exercise prices for each company) than the* Financial Times.

this right to insist that the writer sells the shares at the fixed price of 340p on or before a date in late March will cost another £17.50 (the total premium payable on one option contract is £65 rather than £47.50). This extra £17.50 represents additional **time value**. Time value arises because of the potential for the market price of the underlying to change in a way that creates **intrinsic value**. The intrinsic value of an option is the pay-off that would be received if the underlying were at its current level when the option expires. In this case, there is currently (14 January) no intrinsic value because the right to buy is at 340p whereas the share price is 331.2p. However, if you look at the call option with an exercise price of 330p then the right to buy at 330p has intrinsic value because if you purchased at 330p by exercising the option you could immediately sell at 331.2p in the share market: the intrinsic value is therefore 1.2p per share, or £12 for 1,000 shares. The longer the time over which the option is exercisable, the greater the chance that the price will move to give intrinsic value – this explains the higher premiums on more distant expiry options. Time value is the amount by which the option premium exceeds the intrinsic value.

The two exercise price (also called **strike price**) levels presented in Figure 8.1 illustrate an **in-the-money option** (the 330 call options) and an **out-of-the-money option** (the 340 call options). The underlying share price (331.2p) is above the strike price of 330 and so the 330p call option has an intrinsic value of 1.2p and is therefore in-the-money. The right to buy at 340p is out-of-the-money because the share price is below the call option exercise price and therefore has no intrinsic value. The holder of a 340p option would not exercise this right to buy at 340p because the shares can be bought on the stock exchange for 331.2p. (It is sometimes possible to buy an **at-the-money option**, which is one where the market share price is equal to the option exercise price.)

To emphasise the key points: the option premiums vary in proportion to the length of time over which the option is exercisable (e.g. they are higher for a March option than for a January option). Also, call options with lower exercise prices will have a higher premium.

An illustration

Suppose on 14 January you are confident that Tesco shares are going to rise over the next two months to 380p and you purchase a March 330 call at 10.75p.[2] The cost of this right to purchase 1,000 shares is £107.50 (10.75p × 1,000 shares). If the share rises as expected then you could exercise the right to purchase the shares for a total of £3,300 and then sell them in the market for £3,800. A profit of £500 less the option premium of £107.50 (i.e. £392.50) is made before transaction costs (the brokers' fees, etc. would be in the region of £20–£50). This represents a massive 365 per cent rise before costs.

However, the future is uncertain and the share price may not rise as expected. Let us consider two other possibilities. First, the share price may remain at 331.2p throughout the life of the option. Second, the stock market may have a downturn and Tesco shares may fall to 300p. These possibilities are shown in Figure 8.2.

In the case of a standstill in the share price, the option gradually loses its time value over the two months until, at expiry, only the intrinsic value of 1.2p per share remains. The fall in the share price to 300p illustrates one of the advantages of purchasing options over some other derivatives: the holder has a right to abandon the option and is not forced to buy the underlying shares at the option exercise price – this saves £300. It would have added insult to injury to be compelled to buy at £3,300 and sell at £3,000 after having already lost £107.50 on the premium for the purchase of the option.

Figures 8.3 and 8.4 show the extent to which the purchase of an option gears up the return from share price movements: a wider dispersion of returns is experienced. On 14 January 2014, 1,000 shares could be bought for £3,312. If the value

---

[2] For this exercise we will assume that the option is held to expiry and not traded before then. However, in many cases this option will be sold on to another trader long before the expiry date approaches, at a profit or a loss.

	Assumptions on share price in March at expiry		
	300p	331.2p	380p
Cost of purchasing shares by exercising the option	£3,300	£3,300	£3,300
Value of shares bought	£3,000	£3,312	£3,800
Profit from exercise of option and sale of shares in the market	Not exercised	£12	£500
Less option premium paid	£107.50	£107.50	£107.50
Profit (loss) before transaction costs	loss £107.50	loss £95.50	profit £392.50
Percentage return over 2 months	loss 100%	loss 89%	profit 365%

Figure 8.2   **Profits and losses on the March 330 call option following purchase on 14 January**

rose to £3,800, a 14.7 per cent return would be made, compared with a 365 per cent return if options are bought. We would all like the higher positive return on the option than the lower one available on the underlying – but would we all accept the downside risk associated with this option? Consider the following possibilities. If the share price remains at 331.2p, the return if shares are bought is 0 per cent, while the return if one 330 March call option is bought is –89 per cent (the £107.5 paid for the option declines to its intrinsic value of only £12).[3] If the share prices falls to 300p, then the return if shares are bought is –9.4 per cent, while the return if one 330 January call option is bought is –100 per cent (the option is worth nothing).

The holder of the call option will not exercise unless the share price is at least 330p. At a lower price it will be cheaper to buy the 1,000 shares on the stock market. Break-even does not occur until a price of 340.75p because of the need to cover the cost of the premium (330p + 10.75p). However, at higher prices the option value increases, penny for penny, with the share price. Also the downside risk is limited to the size of the option premium.

---

[3]   £12 is the intrinsic value at expiry: (331.2p – 330p) ×1,000 = £12.

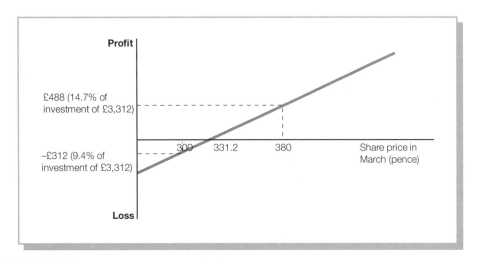

Figure 8.3 Profit if 1,000 shares in Tesco are bought on 14 January 2014 at 331.2p

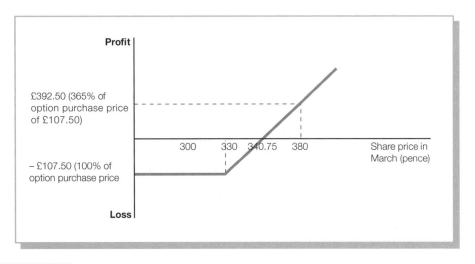

Figure 8.4 Profit if one 330 March call option contract (for 1,000 shares) in Tesco is bought on 14 January 2014 and held to maturity

Call option writers

The returns position for the writer of a call option in Tesco can also be presented in a diagram (see Figure 8.5). With all these examples remember that there is an assumption that the position is held to expiry.

If the market price is less than the exercise price (330p) in March the option will not be exercised and the call writer profits to the extent of the option premium (10.75p per share). A market price greater than the exercise price will result in the option being exercised and the writer will be forced to deliver 1,000 shares for a price of 330p. This may mean buying shares on the stock market to supply to the option holder. As the share price rises this becomes increasingly onerous, and losses mount.

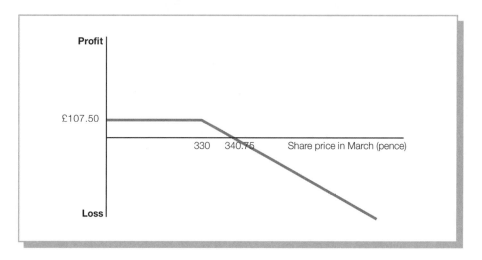

Figure 8.5   Profit to a call option writer of one 330 March call option contract (for 1,000 shares) in Tesco if written on 14 January 2014

Note that in the sophisticated traded option markets of today very few option positions are held to expiry. In most cases the option holder sells the option in the market to make a cash profit or loss. Option writers often cancel out their exposure before expiry – for example, they could purchase an option to buy the same quantity of shares at the same price and expiry date.

An example of an option writing strategy

Joe has a portfolio of shares worth £100,000 and is confident that, while the market will go up steadily over time, it will not rise over the next few months. He has a strategy of writing out-of-the-money (i.e. no intrinsic value) call options and pocketing premiums on a regular basis. Today (14 January 2014) Joe has written one option on March calls in Tesco for an exercise price of 340p (current share price 331.2p). In other words, Joe is committed to delivering (selling) 1,000 shares at any time between 14 January 2014 and the third Friday in March 2014 for a price of 340p at the insistence of the person who bought the call. This could be very unpleasant for Joe if the market price rises to, say, 400p. Then the option holder will require Joe to sell shares worth £4,000 to her for only £3,400. However, Joe is prepared to take this risk for two reasons. First he receives the premium of 6.5p per share up front – this is 2 per cent of each share's value. This £65 will cushion any feeling of future regret at his actions. Second, Joe holds 1,000 Tesco shares in his portfolio and so would not need to go into the market to buy the shares to then sell them to the option holder if the price did rise significantly. Joe has written a **covered** call option – so-called because he has backing in the form of the underlying shares. Joe only loses out if the share price on the day the option is exercised is greater than the strike price (340p) plus the premium (6.5p). He is prepared to risk losing some of the potential upside (above 340p + 6.5p = 346.5p) to gain the premium. He also reduces his loss on the downside: if the shares in his portfolio fall he has the premium as a cushion.

Some speculators engage in **uncovered (naked) option writing**. This is not recommended for beginners as it is possible to lose a great deal of money – a multiple of your current resources if you write a lot of option contracts and the price moves against you. Imagine if Joe had only £20,000 in savings and entered the options market by writing 300 Tesco March 2014 340 calls receiving a premium of 6.5p × 300 × 1,000 = £19,500.[4] If the price moves to £4 Joe has to buy shares for £4 and then sell them to the option holders for £3.40, a loss of £0.60 per share: £0.60 × 300 × 1,000 = £180,000. Despite receiving the premiums Joe has wiped out his savings and is in considerable debt.

LIFFE share options

The *Financial Times* lists about 60 companies' shares in which options are traded – some are shown in Box 8.1.

---

[4] This is somewhat simplified. In reality Joe would have to provide a margin of cash or shares to reassure the clearing house that he could pay up if the market moved against him. So it could be that all of the premium received would be tied up in the margin held by the clearing house (the role of a clearing house is explained in the next chapter).

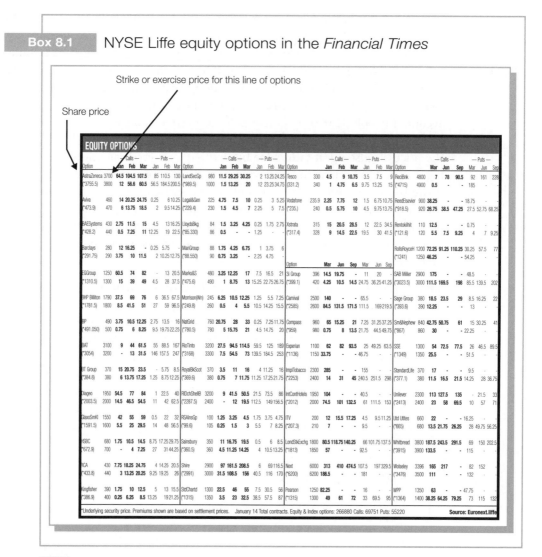

Box 8.1   NYSE Liffe equity options in the *Financial Times*

Source: *Financial Times*, 14 January 2014.

Put options

A **put option** gives the holder the right, but not the obligation, to sell a specific quantity of shares on or before a specified date at a fixed exercise price.

Imagine you are pessimistic about the prospects for Tesco on 14 January 2014. You could purchase, for a premium of 9p per share (£90 in total), the right to sell

1,000 shares before late March 2014 at 330p (see Box 8.1). If a collapse in price subsequently takes place, to 270p, say, you can insist on exercising the right to sell at 330p. The writer of the put option is obliged to purchase shares at 330p while being aware that the put holder is able to buy shares at 270p on the stock market. The option holder makes a profit of 60p per share less the 9p premium (51p per share or £510 in total), a 567 per cent return (before costs).

As with calls, in most cases the option holder would take profits by selling the option on to another investor via NYSE.liffe rather than waiting to exercise at expiry.

For the put option holder, if the market price exceeds the exercise price, it will not be wise to exercise as shares can be sold for a higher price on the stock market. Therefore the maximum loss, equal to the premium paid, is incurred. The option writer gains the premium if the share price remains above the exercise price, but may incur a large loss if the market price falls significantly.

How to trade options

Your existing share dealing broker will probably be able to offer an option (and futures) dealing facility, with or without advice. If not, ask another broker. Minimum commissions are generally £20, but brokers do go lower in special promotional periods when in search of business. Expect to pay a bid–offer spread of between 1p and 3p per share on the premiums. So if a premium were quoted at 35p in the *Financial Times*, this will be a mid-price between the price you would pay if you were buying (offer price), say 36p, and the price you would receive if you were selling (bid price), say 34p.

Traded option prices for over 300 leading European companies are carried on NYSE. liffe's website, https://globalderivatives.nyx.com/en/stock-options/nyse-liffe, continuously updated with a 15-minute delay, as they are on a number of financial websites. The NYSE.liffe site also carries a list of approved brokers. Traders can set limits on the price to pay when making an order. The price limits can be **good for the day** (if not fulfilled in a day, the order is cancelled) or **good till cancelled**.

Gains from option trading are taxable as capital gains. No stamp duty is levied on purchases.

Using share options to reduce risk: hedging

Hedging with options is especially attractive because they can give protection against unfavourable movements in the underlying while permitting the possibility of benefiting from favourable movements. Suppose you hold 1,000 shares in

Tesco on 14 January 2014. Your shareholding is worth £3,312. There are rumours flying around the market that the company may become the target of a takeover bid. If this materialises, the share price will rocket; if it does not, the market will be disappointed and the price will fall dramatically. What are you to do? One way to avoid the downside risk is to sell the shares. The problem is that you may regret this action if the bid does subsequently occur and you have forgone the opportunity of a large profit. An alternative approach is to retain the shares and buy a put option. This will rise in value as the share price falls. If the share price rises you gain from your underlying shareholding.

Assume a 330 March put is purchased for a premium of £90 (see Box 8.1). If the share price falls to 270p in late March you lose on your underlying shares by £612 ((331.2p – 270p) ×1,000). However the put option will have an intrinsic value of £600 ((330p – 270p) ×1,000), thus reducing the loss and limiting the downside risk. Below 330p, for every 1p lost on the share price, 1p is gained on the put option, so the maximum loss is £102 (£12 intrinsic value + £90 option premium).

This hedging reduces the dispersion of possible outcomes. There is a floor below which losses cannot be increased, while on the upside the benefit from any rise in share price is reduced due to the premium paid. If the share price stands still at 331.2p, however, you may feel that the premium you paid to insure against an adverse movement at 9p, or 2.7 per cent of the share price, was excessive. If you keep buying this type of 'insurance' through the year it can reduce your portfolio returns substantially.

Using options to reduce losses

A simpler example of risk reduction occurs when an investor is fairly sure that a share will rise in price but is not so confident as to discount the possibility of a fall. Suppose that the investor wished to buy 10,000 shares in Diageo, currently priced at 2003.5p (on 14 January 2014) – see Box 8.1. This can be achieved either by a direct purchase of shares in the market or through the purchase of an option. If the share price does fall significantly, the size of the loss is greater with the share purchase – the option loss is limited to the premium paid.

Diageo's share price falls to	Losses on 10,000 shares	Losses on 10 call options
1900p	£10,350	£5,450
1800p	£20,350	£5,450
1700p	£30,350	£5,450
1600p	£40,350	£5,450

Figure 8.6   **Losses on alternative buying strategies**

Suppose that 10 March 2000 call options are purchased at a cost of £5,450 (54.5p × 1,000 × 10). Figure 8.6 shows that the option is less risky because of the ability to abandon the right to buy at 2000p.

Index options

Options on whole share indices can be purchased: for example, Standard and Poor's 500 (USA), FTSE 100 (UK), CAC 40 (France), XETRA DAX (Germany). Large investors usually have a varied portfolio of shares so, rather than hedging individual shareholdings with options, they may hedge through options on the entire index of shares. Also speculators can take a position on the future movement of the market as a whole.

A major difference between index options and share options is that the former are **'cash settled'** – so for the FTSE 100 option, there is no delivery of 100 different shares on the expiry day. Rather, a cash difference representing the price change changes hands.

Figure 8.7 shows the April expiry options for the FTSE 100 Index on 16 January 2014. The date of the download was 16 January when the FTSE 100 Index stood at 6827. By convention (so everyone knows where they stand) the index is regarded as a price and each one-point movement on the index represents £10. So if you purchased one contract in April expiry 6,800 calls you would pay an option premium of 149.5 index points × £10 = £1,495.[5] Imagine that the following day, 17 January 2014, the FTSE 100 moved from its level on 16 January 2014 of 6827 to 6870 and the option price on the 6800 call moved to 190 index points (70 points of intrinsic value and 120 points of time value). To convert this into money you could sell the option at £10 per point per contract (190 × £10 = £1,900). In 24 hours your £1,495 has gone up to £1,900, a 27 per cent rise. Large gains can be made when the market moves in your favour. If it moves against you, large percentage losses will occur in just a few hours.

Note that there are many additional option expiry dates stretching months into the future other than the April one shown in Figure 8.7 – the nearest four of March, June, September, December plus such additional months that the nearest four calendar months are always available for trading.

---

[5] Notice that the market makers have a bid/ask (offer) spread. So, if you want to buy the 6800 call option you would pay 149.5 points or £1,495 as a premium, but if you wanted to sell the option to the market maker you would receive 145.5 points or £1,455.

APRIL 2014 PRICES - 16/01/14

	Calls						Strike		Puts					
Settl.	O.I.	Day Vol	Last	Bid	Ask				Bid	Ask	Last	Day Vol	O.I.	Settl.
170.00	138	8	174.00	173.00	177.50	C	6750.00	P	158.00	161.50	–	–	13	165.50
143.50	30	–	–	145.50	149.50	C	6800.00	P	180.00	184.00	183.00	41	14	189.00
119.50	74	–	–	120.50	124.50	C	6850.00	P	204.50	209.50	–	–	30	215.00
98.00	70	4	98.50	99.00	102.00	C	6900.00	P	232.00	237.50	–	–	20	243.00
79.50	34	20	83.00	80.00	83.00	C	6950.00	P	263.00	268.50	–	–	–	274.50

Note: Settlement price is for the trading day CET

Vol – (Volume) is the number of contracts traded in the most recent transaction.

Day's Volume – Number of trades that have taken place so far in the trading day. This figure updates as the day progresses and more trades take place.

+/- Price of last trade compared to yesterday's settlement price.

Settl – The previous day's settlement price.

O.I. – (Open Interest) is the outstanding long and short positions of the previous trading day updated in the morning each day.

Figure 8.7   FTSE 100 index option for April delivery, £10 per index point

Hedging against a decline in the market using index options

An investor with a £136,000 broadly spread portfolio of shares is concerned that the market may fall over the next four months. One strategy to lower risk is to purchase put options on the share index. If the market does fall, losses on the portfolio will be offset by gains on the value of the index put option.

First the investor has to calculate the number of option contracts needed to hedge the underlying. With the index at 6827 on 16 January 2014 and each point of that index settled at £10, one contract has a value of 6827 × £10 = £68,270. To cover an £136,000 portfolio two contracts are needed (investors can trade in whole contracts only). The investor opts to buy two April 6750 puts for 161.5 points per contract.[6] The premium payable is:

---

[6] This is not a *perfect hedge* as there is an element of the underlying risk without offsetting derivative cover.

> 161.50 points × £10 × 2 = £3,230

This amounts to a 2.4 per cent 'insurance premium' (£3,230/£136,000) against a downturn in the market.

Consider what happens if the market does fall by a large amount, say, 15 per cent, between January and April. The index falls from 6827 to 5803, and the loss on the portfolio is

> £136,000 × 0.15 = £20,400

If the portfolio is unhedged, the investor suffers from a market fall. However, in this case the put options gain in value as the index falls because they carry the right to sell at 6750. If the investor closed the option position by selling the put options at a level of 5803, with the right to sell at 6750, a 947-point difference, a gain is made:

> Gain on options (6750 − 5803) × 2 × £10 = £18,940
> Less option premium paid   £ 3,230
>   £15,710

A substantial proportion of the fall in portfolio value is compensated for through the use of the put derivative. Article 8.1 shows a fund manager willing to pay an insurance premium against a fall in the market.

Article 8.1

This is not a hedge fund

By Neil Collins

A fund manager will be forgiven for losing money during a bear market. He may be forgiven a (short) period of underperformance against his benchmark. But woe betide him if he sells and the market then rises. The risk to his mandate if he's caught this way far outweighs the rewards if he's right.

Gervais Williams has not exactly bet the ranch

on a bear market, but last week he bought a little insurance for Diverse Income, the investment trust he manages. He paid 1.6 per cent of its net asset value for a FTSE 100 put option big enough to cover a third of the value of the portfolio. The strike price is 5800 – miles out of the money – but it does run until June 2015.

As Christopher Brown at JPMorgan points

Article 8.1   Continued

out, the option is an imperfect hedge, since Diverse's portfolio is only 8 per cent in FTSE 100 stocks, and if smaller companies perform badly against the big stocks, the option wouldn't offset the portfolio's losses even in a bear market. Nevertheless, it's an unusual and imaginative way for a manager who's apprehensive to hedge his bets.

Source: Collins, N. (2013) This is not a hedge fund, *Financial Times*, 8 November 2013. Courtesy of Neil Collins

Further reading

L. Galitz, *The Financial Times Handbook of Financial Engineering: Using Derivatives to Manage Risk*, 3rd edn (FT Publishing, 2013). A clearly written and sophisticated book on the use of derivatives. Aimed at a professional readership, but some sections are excellent for the novice.

F. Taylor, *Mastering Derivatives Markets*, 4th edn (FT Publishing, 2010). A good introduction to derivatives instruments and markets.

R. Vaitilingam, *The Financial Times Guide to Using the Financial Pages*, 6th edn (Financial Times Prentice Hall, 2010). Explains the tables displayed by the *Financial Times* and some background about the instruments – for the beginner.

Websites

www.advfn.com	ADVFN
www.bloomberg.com	Bloomberg
www.money.cnn.com	CNNMoney
https://derivatives.euronext.com	NYSE Euronext
www.ft.com	Financial Times
www.fow.com	Futures & Options World
www.euronext.com/en/derivatives	Information and learning tools from NYSE Liffe to help
www.reuters.com	Reuters
www.wsj.com	The Wall Street Journal

9

Futures

Futures are contracts between two parties to undertake a transaction at an agreed price on a specified future date. In contrast to buying options, which give you the choice to walk away from the deal, with futures you are committed and are unable to back away. This is a very important difference. In purchasing an option the maximum you can lose is the premium paid, whereas you can lose multiples of the amount you employ in taking a futures position.

A simple example will demonstrate this. Imagine a farmer wishes to lock in a price for his wheat, which will be harvested in six months. You agree to purchase the wheat from the farmer six months hence at a price of £60 per tonne. You are hoping that by the time the wheat is delivered the price has risen and you can sell at a profit. The farmer is worried that all he has from you is the promise to pay £60 per tonne in six months, and if the market price falls you will walk away from the deal. To reassure him you are asked to put money into what the farmer calls a **margin account**. He asks and you agree to deposit £6 for each tonne you have agreed to buy. If you fail to complete the bargain the farmer will be able to draw on the money from the margin account and then sell the wheat as it is harvested at the going rate for immediate (**'spot'**) delivery. So as far as the farmer is concerned the price of wheat for delivery at harvest time could fall to £54 and he is still going to get £60 for each tonne: £6 from what you paid into the margin account and £54 from selling at the spot price.

But what if the price falls below £54? The farmer is exposed to risk – something he had tried to avoid by entering a futures deal. It is for this reason that the farmer asks you to top up your margin account on a daily basis so that there is always a buffer. He sets a **maintenance margin** level of £6 per tonne.

You have to maintain at least £6 per tonne in the margin account. If, the day after buying the future, the harvest-time price in the futures market falls to £57 you have only £3 per tonne left in the margin account as a buffer for the farmer. You agreed to buy at £60 but the going rate is only £57. To bring the margin account up to a £6 buffer you will be required to put in another £3 per tonne. If the price the next day falls to £50 you will be required to put up another £7 per tonne. You agreed to buy at £60; with the market price at £50 you have put a total of £6 + £3 + £7 = £16 into the margin account. By providing top-ups as the price moves against you there will always be at least £6 per tonne providing security for the farmer. Even if you go bankrupt or simply renege on the deal he will receive at least £60 per tonne, either from the spot market or from a combination of a lower market price plus money from the margin account. As the price fell to £50 you have a £10 per tonne incentive to walk away from the deal except for the fact that you have put £16 into an account that the farmer can draw on should you be so stupid or unfortunate. If the price is £50 per tonne at expiry of the contract and you have put £16 in the margin account, you are entitled to the spare £6 of margin.

It is in the margin account that we have the source of multiple losses in the futures markets. Suppose your life savings amount to £10 and you are convinced there will be a drought and shortage of wheat following the next harvest. In your view the price will rise to £95 per tonne. So, to cash in on your forecast you agree to buy a future for 1 tonne of wheat. You have agreed with the farmer that in six months you will pay £60 for the wheat, which you expect to then sell for £95. (The farmer is obviously less convinced that prices are destined to rise than you.)

To gain this right to buy at £60 you need only have £6 for the **initial margin**. The other £4 might be useful to meet day-to-day **margin calls** should the wheat price fall from £60 (temporarily, in your view). If the price does rise to £95 you will make a £35 profit having laid out only £6 (plus some other cash temporarily). This is a very high return of 583 per cent over six months. But what if the price at harvest time is £40? You have agreed to pay £60, therefore the loss of £20 wipes out your savings and you are made bankrupt. You lose three times your initial margin. That is the downside to the gearing effect of futures.

The above example demonstrates the essential features of futures market trading. In reality, however, participants in the market do not transact directly with each other, but go through a regulated exchange. Your opposite number, called a **counterparty**, is not a farmer but an organisation that acts as counterparty to all futures traders, buyers or sellers, called the **clearing house**. This significantly reduces the risk of non-compliance with the contract for the buyer or seller of a future, as it is highly unlikely that the clearing house will be unable to fulfil its obligation.

The exchange provides standardised legal agreements traded in highly liquid markets. The contracts cannot be tailor-made. The fact that the agreements are standardised allows a wide market appeal because buyers and sellers know what is being traded: the contracts are for a specific quality of the underlying, in specific amounts with specific delivery dates. For example, for sugar traded on NYSE.liffe (see Box 9.1) one contract is for a specified grade of sugar and each contract is for a standard 50 tonnes with fixed delivery days in late August, October, December, March and May.

Box 9.1 Commodity spot and futures prices in the *Financial Times*

COMMODITIES

Energy		Price*	Change	Agricultural & Cattle Futures		Price*	Change
WTI Crude Oil †	Feb	94.17	1.58	Corn ◆	Mar	425.75	-5.75
Brent Crude Oil ‡	Feb	107.13	0.74	Wheat ◆	Mar	567.75	-11.50
RBOB Gasoline †	Feb	2.6264	+0.0040	Soyabeans ◆	Mar	1318.00	-21.00
Heating Oil †	Feb	2.9796	+0.0433	Soyabeans Meal ◆	Mar	434.50	-18.00
Natural Gas †	Feb	4.325	-0.044	Cocoa ◈	Mar	£1765	+3
Ethanol ◆	Feb	1.909	-0.009	Cocoa ♥	Mar	2.748	0
Uranium		35.00	0.35	Coffee (Robusta) ◈	Jan	1720	-24
Carbon Emissions ‡	Jan	€4.80	-0.01	Coffee (Arabica) ♥	Mar	117.20	-2.00
Diesel (French)		918.75	+8.75	White Sugar ◈	Mar	416.60	-7.40
Unleaded (95R)		946.00	-10.50	Sugar 11 ♥	Mar	15.23	-0.26
Base Metals (♠ LME 3 Month)				Cotton ♥	Mar	84.79	+1.06
Aluminium		1759.50	-10.50	Orange Juice ♥	Mar	145.15	-2.95
Aluminium Alloy		1795.00	-10.00	Palm Oil	Dec	850.00	-2.50
Copper		7290.00	-29.00	Live Cattle ♣	Feb	139.425	+1.775
Lead		2172.00	-28.00	Feeder Cattle ♣	Jan	169.400	+0.800
Nickel		14290.00	-55.00	Lean Hogs ♣	Feb	86.600	+0.600
Tin		22075.00	-145.00				
Zinc		2050.00	-38.00			**% Chg**	**% Chg**
Precious Metals (PM London Fix)					Jan 14	**Mnth**	**Year**
Gold		1236.00	-15.50	S&P GSCI Spt	610.17	-2.6	-6.1
Silver (US Cents)		2009.00	-18.00	DJ UBS Spt	124.80	-1.2	-9.9
Platinum		1416.00	-17.00	R/J CRB TR	277.37	-1.2	-6.6
Palladium		734.00	-3.00	Rogers RICIX TR 3457.31		-2.0	-6.9
Bulk Commodities				M Lynch MLCX Spt499.37		-1.2	-9.0
Iron Ore (Platts) ±	Feb	127.50	nc	UBS B'berg CMCI TR1196.12		-1.4	-8.1
Iron Ore (TSI) ≠		129.60	+0.10	LEBA EUA Carbon	4.71	-3.3	-23.7
globalCOAL RB Index		84.25	+0.29	LEBA CER Carbon	0.34	-10.5	-29.2
Baltic Dry Index		1370	-25	LEBA UK Power	46.84	-6.5	-11.9

Sources: † NYMEX, ‡ ECX/ICE, ◆ CBOT, ⊞ NYSE Liffe, ♥ NYBOT, ♣ CME, ♠ LME/London Metal Exchange. * Latest prices, $ unless otherwise stated. ± Platts. ≠ The Steel Index.

Source: www.markets.ft.com/research/Markets/Commodities, 16 January 2014.

In examining Box 9.1, it is important to remember that it is the contracts them-selves that are a form of security bought and sold in the market. Thus the March future priced at $416.60 per tonne is a derivative of sugar and is not the same thing as sugar. To buy this future is to enter into an agreement with rights. It is the rights that are bought and sold, not the commodity. But when exercise takes place, it is sugar that is bought. However, as with most derivatives, usually futures positions are cancelled by an offsetting transaction before exercise.

Marking to market and margins

With the clearing house being the formal counterparty for every buyer or seller of a futures contract, an enormous potential for credit risk is imposed on the organisation given the volume of futures traded and the size of the underlying they represent (NYSE.liffe has an average daily volume of millions of contracts worth many hundreds of billions of pounds). If only a small fraction of market participants fail to deliver, this could run into hundreds of millions of pounds. To protect itself the clearing house operates a margining system. The futures buyer or seller has to provide, usually in cash, an initial margin. The amount required depends on the futures market, the level of volatility of the underlying and the potential for default; however, it is likely to be in the region of 0.1–15.0 per cent of the value of the underlying. The initial margin is not a 'down-payment' for the underlying; the funds do not flow to a buyer or seller of the underlying, but stay with the clearing house. It is merely a way of guaranteeing that the buyer or seller will pay up should the price of the underlying move against them. It is refunded when the futures position is closed (if the market has not moved adversely).

The clearing house also operates a system of daily **marking to market**. At the end of every trading day each counterparty's profits or losses created as a result of that day's price changes are calculated. Any counterparty that has made a loss has their **member's margin account** debited. The following morning, the losing counterparty must inject more cash to cover the loss if the amount in the account has fallen below a threshold level, called the maintenance margin. An inability to pay a daily loss causes default and the contract is closed, thus protecting the clearing house from the possibility that the counterparty might accumulate further daily losses without providing cash to cover them. The margin account of the counterparty that makes a daily gain is credited. This may be withdrawn the next day. The daily credits and debits to members' margin accounts are known as **variation margin**.

Worked example showing margins

Imagine a buyer and seller of a future on Monday with an underlying value of £50,000 are each required to provide an initial margin of 10 per cent, or £5,000. The buyer will make profits if the price rises while the seller will make profits if the price falls. In Table 9.1 it is assumed that counterparties have to keep the entire initial margin permanently as a buffer.[1] (In reality this requirement may be relaxed by an exchange.)

Table 9.1   Example of initial margin and marking to market

			Day		
£	Monday	Tuesday	Wednesday	Thursday	Friday
Value of future (based on daily closing price)	50,000	49,000	44,000	50,000	55,000
Buyers' position					
Initial margin	5,000				
Variation margin (+ credited) (– debited)	0	–1,000	–5,000	+6,000	+5,000
Accumulated profit (loss)	0	–1,000	–6,000	0	+5,000
Sellers' position					
Initial margin	5,000				
Variation margin (+ credited) (– debited)	0	+1,000	+5,000	–6,000	–5,000
Accumulated profit (loss)	0	+1,000	+6,000	0	–5,000

At the end of Tuesday the buyer of the contract has £1,000 debited from her member's account. This will have to be handed over the following day or the exchange will automatically close the member's position and crystallise the loss. If the buyer does provide the variation margin and the position is kept open until Friday the account will have an accumulated credit of £5,000. The buyer has the right to buy at £50,000 but can sell at £55,000. If the buyer and the seller closed their positions on Friday the buyer would be entitled to receive the initial margin

---

[1] Initial margin is the same as maintenance margin in this case.

plus the accumulated profit, £5,000 + £5,000 = £10,000, whereas the seller would receive nothing (£5,000 initial margin minus losses of £5,000).

This example illustrates the effect of leverage in futures contracts. The initial margin payments are small relative to the value of the underlying. When the underlying changes by a small percentage the effect is magnified for the future, and large percentage gains and losses are made on the amount committed to the transaction:

$$\text{Underlying change (Monday–Friday)} \quad \frac{55,000 - 50,000}{50,000} \times 100 = 10\%$$

$$\text{Percentage return to buyer of future} \quad \frac{5,000}{5,000} \times 100 = 100\%$$

$$\text{Percentage return to seller of future} \quad \frac{-5,000}{5,000} \times 100 = -100\%$$

Clearly playing the futures market can seriously damage your wealth. This was proved with a vengeance by Nick Leeson of Barings Bank. He bought futures in the Nikkei 225 index – the main Japanese share index – in both the Osaka and the Singapore derivatives exchanges. He was betting that the market would rise as he committed the bank to buying the index at a particular price. When the index fell margin payments had to be made. Leeson took a double or quits attitude: 'a lot of futures traders when the market is against them will double up'.[2] He continued to buy futures. To generate some cash, to make variation margin payments, he wrote combinations of call and put options ('straddles'). This compounded the problem when the Nikkei 225 index continued to fall. The put options became an increasingly expensive commitment to bear – counterparties had the right to sell the index to Barings at a price much higher than the prevailing price. Over £800 million was lost.

Settlement

Historically the futures markets developed on the basis of the **physical delivery** of the underlying. If you had contracted to buy 40,000 lb. of lean hogs, you would receive the meat as settlement. However, in most futures markets today (including that for lean hogs) only a small proportion of contracts result in physical delivery. The majority are **closed out** before the expiry of the contract and all that changes hands is cash. Speculators certainly do not want to end up with 5 tonnes of coffee

---

[2] Nick Leeson in an interview with David Frost reported in the *Financial Times*, 11 September 1995.

or 15,000 lb. of orange juice and so will **reverse their trade** before the contract expires; for example, if they originally bought a future for 50 tonnes of white sugar they later sell a future for 50 tonnes of white sugar for the same future delivery date.

A hedger, say a confectionery manufacturer, may sometimes take delivery from the exchange but in most cases will have established purchasing channels for sugar, cocoa, etc. In these cases they may use the futures markets not as a way of obtaining goods but as a way of offsetting the risk of the prices of goods moving adversely. So a confectionery manufacturer may still plan to buy, say, sugar, at the spot price from its long-standing supplier in six months and simultaneously, to hedge the risk of the price rising, will buy six-month futures in sugar. The position will then be closed before expiry. If the price of the underlying has risen the manufacturer pays more to the supplier but has a compensating gain on the future. If the price falls the supplier is paid less and so the confectioner makes a gain here, but, under a perfect hedge, the future has lost an equal value.

As the futures markets developed it became clear that most participants did not want the complications of physical delivery and this led to the development of futures contracts where cash settlement takes place. This permitted a wider range of futures contracts to be created. Futures contracts based on intangible commodities such as a share index or a rate of interest are now important financial instruments. With these, even if the contract is held to the maturity date one party will simply hand over cash to another (via the clearing house system).

Equity index futures

Equity index futures are an example of a cash settled market. The underlying here is a collection of shares. For example, FTSE 100 futures (see Box 9.2) are notional futures contracts. If not closed out before expiry (by the holder of a future doing the reverse transaction to their first – if they bought the future first, selling will close the position) they are settled in cash based on the average level of the FTSE 100 index between stated times on the last trading day of the contract. Each index point is valued at £10.

Box 9.2 shows futures in indices from stock markets around the world gathered by ft.com for 15 January 2014. We will focus on the line for the FTSE 100 index future. This is very much a cut-down version of the futures available to traders. As well as the March delivery future shown, NYSE.liffe also offers traders the possibility of buying or selling futures that 'deliver' in June, September and December.

Box 9.2 Equity index features table in the electronic version of the *Financial Times* at www.ft.com

EQUITY INDEX FUTURES

Jan 15		Open	Sett	Change	High	Low	Est. vol.	Open int.
DJIA	MAR4	16330.00	16408.00	+109.00	16445.00	16325.00	124	9,561
DJ Euro Stoxx‡	MAR4	3124.00	3163.00	+51.00	3178.00	3120.00	997,646	2,757,441
S&P 500	MAR4	1832.50	1841.60	+8.70	1845.30	1831.70	3,401	140,027
Mini S&P 500	MAR4	1833.00	1841.50	+8.50	1845.75	1831.50	1,252,540	2,868,227
Nasdaq 100	MAR4	3575.50	3598.25	+24.50	3611.00	3571.25	339	10,691
Mini Nasdaq	MAR4	3573.75	3598.25	+24.50	3610.25	3570.75	233,688	430,929
CAC 40	JAN4	4285.00	4330.50	+57.00	4346.00	4281.50	266,958	299,034
DAX	MAR4	9583.00	9727.50	+189.00	9781.00	9573.50	121,597	129,984
AEX	JAN4	407.30	408.60	+2.10	409.35	406.65	69,743	76,033
MIB 30	MAR4	19790.00	20031.00	+287.00	20080.00	19785.00	22,158	49,720
IBEX 35	JAN4	10376.00	10507.90	+174.00	10566.00	10369.00	58,502	67,687
SMI	MAR4	8340.00	8354.00	+41.00	8376.00	8311.00	24,666	130,245
FTSE 100	MAR4	6728.00	6762.50	+50.00	6779.00	6723.50	87,034	574,256
Hang Seng	JAN4	22932.00	22910.00	+139.00	22988.00	22919.00	1,896	97,644
Nikkei 225†	MAR4	15760.00	15780.00	+360.00	15850.00	15700.00	19,107	390,943
Topix	MAR4	1294.50	1295.00	+24.00	1296.00	1288.00	4,043	600,615
KOSPI 200	MAR4	-	255.85	+0.90	-	-	-	103,705

North American Latest. Contracts shown are among the 25 most traded based on estimates of average volumes in 2004. CBOT volume, high & low for pit & electronic trading at settlement. Previous day's Open Interest. † Osaka contract. ‡ Eurex contract.

Source: Financial Times, 15 January 2014.

The table shows the first price traded at the beginning of the day (Open), the settlement price used to mark to market (usually the last traded price), the change from the previous day, highest and lowest prices during the day, the number of contracts traded that day (Est. vol.) and the total number of open contracts (these are trading contracts opened over the last few months that have not yet been closed by an equal and opposite futures transaction).

With each point on the FTSE 100 share index future worth £10, by convention, if the future rises from 6762.5 to 6800 and you bought a future at 6762.5 you have made a 37.5 x £10 = £375 profit if you were to sell now at 6800.

Worked example: hedging with a share index future

It is 15 January 2014 and the FTSE 100 is at 6820. An investor wishes to hedge a £205,000 fund against a decline in the market. A March FTSE 100 future is available at 6762.50 – see Box 9.2. The investor retains the shares in the portfolio and *sells* three index futures contracts. Each futures contract is worth £67,625 (6762.5 points × £10). So three contracts are needed to cover £205,000 (£205,000 ÷ (£10 × 6762.5) = 3).[3]

For the sake of argument assume that in March the index falls by 10 per cent to 6138, leaving the portfolio value at £184,500. The closing of the futures position offsets this £20,500 loss by buying three futures to close the futures position at 6138 producing a profit of:[4]

Able to sell at 6762.5 × 3 × £10	= £202,875
Able to buy at 6138 × 3 × £10	= £184,140
	£ 18,735

These contracts are settled in cash, so £18,735 will be paid to the investor; and he gets back the margin, less broker's fees.

Buying and selling futures

A trader in futures must deal through a registered broker (a 'futures commission merchant'). Many brokers will not accept private clients. You can find out brokers' specialities at www.apcims.co.uk. Those who will accept them insist that traders have enough capital to be able to set aside a proportion for risky futures trading. They will often require a minimum of £20,000 to be set aside, and this is to be no more than 10 per cent of your investment assets (excluding your house) so you have to be fairly wealthy to play in these markets. NYSE.liffe provide a list of designated brokers (these follow rules and codes of conduct imposed by the regulators and the exchange).

Gone are the days of open pit trading and those brightly coloured jackets in the UK. Trades are now conducted over a computer system on LIFFE (LIFFE CONNECT™). You can place a price limit for your trade or make an at-the-market

---

[3] This is an imperfect hedge because we can only deal in whole numbers of futures contracts and £205,000 is not exactly three times £67,625.

[4] Assuming that the futures price is equal to the spot price of the FTSE 100. This would occur close to the expiry date of the future.

order, to be executed immediately at the price determined by current supply and demand conditions. The buyer of a contract is said to be in a **long position** – she agrees to receive the underlying. The seller who agrees to deliver the underlying is said to be in a **short position**.

If the amount in the trader's account falls below the maintenance margin the trader will receive a demand to inject additional money. This may happen every day so the trader cannot buy/sell a future and then go on holiday for a month (unless he leaves plenty of cash with the broker to meet margin calls). Prices are set by competing market makers on LIFFE CONNECT™. Real-time market prices are available on the Internet, as well as historical prices (www.liffe-data.com).

For further reading and a list of websites, see Chapter 8.

10

Spread betting, contracts for difference and warrants

Spread betting

You can bet on the future movements of shares (and other securities) in a similar way to betting on horses. If the share moves the way you said it would, you gain. However, unlike with horses, if it moves against you the loss can be a multiple of the amount you first put down – you lose money for every 1p adverse movement in a share price. So, if you bet that Marks and Spencer's share price will rise, and you punt £10 for every penny rise, if M&S increases by 30p you win £300. However, if M&S falls 30p you have to hand over £300. This is the basic principle, but the actual operation is slightly more complicated. If you believe that the price is destined to rise you will contact (by telephone, or using the Internet) one of the **spread betting** companies. They will quote you two prices (the **spread**), say, 488p–492p, for M&S. The first is called the **'bid' price** and is the relevant price if you are *'selling'* or *'going short'*. The second is the **'offer' price** and is the relevant price if you are *'buying'* or *'going long'*.

Given your optimism about M&S, the relevant price is 492p. You agree to bet £10 per 1p rise in the price. You 'buy' at 492p. Now imagine that you were correct and the spread on M&S moves to 525p–529p. You can close your position by telephoning the spread dealer and *'selling' to close*. The relevant price for you (betting on a rise) on the close is the lower of the two quoted: 525p. So you have made a gain of 33p (525p minus 492p), which translates into £330 given a bet of £10 per penny.

If you had been pessimistic about M&S when the spread quote was at 488p–492p you would have bet by going short at 488p. A movement up to 525p–529p would result in a loss of 41p (529p–488p): £410 at £10 per penny. However, if the spread quote moves to 450p–454p the gain is 488p less 454p = 34p (or £340 if you bet £10 per penny move).

You can see how the spread betting company can make money from the spread: you sell and buy at the least advantageous price on the spread. Presumably there are other investors doing the opposite, if you are 'buying' at 492p they are 'selling' at 488p. The spread betting company's books are balanced but a 4p gain is made.[1] The size of these spreads varies depending on volume of trade and degree of competition between spread betting firms, but they are larger than the market makers' spreads on the underlying shares.

Money up-front

The bookmaker (spread betting company) will require you to demonstrate that you are able to pay should the bet go against you. When you lay a bet you will be asked for a sum of money called the **notional trading requirement** or 'margin', or 'deposit'.[2] This will obviously be a larger sum if you are betting £10 per penny (point) rather than £5 per penny (point) movement in the underlying share (or index), or if the share (or index) is particularly volatile.

Furthermore, if the bet starts to go against you and the position is held open over a number of days you will be asked to top up the funds deposited with the spread betting company through margin calls. Naturally, these will be returned to you if there are moves in your favour.

Imagine you placed an 'up bet' on Vodafone when the spread quote is 203p–204p. You therefore 'buy' at 204p, betting £100 per penny movement. The maximum possible loss occurs when Vodafone goes to zero: 204p loss at £100 per penny is equal to £20,400. The spread betting company requires 10 per cent of this maximum loss (in this particular case), so you deposit £2,040.[3] If the Vodafone spread falls by 5p to 198p–199p the next day, your account will be debited £500

---

[1] If the spread betting company's books are not balanced it may hedge its own position by using futures, or the cash market, or contracts for difference.

[2] Some companies offer credit facilities – useful if you want to leave funds in a high-interest account somewhere else – but you will have to provide reassurance on the liquidity and amount of your funds.

[3] The notional trading requirement (margin) can be as low as 1 per cent for bets on a share index and 5 per cent for individual share bets, but is more usually 10 per cent. However, margins of 40 per cent for small company shares are not unusual.

(5 × £100 = £500). The spread betting company then asks you to top up your account by paying an additional margin of £500. For the next two weeks Vodafone oscillates greatly. On some days your account is credited, on others you are asked for more margin through **'cash calls'**. After 14 days you close your position by telephoning the spread betting company and telling the dealer that you would like to sell Vodafone 'to close'. It is important to make it clear that you are not selling Vodafone 'to open' as that means a fresh separate bet on Vodafone falling.

The spread quoted is 208p–209p. You have gained £400 (sold at 208p and bought at 204p, i.e. a 4p rise at £100 per penny). This is a good return on an initial cash injection of £2,040 (plus a few cash calls during the two weeks). However, the potential risk of it all going wrong was also very high.

An alternative to betting and then being subject to a series of cash calls is to place a 'stop-loss' at the time of the bet. Under a stop-loss the spread betting company closes your position for you if the underlying share moves to the stated stop-loss price. At the time that you place the bet you hand over margin to the spread betting company equal to the maximum loss that could occur should the stop-loss be triggered. For example, if you make an up bet on Pearson when the spread quote is 1280p–1300p at £10 per penny and you set a stop-loss at 1040p (i.e. 20 per cent below the bet level) the maximum loss if the stop-loss is triggered is 260 × £10 + £2,600, so you will be asked to provide £2,600 of margin. This cash may already be in a special account opened when you registered with the spread betting company, or could be transferred by debit card over the telephone/ Internet.

There are two types of stop-loss order. A 'standard' stop-loss is one where the company will *try* to close your position, but if the market is falling like a stone it may not be able to close it before the market price has zoomed past the stop-loss limit. With a 'guaranteed' ('controlled risk') stop-loss the spread betting company will close at the agreed stop-loss price even if the market price has moved beyond this before they were able to act. To have a guarantee you will have to pay a wider spread at the time that the bet is placed. A standard stop-loss does not require a wider spread.

Types of bet

There are three types of share or index bet. An **intraday (cash or spot) bet** is one that starts and is closed in the same trading day. A **futures-based bet** is one on the price of shares (index) on the next month or quarter day or the one after that (quarter days are in late March, June, September and December). So in the above Vodafone example the spread quotes would have been based on the future price for a Vodafone share on the next quarter day.[4] This price is made by the spread betting company but cannot deviate too far from prices in the market place (otherwise arbitrageurs will be given an invitation to make money risk-free by doing opposite transactions in the market and with spread betting companies).

Traditionally, futures-based betting was the way to spread a bet over a few days or weeks. However, spread betting companies have now introduced **rolling cash spread betting (rolling daily bets)**. The spread better 'rolls' his position overnight to the next day.

Uses of spread betting

Spread betting can be used as a kind of insurance. For example, when you hold the underlying shares and you think it possible that the price will fall substantially in the short term, but a potential capital gains tax causes you to hesitate in selling the underlying shares, you could place a bet such that you gain if the share price falls. You will stabilise your position: if the share falls your portfolio declines but you win (an equal amount) on the bet; if the share rises you gain on the portfolio but lose on the bet. You can then select the time when you sell the shares – it might be good to wait a few months until the next tax year when you can use your annual capital gains tax allowance (see Chapter 17).

Spread betting can also be used to take highly leveraged positions where a small movement in the underlying leads to a large percentage gain on the amount initially committed to the bet – as in the Vodafone example.

Finally, spread betting allows you to gain from share (index) falls. You are restricted from shorting shares – selling shares you don't own in anticipation of closing your position by buying the same quantity at a lower price later – in the stock market, but spread betting makes this easy, at least for movements over a few months.

Further points

- All spread bet winnings are free from both income and capital gains tax.
- No stamp duty is payable.
- Brokers' fees are not paid because you go straight to the spread betting companies. They make most of their money from the spread. They also

---

[4] If you want to roll over any quarterly contracts you need to contact the spread betting firm shortly before the expiry date to leave a rollover instruction. The company will close the current trade and then set up a new trade in the same underlying. You will have to pay a spread, but in arranged rollovers this is much less than normal (usually one-half).

charge interest to those betting on a rise on the value of their bet (long position) – a daily financing charge – say 2.5 per cent over the London Interbank Offered Rate, LIBOR (for those holding overnight). Sell bets (going short) could either receive interest or be charged it depending on the level of LIBOR.

■ For tax purposes losses on spread bets cannot be written off against profits made elsewhere in your portfolio.

■ With the market being regulated by the Financial Conduct Authority the investor has some further reassurance. Potential punters must be rigorously vetted to ensure the appropriateness of spread betting for them, e.g. proof of experience with derivatives.

■ In addition to spread betting on shares and share indices, you can spread-bet commodities, bonds, interest rates, currencies, futures, options, house prices and even the outcomes of sporting events.

■ Most spread betting companies quote about 400 companies online, but will give you quotes on many more (smaller ones) if you phone.

■ The spreads are at the discretion of the spread betting firm – when you ask for prices do not reveal whether you are a potential buyer or a seller.

■ Even when the equity markets are closed spread bets can be made, 24 hours a day.

■ Spread betting firms run educational courses and small-scale trial bets to allow punters to gain experience.

■ Over the long term actually buying and holding shares and other investments is better than taking spread betting positions because you avoid regular losses on the spread as you move in and out, and you avoid paying interest on long positions. Being able to offset losses against gains on conventional investing for tax purposes is very useful too.

■ If you are holding a rolling bet long position on a share on the day before it goes ex-dividend the spread betting firm will post a dividend amount to your account just before the market opens on the ex-dividend date (note that shares will generally fall by the dividend amount on ex-dividend day). If you have a short position the dividend will be debited from your account. Some credit only 80 per cent of the dividend to the long holder (reflecting tax deducted by the company paying the dividend) and debit 100 per cent to the short holder; others credit and debit 90 per cent respectively. Prices for quarterly spread betting contracts already include the dividend, so the dividends are not credited or debited on the ex-dividend date.

- Spread betting companies have had difficulties with financial stability because many of their clients lost so much money that they reneged on their deals – see Article 10.1.

Article 10.1

Spread betting groups face stricter rules

Simon Mundy

Spread betting companies are likely to be faced with stricter capital requirements [reserves of money], senior industry figures and analysts say, as the industry's rapid growth brings it under closer scrutiny.

Spread betting has become more popular during the past decade, because it allows users to make profits and losses from betting on minor fluctuations in the prices of securities, by placing relatively small deposits.

However, the industry was hit by a wave of bad debts after the financial crisis in late 2008, and several of the biggest operators have not turned a full-year profit since.

London Capital Group, one of three listed spread betting providers, had to raise £8m in new capital in April, in part to comply with regulatory requirements but also to cover its potential liability for £7.7m ($12m) customer losses.

Spread betting companies require clients to post "margin" to cover any losses, and typically impose automatic "stop-losses" to avoid unsustainable deficits.

But rapid market swings can produce losses that significantly exceed this margin, raising the risk that customers will default. Because the companies cover their exposures to large customer positions by taking corresponding positions in the market, sudden adverse price movements can result in serious losses.

The turbulence raises the chances of "losses that are not covered by the money that customers put up. . . it's possible that a smaller player would run into difficulties," says Andrew Mitchell, an analyst at Collins Stewart.

CMC Markets, the UK's second-largest spread betting group by trading volumes, reported an aggregate pre-tax loss of £51.8m for the three years to March. City Index, recorded an aggregate pre-tax loss of £51.9m in the two years to March 2010.

All the companies said that they had adequate capital and that clients' money was not at risk.

The risks to clients of an operator collapsing have been mitigated by a new rule that came into force this year, obliging companies to segregate client funds. If a company did fail, customers facing losses of up to £85,000 would be covered by the state financial services compensation scheme – but those facing larger losses would be considered ordinary creditors.

About 83,000 people used spread betting platforms in the UK last year.

Spread betting websites (they also offer contract for difference)

www.alpari.co.uk	Alpari
www.cantorcapital.com	Cantor Capital
www.capitalspreads.com	Capital Spreads
www.cityindex.co.uk	City Index
www.cmcmarkets.co.uk	CMC Markets
www.etxcapital.co.uk	ETX Capital
www.finspreads.com	Finspreads
www.ayondo.com	Ayondo
www.ig.com/uk	IG Index
www.intertrader.com	InterTrader
www.spreadex.com	Spreadex
www.saxospreads.com	Saxo Bank

Contracts for difference

Trading in contracts for difference (CFDs) is very similar to spread betting. However, with CFD there is no settlement date – your open position can continue until you choose to close it (or it is closed for you because you have failed to provide margin).

In a CFD contract the buyer and seller agree to pay, in cash, at the closing of the contract, the difference between the opening and closing price of the underlying shares, multiplied by the number of shares in the contract.[5]

For example, imagine that you have a deposit account with a CFD broker. You have placed £40,000 in this account. You are pessimistic about Vodafone's shares and ask for a price quote from the broker.[6] She replies with: '202 bid and 203 offer'. You agree to sell CFDs for 160,000 shares in Vodafone at a price of 202p. Note that with the amount of cash you have (£40,000) you would not be able to purchase this many shares. It is because the CFD brokers permit trading on margins of around 10–20 per cent that you can leverage up the use of the £40,000. If we assume that the CFD broker requires 10 per cent as margin then just over £32,000 of the deposit money will now be held as margin (and not simply as a deposit), leaving you with just under £8,000 as *free equity*. It is good to have some

---

[5] The underlying can also be an equity index, a commodity, bonds or exchange rates.
[6] A high proportion of CFD trade is now conducted online rather than over the telephone.

free equity as you might have to meet margin calls if the price starts to move against you. If the shares now fall to 192 bid and 193 offer you will be showing a gain on your margin account of 202p – 193p = 9p per share, or £14,400. If you close your position your deposit account will then contain the original £40,000 plus £14,400.

On the other hand if Vodafone's share price moves to 213p–214p you lose and the CFD broker will require additional margin. If you close your position at this point your loss will be 214p – 202p = 12p per share or 0.12 × 160,000 = £19,200.

Additional points

■ No stamp duty is charged but you are liable for capital gains tax.

■ Some brokers quote a narrower spread, but then charge up to 0.25 per cent commission on the trade value on both the opening and closing transactions.

■ Stop-losses can be set up, freeing you from monitoring the market every minute to avoid big losses, as your position is automatically closed if the market goes against you.

■ When you sell a CFD as your opening position any dividend due during your period of ownership will be taken from your margin account. Those with a buy ('long') position will receive a payment equivalent to the net dividend.

■ The amount you need to deposit with a CFD broker tends to be at least £10,000 – significantly more than with spread betting.

■ If you take a long position (buy) the CFD trader will charge you interest during the period of holding the CFD (typically LIBOR plus 2–3 per cent). After a few weeks the interest costs start to outweigh the savings you make trading through CFDs rather than the shares (e.g. stamp duty). If you are a long-term holder CFDs are expensive – buy the underlying. If you sell (go short), interest will be added to your account (typically 2–3 per cent below LIBOR).

■ The right to vote at AGMs, etc. is usually not conferred to the CFD holder (although the CFD provider may facilitate the clients wishes, e.g. voting on a merger, in some cases).

■ CFDs are available on most shares, right down to market capitalisations of £10 million.

■ CFD brokers require you to show you are an experienced trader who understands the gearing (leverage) and other risks of CFD.

■ You must carefully monitor your position on a day-to-day basis if you do
not have a stop-loss, as you may have to meet margin calls and/or close out
positions.

■ There have been many complaints against firms offering 'advised CFD
trading'. Some of the advisers have racked up large charges resulting in
the client losing all money put up for CFD margin (the commission can
be 1 per cent of each trade). Be wary: a review by the regulator found that
many smaller stockbrokers advising clients were lacking in knowledge or
authorisation.

Warrants

Warrants give the holder the right to subscribe for a specified number of shares at
a fixed price during or at the end of a specific time period. So, the holder has the
right, but not the obligation, to buy shares. Does this sound familiar? It should.
Warrants are very closely related to call options (see Chapter 8). The main difference is that a warrant is issued by the company whose shares you would be
entitled to buy, whereas options are written by people and organisations unconnected with the company.

Imagine that a company with shares currently trading at 75p chooses to sell warrants, each of which grants the holder the right to buy a share for £1 over the
next five years. If the warrant is exercised the company will issue new shares at
the exercise price (£1) and so raise additional finance.

The amount you pay for a warrant depends on demand from investors. Let us
assume in this case that you purchase one warrant for 10p, which gives you the
right to buy a share for £1. If the share price rises to £1.50 (a 100 per cent rise from
the current price of 75p), the right you hold to buy at £1 now has an intrinsic
value of 50p – you can sell a share for £1.50 in the market that you can purchase
for £1. The warrant value has risen five-fold, from 10p to 50p; it might even be
worth more than 50p if there is still some time before expiry. If the share price
trebles to £2.25 the warrant's intrinsic value rises to £1.25, a 1,150 per cent gain
on the 10p originally paid. This demonstrates the gearing effect of warrants relative to shares. Of course, this works the other way. If the share price falls (stays
the same, or even rises a little) the warrant might expire worthless – a loss of 100
per cent of your investment.

There is no requirement for you to hold the warrant until you exercise or it
expires. You can sell warrants to other investors in an active secondary market
on the London Stock Exchange. Financial websites such as ADVFN carry warrant

prices – search under 'equity warrants'. Most of them are issued by investment trusts (investment companies). A major advantage of warrants over traded options is that they usually hold the right to purchase over many years rather than a few months. Thus you can have a geared exposure to a company's fortune over a much longer time frame.

Note that investors need to keep track of warrants they own, especially those nearing expiry, because if they fail to exercise them the investment becomes worthless.

Covered warrants

Covered warrants are the same as the warrants described in the previous section, except that financial institutions issue them rather than the company itself. The financial institution receives payment (a **'premium'**) selling a warrant in, say, BP shares, and in return grants the warrant holder the right, but not the obligation, to buy or sell an underlying asset (BP shares) at a specified price during, or at the end of, a specified time period. They are *'covered'* because the financial institution (usually an investment bank) that issues them covers its exposure by buying (or selling) the underlying security in the open market.

In 2002 the London Stock Exchange launched its covered warrant market so that even private investors could buy (sell) covered warrants (it was previously a market for professionals only, unless you could prove you understood the risks). Initially 160 covered warrants were made available on leading UK and international companies and international indices – there are now over 1,000.

You can purchase either a call or a put covered warrant. A call gives the right to buy a share. A put gives the right to sell a share. The put rises in value when the share falls – see the description of put options in Chapter 8.

You also have a choice of contract styles. A European-style covered warrant can only be exercised (i.e. share purchase or sale made) at expiry (say, after a year). An American-style covered warrant allows exercise at any time up to expiry.

Example of covered warrant use – releasing cash while maintaining exposure to a share

You own 10,000 shares in Barclays plc, currently priced at 479p, and need to release cash to put a deposit on a house. However, you feel that Barclays are destined to rise over the next few months. You could sell the Barclays shares, releasing £47,900, while simultaneously buying 10,000 Barclays covered warrants, giving the right to buy at 550p (the strike or exercise price). These will expire in nine months. You pay 26.3p for the right to buy one share at 550p – a cost of £2,630. The total cash released is thus £45,270.

If, by expiry of the warrants, Barclays shares have moved to £6, the covered warrants are worth £5,000 (£6 – £5.50 = £0.50 × 10,000). Note the gearing effect; the share moves by 25 per cent but the warrant rises by 90 per cent. You could, of course, sell the covered warrants when they still had time value at any point prior to expiry.

If you are wrong and the Barclays share price stays under £5.50, the covered warrants expire worthless and your loss is limited to £2,630.

Additional points

■ Those covered warrants granting rights on overseas shares can be traded in sterling, thus reducing concern about exchange rate risk.

■ Covered warrants have an average life of 6–12 months, but they can be up to five years.

■ You do not have to hold on until expiry as covered warrants are listed on the London Stock Exchange and prices are provided throughout the trading day. You buy/sell through an ordinary broker in the same way as buying/selling shares (about £10 per trade). Market makers provide bid and offer prices on a continual basis.

■ You can buy either 'call' or 'put' covered warrants on underlying assets ranging from shares, indices, commodities and currencies.

■ With some covered warrants you can either insist on delivery of shares when you exercise or settle for cash – the investor receives cash from the issuer representing the profit they would have made through physical exercise. They are normally settled in cash because this avoids stamp duty.

■ With the Barclays example there is a **conversion ratio** (or **parity**) of one warrant covering one share. However many covered warrants have conversion ratios much higher than this, e.g. three warrants for one share (the holder needs to exercise three warrants to obtain one share), 10:1 or even 100:1.

■ The pay-offs to holders of call or put covered warrants are analogous to those for options in Chapter 8.

■ Potential losses are limited to the amount paid as a premium unlike spread betting, futures and CFDs, where potential losses can be unlimited.

- There is no daily mark-to-market or need to provide margin. You can therefore take a longer-term view – you can go on holiday and not have to keep an eye on the market.

- Covered warrants that are worth something on expiry date are automatically exercised, so you will not lose out if you forget to exercise.

- The Financial Conduct Authority and the London Stock Exchange oversee the market, regulating advisers, issuers and brokers.

- Covered warrant prices and details are available on financial websites such as www.londonstockexchange.com.

- Gains on covered warrant trades are liable for capital gains tax.

- They are settled through CREST, in the same way as shares, two days after the trade.

Further reading

Baltazar, M. *The Beginner's Guide to Financial Spread Betting*, 2nd edn (Harriman House, 2008).

Dragomanovich, V. *Financial Spread Betting For Dummies* (John Wiley and Sons, 2013).

Fieldhouse, S. *The Financial Times Guide to Financial Spread Betting* (Financial Times Prentice Hall, 2011).

Investors Chronicle (www.investorschronicle.co.uk) has numerous articles in its archive.

McHattie, A. *Covered Warrants* (Harriman House, 2000).

Pryor, M. *The Financial Spread Betting Handbook* (Harriman House, 2011).

Pryor, M. *Winning Spread Betting Strategies* (Harriman House, 2009)

Temple, P. *The Investor's Toolbox: How to Use Spread Betting, CFDs, Options, Warrants and Trackers to Boost Returns and Reduce Risk*, 2nd edn (Harriman House, 2007).

Websites

www.advfn.com	ADVFN
www.bloomberg.com	Bloomberg
www.ft.com	Financial Times
www.investorschronicle.co.uk	Investors Chronicle
www.londonstockexchange.com	London Stock Exchange
www.reuters.com	Reuters

part

3

Company analysis

11

Company accounts

Investment in shares requires analysis of companies. To avoid analysis is to end up speculating in shares in an uninformed manner. There is a world of difference between a speculator and an 'investor'.

A subtle blend of two elements is needed for successful analysis: quantitative and qualitative data. An assessment of the company's current financial position, its history of profit growth and other measures of performance are essential quantitative data used to inform the investor trying to gauge future prospects. We compare the current value of projected future business income (per share) with the current share price to draw conclusions about whether the market is over- or undervaluing a company.

Note from this that historical facts about the company are not interesting in and of themselves. They are used to provide clues to enlighten our focus on the *future*: directors' performance in using resources in the past (their 'stewardship' role) may help assess the likelihood of good managerial performance *in the future*; the level of debt relative to the amount of the equity capital in the business may provide a clue on the *future* risk of bankruptcy; the analysis of past cash flow may assist us to assess the extent to which *future* revenues are likely to be swallowed up by investment in plant and machinery rather than being available for distribution to shareholders.

Quantitative data provide a firm, factual base to make these future-orientated judgements, but this is far from sufficient. The really important factors that contribute to future profits of a company are not expressed on a balance sheet, profit and loss account or cash flow statement. These qualitative elements cover a multitude of attributes but can be summarised under the following headings:

- The nature of the industry in which the company is operating, as defined by strategic analysis and the consequent returns on capital employed in that industry.

- The competitive strength of the company within its industry, as defined by its possession (or not) of extraordinary resources that can lead to above industry average returns on capital invested – does the company have a strong business franchise surrounded by a deep and dangerous moat to deter competitors?

- The honesty and competence of the managerial team. Competence on its own is not enough. Honesty is essential, too. You can't, as an investor, sleep easy if you have the most intelligent, experienced and wise managerial team in the world and yet doubt their honesty and sincerity in focusing on shareholder value.

Newspaper articles sometimes have a bias towards providing the reader with a glimpse of some of the key qualitative elements. For example, this fictitious one:

> Sir John Wiseman, the well-respected, highly experienced chief executive of Entrenched plc, yesterday announced the results of his strategic review of the company. It holds a 30 per cent market share in Europe and is building rapidly from its 17 per cent share in the North American market. It is well known that Entrenched has a great deal of power over its customers, the retail chains, because the company's products are 'must have' brands for the supermarkets. The company has also been very careful in sourcing supplies from a wide variety of companies, reducing the potential for a supplier to increase prices in what for the supplier is a highly competitive market. Entrenched has decided not to take over any more competitors but to concentrate on increasing the strength of its brand and raising the research and development budget to £1.1bn per year. This will make it hard for its competitors to challenge Entrenched, either on cost or in its roll-out of innovative products. The management team has recently been strengthened by the appointment of Mike Robinson as finance director, a key figure in the accounting profession's drive for clear and simple accounting and Pat Davis as director with special responsibility for the shareholder value management development programme throughout the organisation. In May Entrenched completed a £700m share buy-back. Sir John said that the company is throwing off cash and shareholders could probably use the money more effectively than the company. 'We

do not want to grow the business just for the sake of growth – we must generate a return greater than our investors could obtain investing elsewhere with that money to justify any expansion.'

On other occasions the journalist concentrates on the quantitative. For example:

Entrenched plc, the consumer products company, reported turnover up from £8.4bn to £9.8bn in the year to the end September. Pre-tax profits have accelerated to £1.8bn, a rise of 10 per cent on last year. This is double the profit of only five years ago. Earnings per share rose from 10p to 11p, which places the shares at their current price of 220p on a price–earnings ratio of 20. This is above the industry average, but, given the strengths of the firm, is regarded as justified.

Many of the technical terms, such as price–earnings ratio, mentioned in these articles will be explained in this part of the book, as will numerous other factors that the serious investor should look for.

The vital factors in company analysis are dealt with as follows. Quantitative analysis is presented in Chapters 11, 12 and 13. The analysis of industries is the subject of Chapter 14. This is followed by the description of a framework for analysing the competitive strength of a company within its industry in Chapter 15.

Oh no! Not numbers again!

Some share pickers never look at the accounts. They are viewed as complex and impenetrable, full of jargon and numbers. The prospect of reading such a boring document is daunting – guaranteed to cure your insomnia.

It has to be admitted that there are more fun ways of spending time, but reading a set of accounts (and the report that goes with them) is a necessary task for an investor. They are a primary source of information permitting company analysis. If you were thinking of buying a corner shop as a going concern you would not see the accounts as a boring irrelevance. Indeed, you would be very keen to know all sorts of things: from the growth in sales to the proportion of sales income that turns into take-away profit; from the market value of the building to the cost of acquiring the stock held in the shop. You could probably think of a dozen fascinating accounting questions before breakfast. What level of debt is the business carrying? Is the profit trend upward or downward? Which areas of the business create profit? And so on. The price you offer for the business would be intimately connected with the numbers you observe in the accounts. And so it is with the price you would pay for shares in larger companies. Firms quoted on stock exchanges present similarly crucial fundamental data. It is just that it looks far more complicated when first encountered.

The key elements of accounting are simple. It really is not necessary for investors to deal with the more complex and obscure accounting issues in order to understand the profit performance of a business or the value of the firm's assets. Indeed, the most successful investor in the history of the world, Warren Buffett, declares that accounts should be easy to follow. If they are presented in such a way that you are finding them difficult then it is probably because the management do not want you to understand. Such a company should be struck from your list of prospective investments simply because you cannot trust the managers.

It is vital that you gain confidence in interpreting the essential financial data. After reading this chapter **and the next two** you will be ready to have a go, and you will gradually gain the confidence to answer key questions. Be prepared for some work, if you want to reduce the chance of making unwise investment decisions.

Be aware that you need to develop a healthy sense of scepticism when examining accounts because, even though they are all drawn up under accounting guidelines, there is plenty of room when compiling the numbers for interpretation, approximation and estimation. The guidelines limit the wriggle-room, but there are still plenty of opportunities for subjectivity and flattery by the managers and their accountants. Despite the element of spurious precision in accounting numbers the report and accounts provide a lot of useful information.

How to obtain reports

Getting hold of a company's report and accounts is very easy these days. For a start, all registered shareholders will generally receive a copy of the annual report and accounts automatically. The word 'generally' is used because some companies produce both a full version and a cut-down version, the **annual review and summary financial statement**. Shareholders then have a choice as to which they would like to receive. The summary rarely contains enough information for investors trying to assess the company, and so reading the full version is necessary.[1]

If you are not a shareholder, you'll need to contact the company if you want a paper copy. You can telephone or write to the *company secretary*, or simply tel-

---

[1] If you hold shares through a nominee account (see Chapter 4), the report and accounts will be sent to the nominee company. If the terms of the nominee account allow, they will be passed on to you – for which there may be a charge.

ephone the head office switchboard. Even if you do not hold any shares in the company, nine times out of ten you'll receive a copy of the report and accounts within a week, at no cost. Most of us these days go to the company website, where we can view not only the most recent figures but also five or more years of data.

It is also possible to obtain reports and accounts from Companies House (www. companieshouse.gov.uk) for all companies, whether quoted or not. A small fee is charged. Some websites provide summary accounting information for some companies that is useful if you are carrying out an initial analysis as a filtering exercise (e.g. www.morningstar.co.uk/uk; www.advfn.com).

The report and accounts

UK companies are required by law to publish a set of accounts annually. They are not obliged to have a December year-end to match the calendar year or a 5 April year-end to match the tax year. Sometimes the year-end is determined by when the company was originally registered. Other companies opt for a year-end that helps the accounts to look healthy – for example, an agricultural business would choose a date just after harvest when debts are low and cash holdings are high.

Registered shareholders are sent the report and accounts a few weeks before the **annual general meeting**, together with details of the meeting and issues on which a vote is required. Voting forms are included so that the votes can be registered and counted prior to the AGM, and in case the shareholder cannot attend the AGM.

The law requires that companies produce a balance sheet, which shows the value of everything the company owns, owes and is owed on the last day of the financial year; a profit and loss account, which shows the company's sales, running costs and the profit or loss it has made over the financial year; notes about the accounts, giving important detail to provide greater understanding of the accounts; a director's report, providing a review of the business and other information; and an auditor's report on the truth and fairness of the accounts.

The **accounting standards** set by the accounting profession clarify the rules and conventions governing the report and accounts. They also changed the naming of parts to some degree; so today they call for '**a statement of financial position**' – many of us have stuck to 'balance sheet' for this, Tesco, for example still uses 'balance sheet'. Under the International Financial Reporting Standards (IFRS) a profit and loss account becomes an **income statement**. The Standards also require a **statement of cash flows**.[2] Furthermore, the United Kingdom Listing Authority insists that listed (Main Market) companies[3] provide more information, as does the London Stock Exchange for Alternative Investment Market (AIM) companies. First, an **interim profit statement** (interim report or **half-yearly report**) describes the company's activities and profit and loss for the first six months of each financial year. Frequently companies also comply with what is considered **best practice**,[4] for the interim report, which means they usually include a balance sheet, a cash flow statement, a statement of total recognised gains and losses and some comment on trading, risks and prospects for the company. They also generally go to the expense of having the figures reviewed by auditors. This is less thorough than the normal audit as it concentrates mainly on whether the numbers have been prepared in a manner consistent with the previous annual accounts. The FCA (UKLA) insists that listed company interim reports are made available within two months of the half-year-end. AIM companies are given three months from the period end. *Interim dividends* are also announced at this time. FT.com lists all the quoted companies which have published interim reports in the previous week – see Box 11.1.

For Main Market companies the UKLA insists on publication of **preliminary annual results (prelims)** for the year. These appear a few weeks after the year-end and provide shareholders with key data such as profits for the year months before the full report and accounts are presented. (The annual report must be issued within four months of the year-end for Main Market listed companies and six months for AIM companies.) The prelims usually receive a great deal of publicity. Be aware, however, that they do not have to be audited, nor do they contain the notes to the accounts, which provide so much vital detail for the investor. The preliminary results announced during the week are listed in the Saturday edition of the *Financial Times* and at FT.com – see Box 11.2. *Financial Times* articles during the week would have provided more detail and some discussion of the prelims.

---

[2] A couple of additional small statements are also required, but these are beyond the scope of this book – see the further reading at the end of this chapter to expand your knowledge.

[3] All listed companies are public, but not all public companies ('plcs') are listed.

[4] This is voluntary, but companies are frowned upon by the Accounting Standards Board and the UKLA if they ignore it. An offender can be ostracised by the financial community.

| Box 11.1 | Interim results shown in the *Financial Times* |

LAST WEEK'S INTERIM RESULTS

Company	Sector	Pre-tax-profit (£m)		Interim dividends[a] per share (p)	
Best of the Best	Unq	0.215	(0.01)	-	(-)
Ebiquity	Unq	1.701	(1.17)	-	(-)
Games Workshop Group	HLPG	7.731	(11.094)	16	(18)
Ideagen	Unq	0.515	(0.23)	0.05	(-)
IG Group Holdings	Unq	95.115	(81.122)	5.75	(5.75)
Ilika	Unq	1.505L	(1.868L)	-	(-)
Leeds Group	AIMFinG	0.975	(0.114)	-	(-)
M & G High Income Inv. Tr.	ConExPrvE	6.501	(23.909)	-	(1.3)
NCC Group	TechS	11.133	(7.535)	1.14	(0.98)
Swan (John) & Sons	Unq	0.087L	(0.135L)	-	(-)

The figure in the first column is for this year.

The figure in the second column is pre-tax profit for the same period last year. 'L' signifies loss

The total interim dividend in pence per share (figures in the second column are for the previous year's interims)

Source: Financial Times, 17 January 2014.

Quoted companies are required to include in the annual report much more than unquoted companies: e.g. a brief biography of each non-executive director, details of directors' interests in the company's shares and options on shares, information on shareholdings greater than 3 per cent, particulars of significant contracts and details of share repurchases. Some companies choose to report quarterly to provide investors with more up-to-date information.

Profit and loss account

The profit and loss account (income statement) records whether the company's sales revenue was greater than its costs. It allows you to compare the latest profit with previous years' profits, or with other companies.

Figure 11.1 shows a typical profit and loss account. The layout and terminology may change from one company to another, but it captures the key figures you are

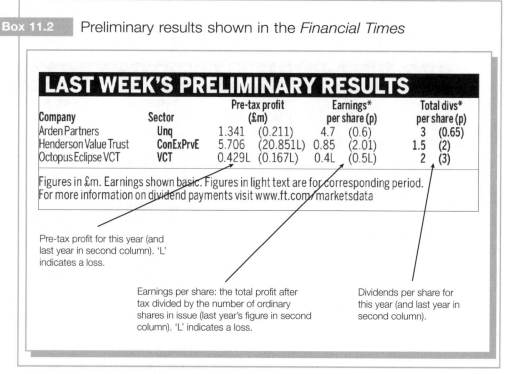

Box 11.2   Preliminary results shown in the *Financial Times*

LAST WEEK'S PRELIMINARY RESULTS

Company	Sector	Pre-tax profit (£m)		Earnings* per share (p)		Total divs* per share (p)	
Arden Partners	Unq	1.341	(0.211)	4.7	(0.6)	3	(0.65)
Henderson Value Trust	ConExPrvE	5.706	(20.851L)	0.85	(2.01)	1.5	(2)
Octopus Eclipse VCT	VCT	0.429L	(0.167L)	0.4L	(0.5L)	2	(3)

Figures in £m. Earnings shown basic. Figures in light text are for corresponding period. For more information on dividend payments visit www.ft.com/marketsdata

Pre-tax profit for this year (and last year in second column). 'L' indicates a loss.

Earnings per share: the total profit after tax divided by the number of ordinary shares in issue (last year's figure in second column). 'L' indicates a loss.

Dividends per share for this year (and last year in second column).

Source: Financial Times, 17 January 2014.

likely to come across. The 'Notes' column points out where in the notes to the accounts to look for more detailed information about a particular item. Brackets are placed around negative numbers.

The accounts of quoted companies with subsidiaries are described as **consolidated** or **group** accounts. This means that all the income, costs, assets and liabilities of all group companies, whether *wholly owned* or *partially owned*, are brought together in the group's consolidated accounts.[5] Quoted companies often operate through dozens of other companies. In most cases they set up these companies and own 100 per cent of the ordinary shares (wholly owned). In other

---

[5] This applies to companies where more than 50 per cent of the shares are held by the parent, or if less than 50 per cent of the shares are held by the parent company but it still exercises control over the majority of director appointments, or exercises a dominant influence over the undertaking.

cases they may have acquired, say, 60 per cent of the shares (partially owned), leaving **minority (non-controlling) shareholders** with the other 40 per cent. Each of these wholly owned or partially owned subsidiaries will have its own accounts, but when the figures are brought together in the consolidated accounts 100 per cent of the income, costs, assets and liabilities are thrown in, even if the controlling company owns only, say, 60 per cent of the subsidiary's shares. A deduction is made later (**minority interests** or **non-controlling interests**) to allow for the 40 per cent owned by outside shareholders.

	Notes	20X2 £m	20X1 £m
Turnover (revenue)	1	230	200
Cost of sales	2	(140)	(120)
Gross profit	3	90	80
Distribution costs	4	(15)	(11)
Administrative costs	5	(10)	(9)
Other costs	6	(10)	(10)
Operating profit		55	50
Less Finance costs (after allowing for finance income)	7	(6)	(5)
Profit before tax		49	45
Less tax on profits	8	(14)	(13)
Profit after tax		35	32
Attributable to:			
Equity shareholders of the parent company	9	34	31
Non-controlling interests (minority interests)	10	1	1
		35	32
Earnings per share	11	68p	62p
Dividends	12	£17m	£15m
Dividends per share		34p	30p
Retained profit for the year		£17m	£16m

Figure 11.1   Typical consolidated income statement (profit and loss account) for the year ending 31 March 20X2

Each of the entries in Figure 11.1 will be explained in turn:

- **Turnover.** This is money received or to be received by the company from the sale of goods or services during the year. Other terms used are *'revenue'* and *'sales'*. This figure is stated net of VAT or sales taxes. Accounting standards require that income statements separate the turnover of continuing operations from activities discontinued during the year and from joint ventures (businesses operated in partnership with other companies). The notes to the accounts will usually give a more detailed breakdown of where sales came from. For example, Tesco separates turnover from the UK, the rest of Europe, Asia, the USA and Tesco Bank.

- Accounts usually show the previous year's figures as well as the latest, which makes comparison over time easier. This is further helped by the five-year summary (described later in this chapter), usually placed at the back of the report. In the example shown, turnover has risen by an apparently healthy 15 per cent, but the analyst would like to know what proportion of that rise was achieved by the existing operations, by new companies acquired in the year, or by **organic** (that is, non-acquisition) capital growth. (For example, did the company borrow a massive amount to open up 100 more shop branches, leading to sales growth? If so, you may be less impressed by a mere 15 per cent rise.) Also, you might also want to take inflation into account when examining change over time.

- **Cost of sales.** The expense incurred for bought-in raw materials or components, and the costs of bringing materials to saleable condition (including costs of production such as factory wages and manufacturing overheads).

- **Gross profit.** Turnover less cost of sales.

- **Distribution costs, administration costs and other costs.** This covers a lot of items, from the expense of employees in head office to the rent paid for a building. **Depreciation** of plant, machinery and other capital items will be included in this section. Depreciation represents the reduction in the stated carrying value of fixed assets in the balance sheet. The method of depreciation will be described in the notes to the accounts.

- **Operating profit (operating income or profit from operations).** This is the income remaining after paying all costs other than interest. It thus focuses on the underlying business return, without the distortionary effect of allowing for how the business was financed (i.e. high or low levels of debt). This may be split between continuing and discontinued operations. At this point, many accounts show an adjustment for **exceptional items.**

These are gains or costs which are part of the company's ordinary activities but are either unusual in themselves or have an exceptionally large impact on profits that year. These one-off items may distort profits in a particular year, so accounts often show results both before and after exceptional items. Examples might include the windfall profits on the sale of an office block, or the exceptional cost of closing down a business activity (e.g. the redundancy costs of closing a subsidiary).[6]

■ **Profit before tax**. Interest paid is deducted, or interest received is added, to arrive at the key profit figure: the one that often receives a lot of attention in the press. This is also referred to as the **pre-tax profit**. In the case of Figure 11.1 net interest paid has risen from £5 million to £6 million between 20X1 and 20X2. Perhaps interest rates rose and/or the amount borrowed increased in 20X2. The notes to the accounts will show a breakdown of borrowings: for example, they will lay out the proportion that is repayable within one year, five years, etc.; the amounts borrowed in different currencies; and the amounts borrowed through various bond issues or bank loans.

■ An analyst might notice that while the turnover of the firm in Figure 11.1 has risen by 15 per cent, costs have grown by a larger percentage, so that pre-tax profit rose by only 9 per cent from £45 million to £49 million.

■ **Taxation. Corporation tax** is payable by UK resident companies on all income and capital gains after all costs. Dividends paid out to ordinary shareholders are not costs, they are a distribution of profits to the owners, the shareholders. The Chancellor of the Exchequer keeps changing the rate of corporation tax, so for illustration we'll stick with 28 per cent. Note, however, that the company is not due to pay 28 per cent of £49 million (which is £13.72 million) in tax. The exact proportion of reported profit paid in tax depends on a number of factors, such as whether tax was paid abroad on income earned abroad. Some companies can pay a very low tax relative to current year earnings because they have tax losses due to trading and other losses made in previous years. When they move into profit they may not have to pay tax for many years. The notes to the accounts (in this case note 8) should provide details on the computation of tax.

---

[6] There may be some additional entries at this point because not all profit comes from operating the underlying business. These additional sources of income may fall under the following headings: (a) income from interests in associated undertakings, and from other participating interests (e.g. if the parent company owns 20 per cent or more of another company and exercises significant influence the group's share of its associates' operating results may be included); (b) income from other investments and other interest receivable (e.g. interest from gilts or dividends).

- **Profit after tax (profit for the period)**. This is also called **net profit**. If there are no minority interests then we can call this the *equity earnings* of the company, which belong to the shareholders. However, in this case one or more of the company's subsidiaries is partly owned by someone else. It is therefore necessary to deduct their slice of the profits. This is shown by the £1 million minority interest figure. The subsidiary that is only partially owned by our large firm has all its revenues and costs included in the figures presented in the upper half of the profit and loss accounts, and it is only at this point in the accounts that we acknowledge that a proportion of the profits actually belong to outsiders. So, after deducting minority interests (and possibly dividends on preference shares) the **profit attributable to equity shareholders of the parent company** of the example company is £34 million in 20X2. This is often called the **'bottom line' figure**. When the dividends paid figure is deducted we are left with the funds which have been ploughed back into the business – the *retained earnings* (or retentions).

- **Earnings per share**. This is the profit attributable to ordinary shareholders (i.e. after minority interests and preference dividends) divided by the number of ordinary shares in issue. The company has issued 50 million shares and so we have earnings per share of £34m/50m = 68p. Earnings per share are a key measure of a company's performance. They allow investors to observe the growth in profits for each share held (it is easy for management to raise total profits if they keep issuing more shares and thereby bring more money into the business; it is not so easy to raise the earnings on each existing share). They are also a measure of the company's ability to pay dividends in a sustainable manner.

- Earnings per share may be presented both before and after exceptional items. There are many adjustments that can be made to earnings per share figures – see Chapter 12 for more details.

- **Dividends per share**. The total amount paid or due to be paid in dividends for the year (interim and final dividend) divided by the number of shares in issue. For 20X2 this is £17m/50m = 34p per share.

Balance sheet (statement of financial position)

The balance sheet provides a snapshot of what the company owned[7], owes and is owed on a particular day in the past: usually the last day of the financial year (or last day of the first half of the year). The balance sheet summarises the assets and

---

[7] Or, in some cases, controlled, as with some leased assets.

the liabilities of the business. The difference between the assets and liabilities is the **net assets** or **equity**.

In reports and accounts you will often see two balance sheets. The first is for the **parent company (holding company)**. This company's numerous wholly or partly owned subsidiaries will be represented on the parent company's balance sheet but not in consolidated form, so this is of limited use for financial analysis. The attention of the investor should be directed at the second balance sheet – the

	Notes	20X2	20X1
		£m	£m
Non-current (fixed) assets			
Tangible assets	13	82	80
Intangible assets	14	18	20
Investments	15	5	5
		105	105
Current assets			
Inventory (stock)	16	35	20
Trade and other receivables (debtors)	17	60	40
Current asset investments and deposits	18	20	20
Cash at bank and in hand	19	10	10
		125	90
Current liabilities	20		
Creditors: amount due within one year		(62)	(49)
Net current assets		63	41
Total assets less current liabilities		168	146
Non-current liabilities			
Creditor amounts due in more than one year	21	(25)	(20)
Provisions for liabilities and charges	22	(14)	(14)
Net assets		129	112
Equity ('Capital and reserves')			
Called-up share capital	23	5	5
Share premium account	24	50	50
Revaluation reserve	25	23	23
Retained earnings	26	46	29
Total attributable to equity shareholders of the parent		124	107
Non-controlling (minority) interests	27	5	5
Total equity		129	112

Figure 11.2   A typical consolidated (group) balance sheet at 31 March 20X2

consolidated (or group) **balance sheet**. This includes all the assets and liabilities of the subsidiary companies and the holding company, whether the parent holds 60, 70 or 100 per cent of the shares in the subsidiary. To explain the terms in a balance sheet we will work through the items shown in Figure 11.2. Note that the assets are shown as positive figures while liabilities are shown in brackets.

■ **Non-current assets (fixed assets)**. The assets are separated into long-term assets (fixed assets or non-current) and short-term assets (current assets). Fixed assets are those that are not held for resale, but for use in the business. The fixed assets are generally displayed under three categories:

– **Tangible assets**. Assets used to earn revenue that have a physical presence (e.g. land, buildings, factories, machinery and vehicles).

– **Intangible assets**. Things you cannot touch, but which have a long life (longer than one year), e.g. copyright and other publishing rights, licences, patents, trademarks, goodwill.

– **Investments** expected to be held for the long term, e.g. shareholdings in other companies (except subsidiary holdings), works of art, and gilts.

■ Most long-term assets wear out, and so allowance has to be made for this. Tangible and intangible assets are therefore usually recorded at **net book value**,[8] which is the original cost of the assets, minus the accumulated depreciation for tangibles, or minus amortisation in the case of intangibles, since their acquisition. Accounting standards require all fixed assets except land to be depreciated (or amortised). Some assets rise in value. If this happens, companies have the possibility of revaluing assets in the balance sheet. As well as being shown in the fixed assets section this is also shown in the **revaluation reserve**. The revaluation reserve represents the accumulated revaluations of fixed assets. In this way a company does not credit the fortuitous increase in value of a fixed asset to the income statement, because this would distort the picture of underlying profitability. (The new International Financial Reporting Standards are less fastidious on this point.)

■ Investments are generally shown at cost, but investments in stock market quoted securities are often shown at market value in the notes to the accounts.

■ **Current assets**. These comprise cash and assets that can be rapidly turned into cash. Inventories of raw materials, partially finished (work in progress) or finished goods are included here as well as the value of **receivables**

---

[8] Under International Financial Reporting Standards some assets may be revalued at 'fair value' which is supposed to relate to some sort of current market value.

(**debtors**) – that is, amounts owed to the business, usually by customers. Investments expected to be sold within the next year are included under current assets (these are normally shown at the lower of cost or net realisable value but can be revalued up to market value or what directors regard as 'fair value').

■ **Liabilities. Current liabilities** are amounts owed that the company expects to have to pay within the next year. Bank loans with less than a year to repayment and overdrafts will be included here, as will outstanding trade **payables (creditors)** (suppliers allowing the firm to pay later for goods supplied) and corporation tax due but not yet paid. The difference between current assets and current liabilities is **net current assets** (commonly known as **working capital**). In our example, on 31 March 20X2 it amounts to £63 million. If we now add on the value of the fixed assets we have the figure of £168 million for the *total assets less current liabilities*.

■ **Net assets**. The net assets figure is the total assets minus all the liabilities. Included in liabilities are those creditor amounts due to be paid after more than a year, non-current liabilities (e.g. long-term bank loans or bonds), and **provisions** for liabilities and charges. A provision is an allowance for a liability if you are unable to be precise about either the amount or when it will be paid. Provisions are often included for items such as pension obligations, restructuring costs (e.g. staff retraining or relocation), environmental damage or litigation.

■ **Equity (capital and reserves)**. The net assets of the company are owned by the shareholders. However, there are two groups of shareholders that we have to allow for in a consolidated balance sheet. Recall that for partially owned subsidiaries we boldly included 100 per cent of the assets and liabilities in the top half of the balance sheet. Some of these net assets are attributable to the holders of the minority fraction of the subsidiaries and not to the holding company shareholders. This amount is represented by the figure for non-controlling (minority) interests. The remainder is the net assets attributable to the holding company's shareholders. This is termed **'equity shareholders' funds'**, or **'shareholders' funds'** for short. In the example equity shareholders' funds are allocated to four categories. The first is **called-up share capital**. If we looked up note 23 we will observe two share capital numbers. The first is the **authorised share capital**. This is the nominal (par) value of the shares that were created when the company was established, or which were subsequently created (with shareholder approval). The nominal value of each share might be, say, 5p, 10p, 25p, 50p or any amount the original founders decided upon. The second is **issued (or called-up) share capital**. This is the total value of the shares issued (sold or allotted to investors) when expressed at nominal value. It is normal to observe a company having many more shares authorised than have actually been sold (issued). The notes usually state both the total number of shares, the nominal value of each share and the total nominal value of all the shares. In this case there are 50 million shares in issue ('called up'), each with a nominal value of 10p at the end of the 20X2 financial year, thus we see a figure of £5 million (the total nominal value) shown in the balance sheet. When shares are sold they rarely sell at nominal value. We saw earlier in the chapter that our example company is now producing earnings per share of 68p and paying a dividend of 34p. Clearly if the company issued more shares they could sell them for more than 10p – I'd be first in the queue with my 10p if I could get an annual dividend of 34p! Even when a company is first established the nominal value is often set below the amount received from the sale of the shares. The **share premium account** records the additional amount (above the nominal value) for which shares were sold.

- The **retained earnings (profit and loss account or revenue reserves)** entry in the balance sheet represents the accumulated retained profits for all the years of the company's existence. Notice that this figure rose by £17 million between 20X1 and 20X2, reflecting the retention of the profits made in 20X2. This is the reserve that can be dipped into to pay dividends.[9] So if our company has a loss-making year in 20X3 and still wishes to pay a dividend it could do so up to an amount of £46 million (minus 20X3's loss).

Cash flow statement

One of the main reasons why companies go into liquidation is that they run out of cash. It is possible for profits to be on a rising trend and yet to see the company going under. The prospect of liquidation is one of the reasons why the analyst needs to examine the cash inflows and outflows of the business over the year.

In addition to assessing the likelihood of corporate failure, examining cash flow statements is very useful for filling in some of the gaps in the picture of the company's performance and strength left after analysing the profit and loss and the balance sheet. It helps answer some key questions such as: what proportion of any increase in profit is swallowed up by ever larger investments in fixed assets, trade receivables and inventories needed to maintain earnings growth? If all the cash is being absorbed, what is going to be left for dividends? If investment in assets year

---

[9] Dividends can also be paid out of the gains made when non-current assets are sold, after netting out tax and losses made on other non-current asset sales.

after year is greater than cash generated by operations, will the directors have to keep asking shareholders for more money or will they borrow more? If borrowings are increasing how does that affect the risk of the ordinary shares? Does the company generate enough cash to pay its interest? And so on.

Furthermore, the cash flow statement is much more difficult for managers to manipulate than the profit and loss account and balance sheet because it is a measure of actual cash movements. It identifies where the company gets its money from and what it spent that money on.[10]

Figure 11.3 shows a typical cash flow statement.

This is for the same company as the profit and loss and balance sheet shown earlier in the chapter. It is divided into a number of areas:

■ **Cash flows from operating activities**. This includes the cash received from the firm's customers in the year (excluding sales made for which cash has not yet been received and sales taxes, e.g. VAT). Cash paid to suppliers, employees, etc., has been deducted. In the reconciliation between the profit and loss and the cash flow statement there will be a recognition that the depreciation expensed in the profit and loss is not a cash outflow. This boosts cash flow compared with profit. However the additional expenditure on more inventory (£15 million – see the balance sheet change between 20X1 and 20X2 in Figure 11.2) and on receivables (£20 million) reduces cash flow relative to profit. If net cash from operating activities is negative we might start to worry because the company is not selling its goods and services for more than they cost or is pumping vast amounts into working capital to keep up its sales level.

■ **Cash flows from investing activities**. This section includes cash used to pay for the acquisition of non-current assets and/or cash generated by the

---

[10] In addition to the cash flow statement there may also be a **reconciliation of operating profit reported in the income statement and the net cash flow from operating activities**. This will disclose separately the movements in inventory, receivables and payables. There will also be a note **reconciling the movement of cash with the movement in net debt**. Furthermore companies are required to produce a **statement of changes in equity** which adds to the profit for the period all the other gains and losses that are not permitted into the profit and loss. For example, surpluses and deficits on the revaluation of fixed assets, currency translation gains and losses (overseas subsidiaries boosting or lowering profits, assets or liabilities in parent company currency due to shifting currency rates). This statement shows the extent to which shareholders' funds have decreased or increased from all gains and losses. Often, following the statement of changes in equity, will be a note reconciling the opening and closing totals of shareholders' funds for the period.

	Notes	£m	£m
Cash flows from operating activities			
Cash generated from operations	28		25
Interest paid	7		(6)
Tax paid			(13)
Net cash from operating activities			6
Cash flows from investing activities			
Purchase of property, plant and equipment	13	(5)	
Proceeds from the disposal of property, plant and equip.		0	
Proceeds/purchases of investments		0	
Interest received		0	
Dividends received		0	
Net cash from investing activities			(5)
Cash flows from financing activities			
Increase (repayment) of borrowings	20,21	14	
Ordinary dividends paid	12	(15)	
Net cash used in financing activities			(1)
Net increase/(decrease) in cash and cash equivalents			0
Cash and cash equivalents at beginning of period			10
Cash and cash equivalents at end of period			10

Figure 11.3   **Consolidated cash flow statement, for the year ending 31 March 20X2**

sale of non-current assets. In this case a net £5 million was spent on long-lived assets – vehicles, equipment, buildings, etc. Cash can also be used to purchase subsidiaries or some of the shares in subsidiaries – cash inflow can increase if these assets are sold. If interest or dividends are received from investments in joint ventures or associated companies then this is included in this section.

■ **Cash flows from financing activities**. The first two sections of the cash flow statement show the amount of cash generated (or absorbed) by the operating business or through investment activities. In this case there is an overall surplus of £1 million. However, the company also paid dividends during the year, which used up £15 million, leaving it short of cash. This gap was filled by borrowing an additional £14 million.

Thus, in this year, the company only just generated enough cash to sustain its investment in working capital items (e.g. inventory and receivables) and fixed capital items (e.g. plant and equipment). It did not produce enough cash to also pay a hefty dividend without borrowing more. This may be a concern to an investor, who may like to explore the potential of the firm to produce cash that can be handed out to shareholders. To look at it from a different angle: as the company grows its turnover, does it need large lumps of cash to bolster working and fixed capital just to stay in the game?

Our example is unusual in showing zero overall cash movement for the year (£10 million in cash at the beginning and at the end). Most will show a significant positive or negative cash balance change.

Note that *'cash'* means notes and coins as well as bank deposits repayable on demand less overdrafts.

'Cash flow' includes payments by cheque, etc.

Cash equivalents are short-term investments which can very quickly and easily be sold at low cost to be turned into cash. They are very safe investments so there is very little doubt about the ability of the issuer of the financial instrument being unable to pay. So, for example it is possible to lend to the UK government by purchasing three-month Treasury bills. These promise to pay £100 to the holder say 90 days from now. These are bought and sold among investors during the 90 days. So, someone might hold a Treasury bill and decide to turn this near cash into cash-in-a-bank-account by selling it for say £99.60. A few days later the buyer will collect £100 from the UK government (if he does not sell to yet another buyer). The difference between £100 and £99.60 provides a small amount of interest.

Example of a *profitable* company forced into liquidation

ABC plc starts the year by obtaining equity capital of £1 million by selling shares, and it borrows £1.5 million from the bank on 1 January. It buys £2 million of machinery and hires 25 workers. The machinery is expected to have a useful life of ten years and is depreciated (an expense) at a rate of £200,000 per year. In the first year the company is profitable (Figure 11.4).

Despite reporting a profit, the company runs out of cash and is forced by its bank into liquidation. It ran out of cash because of a number of factors. It granted its customers the right to pay for goods 60 days after delivery. In the meantime, ABC had to pay its raw material suppliers, labour, machinery and distribution costs while production was taking place. Many customers either paid late (after 60 days) or did not pay at all. Thus the company received only £4 million during the year, not £5 million. Also another machine was purchased half way through the year for £250,000. The cash flow statement for the year in this simple case looks

	£
Sales	5,000,000
Cost of sales	(4,000,000)
Gross profit	1,000,000
Costs	
Labour	(400,000)
Factory and other costs	(300,000)
Depreciation on machine	(200,000)
Operating profit	100,000
Less interest payable	(80,000)
Profit on ordinary activities before taxation	20,000

Figure 11.4   **ABC plc profit and loss account**

	£
Net cash flow from operating activities[a]	(700,000)
Interest paid	(80,000)
Taxation	0
Capital expenditure	(2,250,000)
Equity dividends paid	0
Cash inflow (outflow) before financing	(3,030,000)
Financing : Issue of shares	1,000,000
Increase in debt	1,500,000
Increase (decrease) in cash in the year	(530,000)

[a] Cash received from customers (£4m) minus cash flowing out for operations (£4.7m)
which includes costs of sales, labour, factory and other costs

Figure 11.5   **ABC plc cash flow statement**

far worse than the profit and loss account (Figure 11.5). This company started the year with zero cash and ended with negative £530,000 cash – clearly unsustainable (even if it did manage to limp to the end of the year).

Chairman's statement

The law does not require a chairman's statement, but most companies include one. It can be useful because it helps to put the accounting numbers into context. Events might have occurred which have a significant effect on the profit and loss, balance sheet and cash flow statement, and it is often the chairman's statement that flags these. For example, a major acquisition may have taken place, together with a rights issue and a rise in borrowing impacting on the accounts. Without the comment from the chairman it may not be possible to understand why the accounts show dramatic change from one year to the next.

The statement is also a personal comment from the chairman that will attempt to enlighten the shareholders on the general trading environment that the company coped with in the past and is now faced with. It may also break down the overall performance into constituent parts (e.g. by product line, division or geography) and comment on future prospects for these. Major action, such as factory closures or large investments in new technology, may be referred to. Also some comment will be made on the overall corporate strategy.

Some chairmen take their role as overseer of the company's direction and performance seriously. They examine the firm's actions purely from a shareholder's perspective. They then report to the shareholders in a frank and critical fashion about the quality of stewardship by the directors of shareholders' money and about the future prospects. Unfortunately, all too many chairmen see their role as cheerleaders for the executives, and the statement can appear to be a public relations exercise: long on presenting the positives of executive action and short on balanced critical content. The investor then has to read the statement with particular care and a degree of scepticism. Reading between the lines is the order of the day. Examine the statement not for what it contains, but for what it leaves out.

Chief executive's review

In addition to the chairman's statement (or sometimes instead of one) there is the chief executive's review or operational review. The **chief executive officer (CEO)** is the most powerful director. In the UK this would normally be the managing director. The review will provide more detail on performance, strategy and managerial intentions for each division.

Financial review

The financial review is normally written by the finance director (FD) and contains a discussion centred on the most significant accounting numbers, linking the results to the firm's strategy and the events of the year. The FD will usually break down the sales and trading profit numbers to different geographies and/ or product divisions. She will also discuss the strength of the balance sheet (e.g. 'we have little debt relative to net assets') and some **key performance indicators** (metrics) **KPIs** such as return on capital employed (see Chapter 12) in different areas of the business, to show how close they are getting to their targets.

Directors' report and business review

These are required by law, but directors frequently supply much more information and commentary than either statutes or the Stock Exchange insist on. The business review is either part of the directors' report or cross-referenced to it. Many companies cover many of these discussion points in the CEO's or FD's reports or in other sections of the annual report and so the business review section can be quite thin. The report contains the following (if not covered elsewhere in the report):

- a discussion of activities during the year and discussion of likely future developments;

- important events affecting the company, which have occurred since the year-end;

- details of share buy-backs;

- technical information, e.g. names of directors and their shareholdings, political or charitable contributions made by the company;

- shareholdings of more than 3 per cent (listed companies only);

- a description of research and development activity;

- policies on employment, supplier relationships, risk management and the environment;

- principal risks and uncertainties facing the business and how the management are confronting them.

The review (which may be called 'the operating and financial review, or OFR) provides (ideally) an analysis of the development and performance of the business(es) during the year and a considered, balanced and comprehensive assessment of the position of the company at the year-end. This might touch on corporate strategy and will include a discussion of principal risks and uncertainties. This is where more detailed KPIs, used to assess its progress and efficiency, might be discussed (see Chapter 12 for some of the ratios commonly used).

Auditors' report

The auditors are appointed by the shareholders at the AGM to hold office until the next AGM. It is a legal requirement to appoint auditors (except for very small companies). Their role is to determine whether the company's financial statements are misleading – whether the accounts show a *'true and fair view'*. It is an offence for directors to give false or misleading information to auditors. Auditors have the right of access to the books and accounts at all times. They can insist on additional information and explanations from managers to try to obtain an understanding of the financial position.

If auditors have doubts about the quality of record keeping or they detect a discrepancy between the books and the accounts, or the information and explanations they demand are not forthcoming, they will state the difficulty in their report. That is, they qualify their report. Alarm bells should start to ring when an investor reads the accounts have been qualified.

Auditors also comment on whether the company complies with the code of practice relating to **corporate governance** – that is, the system of management and control of the corporation. Guidelines of best practice were consolidated in the **UK Corporate Governance Code**. Directors have to state in the accounts how the principles of the code have been applied. If the principles have not been followed they have to state why. Among these principles are the following: there should be transparency on directors' remuneration, requiring a remuneration committee consisting of non-executive directors; directors should retire by rotation at least every three years (for largest 350 companies it is every year); the chairman should not also be the chief executive officer to avoid domination by one person (in exceptional circumstances this may be ignored, if a written justification is presented to shareholders); the **audit committee** (responsible for validating financial figures, e.g. by appointing effective external auditors) should consist exclusively of independent[11] non-executive directors and not executive directors, otherwise

---

[11] To be independent the non-executive directors should not, for example, be a customer, supplier or a friend of the founding family or the chief executive. They should not be dependent on the fee from the company for their income.

the committee would not be able to act as a check and balance to the executive directors; at least half the members of the board, excluding the chairman, should be independent non-executive directors; the accounts must contain a statement by the directors that the company is a going concern, that is, it has the financial wherewithal to continue for at least another year; and a senior independent director should be appointed to listen to the views of a range of shareholders and communicate those views to the board.

Five-year summary

Usually placed at the back of the report and accounts is a very useful five- or ten-year summary of key financial data. It is here that you can observe the historic pattern of growth in sales, profits, dividends, earnings per share, and a host of other important variables. An erratic pattern may be less attractive than a smooth one. Fast sales and profit growth with zero earnings per share growth will probably indicate large-scale acquisition of companies combined with regular issuance of shares. This is likely to be less attractive than more pedestrian organic sales and profit growth combined with rising earnings per share.

Beware of relying too much on these summary tables without understanding the detail behind them. Distortions over time can arise because of changes in accounting practice policies, or even accounting standards. Another major source of confusion is the inclusion or exclusion of discontinued activities.

Trading statements

Interim management statements (trading updates) are issued by a company in the middle of each half year. They are a requirement for Main Market companies, and many AIM companies follow suit. They are usually very simple, consisting of a few paragraphs providing a brief description of the firm's trading performance since the last formal report. The financial data supplied is very limited (e.g. in the 12 weeks to 15 January sales were down 2 per cent) and profit figures are not provided. They should highlight material events or transactions that impact on the firm's position.

Throughout the year companies are required to make announcements if they have any information that may, when released, have a significant impact on share price, e.g. losing a major contract.

Further reading

W. McKenzie, *The Financial Times Guide to Using and Interpreting Company Accounts*, 4th edn (Financial Times Prentice Hall, 2009).

E. McLaney and P. Atrill, *Accounting: An Introduction*, 6th edn (Pearson, 2012).

F. Wood and A. Sangster, *Frank Wood's Business Accounting Volume Two*, 12th edn (Financial Times Prentice Hall, 2012).

The first two books provide easy-to-follow introductions to reports and accounts that are much more detailed than those provided in this chapter. Up-to-date information on the various accounting standards is available from the Financial Reporting Council website (https://www.frc.org.uk).

12

Key investment ratios and measures

This chapter explains the jargon used by the financial press when it reports on the performance or the financial health of a company. The investor is bombarded with a bewildering variety of summary statistics about companies. Here we describe the most commonly used and important. So if you don't know your acid test from your NAV, or your PER from your ROCE, then this is the chapter for you.

At the end of it you will not only be able to understand company data in the *Financial Times* but will also be capable of calculating for yourself ratios and other measures from the base data – usually the annual report and accounts. You will then be in a position to analyse a company by focusing on those elements that seem particularly important to you. In other words, you don't have to be reliant on other people's judgement as to which measures are most significant, or how they are calculated (with some measures there is room for selection as to which component numbers to include).

The value of these ratios and other measures is that they help to put into perspective the numbers reported in the profit and loss account, balance sheet and cash flow statements. They often relate one aspect of the accounts (e.g. profits) to another (e.g. the value of all the assets the company is using). For example, if you were told that company A made £10 million profit whereas company B made £20 million, would you automatically conclude that B is the better company? Perhaps you would like to compare the return per pound used by each business. If A had net assets of £40 million at the start and end of the year, while B had £200 million of net assets you would have some useful information about the efficiency with which each company used the assets available to it. Company A produces a 25p profit for every £1 of capital, a 25 per cent return on capital (profit/net assets = £10m/£40m = 0.25) whereas B produces a mere 10p for every £1 of capital it uses (£20m/£200m = 0.10).

These ratios and measures, as well as displaying the relationship between pairs of figures and permitting comparison with other companies, allow an investor to develop a more informed perspective on the firm's performance and financial standing across time. The way in which ratios change over a period of five or ten years can help to build up a picture of the company's progress or decline.

In this chapter the investment ratios and measures are presented in four sections:

▪ Measures that are given daily (or at least weekly) in the financial press. These mostly relate to the share price.

▪ Statistics that measure the company's performance in terms of profit, profitability and efficiency.

▪ Financial health ratios and measures. This section examines the level of debt and solvency ratios.

▪ Forward-looking measures that help in the valuing of shares based on the income flows that a shareholder is forecast to receive.

From the financial pages

Price–earnings ratio

The **price–earnings ratio or PER** (*'P/E ratio'* or **earnings multiple**) compares a company's share price with its latest annual earnings per share (eps). The eps is the profit attributable to shareholders, as shown in the income statement, divided by the number of shares in issue (see Chapter 11).

$$PER = \frac{\text{Current market price of share}}{\text{Last year's earnings per share}}$$

So, for example, if a company has a current market price of £9 for one of its shares and the earnings per share shown in the latest accounts are 68p the PER (**earnings multiple**) is:

$$PER = \frac{900p}{68p} = 13.2$$

The eps figure assumed here came from the income statement shown in Figure 11.1. The profit attributable to the shareholders is £34 million (after subtracting £1 million for minority interests from the profit after tax figure) and the number of shares in issue is 50 million, giving eps of 68p.

The PER shown above should strictly be called the **'historical PER'** (or **trailing PER**) because it is based on earnings that have already happened. This is the PER that receives most attention in the press. However, quite often investors are interested in knowing how high the share price is in relation to the level of projected earnings for next year. This is the **prospective PER** or **forward PER**:

$$\text{Prospective PER} = \frac{\text{Current market price of share}}{\text{Next year's expected earnings per share}}$$

Box 12.1 shows the historical PER for a number of aerospace and defence companies. The PER changes daily as the share price moves up or down. The previous day's PER is shown in the Tuesday to Saturday editions of the *Financial Times*. The Monday edition shows other company/market statistics.

An examination of Box 12.1 shows that investors are willing to buy Avon Rubber shares at 13 times last year's earnings, compared with only 7.4 times last year's earnings for BAe Systems. One explanation for the difference in PERs is that companies with higher PERs are expected to show faster growth in earnings in the future. Avon may appear expensive relative to BAe based on historical profit figures, but the differential may be justified when forecasts of earnings are made. If a PER is high, investors expect profits to rise. This does not necessarily mean that all companies with high PERs are expected to perform to a high standard, merely that they are expected to do significantly better than in the past. Another factor for PERs is the relative risk of the shares.

Some analysts prefer to swap the top and bottom of the PER ratio to create the **earnings yield**. This shows the profits attributable to each £1 invested buying a share:

$$\text{Earnings yield} = \frac{\text{Earnings per share}}{\text{Current market price of share}}$$

So, to take our earlier example, for every £1 spent buying a share last year's company profits are 7.56p (historic earnings yield):

$$\text{Earnings yield} = \frac{68p}{900p} = 7.56\%$$

Box 12.1 London share service extracts, Aerospace and Defence

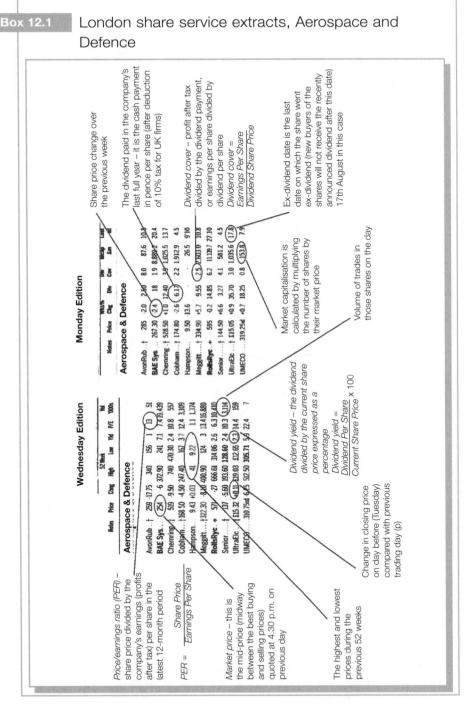

Source: Financial Times.

Historical PERs reported in the financial press are usually based on the latest annual reports and accounts, and are updated on interim figures. So if earnings for the first six months of the year have just been reported these are used instead of the earnings for the first six months of the last full year to calculate the latest 12 months of earnings.[1]

Companies sometimes report **diluted earnings per share**. This takes into account any additional shares that may be issued in the future under executive share option schemes, convertible bonds, convertible preference shares and warrants. The word 'diluted' indicates that the earnings are spread over a larger number of shares so the fully diluted eps will be less than the normal eps reported.

The eps figures used by the press are usually **basic earnings (reported earnings)**. These include a deduction from profit of one-off exceptional items, so they present a warts-and-all picture. They do not allow for future dilution because they only include the weighted average number of ordinary shares outstanding during the period (those at the start of the year adjusted for new shares issued and shares bought back in the year). The weighting gives more weight to those issued earlier in the year – as they were in existence longer.

Companies often like to present the largest eps figure possible and so they highlight the **headline**, **underlying**, **adjusted** or **normalised eps**, which excludes one-off costs, exceptional items and goodwill amortisation. These figures are supposed to show the underlying trend, but some companies seem to have a habit of showing large, supposedly one-off, costs every year. The reassuring titles of these earnings figures belie the fact that directors are able to flatter the company's performance by emphasising these numbers – they neatly sidestep some harsh facts, such as major losses in some of the business's operations.

Earnings per share may also be reported as that from 'continuing operations' (excluding earnings from businesses that have now ceased or been sold off).

The PER on its own does not tell you whether a share is appropriately valued. It merely tells you the profit growth that investors are generally expecting. This can then be compared with your estimate of growth to judge whether the market is being realistic, over-pessimistic or over-optimistic. Perhaps your judgement will be influenced by the PERs of other companies, such as those in the same sector, or

---

[1] A rolling method is used: take the latest full year's earnings, add on the latest six months' figures and deduct the earnings for the six-month period a year ago. For a company that reports earnings every quarter the earnings number used is the sum of the last four quarterly earnings.

the PER for the market as a whole. The *Financial Times* publishes industry group and market-wide PERs.

Dividend yield

The dividend yield is the amount of dividend paid on each share as a percentage of the share price:

$$\text{Dividend yield} = \frac{\text{Dividend per share (pence)}}{\text{Current share price (pence)}} \times 100$$

So, in the case of a company where the dividend paid is 34p per share and the current share price is 900p:

$$\text{Dividend yield} = \frac{34p}{900p} \times 100 = 3.78\%$$

The dividend yields for UK firms shown in the *Financial Times* are calculated after deducting 10 per cent tax from the gross dividend, overseas companies are shown gross.

The dividend figure is the total of all dividend payments declared for the year. There may be two payments: an interim dividend (say, 14p per share) following the first half of the year, and the final dividend (say, 20p). There may be four payments in the case of those companies declaring dividends quarterly.

In Box 12.1 the dividend yield ('yield') includes all the dividends for the last 12 months, which means they are updated for interim (or quarterly) dividends. Suppose a company is more than half way through a financial year and has paid the following dividends:

Last complete financial year dividend payment	22p
Latest interim dividend	7p
Previous interim dividend (last year)	6p
Current share price	500p

Then:

$$\text{Adjusted dividend} = 22p + 7p - 6p = 23p$$

$$\text{Dividend yield} = \frac{23}{500} \times 100 = 4.6\%$$

Dividend yields can be calculated on *historical* figures (based on the most recent 12 months of dividends) or on a *prospective* (*future*) basis, which makes use of the forecast for the next year.

Dividend yield is important because it is the near-term cash return you are actually receiving from a company. You may hope to make capital gains as well, but this is somewhat theoretical – dividend income is real. The yield offered on a share can be compared with other shares, sectors or the market as a whole. It can also be compared with other investments such as government bonds or building society accounts. Government bonds usually give a higher yield than shares. This is acceptable to shareholders despite the higher risk on shares because there is an anticipation that the dividend on shares will grow significantly over the years as profits rise, while coupon payments on bonds are normally a constant amount.[2] Those companies expected to grow their profits at a fast rate will have low dividend yields because investors tend to bid up the share price. These **lower yield** shares are often labelled 'growth shares'. **Higher yield** (or simply **yield**) **stocks** are expected to have low profits growth and are labelled 'value shares'.[3] Shares offering very high yields often indicate market consensus that the dividend will fall as the company heads into difficulties – undertake your own investigation to see if the consensus is wrong, the crowd might have overreacted.

Managers often use dividends to signal to shareholders their confidence in the firm's future. In years when losses are made dividends are often maintained, or even increased, to signal that the firm had an unusually bad year and all will be well soon.

A share designated **cum-dividend** indicates that any buyer of the share at that time will receive a dividend recently announced by the company. There will be a

---

[2] Unusually, in 2014 the yield on 10 year gilts (less than 3 per cent) was actually less than that for the average share (around 3.4 per cent) because of the Bank of England's actions to lower interest rates.

[3] This is an unforgivably crude definition of 'growth' and 'value' shares and should not be taken too seriously – see Glen Arnold, *The Financial Times Guide to Value Investing* (Financial Times Prentice Hall, 2009) for the poor quality of thinking demonstrated by crudely classifying shares as value or growth. You might like to read about up-to-date examples at www.glen-arnold-investments.co.uk.

date set when the share will go **ex-dividend** after which a purchaser will not be entitled to a recently announced dividend – it will go to the old owner.

Dividend cover, payout ratio and retention ratio

Dividend cover is the ratio of profit attributable to ordinary shareholders to dividends. It can be calculated by dividing the earnings per share by the dividend per share:

$$\text{Dividend cover} = \frac{\text{Earnings per share}}{\text{Dividends per share}}$$

Or, for the company as a whole:

$$\text{Dividend cover} = \frac{\text{Profit attributable to ordinary shareholders}}{\text{Total dividend payment}}$$

So, if eps are 68p and the dividend per share is 34p (Figure 11.1) the dividend cover is 2.

The dividend covers in the *Financial Times* are calculated after deduction of 10 per cent tax from the gross dividend (for UK companies).

Dividend cover highlights the affordability of the current level of dividends. It shows the number of the current dividend payments that could be made out of current after-tax profits. The higher the proportion of profits paid out, the less is available for business investment and growth.

Switching around the top and bottom of the ratio gives the **payout ratio**. This is the percentage of after-tax profit paid to shareholders in dividends. What is left in the company is the **retention ratio**:

$$\text{Retention ratio} = \frac{\text{Retained profits}}{\text{Profits attributable to ordinary shareholders}}$$

Companies, on average, maintain payout ratios of around 45–50 per cent, therefore dividend covers are typically around 2 or slightly higher (although they dip in difficult times). However, there is a wide range around this average, as you can see from the Monday *Financial Times* extract in Box 12.1. Some companies pay out all profit and more (e.g. UMECO), others only pay out a small fraction of profits (e.g. Avon Rubber). If the cover drops below 1.5 investors can become concerned that it will only take a modest drop in profits for them to fall below the dividend.

Market capitalisation

The market capitalisation of a company is the number of shares in issue multiplied by the market price. Market capitalisation is useful for comparing the size of companies. Box 12.1 shows that the total value of the ordinary shares in Avon Rubber is only £87.6 million compared with £8,889.2 million for BAe Systems. Note that companies may issue two or more types of shares (e.g. ordinary shares with votes and ordinary shares without votes). These may be quoted separately in the *Financial Times*. The value of the two types would need to be added together to calculate the company's total market capitalisation – this is not always done for you on financial websites, so be careful. You can calculate it yourself by obtaining the number of shares in issue from the notes to the accounts.

Net asset value

Net asset value (NAV) (or book value) is the total assets of a company minus all its liabilities. The NAV is often viewed as the break-up value of the company.[4] Should the company be wound up *and* its assets sold at the balance sheet value *and* the liabilities remain as shown on the balance sheet, then the NAV represents the amount available for shareholders after all other claims have been met. The NAV figure provides a useful indicator of the value of assets underpinning the shares. However, most shares are rarely valued on NAVs because investors are not looking to liquidate the company, but are anticipating a flow of income from holding shares, and this income flow forms the basis for valuation.

Net tangible asset value, NTAV, is the same as NAV except that patents, trademarks, goodwill and other intangible assets are removed, thus focusing on the physical assets only. In many cases it can be unreasonable to include goodwill and so on in the assets when judging managerial return on net assets because this can be an accounting artifact rather than anything the current managerial team have control over.

Market (price) to book ratio (or, inversely, the book to market ratio)

The market to book ratio is the share price divided by net assets per share (book value). This ratio is used by some analysts as an indicator of over- or undervaluation. If the balance sheet assets per share are much larger than the share price,

---

[4] The financial press often uses a different 'break-up value'. This is based on the amount that could be raised by selling the various subsidiaries (rather than individual assets) to other companies, and is usually considerably more than the NAV.

this is taken to be a buy signal. Share prices significantly above net assets values might indicate over-excitement. However, this type of analysis relies on balance sheets providing useful and accurate valuations – close to sale value or the value of replacing the assets. As discussed in the next chapter, balance sheets are not designed for this.

$$\text{Market to book ratio} = \frac{\text{Current market price of share}}{\text{Book value (net asset value) per share}}$$

For the example company in Chapter 11, assets are £129 million and the NAV per share is £2.58 (£129m/50m). Thus the market to book ratio or price to book ratio can be calculated as

$$\frac{900p}{258p} = 3.49$$

A more sophisticated method would be to deduct the £5 million of net assets attributable to minority shareholders (see Figure 11.2), leaving net assets of £124 million and a market to book ratio of 3.63. Some analysts would deduct goodwill as well.

If the NAV is high relative to a share's current market value it gives the shareholder some reassurance about the downside of the share. Of course, this only applies if you can trust the balance sheet values. The chances of being able to sell the assets at the balance sheet values are pretty slim for most companies.

Enterprise value

Enterprise value (EV) is the total of equity market capitalisation and all of the company's debt minus cash the company holds:

$$\text{EV} = \text{Market capitalisation} + \text{total debt} - \text{cash}$$

So, for our example company in Chapter 11, with 50 million shares in issue each trading at 900p, we have total capitalisation of £450 million. The balance sheet shows total debt of £87 million (£62 million due within one year and £25 million due after one year) and £10 million in cash. Thus:

$$\text{EV} = £450m + £87m - £10m = £527m$$

Analysts use EV when comparing relative profit or cash flow. If the profit or cash flow is expressed before deduction of interest payments, then you can compare the company's profits before interest with the total value of the equity and debt held by the business. (In the EV calculation, some analysts add pension provisions, minority interests and other claims on the business.)

Performance ratios and measures

Profit margins

There are different profit margins, and it is important to know which one is being referred to in a particular context.

Gross profit margin (or **gross margin**) is defined as sales minus cost of sales, expressed as a percentage of sales:

$$\text{Gross profit margin} = \frac{\text{Gross profit}}{\text{Sales}} \times 100$$
$$= \frac{\text{Sales} - \text{Cost of Sales}}{\text{Sales}} \times 100$$

So, for the example used in Chapter 11, where sales are £230 million in 20X2 (£200 million in 20X1), and the cost of sales £140 million (£120 million in 20X1), the gross profit margins are:

$$\text{For 20X2: } \frac{90}{230} \times 100 = 39.1\%$$
$$\text{For 20X1: } \frac{80}{200} \times 100 = 40\%$$

Gross profit margin can be used to compare the performance of a company with that of its competitors. If it is low, investigate the reason. It may simply be that the company has a mix of products that have a high level of bought-in raw material costs. It could be that the management are less efficient, or, perhaps, pricing power in the market place is low. Observations of gross profit over time can likewise prompt further investigation.

Operating profit margin (or **operating margin** or **trading margin**) is operating profit as a percentage of sales. The profit figure used here is profit before interest and tax (PBIT) is deducted. It allows for all the expenses of manufacture, distribution, administration, R&D, depreciation, etc., but not for the financing costs or tax.

$$\text{Operating profit margin} = \frac{\text{Operating profit}}{\text{Sales}} \times 100$$
$$= \frac{\text{Sales} - \text{All operating expenses}}{\text{Sales}} \times 100$$

In our example:

For 20X2: $\dfrac{55}{230} \times 100 = 23.9\%$

For 20X1: $\dfrac{50}{200} \times 100 = 25\%$

If the company has a declining operating profit margin over time and/or relative to its competitors, this may be a sign of serious trouble – cost control or pricing power may be deteriorating.

Pre-tax profit margin (or **pre-tax margin**) is profit after all expenses including interest, expressed as a percentage of sales:

$$\text{Pre-tax profit margin} = \frac{\text{Profit on ordinary activities before taxation}}{\text{Sales}} \times 100$$

In our example:

For 20X2: $\dfrac{49}{230} \times 100 = 21.3\%$

For 20X1: $\dfrac{45}{200} \times 100 = 22.5\%$

Again the profit margin worsens over time.[5] This piece of information needs to be combined with others to build up a picture of the company. It must be noted that a pre-tax profit margin of over 20 per cent is still high compared with most firms (mind you, this depends on the industry), so perhaps our company is fundamentally sound but has had a minor downturn in fortunes. We are unable to draw conclusions yet, but we are gaining insight as we gather information.

Return on capital employed

The return on capital employed (ROCE) measures the return (operating profit) per pound invested in assets within the business.

$$\text{ROCE} = \frac{\text{Profit before interest and tax (operating profit)}}{\text{Capital employed}} \times 100$$

There is no hard-and-fast rule to define capital employed. It may be defined as the total of equity shareholders' funds plus all borrowings. If we assume, for the sake of simplicity, all liabilities are borrowings for our example company then:

---

[5] We would normally observe margin changes over at least five years to avoid drawing conclusions from a period that is too short.

$$\text{ROCE} = \frac{\overset{\text{Operating profit}}{55}}{\underset{\text{Shareholders' funds Short-term debt Long-term debt}}{124 + 62 + 25}} \times 100 = 26.1\%$$

Alternatively, capital employed can be defined as equity shareholders' funds plus long-term loans only. Other analysts throw in provisions for liabilities and charges, minority interests and a host of other factors as part of the capital figure. Clearly, you need to know just what definition was used if you are taking someone else's calculation for ROCE. You also need to ensure consistency when comparing figures over the years or between companies.

ROCE measures how successfully a company is at investing the money it takes from investors (and lenders) in real assets. Our example company produces a relatively high ROCE. A return of 26 per cent is likely to be significantly above any cost of borrowing that money or the return that shareholders could get elsewhere for the level of risk associated with holding the shares. If ROCE were less than 8 per cent we would worry, as this is likely to be below the returns achieved by other companies or available elsewhere in the financial markets.

You may observe in practice that some ROCE calculations don't use the end-of-year balance sheet values for capital employed but use an average of two consecutive balance sheets. This is to reflect the fact that the profits were earned over a period of a year – using the quantity of assets available at different points in the year and not just using the assets the company happened to have right at the end of the year. Apart from anything else, the end-of-year balance sheet is likely to be boosted by the retained profits for the year, so the ROCE is unreasonably reduced by the benefit of having lots of retained profits that year.

It might be interesting to look at the return generated for every pound of *equity capital* – leaving out the return to debt holders and the money put in by lenders. This is achieved by calculating the **return on equity (ROE)**:

$$\text{ROE} = \frac{\text{Profit attributable to shareholders}}{\text{Equity shareholders' funds}} \times 100$$

Profit attributable to shareholders is profit after the deduction of interest, tax, minority interests and preference share dividends. Equity shareholders' funds are calculated after the deduction of minority interests and preference share capital. So, for our example company:

$$\text{ROE} = £34m/£124m \times 100 = 27.4\%$$

The ROE may be affected by unusual tax conditions outside management control, and so in using this measure as a comparator care must be taken. Note that some analysts may leave minority interests in the numerator and denominator – if a consistent approach is taken this is not a problem.

Other variations on the theme of profit per pound of capital include **return on capital**, **return on net assets** and **return on shareholders' funds**. Definitions of these vary and often overlap with the measures we have already looked at.

EBITDA

EBITDA (pronounced 'e-bit-dah') became a very popular measure of a company's performance in the late 1990s. It was especially popular with managers of firms that failed to make a profit or private equity companies trying to sell a loss-making business. **EBITDA** means **'earnings before interest, taxation, depreciation and amortisation'**. Managers liked to emphasise this measure in their communications to shareholders because large positive numbers could be shown. Some sceptics have renamed it 'Earnings Before I Tricked the Dumb Auditor'.

If you run an Internet company that makes a £100 million loss and the future looks pretty dim unless you can persuade investors and bankers to continue their support, perhaps you would want to add back all the interest (say, £50 million), depreciation on assets that are wearing out or becoming obsolete (say, £40 million), and the declining value of intangible assets, such as software licences and goodwill amortisation (say, £65 million), so that you could show a healthy positive number on EBITDA of £55 million. And if your loss seems to get worse from one year to the next as your acquisition strategy fails to pay off, it is wonderfully convenient to report and emphasise a stable or rising EBITDA.

Some uses of EBITDA by company directors make political spin doctors look amateurs by comparison. EBITDA is not covered by any accounting standards, so companies are entitled to use a variety of methods – whatever shows the company in the best light.

In the real world directors (and investors) cannot ignore the cost of using up and wearing out equipment and other assets or the fact that interest and tax need to be paid, however much they would want to. Warren Buffett made the comment: 'References to EBITDA make us shudder – does management think the tooth fairy pays for capital expenditures?'[6]

---

[6] Chairman's letter accompanying the 2000 annual report of Berkshire Hathaway Inc.

EBITDA is often used with enterprise value (EV), rather than solely with the equity value (market capitalisation alone). This is because of the 'before interest' character of EBITDA. Thus EV/EBITDA measures the value of the company in terms of both the providers of equity and the providers of debt capital as a multiple of the 'cash' generated, including that generated to provide interest for the debt holders.

$$\text{EV/EBITDA} = \frac{\text{Market value of equity + market value of debt – cash}}{\text{EBITDA}}$$

Typically, multiples of EV/EBITDA are calculated for a sample of comparable quoted companies to, hopefully, establish a stable relationship. These multiples would then be applied to another company to estimate its likely entity value (equity + debt).

Despite its drawbacks as a valuation tool EBITDA does have an important role to play in judging the financial stability and liquidity of a company. It is used particularly in the field of leveraged management buy-outs and acquisitions with high levels of debt. A key measure is the EBITDA interest coverage ratio:

$$\text{EBITDA interest coverage} = \frac{\text{EBITDA}}{\text{Gross interest}}$$

The logic behind observing the metric is that, if required, the company could concentrate on paying interest, and could therefore afford a high leverage by forgoing capital expenditure for a while. That still leaves taxes to be paid, and while capital expenditure is discretionary in the very short run it is not in the long run if the firm wants to maintain its long-term competitive position, its economic franchise, unit volume and finance all value-enhancing projects that might arise (these elements may not be of great interest to some private equity players selling companies into the stock market, who want you to concentrate on EBITDA, of course – so remember *caveat emptor*).

Some analysts use the ratio of market capitalisation to EBITDA. The numerator is an equity value, but the denominator relates to income flowing to both debt and equity holders. Firms with very high levels of debt will look 'cheap' on this ratio compared with other firms, when, in fact, they might be overpriced.

Free cash flow

Free cash flow is a useful measure of the company's cash flow available to return to lenders and shareholders. It takes into account the fact that tax payments and investments in working capital and long-lived assets represent cash that is then not available to return to lenders and shareholders. For our example company we calculate the free cash flow as follows:

	£m
Operating profit	55
plus depreciation and other non-cash items	5
minus cash tax paid	(13)
Cash profits	47
minus investment in fixed assets	(5)
minus investment in working capital	(35)
Free cash flow	7

Out of a company's free cash flow it will have to make interest payments, which may or may not leave some free cash flow available for shareholders.

Small, rapidly expanding companies frequently fail to produce positive free cash flow. This may be good if the company is investing for the future by buying lots of assets to permit growth. However, a mature business with few avenues for profitable capital investment should not show negative cash flow. It should be throwing off cash for shareholders to invest elsewhere.

Also note that if fixed asset (long-lived asset) expenditure is significantly less than depreciation the company may be stinting on investment. This may boost short-term appearances with a nice positive free cash flow – and even high dividends – but in the long run serious damage may be done to the business as it falls behind competitors.

There are other definitions of free cash flow, for example, some companies also deduct dividends paid and cash flowing out to acquire other companies or for share buy backs. So be careful – when using someone else's free cash flow make sure you know how it has been defined.

Owner earnings

Whereas free cash flow reports the *actual* expenditure on new business assets, owner earnings force the analyst to think about the *necessary* level of expenditure *in the future* on these items needed to maintain the firm's competitive position, its unit volume and to invest in all new projects that create value for shareholders. This investment figure is inevitably subjective and imprecise, but then we must acknowledge that the most important aspects of investment are not the quantifiable elements – I'd rather be roughly right than precisely wrong.

Owner earnings represent what can be taken out of the business by shareholders without damaging the company's economic franchise. Owner earnings are defined as:

(a)   earnings after tax;

(b)   *plus* depreciation, depletion (e.g. of natural resources such as oil reserves), amortisation of intangible assets and other non-cash charges;

(c)   *less* the amount of expenditure for plant and machinery, etc., that the business requires to fully maintain its long-term competitive position, its unit volume and its investment in all new value-creating projects;

(d)   *less* any extra amount for working capital that is needed to maintain the firm's long-term competitive position, unit volume and its investment in all new value-creating projects.[7]

An example of share valuation using owner earnings is shown later in this chapter – in the intrinsic value calculation.

Financial health ratios and measures

Gearing (leverage)

We need to avoid some of the confusion possible when using the word 'gearing'. First, we should make a distinction between operating gearing and financial gearing.

Operating gearing (leverage) refers to the extent to which the firm's total costs are fixed. The profits of firms with high operating gearing, such as car or steel manufacturers, are very sensitive to changes in the sales level. They have high *break-even points* (the turnover level at which profits are achieved) but when this level is breached a large proportion of any additional sales revenue turns into profit because of the relatively low **variable costs** (costs that go up and down as company output and sales change).

Financial gearing (leverage) concerns the proportion of debt in the capital structure. The income you receive as a shareholder can decline more dramatically in a company with high borrowings when there is a small change in operating profits. So, for a company with an annual interest bill of £1 million and profits (before deduction of interest) of £3 million, if profits fall by 50 per cent to £1.5 million

---

[7] For more detail see Chapter 8 of Glen Arnold, *The Financial Times Guide to Value Investing* (Financial Times Prentice Hall, 2009) or see www.glen-arnold-investments.co.uk to see it applied to real companies I've invested in.

the income available to shareholders falls from £2 million to £0.5 million, a 75 per cent decline. On the other hand, if profit before interest rose by 50 per cent to £4.5 million, after-interest income grows from £2 million to £3.5 million, a 75 per cent increase. Debt *gears up* profit changes.

There are two ways of putting in perspective the levels of debt that a firm carries. **Capital gearing** focuses on the extent to which a firm's total capital is in the form of debt. **Income gearing** is concerned with the proportion of the annual income stream (i.e. the pre-interest profits) devoted to the prior claims of debt holders, in other words, what proportion of profits is taken by interest charges.

There are alternative measures of the extent to which the capital structure consists of debt. One popular approach is the ratio of long-term debt to shareholders' funds. The long-term debt is usually taken as the balance sheet items 'amounts falling due after more than one year', and shareholders' funds is the net assets (or net worth) figure in the balance sheet.

$$\text{Capital gearing (1)} = \frac{\text{Long-term debt}}{\text{Shareholders' funds}}$$

This ratio is of interest because it may give some indication of the firm's ability to sell assets to repay debts. For example, if the ratio stood at 0.3, or 30 per cent, lenders and shareholders might feel relatively comfortable as there would be, apparently, over three times as much in net assets (i.e. after paying off liabilities) as long-term debt. So, if the worst came to the worst, the company could sell assets to satisfy its long-term lenders. A figure of over 100 per cent would be a matter of concern (for most types of company/industry).

A major problem with relying on this measure of gearing is that the book value of assets can be quite different from the saleable value. This may be because many of the assets have been recorded at historical purchase value (perhaps less depreciation) and have not been revalued over time. It may also be due to the fact that companies forced to sell assets to satisfy creditors often have to do so at greatly reduced prices if they are in a hurry.[8] Also, this measure of gearing can have a range of values from zero to infinity, and this makes inter-firm comparisons difficult. The measure shown below puts gearing within a range of zero to 100 per cent as debt is expressed as a fraction of all long-term capital:

---

[8] The problems also apply to capital gearing measures (2) and (3).

$$\text{Capital gearing (2)} = \frac{\text{Long-term debt}}{\text{Long-term debt + Shareholders' funds}}$$

Many firms rely on overdraft facilities and other short-term borrowing. Technically these are classified as short term. In reality, many firms use the overdraft and other short-term borrowing as long-term sources of funds. Furthermore, if we are concerned about the potential for financial distress, then we must recognise that an inability to repay an overdraft can be just as serious as an inability to service a long-term bond. The third capital gearing measure, in addition to allowing for long-term debt, includes short-term borrowing:

$$\text{Capital gearing (3)} = \frac{\text{All borrowing}}{\text{All borrowing + Shareholder' funds}}$$

To add sophistication to capital gearing analysis it is often necessary to take into account any cash (or marketable securities, e.g. gilts) holdings in the firm. These can be used to offset the threat that debt poses:

$$\text{Capital gearing (4)} = \frac{\text{All debt – cash and short-term deposits}}{\text{Shareholders' funds}}$$

The capital gearing measures rely on the appropriate valuation of net assets either in the balance sheet or in a revaluation exercise. This figure can be badly distorted by, for instance, pension fund surpluses or deficits, the revaluation of assets, provisions and goodwill. As a result many analysts exclude these factors. Furthermore, capital gearing measures focus on a worst-case scenario: 'What could we sell the business assets for if we had to, in order to pay creditors?'

It may be erroneous to focus exclusively on assets when trying to judge a company's ability to repay debts. Take the example of a successful advertising agency. It may not have any saleable assets at all, apart from a few desks and chairs, and yet it may be able to borrow hundreds of millions of pounds because it has the ability to generate cash to make interest payments. Thus, quite often, a more appropriate measure of gearing is one concerned with the level of a firm's income relative to its interest commitments, the **interest cover**:

$$\text{Interest cover} = \frac{\text{Profit before interest and tax}}{\text{Interest charges}} \text{ or } \frac{\text{Operating cash flow}}{\text{Interest charges}}$$

The lower the interest cover ratio the greater the chance of interest payment default and liquidation. The inverse of interest cover measures the proportion of profits paid out in interest – this is known as **income gearing**. As a crude rule of thumb, an interest cover of less than three would be a worry unless the company had exceptionally stable cash flows.

Watch out for interest being 'capitalised' on a balance sheet rather than being treated as an expense and therefore charged to the profit. This can make interest payments seem low when in reality large sums are paid out to lenders. You can check up on this practice by observing cash outflow for interest payments in the cash flow statement and related notes. Capitalisation of interest is discussed in more detail in the next chapter.

Current ratio

It is useful to know if a company has enough cash and other short-term assets that can fairly quickly be turned into cash to meet its short-term liabilities (does it have **liquidity**?). Can the company pay its near-term bills? The current ratio measures this:

$$\text{Current ratio} = \frac{\text{Current assets}}{\text{Current liabilities}}$$

In the case of our example company

$$\text{Current ratio} = \frac{125}{62} = 2.02$$

indicating that it has significantly more short-term assets than short-term liabilities – this would be considered prudent (a current ratio less than 1 is cause for worry), but much depends on the nature of the business.

Quick ratio

A large element of the current assets, that is, inventory (of raw material, half-finished goods, etc.), may not be easy to quickly convert to cash so a tighter measure of immediate **solvency** (the ability to pay debts when they become due) is used, called the **quick ratio**, **liquid ratio** or **acid test**:

$$\text{Quick ratio} = \frac{\text{Current assets} - \text{stock}}{\text{Current liabilities}}$$

So, for our example company:

$$\text{Quick ratio} = \frac{125 - 35}{62} = 1.45$$

If the quick ratio is less than 1 the company could not meet all its current liabilities should they be due immediately. Comparison across an industry is useful for putting the quick ratio figure in perspective. For example, supermarkets frequently show a quick ratio of around 0.2 – for these firms this is acceptable given that so much of their current assets are rapidly moving stock items matched by high levels of trade creditors (a current liability).

Forward-looking measures

Dividend valuation model

To value a share, analysts often estimate all the future dividends. They are not able to simply add these together to calculate a share's value, because a dividend of 34p to be received in five years is not worth the same to the investor as a dividend of 34p received now. Most people, given the choice between the receipt of a sum of money now and the same sum in the future will say 'I'd rather have it now'. Thus money has a **time value**. Given the existence of the time value of money, it makes sense to allow for the fact that people will need to be compensated for giving up money now.

There are three reasons why investors prefer £1 now rather than £1 in the future and therefore three things that have to be compensated for:

- **Inflation**. If there is inflation, then investors need compensation over time for giving up money now.

- **Risk**. If there is a risk that the future payout may not take place or will be less than promised, then investors will want a greater return on their money (greater compensation over time). Company shares carry greater risk than, say, government bonds, and offer a significantly higher rate of return.

- **Impatience to consume**. People like to consume. Compensation will be required for a delay in gratification even in a world without the first two factors, inflation and risk.

Let us assume that the company shares we are analysing present a risk level to investors which means they require an annual rate of return of 10 per cent which incorporates all these elements of compensation (impatience to consume, inflation and risk). Now, if you asked someone who required a 10 per cent rate of return what is the sum of money to be received in one year that is sufficient for you to give up £100 now, they will reply £110. They are indifferent between holding on to the £100 now and giving it up and receiving £110 in 12 months' time. The relationship is explained in the compounding formula:

Future value = Present value $(1 + \text{rate of return})^{\text{number of years}}$

£100 = £100 $(1 + 0.10)^1$

We could use the formula to ask other questions. For example, what sum of money do investors need in three years' time to compensate them for the sacrifice of £100 now if the required rate of return is 10 per cent per year? The answer is:

$$£100 (1 + 0.1)^3 = £100 \times 1.10 \times 1.10 \times 1.10$$
$$= £133.10$$

Investors in this risk class of shares are indifferent between receiving £133.10 in three years' time and keeping £100 because they get a 10 per cent rate of return. If they received £150 in three years the rate of return would be more than 10 per cent and investors would be delighted to receive a surplus above the minimum required.

An alternative way of using the formula is to estimate the future income and then turn it into an equivalent value now. That is, calculate its **present value**. So, if you estimate income of £133.10 in three years and the required rate of return on an investment of that risk is 10 per cent the equivalent present value is £100:

$$\frac{£133.10}{(1 + 0.10)^3} = \frac{£133.10}{1.10 \times 1.10 \times 1.10} = £100$$

This is called '**discounting**' the future income flow. If you estimate the future income to be £150 in three years, the present value is more than £100 because you still discount at 10 per cent (the discount rate is determined by the risk class):

$$\frac{£150}{(1 + 0.10)^3} = £112.70$$

If someone asks you to pay £100 now for an investment that pays £150 in three years, snatch it quick as its equivalent present value is £112.70 (assuming a time value of 10 per cent per year – more risky investments require higher rates of return).

With shares the dividends are not all received at one point in the future. Rather, they arrive at fairly regular intervals. When calculating a share's value we can use the **dividend valuation model**. For the sake of simplicity we will assume dividends are received annually, with the first one due in a year from now. Let us assume that each of the future dividends (which occur every year for ever) will be 34p. Then we can value a share (assuming a 10 per cent discount rate) as follows:

Time dividend received:

$$\begin{array}{ccc} \text{in 1 year} & \text{in 2 years} & \text{in 3 years} \end{array}$$

$$\text{Share value} = \frac{34p}{1 + 0.10} + \frac{34p}{(1 + 0.10)^2} + \frac{34p}{(1 + 0.10)^3} \quad + \ldots + \ldots$$

$$\text{Present value} = 30.91p + 28.10p + 25.5p \quad\quad + \ldots + \ldots$$

Notice the decline in the present value of the dividend the further from the present time it is received.

These dividends stretch to an infinite horizon and so this calculation could take a long time – if we do it this way. Fortunately, we can be rescued from the dire prospect of lengthy calculations because the formula simplifies down to the following if the dividends are constant (the same every year) and are at annual intervals for ever:

$$\text{Share value} = \frac{\text{Dividend}}{\text{Discount rate}} = \frac{34p}{0.10} = £3.40$$

Note here that even though only one year's dividend has gone into the formula it represents all the future dividends – forever.

Dividends are rarely constant year after year. Managers often make great efforts to provide a steadily rising annual dividend. If dividends grow over time by a constant amount each year, say 4.5 per cent per year, then the following formula can be used (if we assume annual dividends for ever):

$$\text{Share value} = \frac{\text{Next year's dividend}}{\text{Discount rate} - \text{Growth rate}}$$

If the recently paid dividend is 34p and the next to be paid, in one year, is bigger by 4.5 per cent then next year's dividend is 35.53p (34p × 1.045). The share value is now:

$$\frac{35.53p}{0.10 - 0.045} = £6.46$$

Notice that even a modest rate of growth in the dividend results in the share value almost doubling from the constant (no-growth) dividend case – from £3.40 to £6.46.[9]

The major difficulty with the discounted valuation method is the estimation of the growth rate. The chapters on industry and strategic analysis (Chapters 14–15) will help you to search for the right factors, but it remains a difficult and uncertain task. One pointer is that companies as a whole do not grow dividends at a faster rate than the economy grows over the long run. So if, say, real economic growth is 2.5 per cent and inflation is 2 per cent don't expect the average company to grow profits at more than 4.5 per cent per year except in short-term bursts (which are likely to be corrected in the next downturn). City analysts often bring out absurd estimates for the corporate sector expecting double-digit growth for many years ahead. If this happened over the long run then corporate profits and dividends would become larger than the entire economy!

Intrinsic value

The intrinsic value of a share is the discounted value of all the owner earnings that can be taken out of the business during its remaining life. Future owner earnings[10] are determined by the strength and durability of the economic franchise (see Chapters 14 and 15), the quality of the management and the financial strength of the business.

Each of the estimated *future* annual owner earnings figures needs to be calculated and then discounted. When these are all totalled we have intrinsic value. While we need to estimate future values, the only solid evidence we have are past accounting numbers. These have to be used as a starting point for our thinking. So, if our example company has reported earnings after tax attributable to shareholders[11] of £34 million and in calculating that figure the non-cash item called depreciation (£5 million) was deducted we can make a stab at last year's owner earnings. This can only be an estimate because items (c) and (d) in the owner earnings calculations (see page 268) are largely subjective. For example, we may estimate that the level of investment needed in fixed capital equipment to maintain long-term competitive position, unit volume and investment in new projects is £5 million per year, but we cannot be mathematically precise. Likewise we may judge that £8 million will be needed for additional

[9] For more on discounted cash flow and the dividend valuation model, see Chapters 2, 16 and 17 of Glen Arnold, *Corporate Financial Management* (Pearson, 2013).

[10] See earlier in this chapter for owner earnings.

[11] After minority interests.

working capital investment.[12] Despite the uncertainty inherent in such judgements these elements are vital and this method preferable to merely using reported historical cash flow. With the assumption that total expenditure on fixed capital assets and working capital is £13 million we have owner earnings of £26 million:

		£m
(a)	Earnings after tax	34
	Plus	
(b)	Depreciation, depletion, amortisation and other non-cash charges	5
		39
	Less	
(c)	and **(d)** Expenditure on plant machinery, working capital, brand maintenance, etc., required to maintain long-term competitive position, unit volume and investment in new projects	13
	Owner earnings	26

If we now make the simplifying assumption that the owner earnings will be the same in all future years we can calculate intrinsic value:

$$\text{Intrinsic value} = \frac{\text{Annual owner earnings}}{\text{Discount rate}}$$

If the appropriate discount rate is 10 per cent, then the intrinsic value is

$$\text{Intrinsic value} = \frac{£26m}{0.1} = £260m$$

or £260m/50m = £5.20 per share.

These shares are currently trading in the stock market at £9, so we would not be buyers based on this calculation.

However, it is possible we have been too pessimistic in assuming that the company will not grow its owner earnings over time. Let us now assume that the company has a series of new projects that will generate returns greater than 10 per cent (the required rate of return for this risk class of shares). By investing in these projects,

---

[12] Notice that this figure is a lot less than that shown in the example company's cash flow statement in Chapter 11. This is because owner earnings estimate the *necessary future* expense, not the *actual* expense in the last reported figures.

owner earnings will rise by 5 per cent in each future year (on the one hand, owner earnings are decreased by the need for additional investment in fixed and working capital, but, on the other, reported earnings after tax are boosted to produce a net 5 per cent growth). With a constant future growth rate we can use the formula (assuming owner earnings for every future year rising from £26m by 5 per cent per year):

$$\text{Intrinsic value} = \frac{\text{Owner earnings next year}}{\text{Discount rate} - \text{Growth rate}}$$

Next years' owner earnings = £26m × (1 + 0.05) = £27.30m

$$\text{Intrinsic value of company} = \frac{£27.30m}{0.10 - 0.05} = £546m$$

$$\text{Intrinsic value per share} = \frac{£546m}{50m} = £10.92$$

Under these circumstances the share does not look overvalued. However, given the uncertainties in the calculation I would want to see a larger 'margin of safety' between my calculated value and the current share price before buying.

When I estimate owner earnings of the past I often look at the accounts going back 5–8 years and calculate the 'owner earnings' on the assumption that what the company *actually spent* on new capital items and additional working capital is what they *needed to spend* in order to maintain a competitive position, unit volume and invest in all value-enhancing projects. Obviously the 'owner earnings' produced through this method bounce around from one year to the next: capital expenditure for instance can double or treble in a year. But if you half close your eyes on the row of, say, six years of 'owner earnings' you might be able to detect a pattern, a normal level or a growing trend. This rough impression when combined with your knowledge of the company's strategic strengths and quality of management may be quite powerful in providing you with a useful owner earnings number or trend for *future years*. It is important to look at more than one year because strange things happen to companies in a period as short as it takes the earth to go around the sun – one-off massive rises in income or massive falls. Obtaining a range of years allows a greater impression of the norm for that company.[13]

---

[13] There is more on the intrinsic value method in G. Arnold, *The Financial Times Guide to Value Investing* (Financial Times Prentice Hall, 2009) and in Chapter 17 of G. Arnold, *Corporate Financial Management* (Pearson, 2013). You might like to see real world examples at www.glen-arnold-investments.co.uk.

Further reading

G. Arnold, *The Financial Times Guide to Value Investing* (Financial Times Prentice Hall, 2009).

G. Arnold, *Corporate Financial Management* (Pearson, 2013).

W. McKenzie, *The Financial Times Guide to Using and Interpreting Company Accounts* (Financial Times Prentice Hall, 2009).

E. McLaney and P. Atrill, *Accounting: An Introduction*, 6th edn (Pearson, 2012).

F. Wood and A. Sangster, *Frank Wood's Business Accounting Volume Two*, 12th edn (Financial Times Prentice Hall, 2012).

B. Vause, *Guide To Analysing Companies*, 5th edn (The Economist Books/Profile Books, 2009).

Free financial website sources of ratios and measures include www.uk.finance.yahoo.com and www.advfn.com.

13

Tricks of the accounting trade

Financial statements are supposed to show the underlying economic performance of a company. The profit and loss account shows the difference between total revenue and total expenses. The balance sheet displays the assets, liabilities and capital of the business at a snapshot moment. What could be simpler than adding a few numbers to get a trustworthy and definitive conclusion? Well, drawing up a set of accounts is far from simple, or unambiguously precise. It is nowhere near as scientific and objective as some people would have you believe. There is plenty of scope for judgement, guesswork or even cynical manipulation. Despite the mountain of accounting rules and regulations there are numerous opportunities to flatter the figures, or at least to offer two or three legitimate estimates of the value of something or the profit generated by an activity. Imagine the difficulty facing the company accountant and auditors of a clothes retailer when trying to value a dress which has been on sale for six months. Let us suppose the dress cost the firm £50. Perhaps this should go into the balance sheet and the profit and loss account would not be affected. But what if the store manager says that he can only sell the dress if it is reduced to £30, and contradicting him the managing director says that if a little more effort was made £40 could be achieved? Which figure is the person who drafts the accounts going to take? Profits can vary significantly, depending on a multitude of small judgements like this.

Consider another simple example. Suppose that there are two identical companies except that during the last year one bought a £10 million factory, while the other spent £10 million on advertising. How are you going to value the assets at the end of the year? The company that acquired the £10 million factory has something tangible to show. Perhaps we should say the year-end value of the asset is £10 million. On the other hand, you may think the asset has decreased in value since it was purchased. Perhaps it should now be valued at only £9 million. So what do you do with the £1 million write-off? Should that be regarded as a cost of doing business and deducted from profit? Or, if the £1 million reduction in value is due to a general downturn in property values, is it best to account for it by stating a separate exceptional charge? The second firm's accounts are even more subject to judgement. Presumably the management believed that expenditure on advertising would create something of value – an enhanced brand, for example. This asset may be more valuable than the physical assets bought by the first company, and yet, because intangibles are usually valued at zero, the entire expenditure becomes a cost for the year, reducing the profit significantly.

Given that accounts are malleable, investors need to be alive to three possibilities:

- Directors and accountants are trying hard to present a picture of the firm's performance and financial standing that is true and fair but are forced to make numerous judgements along the way. They are trying to apply the rules to produce accurate figures. However, if another equally honest and meticulous accountant were making the judgements the figures would look different simply because some of these judgement calls are finely balanced. We do not live in a mathematically precise world – the investor needs to accept that the accounts merely provide no more than ballpark figures. Having said this, for most firms, with accountants conscientiously trying to avoid tipping the balance either way between favourable and unfavourable reporting, the room for judgement should not make more than about 10–20 per cent difference.

- The second possibility is **creative accounting**, in which the letter of the accounting standards is abided by, but there is a deliberate attempt to flatter the figures. When judgement calls are required there is a bias to show a favourable figure. The accounting regulators periodically try to close loopholes to bring accounts back to a true and fair view, but many managers and their accountants are adept at outwitting the rule setters. Every now and again there is the deafening sound of stable doors being slammed long after the horses have bolted.

- Fraud occasionally occurs in which the rules are completely flouted. WorldCom is probably a record holder for both the amount involved and for its brass-necked boldness in committing such a simple fraud. All it did was declare that $3.8 billion of operating expenses were not expenses at all and claim that this money went to create assets of ongoing value to the company. Annual profits were artificially boosted by nearly $4 billion. Over in India the boss of Satyam, India's fourth largest technology firm, wrote a letter in 2009 confessing that he had cooked the books on an epic scale, by creating bogus customer receipts amounting to more than 90 per cent of reported turnover, a total of almost £1 billion. The story of the Gem of Tanzania is an interesting case where the directors claimed a stone was worth £11 million thus bolstering a balance sheet of an otherwise very shaky company – see Article 13.1. The gem was eventually sold for £8,000 and three Wrekin directors, including Mr Unwin, were disqualified from holding such positions.

Article 13.1

Now £11m Gem of Tanzania hits rock bottom

By Jonathan Guthrie

One of the strangest tales in the history of company accounting looks increasingly likely to end with a fabled gem being downgraded to an unusual paper weight.

The Gem of Tanzania, a large ruby whose £11m valuation once underpinned the finances of a failed company with yearly turnover of £103m, may be worth as little as £100.

Rebuffed by large auction houses, administrators to Wrekin Construction, a Shropshire building company, are now planning to advertise the big purple rock in a small magazine whose subjects include New Age crystals.

The police said yesterday that they were considering whether to mount a fraud investigation, while forensic accountants are already on the case.

After Wrekin collapsed in May it emerged that the main asset of the business was an £11m ruby. Derbyshire businessman David Unwin used the jewel, previously valued at £300,000, to revive the balance sheet of Wrekin, which he bought in 2007.

A Financial Times investigation found that the gem was sold to a South African-born businessman for the equivalent of £13,000 in Tanzania in 2002. The jewel was then handled by at least one other intermediary before Mr Unwin bought it through a land deal.

Two key valuation documents acquired by Mr Unwin with the gem were denounced as forgeries by the purported valuers. Mr Unwin has consistently said that he is innocent of any wrongdoing. Supporters say that he would be the victim of any fraud.

It is understood that prestigious London auction houses rejected the gem because its value was too low.

Marcus McCallum, a Hatton Garden gem dealer said: "The Gem of Tanzania may not be worth the cost of the advertisement. A two-kilogram lump of anyolite [a low-grade form of ruby] is probably worth about £100. A valuation of £11m would be utterly bonkers."

This chapter cannot protect you against out-and-out fraud, but it can explain a number of areas of accounting in which judgement calls have to be made and where there is sufficient lack of clarity in the rules for a potential bias to creep in and open up the possibility of producing artificially increasing profits, or higher asset levels than are truly warranted. Following this chapter you should understand the high degree of flexibility in accounting data and the potential for enhancing companies' reported performance through circumventions of the spirit of the accounting regulations. You will view accounts with a questioning mind and make sure you are aware of the company's accounting policies and the implications behind them. Remember: if it looks too good to be true, then it probably is.

Goodwill

When one company acquires another there is usually a difference between the fair value of the assets acquired and the price paid. The difference is termed **goodwill**. The significance of this is best explained through an example. Imagine that Stephenson Brunel Ltd has been operating for 50 years and is making profits of £20 million per year. The assets on its balance sheet have a stated a **fair value**[1] of £100 million after subtracting all liabilities (i.e. £100 million represents the net assets).

You and I are owners of a railway company in another part of the country and we decide to offer £220 million to buy all the shares in Stephenson Brunel. Our offer price is based primarily on the earnings potential of the business, not on its net assets. The offer is accepted. We have paid £120 million above the asset value. This is motivated by our high regard for the company's economic franchise – for example, it has a near monopoly position (economic franchises are discussed in Chapter 15).

Stephenson Brunel now becomes a subsidiary of our company, and consolidated accounts are prepared. But how do we draw up a balance sheet? Prior to the acquisition we held £220 million in cash as one of our assets in the balance sheet. We exchanged this for £100 million of assets. There is a gap of £120 million. To solve this problem the accountant places in the balance sheet a £120 million asset called 'goodwill'. Now the books will balance: £220 million buys £100 million of tangible assets plus £120 million of the intangible asset called goodwill.

---

[1]   The stated value is the value derived from the accounts. The fair value is the amount an asset could be exchanged for in an arm's-length transaction between informed and willing parties.

Goodwill = Price paid – Fair value of assets acquired.

What happens next can make a huge difference to the balance sheet, the profit and loss account and to various measures of performance. In the UK, until 1998 companies were permitted to write off purchased goodwill through the balance sheet. Immediately goodwill seemed to simply vanish from the accounts.[2] Managers liked this approach for two reasons. Firstly, because profits in the year of acquisition and all future profits do not have to suffer the burden of an annual expense of writing off a portion of the goodwill through the profit and loss accounts year by year; it was all written off in one year – moreover, it was written off via the balance sheet, so the profits did not take a hit. Secondly, reducing the net assets of the firm by £120 million makes managers look good when they are judged by a return-on-capital measure, such as return on capital employed. The denominator (capital) is reduced while the numerator (profit) does not suffer. Managers begin to look like geniuses because they appear to be making high profits on a lower capital base.

Accountants pondered these distortions and concluded that, generally, acquired goodwill does in fact decline in value over time, and so needs to be **amortised** (depreciated) in a similar fashion to tangible assets, such as machinery. It should not be assigned a zero value in the year of acquisition. Between 1998 and 2005 the rule was that purchased goodwill should be **capitalised** (i.e. placed in the balance sheet at its purchase value) and then amortised over the asset's useful economic life, up to a maximum of 20 years in most cases.

Now imagine you are a director needing to show good profit figures and you know that £120 million of purchased goodwill has to be apportioned as an expense to the profit and loss account over 'its useful economic life'. You can see there is considerable room for debate on the length of time representing this asset's useful economic life. Would you tend to plump for a write-off over, say, six years, so that £20 million comes off your profit in each of the next six years? Or would you go for the longest period possible, 20 years, in which case only £6 million is amortised each year? Well now, guess what the vast majority of firms 'estimated' the length of 'useful economic life' to be. Yes, it's 20 years! Did this reflect reality in terms of the true value of the intangible assets over time? I doubt it. Obsolescence, competitor action, and changes in the market environment can have a devastating impact, and many firms lose their business franchises in as little as two or three years.

---

[2] However, the rules insisted that some note on accumulated goodwill write-offs be presented in the notes to the accounts.

Also, under these rules, companies can amortise over more than 20 years, or even not amortise at all, if they could show that the balance sheet entry showed a reasonable valuation. (However, if they chose either of these methods the assets must be reviewed each year to see if it is being impaired.) If it was impaired then the goodwill was written down in the balance sheet and the loss shown separately in the profit and loss account (as a goodwill impairment charge). This is all very reasonable. The problem is that the numbers used were based on estimates and forecasts made by the *company*. Many firms claimed values for purchased goodwill that you or I might question.

Since 2005 International Financial Reporting Standards have applied to the consolidated accounts of listed companies on LSE's Main Market. They now also apply to AIM companies. Under these rules there is a prohibition against the systematic annual amortisation of goodwill. Thus 'purchased' goodwill (from an acquisition) is included under 'Intangible fixed assets' at its initial cost. However, this figure must be reviewed at least annually thereafter, to see if the value has been impaired. If there is no impairment then the goodwill remains at its cost figure. With impairment the figure is written down to the lower amount in the balance sheet. Furthermore, an impairment charge is a negative element in that year's profit and loss account, thus depressing reported profits. The £602 million goodwill write down for EMI damaged the company greatly – see Article 13.2

Article 13.2

EMI covenants at risk until 2015, says owner

By Andrew Edgecliffe-Johnson

EMI will fall short of its banking covenants until 2015 and will need a far larger injection of fresh equity next year than the £87.5m ($136m) it received in 2010, according to an assessment by the British music group's private equity owner.

Maltby Capital, the holding company through which Guy Hands' Terra Firma group made its £4.2bn leveraged buy-out of EMI in 2007, outlines strong operational improvements in the business in its annual report.

However, the gains remain insufficient to satisfy tightening banking covenants, raising the pressure for a renegotiation with Citigroup, its sole lender, to avoid breaching the terms of the £3.04bn debt due between 2014 and 2017.

The report shows Maltby lost £512m after tax for the year to March 31, an improvement from the prior £1.57bn loss thanks to lower impairment and restructuring charges, favourable currency movements and operational advances.

A second year of heavy impairment charges to goodwill and the value of the group's catalogues, amounting to £602m compared with £1.04bn a year earlier, was driven in part by reduced expectations for growth in digital music.

Article 13.2   Continued

Maltby expects "continued shortfalls" against its covenants, which monitor the multiple of debt to earnings, requiring further "equity cures".

Directors are getting quite adept at encouraging shareholders to focus on 'under-lying' profits that exclude these charges. The reality is that it is very difficult to know, in most cases, when goodwill has declined in value and by how much. There remains great latitude for the employment of 'judgement' here, so we will have lots of fun and games over the next few years as companies avoid write-downs.

All the discussion so far applies to purchased ('acquired') goodwill. What about goodwill that is generated internally? Most company's shares are worth a lot more than the net assets total shown in the balance sheet. The stock market values a company on the basis of its future earnings, which, in turn, come from *all* its 'assets', including those not measured in a balance sheet, such as extraordinarily good reputations or strong relationships with customers. This internally gener-ated goodwill cannot be shown in the accounts – any figure selected would be too subjective. Stock market investors are left to value this on their own.

There are, however, some intangible assets that can be valued on the balance sheet. These are intangibles for which it is possible to get a reasonably firm grasp on the cost of creating or buying them. For example, while most *research and development* (**R&D**) expenditure is written off in the year in which it occurs (i.e. the profit figure is reduced) it is possible for a UK company to argue that the development expense is for a separately identifiable project for which there is rea-sonable expectation of specific commercial success. In this case the expenditure can be **capitalised**, that is, shown as an asset on the balance sheet, and then the expense to the income statement (amortisation of the asset) is spread out over many years. Copyrights, licences (e.g. bookmakers' licence to operate), patents and trademarks may also be capitalised and amortised over their useful lives.[3]

---

[3] To be capitalised it must be possible to separate these assets from the rest of the business and sell them. There must be a 'readily ascertainable market' for internally generated assets to be valued in the accounts. If the asset is not amortised at all or is amortised over a period greater than 20 years it will be subject to review for impairment annually.

With all of these intangibles there is considerable room for disagreement about appropriate values over time and the amount that should be deducted from the income statement each year.

Points to watch out for when viewing goodwill and other intangibles in accounts include the following:

- Amortisation generally takes place by an arbitrary amount over an arbitrary time period. However, as a safeguard, the policy adopted must be clearly stated in the accounts.

- Goodwill and other intangibles are frequently not **depreciating** assets in the everyday sense of really losing value. When analysing a company it might be advisable to add back the amount of amortisation to the year's income statement to obtain a measure of **normalised earnings**. You could also add back goodwill accumulated over many years to obtain a more realistic net asset figure.

- In some companies goodwill and other intangibles may be eroding much faster than the amortised rate. The analyst will need to reduce the profit and balance sheet asset figures to account for this.

- A company showing significant regular goodwill impairment charges should be viewed with scepticism. This may indicate that the company has a habit of overpaying for acquisitions.

All the above adjustments by the analyst are, of course, subjective and imprecise, but are nevertheless better than simply ignoring the issue. The adjustments can have profound effects on key measures such as net assets, gearing, earnings per share and return on capital employed.

Fair value

When a company is acquired its assets are revalued at fair value on the acquisition date for the purposes of consolidation in the group accounts. Also under International Financial Reporting Standards (IFRS) companies have to value certain assets at fair value whether or not they were acquired through acquisition. In the Stephenson Brunel example we assumed that the fair value of net assets was £100 million (which for the sake of simplicity, is the same as the stated value in Stephenson Brunel's balance sheet). This left £120 million of goodwill. Given the scope for discretion in this area it might be possible for the directors to argue that the assets are in fact worth only £50 million. Auditors might then agree, and £50 million is placed in the consolidated balance sheet. Goodwill in the balance sheet therefore rises to £170 million (£220m – £50m). Perhaps you may say that the directors have acted prudently and made sensible provision for the potential of asset devaluation. But what if next year these assets are sold for £180 million? Well, the income statement gets a boost of £130 million because of the 'profit' on the difference between the 'fair' value of the assets (£50 million) and the sale proceeds (£180 million). Thus profits can be massaged by marking down fair values of acquired assets. There are also (dubious) benefits prior to selling the assets: depreciation is lower and so less is coming off the profit figure each year; undervaluing stock items reduces future cost of sales to enhance profits; undervaluing receivables will help a later year's operating profit if customers eventually pay more than the stated amount owed.

Under the IFRS fair value accounting has become a major area of controversy, particularly for the banks, who, many people said, were threatened with destruction because they were forced to write down a number of their assets (e.g. bonds in other entities that depend on sub-prime mortgagees paying their interest) to the current market value. In the banking crisis it was very difficult to discern the true market value – much subjectivity came into play. See Article 13.3 for a fuller discussion of the difficulties.

Article 13.3

Fair value accounting is a can of worms, but it's a smaller can than the alternatives

By Alistair Blair

I do not willingly immerse myself in the subject of fair value accounting. It is arcane, confusing and sometimes downright counterintuitive. I am not the only victim. It has been reported that, last year, a meeting of the US Financial Accounting Standards Board got so argumentative that it was suspended for a few weeks so that officials could provide board members with a summary of each of their colleagues' views.

And yet I think I have a grasp of the essentials, to whit: if you own something that you are likely to sell, in the meantime, you should value it at what you are likely to get for it based on the best available information. Thus your house is worth what similar properties in the locale have recently sold for. This is only really important if you are planning to sell.

Now, take a bank stuffed with mortgage-backed securities, which it bought from other banks. It paid $10 per security and they have recently been selling for $1.50. Is it really $8.50 poorer (you can add 'bn' to the end of these figures if you like)?

It's time to stroke your chin and ask a few questions. Such as these: "Are the mortgages still being paid? In other words, is the bank receiving the expected income from the securities?" Answer: currently, yes – however,

Article 13.3   Continued

it is expected that at least some of them will go bad, although probably not 85 per cent of them. Maybe only 40 per cent will go bad, and the rest will ultimately be repaid.

"How many have sold for $1.50?" Answer: only a very few. The market has dried up.

"Does the bank need to sell the securities now?" Answer: it needs ready cash now and if things were normal, selling these securities would be a typical way of raising that cash.

These answers point in different directions. The bank is still receiving interest and principal payments, so, from that perspective, it doesn't feel any poorer. The market price is no longer really a valid indicator, unless you are a forced seller. Take the house you were planning to sell. If your estate agent told you to forget the £100,000 valuation you had in mind last year, and to expect only £15,000, you would – in 99.9 per cent of conceivable circumstances – suspend your plan to sell. You'd expect to take a few years before reviving your plan.

These two answers say it would be wrong to consider that the bank is $8.50 poorer.

But a bank is not an average houseowner with the ability to postpone a sale if things get really grim. It is a forced seller. A bank must have the cash required to meet its obligations at all times. That is the essence of a bank. If a bank was a houseowner, it would be very unaverage (the 0.1 per cent) whose circumstances are such that he must sell – the overseas relative who inherits a house, say, and just wants to sell. Or the 85-year-old with no relatives now needing to move to a hospice.

It does not matter that the widespread belief is that only 40 per cent of the mortgages will eventually go bad, and that therefore, in all likelihood, the bank will eventually get $6 for the mortgage-backed security rather than the $1.50 it could get now.

The essential thing about fair value accounting, insofar as it applies to the bank, is that it must value its mortgage-backed securities at $1.50 and include in its profit statement a loss of $8.50. For banks, of course, the consequences of these losses – even though they are 'only accounting losses' are dire – we are witnessing them day by day.

A considerable body of opinion thinks that without fair value accounting – which was introduced over the past few years – we would have had no credit crunch.

Last year, William Isaac, a former head of the US Federal Deposit Insurance Corporation, which stands behind deposits in US banks, told a government agency panel that by forcing banks to write "unrealistic fire-sale prices" into their balance sheets and profit statements, fair value accounting had destroyed bank's capital. He is urging President Obama to suspend fair value accounting. This would on the face of it postpone – and possibly altogether bypass – the reckoning (that part which is to come!).

This would be wrong. Fair value accounting is a can of worms, but it's a smaller can than the alternatives, which are far more open to manipulation and have generated their own severe crises over many years. I'm hoping Obama favours fair value accounting.

Source: Blair, A. (2009) 'Fair value accounting is a can of worms, but it's a smaller can than the alternatives', *Investors Chronicle*, 30 January–5 February 2009.

In response to the problem of taking distressed prices from the market discussed in Article 13.3 the accounting regulators relented and said that for transactions in inactive or illiquid markets prices may be adjusted to be more indicative of orderly transactions – it may be more appropriate to estimate value from a valuation model, e.g. use discounted dividend analysis (as in Chapter 12).

Financial institutions, particularly banks, are allowed to treat financial assets they hold in totally different ways depending on how they are classified. With **'assets held for trading'**, the assets (e.g. securities such as gilts or derivatives) are revalued at each balance sheet date even if not sold, mostly using fair market values. If they have risen between balance sheet dates a gain is recognised in earnings, i.e. profits are boosted. With **'assets available for sale'**, the assets are revalued at each balance sheet date even if not yet sold and any unrealised gains or losses go through the balance sheet without raising or lowering profits. The third category applies if the business has the positive intent and ability to hold to maturity the financial assets, say a bond for 20 years. These **'assets held to maturity'** securities are put in the balance sheet at amortised cost less impairment (amortisation refers to the gradual decline that might occur as, say, coupons are paid and/or the time to maturity lessens). There are calls for more consistency in the treatment of fluctuations of the value of bank assets – see Article 13.4.

Article 13.4

Haldane seeks new bank accounts regime

By Norma Cohen and Brooke Masters

Banks should no longer be allowed to avoid taking losses on loans and bonds by saying they will hold them until repayment is due but should instead disclose their "fair value" to investors, a Bank of England director urged in a speech released on Thursday.

Andrew Haldane, executive director for financial stability, told an accounting conference that banking is so complex and different from other industries that it needs a new accounting regime, which would amount to a "radical departure from the past".

Mr Haldane argued that banks embraced so-called fair value accounting, where they showed assets at market prices, in good times. But in bad times, such as after the 2008 collapse of Lehman Brothers, the sector argued that using fair value accounting would exacerbate instability by showing that many banks were insolvent and forcing them to sell assets at fire-sale prices.

Accounting bodies say banks only need to "mark to market" those securities they intend to sell and can hold others at face value.

But Mr Haldane criticised that distinction by citing the case of a hypothetical bank funded by short-term deposits that bought 50-year securities. If such a bank suddenly experienced a run on deposits "its 50-year best intentions could be invalidated within 24 hours".

"Currently, the regulatory boundary is based on banks' trading intent," Mr Haldane said. "There is a strong economic case for moving away from the existing intent-based convention for differentiating banking and trading books."

Mr Haldane noted that fair value accounting made banks look a lot more profitable during the good years as securities prices were rising, possibly further encouraging banks to load up on them and take excessive risks. But when stock markets crashed, "fair values were seen as more troublemaker than matchmaker", he noted.

Some international regulators share Mr Haldane's concerns about the distinction between assets held for trading purposes and those in the banking book that institutions say they intend to hold.

Non-financial firms may also be affected by alternative treatments of assets held. The IFRS insist that property held by a company as an investment (not for use in manufacturing or commercial process) can be accounted for in either of two ways. First, the balance sheet value is altered to market value and changes in fair value from one year to the next are added to, or deducted from, the income statement. Thus, a company can make a normal operating profit in its manufacturing division or by renting out houses, of say £30 million, but this can be drowned in the reported earnings figure by a massive write-down on the fair value of its properties, say £240 million. During the recession we saw numerous companies report very large losses because of this fair valuation of property assets. The alternative accounting approach permitted is to state investment properties at cost in the balance sheet and depreciate over the useful life. You can imagine that in a property crash many companies would like to follow the second approach. However, the rules are fairly strict on what can be reported under each approach – but that doesn't prevent some flexibility on the determination of a fair valuation.

Another problem arises with the valuation of financial instruments held by non-financial firms. Some are held in the balance sheet at their amortised cost, whereas others are revalued at fair value with the change in value going through the balance sheet, yet others are revalued at fair value with the change in value going through the balance sheet and the income statement. The rules governing these classifications is complex and, as you can imagine, open to much interpretation and judgement.

What was our revenue again?

The basic rules of revenue recognition are that it is recognised in the period when the substantial risks and rewards of ownership are transferred and the amount of revenue can be measured reliably.

The trick of bringing forward revenue from future years into this year is an old one. Sales are not easy to define. Do you recognise sales revenue when the order is placed, when you receive cash from the customer, or when the goods or services are delivered to the customer? For a retailer the issue of revenue recognition is usually simple: a sale takes place when the goods are handed over and payment is received. But revenue is more difficult to allocate to particular years when the revenue bridges different years. For example, imagine a long-term contract to build and service a power station. The order is placed in 2015, construction begins in 2016, the first payments are received in 2017 and ongoing annual service activity is expected from 2018. What revenues do you allocate to each year? Examples of revenue recognition difficulty are shown in Box 13.1.

Box 13.1 | When to recognise a sale?

■ Wiggins, the commercial property developer, recognised a sale of a property once it obtained]planning permission satisfactory to the purchaser (without the planning permission the purchaser could back away). But it was forced to restate the accounts because the sale had not yet been completed – it was completed the next year.

■ Healthcare Locums was forced to change its accounting policy of recognising revenue generated when it placed medical staff at, say, a hospital, from the date of acceptance of the position to the date at which they actually started.

■ Allied Carpets got into trouble for booking sales as soon as an order had been placed ('pre-despatching'). When this 'error' was corrected the accountants found an overstatement of £6.4 million.

■ MFI, the furniture group, had to change its accounting policy. It had been recognising sales on taking an order (with the customer paying merely a deposit) and changed this to 'a dispatch basis'. The effect of the change was to reduce the company's net assets by £19.2 million.

■ Several companies have included revenue in full in the year of receipt, even though some of the revenue related to provision of services after the balance sheet date. For example, with extended warrantees some retailers have taken full credit for revenue from extended warranties in the period in which the sale of the product took place rather than spreading it over the lifetime of the cover. The rules have been tightened so that the revenue should be recognised over the term of the contract (the excess of the money received over the revenue recognised for the first period's P&L should be included in payables as a payment in advance and then this is released as performance takes place).

> ■ Seller of software: a company sells software to a customer and in addition receives payment of £12,000 in relation to a maintenance and support contract covering a period of 12 months. Five months of the period covered falls in the supplier's current year and seven months in the following year. In the past in the UK, and in some other jurisdictions today, the supplier would take £12,000 credit in the current period. Under new UK rules, the income is spread over the period of the contract (only £5,000 in the current period). The balance sheet will show a £7,000 prepayment.

When there is doubt about the veracity of the figures, the analyst will want to look at cash flow to see when the cash from sales actually turns up.

Examples of out-and-out fraud on revenue

These include the following:

■ Telecommunication companies sold useless fibre-optic capacity to each other in order to generate revenues on their income statements (e.g. Global Crossing).

■ Then there is 'channel stuffing' (or 'trade loading'): a company floods the market with more products than its distributors can sell, artificially boosting sales. A few years ago SSL (condom maker) shifted £60 million in excess inventories on to trade customers.

■ 'Round tripping' (or 'in-and-out trading'): two or more traders buy and sell, say, energy contracts among themselves for the same price at the same time. This was one of Enron's tricks – it inflated trading volumes which makes the participants appear to be doing more business than they really are. Sales revenue growth is often taken by investors as an important yardstick and can affect the value they place on the business.

Exceptional items

When companies issue press releases about their results they tend to emphasise 'profit before exceptional items'. This is, profit that does not take account of items which are the result of ordinary activities but are large and unusual (e.g. a large bad debt, windfall profits, merger bid defence costs or losses on the disposal of a subsidiary). Companies are obliged to report both profit before and after deduction of exceptionals. It makes some sense to exclude unusual events so that the underlying trend can be seen. However, directors tend to want to direct your attention to the figure that puts them in the best light. Profit figures feed through to reported earnings per share and if directors can get investors to focus on the 'sustainable', 'maintainable' or 'normalised' earnings which exclude exceptionals then the share price might increase.

There is also the problem of defining what is an exceptional occurrence. It is funny how directors can be persuaded to include or exclude an exceptional item – I wonder if it depends on whether it will have a positive or negative impact on reported figures – see Article 13.5.

Article 13.5

Buttressed builder

LOMBARD COLUMN: Jonathan Guthrie

Consistency of accounting treatment is important for shareholders. It reassures them that they are comparing apples with apples, rather than oranges, and facilitates just comparisons with peers. But looking at the reported operating profit margins at Taylor Wimpey and Persimmon, two of the UK's largest housebuilders, is a bit like comparing apples with penguins. This month, Taylor Wimpey delivered a self-proclaimed sector-beating 9.3 per cent first-half operating margin. The 9 per cent figure Persimmon announced on Tuesday looked a bit measly by comparison. There is, however, a special ingredient to Taylor Wimpey's apparent triumph over its more conservative rival. Included in its profits was a £48.9m gain from land sold for more than its estimated value. But during the recession the impairment on the very same land was deducted as an "exceptional" and was not reflected in the operating margin.

The company has done the accounting equivalent of having its cake and eating it. Discount the yo-yoing of its once "exceptional" slice of British turf and Taylor Wimpey's margins look less healthy at 3.3 per cent. A neat piece of financial footwork. But one that has annoyed peers and will be hard to repeat a second time around.

 Source: Guthrie, J. (2011) Butressed builder, *Financial Times*, 23 August 2011.

Stock (inventory) valuation

Year-end stock displayed in a company's balance sheet normally consists of a mixture of raw materials, work in progress (incomplete items still being worked on) and finished goods ready for sale. The rule on stock valuation is that it should be shown on the balance sheet at cost or net realisable value (what someone might reasonably expect to pay for it),[4] whichever is lower.

---

[4] Net realisable value is calculated after deducting all further cost to complete the item and all costs of the selling process.

Identifying the cost of some items of stock is relatively easy. If the company buys 100 tonnes of steel as a raw material input to its processes then it has invoices to look at. But consider the difficulty of valuing an incomplete car half way down an assembly line. You might be able to isolate the costs of the material actually used, but how much of the factory overheads and the company's general overhead should be allocated to the cost calculation for the car? **Overheads** are business expenses that range over the operations as a whole and are not directly chargeable to a particular part of the work or product. So the costs of the factory managers and the factory rent relate to the costs of all cars produced in the year and not to any particular one. The accountant, when valuing a half-finished car, will add together the easily identifiable direct costs with the difficult-to-apportion production overhead costs. With overhead allocation there is much room for disagreement and also much room for putting on a positive gloss. The higher the year-end value, the lower the cost of manufacturing the cars sold during the year and therefore the higher the profit figures. A £1,000 increase in year-end stock value feeds into a £1,000 rise in profits. Also the balance sheet can be shown in a healthier light, with more assets relative to debts.

Depreciation

Imagine that your company has just purchased a state-of-the-art computer-controlled machine for its manufacturing operations at a price of £20 million. The managing director estimates that it will have a useful economic life of ten years and at the end have a second-hand sale value of £1 million. She is in favour of **straight-line depreciation**, which means that the same amount is charged each year to the profit and loss account for the cost of using the machine.[5] The cost less the residual value is £19 million. This is divided by 10 years to give a depreciation charge of £1.9 million per year.

The production director, on the other hand, thinks that the machine will wear out much more quickly. He prefers to use the **declining (reducing) balance method of depreciation**. He thinks the appropriate rate in this case is 25 per cent per year. Thus the machine will be depreciated each year by 25 per cent of the balance sheet value at the start of the year. In the first year £5 million is charged to the profit and loss (25 per cent × £20 million). In the second year 25 per cent of £15 million (balance sheet value at end of first year) is charged (£3.75 million). In the third 25 per cent of £11.25 million is charged (£2.81 million) and so on.

---

[5] The term 'depreciation' is generally applied to tangible fixed assets, whereas 'amortisation' is used for intangible assets.

Both methods are permitted under the accounting rules, and yet choosing one rather than the other can have a dramatic effect on profit and asset levels. Imagine that profit before the depreciation expense is charged is £8 million per year, the machine represents the only asset the firm has and there is no debt. Then the profit patterns under these two methods look quite different (Table 13.1). Profit appears to be on a rising trend in the second case – soon to overtake the static profit in the first case.

After four years the asset value is still over £12.4 million under the straight-line method, but only £6.33 million under the declining balance method. Imagine that the numbers in Table 13.1 represent two identical firms, and that the only difference is the method used for depreciation of fixed assets. If you were analysing these four years you would need to dig out the notes to the accounts in the hope that you could find the basis on which depreciation was calculated and then make adjustments in order to compare the performance and balance sheet strength of the two. Of course, you should discover that the two, at base, are identical, but frequently there is insufficient information to reach that conclusion and the superficial appearance of the profit and loss account and balance sheet persuades investors that one company is more sound than the other when the only difference is the optimism/pessimism of the management about a long-term asset that may or may not have a 10-year life.

Even worse, although the two depreciation methods shown are the most commonly used, they are not the only ones permitted – there are at least four other methods for managers to choose from at their discretion. In addition, companies can play tricks by being more optimistic on the *residual value* (the sale value of the asset when the company has finished with it). The potential for manipulation is huge, and all within the rules of the game.

Managers sometimes change the depreciation policy, sometimes for legitimate reasons (e.g. the asset suddenly has a new lease of life and should be depreciated in a different way), sometimes simply to make the accounts look better. So what is the investor to do? The answer is to examine the statement on depreciation methodology in the report and accounts. You can also derive evidence on depreciation policy change by comparing the amount of depreciation with the value of assets: do the proportions change over time? A fall from 12 per cent to 5 per cent, for instance, may set alarm bells ringing, as managers may be deliberately underestimating wear and tear and obsolescence of assets.

Table 13.1   Two methods of depreciation

Year	1	2	3	4
	£m	£m	£m	£m
Straight-line method				
Profit before depreciation	8.0	8.0	8.0	8.0
Straight-line depreciation charge	(1.9)	(1.9)	(1.9)	(1.9)
Profit after straight-line depreciation	6.1	6.1	6.1	6.1
Declining balance method				
Profit before depreciation	8.0	8.0	8.0	8.0
Declining balance depreciation charge	(5.0)	(3.75)	(2.81)	(2.11)
Profit after declining balance depreciation	3.0	4.25	5.19	5.89
Effect on the balance sheet at end of year:				
Value of asset under straight-line depreciation	18.1	16.2	14.3	12.4
Value of asset under declining balance method	15.0	11.25	8.44	6.33

Capitalisation

When a company spends money on something there are two possible consequences: either an asset is acquired which then goes into the balance sheet; or
there is an expense to be charged to the profit and loss. It is possible to boost
profit and the balance sheet asset values by taking the view that a greater proportion of spending is for the acquisition of assets rather than for expenses. With
assets such as buildings there is little problem with stating a capital value in the
balance sheet. However, with spending on items like research and development
we have the potential for rose-tinted spectacle distortion. As stated earlier, companies are allowed to capitalise development expenditure for clearly defined projects
with near-certain commercial success – that is, show it on the balance sheet as
an asset. This subjective test is all the flexibility that creative accountants need.

Alongside development expenditure managers are often permitted to capitalise
interest on a project during construction. So a property construction company
that paid £100,000 for building land, £900,000 to build and £200,000 of interest
during construction may have a stated balance sheet value for that property of
£1.2 million. Under the rules capitalisation of interest is supposed to stop after
completion of the building. However, some companies have been known to
extend this period of 'construction' over a considerable time period, thus tying up

more interest as an 'asset' in the balance sheet. Supermarkets often capitalise the interest incurred while building a supermarket. This is then written off gradually under the company's normal depreciation policy. Capitalisation of interest has also been used by ship and aircraft manufacturers, and producers of whisky (a 'good' that takes a long time to 'construct'). The problem is that some managers and acquiescent accountants/auditors have taken the process too far.

The analyst needs to take particular care when calculating the interest cover ratio (see Chapter 12) for a company with a propensity to capitalise interest. The interest paid and charged to the profit and loss can be a small fraction of that sent straight to the balance sheet to be capitalised. You need to add both interest figures together to get a view on the level of payments to lenders relative to profits (look at the interest charge in the cash flow statement).

It is also considered acceptable to capitalise some starting-up costs (e.g. costs of running in new machinery or testing equipment). Again the absence of precise definitions for what can and can't be capitalised provides the loophole some managers and accountants are looking for.

Off-balance-sheet items

Investors may be worried not about the treatment of items that are actually shown in the balance sheet, but about commitments the company has entered into, but which are *not* shown in the balance sheet. These off-balance-sheet items can seem to appear out of the blue to destroy a company. For example, Enron, the disgraced Texas energy trader, used **special-purpose entities** to manipulate its profits and the appearance of its balance sheet. Special-purpose entities are set up as separate organisations and their accounts are not consolidated with the rest of the group – which can be useful if you want to hide a vast amount of debt or expenses. Not all special-purpose entities should be viewed with suspicion; some have legitimate uses, for example, to finance a research and development partnership with another company, or for repackaging some of the company's assets and then selling these on to investors (**securitisation**). However, special-purpose entities are a useful tool in the hands of dishonest managers.

In the UK there have been fewer scandals with special-purpose entities and other off-balance-sheet financing techniques than in the USA. Perhaps this is due to the accounting rules insisting that, regardless of the technical position, managers and accountants are required to report the substance of a transaction. Accounts are supposed to reflect the underlying reality of the situation. Having said that, some grey areas remain. For example, banks take on numerous risks in the derivatives markets. They might have to face significant liabilities if certain events come to pass (e.g. interest rates rise or fall by large amounts – many of these risks do not appear in the accounts).

Another grey area is the presentation of lease commitments. Take a company needing to acquire the use of a new machine. It could go out and buy the machine for £1 million, using a bank loan to do it. A disadvantage of this is that the debt–equity ratio (gearing) rises because of the new loan. An alternative is to lease the machine for say, £10,000 per month. The company has not borrowed £1 million and so the balance sheet is not burdened. However, with many of these lease agreements the company is making a strong legally binding commitment to make regular payments: at least as strong as it would if it was paying off a bank loan. So the substance is much the same, whether the asset is leased or bought with a bank loan. Back in the 1980s the accounting profession made a big step in closing this loophole. If the lease transfers substantially all the risks and rewards of ownership of an asset to the company over the course of the lease then it has to be classified as a **finance lease**, which means the machine is recorded as an asset and the obligation to pay future rentals is recorded as a liability on the balance sheet.

Other leases are referred to as **operating leases**. The assets and liabilities under operating leases do not have to be displayed on the balance sheet. While many lease obligations are made explicit to investors, this remains a tricky area because it is often very difficult to declare one lease as 'transferring substantially all the risk and rewards of ownership' and another lease as not doing so. Airlines, for example, are very adept at signing up for aircraft rentals that just fall into the category of operating leases and thereby clear their accounts of large numbers of aircraft as assets, and the associated leases as liabilities.

Another off-balance-sheet liability used to be the amount companies owe to the *pension scheme* set up for employees. There was much heated discussion as to whether companies should place this as a liability on their balance sheet. The case for ignoring it is that the amount owed varies from one year to the next and so the accounts would become volatile for reasons unconnected with underlying trading. Investors would then be confused by the extra information, and this would lead to wrongly priced shares. This is a self-serving argument in most cases. Some companies have pension liabilities that dwarf the assets of the business. British Airways, for example, has been described as a pension fund with an interesting sideline in flying. Nowadays pension liabilities are generally on-balance-sheet.

Share (stock) options

Imagine you own 50 per cent of the shares in X plc. There are 10 million shares in issue. The company has a share option scheme in which directors are entitled to buy, in three years' time, 1 million shares at £1 each (the same as the current share price). Now imagine that the three years have passed and the share price has risen to £3. The directors have a bonanza. They can now exercise the option to purchase £3 million worth of shares for a third of the price.

This type of scheme is quite common and can be useful to incentivise managers. However, the difficulty comes in accounting for share options. Suppose the company at the end of the three years is making annual profits of £2 million, so before the exercise of the options you, as a 50 per cent shareholder, have a £1 million claim on the profits – 20p per share. If the options are exercised the number of shares in issue rises to 11 million. Then each share has a claim on only £2m/11m = 18.18p. Your claim is 5m × 0.1818 = £909,090. You have lost out because the directors now have a claim on 9 per cent of the company's profits.[6] This is a cost to you, the shareholder.

In the past most companies failed to properly acknowledge share options as a cost to the shareholders – the best that was offered was a note in the accounts. Thousands of directors became very wealthy as a result of share option schemes. That wealth came from somewhere, and yet rarely was the cost to shareholders properly recorded. Sure, the earnings per share figure was 'diluted' to allow for the possibility of the issue of additional shares, but the headline profit reported on the face of the accounts generally ignored the cost.

If managers had been incentivised through a cash bonus scheme of £2 million, this would have been highly visible and profit would have been depressed. Given this, why not express the share-option-based transfer of shareholder wealth as a cost? The accounting regulators now insist that the value of options be assessed at the date they were granted (even if they are 'out of the money' – see Chapter 8) and charged to that year's income statement. This is different to either (a) ignoring option values (as UK companies used to do) or (b) only valuing the option when and if it is exercised, or (c) only valuing the option prior to the exercise if it has intrinsic value, i.e. the option is 'in the money'. The main problem with the solution chosen is that the models used to calculate out-of-the-money option values are complex and full of bold assumptions.

---

[6] Admittedly, directors have boosted the company's cash by £1 million, but this is insufficient to offset the loss.

Missing the profits and assets in investee companies

This is an accounting problem that generally leads to under-reporting of the company's performance. When a company owns say 10 per cent of the shares in another company it will only bring into its consolidated profit the dividends it received and not the full 10 per cent of the investees earnings. Warren Buffett explains this well – see Box 13.2 (GAAP is the US accounting rules 'Generally Accepted Accounting Principles').

Box 13.2   Calculate 'look-through' earnings

Investors must always keep their guard up and use accounting numbers as a beginning, not an end, in their attempts to calculate true "economic earnings" accruing to them.

Berkshire's own reported earnings are misleading in a different, but important, way: We have huge investments in companies ("investees") whose earnings far exceed their dividends and in which we record our share of earnings only to the extent of the dividends we receive. The extreme case is Capital Cities/ABC, Inc. Our 17% share of the company's earnings amounted to more than $83 million last year. Yet only about $530,000 ($600,000 of dividends it paid us less some $70,000 of tax) is counted in Berkshire's GAAP earnings. The residual $82 million-plus stayed with Cap Cities as retained earnings, which work for our benefit but go unrecorded on our books.

Our perspective on such "forgotten-but-not-gone" earnings is simple: The way they are accounted for is of no importance, but their ownership and subsequent utilization is all-important. We care not whether the auditors hear a tree fall in the forest; we do care who owns the tree and what's next done with it.

When Coca-Cola uses retained earnings to repurchase its shares, the company increases our percentage ownership in what I regard to be the most valuable franchise in the world. (Coke also, of course, uses retained earnings in many other value-enhancing ways.) Instead of repurchasing stock, Coca-Cola could pay those funds to us in dividends, which we could then use to purchase more Coke shares. That would be a less efficient scenario: Because of taxes we would pay on dividend income, we would not be able to increase our proportionate ownership to the degree that Coke can, acting for us. If this less efficient procedure were followed, however, Berkshire would report far greater "earnings."

I believe the best way to think about our earnings is in terms of "look-through" results, calculated as follows: Take $250 million, which is roughly our share of the 1990 operating earnings retained by our investees; subtract $30 million, for the incremental taxes we would have owed had that $250 million been paid to us in dividends; and add the remainder, $220 million, to our reported operating earnings of $371 million. Thus our 1990 "look-through" earnings" were about $590 million.

Source: Warren Buffett's 1990 Chairman's Letter to Berkshire Hathaway Shareholders.

Other tricks

■ Companies sometimes emphasise **'pro-forma'** accounting numbers, which are prepared to exclude those items that the manager regards as unusual and non-recurring items for a recent past period, or when stating how much money the company will make on some assumed events and transactions that have not yet occurred. This is often a deliberate distraction tactic employed by companies that are currently making accounting losses. Pro-forma numbers remove many negative items from the profit and loss account in a manner that may not, in any way, comply with the accounting rules. Pay no attention to pro-forma figures. See Article 13.6 for some examples. Note the resistance in US boardrooms to regarding share (stock) options as a cost.

■ Companies sometimes try to load losses on to operations that are going to be discontinued. Because continuing businesses and discontinued businesses are separated in the profit and loss account, it becomes possible to direct investors' attention to the continuing business and then bury losses in the non-continuing businesses section.

■ Firms sometimes fail to **write down (write-off)** worthless assets.

■ Fun and games can also be had with **changes in foreign exchange rates** impacting on assets, liabilities, revenues and costs.

Article 13.6

Accounting exceptionalism has become harder to ignore

By Richard Waters

The costs being stripped out in company results are growing.

Twitter's red-hot IPO and regulatory warnings about the flattering light in which some internet companies like to present their performance have revived memories of the dotcom bubble. With stock prices soaring, it has become tempting for fast-growing companies to stretch conventional accounting rules.

But the biggest perception gap in the technology world involves a group of far more mature companies. As the pace of change in their markets accelerates and some of the industry's best-known names face upheaval in their businesses, this gap looks set to widen further.

Look no further than that model of corporate probity, IBM. It wasn't long ago that IBMers scoffed privately at rivals such as Hewlett-

Article 13.6   Continued

Packard for publishing pro-forma earnings. Such figures, known, inelegantly, as non-GAAP since they deviate from generally accepted accounting principles, tend to exclude costs that companies claim make it harder for investors to understand what's happening in their underlying businesses.

Three years ago, IBM gave in to the prevailing mood and started stripping some costs from its preferred measure of earnings (in its case, some employee retirement costs and charges related to acquisitions.) Like others, IBM is still required to report official earnings with all costs included, but it uses the non-GAAP numbers when talking to Wall Street.

It is not obvious for investors which measure of IBM's profits they should care most about. After its second quarter this year, Big Blue put the spotlight in its press release on an earnings per share figure of $3.91 – a number deemed "most indicative of operational trajectory", since it excluded $1bn in "workforce rebalancing" charges.

But in its official quarterly filing, IBM added back the lay-off charges and settled on a different non-GAAP number of $3.22. Both were higher than the $2.91 a share it recorded under official accounting rules.

The amounts that are being routinely added back to profits have become staggering. For tech companies in the Standard & Poor's 500, they amounted to $40.7bn in 2012. The difference boosted the profits these companies earned under standard accounting rules by 36 per cent, according to Jack Ciesielski.

The companies, and the analysts who follow

them, have largely justified this behaviour on the grounds of tech industry exceptionalism. This argument holds that they are not like other companies due to the larger amounts of stock they issue to attract and reward workers.

Formal accounting rules require this to be deducted from earnings. Most companies argue that issuing shares isn't a direct cost on the company – and that current valuations of the future stock benefits are largely meaningless anyway, so it is better to exclude them.

Whatever side you take on this issue, though, it turns out to be a sideshow. Stock benefits only accounted for a quarter of the costs that tech companies added back to profits in 2012, according to Mr Ciesielski. The other 75 per cent was not so different from the sort of things that companies in all industries face.

The costs added back to earnings last year included: charges related to acquisitions (four companies did this), restructuring costs (three), amortisation of intangibles (two), asset impairments (two) and fines and legal judgments (two).

Individually, and in any given year, the companies that try to gloss over charges such as these might have some success in arguing that they are one-offs.

But collectively, and with the numbers growing from year to year, it becomes much harder to sweep all the industry's bad news under the rug.

Many of these one-off costs are coming to look like business as usual. It is up to investors to decide how much of this they can afford to ignore.

FT   *Source:* Waters, R. (2013) Accounting exceptionalism has become harder to ignore, *Financial Times*, 13 November 2013.

Concluding comments

So what is the time-pressed investor to do, given all this potential for trickery? First of all, don't panic. The vast majority of managers are honest and like to present an accurate picture of the state of affairs of the company. Even those tempted to flatter the figures will be restrained by the accounting standards and the necessity of adding a note to the accounts where they have viewed an element in a particularly favourable light. They are also inclined to integrity by the fact that a lot of the tricks will be revealed to investors over the medium term – they might get away with it for a year or two but eventually the truth will out. Smart managers, with a long-term career to think about, recognise the necessity of straight dealing. Most try to avoid weaving tangled webs.

Having said that, not all managers and accountants are as straight as we would like, so here is a list of what you can do to avoid being taken for a ride:

■ **Pay close attention to the notes to the accounts**. Many analysts read the accounts backwards working from the notes, through the cash flows, balance sheets and profit and loss until finally reaching the points that were supposed to impress (and possibly mislead) them at the front of the annual report and accounts. Reading the notes first will highlight issues tucked away, such as goodwill, amortisation, exceptional items and capitalised interest that will not be presented in the profit and loss, balance sheet and cash flows. When you reach the main accounts you will have the information to allow you to make adjustments so that ratio analysis is more meaningful. When reading the accounts ask yourself which numbers you would manipulate if you wanted to bias the figures.

■ **Get data from other sources**. Brokers' reports can give a critical appraisal of the company's accounts. You can obtain information about the directors' past lives by, say, conducting an Internet search – tap their names into a search engine and see what comes up. Industry analyses are available from the specialist websites such as Dun and Bradstreet (www.dnb.co.uk), but you can find out a lot about an industry for free by simply browsing the web.

■ **Focus on cash**. Being creative with cash flow figures is much more difficult than being creative with profits and balance sheets. Be sceptical about companies that show high and rising profits with low cash flow. A very useful measure is the cash return on capital employed in the business. It suffers far less from biased accounting than earnings-based measures.

■ **Check accounting policies**. If accounting policies (e.g. on depreciation) have changed from the previous year then watch for the effect on profits.

Ask questions such as: does the reduction in depreciation boost profit artificially, or is it justified? If there is not enough information in the accounts then you could ring the investor relations department of the firm to ask for an explanation of the accounting policies.

- **Meet the management**. The issues of creative accounting and fraud are fundamentally issues of trust. If you attend AGMs and regularly scrutinise the directors' public statements you may instinctively sniff out suspicious characters. For instance, if managers one year try to direct your attention to earnings per share, and the next to EBITDA, and in the third year they emphasise operating profits, you may start to suspect that they are more interested in short-term appearances than in creating long-term value. They are certainly not interested in communicating their (inevitable bumpy) progress in a frank and unspun way. If year after year the firm comes up with pathetic excuses such as an 'early Easter' or 'bad weather' for poor performance rather than occasionally putting their hands up and saying that the strategy had gone awry, you have reason to doubt the management's honesty – with themselves, let alone with investors.

- **If in doubt, don't take a punt**. If you are not sure about the quality of the numbers, or cannot see clearly what is going on, then don't allocate some of your precious fund to the company. Investors can afford to let many balls go past them until they get a perfect pitch that they can hit cleanly and relatively safely.

Further reading

W. McKenzie *The Financial Times Guide to Using and Interpreting Company Accounts* (Financial Times Prentice Hall, 2009).

E. McLaney and P. Atrill, *Accounting: An Introduction*, 6th edn (Pearson, 2012).

F. Wood and A. Sangster, *Frank Wood's Business Accounting Volume Two*, 12th edn (Financial Times Prentice Hall, 2012).

B. Vause, *Guide To Analysing Companies*, 5th edn (The Economist Books/Profile Books, 2009).

14

Analysing industries

The examination and analysis of the report and accounts tells us a lot about the company's past performance. The questions we must now ask are: How sustainable is that past performance? What potential is there for improvement in the future? The answers to these questions depend not only on the financial strength of the company, but also on the type of industry or industries in which the company operates, its possession or otherwise of extraordinary resources allowing it to perform well in the industry (i.e. to achieve returns on capital invested in real assets significantly above the industry average) and the honesty and competence of the managerial team. This chapter focuses on the first of these factors: the analysis of industries.

There are some crucial factors that determine the average long-run rate of return on capital employed by firms in an industry. This chapter provides a framework for identifying these factors.[1]

The competitive floor

In a perfectly competitive industry structure, where outside firms can enter the industry at will, companies can only achieve a **'normal' rate of return**. That is, shareholders receive a rate of return that only just induces them to put money into the firm and hold it there. If returns dropped by 0.1 per cent then investors

---

[1] Much of the material for this chapter is condensed from G. Arnold, *The Financial Times Guide to Value Investing,* 2nd edn (Financial Times Prentice Hall, 2009) and is applied further for some companies on my blog – see www.glen-arnold-investments.co.uk.

would withdraw capital from the firm and invest in an alternative with the same risk level providing the full 'normal' rate of return – eventually the firm would go out of business. With perfect competition the rate of return cannot rise above the normal level to give a **supernormal return**. Imagine if an industry did give a very high rate of return temporarily because of, say, a rise in the price of the product. New entrants to the industry, or additional investment by existing competitors, would quickly result in any supernormal return being competed away to take the industry back to the point where the return available is merely that appropriate for the risk level.

Obviously, a perfectly competitive industry is not attractive for investors. Investors need to search for an industry displaying a wide gap between the price of the product and its cost – one producing a high rate of return on the capital taken from shareholders and used by managers. The problem is that competitive forces within industries tend to continually narrow the gap between price and cost – to push it towards the **competitive floor** – and thus put downward pressure on the rate of return on invested capital.

However, there are some industries in which the competitive forces are weak, permitting supernormal returns to persist over a long period. The investor needs to search out those industries in which the average firm has a high degree of durable pricing power.

The five competitive forces

Michael Porter produced a framework for analysing the forces driving returns to the perfectly competitive level. It goes way beyond simply analysing the degree of rivalry between existing competitors and the potential for entry of new competitors. He pointed out that customers, suppliers and substitutes are also 'competitors' to the firms in an industry in the sense that they impose constraints on the firms achieving supernormal returns. For example, Heinz (and other big brand food producers) has few direct competitors, because its brand sets it apart and it has an unrivalled distribution system. It faces little threat from the entry of new competitors because the new entrant would need decades to build the necessary brand image and distribution capability. However, Heinz's management is worried because of the increasing power of its customers, the major supermarket chains. The giant food retailers are in a position to ask for more of the value generated by the sale of the product – to put it more crudely, they can hammer Heinz on price. Take another case: the music distribution industry (record producers and retailers) chief executives here are scared. It is not that particularly strong current competitors are taking greater market share and thereby becoming stronger. This

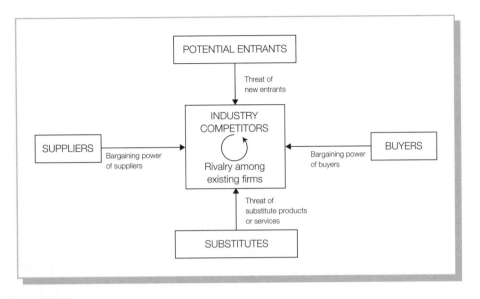

Figure 14.1   The five forces driving industry competition

is happening, but it is not the main cause of sleepless nights. Nor are they worried about the entry of new record labels and retail chains. These have come and gone before, and industry returns have remained high. No, their nightmare comes in the form of a new technology that allows consumers to download music by file-swapping on the Internet for virtually nothing. Thus a substitute distribution system is a competitive threat to the entire industry.

In a perfectly competitive situation entry is free and existing firms have no bargaining power over suppliers or customers. In addition, rivalry between existing firms is fierce because products are identical. In reality, few industries resemble perfect competition. As J.K. Galbraith once observed, the greatest source of insecurity in business is competition, and so managers strive constantly to move as far away from perfect competition as possible. How far they travel is determined by the strength of the five forces shown in Figure 14.1.

Steel

The five forces determine the industry structure, which in turn determines the long-run rate of return for the industry. Some industries have an appalling position *vis-à-vis* the five forces and thus make very poor returns. Take steel production in western Europe, for example. Here are some of the largest and most efficient plants in the world. As things stand, the steel firms could hire the best team of managers in the world but they would still not make good rates of return. All the five forces are against them. The suppliers of raw materials tend to be large groups with strong bargaining power (three producers dominate the world's iron-ore business, for instance). Many of their customers are enormous groups (particularly the big six car makers who are quite prepared to switch steel supplier unless the keenest prices are offered). There are dozens of low-cost new entrants in Asia eager to take market share. Within western Europe there is intense rivalry between the existing players because of the need for each participant to produce at a high volume due to the necessity of spreading high fixed costs.[2] This is exacerbated by the difficulty of achieving *exit* from the industry: many companies are seen as national champions and important employers; they thus receive more than just a sympathetic ear from government. On top of all of this there is continual threat of **substitutes** – for example, the aluminium producers are a constant worry.

Airlines

An industry that has proven to be even worse than steel is airlines. It is astonishing to discover that, after years of management initiatives, cost-cutting, mergers, massive marketing campaigns and all the rest, the cumulative earnings of the industry over its entire history are negative. The fact that passenger numbers grow at a rate other industries would die for (4–5 per cent per year) seems to count for nothing in terms of profitability. Suppliers are often powerful (e.g. pilot unions). Also, if an airline establishes a profitable market segment it is quickly swamped by new entrants, and by existing airlines moving planes from one part of the globe to another. Over-capacity and low prices are the result. Airlines find it difficult to shed capacity in a hurry; they buy aircraft that fly for decades. When passenger demand falls they simply cannot reduce the supply of aircraft. Exit from the industry is also inhibited by national pride, which leads to suspension of normal commercial logic which would allow unprofitable companies to die.

Dynamic approach

It is worth remembering two points before we look in more detail at the framework for the analysis of industry structure. The first is that industries can change. An industry with a poor structure offering low returns can be transformed into an industry with a high rate of return on invested capital. This may come about for any number of reasons, ranging from a technological innovation that alters

---

[2] Those costs that do not change as quantity produced rises.

the entire economics of the industry (e.g. mobile phones and the Internet in the case of telecommunications) to government policy (e.g. allowing mergers to take place in the airline industry that were previously prohibited). We therefore need to obtain a dynamic rather than a static view when enquiring into an industry structure.

Second, when we are talking about rates of return on invested capital we are referring to the rate expected over the long term. Transient boosts to or dampenings of profitability – from an economic boom or recession, for example – should be distinguished from the long-term underlying nature of the industry and its consequent rate of return.

The strength of each of the five forces is influenced by a number of factors. The most important of these are discussed below. This discussion will provide a checklist of factors that the investor needs to investigate.

Threat of entry

If an industry is generating a return above that available in other industries (of comparable risk) it acts as a honey pot – a swarm of hungry insects will try to enter to take away some of the honey. New entrants add to the capacity of the industry as they make a grab for market share. The result is falling prices for every firm in the industry, or the costs of the original industry players rise as they try to maintain sales by spending on marketing, favourable credit terms for customers, etc.

New entry is definitely something that the incumbent firms abhor. There are two things that can stop, or at least slow down, the advance of the insects to the honey pot. First, there could be **barriers to entry** put in the path of the outsiders. Second, a clear message could go out to the aspiring entrants that if they did dare to cross the threshold then they would be subject to a massive retaliatory attack until they were driven out again. Of course, in many industries these two disincentives work in tandem.

Credibility is key to using the threat of retaliation to deter entrants. The following enhance this credibility:

■ If the incumbents have shown themselves to be vigorous defenders of their honey pot in the past.

■ If the incumbents have a large stock of resources with which to fight (cash, borrowing capacity, strong relationships or power over suppliers and customers, etc.).

■ If the incumbents are clearly committed to the industry (e.g. the assets employed within it have few alternative uses).

Examples of industries with strong retaliatory threats include PC software and soft drinks.

Barriers to new entry come in a variety of forms – these may occur singly or in combination:

■ **Large economies of scale and high capital costs**. In some industries firms operating on a small scale are at a competitive disadvantage because the average cost of their product is higher than for those companies producing at the most efficient scale. The aspiring entrant therefore knows that the only way it can survive in the industry is to invest massively. This narrows the field of potential entrants down to a few firms with the required financial resources. If one of these large firms did dare to commit so much money it would risk a severe reaction from the existing firms. Examples of industries protected to some degree by scale economies include brewing, aircraft engines and mid-market automobile assembly. To overcome established brands such as Mars, Coca-Cola or Nike would cost a vast amount in marketing expense. Some industries are also protected by **economies of scope** – that is, the ability to reap economies by sharing costs between a number of product lines. For example, food manufacturers can add additional product lines that make use of the same logistical network, influence with retailers and production equipment. This is one of the main motivators for mergers in this industry.

■ **High risks associated with imitation**. It is not always easy to identify how it is that a successful business manages to do what it does to elevate it above the also-rans. The incumbent(s) may have special capabilities that are very difficult to emulate even if they could all be observed. The **uncertainty** of being able to imitate inhibits firms from entering the competitive arena. For example, it would be very difficult to imitate, in a credible fashion, the McKinsey method or the Goldman Sachs approach.

■ **Access to distribution channels**. The obvious distribution channels are usually tied up by the existing firms. The newcomer will need to somehow break into these relationships to try to secure distribution for its product. This can be very costly. Buyers are likely to ask for substantial price-cutting and other benefits if they are to welcome a new supplier. New food manufacturers, for example, find it very difficult to attract the attention of the large retailers. Incumbents often have strong relationships and a long experience of adapting to customer demands to provide a specialist, high-quality service. These can form a very high barrier to entry. Often the only option open to an outsider is to find a completely new distribution channel (e.g. the Internet).

■ **Switching costs**. It may be prohibitively expensive for the buyers of a firm's output to switch to another supplier. For example, the purchasers of aircraft spend a substantial amount training employees to fly and service the aircraft. They may invest in ancillary equipment to maintain and make best use of the planes. It would be costly to switch to another aeroplane manufacturer in terms of staff training and equipment. New entrants have to make an offer that is so good that it overcomes these switching costs. It would be very expensive for organisations to switch from using Microsoft's operating system and the Office suite. Any potential entrant would need to offer something very special to encourage a switch. Merely offering slightly better performance and a slightly lower price is not good enough.

■ **Differentiation**. Differentiation means that the product offers something of higher value than the competition. The additional features of the offer are valued more highly than the additional cost of those features charged to the customer. For example, there are many chocolate bars on the market, but only one Dairy Milk. Once a reputation is established it is very difficult for others to usurp that position.

■ **Experience**. Over time incumbents learn a great deal about their industry, their suppliers' and their buyer's industries. They develop specialist technical knowledge and a culture adapted to operating in the industry. The experienced firm can often make the product better or more cheaply than anyone else. Intel, for example, has decades of experience in developing microprocessors, which makes it very difficult for new entrants to catch up.

■ **Government legislation and policy**. Patents are the most obvious barriers to entry erected by governments, but there are others. For example, restrictions on take-off and landing slots at airports, controls on over-the-counter pharmaceuticals, tariff and quota barriers keeping out foreign competition, government subsidies to favoured sectors, licensing which forecloses entry, regulation of pricing, fishing quotas, and purchase of defence equipment from domestic suppliers.

■ **Control over raw materials or outlets**. The firms in the industry may have favourable access or outright control over key inputs and outlets. For example, car manufacturers insist on repairs and maintenance being done only with approved parts fitted at approved dealers if you want your warrantee to remain valid.

Intensity of rivalry of existing companies

Investors must concern themselves with the degree of rivalrous behaviour between the existing industry competitors. The more in-fighting there is between the companies for market share and profits, the more rates of return will be depressed. Intense rivalry can erode profits in a number of ways, as firms compete fiercely on price (any move made by one player is quickly matched by rivals), there is a tendency to spend a great deal on marketing, and firms are impelled regularly to improve the product and to introduce new products to try and stay one step ahead.

In highly rivalrous industries there is always at least one maverick trying to get ahead of competitors. They see an opportunity and go for it with all their might. Unfortunately, the advantage is short-lived as other firms follow the price reductions, marketing innovation or new improved product with their own versions. At the end of the process the whole industry can end up less profitable than before.

In industries with few companies competitors usually start to recognise their mutual interdependence and so restrain their rivalry. If the industry develops a dominant competitor, rather than a set of equally balanced competitors, rivalry is reduced – the dominant firm has a strong influence on industry prices and is able to discipline the mavericks. For highly rivalrous industries the financial press is likely to use phrases such as 'cut-throat competition' or 'price wars'. Less rivalrous industries will be described as 'stable', even 'boring' or 'gentlemanly'. Some of the factors that intensify rivalry and which can therefore be taken as bad signs for investors are:

- **Many equally balanced competitors**. Where there is no dominant player there will be fierce fighting for market share and profits. This is great for customers, but the industry would be much more profitable with a dominant player, e.g. electronics retailing.

- **Slow industry growth**. When an industry is growing fast firms can increase sales without necessarily taking sales from other firms. In a slow-growing industry there is a tendency to intense market share rivalry. The mass-market automobile industry is a prime example – car assemblers rarely achieve a good rate of return on their massive investment; much of the time they make losses.

- **High fixed costs**. Firms with high fixed costs need to have a high volume of output to spread costs over a lot of units. There is a high breakeven point. Rivals will cut prices to achieve the turnover required. Paper-making and steel manufacturers are industries that suffer from this problem. A similar tendency to slash prices to achieve rapid throughput is present in industries producing goods and services that are difficult to store (e.g. fruit, air travel).

■ **Products are not differentiated**. If the product (or service) is seen as commodity-like (it is identical to that supplied by other firms) buyers will be attracted purely by price and ancillary services. Margins will be cut and rates of return constrained. For example, bricks, fertiliser, mobile phones, PCs, white goods and various plastics have been *commoditised.*

■ **Extra capacity is added in large increments**. In some industries small increases in capacity are not possible (e.g. bulk chemicals, steel). When a large-scale plant is added chronic industry disruption can occur. Companies are tempted to fill the capacity by reducing prices. Many industries are subject to recurring bouts of over-capacity (e.g. paper, oil and plastics) as new plant is brought on-stream – usually at the peak of business cycles.

■ **When rivals have different strategies, origins, personalities and relationships**. Firms in an industry may have completely different objectives, targets and strategies depending on their background, parent-company goals and corporate personalities. What seems rational action to one appears irrational industry-damaging to others. In their competitive acts they 'continually run head on into each other in the process'.[3] Family-owned firms might have a completely different attitude to public companies or foreign rivals. Tacit collusion becomes extremely difficult as they have great difficulty reading each other's signals. Rules of the game do not become established to allow each firm to earn a high return.

■ **High exit barriers**. In a low-return industry the logical response from managers should be to exit the market and use the resources thus released in another industry where the returns are higher. The reduced supply will benefit the firms that remain and rates of return will rise. In reality, there are often factors that prevent the exit of firms despite sub-normal returns. **Exit barriers** come in many forms:

– *Specialised assets.* If the assets of the business are useful in the one business but have no or little value in any other there may be little incentive to quit. Investment in plant, machinery, and so on may be regarded as sunk and therefore does not contribute to the economic cost of running the business. The textile industry in Europe and North America suffered from the unwillingness of firms to exit that were using increasingly old machinery – the 50-year shake-out is continuing.

---

[3] Michael Porter, *Competitive Strategy* (Free Press, 1980, p.19).

- *Fixed costs of exit.* There may be substantial costs imposed on firms when they exit an industry. For example, they may be obliged to pay large amounts under labour agreements (this is particularly the case in many countries in Europe); the divestment process itself is costly in terms of managerial time, lawyers and accountants; customers may have entitlement to after-sales service or spare parts for many years; employees may need to be retrained and reassigned; and supplier compensation may be payable for broken contracts.

- *Strategic loss.* The business may be part of an overall strategic plan. Its removal might have a severe impact on other parts of the business. Perhaps the business, although not profitable in itself, adds greatly to the image of the firm or the quality of its relationships with customers, suppliers or government, so it is well worth retaining (e.g. newspapers often make a loss, but the political leverage they bring to owners may be useful for other businesses in the group). It may share facilities that would become uneconomic for the parent without the business. Key raw material suppliers to the group may become unwilling to supply in the absence of the subsidiary. The business may be an important link in a vertically integrated chain. For example, the major oil companies have exploration operations, extraction divisions, refining business and retail outlets. One of these businesses could be underperforming (often the retail side), yet it is kept within the fold out of wider strategic considerations.

- *Emotional barriers.* In a stand-alone business the managers will tend not to exit even in the face of economic adversity. They are likely to have an emotional attachment to the business. They take pride in the quality of the product and in the efficiency of the operation. It is a business they know and love – it often has a rich history and tradition. The managers realise that they are ill suited for any other trade. These emotional ties can be especially strong in family-owned firms.

- *Government and social barriers.* Governments often step in to prevent the closure of businesses because of their concern for jobs and the community. As a result, the required capacity reduction in the industry does not take place and companies grimly hang on and battle away. The result is persistent low returns for the entire industry.

The threat from substitutes

The threat from substitutes dampens profit potential. **Substitutes** are products or services that perform the same function (at least in approximate terms). The returns available in the beverage packaging industry have a ceiling because the buyers are able to switch between steel, aluminium, glass and plastic. Book retailers' margins are under threat because the Internet has provided a substitute method of obtaining books. The threat of substitutes is worse if the cost to buyers of switching is low, and the ratio of price to performance is better. That is, the substitute may not be as good at serving the function as the existing product or service, but it is a lot cheaper (e.g. low-cost airlines); or the substitute is slightly more expensive, but significantly more effective.

Buyer (customer) power

Buyer power gives customers the potential to squeeze industry margins by forcing down prices, or pressing for higher quality or more services. Tesco has achieved a great deal of buyer power. It is able to exert huge pressure on the firms in the industries producing food, clothes and electrical items. Buyers are in a strong bargaining position if one or more of the following applies:

■ **There is a concentration of buyers**. If there are a few large firms responsible for the majority of market purchases then their power is likely to be enhanced *vis-à-vis* suppliers. The major automobile assemblers have a great deal of power over component suppliers. The supplier can be threatened with a loss of business if they refuse to co-operate. They are usually desperate to avoid losing a substantial proportion of their sales.

■ **The product is standardised or undifferentiated**. If the product is much the same as that supplied by other companies, then buyers will be confident that they will always be able to obtain the product if a particular supplier refuses to reduce prices or add service features. They are then in a position to play one company against another. This is a particular problem for suppliers of some raw materials.

■ **If the product accounts for a large proportion of buyers' costs**. Purchasers are likely to expend more energy driving down the price of larger-cost items than the price of a product that has an insignificant effect on their overall costs. Buyers are less price-sensitive with incidental products.

■ **If the buyer has low switching costs**. If it is costly for buyers to change suppliers then the suppliers' bargaining power is enhanced.

■ **Buyers suffer from low profitability**. Vehicle assemblers frequently announce that they have developed a plan for survival and for a return to profitability. Invariably, as part of the package of measures, they declare that they have reached an 'agreement' with their suppliers to cut billions of pounds from the components bill. One can only guess at the negotiating stance taken, but it probably goes along the line of 'If you don't reduce prices then we will shut down plant, and even go bankrupt, and you will lose an important customer.' If buyer firms are highly profitable they are less likely to be focused on cost-cutting and may take a greater interest in preserving the long-run health of their suppliers.

■ **If buyers can integrate backwards**. If buyers can credibly threaten to make the product themselves they may have greater leverage over their suppliers. Paint manufacturers are often in a position to manufacture resin themselves should they choose to do so. If the 'make or buy' decision is finely balanced, suppliers have little room for bargaining.

■ **The consequences and risks of product failure are low**. If the quality of the product is crucial to buyers' systems of operations then they are likely to pay less attention to fine-tuning the price. For example, equipment that is used to prevent oil-rig blow-outs is so vital and costs such a small amount compared with the costs of a blow-out that buyers are willing to pay a little extra to be absolutely sure of complete safety. Similar logic applies to medical equipment, legal advice and corporate finance guidance. If quality is unimportant, buyers will be more price-sensitive and shop around among suppliers.

■ **Buyers have plenty of information**. Buyers' leverage can be enhanced if they know a lot about suppliers' margins, costs, and order books. Suppliers will be unable to kid the buyers into thinking that they have inflicted real pain by bargaining down the price when in reality the price agreed is above the suppliers' minimum bargaining price. The old lines such as 'you've cut my prices to the bone' and 'at this rate I'll be losing money on the deal' will not work if the buyer knows the reality of the supplier's costs.

Supplier power

In many ways supplier power is the mirror image of buyer power. Powerful suppliers are able to set prices that are much greater than their production costs; they are able to appropriate a substantial proportion of the value created in the industries they serve. Suppliers exercise the power that they possess by raising prices or reducing the quality of purchased goods and services. Intel is a powerful supplier to the PC assemblers. Sports rights holders and hit TV show producers are powerful suppliers to the TV networks. Coca-Cola sells to an industry (retailers) that is highly fragmented. Most of these buyers have very little power. A few of the large supermarket groups try to exert some authority, but they are up against a powerful brand and a company used to deciding terms (Coke has over 50 per cent of the carbonated soft drinks market worldwide). If the firms in the industry are geared up to obtaining supplies from a particular source and there would be enormous cost of switching suppliers then the supplying firms have power. For example, Judge Thomas Penfield Jackson in his findings on Microsoft in 1999 declared:

> the cost of switching to a non-Intel compatible PC operating system includes the price of not only a new operating system, but also a new PC and new peripheral devices. It also includes the effort of learning to use the new system, the cost of acquiring a new set of compatible applications, and the work of replacing files and documents that were associated with the old applications.... users of Intel-compatible PC operating systems would not switch in large numbers to the Mac OS in response to even a substantial, sustained increase in the price of an Intel-compatible PC operating system.[4]

Industry evolution

The five-forces model is essentially static. However, investors need to develop a view of how favourable the industry structure will be years into the future. Industries change as companies, suppliers and buyers undertake strategic actions to enhance their respective degrees of power. They also change as new technology and government policy shift the basic economic facts of life.

Having completed a static evaluation of the industry – a snapshot in time – the investor must consider the factors that are likely to lead to the evolution of the industry. A firm that currently has strong pricing power can find it slipping away rapidly – one example is IBM's slide in the late 1980s and early 1990s as the PC was exploited more effectively by competitors; another is the way fixed-line telecom companies have been outwitted by mobile companies. Then there are the examples of book shops swept away by Amazon; and BlackBerry and Nokia impacted by leapfrogging competition.

If you have found an industry with excellent current characteristics then, when completing an industry evolution analysis, you will be looking for the potential for the industry to continue to produce high returns. Stability and invulnerability to attack and change are the desired qualities. On the other hand, if the industry has a 'poor' or 'fair' structure you would be interested in evaluating the potential for change to a durable high-return structure.

Long-range structural analysis is used to forecast the long-term rates of return of an industry. The task is to examine the changing strength of each competitive force

---

[4] See http://usvms.gpo.gov/findings_index.html

and to attempt the construction of a probable profit potential for the industry. Of course, this is easier in less complex industry environments. Investors should not try to analyse an industry with many highly uncertain variables. Concentrate on industries that are relatively easy to follow. (You may ignore this point if you have special knowledge of a hard-to-follow industry – exploit your analytical advantage.)

Changes in the environment of the industry are of significance if they affect the five forces. So an analyst will ask questions such as whether the change in technology or government regulations will result in a raising or lowering of entry or exit barriers, or whether a social trend will result in more power accruing to buyers. The driving forces at the root of industry evolution can be classified under the following headings:

- technological change;
- learning within the industry, and by suppliers, buyers and potential entrants;
- economic change;
- government legislation and policy;
- social change.

Technological change

The most visible and pervasive form of change in society is the result of techno-logical developments. New products, processes and materials directly affect people and alter the competitive forces within industries. Just consider the last 100 years. Inventions and innovations in the fields of electricity, communication, transport, pharmaceuticals, computers and satellites, to name a few, have had profound effects on daily lives and industry structure. Given that there are more scientists alive today than have ever breathed in all the previous generations, it seems reasonable to con-clude that technological change is more likely to accelerate rather than decline. This presents a serious challenge to the investor in trying to assess the durability of an industry's rate of return. If you really understand an industry subject to unusually rapid technological change, such as one of the information technology or biotechnology industries, then by all means concentrate your resources on esti-mating likely future profitability. However, most of us will not be able to do this. For us the only hope is to focus on industries that are more predictable. These will still have technological (and social, economic, etc.) change and therefore need an evolutionary assessment; however, the pace of change is likely to be much slower in certain areas. For example, the industry structure for the extraction of rock and gravel is unlikely to alter greatly as a result of invention and innovation. Perhaps new improved and specialist machinery will come along, but there are unlikely to be the seismic shifts that occur in other industries. The production and sale of old favourites such as *The Economist* and Nescafé is likely to continue much as it did before. It is true that all of these firms have to consider developments such as the Internet, but they will be able to adapt without fundamentally changing the method of doing business or, more importantly, the power structure within the industry. The *Financial Times* may develop its website but the paper version will still sell well. Nestlé may use the Internet to coordinate suppliers and drive down prices but will still sell through vending machines, stores and fast food outlets, over which it has tremendous power. Of course, we may be surprised by developments in the industry or in adjacent industries that lead to dramatic technological change, and in the five forces. Despite this uncertainty, evolution analysis is still desirable.

There are a number of ways in which technology can impact on industry structure. For example, the cost and quality of substitutes can change as a result of invention and innovation. This can affect the demand for the product if the cost falls or the quality improves sufficiently to overcome buyer switching costs. Examples of such change include the switch from the purchase of air travel tickets from travel agents to the Internet, and the switch from traditional brokers to Internet brokers for the purchase of shares.

The sales achieved by a particular industry may be influenced by the cost, quality and availability of **complementary products**. If the complementary product is affected by technological change then the industry under examination may experience a shift in the five forces. For example, advances in digital telecommunication speed affects the demand for movie downloads.

Entry barriers have been smashed in a lot of industries as a consequence of using Internet technology. Now small players can establish themselves as music or periodical publishers; a specialist producer of Stilton cheese in England can market the product worldwide, bypassing the powerful retail chains. In other industries rapid and frequent product introduction may create barriers to entry because potential competitors are unable to keep pace with the incumbent firms (e.g. microprocessor design).

The methods of producing the output of the industry might change as new technology is introduced. Banks are switching increasing numbers of customers to Internet/mobile bank accounts. They are under attack from non-banking firms setting up Internet banking operations now that the barriers to entry have been lowered – an extensive branch network is not required.

Technological advancement may lead the industry to change the typical buyers that it serves. For example, mobile telephones were initially very expensive and useful only in a confined geographic area, such as the City of London. Target customers were high-income, time-pressed individuals. Now one of the largest target markets is children who value text messaging and games as well as chatting.

Technological innovation can change the definition of the industry as industry boundaries can be enlarged or contracted. For example, the TV set is being used for communication and the Internet (particularly via cable systems). The convergence of telecommunications, computer technology and televisions will have a profound impact on these industry structures. New rivals appear, buyer power changes (as well as buyer demands) and content provider power may be enhanced.

Learning

Over time the participants in an industry and those with an interest in an industry (e.g. suppliers) accumulate knowledge that can change the industry power balance. Through the regular purchase of a product, buyers develop knowledge of the product's characteristics and qualities, and the cost of competing products. As buyers become more expert and the volume of sales increases, a product can move from being unusual and differentiated to being more commodity-like. Buyers become increasingly demanding, looking for higher specification, additional service, and lower price. When personal computers were first marketed they were novel and differentiated. As more manufacturers extended the industry and buyers accumulated knowledge, the PC increasingly became a commodity item. Also, buyers insisted on even greater computing power, after-sales service and 'free' software. Now many manufacturers make losses or very poor profits in the PC market.

Some industries are developed on the back of specialist knowledge of business processes or products. The firms in possession of this knowledge will guard it jealously to differentiate their product from the current competitors and to keep out potential entrants. However, gradually, as a technology becomes established, diffusion takes place. This may occur because other firms take apart the product and figure out how it was put together, or they may poach key staff; or customers may help create alternative suppliers by deliberate leaking.

Advantages based on the ownership of special knowledge are likely to be eroded. Advantages based on the ability to continually develop new special knowledge can be sustainable. There must be a dynamic managerial response. If a technology-led company is hiding behind patent protection and is not developing a stream of successor products it will not have the durable competitive advantage that the investor is looking for.

Economic change

A slowdown in the growth rate of an industry can have a dramatic effect on the industry structure. This is a particular problem for durable goods producers. When a durable good is first invented there is initially a slow consumer take-up. There follows a rapid growth phase. This starts to tail off as penetration reaches saturation point. A slowdown in the rate of growth is bad enough for firms that are accustomed to large year-on-year increases. But at least they are selling more each year so they continue to add capacity. Then the crunch comes. Once satiation is reached sales can fall dramatically as consumers shift from first-time buying to replacement purchase – for example, some mobile phone handset providers came close to failure because the anticipated growth in demand did not materialise after they borrowed to grow. With durable goods consumers can put off replacement for many years (even decades). This effect can be exacerbated by recession. The power balance in the growth phase can be completely different from that in the falling sales phase. During growth the industry can absorb entrants while each firm remains profitable. The companies are less concerned with pushing down the price of components from suppliers than with reliability and speed of supply. In the downturn new entrants become a great danger to industry profitability. Suppliers are asked to bear a greater share of the burden of the crisis and buyers gain enormous power as they shop around for bargains.

Changes in the price of input costs as a result of economic developments can affect industry structure. For example, in the last 50 years the cost of shipping goods around the world has fallen a great deal. This has widened the potential market for some producers of exported goods and meant an influx of entrants for incumbents in particular countries. The lowering of telecommunications costs has also had a significant effect on industries. For example, India has an enormous software industry – code can be written in India at a fraction of the cost in Silicon Valley and transmitted instantly to anywhere in the world. Other examples of economic events that influence industry structure and the relative strength of the five forces include the liberalisation of world trade, the rise in labour costs and changes in exchange rates.

Government

Changes in government legislation and policy can lead to significant changes in industry structure. The government's attitude towards competitive practices, for example, can vary over time. What is considered an acceptable level of industry concentration of power in the hands of a few firms at one time is regarded as unacceptable at another, and companies are obliged to subject themselves to greater competition. There are some industries whose prices are regulated by governments or government-appointed agencies. Governments also license some firms to enter industries. The other side of that coin is they restrict the entry of other companies. Product quality and safety are also influenced by government organisations (e.g. in food). Government agreements to impose legislation to curtail the emission of greenhouse gases can have enormous impacts on companies, e.g. steel manufacturers in Europe are very worried by the high cost of energy, particularly when the price of gas in the USA has fallen to a fraction of that in Europe due to fracking. Industry structure can be greatly influenced by the imposition or removal of tariffs or import quotas.

Industry structures are changed by a whole series of other government moves from labour law and privatisation to patent law and information disclosure. The investor has the difficult task of trying to evaluate the likelihood of a change in government policy having a significant influence on industry profitability through the power relationships of the five forces.

Social change

Demographic change can influence the size of the buyer pool for an industry. For example, as the proportion of the population over the age of 50 in western countries increases, demand for some products will rise (e.g. golf?) and others will fall (e.g. discos?). The ethnic mix of the population can alter the demand for products, increasing the demand for some (e.g. certain foods) at the expense of others.

Values and cultures can change. Vegetarianism is growing in popularity, which is bound to affect the meat industry. There is greater equality between the sexes, which will affect industries from employment agencies to childcare providers. Shifts are taking place in the perceived appropriate work–life balance, affecting the demand for leisure activities.

Education and health levels can change over a relatively short period of time, particularly in countries with high economic growth. A more highly educated populace is likely to demand more news, books and training courses. Health can rise in some regards, but decline in others, as incomes increase. Concern about weight has become a fixation – slimming foods and exercise/gym businesses have been the beneficiaries.

Income distribution can change over time. For example, the redistribution of income towards the poor can reduce the demand for luxury goods but increase the demand for basics. Even a social issue as simple as the spread of English as the world language can influence industry structure: film and television producers see their buyers and competitors as existing all over the world.

Concluding comments

No industry is perfect for the investor. Each one will be negatively affected to some extent by one or more of the forces described above. The investor should not drop an industry from further consideration just because a negative factor is uncovered. Rather, the investor needs to weigh up the balance of a mixture of positive and negative factors. Some industries display an overwhelming combination of negatives – for example, the firms have low bargaining power over suppliers and customers; they are vulnerable to attack by new entrants; the industry is growing slowly; and it has many aggressively competing players.

On the other hand, there are industries with two or three players who sell to customers unable to easily switch their suppliers. Being the dominant firms, these companies can be very forceful in agreeing terms with suppliers. Prices are kept way above the cost of production, helped by a tacit agreement between the companies that they will not compete on price. Entry by other companies is difficult. Even in an industry with so many positives there may be one or two threats – for example, technological or government rule changes may encourage substitute product makers or encourage entry into the industry.

The investor has to be able to stand back and observe the overall picture. Judgement is required in broad terms rather than in pinpoint precision. Here, we are dealing with subjective probabilities of industry returns on capital in the long term, not definitive objective certainties. Despite the superficial appearance that investment is based on hard numbers, it has to be acknowledged that the key inputs to the process are qualitative, such as the degree of pricing power.

Further reading

Two books that are very easy to read and give more detail on analysing industries are Michael Porter, *Competitive Strategy* (Free Press, 1980), and Glen Arnold, *The Financial Times Guide to Value Investing* (Financial Times Prentice Hall, 2009).

15

The competitive position of the firm[1]

Earlier **(in the previous chapter)** we dealt with identifying industries offering high returns on capital employed. However, identifying a good industry is only the first step. Investors need to seek out companies that beat the average rates of return on capital employed in a good industry. To beat the averages, companies need something special. That something special comes from the bundle of resources that the firm possesses. Most of the resources are ordinary. That is, they give the firm competitive parity. However, the firm may be able to exploit one or two extraordinary resources – those that give a competitive edge. An **extraordinary resource** is one which, when combined with other (ordinary) resources, enables the firm to outperform competitors and create new value-generating opportunities. Critical extraordinary resources determine what a firm can do successfully.

It is the ability to generate value for customers that is crucial for superior returns. High shareholder returns are determined by the firm's ability to offer either the same benefits to customers as competitors but at a lower price, or unique benefits that more than outweigh the associated higher price.

Ordinary resources provide a threshold competence. They are vital to ensure a company's survival. The problem is that mere competitive parity does not produce the returns looked for by investors. In the food retail business, for example, most

[1] Much of the material for this chapter is condensed from G. Arnold, *The Financial Times Guide to Value Investing,* 2nd edn (Financial Times Prentice Hall, 2009) and is discussed further at my seminars – see www.glen-arnold-investments.co.uk.

firms have a threshold competence in basic activities, such as purchasing, human resource management, accounting control and store layout. However, the large chains have resources that set them apart from the small stores: they are able to obtain lower cost supplies because of their enormous buying power; they can exploit economies of scale in advertising and in the range of produce offered.

Despite large retailers having these advantages, it is clear that small stores have survived, and some produce very high returns on capital invested. These superior firms provide value to the customer significantly above cost. Some corner stores have a different set of extraordinary resources compared with the large groups: personal friendly service could be valued highly; opening at times convenient to customers could lead to acceptance of a premium price; the location may make shopping less hassle than traipsing to an out-of-town hypermarket.

The extraordinary resources possessed by the supermarket chains as a group when compared with small shops are not necessarily extraordinary resources in the competitive rivalry *between* the chains. If the focus is shifted to the 'industry' of supermarket chains, factors such as economies of scale may merely give competitive parity – scale is needed for survival. Competitive advantage is achieved through the development of other extraordinary resources – for example, the quality of the relationship with suppliers, the combination of a sophisticated system for collecting data on customers and target marketing, or ownership of the best sites. However, even these extraordinary resources will not maintain a superior competitive position for ever. Many of these can be imitated. Long-term competitive advantage may depend on the ability of the management team to continually innovate and thereby shift the ground from under the feet of competitors. The extraordinary resource is then the coherence, attitude, intelligence, knowledge and drive of the managers in the organisation setting.

Many successful companies have stopped seeing themselves as bundles of product lines and businesses. Instead they look at the firm as a collection of resources. This helps to explain the logic behind some companies going into apparently unconnected product areas. The connection is the exploitation of extraordinary resources. So, for example, Honda has many different product areas: motor boat engines, automobiles, motorcycles, lawn mowers and electric generators. These are sold through different distribution channels in completely different ways to different customers. The common root for all these products is Honda's extraordinary resource, which led to a superior ability to produce engines. Likewise, photocopiers, cameras and image scanners are completely different product sectors and sold in different ways. Yet they are all made by Canon, which has extraordinary capabilities and knowledge of optics, imaging and microprocessor controls.

The TRRACK system

The investor should not be looking for a long list of extraordinary resources in any one firm. It is great if you can find one – it only takes one to leap ahead of competitors and produce supernormal returns. If two are found, then that is excellent. It is very unusual to come across a company that has three or more extraordinary resources. Coca-Cola is an exception with an extraordinary brand, an extensive distribution system with its connected relationships, and highly knowledgeable managers (knowledgeable principally about how to work the systems in countries around the world to keep the competition authorities off their backs while they tighten control over distribution and prices – allegedly).

To assist the thorough analysis of a company's extraordinary resource I have developed the TRRACK system. This classifies extraordinary resources into six categories:

T   Tangible
R   Relationships
R   Reputation
A   Attitude
C   Capabilities
K   Knowledge

Notice that the vast majority of extraordinary resources are intangible. They are qualities that are carried within the individuals that make up the organisation, or are connected with the interaction between individuals. They are usually developed over a long time rather than bought. These qualities cannot be scientifically evaluated to provide objective quantification. Despite our inability to be precise, it is usually the case that these people-embodied factors are the most important drivers of value creation and we must pay most attention to them. Good investment hinges on good judgement rather than the ability to plug numbers into a formula.

Tangible

Occasionally physical resources provide a sustainable competitive advantage. These are assets that can be physically observed and are often valued (or mis-valued) in a balance sheet. They include property, materials, production facilities and patents. They can be purchased, but if they were easily purchased they would cease to be extraordinary because all competitors would go out and buy. There must be some barrier preventing other firms from acquiring the same or similar assets for them to be truly valuable in the long run.

McDonald's makes sure that it takes the best locations on the busiest highways, rather than settling for obscure secondary roads. Many smaller businesses have found themselves with (or made smart moves to secure) the ownership of valuable land adjacent to popular tourist sites. Pharmaceutical companies, such as Merck, own valuable patents giving some protection against rivalry – at least temporarily.

Relationships

Over time companies can form valuable relationships with individuals and organisations that are difficult or impossible for a potential competitor to emulate. Relationships in business can be of many kinds. The least important are the contractual ones. The most important are informal or implicit. These relationships are usually based on a trust that has grown over many years. The terms of the implicit contract are enforced by the parties themselves rather than through the court – a loss of trust can be immensely damaging. It is in all the parties' interests to cooperate with integrity because there is the expectation of reiteration leading to the sharing of collective value created over a long period.

Buyer–seller relationships differ in quality. Many are simply arm's-length, adversarial and involve serious bargaining. This may make sense when selling incidental items, say pencils, to organisations. It is not worth the expense of establishing a more sophisticated interaction. However, many firms have seen the value of developing close relationships with either their suppliers or customers. For example, IKEA and Wal-Mart are moving towards more collaborative relationships with suppliers to improve delivery mechanisms, through joint planning and scheduling, information system management and co-operation on quality and reliability advances.

South African Breweries (now SABMiller plc) has 77 per cent of the beer market in South Africa. It has kept out foreign and domestic competitors because of its special relationships with suppliers and customers. It is highly profitable. Most of South Africa's roads are poor and electricity supplies are intermittent. To distribute its beer it has formed some strong relationships. It helps truck drivers, many of whom are former employees, to set up small trucking businesses. *Shebeens* sell most of the beer. These are unlicensed pubs. Often they are tiny – no more than a few benches. SAB cannot sell directly to the illegal shebeens. Instead it maintains an informal relationship via a system of wholesalers. SAB makes sure that distributors have refrigerators and, if necessary, generators. An entrant would have to develop its own special relationship with truck drivers, wholesalers and retailers. In all likelihood it would have to establish a completely separate and parallel system of distribution. Even then it would lack the legitimacy that comes with a long-standing relationship.

IBM developed close working relationships with many of its customers after they bought its mainframe computers in the twentieth century. Customers needed help with running, maintaining and updating their systems. As computer hardware became increasingly commoditised in the twenty-first century, IBM lost much of its pricing power here, but more than made up for this by building on those long-established relations of trust. IBM's service division was greatly expanded so that it now employs more than half of its 427,000 workforce. The shift towards vast data centres, mobile devices and the cloud, rather than computing on in-house desktops or mainframes, meant that services such as business analytics required that guides were needed in each customer's electronic jungle. It now co-creates products with customers as well helping them to organise their businesses.

Accounting firms, management consultancies and investment banks are particularly keen on 'client-relationship management'. Frequently, it is the quality of the customer relationship that creates the real value for these types of organisations.

Relationships between employees, and between employees and the firm, can give a competitive edge. Some firms seem to possess a culture that creates wealth through the cooperation and dynamism of the employees. Information is shared, knowledge is developed, innovative activity flows, rapid response to market change is natural, and respect for all pervades.

The quality of relationships with government can be astonishingly important to a company. Many of the defence contractors concentrate enormous resources to ensure a special relationship with various organs of government. The biggest firms often attract the best ex-government people to take up directorships or to head liaison with the government. Their contacts and knowledge of the inside workings of purchasing decisions, with their political complications, can be very valuable. A similar logic often applies to pharmaceutical companies, airlines and regulated (e.g. energy, water) companies.

Reputation

Reputations are normally made over a long period. Once a good reputation is established it can be a source of very high returns (assuming that all the necessary ordinary resources are in place to support it).

In the markets for goods and services consumers constantly come up against the difficulty of judging quality before purchase. This is an ancient problem. In medieval times craftsmen banded together in guilds which then sought to establish a quality reputation for every member of the group. If a member fell below the required standard he would be ejected to prevent the image of the group being sullied permanently. This type of arrangement exists today for builders, plumbers and cabinet-makers. Those who deal in gold and silver found, and still find, it worthwhile to spend time and money demonstrating the purity of the metal. They pay for systems to assay to the declared specification.

Customers are willing to pay a premium for product quality assurance when they cannot easily monitor quality for themselves. This premium is not available to the suppliers in many markets (e.g. coal, electricity, sugar, paper) where the buyer is able to quickly and cheaply gauge quality. But in some industries customers will pay a price premium for the assurance of quality. To appreciate the value of reputation it is worth thinking about goods and services as falling into four categories:

■ search goods;

■ immediate-experience goods;

■ long-term-experience goods;

■ no-experience goods.

Reputation is most important in the last two, but it has relevance to many immediate experience goods.

Search goods are those for which the buyer can establish quality by inspection before purchase. So, for example, the quality of bananas can generally be observed in the store. It makes sense for the storekeeper to build up a reputation for quality as this will enable the store to remain on the list of retailers that consumers like to purchase from. But retailers are generally unable to exploit this reputation to charge a significant price premium. If they attempted to do so, consumers would quickly switch to other stores where they could easily assess the quality of the produce.

The second group of products are *immediate-experience goods*. Here quality cannot be established by inspection. So the taste of a soup in a can or the flavour of canned vegetables is only learnt by the consumer after purchase. However, it does not take long to learn about the quality of Campbell's or Heinz soup. Consumers soon develop knowledge of a manufacturer's quality with immediate-experience goods. Once learned, there tends to be some degree of inertia, leading to consumers being reluctant to switch brands (giving some pricing power).

The value of *long-term-experience goods* can only be determined after extensive personal experience. For example, it takes a long time to establish whether a doctor is very able (given that most ailments clear up spontaneously). Only in the long term do you know, if you are relying on personal experience, whether the cancer treatment is working or the heart pills do not have unacceptable side effects. Reputation established with other patients may be key to your decision to accept the advice and treatment of a doctor. When companies are selecting auditing, accounting and other professional services they rarely have an extensive history of dealing with a range of possible suppliers to be able to choose one on the basis of experience. They generally rely on reputation. With car hire in a foreign country the consumer is unable to assess quality in advance. Hertz provide certification for local traders under a franchise arrangement. These local car hirers would see no benefit to providing an above average service without the certification of Hertz because they would not be able to charge a premium price. It is surprising how much more consumers are willing to pay for the assurance of reliable and efficient car hire when they travel abroad, compared with the hiring of a car from an unfranchised local.

There are some goods that are only purchased once (or rarely). These are *no-experience goods*. Examples are funeral services, swimming pools, construction, and specialist legal services. Consumers tend to lean heavily on reputations established with other customers.

The ways in which buyers ascertain the quality of a good (e.g. visual inspection or personal recommendation) can strongly influence the potential for competitive advantage in an industry. The four types of goods and the importance of reputation in attaining reassurance on quality are shown in Table 15.1.

Table 15.1   **Type of good and the importance of reputation**

Type of good	Information on quality	Examples
Search	Obtained by inspection prior to purchase: reputation is of very little importance	Fresh fruit and vegetables Clothing Some furniture
Immediate experience	Obtained quickly after consumption: reputation is of some importance	Tinned food and drink Newspapers Theme parks
Long-term experience	Obtained only after a long period of individual experience: reputation is therefore very important	Professional advice Some medicines Investment advice
No experience	Not possible to obtain from individual experience: reputation is therefore very important	Investment bank advice Funeral services Life assurance

Branding is designed to represent and enhance reputations. Brands generally provide a degree of quality certification for consumers. For immediate-experience and long-term-experience goods the brand provides the assurance of consistency. People buy branded beer because they expect that the next can will taste the same as the ones they bought previously. In many product areas consumers are reluctant to take the risk of buying unbranded products, for fear of inconsistency of quality (e.g. hamburgers, soup, breakfast cereals and shampoo).

The promise of consistency provides a company with a competitive advantage, but the price premium that can be charged for this factor alone is limited because the consistency can be replicated by competitors. There are two other advantages of branded products that permit enhanced pricing power. These are shown in Figure 15.1. A firm may have one, two or all three of these advantages. Naturally, the more the better.

Incumbency can be a powerful quality of a brand. Once a brand is established in the minds of consumers it is very difficult for a rival manufacturer to successfully introduce an alternative product, even if that product offers better value. For example, a rival to Cadbury's Flake may offer a chocolate bar of equivalent quality at a lower price, but few consumers will switch – at least not without a vast marketing spend and a long period of time. Similarly, consumers are attached to dog food brands, ketchup brands and cleaning product brands. Consumer recognition

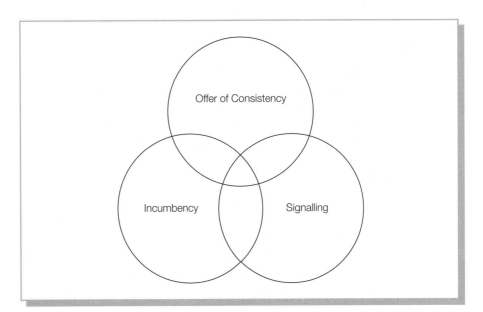

Figure 15.1 **Three powerful advantages of brands**

and acceptance of a new product in the face of a well-established incumbent is extraordinarily difficult. The combination of consistency and incumbency can lead to very high returns. Coca-Cola is aware of the role of these two factors in its success – Douglas Daft, former Chairman and Chief Executive, wrote: 'All our success flows from the strength of our brands, and our ability to relate to people. That's why we have to be the world's best marketers.'[2] He said that Coca-Cola should focus on becoming a 'pure marketing company', presumably in order to entrench the power of consistency and incumbency.

Consumers often use branded products to send *signals* to other people. Nike, Ralph Lauren, Levi's and a host of others exploit this element of human nature and receive a premium price. Signals of high status are generally expensive – Rolls-Royce, Moët et Chandon and Burberry spring to mind. Coca-Cola manages to score on this point as well: in many developing countries its American cultural associations mean that young people, in particular, will pay a premium.

Note that strong brands in and of themselves are not competitive advantages. You need a brand with a barrier to entry. For example, Vauxhall or Ford have many strong brands, but the ease of entry into volume car making means they produce poor returns on capital employed. Even the brand strength of Mercedes has profound limitations in a market that is so heavily contested. Not many customers can be persuaded to pay a high price over production costs when, say, Jaguars, BMWs, etc. are alternatives.

Attitude

Attitude refers to the mentality of the organisation. It is the prevalent outlook. It is the way in which the organisation views and relates to the world. Terms such as 'disposition', 'will' and 'culture' are closely connected with attitude. Every sports coach is aware of the importance of attitude. The team may consist of players with the best technique in the business or with a superb knowledge of the game, they may be the fastest and the most skilful, but without a winning attitude they will not succeed. There must be a will to win and a will to prepare.

Some firms develop a winning mentality based on a culture of innovation. Others are determinedly orientated towards customer satisfaction, while some are quality-driven. 3M has a pervasive attitude of 'having a go'. Testing out wild ideas is encouraged. Employees are given time to follow up a dreamed-up innovation, and they are not criticised for failing. Innovations such as *Post-it* notes have flowed from this attitude.

---

2   D. Daft, 'Back to basic Coke', *Financial Times,* 27 March 2000, p.20.

Capabilities

Capabilities are derived from the company's ability to undertake a *set* of tasks. The term 'skill' can be used to refer to a narrow activity or single task. The word 'capability' is used for the combination of a number of skills. For example, Sony developed a capability in miniaturisation. This enabled it to produce a string of products from the Walkman to the PlayStation. It grew by continually reinforcing the various skills needed for technology-based product innovation. This was complemented by marketing flair and strong brands.

Frequently, it is extremely difficult for a firm to combine its process skills in such a way as to provide a superior capability. The mere fact that it is difficult gives a competitive advantage to a firm that has achieved it, as the combination becomes difficult for rivals to imitate. Static capabilities are less valuable than the ability to move quickly in product markets.

In the 1940s Caterpillar developed a capability for building roads, airstrips and army bases for the US Department of War. It had to develop a wide range of skills as the military needed one supplier that would take on entire projects. Caterpillar offered a worldwide service and supply network for construction equipment at low cost. Having met the challenge set by the military, Caterpillar was in an excellent position after the war to offer a capability rivals could not emulate. It became the dominant firm in the heavy construction equipment industry. Its ability to deliver any Caterpillar part to any location in the world in less than two days was an unbeatable offer.

In some industries the capability to be the lowest-cost producer is vital for superior profitability. Cost leaders must exploit all sources of cost advantage. They tend to sell standard, undifferentiated products with few or no frills. They must be determined to be *the* lowest-cost producer, not just one of many.

Knowledge

The retention, exploitation and sharing of knowledge can be extremely important in the achievement and maintenance of competitive advantage. *Knowledge* is the awareness of information, and its interpretation, organisation, synthesis and prioritisation, to provide insights and understanding. All firms in an industry share basic knowledge. For example, all publishers have some knowledge of market trends, distribution techniques and printing technology. It is not this common knowledge that I am referring to in the context of extraordinary resources. If a publisher builds up data and skills in understanding a particular segment of the market (say, investment books), then its superior awareness, interpretation, organisation, synthesis and prioritisation of information can create competitive advantage through extraordinary knowledge. The company will have greater insight than rivals into this segment of the market.

There are two types of organisational knowledge. The first, *explicit knowledge*, can be written down and passed on to others relatively easily. This is objective knowledge that can be defined and documented. The second, *tacit knowledge*, is very difficult to define. It is subjective, personal, fuzzy and complex. It is hard to formalise and communicate. An example of explicit knowledge would be how to manufacture a component. Explicit knowledge is unlikely to provide competitive advantage: if it is easily defined and codified it is likely be available to rivals. Tacit knowledge, on the other hand, is very difficult for rivals to obtain. Consider the analogy of football: explicit knowledge of tactics is generally available; what separates the excellent from the ordinary player is the application of tacit knowledge (e.g. the instinctive ability to place the ball and an awareness of other members of the team). Tacit knowledge is transmitted by doing: the main means of transferring knowledge from one individual to another is through close interaction to build understanding, as in the master–apprentice relationship.

Nike was started by Phil Knight in 1964. He had a special knowledge of the needs of runners – in the 1950s he had been a middle-distance runner in the University of Oregon's track team. He felt that runners had been badly served by the existing manufacturers. He designed shoes using his special insight, but had no special knowledge of manufacturing, and so this was contracted to Asian suppliers. His new designs were a great success. In the 1980s the company grew from the specialist sports shoe market to the fashion-conscious teenage and youth market. This required an additional set of knowledge attributes. As well as knowledge of how to create innovative sport shoes (e.g. Nike Air) the company became very knowledgeable about its customers, marketing and distributors. For example, image building was vital to sell to this type of consumer. Michael Jordan was featured in its advertising. The amount spent on sports marketing reached $1 billion in 1995. Tiger Woods and the whole of the Brazilian soccer team were signed up. The company's understanding of its target market was second to none. It projected a cool and competitive image that appealed to the young. Its knowledge of product development was built on – in one year it launched 300 new designs! It developed a knowledge of new materials and fabrics. The easily documented elements of Nike's knowledge base are the least important. The key elements are the knowledge that comes from day-to-day interaction between employees and with customers, suppliers and distributors. This knowledge builds up over time and is diffused throughout the organisation in the heads of thousands of individuals.

What makes resources extraordinary?

It is sometimes difficult to identify the extraordinary resources of a company, if indeed it has any at all. This section may help by summarising the characteristics of extraordinary resources. To achieve *sustainable* competitive advantage, the three characteristics must be *durable*. That is, it is expected that the above average return on capital will persist for a very long time because:

■ the resource will be *demanded* (regarded as valuable) by customers far into the future;

■ the resource will continue to be *scarce* (i.e. competitors will not be able to imitate the resource or substitute alternative resources to satisfy customers' needs);

■ as far as can be seen, the additional net income generated by the use of the extraordinary resource is *appropriable* by the firm and not by another organisation or individual(s).

The challenge for the investor is understanding what distinguishes extraordinary resources from those that merely give competitive parity and to recognise when a resource switches from being extremely valuable to being pedestrian (and the likelihood of that switch occurring in the near future). For example, lower priced Swiss watch manufacturers discovered that the extraordinary resources of knowledge accumulated over centuries and a high reputation were not enough to induce consumers to pay a premium when cheap digital watches became available. Similarly, IBM found that it could not resist the onslaught in the PC market as the extraordinary resources it offered (technical design, reputation for bespoke solutions, etc.) became regarded as secondary when customers were offered cheaper PCs with a high specification produced as commodity-type products.

Demanded

The first question to ask is whether the resource produces something of value to the customer, at a price the customer is more than willing to pay. To be extraordinary the resource must fulfil a customer's need, and the customer must be prepared to pay a premium over the cost to obtain that benefit. At any one time, willingness to pay a premium will depend on the alternatives open to the customer. The resource has to meet current and projected needs that cannot be met by competitors.

Firms frequently see themselves as having extraordinary resources that are still demanded by customers, but, in reality, they are deluding themselves. Their belief is often based on success in the past. For example, a manufacturer of metal car bumpers may be the best in the world, with the greatest technical design, cheapest operating costs, brilliant plant managers, etc. But if customer demand has moved from metal automobile bumpers to compressible plastic, those resources are no longer in demand and are therefore not valuable. To take another example, the demand for the resources possessed by skilful tailors has all but disappeared.

There are some resources that are more likely to have a long life than others. For example, Disney's extraordinary resource as a family-orientated entertainment brand will, bar managerial stupidity or accident, produce price premiums long into the future. Each of the leading characters (Mickey Mouse, Snow White, etc.) and the library of movies can be considered extraordinary resources with a long shelf life. The theme parks have a special place in the hearts of many people – they are world-renowned leaders in the field. Each generation will want to share with their children the magic of Disney. They offer something special that competitors find hard to beat. Cadbury and *The Economist* have powerful reputations in their respective fields that are likely to be long-lived because they offer to satisfy customer needs better than alternatives. Of course, the management will need to be vigilant and to invest to stay ahead, but they start from an excellent position.

Scarcity

If the resource is widely available it cannot be extraordinary. It must be in short supply to be valuable. If it is commonplace competitors will acquire it and undercut the price premium. The company must have some protection against the actions of rivals attempting to either imitate its advantage or provide a substitute resource to steal away customers. It must have a deep moat around the competitive advantage to make it sustainable. Resources that have built-in inhibitors to imitation fall into four categories:[3]

- **Physically unique**. A company may have ownership of the best real estate. Rivals cannot imitate this. The firm may have the mineral rights over a piece of land that contains the only economically viable quantity of a metal on a continent. Patent rights (e.g. for drugs) can prevent imitation for a while. However, the company must not rest on its laurels, as patent rights can be bypassed by determined rivals fairly quickly. A more durable extraordinary resource is the ability to produce a *stream* of patentable products. That way

---

[3] Much of this discussion is inspired by work done by David Collis and Cynthia Montgomery; see D.J. Collis and C.A. Montgomery, *Corporate Strategy,* 2nd edn (McGraw-Hill, 2005) for more details.

competitors are always running to catch up. So developing a capability and an attitude that allows rapid knowledge accumulation, innovative thinking, and quick development of products may be sustainable. The physical assets of firms are rarely inimitable. Gillette, for example, took 10 years and spent $1 billion developing its Mach3 triple-blade razor. Within a few months, Asda had produced its own triple-bladed razor selling at a 40 per cent discount. The start-up electronic traders such as CDNOW, eToys and E*Trade thought they had developed unique physical resources – a strong presence on the Internet. However, it has become apparent that the 'space' they occupy can be invaded by the traditional retailers, who found it relatively easy to occupy a 'site' adjacent to the brash upstarts. Furthermore, the old firms were able to apply some other significant advantages such as exploiting relationships established with millions of customers over many years, a strong brand name, tried and tested distribution capability and good relationships with suppliers.

■ **Path dependency**. This is more likely to produce sustainable extraordinary resource than physical assets. Path-dependent resources are created over a long period of time. They are created because of the route that the firm took to get to where it is today. The history of some firms gives them the idiosyncratic attributes that make them unique. Only they can offer the qualities demanded by the customer. So, a technology firm may develop an extraordinary resource in the creation and exploitation of breakthroughs in a scientific discipline. It is the long history of sequentially overcoming scientific barriers by a tight knit group of scientists that provides the firm with superior knowledge and capabilities leading to products that are cutting-edge. Competitors may try to imitate by hiring hundreds of scientists and providing them with vast financial resources, but the new team will lack the long-term perspective, coherence and tacit knowledge of the established team. It takes a long time to develop strong and loyal networks of relationships with suppliers and customers. For example, SABMiller plc is now in a strong position because, over many decades, it worked with suppliers and customers to make the distribution of beer possible in difficult circumstances. Brand name recognition is usually path-dependent. Kellogg's and Heinz have taken over a century to establish themselves in the psyche of consumers. An imitator would find this very difficult to break. Coca-Cola's brand name recognition will not be replicated simply by a rival spending vast sums on marketing. Consumers have long experience of drinking Coke, and their association of the drink with every stage of their lives means that they have a path-dependent attachment to it. This presents a deep moat to rivals.

- **Causal ambiguity**. By this is meant uncertainty over what the extraordinary resource is or how it was created. There are two types of causal ambiguity. The first is where the potential imitator is unable to see clearly which resource is giving the sustainable competitive advantage. The second is where it is difficult to identify the way in which the extraordinary resource was created in the first place: the recipe is not obvious. If the sustainable competitive advantage is created by a single skill, relationship or capability then rivals will usually find it relatively easy to understand the causal mechanism leading to market-place success and abnormally high rates of return on capital used. However, in many cases the competitive advantage relies on a complex set of interacting factors and it is very difficult to disentangle the key elements that create resources and to identify those resources that raise the firm above competitive parity.

  With Google, it is possible to observe the extraordinary resources; therefore, the first type of causal ambiguity is no problem. Google has created a working environment that produces a stream of well-designed innovations. While a rival can observe that Google has these extraordinary resources, it cannot figure out how those resources were created in the first place.

  A multitude of factors embedded in the company's culture, personal interactions of employees, attitudes and skills base enter the melting pot to produce the special something. It is usually the case that the firm with the causally ambiguous extraordinary resources does not itself understand what it is that gives it an advantage. If it did become obvious to those working for the company then rivals would be able to imitate it by hiring away the well-placed knowledgeable managers. The most common reason for causal ambiguity is that the firm's resources are the result of complex social phenomena. The unique formal and informal social structures and interactions develop in that one environment (e.g. Facebook).

- **Economic deterrence**. Rivals may be able to imitate but choose not to do so because they fear the consequences. For example, some industries consist of a few firms operating with very high fixed (and often sunk) costs in large-scale plant. A potential entrant could build a similar massive plant but that would add a lot of additional supply to the market and result in depressed prices. Furthermore, the existing players often have assets specific to that industry – they cannot be redeployed in another industry. The incumbents therefore offer a very credible threat of retaliation to a new rival, as they are quite prepared, at least in the short run, to sell the product at a very low price.

Appropriability

The resource that is supplying value must be one that allows *the company* to capture the value, rather than allowing it to be captured by another organisation or individual(s). In other words, the value is appropriable by the shareholders. For example, films that are successful at the box office are often financially damaging to the studios. The leading actors are able to bargain for such high fees that they leave little for the company. A similar phenomenon occurs in sport where the clubs fail to hold on to the revenue generated as players appropriate a substantial proportion – witness all the loss-making football clubs as players receive thousands of pounds for every game. In investment banking 'star' mergers and acquisition specialists, equity underwriters and bond managers can ask for multimillion-dollar remuneration packages, siphoning off much (or all) of the value they create.

This distribution-of-rewards question will be resolved in favour of the company if it, rather than an external party, owns the property rights to the critical resource. For a company like Disney the critical resources are owned by the organisation – Snow White, the reputation for family orientated entertainment, library of movies, etc. – therefore the company will gain from the exploitation of the resource. From time to time a brilliant director, manager or 'imaginateer' will be found in the organisation, but the value that these individuals can pull away will be small beer compared with the organisation in its entirety.

Another factor influencing appropriability is the degree of bargaining power. The firm's negotiating position will be enhanced if the supplier of a critical resource is one among many – then the company can shop around. (In contrast, Intel and Microsoft are able to appropriate much of the value created by PCs. The manufacturers of PCs battle it out in a fierce market, while these two companies coin it in. However, this may change as ARM chips catch on and mobile systems start to dominate.) Also, if the critical resource owner has few or no alternative uses for the skill, capability, knowledge or whatever, then the company may be able to lower the cost of buying that resource.

Sometimes firms seem to give away the value derived from resources. Perhaps, they come under pressure to pay out the supernormal profits by making excessive payments for inputs. The major European telecommunication firms, such as British Telecom, Deutsche Telekom and France Telecom, saw that high revenues could be expected by developing third-generation (3G) mobile telephone networks. They were right: value was created by this new technology. What is doubtful is whether much of this value was appropriated by the telecommunications companies. They paid over £80 billion to various European governments for licences to set up networks. They then spent the same amount again to build the networks. It is hotly debated as to whether most of the value created by 3G was captured by governments, consumers and equipment suppliers, with little or nothing going to the operators.

Investment in resources

The investor needs to investigate whether the firm is continuing to invest in its resource base. If it is reporting high current earnings because it is running down the resource base, then the shares should be avoided. A good company needs to maintain an approach of dynamic evolution with regard to its extraordinary resources. It has to recognise that it faces a never-ending struggle for competitive advantage. The firm can never rest from continually trying to offer better service to customers if it is to retain a large gap between price charged and cost. If it does not have this sense of urgency, then rivals will soon take action to erode its advantage.

The resources of a firm have been likened to water in a bathtub. The water represents the current stock of resources. Unfortunately, there is a continual leakage from the bottom as resources depreciate (knowledge becomes less relevant, capabilities decline or reputations and brands become less appealing). It is necessary to continually pump in more to maintain the future value to be generated from a sustainable competitive advantage. Failure to spend more to top up the resource base (e.g. by not advertising the brand or by cutting R&D) is perfectly possible for a number of years. Profits will receive a short-term boost. But eventually the tub runs out of water – the company has no extraordinary resources to offer customers. It is condemned to either limp along with low returns or head for corporate death.

Changing the metaphor might help to see what a truly good company looks like. Companies can be viewed as organisations existing in a Darwinian ecology of survival of the fittest and natural selection. Those that have reached the top have created extraordinary resources that enable them to dominate and exploit their part of the ecosystem. They have developed superior ways of doing things. Their capabilities, knowledge, attitudes, etc., have allowed them to survive when less well-endowed rivals failed. But the business world is susceptible to much more rapid change than the biological one. If the company becomes too rigid in relying on the ways of doing things that have stood it in good stead for much of its history then it becomes vulnerable to competitors who are better able to adapt to environmental change, ranging from new technology to social trends. Entire species of companies will die unless they adapt. Some are aware enough, and able enough, to respond; others die, sometimes slowly, sometimes quickly, but usually mystified as to why they are being outcompeted when they used to be so strong.

Leveraging resources and over-exploiting them

Some companies have a powerful ability to leverage their resources into other segments or industries. For example, Disney has leveraged its characters into theme parks, promotions at McDonald's, websites and elsewhere.

Many resources not fully utilised in their original settings offer terrific opportunities for being applied to other fields. For example, a firm may have developed strong relationships and/or reputations with customers, governments and suppliers. These could be used by other parts of the organisation at little additional cost and without impairing the resource. Likewise brands may be used for a wider range of products (e.g. chocolate bar brand used for ice cream). Or knowledge could be leveraged (e.g. the use of technological innovation in more than one business sector). Or coordination of marketing strategies could create value (e.g. a film division might use music from the back catalogues of the music division).

The investor needs to watch out for companies diversifying beyond their extraordinary resource base. Between 1958 and 1974 BIC Pen Corporation had a great time leveraging its resources. It had the extraordinary resources of capability and knowledge in plastic injection moulding, mass marketing and a reputation through its strong brand. It leveraged from disposable pen production to disposable lighters and then to razors. This leveraging went well because the new product lines could make good use of all three of BIC's extraordinary resources. Then, in 1974 it made a mistake. It entered the hosiery market. None of the extraordinary resources were any use at all in producing or selling stockings. Their plastic manufacturing capability was not relevant, the product sold through completely different outlets, and marketing a fashion item required a different approach than selling disposable pens, lighters and razors.

Also watch out for companies over-exploiting a resource. Gucci is a company that realises that one of its key resources is its rarity value. It is careful not to grow too big or to stretch the brand too far. Instead of increasing volume it has added new rarity value brands: Yves Saint Laurent, Boucheron, Sergio Rossi and Alexander McQueen. Gucci had learnt the hard way that over-exploitation of a brand is both possible and potentially fatal. In the 1980s it launched an aggressive strategy of rapid sales growth. It added lower priced goods to its product line and started to sell through department stores and duty-free shops. Its name appeared on a host of products, from sunglasses to perfumes. Sales soared but its image fell, along with sales of its up-market products, reducing overall profitability.

Concluding comments

The investor has quite a long list of factors to consider when trying to identify companies with durable extraordinary resources in an industry with high returns. However, you should not be daunted. A two-stage approach will ease the burden. The first stage is designed to create a short-list of candidates for more in-depth analysis in the second stage. Simply read the financial press on a regular basis, looking out for key phrases that connect with the factors under the TRRACK system. So if you read 'XYZ plc has a dominant market position because of its strong brand' you would recognise that this fits the 'reputation' heading. Cut out the article and place it in a file to be researched later. Also, try to memorise the companies in your short-list file so that you can look out for other articles on them.

The second stage (possibly months or years after the first) is to confirm that the company has the characteristics you are looking for: a presence in an industry with high sustainable returns on capital; at least one durable extraordinary resource; and a management that is competent, honest and reliably shareholder-orientated? Information from many sources needs to be tapped. The Internet can be great for this. Company websites and specialist financial sites, such as www.advfn.co.uk, can provide mountains of information. Newspaper websites, such as www.ft.com, will provide articles going back several years. The annual reports of rival companies will also be on the Internet.

If the written information does not put you off, then you might want to see the management face to face. By buying a small number of shares you will be invited to the AGM of the company where you will hear the directors explain their actions and their future plans – you can even question them (after all, they are the shareholders' servants). If you really want to make sure you have dotted all the i's and crossed all the t's you could attend trade shows or go and talk to the firm's competitors, suppliers and customers to build up a detailed picture of the company's strengths and weaknesses.

Given the amount of time and effort required to invest (rather than speculate), the great investors suggest that we do not try to analyse and subsequently keep track of dozens of companies. If we do, we will never attain the required level of depth of knowledge on any of them. On the other hand, retort thousands of professional investors trained in portfolio theory, it is essential to be well diversified so that if some investments turn south you are protected. By this they generally mean at least 20 holdings, possibly 40. The great investors reply that this approach merely results in diversification to mediocrity, and the biggest threat to investor wealth is the failure to understand the companies they own a part of.

'Analysing' 40 companies means not understanding any of them. Besides, if the fund managers cared to look at the research on portfolio theory they would find that the vast majority of the benefits of diversification (lower portfolio volatility) occur up to a diversification level of five or ten shares. Going from ten to 40 shares has very little effect on volatility, but there is a heavy price to be paid – in terms of moving from buying on intelligence to buying on ignorance.

On top of that we have the phenomenon of **diminishing marginal attractiveness**. Imagine listing all the shares you could buy in order of attractiveness. At the top of the list would go a company in whose prospects and management you feel very confident, and whose share price is well below your calculation of intrinsic value. The next share is very attractive, but not as great as the top one, and so on. The great investors ask: what is the point in investing significant sums in the 40th share on your list when you could move up the diminishing marginal attractiveness curve and buy more of the top five? None of the great investors suggests that we should put all our money in just one or two shares, but they agree that most private investors are unlikely to be able to investigate, understand and follow up the story on more than five to ten companies.

Further reading

Some of the issues discussed in this chapter are explained in more depth in David Collis and Cynthia Montgomery, *Corporate Strategy*, 2nd edn (McGraw-Hill, 2005). Another useful book is John Kay, *Foundations of Corporate Success,* 2nd edn (Oxford University Press, 1993). You could read about this form of analysis in a broader context of disciplined investing in Glen Arnold, *The Financial Times Guide to Value Investing* (Financial Times Prentice Hall, 2009).

part

4

Managing your portfolio

16

Companies issuing shares

Occasionally there are opportunities to buy shares directly from the company, rather than from existing shareholders. The company may be floating its shares for the first time on the stock market and offering new shares to outsiders to, say, raise money for future growth – called a **'new issue'** or **'initial public offering'** (**IPO**). Alternatively, firms that have been on the stock market for some time may need to raise more money for expansion or to replace debt financing (**seasoned equity offerings, SEO**). This can be achieved by selling new shares to existing shareholders in a **rights issue**. Or the company may offer its shares to outsiders in a **placing** or **open offer**. On the other hand, there are times when the directors believe the company has too much equity capital and the best thing to do with the surplus cash is to return it to shareholders by buying in some of their shares.

This chapter will help you to understand the process of new issues, rights issues, other share sales, scrip issues and share buy-backs. It will alert you to the pitfalls and tackle the bewildering jargon associated with this area of investment.

New issues

In a typical week two or three companies obtain a quotation for their shares on the Main Market or the Alternative Investment Market (AIM) of the London Stock Exchange. This is often referred to as companies **'going public'**. This term is accurate in the sense that the shares will now be available to a much wider range of people. But it may mislead if it is thought that the companies are changing their status from **private limited companies** ('Ltd') to **public limited companies** ('plc'). There are many thousands of plcs that choose not to float on the stock market. Being plcs they can, under the law, offer their shares to a wider range of investors than private limited companies. However, plc status on its own does not mean there is a secondary market in the shares on a regulated exchange.

If you are a shareholder in an unquoted plc you will probably find it difficult to sell your shares when you want to. This is one reason why some plcs choose to have their shares quoted on an exchange – it allows existing shareholders to liquidate their holdings (or simply to value their shares). Another reason is to raise money to grow the business.

The sponsor

The United Kingdom Listing Authority (UKLA), a division of the Financial Conduct Authority, is responsible for approval of the prospectuses and admission of companies to the Official List (most of which are on the Main Market of the London Stock Exchange (LSE), although ISDX may also admit Official List companies to its Main Board). The LSE has to separately admit companies to its Main Market. Thus a floating company has to go through two parallel processes: (a) gain a 'listing' with the UKLA; and (b) admission to trading on the Main Market.

When the directors decide it is time to *float* the company they will quickly realise that they lack the expertise needed to bring the project to fruition. They need the help of a number of specialists. The key adviser is the sponsor. This may be an investment bank, stockbroker or other professional adviser (e.g. accountant) approved by the UKLA.

The sponsor (sometimes called the **issuing house**) will discuss with the directors the nature of the business and the aspirations of the management team. They will be probing to see if flotation really is the most suitable route for the company to take. The sponsor usually has a high reputation in the City and will be putting this reputation on the line if it recommends a company to investors – sponsors regularly drop unsuitable companies. One of the key things the sponsor will examine is the management team. There must be a good mixture of talents, rather than reliance on one individual. The sponsor may even – quite forcefully – recommend additional directors, supplementing the team to bring it up to the required standard.

The sponsor will also make sure the company complies with the usual rule of having three years of accounting figures.[1] Another key rule is that the company

---

[1] This rule is relaxed for scientific research-based companies on techMARK, those undertaking major capital projects and those seeking a 'standard listing' – see Chapter 3.

is willing to allow at least 25 per cent of the share capital to be in public hands.[2] Additional tasks for the sponsor include drawing up a timetable for the flotation, advising on the method of flotation (e.g. placing or offer for sale) and coordinating the activities of a raft of other professional advisers involved in the project.

The prospectus

The most important document in the process is the prospectus. The sponsor helps to draft this alongside the directors (who carry ultimate responsibility for its accuracy). It is designed to reveal a lot of facts about the company to investors. It will probably contain far more information about the firm than it has previously dared to put into the public domain. The UKLA lays down stringent requirements for the content of the prospectus. Even without these the company has an interest in producing a stylish and informative document as it acts as a marketing tool to attract investors.

When examining a prospectus, bear in mind the following:

■ A trading record of three years is the minimum requirement, but you will often be presented with detailed accounts going back five years. Examine these carefully – Chapters 11, 12 and 13 of this book should help.

■ Consider the information given about the growth trajectory of the company. Look at its history, its current position and the, no doubt rosy, picture painted by the directors of its prospects. Do you share their optimism about the industry and about this company's competitive strength within the industry?

■ If the company is selling new shares, does it have a sound strategy for spending the money it raises? Or does it sound vague, using phrases such as 'we are raising funds to exploit future business opportunities' or to 'provide working capital'. It could be that the directors are primarily interested in growing the business for themselves (higher status, salaries, etc.) rather than for shareholders and they see a chance of persuading gullible investors to part with their money.

■ All businesses face risks. The writing of the prospectus should have forced the directors to think about and list the risks facing the firm. For example, is the firm heavily dependent on one customer? Does it rely too much on overdrafts rather than long-term loans? Does it have too much debt? Are its sales vulnerable to political change in a volatile part of the world? To

---

[2] This is for a 'premium' listing, which is the normal quality associated with the Main Market – see Chapter 3.

allow investors to assess these risks, the prospectus will lay out details on types of debt (e.g. repayment at short notice or after two, five and 10 years, bank loans versus bonds, currency of interest and capital payments) and state whether there is sufficient working capital. Also all major contracts entered into in the past two years will be detailed. Analysis of sales by geographic area and category of activity will help you assess the riskiness of the businesses, as will the information on research and development and significant investments in other companies. Statements by experts are usually required: valuers confirm the valuation of property, engineers comment on the viability of processes or machinery, accountants comment on profit figures. As a further safeguard, the prospectus is required to bring to the attention of potential shareholders any risk element apparent to the directors or sponsors that has not already been disclosed.

■ Who owns the shares in the company? Is there a dominant shareholder? To help you here, the rule is that all persons holding more than 3 per cent have to be named.

■ Is the dividend policy acceptable to you? Some companies (e.g. hi-tech firms) have a policy of ploughing back all the money generated (if there is any) and so won't pay dividends for some years.

■ Examine the information given on the directors' and senior managers' backgrounds and reward systems. Which other companies have they worked for? Have they set up a number of companies and abandoned them when they faltered? How many were liquidated? How much are they being paid? Are pay and performance linked in a way that means that they do well only if shareholders are doing well? Does the company do business with another company owned by one or more of the directors (e.g. renting a factory owned by a private company associated with a director)?

Finding out about new issues

Each week the *Financial Times* and the *Investors Chronicle* discuss companies that are due to float in the following months. Both the *Financial Times* and *Investors Chronicle* display statistics of recently completed new issues (an example is shown in Box 16.1). The website of the London Stock Exchange (www.londonstockexchange.com) carries details on the new issues. Other websites concerned with new issues include www.morningstar.co.uk, www.iii.co.uk, www.proactiveinvestors.co.uk and www.allipo.com.

Brokers usually offer a new issues service. You will be sent details of all new issues which your broker is willing to apply for. (Many new issues are only open to large

---

New issue tables in the *Financial Times*

UK RECENT EQUITY ISSUES

issue date	issue price p	Sector	Stock code	Stock	Close price p	+/-	High	Low	Mkt cap (£m)
22/1	§7.3	AIM	LENL	Leyshon Energy	6.25	-0.38	6.63	5.65	15.6
17/1	§60	AIM	CFHL	Cityfibre	64.25	0.25	66.25	64	33.6
9/1	§-	-		Conygar	104	-0.50	104.75	104	31.2
5/1	§100	AIM	RM2	RM2 Int	85.50	-1	101	85.50	270.4
28/12	0.7	AIM	KOD	Kodal Minerals	1.15	0.03	2.70	0.78	7.7
23/12	§64	AIM	AHCG	Action Hotels	62	0.50	65	60.50	91.5
17/12	§§10	-	ATMA	Atlas Mara ‡	681.69	14.82	789.68	628	5.1
8/12	70	AIM	JQW	JQW	68	-	76.50	59.50	131.6
8/12	100	-	CCDS	Nationwide Building £120		-	£120	£109	660.0
8/12	100	-	BBOX	Tritax Big Box	104.88	-	105	100.50	209.8
3/12	§62	AIM	SYQ	Syqic	61	-1.50	83	61	14.2
2/12	18	-	SERV	Servelec Grp	233	-1.75	245	207	159.2
28/11	§79	AIM	KLBT	Kalibrate Tech	95.50	-	115.50	82	31.7
26/11	§80	AIM	MCON	Mincon Group	84.25	2.25	84.25	77.25	174.8
25/11	§135	AIM	GAME	Gameaccount Network	176.50	-	178.50	138.50	97.7
20/11	§210	AIM	BON	Bonmarche Holdings	275.50	-13.50	289	220.50	137.8
15/11	§22.6	AIM	EUSP	EU Supply	27.50	-0.75	28.25	21.50	15.9
12/11	225	-	JRG	Just Retirement ‡	240	-9.25	253.25	185	366.1
12/11	§60	-	RSTR	Rightster Group	73	-	83.50	42	85.0
12/11	$9.5	-	SNGR	Romgaz R	601.41	-0.30	678.05	593.61	347.7
7/11	§83	AIM	GWIN	Gowin New Energy	6.75	0.13	16	5.63	23.2

§Placing price. * Introduction. ‡ When issued. Annual report/prospectus available, see London Shares Page. For a full explanation of all other symbols please refer to London Share Service notes.

Source: Financial Times, www.ft.com, 24 January 2014.

buyers, such as pension funds and insurance companies. However, brokers are allowed to collate small-investor applications and then buy shares in bulk in the same way as an institution.)

Underwriting

The sponsor generally **underwrites** the issue. In return for a fee, underwriters guarantee to buy any shares not taken up by the market. This is a kind of insurance for the company – come what may, it will raise the money it needs to fulfil its strategic objectives. The sponsor generally charges a fee of 2–4 per cent of the issue proceeds and then pays part of that fee, say 1.25–3.0 per cent, to *sub-underwriters* (usually large financial institutions) who each agree to buy a certain number of shares if called on to do so. In the vast majority of cases the underwriters do not have to purchase any shares and so walk away with thousands or millions of pounds in fees. However, there are occasional flops when they are forced to buy shares no one else wants, resulting in the shares **overhanging** the market. Attempts have been made by some companies to go below the standard 2–4 per cent cost of underwriting but the majority continue to accept this as the going rate. It is a 'nice little earner' for the City institutions, and they like to keep it that way.

The role of the corporate broker

Brokers play a vital role in advising on share market conditions and the likely demand from investors for the company's shares. They also represent the company to investors to try to generate interest. When debating issues such as the method to be employed, the marketing strategy, the size of the issue, the timing or the pricing of the shares, the company may value the market knowledge the broker has to offer. Brokers can also organise sub-underwriting, and in the years following the flotation may work with the company to maintain a liquid and properly informed market in its shares. Brokers also help with subsequent share issues (e.g. rights issues). When a broker is employed as a sponsor the two roles can be combined. If the sponsor is an investment bank, the UKLA requires that a broker also be appointed.

Methods of flotation

The sponsor will look at the motives for wanting a quotation, at the amount of money that is to be raised, at the history and reputation of the firm, and will then advise on the best method of issuing the shares. There are various methods, ranging from a full-scale offer for sale to a relatively simple introduction. The final choice often rests on the costs of the method of issue, which can vary considerably. Here are the main options:

- **Offer for sale**. The company sponsor offers shares to the public by inviting subscriptions from institutional and individual investors. Sometimes newspapers carry a prospectus and an application form. However, most investors will need to contact the sponsor or the broker to obtain an application form. Normally the shares are offered at a *fixed price* determined by the company's directors and their financial advisers. A variation of this method is an **offer for sale by tender**. Here investors are invited to state a price at which they are willing to buy (above a minimum reserve price). The sponsor gathers the applications and then selects a price which will dispose of all the shares – the strike price. Investors bidding a price at or above this will be allocated shares at the strike price – not at the price of their bid. Those who bid below the strike price will not receive any shares. This method is useful in situations where it is very difficult to value a company – for instance, where there is no comparable company already listed or where the level of demand may be difficult to assess. Many investors are put off offers for sale by tender because they do not want the onerous task of estimating the share's value. (This happened in the case of Google.com in 2004 which received fewer applications than expected in a type of auction system.)

■ **Introduction**. Introductions do not raise any new money for the company. If the company's shares are already quoted on another stock exchange or there is a wide spread of shareholders, with more than 25 per cent of the shares in public hands, the Stock Exchange permits a company to be 'introduced' to the market. This method may allow companies trading on AIM to move up to the Main Market or foreign corporations to gain a London listing. This is the cheapest method of flotation since there are no underwriting costs and relatively small advertising expenditures.

■ **Placing**. In a placing, shares are offered to the public but the term 'public' is narrowly defined. Instead of engaging in advertising to the population at large, the sponsor or broker handling the issue sells the shares to a select group of institutions such as pension and insurance funds. The costs of this method are considerably lower than those of an offer for sale. There are lower publicity and legal costs. A drawback of this method is that the spread of shareholders is going to be more limited. To alleviate this problem the Stock Exchange does insist on large number of placees holding shares after the new issue. In the 1980s the most frequently used method of new issue was the offer for sale. This ensured a wide spread of share ownership and thus a more liquid secondary market. It also permitted all investors to participate in new issues. Placings were only permitted for small offerings when the costs of an offer for sale would have been prohibitive. Today any size of new issue can be placed. As this method is much cheaper and easier than an offer for sale, companies have naturally switched to placings. The majority now choose to use the placing method, thus excluding small investors from most new issues.

■ **Intermediaries offer**. This method is often combined with a placing. Shares are offered for sale to financial institutions such as stockbrokers. Clients of these intermediaries can then apply to buy shares from them. Thus small investors can participate.

■ **Reverse takeover.** Sometimes a larger unquoted company makes a deal with a smaller quoted company whereby the smaller company 'takes over' the larger firm by swapping newly created shares in itself for the shares in the unquoted firm currently held by its owners. Because the quoted firm creates and issues more new shares itself than it had to start with the unquoted firm's shareholders end up with the majority of the shares in the newly merged entity. They therefore now control a quoted company. The only task remaining is to decide on a name for the company – frequently the name of the previously unquoted company is chosen. A reverse takeover is a way for a company to gain a listing/quotation without the hassle of an official new issue. An example is shown in Article 16.1.

Article 16.1

Trinity to test Aim oil venture appetite

By Michael Kavanagh

Trinity Exploration & Production is set to become the first company this year to test the fragile appetite among investors for new oil ventures.

The privately held company plans to join London's junior market in February by effectively reversing into Bayfield Energy, a junior oil explorer that also holds assets in fields across Trinidad and Tobago in the Caribbean.

Shares in Bayfield, which raised £54m when it was quoted on Aim in July last year, were suspended in October, after it announced its intention to merge with Trinity in a deal that valued it at £45m.

Under the terms of the deal, Trinity's shareholders will take up a 55 per cent share of the combined company while Bayfield's shareholders will get 45 per cent of the equity.

Yesterday Trinity confirmed plans for the merged company to be readmitted to Aim under its new moniker.

■ **Book-building.** Selling new issues of shares through book-building is a popular technique in the USA, and is catching on in Europe. Under this method the financial advisers to an issue contact major institutional investors to get from them bids for the shares. The investors' orders are sorted according to price, quantity and other factors such as 'firmness' of bid (e.g. 'we will buy regardless of market conditions'). This information may then be used to establish a price for the issue and the placing of shares.

Timetable for a new offer

The various stages of a new issue will be explained using the example of the flotation of Royal Mail on the Main Market in 2013.

Pre-launch preparation

Royal Mail was separated from the Post Office many years ago, but remained in state ownership. Vince Cable, business secretary, said the privatisation was motivated by giving Royal Mail access to the private capital it needs to modernise (and it raised cash for the Treasury). Despite the doubts over the growth potential of letters it was thought that parcel delivery would be a good bet on the back of online shopping. The government prepared for the sale by freeing 90 per cent of the business from price controls (second class stamp prices are still regulated) and by ensuring that the enormous pension obligations stay with the state. The chief executive, Moya Greene, was appointed three years earlier, with a brief to modernise, and permission to raise prices and profit margins. Pre-tax profit rose 60 per cent at £324 million in the previous year. To counter opposition from unions the government decided to give 10 per cent of the shares free to the workers.

Advisers

In December 2012 Royal Mail appointed three investment banks to advise it – Barclays, Bank of America Merrill Lynch and Goldman Sachs – with their first task being to sound out investing institutions to assist with government decision making on the form and timing of a future sale.

In May 2013 the tender process for an IPO syndicate was underway: Royal Mail began the 'beauty parade' (asking for presentations and proposals) to pick the lead banks as advisers and bookrunners. They selected UBS, Investec, Nomura and RBC to work with the original three. Lazard advised the government and Rothschild was hired solely to explore raising a syndicate of banks to provide financing to Royal Mail prior to the float.

The sponsors and advisers worked on details such as drawing up an accountant's report, the price and method of issue, and organising underwriting. They also had many contacts with investing institutions which helped to drum up demand (that is one of the reasons so many banks were involved). Between six weeks and one week before impact day the sponsors were required to show all the documents to the UKLA for approval.

Preparation to float – several weeks before impact day

On 12 September 2013 it was announced that at least 41 per cent of its shares would be sold off or given away. There were three parts to the sale: (1) an offer to institutions, (2) free shares for Royal Mail employees, and (3) an allocation to a retail offer.

The public were to be able to buy shares in the 'retail offer', through stockbrokers and direct from the government via a special website, where investors could read documentation, register their interest, apply for shares using a debit card, or download and print out an application form. Also, documents and application packs were available at larger post offices, and it was possible to fill in a form and post a cheque. The minimum application size was £750 for members of the public and £500 for employees, who had priority if they wanted to buy extra shares. The estimated market capitalisation of Royal Mail was about £3 billion. As a further enticement it announced a planned final dividend in July 2014 of £133 million.

In the Autumn the directors went on a **roadshow** with their financial advisers – they made presentations to institutional investors at various locations. Roadshows are important not just for marketing the issue, but because they allow sponsors to gather information from investors, such as their opinions of the company and its valuation.

Pathfinder prospectus

On 27 September 2013 the pathfinder prospectus was published and the price range was set at 260p to 330p per share, valuing Royal Mail at between £2.6 billion and £3.3 billion. This is not a firm expectation of the sale price, but a 'test the water' type of price announcement. As a result of the book-building period through late September and early October the book builders built up a picture of what demand was likely to be at different prices.

The government now said it would sell between 40.1 per cent and 52.2 per cent, plus a further 7.8 per cent if demand was high, in addition to the 10 per cent going free to staff.

By 4 October 2013, because of the apparent strong demand, the government was exploring whether it could extract a higher price. They lifted the bottom of the suggested price range to 300p but key institutional investors signalled they would drop out if they had to pay more than 330p a share. The government did not want the 'disaster' of investors experiencing a drop in price immediately after purchasing so they erred on the side of caution and kept the price low.

Impact day

The full prospectus is published on impact day, together with the price in a fixed price offer for sale. In this case the government retained flexibility in pricing to the end, waiting until after receiving all the applications. The final date for receipt of offers was Tuesday 8 October 2013.

(In an offer for sale at a fixed price, up to two weeks is needed for investors to consider the offer price and send in payments. There is a fixed cut-off date for applications. In the case of a placing/book-building the time needed is much shorter as the share buyers have already indicated their interest to the sponsors and managers, and transactions can be expedited between City institutions.)

Vince Cable said on Wednesday 9 October there had been 700,000 individual retail applications – which were seven times oversubscribed. Institutions had placed orders for more than £30 billion of shares. Such a figure had little meaning because institutions, realising demand was heavy, had ramped up orders in the hope of winning just a proportion of them. Only 368 of Royal Mail's 150,000 workers declined the offer of free shares in the company.

Allotment

Investors applied for many more shares than were on offer. The shares are allocated by the sponsors in a placing/book-building depending on commitments made in the book-building process. In an offer for sale, allocation can be achieved in a number of different ways. A **ballot** means that only some investors receive shares (recipients are selected at random). In a **scaledown** applicants generally receive some shares, but fewer than they applied for. A cut-off point might be used in which applicants for large quantities are excluded.

The government confirmed the price for Royal Mail shares was 330p, valuing it at £3.3 billion. Retail investors got 33 per cent of the shares on offer, up on the 30 per cent originally planned, while institutional investors got 67 per cent. All members of the public who applied for the minimum £750 up to £10,000 got 227 shares, paying £749.10, but the 5 per cent of applicants who bid above £10,000 got nothing (because it was felt they would not be satisfied with £749.10 and would be more likely to sell quickly). Most institutional investors got no shares at all, including those that bid below 330p. The government favoured stable investors such as pension funds in the allocation, though some hedge funds with a long-term focus also got shares. The government sold 60 per cent of Royal Mail raising nearly £2 billion.

Dealing begins

Formal dealing in the shares started at 8 a.m. on 15 October 2013. Formal dealing means on the Exchange after the shares have been allocated. However, deals had been made between investing institutions in an informal market from 11 October – buying and selling shares they believed they were to receive (a **'grey market'** in shares).

On 15 October the shares soared by a third, adding £1 billion to the company's value but fuelling accusations that the formerly state-owned postal operator had been sold too cheaply. More than 100 million shares were traded in the first hour. During the morning, more than a quarter of all the shares sold by the government changed hands. A month later retail investors were able to sell at around a £500 profit on the £750 put down.

Underpricing and stagging

The company floating is usually keen to have the offer fully taken up by public investors. To have shares left with the underwriters gives the firm a bad image because the company is perceived to have been associated with an issue which 'flopped'. Furthermore, over the following few months, the underwriters will try to offload their shares, and this action has the potential to depress the price for a long time. The sponsor also has an incentive to avoid leaving the underwriters with large blocks of shares. The sponsoring organisation consists of people who are professional analysts and deal makers, and an issue which flops can be very bad for their image. It might indicate that they are not reading the market signals correctly and that they have overestimated demand. They might have done a poor job in assessing the firm's riskiness or failed to communicate its virtues to investors. These bad images can stick, so both the firm and the sponsor have an incentive to err on the side of caution and price a little lower to make sure that the issue will be fully subscribed. A major problem in establishing this **discount** is that in an offer for sale the firm has to decide the price one or two weeks before the close of the offer. In the period between impact day and first trading the market may decline dramatically. This makes potential investors nervous about committing themselves to a fixed price. To overcome this additional risk factor the issue price may have to be significantly less than the expected first day's trading price. Giving this discount to new shares deprives the firm (or its selling shareholders) of money which it might have received in the absence of these uncertainties, and can therefore be regarded as a cost to the firm but an opportunity for buyers in a new issue. They can buy the shares from the company and then sell immediately following receipt. This is called **stagging**.

Stagging for private investors is rarely possible these days as most new issue shares go to institutions in a placing. However, there are occasional opportunities in intermediaries' offers or (rare) offers for sale.

Stagging is not always profitable as many shares fall in price soon after flotation (e.g. Debenhams, Ocado and Facebook).

How does an AIM flotation differ from one on the Official List?

The AIM's rules are kept as relaxed as possible to encourage a wide variety of companies to join and keep costs of membership and capital raising to a minimum. However, it is felt necessary to have some vetting process for firms wishing to float on the AIM. This policing role was given to **nominated advisers** who are paid a fee by the company to act as unofficial 'sponsors' in investigating and verifying its financial health. When the nominated adviser's fee is added to those of the stock exchange, accountants, lawyers, printers and so on, the cost can be as much as 10–40 per cent of the amount being raised. The AIM was designed so that the cost of joining was in the region of £40,000–£50,000. But this figure has now risen so that frequently more than £500,000 is paid. Most of the additional cost is for raising funds by selling newly created shares rather than just joining the AIM, which costs about £100,000 to £200,000. The nominated advisers argue that they are forced to charge firms higher fees because they incur more investigatory costs due to the emphasis put on their policing role by the Stock Exchange.

Rights issues

A rights issue is an invitation to existing shareholders to purchase additional shares in the company. This is a very popular method of raising new funds. It is easy and relatively cheap (compared with new issues). Directors are not required to seek the prior consent of shareholders,[3] and the London Stock Exchange will only intervene in larger issues (to adjust the timing so that the market does not suffer from too many issues in one period). The UK has particularly strong

---

[3] However, there may not be enough authorised share capital to permit the issue of more shares. In this case the company needs to convene an Annual General Meeting or an Extraordinary General Meeting (EGM) to increase the authorised share capital. Directors also need the authority to allot shares from the shareholders. Companies will also need to publish a prospectus which must be vetted by the UKLA for listed firms (time-consuming and expensive – it can take two or three months for planning, writing documents, verification and legal processes) whereas for placings (see below) the whole process can be completed in about a week.

traditions and laws concerning **pre-emption rights**. These require a company raising new equity capital by selling shares to offer those shares to the existing shareholders first. The owners of the company are entitled to subscribe for the new shares in proportion to their existing holding. This will enable them to maintain their existing percentage ownership of the company – the only difference is that each slice of the company cake is bigger because it has more financial resources under its control.

The shares are usually offered at a significantly discounted price from the market value of the current shares – typically 10–40 per cent. This gives the illusion that shareholders are getting a bargain. But, as we shall see, the benefit from the discount given is taken away by a decline in value of the old shares.

Shareholders can either buy these shares themselves or sell the 'right' to buy to another investor. For further reassurance that the firm will raise the anticipated finance, rights issues are usually underwritten by financial institutions.

Shareholders will receive Provisional Allotment Letters (PALs), which are temporary documents of title showing each shareholder the number of new shares they can apply for. To accept, the shareholder fills in and returns the PAL with a cheque or banker's draft for the full amount. They have 10 business days to do this.

Example

Take the case of the imaginary listed company, Getbigger plc, with 100 million shares in issue. It wants to raise £25 million for expansion but does not want to borrow it. Given that its existing shares are quoted on the stock market at 120p, the new rights shares will have to be issued at a lower price to appeal to shareholders because there is a risk of the market share price falling in the period between the announcement and the purchasing of new shares. The offer must remain open for at least two weeks (10 working days) to allow shareholders time to decide whether to buy the new shares and send in payment. During that time there is a greater risk of the market price falling below the rights issue price if they are close together to start with. Getbigger has decided that the £25 million will be obtained by issuing 25 million shares at 100p each. Thus the ratio of new shares to old is 25:100. In other words, this issue is a 'one-for-four' rights issue. Each shareholder will be offered one new share for every four already held. The discount on these new shares is 20p or 16.7 per cent of £1.20.

If the market price before the issue is 120p, valuing the entire company at £120 million and another £25 million is pumped into the company by selling 25 million shares at £1, it logically follows that the market price after the rights issue cannot remain at 120p (assuming all else equal). A company that was previously valued at £120 million which then adds £25 million of value to itself (in the form of cash) should be worth £145 million. This company now has 125 million shares, therefore each share is worth £1.16 (i.e. £145 million divided by 125 million shares).

An alternative way of calculating the *ex-rights* price is as follows:

Four existing shares at a price of 120p	480p
One new share for cash at 100p	100p
Value of five shares	580p
Value of one share ex-rights = 580p/5	116p
Investors call this the theoretical ex-rights price, TERP	

Shareholders have experienced a decline in the price of their old shares from 120p to 116p. A fall of this magnitude necessarily follows from the introduction of new shares at a discounted price. However, the loss is exactly offset by the gain in share value on the new rights issue shares. They cost 100p but have a market price of 116p. This can be illustrated through the example of Sid, who owned 100 shares worth £120 prior to the rights announcement. Sid loses £4 on the old shares – their value is now £116. However, he makes a gain of £4 on the new shares:

Cost of rights shares (25 × £1)	£25
Ex-rights value (25 × £1.16)	£29
Gain	£4

When journalists talk glibly of a rights offer being 'very attractively priced for shareholders' they are generally talking nonsense. Whatever the size of the discount the same value will be removed from the old shares to leave the shareholder no worse or better off. Logically value cannot be handed over to the shareholders from the size of the discount decision. Shareholders own all the company's shares before and after the rights issue – they can't hand value to themselves without also taking value from themselves. Of course, if the prospects for the company's profits rise because it can now make brilliant capital expenditures, which lead to dominant market positions, then the value of shares will rise – for both the old and the new shares. But this is value creation that has nothing to do with the level of the discount.

Article 16.2 discusses a 'rescue rights issue' for a company that got itself into trouble.

Article 16.2

Severfield-Rowen boosted by fund backing

By Mark Wembridge

Severfield-Rowen's balance sheet received a much-needed boost on Friday after shareholders in the lossmaking provider of structural steel overwhelmingly backed a £48m emergency fundraising.

The engineer – whose steel can be found in London's Shard building, the 2012 London Olympic Stadium and the retractable roof over Wimbledon's centre court – said that more than 93 per cent of shareholders had taken up their rights in the deeply discounted placement.

The rights issue was priced at 23p, a 40 per cent discount to Severfield-Rowen's theoretical ex-rights price of 37p, and two-thirds lower than the 71.5p price before the move was announced. Two years ago, Severfield-Rowen shares traded above 330p.

The rights issue, which was underwritten by Jefferies, raised a net £44.8m, which the steel provider will combine with existing cash to pay down its £44m net debt and bolster its balance sheet.

Earlier this year, Severfield-Rowen swung to an annual loss of £23m after announcing three profit warnings in as many months.

The company's finances took a hit of almost £10m after it underquoted in nine contracts including a deal to supply steel to the Cheesegrater, the 225-metre high building designed by Lord Rogers at 122 Leadenhall in the City of London.

Severfield-Rowen shares edged up 2.5 per cent to 41p, valuing the group's equity at £120m.

Source: Wembridge, M. (2013) Severfield-Rowen boosted by fund backing, *Financial Times*, 5 April 2013. © The Financial Times Limited 2013. All Rights Reserved.

What if a shareholder does not want to take up the rights?

As owners of the firm, all shareholders must be treated in the same way. To make sure that some shareholders do not lose out because they are unwilling or unable to buy more shares, the law requires that shareholders have a third choice, other than to buy or not buy the new shares. This is to sell the rights on to someone else on the stock market – **selling the rights nil paid**.

Take the case of the impoverished Sid, who is unable to find the necessary £25. He could sell the rights to subscribe for the shares to another investor and not have to go through the process of taking up any of the shares himself. Indeed, so deeply enshrined are pre-emption rights that even if the shareholder does nothing the company will sell his rights to the new shares on his behalf and send the proceeds to him.[4] Thus, Sid would benefit to the extent of 16p per share or a total of £4 (if the market price stays constant), which adequately compensates for the loss on the 100 shares he holds. But the extent of his control over the company has been reduced – his percentage share of the votes has decreased.

The *value* of a right on one new share is:

Theoretical market value of share ex-rights – Subscription price =
116p – 100p = 16p.

Ex-rights and cum-rights

Old shares bought in the stock market and designated **cum-rights** carry with them the right to subscribe for the new shares in the rights issue. After a cut-off date the old shares go ex-rights, which means that any purchaser of old shares during that period will not have the right to purchase any new shares in the rights issue – they remain with the former shareholder.

The price discount decision

It does not matter greatly whether Getbigger raises £25 million on a one-for-four basis at 100p or on a one-for-three basis at 75p per share, or on some other basis. As Figure 16.1 shows, whatever the basis of the rights issue, the company will receive £25 million and the shareholders will see the price of their old shares decrease, but this will be exactly offset by the value of the rights on the new shares.

Rights basis	Number of new shares (m)	Price of new shares (p)	Total raised (£m)
1 for 4	25	100	25
1 for 3	33.3	75	25
1 for 2	50	50	25
1 for 1	100	25	25

Figure 16.1 **Comparison of different rights bases**

[4] Another possibility is for the shareholder to sell some of the rights to provide finance to purchase the remainder – called 'swallowing the tail'.

However, the ex-rights price will change. For a one-for-three basis it will be £108.75:

Three old shares at 120p	360p
One new share at 75p	75p
Value of four shares	435p
Value of one share = 435p/4	108.75p

If Getbigger chose the one-for-one basis this would be regarded as a **deep-discounted rights issue** (current share price 120p, new shares sold at 25p). With an issue of this sort there is only a minute probability that the market price will fall below the rights offer price and therefore there is almost complete certainty that the offer will be taken up. It seems reasonable to suggest that the underwriting service provided by the institutions is largely redundant here and the firm can make a significant saving. Yet most rights issues are underwritten, sometimes involving 100 sub-underwriters. The underwriting fees used to be a flat 2 per cent of the offer. Of this the issuing house received 0.5 per cent, the broker received 0.25 per cent and the sub-underwriters 1.25 per cent. However, fees have risen recently to around 3 per cent. The underwriters do not always win though – over the past few years many of them have been forced to buy shares when the price of the old shares fell below the discounted right issue shares. Note that a deep discount can sometimes be a disadvantage for private investors – for instance, if they sell the rights nil-paid they may face a capital gains tax bill.

Other equity issues

Some companies argue that the lengthy procedures and expense associated with rights issues (e.g. the time and trouble it takes to get a prospectus prepared and approved by the UKLA) frustrate directors' efforts to take advantage of opportunities in a timely fashion. Firms in the USA have much more freedom to bypass pre-emption rights. They are able to sell blocks of shares to securities houses for distribution elsewhere in the market. This is fast and has low transaction costs. If this were permitted in the UK there would be a concern for existing shareholders: they could experience a dilution of their voting power and/or the shares could be sold at such a low price that a portion of the firm is handed over to new shareholders too cheaply. The UK authorities have produced a compromise, under which firms must obtain shareholders' approval through a **special resolution** (a majority of 75 per cent of those voting) at the company's AGM, or at an EGM, to waive ('disapply') the **pre-emption right**.

Even then the shares must not be sold to outside investors at more than a 5, 7.5 or 10 per cent discount to the share price. While the maximum discount for premium listed Main Market companies under the listing rules is 10 per cent (does not apply to AIM, ISDX companies or standard listed firms) the Association of British Insurers (ABI) guidelines are for a maximum of 5 per cent for placings (see below) and 7.5 per cent for open offers[5] (see below). This is an important condition. It does not make any difference to existing shareholders if new shares are offered at a deep discount to the market price as long as they are offered to them. If external investors get a discount there is a transfer of value from the current shareholders to the new.

Placings and open offers

In **placings**, new shares of companies already quoted are sold directly to a narrow group of external investors, usually without the need for a prospectus,[6] and in one or two days. The institutions, as existing shareholders, have produced guidelines to prevent abuse, which normally allow a placing of only a small proportion of the company's capital – a maximum of 5 per cent in a single year, and no more than 7.5 per cent is to be added to the company's equity capital over a rolling three-year period[7] – in the absence of a **clawback**.

Under clawback, existing shareholders have the right to reclaim the shares as though they were entitled to them under a rights issue. They can buy them at the price they were offered to the external investors. With a clawback the issue becomes an **'open offer'**, although many open offers stand on their own without being linked to a placing. Under an open offer companies can increase their share capital by between 15 per cent and 18 per cent.[8] Beyond that the investors (e.g. ABI) prefer a rights issue. The major difference compared with a rights issue is that if they do not exercise this clawback right they receive no compensation for

---

[5] Even though the ABI rules are targeted primarily at the premium listed Main Market companies the organisation indicates that it 'prefers' that they also apply to AIM and standard listed firms.

[6] If under 10 per cent of equity capital and offered to financial institutions rather than the public.

[7] The National Association of Pension Funds has indicated that it will accept a 10 per cent (one-tenth of current shares) annual disapplication of pre-emption rights for AIM companies and, on a case by case basis, small companies on the Main Market.

[8] The 15–18 per cent rule applies to premium listed Main Market companies and the ABI prefers it to apply to AIM companies, but are merely 'encouraging' its adoption rather than insisting.

any reduction in the price of their existing shares – there are no nil-paid rights to sell.[9]

Shareholders on the share register at the time of the announcement of an open offer will receive a document indicating how many shares they can apply for and a timetable. Shareholders generally have 10 business days (two weeks) to complete application forms and make payments. Trading in the new shares will start a week or so after the final deadline for applications.

The ABI has indicated that it prefers a premium listed company select a rights issue rather than an open offer if the discount is greater than 7.5 per cent. However, the regulations on the Main Market state a cut off at 10 per cent. While this 10 per cent discount off the current share price in a placing and open offer rule does not strictly apply to AIM or PLUS-quoted shares, the main investor groups (e.g. ABI) say AIM companies are encouraged to apply the same restrictions, but recognise that greater flexibility is likely to be justified in the case of smaller companies (they seem to be *ipso facto* equally flexible when it comes to Main Market companies outside of the FTSE All-Share).

Vendor placing

If a company wishes to pay for an asset such as a subsidiary of another firm or an entire company with newly issued shares, but the vendor does not want to hold the shares, the purchaser could arrange for the new shares to be bought by institutional investors for cash. In this way the buyer gets the asset, the vendor (e.g. shareholders in the target company in a merger or takeover) receive cash and the institutional investor makes an investment. There is usually a clawback arrangement for a vendor placing. If the issue is more than 10 per cent of market capitalisation of the acquirer or sold for more than a 5 per cent discount shareholder consent at a meeting is required unless a clawback is offered to shareholders.

Bought deal

Instead of selling shares to investors, companies are sometimes able to make an arrangement with a securities house whereby it buys all the shares being offered for cash. The securities house then sells the shares on to investors included in its

---

[9] However it is possible to structure the open offer in a way that gives compensation to current shareholders who do not buy shares in an open offer. They receive any value above the subscription price achieved by the underwriters in selling those shares not taken up.

distribution network, hoping to make a profit on the deal. Securities houses often compete to buy a package of shares from the company, with the highest bidder winning. The securities houses take the risk of being unable to sell the shares for at least the amount that they paid. Bought deals are limited by the 5 or 10 per cent pre-emption rules.

Scrip issues

Scrip issues do not raise new money: a company simply gives shareholders more shares in proportion to their existing holdings. In theory, the value of each shareholding does not change, because the share price drops in proportion to the additional shares. They are also known as **capitalisation issues** or **bonus issues**. The purpose is to make shares more attractive by bringing down the price. British investors are thought to consider a share price of £10 and above as less attractive than one in single figures. So a company with shares trading at £15 on the market might distribute two 'free' shares for every one held – a two-for-one scrip issue. Since the amount of money in the firm and its economic potential are constant, the share price will theoretically fall to £5.[10] Scrip issues are often regarded as indicating confidence in future earnings increases. If this new optimism is expressed in the share price it may not fall as much as theory would suggest. However, many people are sceptical about the benefits of scrips, especially in light of the transaction costs.

A number of companies have an annual scrip issue while maintaining a constant dividend per share, effectively raising the level of profit distribution. For example, if a company pays a regular dividend of 20p per share but also has a one-for-10 scrip, the annual income will go up by 10 per cent. (A holder of 10 shares who previously received 200p now receives 220p on a holding of 11 shares.)

Scrip dividends are slightly different: shareholders are offered a choice between receiving a cash dividend and receiving additional shares. This is more like a rights issue because the shareholders are making a cash sacrifice if they accept the scrip shares. Shareholders are able to add to their holding without paying stockbroker's commission. Companies are able to raise additional equity capital without the expense of a rights issue.

A **'share split'** (stock split) means that the nominal value of each share is reduced in proportion to the increase in the number of shares, so the total book value of shares remains the same. So, for example, a company may have 1 million shares

---

[10] Scrip issues are achieved by taking reserves on the balance sheet and capitalising them. For example, taking £10 million from the 'share premium account' or the 'profit and loss reserves' and transferring this amount to the 'called up share capital' account.

in issue with a nominal value of 50p each. It issues a further 1 million shares to existing shareholders with the nominal value of each share reducing to 25p, but total nominal value remains at £500,000. Of course, the share price will halve – assuming all else is constant. However, not all else is always constant because, as with a scrip issue, a share split often has a psychological effect on shareholders: it is taken as a sign of confidence that the company is going to perform well in the future. Therefore, the share price does not reduce as much as we might expect.

If the share price goes too low, say 15p, companies may decide to pursue **consolidation of shares**. This is the opposite of a split: the number of shares is reduced and the nominal value of each remaining share rises. If the nominal (par) value is 5p the company could consolidate on the basis of five shares for one. A 25p nominal share would replace five 5p nominal shares and the new share would then trade in the market at 5 × 15p = 75p (or slightly more if investors are more attracted to shares within a 'normal' price range). Much scepticism greeted the share consolidation of RBS – see Article 16.3.

Article 16.3

RBS share move raises doubts

By Kate Burgess

This week Royal Bank of Scotland, which is four-fifths owned by UK taxpayers, announced plans to transform its share price in one fell swoop from 23p to £2.30. If approved by investors at the annual meeting next month, the bank will swap 10 shares for one.

However, the move has left analysts scratching their heads about what it really does for shareholders.

In the US, many companies have consolidated shares for fear of share prices falling below regulatory thresholds, which would force them to delist. In Britain, most share mergers are done by deadbeat stocks whose shares have fallen below a penny. It is highly unusual among big UK companies, say market watchers.

Some research suggests consolidations improve the liquidity of shares while cutting trading

activity and volatility. But academics warn the evidence is limited.

RBS' arguments for merging its shares centre round the view that most FTSE stocks trade between £2 and £4 and hopes the move will help to anchor down the RBS share price. "That is wishful thinking," says Paul Marsh, emeritus professor at the London Business School. He points out most share prices move in fractions of a penny and says RBS shares will be just as volatile at £2 as they are at 20p.

Veterans of the UK stock market are similarly sceptical. "There is no economic rationale. It is cosmetic," says one leading institutional investor. "Boards, particularly of big companies, don't like their shares being described as penny stocks. But the benefits are merely emotional." And like cosmetic surgery, the costs may outweigh the benefits, he adds.

Share buy-backs and special dividends

Occasionally directors conclude that the company has too much equity capital and that it would be appropriate to hand back some of the cash to shareholders. It could be that the company is able to generate higher returns on each remaining share by borrowing more to reduce the number of shares by self-purchase. It could be that the directors think the shares are undervalued, and by reducing the quantity on the market the price will rise. It could be that the directors are aware of the tendency of companies to squander surplus cash on value-destroying mergers, and they want to avoid the temptation.

Buy-backs may also be a useful alternative when the company is unsure about the sustainability of a possible increase in the normal cash dividend. A stable policy may be pursued on dividends, and then shares are repurchased as and when surplus cash is available. This two-track approach avoids sending an over-optimistic signal about future growth through changing underlying dividend levels.

It is necessary for companies to ask shareholders'[11] permission to buy back. Many companies now regularly vote at AGMs (an ordinary resolution – 50 per cent of votes) to allow buy-backs of up to 10 per cent of share capital in the following 12 months. The directors then have the freedom to choose when, and if, they will buy in shares.

A second possible approach to returning surplus funds is to pay a special dividend. This is the same as the normal dividend, but bigger and paid on a one-off basis. A special dividend has to be offered to all shareholders. However, a share repurchase may not always be open to all shareholders as it can be accomplished in one of three ways:

■ purchasing shares in the stock market;

■ all shareholders are invited to tender some or all of their shares;

■ an arrangement with particular shareholders.

Many investors take buy-backs as an indicator of a management team that is owner-orientated because it is volunteering to reduce the size of its empire. The team would rather hand back cash for shareholders to employ elsewhere than go on investing in projects and acquisitions producing ever smaller returns. Other commentators see buy-backs as an admission of managerial failure to develop avenues for expansion. Personally, I would rather back a management team that

---

[11] And warrant holders, share option holders and convertible bond/preference share holders.

sticks to where it has a competitive advantage and refuses to expand beyond its circle of competence than one that is so full of hubris that it can always find a use for any amount of shareholders' money. However, in the 1990s–2000s share buy-backs became a management fad with the aim of providing short-term boosts to the share price and earnings per share rather than for rational long-term shareholder wealth enhancement reasons. This was overlaid with another fad – that for high borrowings relative to the equity capital of the business. This can enhance returns to shareholders in stable circumstances but can be very risky if the underlying cash flows of the business decline – as they did for many in the recession. Thus, we had the spectacle of 2007 (boom time) buy-backs at, say, £5 per share followed by a desperate attempt to reinforce the business through selling shares at, say, £1 per share in 2008 (the crash). Existing shareholders were not pleased when a portion of the company was handed over to outsiders for such a small amount. So when viewing (and voting on) buy-backs, consider the overall debt levels that would result.

17

Taxation and investors

If you are fortunate enough to receive income or capital gains from your investments then Her Majesty's Revenue and Customs (HMRC) will be interested in hearing about it. It is illegal to **evade** tax (i.e. deliberately making a false statement or omitting a relevant fact) so you need to keep careful records and declare gains at the appropriate time (e.g. on an annual self-assessment tax return).

The heart sinks at the prospect of handing over large sums, but don't despair. There are many ways of *avoiding* tax – 'avoiding' is OK, it's legal. You can take advantage of various tax breaks introduced by government – usually to encourage people to act in particular ways (e.g. to save more, or to buy shares in companies just starting up). Thus, there are 'tax-efficient' actions that investors can take to reduce the size of the cheque sent to HMRC. Be careful though: some of these tax wrappers and other structures can cost more than they are worth. In other words, don't let the tax tail wag the investment dog. This chapter describes the main forms of taxation investors have to bear, as well as methods of reducing tax, together with some thoughts on whether these breaks are worth taking advantage of.

Tax rules and allowances change from year to year. The material below is informed by the 2014 tax rules. You might like to consult an expert to understand your position in another year. HMRC's website (www.hmrc.gov.uk) can be useful for keeping you up to date and the Directgov website has some easy-to-follow web pages (www.direct.gov.uk).

Stamp duty

A tax that you have to pay regardless of whether you are a successful investor is stamp duty. A charge of 0.5 per cent of the value of Main Market share purchases (and other marketable securities) is levied at the time of purchase.[1] The tax is automatically added to the bill that you receive from your broker.

Some people get quite hot under the collar about stamp duty, saying that it discourages investment in UK shares, is unfair because it is not based on income, eats into pensions and makes the cost of equity capital greater for companies. The government raises around £3–£4 billion per year from it and has shown little interest in abolishing it.

Tax on dividends

Dividends, whether from a company, unit trust or open-ended investment company, are subject to income tax. Dividends are paid out of company profits after tax has been deducted; the company has paid or is due to pay corporation tax on those profits. Out of the overall corporate tax bill the company is allowed to assign some of it to dividends as though the shareholders paid the tax. Thus when the company sends you a dividend it has already deducted 10 per cent for taxes (which is part of its overall corporation tax bill) – you simply receive the net amount after tax. The 10 per cent deduction is actually called a 'tax credit' and you can use this as an offset against any of your income tax. The dividend you are paid represents 90 per cent of your 'dividend income'. The remaining 10 per cent of the dividend income is made up of the tax credit.

Unfortunately, if you are not a taxpayer you are unable to reclaim the tax paid. If you are a standard rate tax payer (20 per cent tax rate) you will have no further tax to pay on the dividend. If you are a higher rate taxpayer (40 per cent marginal rate) you will be chargeable for tax on dividends at a rate of 32.5 per cent. Because 10 per cent of the *gross* (before tax) dividend has already been imputed you will have to pay an additional 25 per cent of the *net* (after 10 per cent) dividend received from the company at a later date (after completing your tax return).[2]

---

[1]   The tax was scrapped for AIM and ISDX shares in April 2014.
[2]   A 45 per cent marginal rate tax payer (taxable income over £150,000) pays a further additional amount.

> ### Example
>
> Martin receives a dividend of 20p per share on his 1,000 shares, a total of £200. He also receives a tax credit for 10 per cent of the gross amount of the dividend amounting to £22.22. This represents 10 per cent of the gross dividend which is £222.22:
>
> £200 + £22.22 = £222.22.
>
> Martin is a higher rate taxpayer and will have to pay tax of 32.5 per cent of the gross dividend: £222.22 × 0.325 = £72.22. He is deemed to have paid £22.22 of this already (the company did it on his behalf) so he has to pay a further £50 (25% of the net dividend or 22.5% of the gross). Martin therefore walks away with £150.

You will receive a voucher with the dividend payment showing the tax paid. Hold on to the voucher because you will be asked to declare dividend income and tax payments made on your tax return. It is your responsibility to contact HMRC if you believe you have taxable income (or gains) to declare.

If you choose to receive shares instead of a cash dividend (called a 'scrip dividend' or 'stock dividend' – see Chapter 16) the shares are valued as income equal to the alternative cash dividend for income tax purposes. If there is no cash alternative to the scrip the market value is used. If the cash alternative differs from the market value of the shares by 15 per cent or more the market value will be used. Again, tax is deemed to have been paid at the 10 per cent rate, so if you are a basic rate taxpayer no more tax is payable. A higher rate taxpayer will have to pay more.

Capital gains tax

If you sell an asset for more than it cost, you may be liable for capital gains tax (CGT). This includes shares, unit trusts, OEICs and some bonds.[3] However, you will not be liable for tax on all the difference between the purchase price and the sale value. For a start you can deduct various expenses (e.g. stamp duty and brokers' fees). Second, you can offset capital losses made in the same year (or carried forward from an earlier year) on other assets against the gain. Third, and perhaps most importantly, you are permitted to make annual gains of £11,000 (in 2014–15) tax free (called an **'annual exempt amount'**) – so you only pay tax on gains made above this figure.

Basic rate taxpayers pay CGT at 18 per cent, but higher rate taxpayers are charged 28 per cent on any gains that push them into the higher rate tax bracket when

---

[3] Gilts are exempt from CGT. Most sterling bonds, debentures, loan notes and loan stock are 'qualifying corporate bonds', which are also exempt.

added to income. CGT is worked out for each tax year (from 6 April to the next 5 April). You are required to report gains made on your normal tax return and any tax due must be paid by 31 January after the end of each tax year.

Example

In 2014–15 Frank has taxable income, after personal allowances, of £26,000. He also makes capital gains on shares bought in 2008, after expenses and offsetting losses, of £16,000. We deduct his £11,000 **annual exempt amount** to arrive at the chargeable gain of £5,000. This will be taxed at 18 per cent. Thus £900 is payable 31 January 2016.

Tips on reducing CGT

For the majority of private investors the annual allowance of £11,000 will be more than enough to avoid paying any CGT. However, if you are fortunate enough to make substantial gains you might like to know about tax-efficient steps you can take:

- You could *transfer* (sell or give) shares to your spouse or civil partner who could then make use of their annual £11,000 allowance. You have £22,000 of allowance between you. Transfers between spouses and civil partners are not taxed.

- **'Bed and breakfasting'** used to be a very popular way of reducing CGT. If you expected to hold shares for a long time there might be many years when you are not using up the annual CGT allowance. Then, when you do sell, the (say) £50,000 capital gain can be offset against only the final year's allowance – so you face a large tax bill. To get around this investors would sell shares to realise a capital gain (bed) and then repurchase these the next day (breakfast) in each of the intervening years (or at least those when they made a gain). Then the capital gain in the final year is the gain made over merely the last 12 months or so. The loophole is now closed. You now have to leave a gap of 30 days before repurchasing if you wish HMRC to crystallise the capital gain. The exposure to share price change over the 30 days reduced the attractiveness of this technique. The 30-day rule does not apply if you sell the shares and then buy identical shares within an individual savings account (**'bed-and-ISA'**) – in an ISA there is no capital gains tax. Nor does it apply if you sell the shares and then buy identical shares for a self-invested personal pension (SIPP) (a **'bed-and-SIPP'**). Alternatively you can reduce your risk exposure over the 30 days by buying a derivative instrument, the value of which goes up and down with the underlying share price (e.g. traded option, spread bet, contracts for difference – see Chapters 8, 9 and 10 for details).

■ If your losses in a tax year outweigh your gains, make sure you keep a careful record. You have to let HMRC know that you are offsetting *carry-forward losses* against gains in later years. Losses must be registered with HMRC within four years of the loss. Note you cannot offset capital losses against income – only against capital gains.

■ If you know you would like to sell out of a company over the next few months, consider the possibility of spreading the gain over two tax years by selling some shares before 5 April and some after that date. Of course, do not take the risk of delay if you think that the shares are destined to plunge or you need the cash.

One trick you cannot get away with is to give away the shares or sell them at an artificially low price to an accomplice who then sells them for you. HMRC are on to this one – they will value the disposal at the proper market price for CGT purposes.

Interest-bearing instruments

Interest from bank and building society accounts (and from unit trusts and OEICs) is taxed at 20 per cent unless you are liable for higher rate tax, in which case you are required to declare this income and it will be subject to 40 per cent tax ('additional rate' taxpayers pay at 45 per cent). The 20 per cent tax will normally be deducted *at source* by the bank and passed on to HMRC. If you have a low income you may be able to claim tax back. Your savings income is added to your other income and taxed after your tax-free allowances – for example the personal allowance – have been taken into account.

Interest on gilts is payable gross, without deduction of tax. Interest received is taxable and must be declared on tax returns as part of your income. Private investors pay no tax on capital gains made on gilts. Interest on corporate bonds is normally subject to deduction of tax at source (at 20 per cent), but higher rate taxpayers will have to pay more. Some corporate bonds are exempt from capital gains tax.

Inheritance tax

Inheritance tax (IHT) is a tax payable on transfers made on an individual's estate at the time of death (it also covers some gifts made during the individual's lifetime). Transfers of less than £325,000 are free of tax. For every £1 over this threshold 40 per cent goes in tax. Gifts made to survivors more than seven years before death are generally exempt – subject to a maximum of £3,000 per donor per year. Gifts made within seven years of death are taxed at 40 per cent reduced by the following percentages:

Years before death	0–3	3–4	4–5	5–6	6–7	more than 7
Reduction in tax on gifts	0%	20%	40%	60%	80%	100%

Note that the tax is deducted from the estate before the residual is passed on to heirs. The total exemption is £325,000 on the estate; not £325,000 per heir.

Any gifts you make to a 'qualifying' charity – during your lifetime or in your will – will be exempt from IHT. Also, people who leave 10 per cent or more of their net estate to charity can choose to pay a reduced rate of IHT of 36 per cent.

Transfers to spouses or civil partners are exempt from IHT. Setting up a trust is another way to gain exemption, but requires specialist knowledge – consult a professional (e.g. a solicitor). Shares in trading companies listed on AIM or ISDX are exempt from IHT after a two-year holding period, and so the value of these shares is effectively removed from your estate for IHT purposes.

Individual savings accounts

Individual savings accounts (ISAs) are run by financial institutions such as platforms (see Chapter 5), brokers and banks, who impose charges. They should not be viewed as investments in themselves: they are 'wrappers' or 'baskets' which contain the underlying investments. These tax shelters protect your investments from some elements of tax. The underlying investments can be shares (including those on AIM and ISDX), unit trusts, investment trusts, open-ended investment companies, exchange traded funds, life insurance policies, corporate bonds and gilts. You can also keep money as cash in an ISA wrapper. Thus it could be with banks, building societies, credit unions or National Savings products earning interest. Some of these accounts have quick access, others require notice to withdraw your money. If you are willing to lock away your money for years then you can achieve a higher interest rate, but there are severe penalties if you want to access your money before the fixed term is up

The tax benefits of ISAs are as follows:

■ There is no capital gains tax to pay on investments held in the ISA.

■ Tax is not deducted from interest paid from, say, ISA bank accounts.

■ All tax on bonds can be reclaimed.

■ Higher rate taxpayers do not pay additional tax on dividends beyond the imputed 10 per cent.

Unfortunately, one of the former benefits of ISAs has been removed: now dividends on shares (and unit trusts, etc.) will be taxable in the normal way for a basic rate taxpayer. That is, the 10 per cent tax paid on dividend income from the company cannot be reclaimed.

You can put up to £15,000 each year into an ISA to shelter the returns from tax. You can transfer money from one ISA manager to another. However, be very careful not to withdraw the money and then open another ISA because you will lose the future tax benefits. Instead fill in a transfer form supplied by your new ISA provider.

You do not have to invest the full amount all in one go – you can make regular payments (say £50 per month) or send irregular lump sums through the year, just so long as the total does not breach the annual limits. The amount you can put into ISAs each year is not increased if you also withdraw some money in the same tax year. So, if you put £15,000 into an ISA in November and then withdraw £1,800 in December, you cannot put another £1,800 in that tax year – you have already used your £15,000 allowance for the tax year. You are permitted to withdraw from an ISA at any time without incurring a tax charge; however, the ISA provider may impose penalties or restrict your freedom of action (e.g. if you agreed to lock your money into a bank's cash ISA for a year).

You cannot set up an ISA on your own. It is necessary to purchase the ongoing wrapper service from an ISA provider. Fund supermarkets (see Chapter 5) provide ISA wrappers within which it is possible to invest in many different funds, shares and other securities. Overseas shares traded on main national exchanges can also be held. The **self-select ISA** allows you decide which shares, gilts, OEICs, corporate bonds, etc. should be bought for your funds. Not all ISA managers offer this option, so you may have to shop around. Be wary of the charges levied by the providers of self-select ISAs. In addition to dealing charges for buying the shares (say £10), etc., an annual fee is levied linked to the value of the fund – often 0.35 per cent or more. Alternatively a flat annual management charge will be made, say £12 per quarter. You need to examine each platform's charges page to see what the charges are (including share dealing charges and dividend reinvestment charges) and then consider whether a percentage or flat fee is best for you.

Many people doubt the wisdom of holding share ISAs. Most private investors are unlikely to be caught by CGT given the £11,000 annual allowance. Buying an equity ISA wrapper for your share investments can therefore mean annual charges to a platform of say 0.45 per cent for the perhaps insignificant tax advantage that if you are a higher rate taxpayer you will not pay additional tax on dividend income.

On the other hand, many people have now become 'ISA millionaires' by putting the maximum allowed each year and through wise investing they now have over £1 million in ISAs. For these people there is a fairly high likelihood that they will make capital gains of over £11,000 in most years; a few takeover bids and a few share sales at decent profits can easily add up to a large CGT bill. Thus a flat charge of say £4 per month for the ISA wrapper is a small price to pay relative to the tax saved.

Even if you managed to put away 'only' £100,000 or so into your ISA you will start to notice the benefits of the CGT shelter. It is perfectly possible for one or two of your investments to produce gains of over £11,000. Selling them outside of an ISA can result in a painful 18 or 28 per cent tax.

ISAs are regarded as a good home for temporary cash holdings. No charges are applied and you can usually get at your money within a day or so. It is also a very competitive market, so the interest rates offered are good.

If your ISA provider is authorised by the FCA you will be entitled to compensation under the FSCS – see Chapter 19 – your cash ISA money is protected up to £85,000 and your stocks and shares ISA money up to £50,000.

Personal pensions

Personal pensions are very tax-efficient if you are saving/investing for the long term:

- The money you put in (your contribution) qualifies for full tax relief. This means that if you contribute say £2,880 from taxed earnings the government then adds back tax (at 20 per cent) to the fund amounting to £720, meaning that £3,600 is added to your pension pot. Higher rate taxpayers get additional tax relief – they claim back the other 20 per cent of tax paid.

■ Once the money is in the fund it can grow without tax being levied on interest income, or on capital gains (however, the imputed 10 per cent dividend tax cannot be reclaimed).

■ When you reach retirement you can take 25 per cent of the fund in cash, tax-free. The rest may be put into a fund that will provide you with an **annuity** – regular payments for the rest of your life. You can shop around for the best annuity rates, i.e. the annual payout to you for handing over say £100,000 to an insurance company at the outset. Alternatively, you can keep it invested under your control and can then withdraw as much or as little money as you like, when you like.

You are permitted to start receiving the pension after the age of 55. Opening a number of schemes allows you to begin drawing benefits at different points. You do not have to stop work to start receiving benefits under these schemes.

There is a wide range of type of funds, e.g. shares (UK or overseas, passive/tracker funds or actively managed), corporate bonds and gilts, cash. You can put money into a fund that invests in a mixture of securities – for example, a **lifestyle pension** scheme invests mostly in equities when you are many decades away from retirement and then gradually switches to cash and bonds when you are less than 10 years away.

You can save a regular amount into a personal pension (the minimum is usually £20 or £50 a month) or pay in lump sums on an *ad hoc* basis.

You can now contribute up to £40,000 per year to any number of pension schemes and gain tax relief. These can be a mixture of a company scheme and personal pension schemes. Thus you can gain tax relief on pension contributions up to 100 per cent of your taxable earnings annually subject to a lifetime limit of £1,250,000 of tax relieved pension savings. There is no upper limit to the amount of pension saving you can build up.

Stakeholder pensions

Stakeholder pensions are similar to standard personal pensions except that you pay low management charges (no more than 1.5 per cent in the first 10 years falling to 1 per cent thereafter of the value of the pension fund). Contributions can be very small (minimum contribution no higher than £20), you can start and stop payments whenever you want and you can move the scheme to another provider without penalty. They may be taken out through an employer or individually (e.g. self-employed). The most significant advantage is that whatever you pay in (which is a maximum of £3,600 grossed-up contributions per year) is treated as though it has been subject to basic rate tax. The stakeholder scheme provider can claim this 'tax' back for you even if you are a non-taxpayer (e.g. non-working spouse) and therefore did not actually have tax deducted in the first place. Higher rate taxpayers can claim extra relief.

Self-invested personal pension

A disadvantage of standard personal pensions is that you have no choice over the specific investments held in the fund – this is left up to the fund manager, who also has to be paid. If you are confident about your share/securities selection capabilities then you may like to opt for a **self-invested personal pension (SIPP)**. These allow you to instruct the fund administrator, e.g. a platform (see Chapter 5), to buy and sell shares and other investments on your behalf within the SIPP wrapper. You gain the same tax advantages as for a standard personal pension and you have control over the investment performance.

There are two types:

- Basic low-cost SIPPs are normally web-based (although you can use the phone). Even these allow a wide variety of funds (often over 2,000 unit trusts, investment trusts, ETFs, OEICs to choose from) and a wide variety of shares, bonds, etc.

- Full SIPPs allow you to invest in a very wide variety of asset classes. As well as shares, funds and bonds you can choose commercial property, cash, gold bullion, unquoted shares, even copyrights and other intellectual property. The full SIPP providers generally require you to invest through a financial adviser rather than independently and so you are unlikely to be managing it entirely yourself over the Internet.

You need to set up a SIPP through an administration company plus a trustee, which can both be part of the same group. It may sound complicated, but in reality the investment platforms and other SIPP providers organise this for hundreds of investors daily.

You can invest in SIPPs after retirement until you are 75. The rule that 25 per cent of a pension pot can be taken a cash-free lump sum applies to SIPPs as well.

SIPPs can be taken out for a non-tax-paying relative – HMRC will top up the fund at the basic rate of tax. The limit for this is a grossed-up £3,600 per year – so you would put in a maximum of £2,880.

Basic low-cost SIPPs

Most low-cost SIPP providers do not levy an initial charge for putting money into the fund (a 'set-up fee') but they charge you annual fees of about 0.2–0.45 per cent of the fund per year. Other providers will charge you fixed annual fees of £48–£200. Buying or selling securities within the fund would also be subject to the platform's brokers' fees of £10–£30. These low-cost SIPPs are usually execution only, without providing advice, however, many of the platform websites have useful articles to provide some guidance. Most online SIPP providers will give you a real-time valuation of your holdings. See the list of platforms in Chapter 5.

Full SIPPs

By investing in commercial property you could, for example, use SIPP money to buy an office which you then rented out (maybe even to yourself) on a commercial basis, building up tax-free rental income and capital gains in your retirement fund. (You can borrow a high proportion of the money for the property purchase and use other assets in the SIPP fund as security for the borrowing.) SIPPs have been particularly popular with doctors, lawyers and accountants to purchase the properties they occupy. The rent paid is a tax-deductible expense of their businesses. The rent received by the SIPP is not taxed in the fund. You cannot use a SIPP to buy residential property.

The charging structure for full SIPPs varies enormously, but many of them are around £400 to set up with annual fees of 1.5 per cent of funds under management or a flat £500 per year, plus costs of trading (say £30 per stock market transaction, much more for purchasing commercial property). SIPP administrators often insist on a high minimum initial investment: £50,000 is fairly typical. Indeed, given the high charges you would not want to select a full SIPP unless you had many tens or hundreds of thousands to put in it.

A list of all SIPP providers is available on the website of their umbrella group, the Association of Member-Directed Pension Schemes (www.ampsonline.co.uk).

Warnings on pensions

■ Equities are riskier than bonds or cash, so it can be dangerous to be only 5–10 years away from retirement and be holding your entire pension fund in a handful of shares – they can fall 40 per cent in a year. To avoid the possibility of retiring just after a collapse in share prices it makes sense to shift the weighting of your fund gradually towards bonds and cash-type (e.g. deposit account) holdings, with perhaps a proportion of the fund in property. Unless, of course, bonds and/or property markets are in a bubble, with prices artificially high.

■ Be careful that you don't lose half of your fund in management charges of one sort or another. For example, you could end up paying high charges to a unit or investment trust manager as well as fees to the SIPP provider.

■ Don't trade frequently. You are likely to lose a tremendous amount in dealing costs for little gain.

■ Providers can, and sometimes do, introduce new charges on SIPPs. Remain vigilant.

■ Make sure that it is relatively cheap and painless to transfer your pension to another provider if the service is poor.

■ Interest rates on cash balances held by a SIPP provider may be low. Shop around and ask before you sign up. Any cash deposited with a SIPP provider is protected under the Financial Services Compensation Scheme – see Chapter 19.

■ When you start to withdraw money from a personal pension this will be subject to income tax.

■ Insurance companies have launched SIPPs, but they tend to be very limiting in the range of investments available to the holder. Their main focus is the insurance firm's in-house products.

Enterprise Investment Scheme

The Enterprise Investment Scheme (EIS) is a government initiative to encourage the flow of risk capital to smaller companies. Income tax relief at 30 per cent is available for investments of up to £1,000,000 made directly into qualifying company ordinary shares.[4] By putting £10,000 into an EIS qualifying company an investor will pay £3,000 less tax, so the effective cost is only £7,000. There is also capital gains tax relief.[5] No capital gains tax is payable on the disposal of shares in an EIS company after holding for three years (or after three years of com-

---

[4] It is also possible to 'carry-back' the investment to the previous tax year – offsetting the invested amount against tax paid then – so tax can be reclaimed.

[5] CGT on any gains realised on other assets in the period up to 36 months prior to, and 12 months after, the EIS shares are allotted can be deferred. This applies to gains up to the amount put into the EIS fund. If you made a chargeable gain of £20,000 on some other investment and put £18,000 into the EIS, then you are liable to CGT on only £2,000 in the immediate future.

mencement of trading, if later). Losses within an EIS are allowable against income tax or capital gains. Furthermore, the value of EIS investments is not counted for inheritance tax after only two years.

'Direct investment' means investing when the company issues shares. It does not mean buying shares in the secondary market from other investors. The tax benefits are lost if the investments are held for less than three years. To raise money from this source the firm must have been carrying out a 'qualifying activity' – this generally excludes financial investment and property companies. The company must not be on the Official List and the most it can raise under the EIS in any one year is usually £5 million. Alternative Investment Market and ISDX companies frequently qualify for EIS. The company must not have gross assets worth more than £15 million or more than 250 employees. For the investor to claim the various tax reliefs they must not hold more than 30 per cent of the share capital or votes (or share and loan capital taken together). Also the investor cannot be a partner, director or employee (except a director who receives no remuneration). Funds investing in a range of EIS companies are springing up to help investors spread risk.

Many of the companies that sell shares to investors under the EIS are high-risk ventures. You must assess the viability of the underlying business and not be mesmerised by the tax reliefs. Only invest if you can afford to lose the lot.

Once the shares are bought you may find yourself with a financial asset that is difficult to sell. This can be the case if the company is on the AIM or ISDX, let alone a company with no secondary market trading facility for its shares.

Seed Enterprise Investment Scheme (SEIS)

There are even better tax breaks for investing in small, early-stage companies, those with fewer than 25 employees and gross assets under £200,000, with the SEIS. An investor can buy up to £100,000 shares per year and gain 50 per cent tax relief; so if you invest £10,000 you get £5,000 back on your income tax (if you have a UK tax liability against which to set the relief). The shares must be held for a period of three years from date of issue for relief to be retained. Only qualifying trades are permitted (notably excludes property and finance) and the trade being carried on by the company at the date of issue of the relevant shares must be less than two years old.

If you make a gain on selling your shares there is no CGT on the sale after three years. If the company fails you are likely to be able to offset your loss against your income tax. So if you originally bought £10,000 of shares you already received £5,000 back from HMRC. Now, if the remaining £5,000 is lost you can use this to reduce your tax. The investor is allowed a maximum proportion of the company's shares/votes/right to assets in winding up of 30 per cent. The investor must not be an employee. Finally, the company can only receive £150,000 under SEIS.

Venture capital trusts

Venture capital trusts (VCTs) are quoted companies that gather together a pot of investment money by selling their shares to investors. This pot of money is then used to buy shares in smaller unquoted trading companies. They operate in a similar way to investment trusts – see Chapter 5.

There are valuable tax breaks for investors putting money into VCTs:

- There is an immediate relief on their current year's income tax at 30 per cent (even if you are a lower or basic rate taxpayer), e.g. if you put £10,000 into a VCT you can claim £3,000 back on your tax return. Individuals claiming tax relief for money put into a VCT are limited to a maximum of £200,000 placed with VCTs per year. The benefit of the initial income tax relief is only available to investors buying new VCT shares (not VCT shares bought from other investors in the secondary market) who hold the investment for at least five years.

- The returns (dividend income and capital gains) on a VCT are free of tax. The dividend relief and capital gains tax exemption are available to you for both newly issued shares and second-hand shares acquired, for example, through the Stock Exchange.

The gross assets of the investee companies must not exceed £15 million and they must have fewer than 250 employees. The term 'unquoted' is used rather loosely and includes AIM and ISDX companies. Investee companies can raise only £5 million per year through VCTs.

These trusts offer investors a way of investing in a broad spread of small firms with high potential, but with greater uncertainty, in a tax-efficient manner. They also offer the possibility of being able to sell the VCT shares in the secondary market on the London Stock Exchange – however, for some VCTs there is little demand and so you may have difficulty selling.

VCTs can have several charges applied including an initial charge, an annual management charge, additional expenses and incentive bonuses to the fund manager. Total fees are around 3.5 per cent per year. Check out five-year return performances of existing VCTs before buying into a new fund – see Article 17.1 for a sceptic's view on these schemes. Note there is no protection under the Financial Service Compensation Scheme – see Chapter 19 – for VCTs (or the EIS and SEIS).

Never invest just to avoid tax

By Terry Smith (chief executive of Tullett Prebon and of Fundsmith LLP)

The tax year ends this coming week and if your mail is anything like mine, you are being inundated with offers of investments which qualify for tax relief provided you invest on or before April 5.

Some of these offers make sense. They are the ones in which tax relief is available for investment through a so-called "wrapper" such as an individual savings account (Isa) or a self invested personal pension (Sipp). You don't pay any tax on capital gains realised or dividends received in your Isa, or on any funds withdrawn from it, and you can also get tax relief on contributions into Sipp. You can put sensible investments into Isas – stocks, cash, mutual funds, and an even wider range of assets in Sipps, including commercial property.

The problem comes when you invest mainly to obtain the tax relief, rather than because of a genuine desire to invest in the underlying assets. With enterprise investment schemes, film finance schemes and venture capital trusts, I suspect that the main object of most investors is to avoid or defer tax rather than to access the highly restricted and specialised investments which these schemes involve.

Do you really want to invest in unquoted companies with less than £15m of gross assets, which is what is required to qualify for an EIS or a VCT? And should anyone invest in movies? Last year, Disney, which is not exactly inexperienced in the movie business, lost more than $200m on the movie *John Carter*.

We are often blinded by the ability to avoid tax. Not only does this lead us to invest in assets which we would not normally consider, it means we tend not to look as closely at the fees which are charged. From a selection of EISs and VCTs

I found initial fees which ranged from 2 per cent to 7.5 per cent of the amount invested, charges of 2–3 per cent each year and performance fees, typically at 20 per cent on any gains, albeit over a hurdle rate. A product with such a rich fee structure generates a lot of sales effort, as you may also have spotted from your mailbox.

This combination of tiny, illiquid companies and high fees produces an inevitable result. Out of 131 VCTs, only 17 have a net asset value higher than the subscription price. Worse than that, the only way you can realise your investment in a VCT is to sell the shares. That is usually done not at net asset value but at the share price which typically trails the NAV by some margin. Only five of the 131 had a share price above their issue price, partly because purchases in the secondary market don't attract tax relief.

To be fair, a lot of VCTs distribute dividends, as they are also exempt from tax, but if I look at the only VCT which I have ever invested in, the cumulative total of dividends plus NAV barely gets me back above the price at which I subscribed for the shares seven years ago. A prospectus inviting new subscriptions this tax season shows the total return since subscription excluding subscription costs as 8 per cent. That's not 8 per cent per year, it's 8 per cent *in total*.

You might object that I was unlucky or chose badly. But the VCT in question features in the middle of the 131 VCTs in NAV terms, and scored 86 out of a possible 100 in Tax Efficient Review in February.

Managers of tax-based investments seem to want investors to focus on returns after tax relief. So if you got 30 per cent income tax relief on your VCT subscription they will try

➡

Article 17.1   Continued

to get you to focus on the return from the 70p each £1 invested cost you after tax relief (even though the tax relief is actually applied to your tax code through self-assessment, not added to your investment as basic-rate pension tax relief is).

The flaw in this argument is that the 30p was supplied by the taxman, not by the manager, who had 100p to invest, before the not-inconsiderable fees, of course.

Rather than investing in assets you would not normally want to own through these complex, illiquid and expensive vehicles, purely to avoid tax, it is usually better to invest in things you really want to own and pay the tax due on any profits you make.

Tax-efficient charitable gifts

Imagine that you have done really well as an investor and are now in the position to be generous to others less fortunate. Then you can give your shares to charity, which means that you can take advantage of some tax breaks.

If you give shares, unit trusts or OEICs or sell them to a charity at less than their market value, you can claim income tax relief and lower your tax bill, as well as getting CGT relief. Shares allowed under this scheme include those of the LSE's Main Market and AIM as well as ISDX and many overseas shares.

If you bought some shares for £10,000 and they are now worth £20,000 you could hand them over to the charity of your choice and then deduct the market value from your normal taxable income. So for 40 per cent taxpayers the charity benefits from the ownership of £20,000 of shares and the giver pays £8,000 less tax that year.

If you have made a large capital gain and are therefore expecting to pay CGT, you can give the shares to a charity that will not have to pay the tax – nor will you.

You need to complete a stock transfer form (from the company's registrar) to take the shares out of your name and put them into the charity's name. The charity will then give you a certificate stating that they have acquired them.

When you complete an annual self-assessment tax return you can make your claim on the form. Alternatively, if you pay tax through PAYE you can write to your tax office with details of your gift or sale to a charity and how much tax relief you would like to claim. HMRC will change your tax code for the current year reducing your monthly tax bill, or give you a refund for an earlier year.

18

Mergers and takeovers

This chapter examines the reasons why the managers of your company may want to merge it with another, and the ways in which mergers are financed. Then the merger process itself is described, along with the rules and regulations designed to prevent unfairness to shareholders. A major question to be addressed is: who gains from mergers? Is it shareholders, managers, advisers, etc.? Shockingly, the evidence suggests that in less than half of corporate mergers do the shareholders of the acquiring firm benefit.

Many people, for various reasons, differentiate between the terms **'merger'**, **'acquisition'** and **'takeover'** – for example, for accounting and legal purposes. However, like most commentators, this book will use the three terms interchangeably, and with good reason. It is sometimes very difficult to decide if a particular unification of two companies is more like a merger – in the sense of being a coming together of roughly equal sized firms on roughly equal terms, in which the shareholders remain as joint owners and both teams of managers share in the managerial duties – or whether the act of union is closer to what some people would say is an acquisition or takeover – a purchase of one firm by another with the associated implication of financial and managerial domination.

Merger motives

In the interests of shareholders

Firms decide to merge with other firms for a variety of reasons. The classic word associated with merger announcements is **'synergy'**. The idea underlying this is that the combined entity will have a value greater than the sum of its parts.

The increased value comes about because of boosts to revenue and/or the cost base. Perhaps complementary skills or complementary market outlets enable the combined firms to sell more goods. Sometimes the ability to share sources of supply or production facilities improves the competitive position of the firm. One of the most important forces driving mergers is the attempt to increase **market power**. This is the ability to exercise some control over the price of the product. It can be achieved through either (a) monopoly, oligopoly (a small number of producers) or dominant producer positions, etc., or (b) collusion between the firms in the industry. If a firm has a large share of a market it often has some degree of control over price. It may be able to push up the price of goods sold because customers have few alternative sources of supply. Even if the firm does not control the entire market, a reduction in the number of participating firms to a handful makes collusion easier. Whether openly or not, the firms in a concentrated market may agree among themselves to charge customers higher prices and not to undercut each other. The regulatory authorities are watching out for such socially damaging activities and have fined a number of firms for such practices – for example, in the cement, steel and chemicals industries.

An important contributor to synergy is the ability to exploit economies of scale. Larger size often leads to lower cost per unit of output. Rationalising and consolidating manufacturing capacity at fewer, larger sites can lead to production utilising larger machines. Economies in marketing can arise through the use of common distribution channels or joint advertising. There are also economies in administration, research and development, purchasing and finance.

If a firm has chosen to enter a particular market but lacks the right know-how, the quickest way of establishing itself may be through the purchase of an existing player in that product or geographical market. To grow into the market organically – by developing the required skills and market strength through internal efforts alone – may mean that for many years the firm will not have the necessary critical size to become an effective competitor. Furthermore, creating a new participant in a market may result in over-supply and excessive competition, leading to the danger of a price war and thus eliminating profits.

One of the primary reasons advanced for **conglomerate mergers** (involving unrelated business areas) is that the overall income stream of the holding company will be less volatile if the cash flows come from a wide variety of products and markets. At first glance the pooling of unrelated income streams would seem to improve the position of shareholders. They obtain a reduction in risk without a decrease in return. The problem with this argument is that investors can obtain the same risk reduction in an easier and cheaper way. They could simply buy a range of shares in the independent, separately quoted firms. In addition, it is said that conglomerates lack focus – with managerial attention and resources being dissipated.

A further reason for mergers which favours shareholders is that the management of firm X may be more efficient than the management of firm Y, resulting in a gain produced if X's management is dominant after the unification.

Many people believe that stock markets occasionally underestimate the true value of a share and so bargains appear for managers of other firms on the prowl for targets. It may well be that the potential target firm is being operated in the most efficient manner possible and productivity could not be raised even if the most able managerial team in the world took over. Such a firm might be valued low by the stock market because the management are not very aware of the importance of a good stock market image. Perhaps they provide little information beyond the statutory minimum and in this way engender suspicion and uncertainty. Investors hate uncertainty and will tend to avoid such a firm. On the other hand, the acquiring firm might be very conscious of its stock market image and put considerable effort into cultivating good relationships with the investment community.

Managerial motives

The reasons for merger described in this section are often just as rational as the ones which have gone before, except, this time, the rational objective may not be shareholder wealth maximisation but manager wealth maximisation.

One group that seems to do well out of merger activity is the management team of acquiring firms. When all the dust has settled after a merger they end up controlling a larger enterprise. And, of course, having responsibility for a larger business means that the managers *have* to be paid a lot more money. Not only must they have higher monthly pay to induce them to give of their best, they must also have enhanced pension contributions and myriad perks. Being in charge of a larger business and receiving a higher salary also brings increased status. Some feel more successful and important, and the people they rub shoulders with tend to be in a more influential class.

As if these incentives to grow rapidly through mergers were not enough, some people simply enjoy putting together an empire – to create something grand and imposing gives a sense of achievement and satisfaction. To have control over ever larger numbers of individuals appeals to basic instincts – some measure their social position and their stature by counting the number of employees under them. Warren Buffett comments:

The acquisition problem is often compounded by a biological bias: Many CEO's [chief executive officers] attain their positions in part because they possess an abundance of animal spirit and ego. If an executive is heavily endowed with these qualities – which, it should be acknowledged, sometimes have their advantages – they won't disappear when he reaches the top. When such a CEO is encouraged by his advisors to make deals, he responds much as would a teenage boy who is encouraged by his father to have a normal sex life. It's not a push he needs.[1]

John Kay points out that many managers enjoy the excitement of the merger process itself:

For the modern manager, only acquisition reproduces the thrill of the chase, the adventures of military strategy. There is the buzz that comes from the late-night meetings in merchant banks, the morning conference calls with advisers to plan your strategy. Nothing else puts your picture and your pronouncements on the front page, nothing else offers so easy a way to expand your empire and emphasise your role.[2]

These first four managerial motives for merger – empire building, status, power and remuneration – can be powerful forces impelling takeover activity. But, of course, they are rarely expressed openly, and certainly not shouted about during a takeover battle.

The fifth reason, hubris, is also very important in explaining merger activity. It may help particularly to explain why mergers tend to occur in greatest number when the economy and companies generally have had a few good years of growth, and management are feeling rather pleased with themselves.

'Hubris' means over-weaning self-confidence or, less kindly, arrogance. Managers commit errors of over-optimism in evaluating merger opportunities due to excessive pride or faith in their own abilities. The suggestion is that some acquirers do not learn from their mistakes and may be convinced that they can see an undervalued firm when others cannot. Also, that they have the talent, experience and entrepreneurial flair to shake up almost any business, and generate improved profit performance. Here's what Warren Buffett has to say on the subject of hubris:

---

[1] Chairman's letter accompanying the 1994 annual report of Berkshire Hathaway Inc. Reprinted by kind permission of Warren Buffett. © Warren Buffett.

[2] John Kay, 'Poor odds on the takeover lottery', *Financial Times*, 26 January 1996.

On Toads and Princesses

Many managements apparently were overexposed in impressionable childhood years to the story in which the imprisoned handsome prince is released from the toad's body by a kiss from the beautiful princess. Consequently, they are certain their managerial kiss will do wonders for the profitability of the Company T(arget).

Such optimism is essential. Absent that rosy view, why else should the shareholders of Company A(cquisitor) want to own an interest in T at the 2X takeover cost rather than at the X market price they would pay if they made direct purchases of their own?

In other words, investors can always buy toads at the going price for toads. If investors instead bankroll princesses who wish to pay double for the right to kiss a toad, those kisses better pack some real dynamite. We've observed many kisses but very few miracles. Nevertheless, many managerial princesses remain serenely confident about the future potency of their kisses – even after their corporate backyards are knee-deep in unresponsive toads.[3]

Note that the hubris hypothesis does not require the conscious pursuit of self-interest by managers. They may have worthy intentions but can make mistakes in judgement.

It is generally observed that mergers tend to take place with a large acquirer and a smaller target. Potential target managements may come to believe that the best way to avoid being taken over and then sacked or dominated is to grow large themselves, and to do so quickly. Thus mergers can have a self-reinforcing mechanism or positive feedback loop – the more mergers there are the more vulnerable managements feel and the more they are inclined to carry out mergers. Firms may merge for the survival of the management team and not primarily for the benefit of shareholders.

Third-party motives

There are many highly paid individuals who benefit greatly from merger activity. Advisers charge fees to the bidding company to advise on such matters as identifying targets, the rules of the takeover game, regulations, monopoly references,

---

[3] Chairman's letter accompanying the 1981 annual report of Berkshire Hathaway Inc. Reprinted by kind permission of Warren Buffett. © Warren Buffett.

finance, bidding tactics, stock market announcements, and so on. Typical fees are between 0.125 and 0.5 per cent of the value of the target company for advisory work and another 3–4 per cent of any money raised to finance the merger. That can add up to many tens of millions. Advisers are also appointed to the target firms. Other groups with a keen eye on the merger market include accountants and lawyers.

It seems reasonable to suppose that professionals engaged in the merger market might try to encourage or cajole firms to contemplate a merger and thus generate turnover in the market. Some provide reports on potential targets to try and tempt prospective clients into becoming acquirers. Of course, the author would never suggest that such esteemed and dignified organisations would ever stoop to promote mergers for the sake of increasing fee levels alone. You may think that, but I could not possibly comment!

There is also the press, ranging from tabloids to specialist publications. Even a cursory examination gives the distinct impression that they tend to have a bias of articles emphasising the positive aspects of mergers. It is difficult to find negative articles, especially at the time of a takeover. They like the excitement of the merger event and rarely follow up with a considered assessment of the outcome. Also the press reports generally portray acquirers as dynamic, forward-looking and entrepreneurial.

Financing mergers

In order that the acquiring company can take control of the destiny of the target company it needs to buy the majority of its shares. To induce the target shareholders to sell their shares it usually offers cash, newly minted shares in the acquirer, or some other financial security, such as convertible bonds. Sometimes the acquirer offers a package of cash and/or shares and/or other securities.

Cash

One of the advantages of using cash for payment is that the acquirer's shareholders retain the same level of control over their company. That is, new shareholders from the target do not suddenly take possession of a proportion of the acquiring firm's voting rights, as they would if the target shareholders were offered shares in the acquirer. Sometimes it is very important to shareholders that they maintain control over a company by owning a certain proportion of the firm's shares. Someone who has a 50.1 per cent stake may resist attempts to dilute that holding to 25 per cent even though the company may more than double in size.

The second major advantage of using cash is that its simplicity and preciseness give a greater chance of success. The alternative methods carry with them some uncertainty about their true worth. Cash has an obvious value and is therefore preferred by vendors, especially when markets are volatile.

From the point of view of the target's shareholders, cash has the advantage – in addition to being more certain in its value – that it allows the recipient to spread their investments through the purchase of a wide-ranging portfolio. The receipt of shares or other securities means that the target shareholder either keeps the investment or, if diversification is required, has to incur transaction costs associated with selling the shares.

A disadvantage of cash for the target shareholders is that they may be liable for capital gains tax. This is payable when a gain is 'realised'. If the target shareholders receive cash on shares which have risen in value they may have to pay tax. If, on the other hand, the target shareholders receive shares in the acquiring firm then their investment gain is not regarded as being realised and therefore no capital gains tax is payable at that time. The tax payment will be deferred until the time of the sale of the new shares – assuming an overall capital gain is made.

Other disadvantages are that finding the cash may put a strain on the acquiring company's cash flow and overstretch its financial gearing ratio. Also, any risk of misvaluing of the target rest wholly with the acquirer – if shares are accepted by the target's shareholders then they take some of the misvaluing risk.

Shares

The main advantage for target shareholders of receiving shares in the acquirer rather than cash, apart from postponement of capital gains tax, is that they maintain an interest in the combined entity. If the merger offers genuine benefits, the target shareholders may wish to own part of the combined corporation.

To the acquirer an advantage of offering shares is that there is no immediate outflow of cash. In the short run this form of payment puts less pressure on cash flow. However, the firm may consider the effect on the capital structure (amount of debt relative to share capital) of the firm and the dilution of the position of existing shareholders.

Another reason for using shares as the consideration is that the **price–earnings ratio (PER) game** can be played. Through this companies can increase their earnings per share (eps) by acquiring firms with lower PERs than their own. The share price can rise (under certain conditions) despite there being no economic value created from the merger.

Imagine two firms, Crafty plc and Sloth plc. Both earned £1 million last year and had the same number of shares. Earnings per share on a historic basis are therefore identical. The difference between the two companies is the stock market's perception of earnings growth. Because Crafty is judged to be a dynamic go-ahead sort of firm with management determined to improve eps by large percentages in future years, it is valued at a high PER of 20. Sloth, on the other hand, is not seen as a fast-moving firm by investors. It is considered to be rather sleepy. The market multiplies last year's eps by only a factor of 10 to determine the share price – see Table 18.1.

Because Crafty's shares sell at a price exactly double those of Sloth it would be possible for Crafty to exchange one of its shares for two of Sloth's. (This is based on the assumption that there is no bid premium, but the argument that follows works just as well even if a reasonable bid premium is paid.) If Crafty buys all the shares in Sloth its share capital rises by 50 per cent, from 10 million shares to 15 million shares. Earnings per share are one-third higher. If the stock market still puts a high PER on Crafty's earnings, perhaps because investors believe that Crafty will liven up Sloth and produce high eps growth because of their more dynamic management, then the value of Crafty increases and Crafty's shareholders are satisfied.

Table 18.1   The price–earnings ratio game

	Crafty	Sloth	Crafty post-merger
Current earnings	£1m	£1m	£2m
Number of shares	10m	10m	15m
Earnings per share	10p	10p	13.33p
Price–earnings ratio	20	10	20
Share price	£2	£1	£2.67

Each old shareholder in Crafty has experienced an increase in eps and a share price rise of 33 per cent. Also, previously Sloth's shareholders owned £10 million of shares in Sloth; now they own £13.33 million of shares in Crafty (see Table 18.1).

This all seems rational and good, but shareholders are basing their valuations on the assumption that managers will deliver on their promise of higher earnings growth through, for example, operational efficiencies. Managers of companies with high PER may see an easier way of increasing eps and boosting the share price. Imagine you are managing a company that enjoys a high PER. Investors in your firm are expecting you to produce high earnings growth. You could try to achieve this through real entrepreneurial/managerial excellence – for example, by product improvement, achieving economies of scale, or increased operating efficiency, etc. Alternatively, you could buy firms with low PERs and not bother to change operations. In the long run you know that your company will produce lower earnings because you are not adding any value to the firms that you acquire, you are probably paying an excessive bid premium to buy the present earnings and you probably have little expertise in the new areas of activity.

However, in the short run, eps can increase dramatically. The problem with this strategy is that in order to keep the earnings on a rising trend you must continue to keep fooling investors. You have to keep expanding at the same rate to receive regular boosts. One day expansion will stop; it will be revealed that the underlying economics of the firms bought have not improved (they may have even worsened as a result of neglect), and the share price will fall rapidly. The Americans call this the **bootstrapping game**. It can be very lucrative for some managers who play it skilfully. However, there can be many losers – society, shareholders and employees.

Another danger in paying with shares is that the acquiring managers do not properly value what they are giving away relative to what they are receiving in exchange. If acquiring company shareholders own 100 per cent of the shares before the merger and only 50 per cent after the creation of more shares to give away to target shareholders, then the half of the business that they now own should be worth at least as much as the whole business they used to own. Many managers get carried away and sell such a high proportion of the shares in exchange for a mediocre business that value falls for each share, destroying the wealth of the original shareholders. Or they buy an excellent business at a time when their own shares are undervalued on the stock market and therefore have to give away an excessive proportion of the company. It is important to receive as much intrinsic value (see Chapter 12) as you are giving away. Thus, if the acquiring company has intrinsic value of £1,000 million before the merger it will be giving away £500 million of intrinsic value if it creates more shares equal to the number of existing shares to buy a target. If the intrinsic value of the newly acquired target is less than £500 million the intrinsic value of each of the original acquirer's shares will fall. This happens all too often.

Other types of finance

Alternative forms of payment for target shares – corporate bonds, convertible bonds and preference shares – are relatively unpopular largely because of the difficulty of establishing a rate of return on these securities which will be attractive to target shareholders. Also, these securities often lack marketability and voting rights over the newly merged company.

Deferred payment, in which the total to be paid over the next few years depends on performance targets being achieved, is a useful way of tying-in key personnel to the combined company (they might be offered an **'earn-out'** deal). Another, obvious, advantage of deferring payment is the reduced cash flow strain.

The rules of the takeover game

The regulatory bodies

The **City Panel on Takeovers and Mergers** provides the main governing rules for companies engaged in merger activity. It is often referred to as **'The Takeover Panel'** or simply the **'Panel'**. Its rules are expressed in the **City Code on Takeovers and Mergers** (the *'Takeover Code'* or *'Code'*).

The Takeover Panel was originally set up by City institutions, bankers, accountants, the London Stock Exchange, LSE, and the Bank of England as a self-regulatory non-statutory organisation in 1968. It was viewed as a model of self-regulation around the world because it could be very quick in making decisions and enforcing them. Also, because it was run by very knowledgeable practitioners from the City, it could maintain a high degree of flexibility, e.g. it could quickly change the rules to meet new challenges – especially when clever financiers thought they had found a way around the current restrictions. It could also maintain a degree of informality in providing companies with guidance on what is acceptable and what is not – a 'word-in-the-ear' or a 'raised eyebrow' could prevent many actions that would have been against the spirit of the Panel's rules. The alternative approach (adopted in many countries), one based on statute and lawyers, was seen as bureaucratic, expensive and slow.

Somehow the Panel has managed to hold onto its old speed, flexibility and informality despite it now having statutory backing (under the Companies Act 2006 and the EU's Directive on Takeover Bids). It has some strong legal powers, such as the right to insist on receiving information from anyone involved in a bid. Panel decisions are legally enforceable. However, it still operates with a high degree of self-regulation and independence of the state; for example, it can amend its own rules.

It also still relies on an informal relationship with the regulated community, and uses subtle power and influence, rather than a rigid set of statutory rules subject to constant challenge in the courts. Even now it very rarely goes to court to enforce or defend a decision – the courtroom is seen very much as a last resort. The litigation culture that bedevils a lot of other countries is something the City and the government have tried to avoid.

Thus, we still have a 'light-touch' regulatory system with an emphasis on the spirit of the rules, with the Panel seen as approachable for consultation, guidance and negotiation, rather than a heavy-handed rule enforcer.

The sanctions it employs are largely the same as those used before it received statutory backing. These range from private or public reprimands (embarrassing and potentially commercially damaging to bidder, target or adviser) to the shunning of those who defy the Code by regulated City institutions – the Financial Conduct Authority (FCA) demands that no regulated firms (such as a bank, broker or adviser) acts for a client firm that seriously breaks the Panel's rules ('cold-shouldering'). Practitioners in breach of the Code may be judged not fit and proper persons to carry on investment business by the FCA, so there is considerable leverage over City institutions that might otherwise be tempted to assist a rule-breaker. The Panel may give a ruling restraining a person from acting in breach of its rules. It may also insist on compensation being paid. The FCA can also take legal action under market abuse legislation – e.g. when there is share price manipulation. In rare cases the Panel may temporarily remove voting rights from particular shareholders.

Note, however that the Panel does not offer a view on either the commercial merit of the bid nor on competition or other public policy issues that might arise.

The fundamental objective of the Takeover Panel regulation is to ensure fair and equal treatment for all shareholders. The main areas of concern are:

■ shareholders being treated differently (e.g. large shareholders getting a special deal);

■ insider dealing (this is assisted by statutory rules);

■ target management action that is contrary to its shareholders' best interests (e.g. the advice to accept or reject a bid must be in shareholders' best interest not their own);

■ lack of adequate and timely information released to all shareholders equally;

■ artificial manipulation of share prices (e.g. an acquirer offering shares cannot make the offer more attractive by getting friends to push up its share price);

■ the bid process dragging on and thus distracting management from their proper tasks.

The **Office of Fair Trading (OFT)** also takes a keen interest in mergers to ensure that they do not produce 'a substantial lessening of competition'. The OFT can clear a merger on competition grounds. An OFT initial screening may or may not be followed by a **Competition Commission** (CC) investigation. This may take several months to complete, during which time the merger bid is put on hold. In 2014 the OFT and CC were merged into the **Competition and Markets Authority** – it will still have a two-phase approach. Another hurdle has been put in the path of large mergers, with intra-European-Union mergers being considered by the European Commission in Brussels. Furthermore, companies operating in dozens of countries may find that anti-monopoly regulators or governments enforce restrictions in many of them to prevent excess power or to protect sensitive sectors from foreigners, e.g. telecommunications infrastructure or defence.

Pre-bid

Figure 18.1 shows the main stages of merger. The acquiring firm usually employs **advisers** to help make a takeover bid. Most firms carry out mergers infrequently and so have little expertise in-house. The identification of suitable targets may be one of the first tasks of the advisers. Once identified, there would be a period of appraising the target. The strategic fit would be considered, alongside a detailed analysis of what would be purchased. The product markets and types of customers could be investigated, and there would be financial analysis showing sales, profit and rates-of-return history. The assets and liabilities would be assessed, as would assets that are truly valuable but are never recorded on a balance sheet (e.g. employees' extraordinary abilities when working as a team).

If the appraisal stage is satisfactory, the firm may approach the target. Because it is often cheaper to acquire a firm with the agreement of the target management, and because the managers and employees have to work together after the merger, in the majority of cases discussions take place that are designed to produce a set of proposals acceptable to both groups of shareholders and managers.

During the negotiation phase the price and form of payment have to be decided upon. In most cases the acquirer has to offer a **bid premium** – this tends to be in the range of 20 per cent to 100 per cent of the pre-bid price. The average is about 30–50 per cent. The timing of payment is also considered – for example, some mergers involve **'earn-outs'** in which the selling shareholders (usually the same individuals as the directors) receive payment over a period of time dependent on the level of post-merger profits. The issue of how the newly merged entity will be managed will also be discussed – who will be chief executive? Which managers will take particular positions? The pension rights of the target firm's employers and ex-employees have to be considered, as does the issue of redundancy, especially the removal of directors – what pay-offs are to be made available?

If agreement is reached then the acquirer formally communicates the offer to the target's board and shareholders. This will be followed by a recommendation from the target's board to its shareholders to accept the offer.

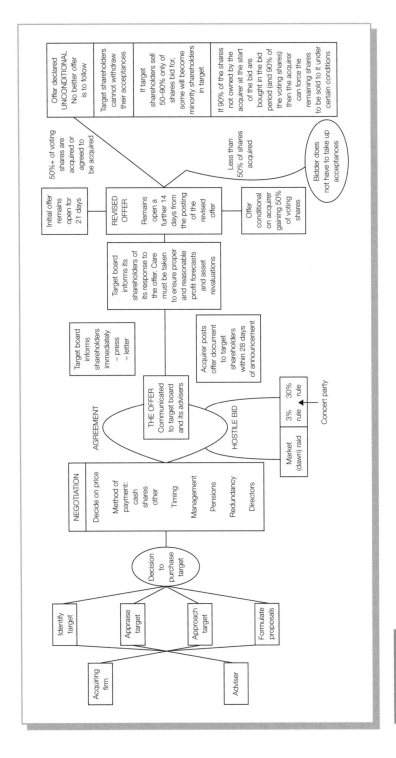

Figure 18.1 The merger process

If, however, agreement cannot be reached and the acquirer still wishes to proceed, the interesting situation of a **hostile bid battle** is created. One of the first stages might be a **'dawn raid'**. This is where the acquirer acts with such speed in buying the shares of the target company that the raider achieves the objective of obtaining a substantial stake in the target before the target's management have time to react. The acquirer usually offers investors and market makers a price which is significantly higher than the closing price on the previous day. This high price is only being offered to those close to the market and able to act quickly.

An important trigger point for **disclosure of shareholdings** in a company, whether the subject of a merger or not, is the 3 per cent holding level. If a 3 per cent stake is owned then this has to be publically declared to the company. Following the formal notice the information is posted on free financial websites. This disclosure rule is designed to allow the target company to know who is buying its shares and to give it advanced warning of a possible takeover raid. The management can then prepare a defence and present information to shareholders should the need arise. (The 3 per cent rule also applies to holdings via derivatives such as contracts for difference.)

If a person or a company builds up a stake of more than 30 per cent of the voting rights, the Takeover Panel rules usually oblige it to make a cash bid for all of the target company's shares (or a share offer with a cash alternative) at the highest price paid in the previous 12 months (a **'mandatory bid'**). A 30 per cent stake often gives the owner a substantial amount of power. It is thought that the shareholders need to be given the opportunity to decide if they want to continue to hold their shares in a company with a dominant shareholder. It is very difficult for anyone else to bid successfully for the firm when someone already has 30 per cent. It is surprising how often one reads in the financial press that a company or individual has bought a 29.9 per cent holding so that they have as large a stake as possible without triggering a mandatory bid.

Sometimes, in the past, if a company wanted to take over another to avoid declaring at the 3 per cent level (or 5 per cent as it was then), or to avoid bidding at the 30 per cent level it would sneak up on the target firm's management and shareholders. It would form a **'concert party'** by persuading its friends, other firms and individuals, to buy stakes in the target. Each of these holdings would be below the threshold levels. When the acquirer was ready to pounce it would already have under its control a significant controlling interest, if not a majority. Today all concert party holdings are lumped together for the purposes of disclosure and trigger points.

Once a company becomes a bid target, any dealings in the target's shares by the bidder (or an associate) must be publically disclosed no later than 12 noon on the business day following the transaction. Furthermore, once an offer is underway, any holder of 1 per cent or more of either the bidder or target must publicly disclose dealings by midday of the next business day. An investor holding 1 per cent must disclose dealings in the bidder's or the target's shares, warrants, convertibles, contracts for difference, options, other derivatives and all other securities in the companies.

A tactic that has become common is for a potential bidder to announce that they are thinking of making a bid rather than actually doing it – they make an **'indicative offer'** (dubbed a **'virtual bid'**) saying they might bid but not committing themselves to the expense and strict timetable of a formal offer. Shareholders in targets may gain from having potential bidders announce an interest in buying their shares and are in favour of allowing time for the bid to be put together. On the other hand, it is not in the shareholders' interest for the management to continually feel under siege. The Takeover Panel permits indicative offers, but within 28 days of an approach to the target a formal bid must be brought (a 'put up or shut up' rule) or the company must confirm that it does not intend to make an offer. It cannot return for at least six months without the target board's consent.

The bid

In both a friendly and a hostile bid the acquirer is required to give notice to the target's board and its advisers that a bid is to be made. The press and the Stock Exchange are usually also informed. The target management must immediately inform their shareholders (and the Takeover Panel). This is done through an announcement to the Stock Exchange and a press notice, which must be quickly followed by a letter explaining the situation. In a hostile bid the target management tend to use phrases like 'derisory offer' or 'wholly unacceptable'. The target is now in an 'offer period', which restricts the firm's actions such as not being able to issue new shares to make the merger more difficult.

If the bidder buys shares carrying 10% or more of the voting rights in the offer period and the previous 12 months combined, the offer must include a cash alternative at the highest price paid by the bidder in that period.

Within 28 days of the initial notice the **offer document** has to be posted to each of the target's shareholders. Details of the offer, the acquirer and its plans will be given. If the acquisition will increase the total value of the acquirer's assets by more than 15 per cent, the acquirer's shareholders need to be informed about the bid. If the asset increase is more than 25 per cent then shareholders must vote in favour of the bid proceeding. They are also entitled to vote on any increase in the authorised share capital.

The target management have 14 days from the dispatch of the offer document in which to respond by writing to all its shareholders ('defence document'). Assuming that they recommend rejection, they will attack the rationale of the merger and the price being offered. They may also highlight the virtues of the present management and reinforce this with revised profit forecasts and asset revaluations. There follows a period of attack and counter-attack through press releases and other means of communication. Public relations consultants may be brought in to provide advice and plan tactics.

The offer remains open for target shareholders to accept for 21 days from the date of posting the offer document. If the offer is revised it must be kept open for a further 14 days from the posting date of the revision.[4] However, to prevent bids from dragging on endlessly the Panel insists that the maximum period for a bid is 60 days from the offer document date (posting day). The final revision of the offer date is day 46, which allows 14 days for acceptances. There are exceptions: if another bidder emerges, then it has 60 days, and its 60th day becomes the final date for both bidders; if the Board of the target agrees to an extension; if the bid is referred to the Competition and Markets Authority it can 'stop the clock', allowing it to proceed only after it has been approved. If the acquirer fails to gain control within 60 days then it is forbidden to make another offer for a year, to prevent continual harassment.

During the bid period, if the bidder buys shares for cash at a price higher than the offer price, the offer must be raised to that level.

Defence tactics

Here are a few of the tactics employed by target managers to prevent a successful bid or to reduce the chances of a bid occurring:

- **Attack the logic of the bid**. Also attack the quality of the bidder's management.
- **Improve the image of the firm**. Use revaluation, profit projections, dividend promises, public relations consultants.
- **Try to get a Competition and Markets Authority inquiry**.
- **Encourage unions, the local community, politicians, customers and suppliers to lobby on your behalf**.
- **White knight**. Invite a second bid from a friendly company.

[4] If an offer is revised all shareholders who accepted an earlier offer are entitled to the increased payment.

■ **Employee share ownership plans**. These can be used to buy a substantial stake in the firm which may make it more difficult for a bidder to take it over.

■ **Share repurchase**. Reduces the number of shares available in the market for bidders.

The following tactics are likely to be frowned upon by the Takeover Panel in the UK but are used in the USA and in a number of European countries:

■ **Poison pills**. Make yourself unpalatable to the bidder by ensuring additional costs should it win, e.g. target shareholders are allowed to buy shares in target or acquirer at a large discount should a bid be successful.

■ **Crown jewels defence**. Sell off the most attractive parts of the business.

■ **Pac-Man defence**. Make a counter-bid for the bidder.

■ **Asset lock-up**. A friendly buyer purchases those parts of the business most attractive to the bidder.

■ **Golden parachutes**. Managers get massive pay-offs if the firm is taken over.

■ **Give in to greenmail**. Key shareholders try to obtain a reward (e.g. the repurchase of their shares at premium) from the company for not selling to a hostile bidder or becoming a bidder themselves. (Green refers to the colour of US dollar bills.)

Post-bid

Usually an offer becomes **unconditional** when the acquirer has bought or has agreed to buy between 50 and 90 per cent of the target's shares. Prior to the declaration of the offer as unconditional the bidding firm would have said in the offer documents that the offer is conditional on the acquirer gaining 90 per cent (or whatever figure they select above 50 per cent) of the voting shares. This allows the bidding firm to receive acceptances from the target shareholders without the obligation to buy.[5] Once the bid is declared unconditional the acquirer is making a firm offer for the shares which it does not already have, and that no better offer is to follow. Before the announcement of unconditionality those target shareholders who accepted the offer are entitled to withdraw their acceptance – after it, they are forbidden from doing so.

---

[5] If 90 per cent of the target shares are offered to the bidder then it must proceed (unless there has been a material adverse change of circumstance). At lower levels of acceptance, it has a choice of whether to declare unconditionality.

Usually in the days following unconditionality the target shareholders who have not already accepted quickly do so. The alternative is to remain a minority shareholder – still receiving dividends (if management and the majority shareholders choose to pay dividends), but with power concentrated in the hands of a majority shareholder. There is a rule to avoid the frustration of having a small group of shareholders stubbornly refusing to sell. If the acquirer has bought nine-tenths of the shares it bid for (and 90 per cent of the voting shares), it can, within three to six months of the last date on which the offer can be accepted, insist that the remaining shareholders sell at the final offer price.

If the bid has lapsed or not been declared unconditional the bidder cannot bid again for a 12-month period. However, this rule is null and void if another company bids for the target or the original bidder has persuaded the board of the target to accept an offer.

Scheme of arrangement

There is a quick and cheap way of combining two companies called a scheme of arrangement, whereby the target managers and the acquiring managers agree to allow the target shareholders to vote on a merger. If three-quarters of them vote in favour, and the arrangement is sanctioned by a court, then the scheme is binding on all shareholders. All the target shareholders are then required to sell to the acquirer. Thus the acquirer can avoid a situation where a rump minority hang onto their shares.

Information

The *Financial Times* regularly reports the initiation and progress of merger bids. The Saturday edition and www.ft.com summarise current bids, as does the weekly *Investors Chronicle*. Most financial websites display news announcements. The Takeover Panel publishes a table (the disclosure table) listing bidders (offerors) and targets (offerees) which is updated daily (www.thetakeoverpanel. org.uk).

Who wins from mergers?

- **Do the shareholders of acquirers gain from mergers?** An overview of the evidence on the effects of acquisitions on the shareholders of the bidding firm is that in around half of cases they benefit, but many acquiring firms give their shareholders poorer returns than firms that are not acquirers. Even studies that show a gain to acquiring shareholders tend to produce very small average gains. This helps to explain why the share prices of acquirers generally fall when a merger intention is announced.

■ **Do target shareholders gain from mergers?** Acquirers usually have to pay a substantial premium over the pre-bid share price to persuade target shareholders to sell. The evidence in this area is overwhelming – target shareholders usually gain from mergers.

■ **Do the employees gain?** In the aftermath of a merger it sometimes happens that large areas of the target firm's operations are closed down, with a consequent loss of jobs. Often operating units of the two firms are fused and overlapping functions are eliminated, resulting in the shedding of staff. However, sometimes the increased competitive strength of the combined entity saves jobs and creates many more.

■ **Do the directors of the acquirer gain?** Yes, they often gain increased status and power. They also, generally, receive increased remuneration packages.

■ **Do the directors of the target gain?** We do not have a definitive answer as to whether the directors of the target gain. In the press they are often unfairly described as the failed managers and therefore out of a job. They are the losers in the 'market for managerial control'. In reality they often receive large pay-offs on their lengthy employment contracts and then take on another highly paid directorship.

■ **Do the financial institutions gain?** This group benefits greatly from merger activity. They usually receive fees, regardless of whether they are on the winning side in a bid battle.

Final comment: why do mergers fail?

Mergers frequently fail to produce good returns for acquiring shareholders for a variety of reasons. This is an area where managers are very prone to tripping up. The most common stumbling blocks are: the strategy is misguided (the company should not be going into this area of business); the managers are over-optimistic about the future potential of their acquisition, while underestimating the costs associated with the resistance to change in the target and the counter-actions of competitors; there is a failure to prepare integration plans and implement an integration programme that engenders the commitment of the acquired workforce.[6]

---

[6] There is more on the management of mergers in Glen Arnold, *Corporate Financial Management* (Financial Times Prentice Hall, 2013).

Further reading

Sudi Sudarsanam's book (*Creating Value from Mergers and Acquisitions*, 2nd edn, Financial Times Prentice Hall, 2010) provides an excellent overview of the many aspects of merger and is easy to read and comprehensive. *Acquisition Essentials* (FT Publishing, 2014) by Denzil Rankine and Peter Howson is also useful. The rulebook (*The Takeover Code*) is available from the Panel on Takeovers and Mergers at www.thetakeoverpanel.org.uk. Be warned though, it is written for lawyers who enjoy navigating their way through complicated mazes.

19

Investor protection

Investing in shares and other financial instruments is, by nature, risky. If the business goes into liquidation your investment can become worthless. This is a risk all investors have to face. However, there are risks investors should not have to face: firstly, the risk of incompetence by advisers or financial service firms with control over investors' money; secondly, the risk of fraud. There is an extensive system of regulations designed to protect you from the unscrupulous, ignorant and incompetent. There are also systems to enable you to claim compensation should you suffer. This chapter describes both the protection systems and the fall-back compensation systems, as well as giving some advice on steps you can take to protect yourself against being taken for a ride.

There are four levels of protection for UK investors:

■ protection from wayward financial services professionals;

■ regulation of markets;

■ regulation of companies;

■ self-protection.

Protecting investors from wayward financial services professionals

At the centre of UK investor protection is the watchdog, the **Financial Conduct Authority**. The FCA is described as a 'super-regulator' because it regulates so many different aspects of the financial system from stockbrokers, banks and

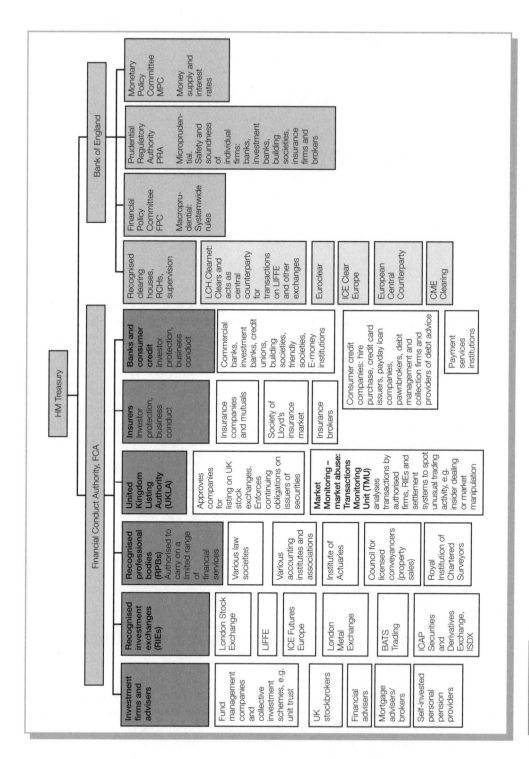

Figure 19.1 UK financial services industry regulation

stock markets to independent financial advisers – see Figure 19.1. The FCA can be described as semi-detached from government: it is financed by the industries it regulates but its powers come from legislation; it often consults the financial services companies before deciding on rules and codes of conduct but it has basic principles approved by the government and it is answerable to the Treasury which appoints its board.

The FCA has been given the objectives of maintaining confidence in the financial system, protecting consumers, preserving market integrity, reducing financial crime (e.g. fraud, insider dealing and money laundering), financial stability of the UK system and helping people to gain the knowledge, aptitude and skills to manage their financial affairs effectively by promoting public understanding of the financial system.

Authorisation

All firms or individuals offering financial advice, products or services in the UK must be authorised by the FCA.[1] Engaging in a regulated activity without authorisation can result in a two-year prison sentence. The FCA insists on high standards when assessing for authorisation. These require competence, financial soundness and fair treatment of customers. They must be 'fit and proper', of good character. Firms are authorised to carry out specific activities, e.g. giving financial advice only, or managing a client's money in a fund, or stockbroking.

Monitoring

Even after initial approval, firms cannot relax as the FCA continues to monitor the adequacy of management, financial resources and internal systems and controls. It also insists that any information provided to investors is clear, fair and not misleading. If there is a failure to meet these standards the firms can be fined or even stopped from doing business. The FCA also works closely with the criminal authorities and uses civil and criminal powers. The following are some of the rules it enforces:

■ Financial advisers have to ensure the product sold to an investor is suited to their needs – this requires knowledge of the consumer's personal and financial situation. See Article 19.1 for an example of failure here.

---

[1] Or have special exemption. You can check the list of those registered as authorised by the FCA at www.fca.org.uk.

Article 19.1

HSBC compensates customers for poor advice

By Elaine Moore

More than 200,000 HSBC customers could be in line for compensation after receiving unsuitable investment advice in the bank's UK branches. About £18m is earmarked to compensate affected customers.

The bank said it would write to all customers who received advice in its branches between August 2008 and October 2012. Advice generally related to investment funds.

"The bank does not expect the number of unhappy customers to be large, as stock markets generally rose during this period, meaning that even clients who received poor advice are unlikely to have lost money. We don't envisage it to be a significant redress programme."

HSBC has become the first lender to set aside money to look into failings in its wealth management advice sector after six banks were investigated by the financial regulator in a mystery shopping exercise.

Over the course of more than 200 branch visits the Financial Services Authority (the precursor to the Financial Conduct Authority) found that advisers were providing unsuitable advice in 11 per cent of cases and that in a further 15 per cent they had failed to collect enough information to make sure their advice was suitable. The FSA said it had found evidence of a "high level of poor advice".

Santander, one of the other banks involved, has already been referred to the regulator's enforcement division.

HSBC has already removed or retrained the advisers.

HSBC was hit with a £10.5m fine in 2011 for selling investment bonds to elderly clients with investment timeframes longer than their life expectancy.

Axa Wealth was fined £1.8m this year for failing to give suitable stocks and shares Isa investment advice in Clydesdale Bank, Yorkshire Bank and the West Bromwich Building Society branches.

- The firm must have a complaints procedure and a system for compensating those unfairly treated.

- Insurance companies, especially those providing with-profits policies, endowments and other savings products, should have significantly more assets than they owe to customers under the policies they have sold them.

- Market 'abuse' is not allowed. For example, individuals are not allowed to trade on inside information or to manipulate share prices by, for example, providing misleading information to the market.

■ There must be a clear separation of clients' money from the firms' money ('ring fencing').

If you have a complaint

There are three steps you should take if you have a grievance.

■ **Raise the issue with the financial service company**. All firms should have a formal complaints procedure, and you are encouraged by the FCA to start here, giving the firm a chance to right the wrong. After all, the firm is best placed to check its records and see what happened. So, ask for the details of the complaints procedure and try to contact the person you originally dealt with because they are most likely to be able to clear up the problem. If you do not get a satisfactory response at this level, go to the top – the chief executive (his or her name should be on company literature, on the company website or at a public library). Most regulated firms have **compliance officers** whose job it is to ensure the FCA rules are being followed. Send a copy of your complaint letter to him or her. (If the company has ceased to trade then call the FCA help line on 0800 111 6768 for advice.)

Here are some tips to follow when complaining. Letters should be in black or blue ink (for photocopying). Write 'complaint' at the top of the letter. Describe the events clearly, in order, with relevant dates. Include reference numbers (e.g. customer reference) and photocopies of documents (hold on to the originals). Be firm but remain polite. Keep a copy of your complaint letter(s). If you phone to complain, note the name of the person who took the call, the main points made, and the date and time. Regulated financial firms must respond in writing to your complaint within eight weeks.

Be wary of using complaints management companies, CMCs (claim handlers, claims firms) – they can be expensive.

Roughly three out of four complainants dissatisfied with the response of the company choose not to pursue it further, believing it would be futile to do so. However, there are further positive steps you could take:

■ **Independent complaints scheme**. Most financial services firms belong to an independent complaints scheme – the FCA insists in most cases.[2] Your complaint will be investigated and, if found to be justified, the firm will be ordered to put matters right. You can only go to the independent complaints scheme if you have exhausted the possibility of direct settlement with the

---

[2] The firm's literature should set out its regulatory body and scheme.

firm. You know this has happened when you receive a letter from the firm saying it cannot reach agreement with you – a **'letter of deadlock'**. The FCA usually allows the firm up to two months to reach this point. If this letter (or agreement) is not forthcoming within this time, complain to the Financial Ombudsman Scheme.

Under the **Financial Ombudsman Scheme**[3] **(FOS)** the ombudsman collects together the facts of the case and arrives at what seems to him or her a reasonable and fair settlement allowing for 'common-sense' factors of fairness. The firm and the complainant are then under an obligation to accept the decision.[4] The service is free to consumers. You have six months from the date of the company's final letter to take your complaint to the ombudsman. If the FOS finds in your favour it can order a firm to pay compensation up to a maximum of £150,000 plus interest and costs.

■ **Go to court**. Litigation is often expensive, time-consuming and frustrating, and so should only be contemplated as a last resort. A relatively fast and informal service is provided by the small claims track or the small claims court (maximum claim in England and Wales £10,000, in Northern Ireland and Scotland £3,000). You do not need a solicitor, and court fees are low. You may not even have to attend the court as judges can make judgments on the paper evidence. The Citizens Advice Bureau may be able to guide you on your options.

Compensation

The complaint steps are all well and good if the firm that has treated you badly is still in existence. But what if it is defunct? The **Financial Services Compensation Scheme (FSCS)**[5] can compensate consumers (and small companies) if an *authorised* company is unable to pay money it owes you (note that if you do business with an unauthorised firm, e.g. an offshore company, you are not covered by the FSCS or the complaints procedure). The service is free for consumers and small businesses.

The FSCS covers your investments (e.g. bad advice, bad investment management), money deposited in accounts (at banks, building societies and credit unions) and insurance products (e.g. car insurance, life insurance).

---

[3] www.financial-ombudsman.org.uk or telephone 0800 023 4567.
[4] Although they can appeal through the courts they can only do so on grounds of the way in which the ombudsman arrived at the decision, not on the facts and merits of the case.
[5] www.fscs.org.uk or telephone 0800 678 1100.

The part of the FSCS focused on investment products and services covers shares and bonds, unit trusts, futures and options, personal pension plans and long-term insurance policies such as endowments. For investments the maximum payout is £50,000 per person. For deposit claims the scheme pays up to £85,000 per person (per firm). For insurance the scheme pays 90 per cent of the loss (100 per cent for compulsory insurance).

If your stockbroker, ISA provider or SIPP provider holds your shares in a CREST nominee account (see Chapter 4) and then goes bust, don't panic. The nominee holdings should be ring-fenced (legally separate) and not combined with the broker's assets. You may still be frustrated by the length of time it takes to separate assets though.

Regulation of markets

Financial markets need high-quality regulation in order to induce investors to place their trust in them. There must be safeguards against unscrupulous and incompetent operators. There must be an orderly operation of the markets, fair dealing and integrity. However, the regulations should not be so restrictive as to stifle innovation and prevent the markets from being competitive internationally. London's financial markets have a unique blend of law, self-regulation and custom to regulate and supervise their members' activities.

The FCA oversees exchanges, conducts market surveillance and monitors transactions on six **recognised investment exchanges (RIEs)** – see Figure 19.1. The RIEs work with the FCA to protect investors and maintain the integrity of markets. Much of the monitoring and enforcement is delegated to the RIEs. The London Stock Exchange, for example, vets new stockbrokers and tries to ensure compliance with LSE rules, aimed at making sure members (e.g. market makers and brokers) act with the highest standards of integrity, fairness, transparency and efficiency. It monitors market makers' quotations and the price of actual trades to ensure compliance with its dealing rules. It is constantly on the look-out for patterns of trading that deviate from the norm with the aim of catching those misusing information, e.g. insider dealing, creating a false or misleading impression to the disadvantage of other investors or some other market distorting action – see Article 19.2. The LSE, in partnership with the FCA, also requires companies to disseminate all information that could significantly affect their share prices. It insists on timely and accurate director statements to the stock market so that there is not a false market in the company's shares.

Traders' tools turn tables on dodgy deals

By Brooke Masters

Set a thief to catch a thief, the adage goes. When it comes to catching insider traders, the UK financial watchdog hasn't gone quite that far, but it is turning to traders' tools.

Under the leadership of Patrick Spens, a former Citigroup and hedge fund manager, the market monitoring division of what is now the Financial Conduct Authority has launched a data-based attack on suspicious trading.

First the FCA stepped up the pressure on City banks and brokers to do a better job of getting information to the regulator both about ordinary trades and those that looked suspicious.

Under UK law, banks and brokers must report every single transaction in a regulated security to the FCA every day. But many groups fell short of their responsibilities until the watchdog fined Barclays and eight other companies a combined £8m and forced them to go back and re-report everything they had missed.

Now the watchdog gets 13m detailed transaction reports every day with details of who bought, who sold and for how much. It is thought to be the most comprehensive regulatory database in the world.

Next Lord Spens, who has a hereditary title, stepped up the pressure on banks and brokers to live up to their duty to flag up unusual trading. After much prodding of companies,

the watchdog also received 1018 "suspicious transaction reports" last year, nearly double the previous total.

But data are only as good as the ability to interpret it, so the FCA hired a team of quantitative analysts and set them to work writing algorithms. Some of these "technologists" come from industry; others have PhDs in maths or statistics. Bolstered by the latest in high-end analytics servers as well as commercial surveillance software from Nasdaq OMX, the quants are writing programmes to comb the transaction data alongside news feeds to identify timely trades and unusual patterns.

The quants represent a small share of the 60-person market monitoring programme and their special project budget is in the millions of pounds.

"By marrying the algorithms with the STRs received, we can self-police the quality of STR submissions and create a virtuous circle of surveillance," he says.

Enforcement cases take years – several City professionals first arrested with great fanfare in 2010 won't go on trial until September 2014.

But knowing someone is watching appears to be having a deterrent effect. Suspicious trading before UK mergers and acquisitions fell to the lowest level in more than a decade last year.

Regulation of companies

If you invest in a company by buying its shares or bonds, you have a right to receive information about that company, and to expect that there are laws and other pressures to discourage the management from going astray and acting against your interests. There are various checks and balances in the corporate world:

■ The most important are the requirements under the **Companies Acts,** which are a powerful restraint on behaviour.

■ Accountants and auditors also function, to some extent, as regulators, helping to ensure companies do not misrepresent their position.

■ Furthermore, any member of the public may access the accounts of any company easily and cheaply at Companies House (www.companieshouse. gov.uk).

■ The media keep a watchful stance – always ready to reveal stories of fraud, greed, foul play, poor service, incompetence and chicanery.

■ In the case of mergers of listed or other public limited companies, the City Panel on Takeovers and Mergers acts to ensure fairness for all shareholders.

■ The Competition and Markets Authority investigate, rule on and enforce remedies with regard to anti-competitive behaviour.

■ The FCA is one of several UK organisations that investigates and responds to suspicions of fraud. The **City of London Police** is, however, the 'National Lead Force' for fraud with a remit to create a centre of excellence for fraud investigations and to use its expertise to help police forces across the UK. It is particularly concerned with organised crime groups such as boiler room scammers (see later) and securing major convictions.

■ The **Serious Fraud Office (SFO)** investigates and prosecutes serious or complex fraud and corruption exceeding £1 million in value. It is a part of the criminal justice system, but remains an independent government department (with a high degree of autonomy from political control). If a suspected fraud is likely to give rise to widespread public concern, be complex and thus require specialist knowledge to investigate, or be international in scope, then the SFO is inclined to be the organisation that tackles it.

Self-protection

Even with the complex and sophisticated structure of modern financial and corporate regulation, there is still a heavy responsibility on the ordinary investor to take precautions. It still boils down to 'buyer beware'. Here are some tips:

- If you want cover under the FCA rules and compensation scheme, make sure the financial service company is authorised.[6]

- If it sounds too good to be true, it probably is. Don't be taken in by promises of high returns way beyond the norm.

- Make sure you understand the risks of the underlying investments.

- Do not put all your money with one organisation. By splitting between a number if one goes bust or becomes rotten you have others to fall back on.

- Don't be afraid to ask questions if you don't understand.

- Make sure that your broker or independent financial adviser ring-fences your money – separates it from their own – so if they do go bust your money is safe.

- If you want your brokers to make investment decisions on your behalf make sure they are well informed about your investment aims, attitude to risk and tax position.

- Check what 'guaranteed' means for an investment product. Who is giving the guarantee, and are they sound? A common trick is that the income is guaranteed but your capital diminishes.

- When considering advice from financial advisers, brokers or insurance product sales people, ask how they are remunerated. If it is by receiving a commission on sales made you may view the advice differently. You might be even more sceptical if the level of commission varies depending on which product is sold. A product that might be ideal for you may not be mentioned if there is no commission to the sales person.

- Given the upper limits on compensation under the Financial Services Compensation Scheme, it might be wise to place a maximum of £50,000 of investments with any one provider.

- Ask your brokers what insurance they have against breach of professional duty (such as going outside your stated investment parameters or buying the

---

[6] See the FCA register at www.fca.org.uk or telephone 0800 111 6768.

wrong shares), insolvency, employee fraud, third-party fraud, and computer fraud.

■ Avoid being classed as an experienced investor, as many of the safeguards outlined in the chapter will not apply.

■ Don't be rushed into buying anything. There is generally a cooling-off period for pooled funds (e.g. with-profits policies).

Scams

Fore-warned is fore-armed; so here are couple of popular scams.

Boiler room

Imagine the scene. You have made a decent amount of money with your investments over the years. You have done your usual morning check on your portfolio and the market. While enjoying your morning coffee you get a call from a very nice-sounding man asking you about your investments and aspirations. He's particularly interested in your triumphs and what sort of size your fund has grown to.

And would you know it, he has an amazing opportunity that you really ought to invest in! But he is too polite to push you there and then to buy. Perhaps he can phone back in a week or two, when you have had time to digest the written material he will kindly email to you. No high pressure there then. Could he really be a conman?

Maybe to make sure you check out some details about the company he said was a sure winner on the Internet. It is a relief to find that it does actually exist. And, would you believe it, everything on the website(s) gives a glowing account of its prospects. Message board postings are full of praise.

So what if it is traded on an obscure market in a far-away country. That is exactly what your gentleman caller had said. After all that's where the opportunities are: mines in South America, hi-tech in America or new companies in the leading developing countries. That's where the money is! That's where the future lies! Not in old fashioned boring UK companies that produce pedestrian returns of 10 per cent or so a year.

What did he say? His top-pick forestry company in Indonesia had given its shareholders 120 per cent increases last year, and the year before. Better for you to jump in before everyone else hears about this and the price goes through the roof.

Two weeks later he calls you again. He politely asks you how you are doing, chats about the markets and casually mentions the company again. He is astonished that others in the market have not heard about this one. Don't they know that it is bound to rise at least 100 per cent in the next few months? What's more, because he has got along with you so well he will tell you about a way into this company at an even lower price than other investors. All you need to do is send him a cheque and he'll do the rest. Expect to see your money doubled in no time! Who knows, maybe in a few months he'll have another great opportunity for you. By which time you will have received statements showing the value of your first investment doing very nicely.

But, how much is a statement worth? Can you turn it into cash? 'Ah well ...', says the voice on the other end of the phone, 'that may take some time'.

You have been the victim of a boiler room scam. They are very convincing, very persuasive and very immoral. They are also annoyingly persistent. As much as £200 million is taken off UK investors each year. Many are elderly, who desperately need their savings. I'm always amazed at how apparently sophisticated and experienced investors fall for these scams. Some get so determined to recover the money previously lost that they use credit cards when they have gone through all their cash. While some end up losing their homes, the average loss is £20,000 (but one person lost £6 million).

Quite often, the shares do actually exist. It is just that they are traded on illiquid stock markets (if you can call them stock markets) in unsavoury parts of the world or on developed country markets that the locals are very wary of because of the lack of proper regulation to prevent widespread rip-offs. When you come to sell there is no one around willing to buy. Yes, but who sold you the shares in the first place? Well, the scammer of course, or an accomplice, at a highly inflated price. The company may, in reality, be almost worthless, but you have paid a price that would make a Mayfair antique dealer blush.

Alternatively, the company may not have obtained a quotation on a stock market yet. But it will do soon, you know. If you buy now then you pay a bargain basement price for your shares and multiply your money 2-, 5-, 10-fold when it does float. Of course, it never does. Or if it does it is worth nothing.

The scammers often have a close relationship with the directors of the company being promoted. They operate from overseas, out of the sight and control of the UK regulators and prosecution authorities in places such as Spain, Dubai and South Asia. Quite often they will tell you a blatant lie that they are based in London and regulated by the authorities there. 'Look! you can check the telephone number, and the website, and the company literature.' Definitely London then.

Telephones are not their only tools to trap investors. They also use word of mouth, post, advertise in newspapers and seminars. They may offer you a free research report into a company you already hold shares in, or a free gift or discount on their dealing charges.

Action you can take

■ Do not respond to cold-callers. Real stockbrokers and properly regulated financial advisers do not cold-call. Tell the crooks that they are conmen and immoral, and hang up.

■ Only deal with financial service firms that are authorised and regulated by UK regulators. You'll have to verify by calling them back on the number you find on the FCA's website (they may use the name of a high-reputation/regulated firm).

■ The golden rule for all investments: always understand what you are investing in. Do not be intimidated into being afraid to show your ignorance by asking key questions about the securities you are being asked to buy before you commit. How does the company make money? What are the risks? What safeguards are there?

Scammers are nothing if not inventive – see Article 19.3.

Article 19.3

UK regulator warns on graphene 'investment' schemes

By Jonathan Eley

Financial regulators in the UK have warned that consumers are increasingly being targeted by "dubious" companies offering investment opportunities in graphene, the carbon-based wonder material with a vast range of potential applications.

The Financial Conduct Authority will on Monday post new warnings on its website relating to "unscrupulous brokers" who "appear to be taking advantage of the hype surrounding graphene and are using uncertainty about its future as a way to entice consumers to invest".

It decided to take action after finding details relating to a graphene investment company on the computer servers of a suspected UK 'boiler room' operation that it investigated.

Although governments and companies are pouring billions of dollars into graphene research and development it is unlikely to be used commercially on a significant scale until around 2020.

Article 19.3   Continued

"The scam we are highlighting relies on the fact that although many people will have heard of graphene, they may be unaware it will be some time before graphene-based products hit the market," said Tracey McDermott, director of enforcement and financial crime at the FCA. "Finding an accurate price for graphene is very difficult, and its value is expected to fall over the coming years."

Unlike shares and funds, graphene is not a regulated product and companies promoting it as an investment do not have to be authorised by the FCA. Consumers who deal with unauthorised companies do not have access to the Financial Ombudsman Service, which resolves disputes between financial services companies and consumers, nor are they covered by the Financial Services Compensation Scheme, which provides some security for investors against companies that fail.

The FCA said it suspects the companies or individuals promoting investments in graphene have previously been involved in selling other unregulated products such as carbon credits, rare earth metals and overseas land and crops, in which investors have lost considerable sums. It added there is a danger that what is being sold as graphene might actually be something else, such as carbon solutions, graphite or carbon nanotubes.

"The unscrupulous individuals behind scams are always on the lookout for new ways to part people from their money. They're inventive and they'll create investment schemes based on what is being talked about in the media," Ms McDermott added.

Advanced fee scam

The fraudster finds out that you own shares in a company. He then offers to buy them from you at a higher price than their market value. 'What is wrong with that?' you ask. He will ask for money up front as a bond or other form of security. You will get this back if the sale does not go ahead, he says. Of course, you never hear from him again.

20

Measuring performance: indices and risk

When judging the performance of your share portfolio, in addition to examining the absolute returns, you might like to observe how well you did against the market as a whole, or a particular sector of the market (e.g. technology shares). Furthermore, you may be interested in judging performance in relation to the risk of your portfolio. You may have outperformed the market, but did you take on a very high risk to do it? And, is that level of risk acceptable, given the extra return?

This chapter describes the main indices used to compare performance over time. It also explains the most commonly used measures for calculating share and portfolio risk.

Indices

Information on individual companies in isolation is less useful than information set in the context of the firm's peer group, or in comparison with quoted companies generally. For example, if Marks & Spencer's shares fall by 5 per cent on a particular day, an investor might be keen to learn whether the market as a whole rose or fell on that day, and by how much.

How are indices calculated?

A market index is simply an aggregate value of a group of shares tracked over time. But the way in which these are calculated varies; you can do the aggregating in different ways.

The Dow Jones

The first index, the Dow Jones Industrial Average (DJIA, the Dow), was created over 100 years ago. Charles Henry Dow gathered together the prices of 12 large US shares and simply averaged the prices (the statistic was published in *The Wall Street Journal*).

If one company in that list had a market capitalisation 20 times greater than another, that was ignored – it was purely based on share price. Later, the metric was expanded so that now 30 shares are included in the Dow. To be precise we should say that the Dow is not an index at all, but an average, although people tend not to be so pedantic.

Price weighted index versus a market-value weighted index (market-cap weighted)

There are difficulties with using only prices to represent the market, a **price weighted index**.

Example

Imagine the simple case of an index consisting of two companies, Farmbrough plc and Nunn plc. Farmbrough is priced at £3 per share and Nunn is priced at £6 per share. In a price weighted average Nunn takes a greater proportion of the index – two-thirds, in fact.

Thus, if the index starts at £4.50 and the next day the price of Farmbrough rises by 40 per cent to £4.20 while the price of Nunn rises by 10 per cent to £6.60 the overall index moves from £4.50 to £5.40. This is a 20 per cent rise. (The opening average price was £3 × 0.5 + £6 × 0.5 = £4.50. The closing average is £4.20 × 0.5 + £6.60 × 0.5 = £5.40.)

However, if it is Farmbrough that rises by 10 per cent and Nunn that rises by 40 per cent we see a much bigger jump in the index: Farmbrough is now at £3.30 and Nunn is at £8.40, moving the price weighted average to £5.85 (that is £3.30 × 0.5 + £8.40 × 0.5). The 'market' has moved up by a greater percentage (30 per cent) simply because the larger weighted share had the bigger move.

It occurred to index compilers that a more representative method is to weight according to the size of the company. Thus a 10 per cent movement in the share price of a large company has a greater effect on an index than a 10 per cent change in a small company's share price.

> **Example**
>
> If we now know that Farmbrough has 1000 million shares in issue, but Nunn has only 50 million shares held by shareholders the market capitalisations are 1000 million x £3 = £3,000 million for Farmbrough and 50 million x £6 = £300 million for Nunn. For a market-capitalisation weighted index Farmbrough will represent 90.9 per cent of the index, whereas Nunn will contribute only 9.1 per cent.
>
> So, if we go back to a 10 per cent rise in the price of Farmbrough and a 40 per cent rise for Nunn the market-cap weighted index rises by only 12.7 per cent, being dominated by the larger company (that is, 10% x 0.909 + 40% x 0.091 = 12.7%). If Nunn had the larger capitalisation then the rise in the index would be much nearer to 40 per cent.

Most modern indices are market-cap weighted so that companies such as Shell or Vodafone have much greater influence on the index than say a medium-sized engineering company with a tenth of their market capitalisation.

Notice that we have only allowed for share price changes, ignoring dividends. The main indices discussed below tend to be calculated both as market-capitalisation weighted price change only indices, and as 'total return' versions, which include dividend returns as well.

But, most charts you will see, and news broadcasts, concentrate on the version that leaves out the dividends. This does not make much difference over a short period; but when comparing performances over many years you must include the dividends. Certainly, over the 14 years to 2014 when share prices went nowhere we get a distorted view of the returns on shares if we exclude the dividends (around 3–4 per cent per year – over 14 years that adds up).

The major UK market indices

The *Financial Times* (FT) joined forces with the Stock Exchange (SE) to create FTSE International in 1995, which has taken over the calculation (in conjunction with the Faculty and Institute of Actuaries) of a number of equity indices. These indicate the state of the market as a whole, or selected sectors of the market. The indices in Box 20.1 are market-capitalisation weighted.[1]

---

[1] The weighting for some shares is reduced if a high proportion of the shares are held not in a free float but in the hands of people closely connected with the business (e.g. directors, major shareholders).

Box 20.1   The main UK share indices shown in the *Financial Times*

FTSE ACTUARIES SHARE INDICES
Produced in conjunction with the Institute and Faculty of Actuaries

UK SERIES
www.ft.com/equities

	£ Stlg Feb 11	Day's chge%	Euro Index	£ Stlg Feb 10	£ Stlg Feb 7	Year ago	Div. yield%	Cover	P/E ratio	Xd adj	Total Return
FTSE 100 (100)	6672.66	1.23	6266.39	6591.55	6571.68	6338.38	3.51	2.14	13.32	6.48	4869.19
FTSE 250 (250)	16078.28	1.05	15099.36	15910.72	15865.12	13476.01	2.39	1.91	21.94	13.70	10630.41
FTSE 250 ex Inv Co (207)	17525.38	1.09	16458.36	17337.26	17290.80	14444.75	2.40	2.03	20.55	12.96	11805.84
FTSE 350 (350)	3643.97	1.20	3422.11	3600.64	3589.87	3399.03	3.34	2.11	14.17	3.47	5376.69
FTSE 350 ex Inv Co (307)	3629.07	1.21	3408.12	3585.66	3575.01	3385.50	3.36	2.13	13.99	3.41	2755.83
FTSE 350 Higher Yield (89)	3627.16	1.31	3406.33	3580.44	3572.61	3386.82	4.55	1.91	11.50	4.19	5352.00
FTSE 350 Lower Yield (261)	3301.84	1.10	3100.81	3266.05	3253.50	3075.79	2.05	2.60	18.79	2.45	3352.90
FTSE SmallCap (266)	4511.45	0.50	4236.77	4489.22	4481.90	3692.01	2.21	1.05	43.10	7.45	5883.48
FTSE SmallCap ex Inv Co (135)	4164.57	0.45	3911.01	4145.75	4146.52	3097.50	2.23	1.13	39.84	4.14	5707.81
FTSE All-Share (616)	3582.50	1.18	3364.38	3540.62	3530.17	3330.80	3.30	2.09	14.45	3.49	5350.32
FTSE All-Share ex Inv Co (442)	3556.86	1.20	3340.30	3514.74	3504.49	3307.85	3.34	2.12	14.14	3.35	2746.64
FTSE All-Share ex Multinatl (546)	1154.64	0.56	898.72	1148.24	1145.23	982.43	2.81	2.61	13.62	0.95	1860.74
FTSE Fledgling (107)	6733.46	0.61	6323.50	6692.56	6675.33	5144.23	2.46	-2.75	‡	5.32	11571.33
FTSE Fledgling ex Inv Co (67)	8299.63	0.84	7794.31	8230.85	8201.54	5722.76	2.27	-5.58	‡	0.48	13960.23
FTSE All-Small (373)	3109.20	0.50	2919.90	3093.66	3088.43	2532.99	2.23	0.78	57.24	4.96	5206.84
FTSE All-Small ex Inv Co (202)	3067.46	0.48	2880.69	3052.80	3052.60	2269.43	2.23	0.66	67.69	2.86	5328.67
FTSE AIM All-Share (809)	868.23	0.26	815.37	865.97	863.47	747.86	0.86	0.25	†	0.47	912.37
FTSE Sector Indices											
Oil & Gas (26)	8504.74	1.66	7986.93	8365.74	8332.29	8559.79	4.05	1.87	13.20	-	6502.62
Oil & Gas Producers (18)	8034.84	1.63	7545.64	7905.79	7879.87	8056.41	4.10	1.86	13.11	-	6348.20
Oil Equipment Services tion (7)	23021.99	2.42	21620.30	22478.59	21977.40	25339.75	2.82	2.23	15.90	-	15761.63
Basic Materials (35)	5553.50	2.17	5215.37	5435.30	5415.22	6388.08	3.20	2.59	12.05	0.85	5031.85
Chemicals (8)	11702.88	2.39	10990.35	11429.34	11399.24	9770.37	2.07	2.06	23.45	19.27	9671.65
Forestry & Paper (1)	11494.95	1.14	10795.09	11365.66	11289.27	9438.08	2.51	3.06	13.01	-	11310.88
Industrial Metals & Mining (4)	1203.36	3.08	1130.09	1167.40	1160.26	3403.42	0.78	-0.57	‡	-	1033.92
Mining (22)	16489.07	2.17	15485.14	16138.56	16078.51	19540.97	3.35	2.62	11.39	-	7770.42
Industrials (111)	4580.86	1.11	4301.96	4530.72	4529.28	3796.36	2.21	1.87	24.23	1.02	4330.60
Construction & Materials (12)	4758.77	1.18	4469.03	4703.20	4714.71	3821.26	3.30	0.27	†	-	4586.04
Aerospace & Defense (9)	5486.35	1.16	5152.31	5423.32	5384.24	4306.41	1.89	2.52	21.00	1.03	5421.51

The indices in the first column ('£ Sterling Feb 11') are price indices only (share price movements only are reflected in the indices). The final column, 'Total return', shows the overall performance with both the combined share price rises and dividends reinvested in the portfolio.

Source: www.ft.com, 11 February 2014.

FTSE 100

The Footsie™ index is based on the 100 largest companies with a premium listing (generally with over £2.5 billion market capitalisation) which make up approximately 80 per cent of the total market capitalisation of the LSE's Main Market. Large and relatively safe companies are referred to as **'blue chips'**. This index has risen sixfold since it was introduced at the beginning of 1984 at a value of 1,000. This is the measure most watched by investors. It is calculated in real time and so changes can be observed throughout the day – see free websites.

Box 20.2	The list of FTSE 100 companies in the *Financial Times*

FTSE 100 SUMMARY

FTSE 100	Closing price	Day's change	FTSE 100	Closing price	Day's change
Aberdeen AM	426	+4.50	LSE	£19.39	+0.30
Admiral Group	£14.38	+0.19	Marks & Spencer	485.60	+15.30
Aggreko	£15.87	+0.18	Meggitt	530.50	+6.50
AMEC	£11.12	+0.39	Melrose	305	+4.60
Anglo American	£15.26	+0.25	Mondi	978	+11
Antofagasta	903	+5.50	Morrison Supermk	237.20	-3.10
ARM Holdings	937	+21	National Grid	813.50	+13
Ashtead Gp	815.50	+7	Next	£63.60	+1.25
ABF	£28.05	-0.05	Old Mutual	181.10	+3.10
AstraZeneca	£39.75	+0.60	Pearson	£11.30	+0.16
Aviva	457.70	+1.80	Persimmon	£14.34	+0.41
Babcock International	£13.95	+0.53	Petrofac	£12.61	+0.29
BAE Systems	435.90	+5.10	Prudential	£13.09	+0.31
Barclays	264.70	-10.30	Randgold Resourc	£47.05	+1.75
BG Group	£10.67	+0.07	Reckitt Benckise	£48.27	+0.51
BHP Billiton	£18.49	+0.34	Reed Elsevier	906.50	+20.50
BP	491.75	+9.70	Resolution	366.10	+2.20
Brit Am Tobacco	£29.93	+0.27	Rexam	508.50	+2.50
British Land	678.50	+6.50	Rio Tinto	£34.60	+0.78
B Sky B	900	+10.50	Rolls-Royce Hldgs	£12.05	+0.16
BT Group	395.50	+3.50	Royal Bank Scot	343.20	+5.60
Bunzl	£13.91	+0.04	Royal Dutch Shel A	£21.44	+0.38
Burberry Group	£15.16	+0.22	Royal Dutch Shel B	£22.75	+0.38
Capita	£10.24	+0.10	Royal Mail Grp	596.50	+6
Carnival	£25.49	+0.12	RSA Insurance	99.10	-3.40
Centrica	312.80	+3.90	SABMiller	£27.79	+0.40
Coca-Cola HBC	£15.78	-0.23	Sage Group	428.10	+8.10
Compass Group	907	+16	Sainsbury	348.90	-7.30
CRH	£16.54	+0.21	Schroders	£25.68	+0.35
Diageo	£18.48	+0.19	Shire	£31.63	+0.18
Easyjet	£17.31	+0.22	Smith & Nephew	928.50	+11.50
Experian	£10.89	+0.20	Smiths Group	£13.91	+0.05
Fresnillo	911.50	+49	Sports Direct Int	708	+23
GKN	407.90	+2.50	SSE	£13.65	+0.14
GlaxoSmithKline	£16.43	+0.36	Standrd Chartrd	£12.70	+0.29
Glencore	332.85	+6.80	Standard Life	384.90	+6.20
G4S	234.20	+5.20	Tate & Lyle	786	+3
Hammerson	544	+6	Tesco	318.70	-5
Hargreaves Lansdown	£13.28	+0.24	TravisPrk	£18.81	+0.34
HSBC	635.40	+11.30	TUI Travel	436.90	+3.90
IAG	428.10	+4.60	Tullow Oil	845.50	+5
IMI	£14.95	+0.15	Unilever	£23.96	+0.21
Imperial Tobacco	£22.47	+0.05	United Utilities	752.50	+14
Intercont Hotels	£19.83	+0.32	Vodafone Group	221.50	-0.50
Intertek Group	£29.33	+0.48	Weir Group	£22.26	+0.22
ITV	206	+4.90	Whitbread	£40.67	+0.97
Johnson Matthey	£32.80	+1.02	WilliamHi	353.10	+9.90
Kingfisher	376.80	+11.70	Wolseley	£33.44	+0.16
Land Secs Group	£10.60	+0.12	WPP	£13.34	+0.27
Legal & General	227.60	+4.30			
Lloyds Banking G	83.38	+0.51			

Source: ThomsonReuters

Source: www.ft.com, 11 February 2014.

Box 20.2 shows the constituents of the Footsie in February 2014. Note that as some companies lose market value they may be overtaken by fast growing ones and so the list of the largest 100 changes regularly. To keep up with this, every three months the FTSE reviews to see if it is necessary to take companies out and place others into the index (It is not so strict as to remove and replace the moment a share falls below the top 100 capitalisation – that would be too disruptive – there is some judgement and watching along the way, to see if the fall is temporary. Thus, technically, the index is not purely the largest 100 because at the threshold it takes time to promote or demote companies in the index.)

For the first 16 years of its life the FTSE 100 zoomed away: these were great times for investors. The period following the dotcom crash of 2000 was a less blessed period with some big ups and downs – see Box 20.3.

Box 20.3   The progress of the FTSE 100 index (price only)

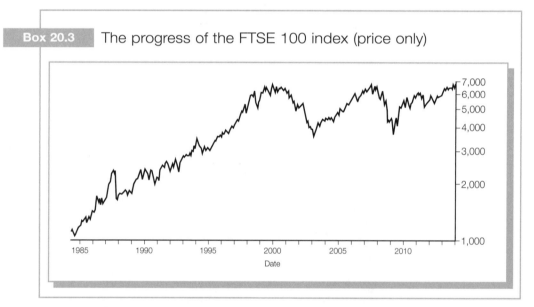

Source: uk.finance.yahoo.com. Reprinted with permission from Yahoo. © 2014 Yahoo.

When judging your portfolio performance it is important to compare like with like. Thus, if you do not have any (or not many) top 100 companies, instead preferring to operate in the mid cap (middle-sized capitalisation firms) then the next index is probably the one for you to use as a comparison. You can do this easily on free websites which will take your portfolio performance over the past few years and place it on a chart alongside a graph of the FTSE 250 index (or other indices you choose).

FTSE 250

No, it is not the top 250. It is based on the largest 250 Main Market firms which are in the next size range after the top 100, representing 15–16 per cent of the total UK market capitalisation. Capitalisations are generally between £500 million and £2.5 billion.

FTSE All-Share

This index is the most representative in that it reflects the average movements of about 800 shares on LSE's Main Market representing approximately 98–99 per cent of the value of London's Main Market. Note that not 'all' shares are included, merely about 70–80 per cent of those on the Main Market. This index is broken down into a number of commercial and industrial sectors, so that investors and companies can use sector-specific yardsticks, such as those for mining or chemicals. Because it is market-cap weighted, the top 10 companies account for over 35 per cent of the index. Companies in the FTSE All-Share index have market capitalisation above £50 million (roughly). It is an aggregation of the FTSE 100, FTSE 250 and the FTSE SmallCap.

FTSE 350

This index is based on the largest 350 Main Market companies. It combines the FTSE 100 and the FTSE 250. This cohort of shares is also split into two to give high and low dividend yield groups. A second 350 index excludes investment trusts.

FTSE SmallCap

This index covers companies included in the FTSE All-Share but excluded from the FTSE 350, with a market capitalisation of between about £50 million and £500 million.

FTSE Fledgling

This index includes companies listed on the Main Market but too small to be in the FTSE All-Share index.

FTSE AIM All-Share

An index of all AIM companies (except those with a low free-float and low liquidity).

FTSE All-Small

This index combines companies in the FTSE SmallCap with those in the FTSE Fledgling.

Comparing collective investment performance

Some monthly financial magazines (e.g. *Money Management* or *What Investment*) carry performance tables showing how particular unit trusts, OEICs and investment trusts have performed over periods of one, three, five and 10 years – also see www.morningstar.co.uk and www.ft.com.

Venturing abroad – international indices

USA

The *Standard & Poor's 500 (S&P 500)* index tracks the performance of the US's 500 leading companies, and so is more representative of US shares than the 30-share Dow. It covers firms listed on Nasdaq (see below), such as Microsoft and Apple, as well as those on the New York Stock Exchange, capturing 75 per cent of the value of US quoted shares. The index was first published in 1957.

Professional investors pay more attention to this index rather than the deeply flawed Dow – the news broadcasters are yet to catch up. The top 10 companies account for 21 per cent of the index and include Exxon Mobil, IBM, GEC, AT&T, Chevron, Johnson & Johnson, Coca-Cola and Wells Fargo, as well as the two computer giants.

The NASDAQ[2] market was started as an alternative trading venue to the NYSE in 1971. It is now the second largest exchange in the world. It tends to attract a greater proportion of hi-tech companies.

The composite index covers around 3,000 companies and contains companies from many industrial sectors, but its greatest components are the technology, telecoms and Internet companies (e.g. Facebook). It is market-cap weighted.

NASDAQ-100 tracks the largest 100 companies on the NASDAQ – this really does have a bias toward hi-tech (e.g. Amazon, Dell and Google).

Japan

Japan is home to one of the world's best known indices, the *Nikkei 225*. The

---

[2] The name originally stood for National Association of Securities Dealers Automated Quotations, but now it is NASDAQ in its own right

Nikkei was established in September 1950. It is one of the few price weighted indices, comprising 225 of the leading companies on the Tokyo Stock Exchange.

Other important indices

There are many other agencies calculating indices all over the world. The main benchmarks are shown in Table 20.1.

Table 20.1   Important stock market indices

Index	Country
NASDAQ Comp	US
Dow Jones Ind.	US
S&P 500	US
FTSE MIB	Italy
Xetra DAX	Germany
Euro Stoxx 50	Eurozone
CAC 40	France
AEX	Netherlands
BEL20	Belgium
PSI General	Portugal
Nikkei 225	Tokyo
Hang Seng	Hong Kong
BSE Sensex	India
Bovespa	Brazil
FTSE Straits Times	Singapore
Shanghai A	China
ASX All Ordinaries	Australia
IBEX 35	Spain
FTSEurofirst 300	Europe
FTSE All-World	World

Risk

The greatest risk of all comes about because share buyers do not understand what they are buying. Frequently, they don't have a clue as to what makes the business tick. The great investors tell us that the best way to reduce risk is to investigate what you are buying into.[3] Don't flail around buying this, that or the other on a whim, a tip or even broker advice. Find out about the people you are handing your money over to (the directors of the company), about the state of the industry (see Chapter 14), whether the company has any extraordinary resources (see Chapter 15) and the financial standing of the firm (see Chapters 11, 12 and 13).

Risk is proportional to ignorance more than it is proportional to any other factor.

Set against the issue of ignorance of what punters are buying, the technical measures described below are pretty unimportant. Nevertheless, they are referred to by many analysts and journalists, and so you need to know what they are talking about. Later we will look at the measures of risk used by the great investors – you'll find that they are not technical at all, they are qualitative, requiring keen judgement rather than mathematical formulas with Greek letters in them.

Diversification – the nearest thing to a free lunch in investing

We have all heard the adage 'don't put all your eggs in one basket'. This applies to your portfolio as much as to other aspects of life. If you place all your money in one company you are vulnerable to adverse news (e.g. a product failure, chief executive's resignation, government rule change) causing a plummet in price. Holding one company's shares in your portfolio will typically result in volatility.

If you split your fund between two companies, at any one time there is a fair chance that bad news affecting one is offset by good news affecting the other, so that overall portfolio returns do not oscillate as much. This principle works even better if you have three, four or five shares in your portfolio.

Ice cream and umbrellas

To illustrate the benefits of diversification let us take an extreme example. My aim here is to eliminate all volatility in profits so that year after year the same return

---

[3] See Glen Arnold, *The Financial Times Guide to Value Investing*, 2nd edn (Financial Times Prentice Hall, 2009) – or www.glen-arnold-investments.co.uk.

comes through to shareholders regardless of the underlying circumstances. Thus there is no bobbing about at all, returns remain perennially good.

Start by imagining that you own an ice cream business in a seaside town. If the summer is hot profits are very high. If the summer is cold you lose money – a lot of hard work for no return that year.

If the summer is typically British, with a mixture of showers and sun, then you make modest profits. These modest profits are perfectly acceptable as a rate of return on your money invested.

Of course, when you bought this business you had no idea what the weather would be over the next 10 years; just that you have to take the rough with the smooth. Profits from year to year are going to be volatile, but over say a decade you will make an acceptable return on the money invested – it will average out OK.

Now I'll demonstrate the benefits of diversification. Instead of putting all your money into the ice cream business you devote half to ice cream and half to the selling of umbrellas. Now what happens? When it is sunny your ice cream business makes bumper profits, but your umbrella business loses money resulting in an overall average return, acceptable but not brilliant. When it is wet the umbrella business has a great time of it, but you lose money on the ice creams resulting, again, in acceptable profits overall. When the weather is mixed both businesses produce acceptable returns.

Thus we have a free lunch: investing purely in ice cream results in 'an acceptable return', say 10 per cent averaged over a lot of years. So does investing in a portfolio of two business: 10 per cent return per year. However, the portfolio gives you something else: without having to sacrifice any return (over a span of years) you bring volatility down to zero.

The stock market is a little different in that the returns between two companies, say M&S and Rolls-Royce, do not move exactly in opposite directions from one year, or one month, to the next. There is generally a small degree of different movement but not much. Nevertheless this is enough, if the portfolio gets to around 10–15 shares, for the effects of portfolio diversification to be very beneficial. You will not eliminate all volatility but you will reduce it without sacrificing overall return.[4]

The typical effects of stock market diversification are illustrated in Figure 20.1.

---

[4] Remarkably, the benefits of diversification work even when the shares move together in the same direction. This co-movement cannot be 'perfect' though – see below for perfect positive correlation

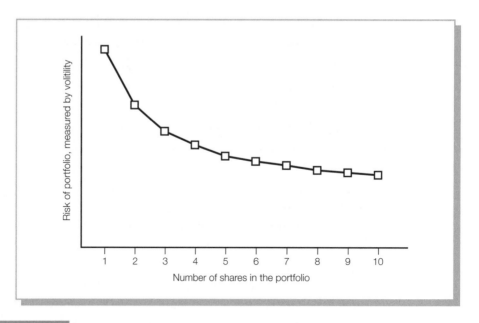

Figure 20.1   Decreasing risk by portfolio diversification

Diversification is a cheap and practical way of reducing your risk. You are highly recommended to do it. However, note that in Figure 20.1 the benefits of further diversification after a handful of different shares are held in the portfolio tail off – you can keep on reducing risk but the additional benefit starts to become very small.

I suggest that private investors should not over-diversify because the benefits of additional diversification become tiny and yet the disadvantage of not being able to understand all the companies you are buying a portion of starts to loom large. Not only do you sacrifice the ability to understand the companies at the time of share purchase, but you are unable to follow the unfolding stories thereafter if you are trying to keep track of dozens of shares.

Note also that the benefits of diversification are very much reduced if you buy shares all in the same sector of the market (e.g. all telecommunications shares). These are likely to go up and down together.

Volatility

Let's take a closer look at this term 'volatility'. Warning: this is about to get mathematical – you can skip the detail of the calculations without losing much comprehension of the volatility measures.

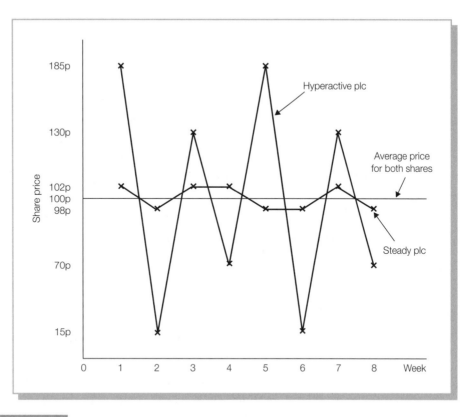

Figure 20.2 Volatility of share prices

Figure 20.2 shows the share prices for two companies over a period of eight weeks. It is obvious from the chart that shares in Hyperactive plc are much more volatile than shares in Steady plc. Volatility describes the way in which the share price wanders around its average (in this case the average price for both shares is £1).

Observing the higher degree of movement in Hyperactive's shares around its average share price is very easy in this case. However, it might be useful to summarise the degree of movement in a number (a statistic), particularly if we were looking at more subtle cases and could not gauge relative volatility by looking at a chart. The measure of this bobbing about the average that is most often used is called the **standard deviation**. The way in which it is calculated is by looking at the difference between the average share price over the entire study period (eight weeks in this case) and the actual share price in each week. In the case of Steady plc the difference is 2p in each week (102p–100p or 100p–98p). Each of these differences (deviations) is squared and then the squares are added together:

$$2 \times 2 + 2 \times 2 + 2 \times 2 + 2 \times 2 + 2 \times 2 + 2 \times 2 + 2 \times 2 + 2 \times 2 = 32$$

The number 32 is then divided by the number of occasions; in this case 8 (weeks). This gives us the **variance** of the share price of Steady, 4, over the period of eight weeks and is a measure of risk in its own right.

This is a large number compared with the size of the weekly movements around the average – only 2 pence. This is because we squared the weekly deviations. So, what we do to bring us back to the same units as the original data is to take the square root of the variance. The square root of 4 is 2. This is called the standard deviation (in pence).

If we follow the same procedure for Hyperactive:

$$85 \times 85 + 85 \times 85 + 30 \times 30 + 30 \times 30 + 85 \times 85 + 85 \times 85 + 30 \times 30 + 30 \times 30 = 32{,}500.$$

Dividing 32,500 by 8 we get 4062.5p, the variance, and, then, taking the square root, a standard deviation of 63.7p.

So now, instead of having a general impression of Hyperactive's higher volatility we have precise measures: Hyperactive's standard deviation, at 63.7 pence, has been many times greater than Steady's, at a mere 2 pence. High standard deviation is regarded as a bad thing because investors do not like to be caught out with a downswing in the market price. They like the upswing, but given a fixed overall return, would prefer a degree of movement that is closer to the average. They 'feel the pain' of the underperformance more than the joy of the equal-sized out-performances.

In reality, when calculating standard deviation analysts will examine more than eight periods. So they might use three years of monthly data, one year of daily data or two years of weekly data, for example. Also total return (including dividends as well as price movement) rather than share price could be analysed.

There is a rough rule of thumb you can use with standard deviation:[5] for a series of returns subject to volatility the likelihood of any one period's returns being within one standard deviation of the average (the mean) is 70 per cent. Thus, if a share has shown an average annual return of 10 per cent and a standard deviation

---

[5] This is if you can assume a 'normal distribution' of the return observations (the bell-shaped curve). Clearly, the returns for Hyperactive and Steady are far from being normally distributed.

of 4 per cent over the past 20 years there is a 70 per cent chance that its return in any one year was between 6 per cent and 14 per cent (if the returns are normally distributed the chance of an outcome below 6 per cent is 15 per cent and the chance of an outcome greater than 14 per cent is 15 per cent). There is a 95 per cent chance for two standard deviations: thus 95 per cent of returns should be between 2 per cent and 18 per cent.

Be aware that, as investors, we are interested in the likelihood of loss in the *future*. Variance and standard deviation tell you about *past* volatility. It is a leap of faith to then assume that the future will be like the past. You need to examine the circumstances to see if such faith can be justified. It is remarkable how measures of standard deviation change over time for the same company. Often a measure of volatility calculated two years ago puts the company into the low-risk category but one calculated last month puts it into the high-risk category (and vice versa). Standard deviation also changes depending on whether your data consists of daily, weekly, monthly, quarterly or yearly movements.

Correlation

Correlation measures the degree to which the returns of two assets move together. Correlations are described on a scale that stretches from –1 to +1. A perfect positive correlation (+1) means that the two assets move in lock step with one another. So, if over time and consistently Tesco's share price went up or down by a certain percentage and Sainsbury's always went up or down by the same percentage then Tesco and Sainsbury would have perfect positive correlation. There is no reduction in volatility for a portfolio of perfectly correlated shares – it is merely averaged.

A correlation of –1 is perfect negative correlation. This time the movements are exact opposites, as in the case of our umbrella company and ice cream company. If they moved in opposite directions most of the time but not perfectly, then the correlation coefficient could be say –0.5. Assets that do not have any co-movement at all – if one goes up the other may either go up or down – show a correlation of 0.

Diversification is going to be most effective with shares that are negatively cor-related. You may have noticed that when the London equity market is up the equity markets in the US and in Europe are also (generally) up. This impression is confirmed by the calculation of correlations which turn out to be around 0.6–0.9.

Beta and alpha

Beta measures the extent to which a share has, historically, gone up when the market as a whole rose, and gone down when the market went down. It is a share's sensitivity to the market movements. A beta of 1 indicates that generally (on average) in the past when the market rose by 10 per cent this share rose by 10 per cent. A beta of, say, 2 indicates a high sensitivity to market movements in the past. If the market rose by 10 per cent this share tends to rise by 20 per cent. This is fine if things are going well – you outperform the market. On the other hand, if the market fell by 10 per cent your share showed a tendency to exaggerate the market movement by falling 20 per cent. Shares with betas less than 1 have historically been more stable than the market as a whole. So, a share with a beta of 0.5 generally responded to a 10 per cent fall in the market by only falling 5 per cent.

The danger of relying on beta for future-orientated investment decisions is that you have to assume that the relationship with market returns will continue. This is often not the case.[6]

Alpha is a measure of performance greater or less than the market as a whole after allowing for beta. It is the portion of a share's return that cannot be explained by its responsiveness to moves in the market as a whole.

Sharpe's ratio

Investors cannot simply look at performance figures and judge whether one portfolio or one fund manager has done better than another. They need to take account of the level of risk to which each portfolio was subject. For example imagine fund manager X achieved a return of 10 per cent over the same period that fund manager Y achieved a return of 11 per cent. We cannot automatically award manager Y the rosette for best performance. It could be that manager Y exposed the investor's money to much higher risk. It happened to pay off this year, but may not do so in future years. The Sharpe ratio (also called the 'reward-to-variability ratio') judges performance in relation to risk. It is the extent to which the portfolio's return has been greater than that on a risk-free asset (e.g. lending to the UK government by buying its treasury bills) divided by its standard deviation. So if the risk-free return is currently 4 per cent and manager X's fund had a standard deviation of 5 per cent whereas manager Y's fund had a standard deviation of 9 per cent, we see that fund manager X outperformed on a 'risk-adjusted' basis:

---

[6] For a discussion of the profound difficulties with relying on beta as a measure of risk see the eighth chapter of the fifth edition of Glen Arnold, *Corporate Financial Management* (Pearson Education, 2013).

Manager X: (10–4)/5 = 1.2

Manager Y: (11–4)/9 = 0.78

Treynor's ratio

Treynor's ratio (also called the 'reward-to-volatility ratio') adjusts performance by beta (rather than standard deviation as in Sharpe's ratio). Treynor's ratio is return minus the risk-free rate of return divided by beta. A higher Treynor ratio indicates that the portfolio or fund has managed a stronger performance relative to the risk it has taken. (If risk can be taken to be beta – many academics and even more practitioners doubt that beta is a good measure of risk.)

Some more types of risk

■ **Liquidity risk.** Liquidity is the degree to which an asset can be sold quickly and easily without loss in value. Property investment assets are relatively illiquid because they may take weeks to sell. If a quick sale is needed, a reduction in price is usually required. Shares are generally more liquid than property, but it can still be hard to sell quickly and without moving the price against you. If other investors and market makers see you coming with a lot of shares that are infrequently traded they may well drop the price. Smaller company shares tend to be most illiquid. There are medium-sized firms where the majority of shares are held by a family or a few close associates. Trading here can be thin and illiquid. Some stock market listed companies see only one trade per month.

■ **Event risk.** September 11, the war in Iraq and the 2008 crisis were events that had profound impacts on airline companies. Event risk is the risk of suffering a loss due to unforeseen events. It could be less dramatic than war, and more specific to a company, e.g. a merger, a loss of a major contract.

■ **Political risk.** Changes in government or government policies may affect investors. This is more usually the case in developing countries where confiscation or forced nationalisation could take away all value from an overseas share holding. In 2012 the Argentine government simply took an oil company from the Spanish firm Repsol. Even limits on dividends can have an impact. Note that investors in UK listed companies conducting activities abroad can be affected by political events in other countries.

■ **Exchange rate risk.** It is possible to lose money on investments abroad simply because the foreign exchange rate moves against you even if the value of the shares (when valued in the overseas currency) remains constant. However, if you are diversified internationally you may be able to take a swings-and-roundabout attitude to this risk.

- **Market risk**. Your investment could be affected by a general slide in the whole stock market. Shares should not be seen as short-term investments because unexpected downward movements in the markets happen regularly – you must allow time for shares to perform well.

- **Manager risk**. Most fund managers (of ISAs, unit trusts, OEICs, investment trusts, pensions, etc.) do not consistently beat the market index average. Given this fact, you might like to save on the high fees of 'active' fund managers and either manage your own investments or go for low-fee 'tracker' funds or exchange traded funds.

- **Inflation risk**. If you select 'safe' investments such as building society accounts or government bonds you may suffer from inflation risk. That is, what seems like a reasonable return when inflation is 2 per cent loses purchasing power if inflation rises in the future to, say, 10 per cent. Investors in government securities were very badly hit in the 1970s as inflation rose to over 20 per cent: they had fixed their 'safe' returns at around 5–6 per cent. In 2014 bond investors are accepting a locked-in rate of return of around 2.7 per cent over 10 or more years. It seems to me that they are taking a big bet on inflation (and therefore interest) rates remaining low. The safer approach to dealing with inflation risk is to buy shares at reasonable prices relative to their long-term prospects. There are occasions in financial history when the riskier investments are bonds. I know, this is the opposite of conventional thinking.

Great investors' views on risk

What do the great investors regard as the best measure of risk? Surprisingly, perhaps, they do not use the mathematically-based measures so much talked about by those bright young graduates in the markets. Are they just old fuddy-duddys with a simplistic homespun view of risk unable to cope with the magnificence of the mathematical models created in recent times? Perhaps.

Or are they really on to something more profound by concentrating on factors which, while impossible to measure with great precision, are nevertheless more important? Personally, I'd rather be roughly right than precisely wrong so I'll stick with the subjective measures of risk. Apart from anything else, they are focused on losses over the long term rather than over a span of days or weeks (as the mathematical measures are). Investors, by definition, should be long-term focused.

Warren Buffett

In our opinion, the real risk that an investor must assess is whether his aggregate after-tax receipts from an investment (including those he receives on sale) will, over his prospective holding period, give him at least as much purchasing power as he had to begin with, plus a modest rate of interest on that initial stake. Though this risk cannot be calculated with engineering precision, it can in some cases be judged with a degree of accuracy that is useful. The primary factors bearing upon this evaluation are:

1 The certainty with which the long-term economic characteristics of the business can be evaluated;

2 The certainty with which management can be evaluated, both as to its ability to realize the full potential of the business and to wisely employ its cash flows;

3 The certainty with which management can be counted on to channel the rewards from the business to the shareholders rather than to itself;

4 The purchase price of the business;

5 The levels of taxation and inflation that will be experienced and that will determine the degree by which an investor's purchasing-power return is reduced from his gross return.

These factors will probably strike many analysts as unbearably fuzzy, since they cannot be extracted from a data base of any kind. But the difficulty of precisely quantifying these matters does not negate their importance nor is it insuperable.

Is it really so difficult to conclude that Coca-Cola and Gillette possess far less business risk over the long-term than, say, *any* computer company or retailer? Worldwide, Coke sells about 44% of all soft drinks, and Gillette has more than a 60% share (in value) of the blade market. Leaving aside chewing gum, in which Wrigley is dominant, I know of no other significant businesses in which the leading company has long enjoyed such global power.

..... The might of their brand names, the attributes of their products, and the strength of their distribution systems give them an enormous competitive advantage, setting up a protective moat around their economic castles. The average company, in contrast, does battle daily without any such means of protection.

The competitive strengths of a Coke or Gillette are obvious to even the casual observer of business. Yet the beta of their stocks is similar to that of a great many run-of-the-mill companies who possess little or no competitive advantage. Should we conclude from this similarity that the competitive strength of Coke and Gillette gains them nothing when business risk is being measured? Or should we conclude that the risk in owning a piece of a company – its stock – is somehow divorced from the long-term risk inherent in its business operations? We believe neither conclusion makes sense and that equating beta with investment risk also makes no sense.

> Buffett, W. (1993) Letter accompanying the Annual Report for
> Berkshire Hathaway Inc. for 1993.

Benjamin Graham

We should like to point out that the words 'risk' and 'safety' are applied to securities in two different senses, with a resultant confusion in thought.

A bond is clearly proved unsafe when it defaults its interest or principal payments. Similarly, if a preferred stock or even a common stock is bought with the expectation that a given rate of dividend will be continued, then a reduction or passing of the dividend means that it has proved unsafe. It is also true that an investment contains a risk if there is a fair possibility that the holder may have to sell at a time when the price is well below cost.

Nevertheless, the idea of risk is often extended to apply to a possible decline in the price of a security, even though the decline may be of a cyclical and temporary nature and even though the holder is unlikely to be forced to sell at such times.... But we believe that what is here involved is not a true risk in the useful sense of the term. The man who holds a mortgage on a building might have to take a substantial loss if he were forced to sell it at an unfavorable time. That element is not taken into account in judging the safety or risk of ordinary real-estate mortgages, the only criterion being the certainty of punctual payments. In the same way the risk attached to an ordinary commercial business is measured by the chance of its losing money, not by what would happen if the owner were forced to sell...

...[T]he bona fide investor does not lose money merely because the market price of his holdings declines; hence the fact that a decline may occur does not mean he is running a true risk of loss. If a group of well-selected common-stock investments shows a satisfactory overall return, as measured through a fair number of years, then this group investment has proved to be 'safe'. During that period its market value is bound to fluctuate, and as likely as not it will sell for a while under the buyer's cost. If that fact makes the investment 'risky', it would then have to be called both risky and safe at the same time. This confusion may be avoided if we apply the concept of risk solely to a loss of value which either is realised through actual sale, or is caused by a significant deterioration in the company's position – or more frequently perhaps, is the result of the payment of an excessive price in relation to the intrinsic worth of the security.

From Graham, B., The Intelligent Investor: The Definitive
Book on Value Investing – A Book of Practical Counsel
(HarperBusiness, 2006)

Websites

Volatility measures for shares are provided on most free financial websites.

The following provide risk information on collective funds: http://funds.ft.com/uk, www.morningstar.co.uk, http://www.standardandpoors.com/ratings/funds-main/en/eu.

Further reading

Portfolio theory, beta, alpha and the efficient markets hypothesis are explained in detail in Glen Arnold *Corporate Financial Management*, 5th edn (Pearson, 2013).

R. Vaitilingam, *The Financial Times Guide to Using the Financial Pages*, 6th edn (Financial Times Prentice Hall, 2010) provides an excellent overview of indices.

The website of the FTSE (www.ftse.com) has a lot of very useful descriptions and explanations to download, as do many of the websites listed above.

21

Investment clubs

Investing can be great fun. Looking for bargains unrecognised by the mass of investors, buying them and following their fortunes is exhilarating. Some people become so enthusiastic about investing that it becomes a hobby as well as a way of building up capital. It can be even more exciting if you can share the ups and downs, triumphs and disasters with fellow enthusiasts.

Investment clubs are groups of people who each contribute a few pounds per month (usually £25 to £40), which is then pooled to buy shares for the club. There are now over 12,000 investment clubs in the UK, with over 100,000 members.

The social aspect is very important – most members of a club are friends, or work colleagues, and about half of the clubs meet in a pub! There is generally a lot of light-hearted banter and, frequently, social events beyond the regular meetings – annual dinners, even club trips abroad.

An investment club is a great place to start if you feel daunted by the prospect of investing as an individual. You can learn a lot from the others and you can enjoy the thrills and spills without betting your life savings. Even experienced investors value clubs for the ability to socialise with like-minded people and the chance to share tips and ideas. Many members, in addition to their monthly contribution to the club, set up their own personal portfolio to gain greater exposure to shares they feel are particularly undervalued.

Club members often have years of experience of particular industries from their working lives and so may have special insight to offer at club meetings. Some clubs encourage members to agree to look at different companies or sectors to enable them to gain a depth of knowledge rather than trying to be jacks-of-all-trades.

How to set up a club

Investment clubs are usually begun when two or three friends think it would be a good idea to meet regularly to discuss investments. Each of these people, in turn, probably know two or three others who would like to join, and soon you have a club of between 10 and 20 members. Most clubs do not go beyond 20 members (the average is 11). This is because the friendly atmosphere can be lost and meetings can become unwieldy.

At the first meeting you need to agree how frequently you should meet and where (members' houses and pubs are the favourite options). You must also agree on the rules for recruiting additional members – there must be trust and a certain rapport within the club, so care is needed when extending the invitation to join. The monthly subscription also needs to be agreed – it can be as little as £10. Also, clubs often start with an initial lump-sum payment by members so that investments of hundreds or thousands of pounds can be made right away without having to wait until the monthly subscription builds up.

You will need to appoint three club officers: a chairman to chair meetings; an honorary secretary to record proceedings and produce minutes; and an honorary treasurer to receive monthly subscriptions (usually by standing order) and pay brokers. These officers should not have to put in more than one hour per month. They are elected by simple majority at the inaugural meeting or subsequently at a general meeting of the club. They are required to resign at the AGM but are entitled to stand again for re-election. The club is able to create other administrative posts as the need arises.

You need to decide on a name for the club and discuss the general investment philosophy and boundaries (e.g. long-term or short-term trading focus, whether to invest in overseas shares, or in traded options).

A rulebook or constitution needs to be drawn up to deal with practical issues. For example: what happens when a member leaves? How much notice should a member give before leaving? How do you calculate what is due to a member on departure? What are the rules for changing the constitution? What size majority is needed to agree investment decisions? How do you elect new members?

The *ProShare Investment Clubs Manual* contains a draft constitution, which you could adopt with or without modification.

The unit valuation system

It is important that every member is clear about how the value of their portion of the clubs' pot is calculated. ProShare, the leading support organisation for investment clubs in the UK, recommends the unit valuation system. When the club is established each £1 contributed gives a member one unit. Thereafter, to calculate the value of units you divide the club's net assets by the number of units. Each month the fund is revalued to create a new unit value. This is then used to work out the number of units to be purchased with each month's cash subscriptions. This system allows new members to join and existing members to buy extra units should they wish to do so. It is also possible for members to sell a portion of their holdings; after a few years a member may be holding £20,000 or so in the club and may wish to turn some of that into cash.[1] ProShare can provide you with a computer program to operate the unit system. The time to trade website (www. timetotrade.eu) provides much more detail on the unit valuation system and other aspects of investment clubs.

Bank account

High street banks offer special accounts for clubs (e.g. 'Clubs and Societies' or 'Treasurers') in which two signatories are usually required. Some accounts pay interest and some provide cheque facilities.

Brokers

Many stockbrokers are keen to help investment clubs. The charges are the same as for individuals. Clubs usually opt for nominee stockbroking accounts (see Chapter 4) because of the ease and efficiency of dealing. Clubs usually select an 'execution-only' service which is cheap and allows the club members to make investment decisions. (Make sure you don't lose your shareholder rights, e.g. to receive company communications and reports, to vote and to attend shareholder meetings.) Brokers usually ask to see a copy of the investment club constitution

---

[1] A disadvantage with the unit valuation system is that after a few years old members might have a large interest, say £25,000 each. If a member leaves this can unbalance the club because a new member might only be able to put in £1,000 or so. This can lead to dominance of discussion by those with most at stake, and tension. One alternative that has been tried is to ask the new member to match the stake of the old members. Another is to lower the stakes of all members to say £1,000–£2,000 when one leaves – this can help maintain a sense of camaraderie, equality and fun.

in case a disagreement arises within the club. The club appoints two members to act on behalf of the club, and both their signatures are required for all documents. The website www.proshareclubs.co.uk list stockbrokers offering services specifically for investment clubs accredited by ProShare.

Tax

There are no special tax advantages in investing through a club. Each member is taxed individually and everyone is liable to pay income tax on his or her share of dividends and capital gains tax on share price rises (when they are realised). The treasurer or secretary will provide to each member the details of his or her profits or losses made and dividends received for the year. It is up to the members to declare their club profits or losses on their individual tax returns. The local HM Revenue and Customs office will expect you to notify them of the club's existence and to make returns for the club each year.

Further reading

The ProShare Investment Club website (www.proshareclubs.co.uk).

T. Bond, *The Company of Successful Investors* (Financial Times Prentice Hall, 2001).

www.timetotrade.eu has a good section on the unit valuation system.

What did you think of this book?

We're really keen to hear from you about this book, so that we can make our publishing even better.

Please log on to the following website and leave us your feedback.

It will only take a few minutes and your thoughts are invaluable to us.

www.pearsoned.co.uk/bookfeedback

Glossary

'A' shares Sometimes the 'A' shares are the ordinary shares that carry fewer or no votes. However, in many companies 'A' shares carry more votes than the 'B' shares. The shares may also differ with regard to the size of the dividend.

Abandon The choice made by a holder of a warrant or option to allow it to expire without exercise.

Abnormal return (residual return) A return greater than the market return after adjusting for differences in risk.

Accounting rate of return A measure of profitability based on accounting numbers. Profit divided by assets devoted to the activity (e.g. project, entire business) as a percentage.

Accounting standards A set of formal rules and conventions set by the accounting profession to calculate accounting numbers.

Accounts payable *See* Trade credit.

Accounts receivable *See* Debtors.

Accumulation (Acc) units Unit trust units that reinvest income (e.g. dividends) earned from a portfolio, on behalf of unit holders, in more units. Also applies to open-ended investment companies.

Acid test *See* Quick ratio.

Acquisition *See* Takeover.

Actively managed fund The managers of the fund spend time and effort carefully selecting shares or other investments (the costs of this are passed on to investors) to try to outperform the market index.

Activist strategy Buying shares in a company and then pressing for changes in management policy which will result in a profit on the shares, e.g. raising dividends, selling off assets.

Actuary A person who makes a judgement on whether a fund has enough assets to deliver on its promises (e.g. to pensioners). The actuary is then able to suggest appropriate premium levels to raise or lower total assets.

Adjusted earnings per share *See* Headline earnings per share.

Administered prices Prices controlled by some authority (e.g. government).

Administration An administrator, 'administrative receiver', takes over the running of a distressed company to help it survive and avoid liquidation. This follows the company's failure to abide by loan agreements. Administrators often keep the business running as a going concern, but may conclude that they have no alternative to liquidation to release money for the creditors.

Admission document for the Alternative Investment Market This is required for a company to be admitted to trade on AIM in the first instance. It is similar to a prospectus.

Advisory service A type of service provided by a stockbroker in which the broker will offer advice prior to the investor's purchase or sale. The decision on whether to carry out a transaction still rests with the investor, unlike with a discretionary service.

Affirmative covenants Loan agreement conditions that require positive action on the part of the borrower, e.g. a statement that a bond will pay regular dividends, or that information will be regularly distributed.

Agency Acting for or in the place of another with his/her/its authority.

Aggressive shares Shares having a beta value greater than 1.

AGM *See* Annual general meeting.

AIC, Association of Investment Companies. Trade body for the closed-ended investment company industry (e.g. investment trusts, venture capital trusts).

AIM *See* Alternative Investment Market.

Allocation of capital (or resources) The mechanism for selecting competing investment projects leading to the production of a mixture of goods and services by a society. This can be influenced by the forces of supply and demand, and by central authority direction. The term may also be used for the selection of securities (e.g. shares) by investors, or business units and activities by managers.

Allocational efficiency of markets Efficiency in the process of allocating society's scarce resources between competing real investments.

Allotment In a new issue of shares, if more shares are demanded at the price than are available, they may be apportioned (allotted) between the applicants.

Allowance *See* Tax allowance.

All-paper deal When a bidder offers to buy shares in a target the payment is entirely in the form of shares in the bidder.

Alpha (alpha coefficient α) A measure of market outperformance (underperformance) after allowing for beta. That portion of a share's return that cannot be explained by its responsiveness to moves in the market as a whole. Sometimes called stock-specific return.

Alternative investment Outside of the mainstream (e.g. art, stamps, coins, wine, hedge funds, venture capital).

Alternative Investment Market (AIM) The lightly regulated share market operated by the London Stock Exchange, focused particularly on smaller, less well-established companies.

American Depositary Receipts Depositary receipts issued in the USA.

American-style option (American option) An option which can be exercised by the purchaser at any time up to the expiry date.

AMEX The American Stock Exchange. Trades equities, options and exchange traded funds. It is now part of NYSE Euronext which is part of Intercontinental Exchange. (Also used for American Express.)

Amortisation (1) The repayment of a debt by a series of instalments; (2) the balance sheet value of intangible assets that are gradually written off, such as goodwill.

Amortised *See* Amortisation.

Analyst A researcher of companies' prospects and predictor of their share price performance. Also analyses other securities.

Angel *See* Business angel.

Annual bonus The bonus given by an insurance company to with-profits policy holders.

Annual Equivalent Rate (AER) *See* Annual percentage rate.

Annual exempt amount Under the capital gains tax rules of the UK Her Majesty's Revenue and Customs permits this tax-free allowance. Those that have made a capital gain only pay tax on total realised gains above this amount.

Annual general meeting (AGM) A limited company must hold in each calendar year an annual general meeting. This is an opportunity for shareholders to meet and talk with each other and with those who run the company on their behalf. The managers give an account of their stewardship. All shareholders are entitled to attend and vote. Election of directors may take place.

Annual management charge (AMC) Collective (pooled) investment fund managers deduct a fee to pay for their time plus other costs of running the fund.

Annual percentage rate (APR) The true annual interest rate charged by a lender, it takes full account of the timing of payments of interest and principal.

Annual results Annual company accounts. This term is often used for the preliminary results.

Annuity (1) (General) An even stream of payments (same amount each time) over a given period of time with a fixed frequency of payments (usually annual). (2) (Insurance) In return for either regular payments or a lump sum payment, which is invested by the receiving company, the insured or their spouse will receive regular income payments either for a set time or until death.

Annuity due An annuity where the cash flows occur at the start of each period rather than at the end – the first payment is due now, not in one year's time.

APCIMS, Association of Private Client Investment Managers and Stockbrokers. Former name of the Wealth Management Association.

Appropriable resource The resource which supplies value must be one that allows the company to capture the value rather than allow it to be captured by another organisation or individual(s).

Arbitrage The act of exploiting price differences on the same instrument or similar securities by simultaneously selling the overpriced security and buying the underpriced security.

Arbitration An arbitrator decides on a just settlement between a complainant and a financial services firm. The decision is binding on both parties.

Arrangement fee A fee for agreeing and setting up a financial transaction such as a bank loan.

Articles of association Internal rules governing a company. These can be unique to the company if true to company law.

Asset In the financial market, anything that can be traded as a security (e.g. share, option, commodity, bond).

Asset allocation An investment methodology which specifies the proportion of funds to be invested in different asset classes (e.g. property, shares, bonds).

Asset-backed securities *See* Securitisation.

Asset backing The value of the assets held in the business – often measured on a per share basis.

Asset class Asset type (e.g. bonds, shares).

Asset liquidity The extent to which assets can be converted to cash quickly, at a low transaction cost and without lowering the price.

Asset lock-up In a hostile takeover situation, the target sells to a friendly firm those parts of the business most attractive to the bidder.

Asset securitisation *See* Securitisation.

Asset stripping Taking over a company and selling off all or some of the assets.

Asset transformers Intermediaries who, by creating a completely new security – the intermediate security – mobilise savings and encourage investment. The primary security is issued by the ultimate borrower to the intermediary, who offers intermediate securities to the primary investors.

Assets-available-for-sale In this category assets are revalued at each balance sheet date and any unrealised (not yet actually sold) gains or losses go through the balance sheet without raising or lowering profits for the period between two balance sheets.

Assets held for trading A category of balance sheet assets which are revalued at each balance sheet date even if not sold, mostly using fair value estimates. Any gain between balance sheet dates is recognised in earnings, i.e. profits are boosted.

Assets-held-to-maturity Assets such as many financial securities are put in a company's balance sheet at amortised cost less impairment.

Associated company A company in which an investor (usually a holding company) holds a participating interest and exercises significant influence. 'Interest' includes shares, options and convertible securities. 'Participating' means the interest is held on a long-term basis and there is significant influence. Usually a 20 per cent or more holding of the shares is presumed to be participating.

Association of investment companies *See* AIC.

Asymmetric information Situation where one party in a negotiation or relationship is not in the same position as other parties, being ignorant of, or unable to observe, some information which is essential to the contracting and decision-making process.

At best A type of buy or sell instruction given by an investor to a broker. The trade is to be completed immediately at the best price available.

At-the-money option The current underlying price is equal to the option exercise price.

Attribute markets Subsections of London Stock Exchange's Main Market consisting of firms with common characteristics – for example, technologically led as with techMARK.

Audit committee A committee of company independent non-executive directors responsible for validating their company's financial figures (e.g. by appointing effective external auditors).

Auditor An auditor determines whether a company's financial statements are misleading and whether the accounts present a true and fair picture.

AUT *See* Authorised unit trust.

Authorised but unissued ordinary share capital Shares that have not yet been sold by the company to investors. However, they have been created (authorised by shareholders) and may be sold or given to existing shareholders or sold to new shareholders.

Authorised corporate director (ACD) Manages and invests the funds in an open ended investment company.

Authorised participants At the heart of the creation of exchange traded funds are authorised participants (often market makers) who exchange a portfolio of underlying securities, e.g. shares of the FTSE 100 index, for ETF shares delivered by the ETF. The authorised participant can then sell the ETF shares in the market. Authorised participants can also sell ETF shares to the fund to receive the underlying securities.

Authorised share capital The maximum amount of share capital that a company can issue. The limit can be changed by a shareholder vote.

Authorised unit trust (AUT) One approved by the Financial Conduct Authority for sale in the UK.

Back office That part of a financial institution which deals with the settlement of contracts, accounting, regulatory matters and management information processes.

Bad debts Debts that are unlikely to be paid.

Balance sheet Summary of assets and liabilities, showing what a company owns, owes and is owed on a particular day in the past.

Ballot In a new issue of shares when a company floats on a stock exchange, if the demand is greater than supply, the shares are allocated to some applicants but not others, selected at random.

Bancassurance Companies offering both banking and insurance.

Bank covenant *See* Covenant.

Bank for International Settlements (BIS) Controlled by central banks, the BIS was established to assist international financial coordination. It promotes international monetary coordination, provides research and statistical data, coordination and trusteeship for intergovernmental loans, and acts as a central bank for national central banks, accepting deposits and making loans.

Bank of England The central bank of the United Kingdom, responsible for monetary policy and the safety and soundness of banks, clearing houses and other financial institutions, as well as the financial system as a whole. It issues banknotes and coins, manages the national debt and exchange rate, and is lender of last resort.

Bankruptcy Commonly used to describe an individual or company that cannot meet its fixed commitments on borrowing which leads to legal action. However, technically, in the UK, individuals become bankrupt whereas companies become insolvent and liquidated.

Bargain A term used interchangeably with the term 'a contract to buy/sell shares'.

Barriers to entry The obstacles that a company entering a market for the first time has to overcome to do well in that market.

Base rate The reference rate of interest that forms the basis for interest rates on bank loans, overdrafts and deposit rates.

Basic earnings per share Includes deductions from profit of one-off exceptional items.

Basis point (bp) One-hundredth of 1 per cent, usually applied to interest rates.

BATS Chi-X Europe In 2011, of the two leading pan-European multilateral trading facilities (MTFs), BATS Europe and Chi-X Europe came together, to offer trading in more than 3,600 securities across 15 major European markets, over one platform.

Bear An investor who takes the view that prices are likely to fall.

Bear fund Designed to do well when shares are falling in price.

Bearer bond The ownership of a bond is not recorded on a register. Possession of the bond is sufficient to receive interest, etc.

Bed and breakfasting shares Selling shares to realise a gain below the annual threshold for capital gains tax. This is followed by a repurchase the next day.

Bed and ISA Selling shares (or funds) in an investment account and then purchasing identical shares in an ISA account. This can take advantage of annual capital gains tax allowances.

Bed and SIPP Selling shares (or funds) in an investment account and then purchasing identical shares in a self-invested personal pension. This action can take advantage of annual capital gains tax allowances.

Bed and spousing Selling shares to realise a gain below the annual threshold for capital gains tax. This is followed by a spouse (or civil partner) repurchasing the shares in the market.

Bells and whistles Additional features placed on derivatives or securities (such as bonds) that are designed to attract investors or reduce issue costs.

Benchmark index An index of shares or other securities that sets a standard for fund manager performance; for example, a fund manager controlling a portfolio of pharmaceutical shares would measure performance against a pharmaceutical index. This is calculated by an independent person to be representative of the sector.

Best execution A broker must carry out a transaction on behalf of a client at the best possible price available at the time.

Beta This measures the systematic risk of a financial security. It is a measure of sensitivity of a financial security's return to market movements. In practice a proxy (e.g. the FTSE 100 index) is used for the market portfolio.

Bid–offer spread ('Bid-ask spread' in the USA) The difference between the market maker's buy and sell prices.

Bid premium The additional amount an acquirer has to offer above the pre-bid share price in order to succeed in a takeover offer.

Bid price The price at which a market maker will buy shares or a dealer in other markets will buy a security or commodity.

Bid yield The yield to maturity on a bond given the market price at which the market makers will buy from investors.

Big Bang A term used for a collection of deregulatory and liberalising reforms to the running of share trading in the UK implemented in 1986.

Bill of exchange A document which sets out a commitment to pay a sum of money at a specified point in time (e.g. an importer commits itself to paying a supplier). Bills of exchange may be discounted – that is, sold before maturity for less than face value.

BIMBO Buy-in management buy-out: a combination of a management buy-out and a buy-in. Outside managers join forces with existing managers to take over a company, subsidiary or unit.

Binary bets Book makers (spread betting firms) accept bets from punters on financial movements. The spread quoted is calculated as a market movement in a chosen direction – up or down within a time frame, say one day, e.g. the quoted spread on the FTSE 100 is 60–61. If you make an 'up' bet (the FTSE will end the day higher) then you will win 100 – 61 = 39 times your stake. If the index falls you lose 60 times the stake.

Black Monday 19 October 1987, the date of a large fall in stock market prices. Also Monday 28 October 1929 in the USA.

Blue chip A company/share regarded as of the highest quality; regarded (often mistakenly) as safest.

Board of directors People elected by shareholders to run a company.

Boiler room scam Fraudsters telephone and email people to persuade them, through hard sell, to buy worthless or near-worthless shares. They base themselves in a country beyond the reach of the regulators and criminal authorities and ask people to transfer money to their bank accounts conveniently located in a place (country) where the police cannot easily track.

Bond A debt obligation with a long-term maturity (more than one year), usually issued by firms and governments.

Bond covenant *See* Covenant.

Bonus issue *See* Scrip issue.

Book-building A book runner (lead manager) invites major institutional investors to suggest how many shares, bonds, etc. they would be interested in purchasing and at what price in a new issue or secondary issue of securities. This helps to establish the price and allocate the financial assets.

Book-to-market ratio (Book-equity to market-equity ratio) The ratio of a firm's balance sheet net asset value to the total market value of its shares.

Book value Balance sheet value as in 'net assets'. This can be expressed on a per share basis.

Bootstrapping game *See* Price–earnings ratio game.

Borrowing capacity Limits to total borrowing levels imposed by lenders, often determined by available collateral.

Bottom fishing Looking for value among shares that have fallen sharply.

Bottom line Profit attributable to the shareholders produced by a company over a period of time, e.g. one year.

Bottom up Analysis of shares or markets where priority is given to individual firm prospects rather than macroeconomic prospects and asset allocation.

Bought deal An investment bank (the 'lead manager', perhaps together with co-managers of the issue), buys an entire security issue (e.g. shares) from a client corporation raising finance. The investment bank usually intends to sell it on to institutional clients within hours.

Bourse Alternative name for a stock exchange. A French word, but used in other countries, particularly in Continental Europe.

Break-even analysis Analysing the level of sales at which a project, division or business produces a zero profit (accounting emphasis).

Break-out In chartism the point where a share breaks out of an established pattern.

Break-up value The total value of separate parts of the company if the parts are sold off to the highest bidder.

Broker/brokerage Assists in the buying and selling of financial securities by acting as a 'go-between', helping to reduce search, transaction and information costs – also *see* Corporate broker for a different type.

Broker-dealer An individual acting as agent for buyers and sellers, but who, at the same time, trades for his own account and may be a market maker.

Broking account An account with a stockbroker used by an investor to deposit and withdraw cash in the course of share and other security transactions.

Bubble An explosive upward movement in financial security or other asset prices not based on fundamentally rational factors, followed by a sharp decline (a crash).

Bubble stock Shares buoyed up by market optimism. Such optimism is not based on any rational standards of value.

Budget (national) Sets out government expenditure and revenue for the financial year. In the UK it is presented to Parliament by the Chancellor of the Exchequer.

Building society A UK financial institution, the primary role of which is the provision of mortgages. Building societies are non-profit-making mutual organisations. Funding is mostly through small deposits by individuals.

Bulge bracket A leading investment bank.

Bull An investor taking the view that prices will rise.

Bull market A market of rising prices.

Bulldog A foreign bond issued in the UK.

Bullet bond A bond where all the principal on a loan is repaid at maturity.

Bulletin board Financial websites often host these for each stock market quoted company, allowing investors to post discussion points for others to read and respond to.

Business angel (informal venture capitalist) Wealthy individual prepared to invest about £10,000 to £250,000 in a start-up, early-stage or developing firm. They will often have managerial and/or technical experience to offer the management team as well as equity and debt finance. This is medium- to long-term investment in high-risk situations.

Business review Required by all UK companies other than the small ones, the business review in the annual report provides an analysis of the development and performance of the business(es) during the year and an assessment of the position of the firm at the year-end in terms of strategy, risk, efficiency and progress.

Business risk The risk associated with the underlying operations of a business. The variability of the firm's operating income before interest: this dispersion is caused purely by business-related factors and not by the debt burden.

Buy-and-hold investor Investor who tends to trade infrequently.

Buyers' strike When there are many sellers of a financial security and buyers are difficult or impossible to find.

Buy-side Investors, and those who act or advise on their behalf (e.g. investment institutions), who purchase securities and the services offered by the sell-side institutions.

BVCA, British Private Equity and Venture Capital Association. The UK industry body and public policy advocate for the private equity and venture capital industry.

CAC 40 A stock market index of French shares quoted in Paris.

Cadbury report The Committee on the Financial Aspects of Corporate Governance, chaired by Sir Adrian Cadbury, made recommendations on the role of directors and auditors, published in 1992.

Call-back feature The issuer of a bond has the right but not the obligation to buy back on specified terms.

Called-up (issued) share capital The total value of shares sold by a company when expressed at par (nominal) value.

Call option This gives the purchaser the right, but not the obligation, to buy a fixed quantity of a commodity, financial instrument or some other underlying asset at a given price, at or before a specified date.

Cap (1) An interest rate cap is a contract that effectively gives the purchaser the right to set a maximum level for interest rates payable. Compensation is paid to the purchaser of a cap if market-set interest rates rise above an agreed level. (2) (Derivatives) Any feature that sets a maximum return, payout or cost.

Capex *See* Capital expenditure.

Capital (1) Funding for a business – can be equity only or equity plus debt; (2) another term for net worth – total assets minus total liabilities.

Capital asset pricing model (CAPM) An asset (e.g. share) pricing theory which assumes that financial assets, in equilibrium, will be priced to produce rates of return which compensate investors for systematic risk, as measured by the covariance of the assets' return with the market portfolio return (i.e. beta).

Capital budgeting The process of analysing and selecting long-term capital investments.

Capital expenditure (Capex) The purchase of long-lived (more than one year) assets (i.e. fixed assets).

Capital gain A gain made when an asset has increased in value and is then sold.

Capital gearing The extent to which a firm's total capital is in the form of debt.

Capital lease *See* Finance lease.

Capital market Where those raising finance can do so by selling financial investments to investors (e.g. bonds, shares).

Capital restructuring (reconstruction) Altering the shape of the firm's liabilities profile, e.g. decreases/increases in the amount of equity or debt, or lengthening/shortening debt maturities.

Capital shares *See* Split-capital investment trusts.

Capital structure The proportion of the firm's capital which is equity or debt.

Capitalisation (1) An item of expenditure is taken on to the balance sheet and capitalised as an asset rather than written off against profits. (2) Short for market capitalisation.

Capitalisation factor A discount rate.

Capitalisation issue *See* Scrip issue.

Capitalisation rate Required rate of return for the class of risk.

Capitalised *See* Capitalisation.

Capped bonds The floating interest rate charged cannot rise above a specified level.

Cartel A group of otherwise competing firms supplying the same market entering into an agreement to set mutually acceptable prices, output levels and market shares for their products.

Cash cow A company with low growth, stable market conditions and low investment needs. The company's competitive strength enables it to produce surplus cash.

Cash dividend A normal dividend from a company, paid in cash rather than a scrip dividend.

Cash flow statement The formal statement of a company's cash movements over a period.

Cash fund Funds that invest in money market investments.

Cash settled In the derivative market some contracts are physically settled at expiry date (e.g. copper is delivered in return for cash under the derivative contract). However, many derivatives are not physically delivered, rather a cash difference representing a gain or loss on the closed derivative position changes hands.

Causal ambiguity A potential imitator is unable to clearly see which resource is giving the sustainable competitive advantage to a firm, or it is difficult to identify the way in which the extraordinary resource was created in the first place.

Central bank A bankers' bank and lender of last resort which controls the credit system of an economy (e.g. controls note issue), acts as the government's bank, controls interest rates and regulates the country's banking system.

Central counterparty (CCP) clearing house An organisation that acts as a buyer to every seller and a seller to every buyer. This is designed to eliminate the risk of failure to complete a deal by guaranteeing that securities will be delivered against payment and vice versa. The London Stock Exchange runs the Central Counterparty Service, operated through LCH.Clearnet or SIX x-clear. Central counterparting can also offer a 'netting facility'. Thus if a large bank conducts numerous buy trades in a single company in a day, amounting to say £10 million, and numerous sells amounting to £8.5 million, only £1.5 million (the net amount) is cleared and settled. A central counterparty system also allows the buyers and sellers to remain anonymous (they are known to the clearing house but not to each other).

CEO (Chief Executive Officer) The director with the highest power over the actions of the firm.

Certificate of deposit (CD) A deposit is made at a bank. A certificate confirming that a deposit has been made is given in return, to the lender. This certificate is normally a bearer security. Most CDs can then be sold in the secondary market whenever the depositor needs cash.

CGT (Capital gains tax) A tax on gains made when assets held are sold for more than cost, less some allowances and expenses.

Chairman's statement A company's annual report and accounts usually has a chairman's statement commenting on the results and progress.

CHAPS (Clearing House Automated Payment System) The UK same-day interbank clearing system for sterling payments.

Chartism Investment analysis that relies on historic price charts (and/or trading volumes) to predict future movements.

Chasing the trend Buying financial securities after a recent upward trend in prices and selling after a recent downward trend.

Chicago Board of Trade (CBOT) The futures and options exchange in Chicago, USA – the world's oldest (established 1848). Now part of CME Group.

Chicago Board Options Exchange (CBOE) The largest options exchange in the world, trading options on shares, indices and interest rates.

Chief executive's review A comment, contained in a company's annual report and accounts, on performance, strategy and managerial intentions.

Chief Financial Officer (CFO) The manager/director in overall charge of the financial affairs of the business.

Chinese walls Barriers within a financial service company designed to prevent sensitive information being passed on to another branch of the organisation.

Churn Buying and selling shares frequently. Fund managers are sometimes accused of doing this to generate fees or just in the vain search for higher returns.

Circle of competence The business areas that an individual thoroughly understands and is equipped to analyse.

City Code on Takeovers and Mergers Provides the main governing rules for companies engaged in merger activity. Largely self-regulated and administered by the Takeover Panel.

City of London A collective term for the financial institutions located in the financial district to the east of St Paul's Cathedral in London (also called the Square Mile). However, the term is also used to refer to all UK financial institutions, wherever they are located.

City of London Police Lead the battle against financial fraud.

City Panel on Takeovers and Mergers The organisation that provides and enforces the rules governing behaviour in companies engaged in merger activity in the UK. The rules apply to unquoted and quoted public limited companies (plcs). Often shortened to 'The Takeover Panel', or 'The Panel'.

Clawback Existing shareholders often have the right to reclaim shares sold under a placing as though they were entitled to them under a rights issue.

Clean fund (unbundled) A collective investment fund where the annual management charge does not include the commission (initial or trail) passed on to sales organisations such as independent financial advisers or fund platforms.

Clean price On a bond the prices are generally quoted 'clean', that is, without taking account of the accrued interest since the last coupon payment.

Clearing a trade The stock exchange (or other market clearer) ensures that (a) all reports of a trade are reconciled to make sure all parties are in agreement as to the number of shares traded and the price; and (b) that the buyer and seller have the cash and securities to do the deal. See Central Counterparty (CCP) clearing house for a linked service.

Clearing bank Member of the London Bankers' Clearing House, which clears cheques, settling indebtedness between two parties.

Clearing house An institution which registers, monitors, matches and settles mutual indebtedness between a number of individuals or organisations. The clearing house may also act as a counterparty. *See* Central counterparty.

Closed-end funds Collective investment vehicles (e.g. investment trusts) that do not create or redeem shares on a daily basis in response to increases and decreases in demand. They have a fixed number of shares for lengthy periods.

Closet indexing (closet tracking) Fund managers declare themselves as active (i.e. searching out bargains) but really construct portfolios that are close to the market benchmark indices.

Closing out a futures position Taking a second action in the futures market (say, selling the future) which is exactly opposite to the first action (say, buying the future). Also called 'reversing the trade'.

CME An exchange which trades a wide range of currency futures and options, interest rate futures and options, commodity futures and options, and share index futures and options. Within the CME Group are CME, CBOT, NYMEX and COMEX.

CME Clearing Europe (CMECE) A London-based clearing house which clears OTC transactions in a broad range of derivative products in an English law and European regulatory environment. Acts as the central counterparty to every trade cleared.

Code *See* City Code on Takeovers and Mergers.

Codes *See* Stock symbols.

Collateral Property and/or other assets pledged by a borrower to protect the interests of the lender – they may be seized if the borrower reneges.

Collective funds *See* Pooled funds.

Combined Code of Corporate Governance A set of guidelines for best practice corporate governance (e.g. majority of board to be independent non-executive directors). The UKLA requires compliance with the Code or an explanation for non-compliance.

Commercial banking A range of banking services for retail and commercial clients, including taking deposits and making loans, chequing facilities, trustee services and security advisory services.

Commercial bill (bank bill or trade bill) A document expressing the commitment of a bank or firm to repay a short-term debt at a fixed date in the future.

Commercial paper (CP) An unsecured note promising the holder (lender) a sum of money to be paid in a few days – average maturity of 40 days. If they are denominated in foreign currency and placed outside the jurisdiction of the authorities of that currency, then the notes are euro-commercial paper.

Commission Fee charged by brokers, usually a percentage of the amount of the transaction.

Commitment fee A fee payable in return for a commitment by a bank to lend money payable even if no borrowing subsequently takes place.

Commodity product (1) Undifferentiated compared with competitor offerings in any customer-important way by factors such as performance, appearance, service support, etc. For example, many personal computers are said to be commodity products. (2) Raw materials and foodstuffs.

Common stock Term used in the USA to describe ordinary shares in a company.

Companies Acts The series of laws enacted by Parliament governing the establishment and conduct of incorporated business enterprises. The Companies Act 2006 consolidated the Acts that preceded it.

Companies House The place where records are kept of every UK company. These accounts etc. are then made available to the general public.

Company registrar *See* Registrar.

Company secretary Responsible for ensuring that the company complies with standard financial and legal practice and maintains standards of corporate governance. Acts as a point of communication between the board of directors and company shareholders, reporting in a timely and accurate manner on company procedures and developments.

Comparative advantage A firm or a country has a comparative advantage in the production of good X if the opportunity cost of producing a unit of X, in terms of other goods forgone, is lower in that country compared with another country, or in that firm compared with another firm.

Competition and Markets Authority (CMA) Established in 2014 as the main UK regulator of markets and firms focused on where there is a substantial lessening of competition leading to anti-competitive behaviour to the detriment of buyers of goods and services. In 2014 it incorporated the Office of Fair Trading and the Competition Commission.

Competition Commission Now merged into the Competition and Markets Authority, the Commission formerly obtained any information needed to investigate possible monopoly anti-competitive situations referred to it. It may recommend competition-enhancing remedies such as blocking a merger.

Competitive advantage (edge) The possession of extraordinary resources that allow a firm to rise above the others in its industry to generate exceptional long-run rates of return on capital employed.

Competitive floor Where shareholders receive a rate of return that only just induces them to put money into the firm and hold it there. This minimal rate of return occurs because of the high level of competition in the market for the firm's product, or because of value being reduced to the minimum by one or more of the other of the Porter's five forces.

Competitive position The competitive strength of the firm *vis-à-vis* rivals, suppliers, customers and substitutes, in a market.

Complementary product One that is generally bought alongside the product in question.

Compliance officers Financial service firms regulated by the Financial Conduct

Authority often have a designated compliance officer who is supposed to ensure that any legal and supervisory rules are followed.

Compound interest Interest is paid on the sum which accumulates, whether or not that sum comes from principal or from interest received at intermediate dates.

Compound return The income received on an investment is reinvested in the investment and future returns are gained on both the original capital and the ploughed-back income.

Concentration When there are few investments in a portfolio, it is said to be concentrated.

Concert party A group of investors who, pursuant to an agreement or understanding (whether formal or informal), co-operate to obtain or consolidate control of a company or to frustrate the successful outcome of a takeover offer for a company.

Conglomerate bank A bank with a wide range of activities, products and markets.

Conglomerate merger The combining of two firms which operate in unrelated business areas.

Consideration The price paid for something.

Consolidated (group) accounts All the income costs, assets and liabilities of all group companies, whether wholly or partially owned, are brought together in the consolidated accounts. Consolidation must take place if 50 per cent or more of the subsidiary's shares are held by the parent. If less than 50 per cent of the shares are held, consolidation may still be required.

Consolidation of shares Reduction in the number of shares so that the nominal value of each remaining share rises.

Consumer price index (CPI) A measure of general inflation.

Continuing obligations Standards of behaviour and actions required of firm's quoted on the London Stock Exchange, enforced by the United Kingdom Listing Authority.

Continuous order book Throughout the trading of securities orders are automatically matched and executed against one another.

Contract for difference (CFD) The buyer and seller agree to pay, in cash, at the closing of the contract, the difference between the opening and closing price of the underlying shares (or some other underlying), multiplied by the number of shares in the contract.

Contract note A statement from a broker to an investor stating the price, the time of deal, the number of shares, the broker's commission and the stamp duty for a recent share transaction.

Contrarians Those taking the opposite position to the generality of investors.

Controlling shareholder Any shareholder able to control the composition of the board of directors and therefore the direction of the company. Strictly speaking this is 50 per cent, but even a 30 per cent shareholder can exercise this degree of power, and therefore 30 per cent is used as the cut-off point for some purposes.

Convergence The coming together of the futures price and the underlying share price as the final trading day of a futures contract approaches.

Conversion premium With convertible bonds, it is the difference between the current share price and the conversion price, expressed as a percentage of the current share price.

Conversion price The share price at which convertible bonds may be converted.

Conversion ratio (1) The nominal (par) value of a convertible bond divided by the conversion price. The number of shares available per bond. (2) The ratio of the number of warrants that must be held and exercised in order to buy or sell a single unit of the asset (e.g. one share).

Conversion value The value of a convertible bond if it were converted into ordinary shares at the current share price.

Convertible bonds Bonds which carry a rate of interest and give the owner the right to exchange the bonds at some stage in the future into ordinary shares according to a prearranged formula.

Convertible loan stock *See* Convertible bonds.

Convertible preference share/stock *See* Preference shares.

Corporate acquisition The purchase of one company by another – buying the shares.

Corporate advisers These professional financial service firms (e.g. investment banks, accountants) advise companies gaining a quotation for their shares on ISDX to ensure knowledge and compliance with the rules and responsibilities of being on ISDX. They provide reassurance to investors that the company meets certain basic standards of financial record keeping, reporting and corporate governance.

Corporate bond A bond issued by a company.

Corporate broker Stockbrokers who act on behalf of companies quoted on an exchange (e.g. providing advice on market conditions or representing the company to the market). Corporate brokers are knowledgeable about the share and other financial markets. They advise companies on fund raising (e.g. new issues). They try to generate interest among investors for the company's securities, and stand prepared to buy and sell companies' shares.

Corporate finance department of investment banks The department assisting firms in raising funds (e.g. rights issues, bond issues) and managing their finances.

Corporate governance The system of management and control of the corporation.

Corporate raider An organisation that makes hostile takeover approaches for quoted companies.

Corporate venturing Large companies fostering the development of smaller enterprises through, for example, joint capital development or equity capital provision.

Corporation tax A tax levied on the profits of companies.

Correction A minor fall during a market rise.

Correlation coefficient A measure of the extent to which two variables show a relationship, expressed on a scale of –1 to +1. A correlation of –1 implies that two share prices, two markets, etc., move in opposite directions by the same percentages.

Cost leadership strategy Emphasis on standard no-frills product, exploiting scale economies and other cost advantages.

Cost of capital The rate of return that a company has to offer finance providers to induce them to buy and hold a financial security.

Cost of sales The expense incurred for bought-in raw materials or components.

Counterparty The buyer for a seller, and the seller for a buyer.

Counterparty risk The risk that a counterparty to a contract defaults and does not fulfil obligations.

Coupon An attachment to a bond or loan note document which may be separated and serve as evidence of entitlement to interest. Nowadays it refers to the interest itself: the nominal annual rate of interest expressed as a percentage of the principal value.

Covariance A measure of the extent to which two variables move together.

Covenant A solemn agreement.

Cover Offsetting one position in a financial security with an equal and opposite transaction in the same or linked (e.g. derivative) security.

Covered call option writing Writing a call option on an underlying when the writer owns at least the number of underlying securities included in the option.

Covered warrants The same as warrants, except that financial institutions issue them, selling the right to buy or sell shares in industrial and commercial companies.

Creation units of ETF shares Shares issued by an ETF provider which represent, and can be exchanged for, a bundle of securities, e.g. shares tracking an index or other assets.

Creative accounting The drawing up of accounts which obey the letter of the law and accounting body rules, but which involve the manipulation of accounts to show a more favourable profit and balance sheet.

Credit A contractual agreement in which a borrower receives something of value now and agrees to repay the lender at some date in the future.

Credit period The average length of time between the purchase of inputs and the payment for them. Equal to the average level of creditors divided by the purchases on credit per day.

Credit rating An estimate of the quality of a debt from the lender viewpoint in terms of the relative likelihood of interest and capital not being paid and of the extent to which the lender is protected in the event of default. Credit rating agencies are paid fees by companies, governments, etc., wishing to attract lenders.

Credit risk The risk that a counterparty to a financial transaction will fail to fulfil their obligation, e.g. be unable to pay interest when due.

Credit union A non-profit organisation accepting deposits and making loans, operated as a cooperative.

Creditor One to whom a debt is owed.

Creditors (accounts payable) Amounts owed by a company to suppliers and others.

CREST or Crest An electronic means of settlement and registration of shares and other securities following a sale on the London Stock Exchange, operated by CRESTCo.

CREST nominee account *See* Nominee company.

Crowdfunding (crowdsource) Websites connect entrepreneurial firms seeking equity or debt funding with investors. An investor can go to one of the crowdsource websites and commit to investing online.

Crown jewels defence In a hostile merger situation, the target sells off the most attractive parts of the business.

Cum-dividend (cum-coupon) (1) When an investor buys a government bond when it is still designated cum-coupon, they are entitled to the accrued interest since the last coupon was paid. (2) A share designated cum-dividend indicates that the buyer will be entitled to a dividend recently announced by the company.

Cum-rights Shares bought on the stock market prior to the ex-rights day are designated cum-rights and carry to the new owner the right to subscribe for the new shares in the rights issue.

Cumulative If a payment (interest or dividend) on a bond or preference share is missed in one period those securities are given priority when the next payment is made. These arrears must be cleared up before shareholders receive dividends.

Cumulative preference share *See* Preference shares.

Currency swap *See* Swap.

Current asset value (net) Current assets (cash, accounts receivable, inventory) minus current liabilities (also called working capital).

Current assets Cash and other assets that can be rapidly turned into cash. Includes inventory (stocks) of raw materials, partially finished goods and finished goods, receivables (debtors) and investments expected to be sold within one year.

Current liabilities Amounts owed that the company expects to have to pay within the next year.

Current ratio The ratio of current assets to the current liabilities of a business.

Current yield (flat yield, income yield or running yield) The ratio of the coupon on a bond to its current market price.

Custodian/custody An organisation that acts for investors in an administrative capacity, managing the holding of shares and other financial securities. The custodian may handle dividend payments and carry out various other administrative duties for the investor.

Cyclical companies (or industries, or shares) Those companies in which profits are particularly sensitive to the growth level in the economy, which may be cyclical.

Daily Official List (DOL) The daily record setting out the prices of all trades in securities conducted on the London Stock Exchange. *See also* SEDOL.

Dark pool Trading venue where large orders can be placed anonymously to reduce the effect of the trade on market prices.

Darling A stock market darling is one which receives a lot of attention and is regarded as very attractive.

Dawn raid Situation where an acquirer acts with such speed in buying the shares of the target company that the raider achieves the objective of accumulating a substantial stake in the target before its management has time to react.

DAX 30 (Deutscher Aktien Index) A stock market index of 30 German shares quoted on the Deutsche Börse.

Day trader Someone who trades in and out of a share in one day. They may have both buy and sell trades for many shares in the same day.

Dead cat bounce Traders' humour: even a dead cat thrown from a tall building will bounce. Likewise, a market may rally a little, but this is temporary. Also known as a sucker's rally.

Debentures Bonds issued with redemption dates a number of years into the future (or irredeemable). Usually secured against specific assets (mortgage debentures) or through a floating charge on the firm's assets (floating charge debentures). In the USA and Canada debenture means an unsecured debt with a fixed coupon.

Debt capital Capital raised with (usually) a fixed obligation in terms of interest and principal payments, e.g. loans, bonds.

Debt Management Office (DMO) Organises the sale of gilts. An Executive Agency of the UK Treasury.

Debt maturity The length of time left until the repayment of principal on a debt becomes due.

Debt restructuring Negotiating with lenders to vary the terms of the debt in time of difficulty.

Debt-to-equity ratio The ratio of a company's long-term debt to shareholders' funds.

Debtor One who owes a debt.

Debtor conversion period The average number of days to convert customer debts into cash. Equal to the average value of debtors divided by the average value of sales per day.

Debtors (accounts receivable) When goods are sold by a company on credit its customers owe it money. They are debtors or trade debtors.

Decentralisation (Fund management) Delegating decision making to multiple managers.

Declining (reducing) balance method of depreciation The amount an asset is depreciated declines from one year to the next as it is determined by a constant percentage of the asset's (depreciated) value at the start of each year.

Deep (depth) financial markets With many buyers and sellers and therefore a great deal of activity.

Deep discounted bonds Bonds sold well below par value, usually because they have little or no coupon.

Deep discounted rights issue A rights issue priced much lower than the present market price of the old shares.

Default A failure to make agreed payments of interest or principal, or failure to comply with some other loan agreement provision.

Defensive industries Those industries where profits are not particularly sensitive to the growth rate of the economy.

Defensive shares Having a beta value of less than 1.

Deferred interest accounts Similar to offshore roll-up funds.

Deferred ordinary shares (1) These rank below preferred ordinary shares for dividends. So, if profits are low, holders of deferred ordinary shares may not receive a dividend. However, if the company achieves a predetermined level of profit or other performance target the deferred ordinary shares often entitle the owner to a higher than normal dividend. (2) The right to the dividend is deferred for a set period, after which the holders rank equal with ordinary shareholders.

Deferred tax With a fixed asset on a company's balance sheet, the writing down allowance, which can be used to reduce current tax payable, is often greater than the depreciation charge as determined by the company's accounting policy. The difference is called a timing difference. A deferred tax provision is the difference between (1) the corporation tax actually payable on the taxable trading profit and (2) the tax that would have been payable if the taxable trading profit is the same as the accounting profit (using normal depreciation, not writing-down allowances).

Defined benefit A pension pays out a fixed amount monthly in retirement based on years worked (contributed to fund) and final salary or some average salary over a number of years.

Defined contribution A pension into which the worker puts regular or irregular amounts during a career. The pension paid out is linked to the investment returns made by the pension fund, not related to salary.

Dematerialisation Traditionally the evidence of financial security ownership is by written statements on paper (e.g. share certificates). Increasingly such information is being placed in electronic records and paper evidence is being abandoned.

Demerger The separation of companies or business units that are currently under one corporate umbrella. It applies particularly to the unravelling of a merger.

Depletion A reduction in the value of a natural resource, e.g. oil in the ground, owned by a company.

Depositary Acts for an open ended investment company, OEIC, safeguarding the assets in a similar way to a trustee for a unit trust.

Depositary receipts Certificates representing evidence of ownership of a company's shares (or other securities) held by a depository. Depositary receipts (DRs) are negotiable (can be traded) certificates which represent ownership of a given number of company shares. The DRs may be listed on a stock market and traded independently from the underlying shares. There are a number of forms of DRs including American depositary receipts (ADRs), global depositary receipts (GDRs), euro depositary receipts (EDRs) and retail depositary receipts (RDRs).

Depository Person or firm, often a large bank, entrusted with safekeeping of funds, securities, or other valuable assets.

Depreciation The reduction in the stated value of assets with a useful life of more than one year that are not bought and sold as part of normal trading. The reduction may be due to wearing out, using up, effluxion of time or obsolescence.

Derivative A financial asset, the performance of which is based on (derived from) the behaviour of the value of an underlying asset.

Deutsche Börse The German Stock Exchange based in Frankfurt.

Differentiated product One that is slightly different in significant ways than those supplied by other companies. The unique nature of the product/service offered allows a premium price to be charged.

Diluted earnings per share This takes into account any additional shares that may be issued in the future under executive share option schemes and other commitments.

Dilution The effect on the earnings and voting power per ordinary share from an increase in the number of shares issued without a corresponding increase in the firm's earnings.

Dilution levy When there are large numbers of buyers or sellers of shares in an open ended investment company, OEIC, the fund may incur high costs to buy/sell the underlying securities. To balance the interests of the old and new shareholders the new members may be charged an extra fee (say 0.5–2 per cent) which is then added to the fund.

Diminishing marginal attractiveness If shares are listed in order of attractiveness based on the difference between their value and current price, then the marginal (next stock) on the list would be less attractive.

Direct foreign investment The purchase of commercial assets such as factories and industrial plant for productive purposes by overseas organisations.

Direct market access (DMA) These systems allow private investors to trade directly in the stock market, placing buy and sell orders into the LSE electronic order book alongside the professionals.

Directors' dealings Directors' purchase or sale of shares in their own company. This is legal (except at certain times of the company's year). Some investors examine directors' dealings to decide whether to buy or sell. Dealings are shown on free financial websites.

Directors' report Information and commentary on company performance and other matters. Presented in a company's annual report and accounts.

Dirty price, full price, invoice price On a bond a buyer pays a total of the clean price and the accrued interest since the last coupon payment.

Disclosure of shareholdings If a stake of 3 per cent or more is held by one shareholder in a UK public company, then this has to be declared to the company.

Discount (1) The amount below face value at which a financial claim sells (e.g. bill of exchange or zero coupon bond). (2) The extent to which an investment trust's shares sell below the net asset value. (3) The amount by which a future value of a currency is less than its spot value. (4) The action of purchasing financial instruments (e.g. bills) at a discount. (5) The degree to which a security sells below its issue price in the secondary market. (6) The process of equating a cash flow at some future date with today's value using the time value of money. (7) The deduction from the normal price or value, the opposite of premium.

Discount rate (1) The rate of return used to discount cash flows received in future years. This is the opportunity cost of capital given the risk class of the future cash flows. (2) The rate of interest at which some central banks lend money to the banking system.

Discount to net asset value Shares (e.g. investment trust shares) sometimes sell at a value less than the per share net asset value of the companies.

Discounted cash flow Future cash flows are converted into the common denominator of time zero money by adjusting for the time value of money.

Discounting The process of reducing future cash flows to a present value using an appropriate discount rate.

Discretionary service A type of service provided by a stockbroker in which the broker will manage the investor's portfolio at the broker's discretion – the investor is not consulted on every deal.

Disintermediation Borrowing firms bypassing financial institutions and obtaining debt finance directly from the market.

Disinvest To sell an investment.

Distribution bonds A type of insurance company bond which invests in a mixture of equity, fixed-income securities and property, but biased toward fixed-income investments.

Distribution units *See* Income ('Inc') units.

Diversifiable risk *See* Unsystematic risk.

Diversification Investing in varied projects, enterprises, financial securities, products, markets, etc., in a portfolio.

Divestiture (divestment) The sell-off of assets or subsidiary businesses by a company or individual.

Dividend That part of profit paid to ordinary shareholders, usually on a regular basis.

Dividend cover The number of times net profits available for distribution exceed the dividend actually paid or declared. Defined as earnings per share divided by dividend per share, *or* total post-tax profits divided by total dividend payout.

Dividend discount model *See* Dividend valuation models.

Dividend payment ratio (payout ratio) The percentage of a company's earnings after tax deduction paid out as dividends.

Dividend per share The total amount paid or due to be paid in dividends for the year (interim and final), divided by the number of shares in issue.

Dividend policy The determination of the proportion of profits paid out to shareholders, over the longer term.

Dividend reinvestment plan (DRIP) A shareholder receives shares in lieu of a cash dividend. This avoids the cost and trouble of receiving cash and then reinvesting.

Dividend valuation models (DVMs) These methods of share valuation are based on the premise that the market value of ordinary shares represents the sum of the expected future dividend flows, to infinity, discounted to present value.

Dividend yield The amount of dividend paid on each share as a percentage of the share price.

Divorce of ownership and control In large corporations shareholders own the firm but may not be able to exercise control. Managers often have control because of a diffuse and divided shareholder body, proxy votes and apathy.

DMO *See* Debt Management Office.

Domestic bond A bond denominated in the issuer's local currency and offered to local investors.

Dow/Dow Jones Industrial Average (DJIA) The best known index of movements in the price of US stocks and shares. There are 30 shares in the index.

Dow theory A method of predicting share price trends by identifying primary trends from historic share price data.

Drawdown arrangement A loan facility is established and the borrower uses it (takes the money available) in stages as the funds are required.

Drawdown (pension) (income drawdown) With a personal pension, instead of taking benefits in the form of an annuity, you can draw money from your pension pot.

Dual capital trusts *See* Split-capital investment trusts.

Dual-class Shares in the USA and some other countries which divide into two or more classes, each with different voting rights.

Due diligence A detailed investigation of a company to ensure that it is in a satisfactory condition for the purpose of the transaction, e.g. in a merger the target is examined by accountants, lawyers, managerial consultants, etc. to reveal risks and other information.

Durable good One with an expected life of more than one year.

E-money Also known as electronic money, as e-currency, electronic cash, digital money, digital cash, digital currency, cyber currency. Money transferred by electronic means.

E-money institutions Issuers of electronic money, e.g. pre-paid cards and electronic pre-paid accounts for use online.

Early-stage capital Funds for initial manufacturing and sales for a newly formed company. High-risk capital available from entrepreneurs, business angels and venture capital funds.

Earn-out The purchase price of a company is linked to the future profits performance. Future instalments of the purchase price may be adjusted if the company performs better or worse than expected.

Earning power The earning (profit) capacity of a business in a normal year, that is, what the company might be expected to earn year after year if business conditions continue unchanged.

Earnings Profits, usually after deduction of tax.

Earnings guidance A company guiding analysts to estimates of profits for the current period.

Earnings multiple *See* Price–earnings ratio.

Earnings per share (eps) Profit after tax and interest divided by number of shares in issue.

Earnings yield Earnings per share divided by current market price of share.

EBIT A company's Earnings (profits) Before Interest and Taxes are deducted.

EBITDA Earnings Before (deduction of) Interest, Taxation, Depreciation and Amortisation.

EBITDA interest coverage ratio EBITDA divided by gross interest.

Economic franchise Pricing power usually facilitated by strong barriers to entry. The strength and durability of an economic franchise is determined by (a) the structure of the industry, and (b) the ability of the firm to rise above its rivals in its industry and generate exceptional long-run rates of return on capital employed.

Economic profit The amount earned by a business after deducting all operating expenses and a charge for the opportunity cost of the capital employed.

Economies of scale Producing a larger output results in lower unit cost.

Economies of scope The ability to reduce unit costs of an item by sharing some costs between a number of product lines (e.g. using the same truck to deliver both ketchup and beans to a store).

Efficient stock market Prices rationally reflect available information. The efficient market hypothesis implies that new information is incorporated into a share price (a) rapidly, and (b) rationally. In an efficient market no trader will be presented with an opportunity for making an abnormal return, except by chance.

EGM *See* Extraordinary general meeting.

EIS *See* Enterprise Investment Scheme.

Electronic platform/trading system A trading system matching buyers and sellers together using computers, communication links and/or the Internet.

Electronic settlement Transferring shares from sellers to buyers without certificates – computer entry only.

Emerging markets Security markets in countries with relatively low/middle incomes but with rapid economic growth, or in countries with fairly high income levels but relatively underdeveloped stock markets and limited internationalisation of financial markets.

Employee share ownership plans (ESOPs) Schemes designed to encourage employees to build up a shareholding in their company.

Endowment policies (saving schemes) Life assurance schemes with the additional feature of a lump-sum payment, either at the end of the term of the policy or on death. One important use is for the repayment of house mortgages.

Enfranchisement Granting voting rights to holders of non-voting shares.

Enterprise Investment Scheme (EIS) Tax relief is available to investors in qualifying UK company shares (unquoted firms not focused on financial investment and property).

Enterprise value The sum of a company's total equity market capitalisation and borrowings minus the cash it holds. (Some analysts add pension provisions, minority interest and other claims on the business.)

Enterprise value to EBITDA ratio The total of the market value of equity plus the market value of debt (minus cash holdings) divided by earnings before deduction of interest, tax, depreciation and amortisation.

Entrepreneur Defined by economists as the owner-manager of a firm. Usually supplies capital, organises production, decides on strategic direction and bears risk.

EPIC code *See* Stock symbols.

Equilibrium in markets When the forces of supply and demand are evenly balanced.

Equities, Equity, Equity capital An ownership share of a business; each equity share (of the same class) represents an equal stake in the business. Capital invested in the business in the form of shares, not set to be repaid, but share owners can sell their shares to other investors, or vote for a liquidation of all the firm's assets to release the capital to them after meeting all other obligations.

Equitisation An increasing emphasis placed on share (equity) finance and stock exchanges in economies around the world. A growing equity culture.

Equity indices Baskets of shares indicating the movement of the equity market as a whole or sub-sets of the market.

Equity kicker (sweetener) The attachment of some rights to participate in and benefit from a good performance (e.g. exercise option to purchase shares) to a bond or other debt finance. Used with mezzanine finance or high-yield bonds.

Equity-linked bond A bond with features of both debt and equity. It contains an option to purchase (or to exchange a bond for) an equity stake in the issuer, its parent or another company. This option can be by way of a right to convert the bond into equity or by way of warrant attached to the bond giving the right to purchase shares.

Equity long/short An investment strategy taking both a long (benefit from a rise in price) and short (benefit from a fall in price) position in shares or other securities.

Equity risk premium The additional average annual rate of return for an averagely risky share over the return on a risk-free asset (e.g. a reputable government bond). It is the average extra return over many decades – a short period of observation will lead to a biased estimate.

Equity shareholders' funds *See* Shareholders' funds.

Equity warrant *See* Warrant.

Ethical investment The avoidance of securities that benefit from activities viewed as unethical (e.g. tobacco shares, genetically modified agriculture, arms sales).

Euribor (Euro Interbank Offered Rate) Short-term interest rates in the interbank market (very stable banks lending to each other) in the currency of euros.

Euro The name of the single European currency in use since 1999.

Eurobond Bond sold outside the jurisdiction of the country in whose currency the bond is denominated (e.g. a bond issued in yen outside Japan).

Euroclear A Belgium based settlement system to help settle domestic and cross-border financial transactions and reduce risk for clients.

Euro-commercial paper *See* Commercial paper.

Eurocurrency Currency held outside its country of origin (e.g. Australian dollars held outside of Australia). Note: this market existed long before the creation of the euro, and has no connection with the currency in the eurozone.

Eurocurrency banking Transactions in a currency other than the host country's currency (e.g. transactions in Canadian dollars in London). No connection with the currency in the eurozone.

Eurodollar A deposit or credit of US dollars held outside of the regulation of the US authorities, say in Tokyo, London or Paris. No connection with the currency in the eurozone.

Euromarkets Markets outside of the jurisdictions of any country; often termed international securities markets. Euromarkets began in the late 1950s.

Euro medium-term notes (EMTN) *See* Medium-term note.

Euronext The combined financial stock market comprising the French, Dutch, Belgian and Portuguese bourses. Now part of NYSE Euronext, which is part of the Intercontinental Exchange, ICE.

European Central Counterparty A pan-European clearing and settlement service for financial transactions.

European Monetary Union (EMU) A single currency with a single central bank having control over interest rates being created for those EU member states which join the euro.

European-style options (or European options) Options which can only be exercised by the purchaser on a predetermined future date.

Euro-security markets Informal (unregulated) markets in money held outside the jurisdiction of the country of origin (e.g. Swiss franc lending outside of the control of the Swiss authorities – perhaps the francs are in London).

Eurosterling bond A bond issued in sterling outside of the control of the UK authorities.

Eurozone Those countries that joined together in adopting the euro as their currency.

Event risk The risk that some future event may negatively affect the return on a financial investment (e.g. an earthquake event affects returns on Japanese bonds, or the resignation of a CEO endangers the company).

Ex-ante Intended, desired or expected before the event.

Ex-coupon A bond sold without the right to the next interest payment.

Ex-dividend When a share or bond is designated ex-dividend a purchaser will not be entitled to a recently announced dividend or the accrued interest on the bond since the last coupon – the old owner will receive the dividend (coupon).

Ex-post The value of some variable after the event.

Ex-rights When a share goes 'ex-rights' any purchaser of a share after that date will not have a right to subscribe for new shares in the rights issue.

Ex-rights price of a share The theoretical market price following a rights issue.

Exceptional items Gains or costs which are part of the company's ordinary activities but are either unusual in themselves or have an exceptionally large impact on profits that year.

Exchange controls The state controls the purchase and sale of currencies by its residents.

Exchange rate The price of one currency expressed in terms of another.

Exchange rate risk The possibility of losing money on investments abroad because the foreign exchange rate moves against you.

Exchange market size (EMS) *See* Normal market size.

Exchange traded commodities (ETCs) Similar to exchange traded funds except the underlying securities are commodities or derivatives of commodities.

Exchange traded funds (ETFs) Funds (companies) that issue shares using the proceeds to invest in the range of shares (or other securities such as bonds) in a particular stock market index or sector, such as the FTSE 100 index. Alternatively derivatives may be purchased which reflect the movements of the index or sector.

Exchange trading Trading of financial instruments on regulated markets.

Exchangeable bond A bond that entitles the owner to choose at a later date whether to exchange the bond for shares in a company. The shares are for a company other than the one that issued the bonds.

Exclusive franchise *See* Economic franchise.

Execute and eliminate A type of buy or sell order instruction given by an investor to a broker. A price limit is set and the transaction is completed in part or in whole immediately and then expires on the spot. If only some of the order is fulfilled the remainder expires.

Execution-only broker A stockbroker who will buy or sell shares cheaply but will not give advice or other services.

Executive directors Manage day-to-day activities of the firm as well as contributing to boardroom discussion on company-wide policy and strategic direction.

Exercise price (strike price) The price at which an underlying will be bought (call) or sold (put) under an option contract.

Exit (1) The term used to describe the point at which a venture capitalist or private equity company can recoup some or all of the investment made. (2) The closing of a position created by a transaction.

Exit barrier A factor preventing firms from stopping production in a particular industry.

Exit charge Unit trusts may charge the investor when the units are sold.

Exotic A term used to describe an unusual financial transaction (e.g. exotic option, exotic currency), i.e. one with few trades.

Expansion capital Companies at a fast-development phase needing capital to increase production capacity, working capital and capital for the further development of the product or market. Venture capital is often used.

Expected return The mean or average outcome calculated by weighting each of the possible outcomes by the probability of occurrence and then summing the result.

Experience curve The cost of performing a task reduces as experience is gained through repetition.

Expert investor Legal term denoting an investor who may by their previous experience be taken to fully understand the nature of investment undertaken. An expert investor is given less protection under the financial regulatory regime.

Expiry date of an option The time when the rights to buy or sell under the option contract cease.

Exposure The amount of a portfolio invested in a particular area (e.g. a £50,000 portfolio with £25,000 in overseas shares has 50 per cent overseas exposure).

External finance Outside finance raised by a firm, i.e. finance that it did not generate internally, for example through profit retention.

Extraordinary general meeting (EGM) A meeting of the company (shareholders and directors) other than the annual general meeting. It may be convened when the directors think fit. However, shareholders holding more than 10 per cent of the paid-up share capital carrying voting rights can insist on the directors calling a meeting (if at least 12 months have elapsed since the last general meeting, the request may be made by only 5 per cent). If the directors do not call a meeting as properly requested, the members who requested it (or half of them by voting rights) may call the meeting themselves.

Extraordinary resources Those that give the firm a competitive edge. A resource, which when combined with other (ordinary) resources enables the firm to outperform competitors and create new value-generating opportunities. Critical extraordinary resources determine what a firm can do successfully.

Extrapolate To estimate values beyond the known values by the extension of a curve or line.

Face value *See* Par value.

Fair game In the context of a stock market, the situation where some investors and fundraisers are not able to benefit at the expense of other participants. The market is regulated to avoid abuse, negligence and fraud. It is cheap to carry out transactions and the market provides high liquidity.

Fair value (Fair market value) The amount an asset could be exchanged for in an arm's-length transaction between informed and willing parties.

Fallen angel Debt which used to rate as investment grade but which is now regarded as junk, mezzanine finance or high-yield finance.

Fallen angel risk The risk that a bond currently rated as 'investment-grade' is downgraded to junk-grade. The bond price falls due to increased default risk and the fact that many institutions, banned from holding high-yield bonds, are forced to sell.

Fat-finger trades With direct market access systems investors have been known to make trades they did not mean to do. For example: buy instead of sell (or vice versa), trade 10 times the amount they meant to, or accidentally put in a silly price, such as selling a share at a fraction of its true value.

Fill or kill A type of buy or sell instruction given by an investor to a broker. If the deal cannot, in its entirety, be executed at the maximum (minimum) price stated by the investor (or better) then the entire order expires.

Final dividend The dividend announced with the annual accounts. The final dividend plus the interim dividend make the total dividend for the year for a company that reports results every six months.

Finance house A financial institution offering to supply finance in the form of hire purchase, leasing and other forms of instalment credit.

Finance lease ('capital lease', 'financial lease' or 'full-payout lease') The lessor expects to recover the full cost (or almost the full cost) of the asset plus interest, over the period of the lease.

Financial assets (securities, instruments or financial claims) Contracts that state agreement about the exchange of money in the future, e.g. shares, bonds, bank loans, derivatives.

Financial binary bets *See* Binary bets.

Financial Conduct Authority (FCA) The chief financial services regulator in the UK from 2013.

Financial distress Obligations to creditors are not met or are met with difficulty.

Financial gearing (leverage) *See* Gearing (financial gearing).

Financial Ombudsman Scheme (FOS) The UK ombudsman tries to find a just settlement between a complainant and a financial service company.

Financial Policy Committee The part of the Bank of England responsible for macro-prudential regulation – trying to reduce risks in the financial system as a whole rather than in individual banks and other financial institutions.

Financial Reporting Council (FRC) The UK's independent regulator responsible for ensuring high-quality corporate reporting, accounting and governance.

Financial review An explanation of financial performance and strategy contained in a company's annual report and account. The finance director usually breaks down turnover, profits, assets and liabilities into geographical and/or product divisions, discusses the balance sheet strengths and some key performance indicators.

Financial risk The additional variability in a firm's returns to shareholders and the additional risk of insolvency which arises because the financial structure contains debt.

Financial Services and Markets Act The 2000 Act (and orders made under it) form the bedrock of financial regulations in the UK.

Financial Services Authority (FSA) The chief financial services regulator in the UK until 2013.

Financial Services Compensation Scheme (FSCS) If a dishonest or incompetent financial services company is unable to pay money owed to a complainant (e.g. it has been liquidated) the FSCS will pay the customer (up to fixed limits) to compensate for loss if the financial services company was authorised by the Financial Conduct Authority.

Financial slack Having cash (or near-cash) and/or spare debt capacity available to take up opportunities as they appear.

Financing gap The gap in the provision of finance for medium-sized, fast-growing firms. Often these firms are too large or growing too fast to ask the individual shareholders for more funds or to obtain sufficient bank finance. Also they are not ready or not willing to launch on the stock market.

Firm prices Market makers are required to trade at the prices posted on the London Stock Exchange's system, unless the transaction is above the normal market size.

Fixed assets (non-current assets) Those not held for resale, but for use in the business.

Fixed charge (e.g. fixed charge debenture or loan) A specific asset(s) is assigned as collateral security for a debt.

Fixed cost A cost that does not vary according to the amount of goods or services that are produced, and has to be paid regardless of the firm's turnover and activity.

Fixed exchange rate The national authorities act to ensure that the rate of exchange between two currencies is constant.

Fixed-interest securities Strictly, as the term applies to securities such as bonds on which the holder receives a predetermined interest pattern on the par value (e.g. gilts, corporate bonds, Eurobonds). However, the term is also used for debt securities even when there is no regular interest, e.g. zero-coupon bonds, and when the interest varies, as with floating rate notes, for example.

Fixed-rate borrowing (fixed interest) The interest rate is constant throughout the loan period.

Fixed-odds trading For those who want to speculate on the movements of markets a fixed-odds trading firm will offer you an amount that you can take from them if your bet turns out to be right. For example, they pay you 200 per cent of the amount you put down if the FTSE falls by more than 10 per cent in the next 30 days. If you lose you forfeit your initial stake and no more.

Flat yield *See* Yield.

Float (for insurance companies) A pool of money held in the firm in readiness to pay claims.

Floating *See* Flotation.

Floating charge The total assets of the company or an individual are used as collateral security for a debt. There is no specific asset assigned as collateral.

Floating exchange rate A rate of exchange which is not fixed by national authorities but fluctuates depending on demand and supply for the currency.

Floating-rate bond *See* Variable-rate bond.

Floating-rate borrowing (floating interest) The rate of interest on a loan varies with a standard reference rate (e.g. LIBOR).

Floating-rate notes (FRNs) Notes (legal contracts for borrowing) in which the coupon fluctuates according to a benchmark interest rate charge (e.g. LIBOR). With **reverse floaters** the interest rate declines as LIBOR rises.

Flotation The issue of shares in a company for the first time on a stock exchange.

'Footsie™' Nickname for the FTSE 100 index.

Foreign banking Transactions in the home currency with non-residents.

Foreign bond A bond denominated in the currency of the country where it is issued when the issuer is a non-resident.

Foreign exchange control Limits are placed by a government on the purchase and sale of foreign currency.

Foreign exchange (forex or FX) markets Markets that facilitate the exchange of one currency into another.

Forex A contraction of 'foreign exchange'.

Forward agreement A contract between two parties to undertake an exchange at an agreed future date at a price agreed now.

Forward basis The price investors pay for unit trust units will be fixed at a particular time of day (usually 12 noon) that is yet to come.

Forward PER Current share price divided by the anticipated earnings for the current year.

Forward-rate agreement (FRA) An agreement about the future level of interest rates. Compensation is paid by one party to the other to the extent that market interest rates turn out to deviate from the 'agreed' rate.

Founders' shares Dividends are paid on these shares only after all other categories of equity shares have received fixed rates of dividend. They usually carry a number of special voting rights over certain company matters.

Free cash flow Cash generated by a business not required for operations or for reinvestment. Profit before depreciation, amortisation and provisions, but after interest, tax, capital expenditure on long-lived items and increases in working capital. These deductions can be made from the historic facts presented by the company of actual spending, or they can be based on estimates of the expenditures necessary to maintain the company's competitive position, unit volume and investment in all value generating projects.

Free float (free capital) The proportion of a quoted company's shares not held by those closest (e.g. founding directors' families) to the company who may be unlikely to sell their shares.

Free plus A return an investor enjoys over and above initial expectations.

Friendly merger Merger to which the two companies agree.

Friendly Society A mutual (cooperative) organisation involved in saving and lending.

Front-end charge A charge made when an investment is first made (e.g. by a unit trust manager when an investor first buys the units). Also called initial charge or sales charge.

Frontier market Financial markets that tend to be small, with few companies, low turnover and often government restrictions on investors. They are usually in poor countries.

FRS 3 earnings *See* Basic earnings per share.

FTSE 100 share index An index representing the UK's 100 largest listed shares.

FTSE 250 index This is an index of UK shares quoted on the London Stock Exchange constructed by the FTSE. Based on the largest 250 firms which are the next size range after the top 100: representing 15–16 per cent of the UK market capitalisations. Capitalisations are generally between £500 million and £2.5 billion. Also calculated with investment trusts excluded.

FTSE 350 index This is an index of UK shares quoted on the London Stock Exchange constructed by the FTSE. Based on the largest 350 quoted companies. It combines the FTSE 100 and the FTSE 250. This cohort of shares is also split in two to give high and low dividend yield groups. A second 350 index excludes investment trusts.

FTSE AIM All-Share This is an index of UK shares quoted on the London Stock Exchange constructed by the FTSE of all Alternative Investment Market companies except those with a low free-float and low liquidity.

FTSE All-Share index (the 'All-Share') This is an index of UK shares listed on the London Stock Exchange constructed by the FTSE. The most representative index reflecting the average movements of about 800 shares representing 98–99 per cent of the value of the London market. Broken down into a number of commercial and industrial sectors. Companies in the FTSE All-Share index have market capitalisation above roughly £50 million. It is an aggregation of the FTSE 100, FTSE 250 and the FTSE SmallCap.

FTSE All-Small An index of UK shares quoted on the London Stock Exchange constructed by the FTSE which combines companies in the FTSE SmallCap with those in the FTSE Fledgling.

FTSE All-World Index Series A share index containing 2,800 large and middle capitalisation size companies from the FTSE Global Equity Index Series. It covers 90–95 per cent of the investable market capitalisation in the world. The series is divided into developed and emerging segments, including sub-indices calculated at regional, national and sector level.

FTSEurofirst 300 An index of large European shares constructed by the FTSE.

FTSE Fledgling An index of UK shares quoted on the London Stock Exchange constructed by the FTSE. Includes companies listed on the Main Market but too small to be in the FTSE All-Share.

FTSE International This organisation calculates a range of share indices published on a regular (usually daily) basis.

FTSE SmallCap index An index of UK shares quoted on the London Stock Exchange constructed by the FTSE. Covers companies included in the FTSE All-Share but excluded from the FTSE 350, with a market capitalisation of between *c.* £50 million and £500 million.

Full price (bonds) *See* Dirty price.

Full-payout lease *See* Leasing and Finance lease.

Fully automated trading *See* Real-time dealing.

Fully paid The holder of shares has paid the full price and does not owe an instalment(s).

Fund management Investment and administration of a quantity of money (e.g. pension fund, insurance fund) on behalf of the fund's owners.

Fund of funds A fund that then invests the money raised from investors in a range of funds (e.g. hedge funds).

Fund platform *See* Platform.

Fund supermarkets *See* Platform.

Fundamental analysts Individuals who try to estimate a share's true value, based on future returns to the company. Data from many sources are used, e.g. company accounts, economic and social trends, technological changes, etc.

Fundraising Companies can raise money through rights issues, etc.

Fungible Interchangeable securities; can be exchanged for each other on identical terms.

Future A standardised contract between two parties to undertake a transaction at an agreed price on a specified future date.

Futures-based bet A bet with a spread betting company placed on the price of shares or the level of an index on the next quarter day or the one after that.

FX A contraction of foreign exchange.

GAAP Generally accepted accounting principles. Accounting rules for reporting results.

GDP (nominal, real) Gross domestic product, the sum of all output of goods and services produced by a nation. Nominal GDP includes inflation, and real excludes it.

Gearing (financial gearing) The proportion of debt capital in the overall capital structure. Also called 'leverage'. High gearing can lead to exaggeratedly high returns if things go well or exaggerated losses if they do not go well.

Gearing (operating gearing) The extent to which the firm's total costs are fixed. This influences the break-even point and the sensitivity of profits to changes in sales level.

General inflation The process of steadily rising prices resulting in the diminishing purchasing power of a given nominal sum of money. Measured by an overall price index which follows the price changes of a 'basket' of goods and services through time.

General insurance Insurance against specific contingencies (e.g. fire, theft and accident). The term excludes life insurance.

Gilt-edged market makers (GEMMs) These organisations are at the centre of trading in UK government bonds. They stand ready to buy from or sell to investors at all times (when markets are open) quoting bid and offer prices.

Gilts (gilt-edged securities) Fixed-interest UK government securities (bonds) – a means for the UK government to raise finance from savers. They usually offer regular interest and a redemption amount paid years in the future.

Global depositary receipts (GDRs) Certificates which represent ownership of a given number of a company's shares and which are traded independently of the underlying shares.

Globalisation The increasing internationalisation of trade, particularly financial product transactions. The integration of economic and capital markets throughout the world.

Goal congruence The aligning of the actions of senior management with the interests of shareholders.

Going concern A judgement as to whether a company has sufficient financial strength to continue for at least one year. Accounts are usually drawn up on the assumption that the business is a going concern.

Going long Buying a financial security (e.g. share) in the hope that its price will rise.

Going public A phrase used when a company becomes quoted on a stock exchange (the company may have been a public limited company for years before this).

Going short *See* Short selling.

Golden handcuffs Financial inducements for managers to remain working for a firm.

Golden parachutes In a hostile merger situation, managers will receive large pay-offs if the firm is acquired.

Golden shares Shares with extraordinary special powers over the company (e.g. power of veto over a merger).

Good for the day A buy or sell order for a financial security has a limit above/below which the investor does not want the broker to go. If the order is not completed that day it is cancelled.

Good till cancelled A buy or sell order for a financial security has a price limit. The order stays in place (up to 90 days) until the investor tells his/her broker that it is cancelled it or it has been satisfied by a trade.

Goodwill An accounting term for the difference between the amount that a company pays for another company and the fair value of the other company's assets (after deducting all liabilities). Goodwill is thus an intangible asset representing such things as the value of the company's brand names and the skills of its employees.

Grace period A lender grants the borrower a delay in the repayment of interest and/or principal at the outset of a lending agreement.

Greater fool investing The object is to pass on a share which is currently of great interest to the market speculators and traders after making a return on the 'investment' without really bothering to understand the fundamentals of the business.

Greenbury Committee report (1995) Recommendations on UK corporate governance.

Greenmail Key shareholders try to obtain a reward (e.g. the repurchase of their shares at a premium) from the company for not selling to a hostile bidder or becoming a bidder themselves.

Greenshoe An option that permits an issuing house, when assisting a corporation in a new issue, to sell more shares than originally planned. They may do this if demand is particularly strong.

Grey market A market in shares which have not yet come into existence (e.g. in the period between investors being told they will receive shares in a new issue and the actual receipt they may sell on the expectation of obtaining them later).

Gross dividend yield The gross (before tax) dividend per share as a percentage of share price.

Gross domestic product *See* GDP.

Gross margin *See* Gross profit margin.

Gross profit Turnover less cost of sales.

Gross profit margin (gross margin) Profit defined as sales minus cost of sales, expressed as a percentage of sales.

Gross redemption yield (gross yield to redemption) A calculation of the redemption yield (*see* Yield) before tax is deducted.

Group accounts *See* Consolidated accounts.

Growth industries Those industries which grow almost regardless of the state of the economy.

Growth stock Where the company has performed better than average (in growth in earnings per share) for a period of years and is expected to do so in the future.

Second-rate investors call some companies growth stocks even if there is no
history of good performance growth.

Guaranteed equity bonds Offered by insurance companies, banks, building
societies and other investment firms, they provide a return linked to stock market
indices. The investor commits to holding the bond for, say, five years and is
guaranteed a minimum amount back and may also benefit from a rise in the
stock market.

Guaranteed income bonds (GIBs) *See* Insurance company bonds.

Guaranteed loan stock (bond) An organisation other than the borrower
guarantees to the lender the repayment of the principal plus the interest
payment.

Haircut A loss of value of a debt instrument due to some form of default.

Half-yearly report *See* Interim report.

Hampel report A follow-up to the Cadbury and Greenbury reports on corporate
governance. Chaired by Sir Ronald Hampel and published in 1998.

Hang Seng index Main index for Hong Kong shares.

Hard currency A currency traded in a foreign exchange market for which
demand is persistently high. It is unlikely to depreciate by large percentages.
The major currencies (e.g. the US dollar, euro and sterling) are considered hard
currencies.

Head and shoulders formation A chartist's (technical analyst's) share price
pattern in which the chart line resembles a shoulder followed by a head (a rise in
price to a peak, followed by a fall) and then another shoulder.

Headline (underlying, adjusted or normalised) earnings per share Directors
produce these profit per share numbers by excluding one-off costs, exceptional
items and goodwill amortisation to show underlying profit-per-share trend (or
just to make the managerial performance look better).

Hedge fund A collective investment vehicle that operates relatively free from
regulation, allowing it to take steps in managing a portfolio that other fund
managers are unable to take (e.g. borrowing to invest, shorting the market).

Hedge or hedging Reducing or eliminating risk by undertaking a countervailing
transaction.

Her Majesty's Revenue and Customs (HMRC) The principal tax-collecting
authority in the UK.

Herstatt risk In 1974 the German bank Herstatt was closed by the authorities.
It had entered into forex transactions and received Deutschmarks from
counterparties in European time, but had not made the corresponding transfer of

US dollars to its counterparties in New York time. It is the risk that arises when forex transactions are settled in different time zones.

High-frequency trading (HFT) Ultra-fast Internet trading using computers programmed with algorithms to enter and exit the market automatically in a fraction of a second.

High Growth Segment Companies can be admitted to this part of the London Stock Exchange's Main Market only subject to the EU minimum standards and the HGS rulebook issued by London Stock Exchange, e.g. only 10 per cent of shares need to be in a free float rather than 25 per cent for a Premium Listing. The segment is designed specifically for high growth, revenue generating businesses incorporated in a European Economic Area (EEA) state, that over time are aspiring to join the Premium segment.

High watermark Many collective investment funds (e.g. unit trusts) increase the fees going to the fund manager if the fund outperforms. These performance fees are usually subject to a high-watermark rule whereby if it underperforms in a year (or a few years) then this has to be made up first before consideration of a performance fee for the current year.

High-yield debt *See* Mezzanine finance; Junk bonds.

High-yield shares (yield stocks, high yielder) Shares offering a high current dividend yield because the share price is low due to the expectation of low growth in profits and dividends, or because of perceived high risk. Sometimes labelled 'value shares'.

Hire purchase (HP) The user (hiree) of a good pays regular instalments of interest and principal to the hire purchase company over a period of months. Full ownership passes to the hiree at the end of the period. The hiree is able to use the good from the outset.

Historic basis The price that an investor in unit trusts pays is determined by the price calculated at a specific time that has already past – usually 12 noon today or the previous day.

Historical price–earnings ratio (PER) *See* Price–earnings ratio.

HMRC *See* Her Majesty's Revenue and Customs.

Holding company *See* Parent company.

Holding period returns Total holding period returns on a financial asset consist of (a) income (e.g. dividend paid), and (b) capital gain – a rise in the value of the asset.

Horizontal merger The two companies merging are engaged in similar lines of activity.

Hostile merger The target (acquired) firm's management is opposed to the merger.

Hot shares/sectors Those currently receiving a lot of attention from the press and investors.

Hubris Overweening self-confidence.

Hurdle rate The required rate of return. The opportunity cost of the finance provider's money. The minimum return required from a position, making an investment or undertaking a project.

Hybrid finance A debt issue or security that combines the features of two or more instruments, e.g. a convertible bond is a package of a bond with an option to convert. Also used to indicate that a form of finance has both debt risk/return features (e.g. regular interest and a right to receive principal at a fixed date) and equity risk/return features (e.g. the returns depend to a large extent on the profitability of the firm).

ICAP Securities and Derivatives Exchange (ISDX) A provider of primary and secondary equity market services independent of the London Stock Exchange (formerly PLUS Stock Exchange).

ICE Clear Europe Established in 2008 to provide central clearing services for ICE's global energy markets (e.g. crude oil and refined oil futures). Also the clearing house for ICE Endex energy derivatives contracts, European credit default swaps (CDS) and the London derivatives market of NYSE Liffe.

ICE Futures Europe Established in 1981 as the International Petroleum Exchange of London (IPE), and acquired by ICE in 2001, it offers trading in energy (e.g. Brent crude oil, coal, gas) and carbon emissions futures and options contracts.

ICE, Intercontinental Exchange Operates some of the world's leading regulated exchanges (e.g. New York Stock Exchange), trading platforms and clearing houses. Deals in shares, futures and other derivatives.

Iceberg order If a seller of a large quantity of shares, say 1 million, wants to disguise the size of the sale a popular technique is to leave an order to sell on the order-driven trading system, such as LSE's SETS, for say 10 tranches of 100,000 shares. The system permits the automatic reloading of the next tranche each time one is sold, until the 1 million shares are all sold. An iceberg order may also be used by buyers.

Idiosyncratic risk An alternative name for unsystematic risk.

Immediate solvency The ability of a firm to pay its short-term liabilities on time.

Impact day The day during the launch of a new issue of shares when the price is announced, the prospectus published and offers to purchase solicited.

Impairment The writing down of fixed assets and goodwill in the balance sheet if they are judged to have become permanently impaired (not expected to earn at least a satisfactory return). Impairments may also impact the profit and loss account.

Imperfect hedge The hedge position will partly, but not exactly, mirror the change in the underlying.

In-house share trading A broker is allowed to complete a share transaction without going to the stock exchange by taking on the deal himself if he can match the best prices offered by the market makers.

In-the-money option An option with intrinsic value. For a call option the current underlying price is more than the option exercise price. For a put option the current price of the underlying is below the exercise price.

Income drawdown (pension) *See* Drawdown (pension).

Income gearing (income leverage) The proportion of the annual income streams (i.e. pre-interest profits or cash flow) devoted to the prior claims of debt holders. The reciprocal of income gearing is the interest cover.

Income ('Inc') units (Distribution units) Unit trust units that pay out all income after deducting charges on set dates. Also applies to open-ended investment companies.

Income reinvested The performance of shares, other securities or portfolios is usually expressed as 'total return' including both capital gains or losses and the benefits of periodic reinvestment of income received in further shares, securities or units of the same kind as the original investment.

Income shares One where the investors anticipate a relatively high regular income from dividends but do not expect high capital growth (share price appreciation). Often found in slow-growing stable industries. *See also* Split-capital investment trusts.

Income statement *See* Profit and loss account.

Income yield *See* Yield.

Incorporation The forming of a company (usually offering limited liability to the shareholders), including the necessary legal formalities.

Independent complaints scheme Financial service companies generally belong to an independent complaints scheme, either an arbitration scheme or Ombudsman scheme. This permits customers to have their complaints looked into by an independent body.

Independent director One who is not beholden to the dominant executive directors. Customers, suppliers or friends of the founding family are not usually regarded as independent, for example.

Independent financial advisers (IFAs) Individuals authorised by the Financial Conduct Authority to provide financial advice.

Independent variables Two variables which are completely unrelated and show no co-movement.

Index *See* Market index.

Index huggers 'Active' investment managers of collective funds pretending to sift companies to select only the most underpriced, when in reality they are creating portfolios that are similar to a broad cross-section of the market.

Index-linked stocks (gilts) The redemption value and the coupons rise with inflation over the life of the UK government bond.

Index option An option on a share index (e.g. FTSE 100 or Standard & Poor's 500).

Index trackers (indexed funds) Collective investment funds (e.g. unit trusts) which try to replicate a stock market index rather than to pick winners in an actively managed fund.

Indicative offer *See* Virtual bid.

Indices *See* Market index.

Individual Savings Account (ISA) A savings account with special tax privileges. The saver can invest savings in cash deposits, shares, insurance products and/or other securities.

Industry attractiveness The economics of the market for the product(s), part of which is determined by industry structure.

Industry structure The combination of the degree of rivalry within the industry among existing firms; the bargaining strength of industry firms with suppliers and customers; and the potential for new firms to enter and for substitute products to take customers. The industry structure determines the long-run rate of return on capital employed within the industry.

Inevitable A company likely to dominate its field for an investment lifetime due to its competitive strength. A term used (invented?) by Warren Buffett.

Inflation The process of prices rising resulting in the fall of the purchasing power of one currency unit.

Inflation risk The risk that the nominal returns on an investment will be insufficient to offset the decline in the value of money due to inflation.

Informal venture capitalist *See* Business angel.

Information asymmetry *See* Asymmetric information.

Informed investors Those who are highly knowledgeable about financial securities and the fundamental evaluation of their worth.

Inheritance tax (IHT) A tax payable on transfers made on an individual's estate at the time of death (it also covers some gifts made during the individual's lifetime).

Inherited estates *See* Orphan assets.

Initial charge (sales charge, front-end charge) A charge to an investor when he/she buys securities to cover administration costs.

Initial margin An amount that a derivative contractor has to provide to the clearing house when first entering upon a derivative contract.

Initial public offering (IPO) (New issue) The offering of shares in the equity of a company to the public for the first time.

Insider trading (dealing) Trading shares, etc., on the basis of information not in the public domain.

Insolvent (1) A company unable to pay debts as they become due. (2) Having liabilities in excess of a reasonable market value of assets.

Institute of Actuaries The UK professional body for educating, developing and regulating actuaries who evaluate, manage and advise on financial risks. Knowledgeable about business and economics as well as probability theory, statistics and investment theory, they can provide strategic, commercial and financial advice. The core of actuarial work lies within pensions and insurance funds.

Institutional imperative An insidious and dangerous unseen force at work in companies. It is the tendency of organisations to stray from the path of rationality, decency and intelligence.

Institutional neglect Share analysts, particularly at the major institutions, may fail to spend enough time studying small firms, preferring to concentrate on the larger 100 or so.

Institutional shareholder committee A grouping of UK institutional investors (e.g. pension funds, insurance companies) which works in partnership to impose codes of conduct on companies and on its own members.

Institutionalisation The increasing tendency towards investment through organisations, as opposed to individuals investing money in securities (e.g. pension funds and investment trusts collect the savings of individuals to invest in shares).

Instrument A general term for all types of financial documents, such as shares, bonds, etc.

Insurance company bonds A lump-sum investment is made with an insurance company for a fixed period, say five years. Guaranteed income bonds (GIBs) pay regular income (the money is invested in a portfolio of low-risk bonds such as gilts). With growth bonds the interest accumulates until the maturity date.

Intangible assets Those that you cannot touch, they are non-physical (e.g. goodwill).

Intelligent speculation A focus on information that is quantifiable. Based on a calculation of probabilities. Keeping the speculative element within minor limits. The odds are strongly in favour of success. (A term used by Benjamin Graham.)

Interbank brokers Brokers in the forex markets who act as intermediaries between buyers and sellers. They provide anonymity to each side.

Interbank market The money market in short-term money and foreign exchange in which banks borrow and lend among themselves. It is now extended to include large companies and other organisations.

Intercontinental Exchange *See* ICE.

Interest cover The number of times the income (or operating cash flow) of a business in a period exceeds the interest payments made to service its loan capital in that period.

Interest rate risk The risk that changes in interest rates will have an adverse impact.

Interest rate swap *See* Swap.

Interest-withholding tax *See* Withholding tax.

Interest yield *See* Yield.

Interim bonus The annual bonus given by an insurance company to with-profits policyholders.

Interim dividend A dividend related to the first half-year's (or quarter's) trading, announced at the time of the interim profit statement.

Interim management statement (or trading update) Issued by a company in the middle of each half year, consisting of a few paragraphs providing a brief description of the firm's trading performance since the last formal report.

Interim payment *See* interim dividend.

Interim report (statement) Describes the company's activities and profit and loss, balance sheet and cashflow statement for the first six months of the financial year. Unaudited.

Intermediaries offer A method of selling shares in the new issue market. Shares are offered to financial institutions such as stockbrokers. Clients of these intermediaries can then apply to buy shares from them.

Intermediate debt *See* Mezzanine finance; Junk bonds.

Internal finance Funds generated by the firm's activities, and available for investment within the firm after meeting contractual obligations.

Internal rate of return (IRR) The discount rate that makes the present value of a stream of cash flows equal to the initial investment(s).

International bonds Some people use the term to mean the same as Eurobonds, others extend the definition to encompass foreign bonds as well.

International Capital Market Association (ICMA) A self-regulatory organisation designed to promote orderly trading and the general development of the international debt markets.

International Financial Reporting Standards (IFRS) Accounting standards issued by the International Accounting Standards Board (IASB) adopted by dozens of countries. Companies listed on London's Main Market and on AIM have now adopted IFRS. Other UK companies may presently adopt either UK GAAP (generally accepted accounting principles) or IFRS.

International Petroleum Exchange The energy futures and options exchange in London. Now part of ICE.

Intraday (cash or spot) bet A bet with a spread betting company that starts and is closed in the same trading day.

Intrinsic value (company) The discounted value of the cash (owner earnings) that can be taken out of a business during its remaining life.

Intrinsic value (options) The pay-off that would be received if the underlying is at its current level when the option expires.

Introduction A company with shares already quoted on another stock exchange, or where there is already a wide spread of shareholders, may be introduced to the market, without underwriting costs. This allows a secondary market in the shares even though no new shares are issued.

Inventory *See* Stock.

Inverse ETFs Exchange traded funds whose returns move inversely with the returns on the underlying securities.

Investment bank Banks that carry out a variety of financial services, usually excluding high street banking. Their services are usually fee-based (e.g. fees for merger advice to companies).

Investment club A group of people who each contribute a few pounds per month which is then pooled to buy shares (or other financial securities) for the club.

Investment committees (ICs) Representative groupings of institutional investors. The main two are the Association of British Insurers (ABI) and the National Association of Pension Funds (NAPF). The ICs provide lobbying power and can guide corporate managers on what they regard as acceptable behaviour, e.g. they sometimes recommend the voting down of a director's remuneration report.

Investment grade debt Debt with a sufficiently high credit rating (BBB– or Baa or above) to be regarded as safe enough for institutional investors who are restricted to buying safe debt only.

Investment-linked insurance plans A term covering with-profits policies, unit-linked policies and others supplied by insurance companies.

Investment Management Association UK trade association for investment management service companies who provide services to life assurance companies, pension funds, individual companies and private investors.

Investment operation One that, upon thorough analysis, promises safety of principal and a satisfactory return. If these criteria are not met then you are speculating.

Investment platform *See* Platform.

Investment trusts (investment companies) Collective investment vehicles set up as companies selling shares. The money raised is invested in assets such as shares, gilts, corporate bonds and property.

Invoice An itemised list of goods shipped, usually specifying the terms of sale and price.

IOU A colloquialism intended to mean 'I owe you'. The acknowledgement of a debt.

IPO *See* Initial public offering.

Irredeemable (perpetual) Financial securities with no fixed maturity date at which the principal is repaid.

ISA *See* Individual Savings Account.

ISDX *See* ICAP Securities and Derivatives Exchange.

iShares A type of exchange traded fund (ETF) created by Barclays Global Investors but now owned and run by BlackRock.

Issued share capital That part of a company's share capital that has been subscribed by shareholders, either paid up or partially paid up. *See also* Called-up share capital.

Issuing house *See* Sponsor.

Joint stock enterprise The ownership (share) capital is divided into small units, permitting a number of investors to contribute varying amounts to the total. Profits are divided between stockholders in proportion to the number of shares they own.

Joint venture A business operation (usually a separate company) is jointly owned by two or more parent firms. The term also applies to strategic alliances between companies where they collaborate on, for example, research.

Junior debt (junior security) *See* Subordinated debt.

Junk bonds Low quality, low credit-rated, company bonds rated below investment-grade (below BBB− or Baa). Risky and with a high yield.

Key investor information document (KIID) Produced by a collective investment fund, e.g. unit trust, and sets out the most important facts about the fund (e.g. fees) in standardised, jargon-free way, allowing comparison between funds to allow investors to assess which funds might suit their investment needs at a reasonable cost.

Key performance indicators (KPIs) Most companies include a number of KPIs in their reports and accounts, comparing actual performance based on these metrics against targets and against previous years, accompanied by a discussion of outcomes and aspirations. Examples: return on capital employed, customer satisfaction ratings.

Kicker *See* Equity kicker.

Kick-out plans Investment deals offered by financial institutions which pay the investor their original capital plus a coupon if the share index (e.g. FTSE 100) is above its level at the beginning of the plan. If it is not, the payout occurs at subsequent anniversaries if the index has at least maintained its start level.

LCH:Clearnet (LCH) Settles mutual indebtedness between a number of organisations. It settles trades for equity traders, derivative traders, bond traders and energy traders and guarantees all contracts. It often acts as counterparty to all trades on an exchange.

Lead manager In a new issue of securities (e.g. shares, bonds, syndicated loans) the lead manager controls and organises the issue. There may be joint lead managers, co-managers and regional lead managers.

Lead steer A term used to describe a dominant person with the power to induce others to follow.

Leasing The owner of an asset (lessor) grants the use of the asset to another party (lessee) for a specified period in return for regular rental payments. The asset does not become the property of the lessee at the end of the specified period. *See also* Finance lease; Operating lease.

Level 2 data (Level II) Online brokers provide streaming data on share prices. Level 2 data allow the investor to observe a lot of detail about trades (e.g. market makers' transactions as they take place or the limit price which that investor put into the system in the search for a counterparty to buy or sell), allowing the investor a better feel for the supply and demand balance in the market.

Leverage *See* Gearing.

Leveraged buyout (LBO) The acquisition of a company, subsidiary or unit by another, financed mainly by borrowings.

Leveraged recapitalisation The financial structure (debt–equity ratio) of the firm is altered in such a way that it becomes highly geared.

LIBOR (London Inter-Bank Offered Rate) The rate of interest obtainable by highly rated (low-risk) banks in the London interbank market for a specific period (e.g. three months). Used as a reference rate for other loans.

Life insurance or life assurance Insurance against death. Beneficiaries receive payment upon death of the policyholder or other person named in the policy. Endowment policies offer a savings vehicle as well as cover against death.

Lifestyle pension fund Invests mostly in equities when the investor is decades away from retirement and then gradually switches to cash and bonds as retirement approaches.

LIFFE (London International Financial Futures and Options Exchange) The main derivatives exchange in London, now owned by the Intercontinental Exchange.

LIFFE CONNECT™ The computer system used by LIFFE for trading derivatives.

Limit order A type of buy or sell order instruction given by an investor to a broker to buy a quantity of a security at or below a specified price or to sell at or above a specified price.

Limited company (Ltd) 'Private' company with no minimum amount of share capital, but with restrictions on the range of investors who can be offered shares. Limited liability for the debts of the firm is granted to the shareholders. It cannot be quoted on the London Stock Exchange.

Limited liability The owners of shares in a business have a limit on their loss, set as the amount they have committed to invest in shares.

Liquid ratio *See* Quick ratio.

Liquidation The winding up of the affairs of a company when it ceases business. This could be forced by an inability to make payment when due or it could be voluntary when shareholders choose to end the company. Assets are sold, liabilities paid (if sufficient funds) and the surplus (if any) is distributed to shareholders.

Liquidity The degree to which an asset can be sold quickly and easily without loss in value.

Liquidity risk (1) The risk that an organisation or individual may not have, or may not be able to raise, cash funds when needed. (2) For an equity investor liquidity may arise because it becomes difficult to sell a shareholding quickly without moving the price against you.

Listed companies Those on the Official List of the United Kingdom Listing Authority.

Listed private equity (LPEQ) Funds which are companies investing in unquoted companies, but which have their own shares quoted on an exchange. A subset are private equity investment trusts.

Listing agreement The UK Listing Authority insists that a company signs a listing agreement committing the directors to certain standards of behaviour and levels of reporting to shareholders.

Listing particulars *See* Prospectus.

Listing rules The regulations concerning the initial flotation of a listed company on a regulated stock market and the continuing requirements the company must meet.

Lloyd's Insurance Market A medium-sized insurance business in London founded over two centuries ago. 'Names' supply the capital to back insurance policies. Names can now be limited liability companies rather than individuals with unlimited liability to pay up on an insurance policy.

LME *See* London Metal Exchange.

Loan stock A fixed-interest debt financial security. May be unsecured.

Local authority deposits Lending money to a UK local government authority.

London Metal Exchange (LME) Trades metals (e.g. lead, zinc, tin, aluminium and nickel) in spot, forward and option markets.

London Stock Exchange (LSE) The London market in which securities are bought and sold.

Long bond Often defined as bonds with more than 15 years to maturity, but there is some flexibility in this, so a 10-year bond is often described as being long.

Long-form report A report produced by accountants for the sponsor of a company being prepared for flotation. The report is detailed and confidential. It helps to reassure the sponsors when putting their name to the issue and provides the basis for the short-form report included in the prospectus.

Long position A positive exposure to a quantity. Owning a security or commodity; the opposite of a short position (selling).

Long-range structural analysis A process used to forecast the long-term rates of return of an industry.

Long/short strategy An investment strategy that takes long positions in some securities and short positions in others.

Long-term incentive plan (LTIP) A scheme designed to motivate senior managers and directors of a company by paying bonuses if certain targets are surpassed (e.g. share price has risen relative to market index).

Look-through earnings (true economic earnings) The profits for a holding company with small percentage stakes (of the ordinary shares) in other companies not only includes the dividends received from those investees but also adds the retained earnings attributable to the holding company given its percentage stake. Thus a company owning 10 per cent of another company will add 10 per cent of the investee's profits that year to derive look-through earnings. The accounting rules only permit the addition of dividends paid to investors and thus look-through earnings is not recognised by accountants, nor is it generally published.

Lot (piece) A standard unit of trading (e.g. only multiples of 1,000 bonds are traded, each 1,000 being a 'lot').

Low-grade debt *See* Mezzanine finance; Junk bonds.

Lower-yield shares (stocks) Shares offering a relatively low dividend yield expected to grow rapidly. Often labelled 'growth stocks'.

LPEQ *See* Listed private equity.

LSE *See* London Stock Exchange.

Ltd *See* Limited company.

M&A Merger and acquisition.

Macroeconomics The study of the relationships between broad economic aggregates: national income, saving, investment, balance of payments, inflation, taxation, etc.

Main Market The Official List of the London Stock Exchange, as opposed to the Alternative Investment Market.

Maintenance margin (futures) The level of margin that must be maintained on a futures account (usually at a clearing house). Daily marking to market of the position may reveal the necessity to put more money into the account to top up to the maintenance margin.

Making a book Market makers offering two prices: the price at which they are willing to buy (bid price) and the price they are willing to sell (offer price).

Managed fund A collective investment fund that allocates different proportions of the fund to UK equities, overseas equities, bonds, property and cash depending on the manager's view on market returns.

Management buy-in (MBI) A new team of managers makes an offer to a company to buy the whole company, a subsidiary or a section of the company, with the intention of taking over the running of it themselves. Private equity organisations often provide the major part of the finance.

Management buy-out (MBO) A team of managers makes an offer to its employers to buy a whole business, a subsidiary or a section so that the managers own and run it themselves. Private equity is often used to finance the majority of the purchase price.

Managementism/managerialism Management not acting in shareholders' best interests by pursuing objectives attractive to the management team. Three levels can be distinguished: (1) dishonest managers; (2) honest but incompetent managers; (3) honest and competent managers, but subject to the influence of conflicts of interest.

Manager risk The risk that you may choose a poor manager (e.g. of ISAs, OEICs) to invest your money.

Managing director (MD) An executive responsible for running a business.

Mandatory bid If 30 per cent or more of the shares of a company are acquired, the holder is required under Takeover Panel rules to bid for all the company's shares.

Margin call A demand by a clearing house for a futures position taker to top up the margin held at the clearing house as the underlying moves unfavourably for the position holder.

Margin (futures) Money placed aside to back a futures purchase or sale. This is used to reassure the counterparty (effectively the clearing house in most cases) to the future that money will be available should the purchaser/seller renege on the deal.

Margin (market makers) The difference between the bid and offer prices announced by market makers.

Margin of safety A share should only be purchased when the value of a share is well in excess of the price paid. A probability of protection against loss under all normal or reasonably likely conditions or variations.

Market capitalisation The total value at market prices of the ordinary shares in issue for a company (or a stock market, or a sector of the stock market).

Market entry Firms that previously did not supply goods or services to this industry now do so.

Market index A sample of shares is used to represent a share (or other security) market's level and movements as a benchmark against which individual shares are judged.

Market in managerial control Teams of managers compete for control of corporate assets (e.g. through merger activity).

Market maker A person or organisation that stands ready to buy and sell shares (or other securities) from investors on their own behalf at the centre of the London Stock Exchange's quote-driven system of share trading. Also known as a dealer.

Market order An investor instructs a broker to buy/sell at whatever is the current market price.

Market portfolio In finance theory it is a portfolio that contains all assets. Each asset is held in proportion to the asset's share of the total market value of all the assets. A proxy for this is often employed (e.g. the FTSE 100 index).

Market power The ability to exercise some control over the price of the product.

Market risk *See* Systematic risk.

Market-to-book ratio Share price divided by capital invested per share ('Capital invested' is usually taken to be the balance sheet net assets).

Market value reduction (MVR) (Market value adjustor) An exit penalty that may be imposed on a with-profits policyholder should he/she withdraw money from the fund.

Market weightings The capitalisation of all the firms in an industry as a proportion of the total capitalisation of all the shares on the stock market.

Marking down Market makers adjust down bid and offer prices in response to news in anticipation of a high volume of sell orders at the previous price.

Marking to market The losses or gains on a derivative contract are assessed daily in reference to the value of the underlying price.

Matador A foreign bond issued in Spain.

Matched-bargain system *See* Order-driven trading system.

Maturity (Maturity date or Final maturity or Redemption date) The time when a financial security (e.g. a bond) is redeemed and the par value is paid to the lender.

Maturity structure The profile of the length of time to the redemption and repayment of a company's various debts.

Maturity transformation Intermediaries offer securities with liquid and low-risk characteristics to induce primary investors to purchase or deposit funds. The money raised is made available to the ultimate borrowers on a long-term, illiquid basis.

Maximisation of long-term shareholder wealth The assumed objective of the firm in finance theory and the objective generally mouthed by executives.

Mean reversion *See* Reversion to the mean.

Medium-term note (MTN) A document setting out a promise from a borrower to pay the holders a specified sum on the maturity date and, in many cases, a coupon interest in the meantime. Maturity can range from nine months to 30 years. If denominated in a foreign currency, they are called euro medium-term notes.

Memorandum of Association Lays down the rules which govern a company and its relations with the outside world (e.g. states the objective of the company).

Merchant bank *See* Investment bank.

Merger The combining of two business entities under common ownership.

Mezzanine finance Unsecured debt or preference shares offering a high return with a high risk. Ranked behind secured debt but ahead of equity. It may carry an equity kicker.

Mid-market price A price between the offer and bid prices of a market maker at which shares are bought and sold.

MiFID, the Markets in Financial Instruments Directive A European Union set of rules (launched in 2007) designed to engender greater competition in share trading in Europe. Brokers need to demonstrate they are achieving the keenest price and using the most efficient, cost-effective clearing and settlement systems. New exchanges (such as BATS Chi-X and Turquoise) sprang up to compete with the traditional national exchanges. These multilateral trading facilities (MTFs) have taken a significant share of trading in the large companys' shares. MiFID also insists that some investors have to provide sufficient information to brokers to prove they have sufficient experience needed to invest in 'complex' structures such as hedge funds and derivatives.

Mini-bonds A class of corporate bonds aimed at retail investors issued in small amounts usually by small companies. They are not vetted by the Financial Conduct Authority and have no secondary market.

Minority shareholder A shareholder who owns less than 50 per cent of the voting shares of a company.

MM Main Market on the London Stock Exchange.

Mobilisation of savings The flow of savings primarily from the household sector to the ultimate borrowers to invest in real assets. This process is encouraged by financial intermediaries.

Model Code for Directors' Dealings London Stock Exchange rules for directors dealing in shares of their own company.

Momentum investing Buying shares that have recently risen and selling shares that have recently fallen.

Monetary policy The deliberate control of the money supply and/or rates of interest by the central bank.

Money market Wholesale (large-volume) financial markets in which lending and borrowing take place on a short-term basis (less than one year). Example of instruments include Treasury bills, commercial paper and certificates of deposit.

Money rate of return The rate of return which includes a return to compensate for inflation.

Monopoly One producer in an industry. However, for Competition and Markets Authority purposes a monopoly is defined as a market share of 25 per cent.

Moral hazard The presence of a safety net (e.g. insurance policy) encourages adverse behaviour (e.g. carelessness). An incentive to take extraordinary risks (risks that tend to fall on others) aimed at rectifying a desperate position. The risk that a party to a transaction is not acting in good faith by providing misleading or inadequate information.

Mortgage-backed securities Securitised bonds backed by a collection of mortgage payments. *See* Securitisation.

Mortgage debentures Bonds secured using property as collateral.

Multi-bagger A share that rises to a multiple of the buying price.

Multilateral Trading Facilities (MTFs) *See* MiFID.

Mutual fund A collective investment vehicle for shares or other financial securities. Many investors own stakes in the mutual fund which then invests in securities.

Mutually owned organisations Organisations run for the benefit of the members (usually the same as the consumers of the organisation's output) and not for shareholders. Examples include some insurance organisations, building societies and the co-operative societies.

Naked (or uncovered) Long or short positioning in a derivative without an offsetting position in the underlying. *See also* Uncovered call option writing.

NASDAQ OMX A series of computer-based information services and order execution system for US shares market plus the Scandinavian and Baltic countries.

NASDAQ 100 A stock market index that tracks the 100 largest companies on the United States NASDAQ share market.

NASDAQ Composite An index of shares on the United States NASDAQ share market containing about 3,000 shares.

National Fraud Authority Coordinates and oversees the fight against fraud in the UK.

National Savings Lending to the UK government through the purchase of bonds, and placing money into savings accounts.

NAV Net Asset Value.

Near-cash (near-money, quasi-money) Highly liquid financial assets but which are generally not usable for transactions such as buying an ice cream and therefore cannot be fully regarded as cash, e.g. Treasury bills.

Negative (restrictive) covenants Loan agreements conditions that restrict the actions and rights of the borrower until the debt has been repaid in full.

Negotiable (1) Transferable to another – free to be traded in financial markets. (2) Capable of being settled by agreements between the parties involved in a transaction.

Net asset value (net worth) (NAV) Total assets minus all the liabilities. Fixed assets, plus inventory, receivables (debtors), cash and other liquid assets, minus long- and short-term liabilities.

Net book value The original cost of an asset minus the accumulated depreciation for tangible assets or minus the amortisation for intangibles since their acquisition.

Net current assets The difference between current assets and current liabilities.

Net interest yield Gross yield on a debt instrument less the tax payable on that interest.

Net operating cash flow Profit before depreciation, less periodic investment in net working capital.

Net present value (NPV) The present value of the expected cash flows associated with a project or other investment after discounting at a rate which reflects the value of the alternative use of the funds.

Net profit (net income) Profit after interest, tax and extraordinary charges and receipts.

Net realisable value What someone might reasonably be expected to pay less the costs of the sale.

Net worth *See* Net asset value.

New entrant A company entering a market area to compete with existing players.

New issue The sale of securities (e.g. debentures or shares), to raise additional finance or to float existing securities of a company on a stock exchange for the first time.

Niche company A fast-growing small to medium-sized firm operating in a niche business with high potential.

Nifty fifty Fifty stocks declared in the late 1960s and early 1970s to have such a marvellous future that supposedly almost any multiple of current income could be justified as a share price.

Nikkei index or Nikkei 225 Stock Average A share index based on the prices of 225 shares quoted on the Tokyo Stock Exchange.

Nil paid rights Shareholders may sell the rights to purchase shares in a rights issue without having paid anything to obtain these rights.

Noise trading Uninformed investors buying and selling financial securities at irrational prices, thus creating noise (strange movements) in the price of securities. 'Noise' is derived from natural science: random interference in physical processes.

Nomad *See* Nominated adviser.

Nominal return (or nominal interest rate) The return on an investment including inflation. If the return necessary to compensate for the decline in purchasing power of money (inflation) is deducted from the nominal return we have the real rate of return.

Nominal value *See* Par value.

Nominated adviser (Nomad) Each company on the Alternative Investment Market has to retain a nomad. They act as quality controllers, confirming to the London Stock Exchange that the company has complied with the rules. They also act as consultants to the company.

Nominated brokers Each company on the Alternative Investment Market has to retain a nominated broker, who helps to bring buyers and sellers together and comments on the firm's prospects and advises the company on investor relations and market conditions for fund raising.

Nominee accounts An official holder of an asset is not the beneficial owner but merely holds the asset in a nominee account for the beneficiary. In the stock market, the most common use of nominee accounts is where execution-only brokers act as nominees for their clients. The shares are registered in the name of the broker, but the client has beneficial ownership of them.

Nominee company Brokers and investment managers hold investors' shares electronically in a nominee company which appears as the registered owner. *See also* Dematerialisation and Nominee accounts.

Non-controlling (minority) shareholder One who has an insufficient percentage of the voting rights to control the composition of the board and how the company is run. Usually the cutoff is at 50 per cent of the votes, but in many cases shareholders with less than 50 per cent are deemed controlling shareholders. For accounting: a shareholder in a subsidiary other than the parent company.

Non-executive (outside) director (NED) A director without day-to-day operational responsibility for the firm.

Non-voting shares A company may issue two or more classes of ordinary shares, one of which may not carry any votes.

Non-UCITS Retail Scheme (NURS) Funds authorised to be sold to the public in EU member states that are not governed by European regulation under the 'UCITS directive', because they invest in assets that the Directive does not permit or comply with different concentration limits. They only comply with domestic country regulations.

Normal market size (NMS) The threshold below which the market makers have to sell/buy shares at the prices they posted on the London Stock Exchange systems without modification. It is normally set at 2.5 per cent of the average daily customer turnover of a share on the LSE in the previous year. The term exchange market size (EMS) is an alternative.

Normal rate of return A rate of return that is just sufficient to induce shareholders to put money into the firm and hold it there.

Normalised earnings per share *See* Headline earnings per share.

Note (promissory note) A financial security with the promise to pay a specific sum of money by a given date (e.g. commercial paper, floating rate notes). Usually unsecured.

Notional trading requirement A sum of money that has to be deposited by an investor with a spread betting company to reassure the company that the investor will not renege on the deal should the bet start to go against him or her.

NYSE The New York Stock Exchange.

NYSE Euronext The combined financial stock markets of New York, Paris, Amsterdam, Brussels and Lisbon, plus Euronext.liffe. Now part of Intercontinental Exchange.

Off-balance-sheet finance Assets are acquired in such a way that liabilities do not appear on the balance sheet (e.g. some lease agreements permit the exclusion of the liability in the accounts).

Off-market transfer The transfer of ownership of shares and other securities without the use of a broker or the stock market. A stock transfer form can be used.

Offer document (1) A formal document sent by a company attempting to buy the shares of a target firm to all the shareholders of the target, setting out the offer. (2) The legal document for an offer for sale in a new issue (IPO).

Offer for sale A method of selling shares in a new issue. The company sponsor offers shares to the public by inviting subscriptions from investors. In an offer for sale by fixed price, the sponsor fixes the price prior to the offer. In an offer for sale by tender, investors state the price they are willing to pay. A strike price is established by the sponsors after receiving all the bids. All investors pay the strike price.

Offer for subscription A method of selling shares in a new issue. The issue is aborted if the offer does not raise sufficient interest from investors.

Offer price (1) The price at which a market maker in shares will sell a share, or a dealer in other markets will sell a security or asset. (2) The price of a new issue of securities e.g. a new issue of shares.

Office of Fair Trading (OFT) Now merged into the Competition and Markets Authority (CMA), it had wide powers to monitor, investigate and correct anti-competitive behaviour and to refer monopoly or anti-competitive situations to the Competition Commission.

Official List (OL) The daily list of securities admitted for trading on the UK's regulated markets by the UK Listing Authority. Most are on the London Stock Exchange's Main Market. It does not include securities traded on the Alternative Investment Market (AIM) or most of those on ISDX.

Offshore investment Outside investors' home country jurisdiction and financial regulation, usually in tax havens, such as the Cayman Islands.

Offshore roll-up funds Savers can deposit money in these outside their country of residence to reduce tax paid on interest or dividends. The interest/dividends are kept within the fund until the saver partially or wholly encashes it. This may be done when the investor enters a phase of life as a low-rate tax payer.

Oligopoly A small number of producers in an industry.

OMX Scandinavian and Baltic group of stock exchanges, now merged with the United States' NASDAQ.

Ongoing charge Collective (pooled) investment funds, e.g. unit trusts need to pay for the management of the fund and numerous other annual costs. The annual ongoing charge, expressed as a percentage of funds under management, is usually 0.2 to 0.5 percentage points greater than the annual management charge and covers, for example, administration, custody, legal and audit, as well as the management charges for selecting shares and running the fund. The ongoing charge bears a close resemblance to the former 'all-encompassing' annual set of fees called the total expense ratio (TER).

Onshore fund A fund authorised and regulated by the regulator in the investor's home country.

Open-ended fund The size of the fund and the number of units depends on the amount investors wish to put into the fund, e.g. a unit trust. The manager adds to or liquidates part of the assets of the fund depending on the level of purchases or sales of the units in the fund.

Open-ended investment companies (OEICs) Share-issuing collective investment vehicles with one price for investors. OEICs are able to issue more shares if demand increases from investors, unlike investment trusts. OEICs invest the finance raised in securities, primarily shares.

Open interest The sum of outstanding long and short positions in a given futures or option contract. Transactions have not been offset or closed out, thus there is still exposure to movements in the underlying.

Open offer New shares created by a company are offered to a wide range of external investors (not the generality of current shareholders). However, under clawback provisions, existing shareholders can buy the shares at the offer price if they wish.

Open outcry Where trading is through oral calling of buy and sell offers and hand signals by market members.

Operating and financial review (OFR) *See* Business review.

Operating gearing *See* Gearing.

Operating lease The lease period is significantly less than the expected useful life of the asset and the agreed lease payments do not amount to more than 90 per cent of the present value of the asset.

Operating margin *See* Operating profit margin.

Operating profit (operating income) The income remaining after paying all costs other than interest and tax.

Operating profit margin (operating margin, trading margin) Operating profit as a percentage of sales.

Operational efficiency of a market Relates to how the market minimises the cost to buyers and sellers of transactions in securities on the exchange.

Opportunity cost The value forgone by opting for one course of action; the next best use of, say, financial resources.

Option A contract giving one party the right, but not the obligation, to buy or sell a financial instrument, commodity or some other underlying asset at a given price, at or before a specified date.

Option premium The amount paid by an option purchaser (holder) to obtain the rights under an option contract.

Order book for retail bond (ORB) The London Stock Exchange's venue for the trading of a dozens of corporate bonds and gilts in transaction sizes suitable for retail investors.

Order book system *See* Order-driven trading system.

Order-driven trading system (matched bargain or order book system) Buy and sell orders for securities are entered on a central computer system, and investors are automatically matched according to the price and volume they entered. SETS is an example.

Order placing service An online brokerage service. The investor emails the broker with an order who then trades with market makers.

Ordinary resources Those that give the firm competitive parity. They provide a threshold competence.

Ordinary shares The equity capital of the firm. The holders of ordinary shares are the owners and are therefore entitled to all distributed profits after the lenders and preference shares have had their claims met. They are also entitled to control the direction of the company through the power of their votes – usually one vote per share.

Organic growth Growth from within the firm rather than through mergers.

Orphan assets (inherited estates) Reserves that an insurance company has held back from with-profits policyholders to act as a buffer should the market decline. Critics claim that the insurance companies have been too cautious and should give the majority of these assets back to policyholders.

Out-of-the-money option An option without intrinsic value. For a call option the current price of the underlying is less than the exercise price. For a put option the current price of the underlying is more than the exercise price.

Over-allotment issue *See* Greenshoe.

Over-capacity An industry or company has significantly more capacity to supply product than is being demanded.

Over-subscription In a new issue (IPO) of securities investors offer to buy more securities (e.g. shares) than are made available.

Over-the-counter (OTC) trade Securities trading carried on outside regulated exchanges. These bilateral trades allow tailor-made transactions.

Overdraft A permit to overdraw on an account (e.g. a bank account) up to a stated limit; to take more out of a bank account than it contains.

Overhang Blocks of securities or commodities that are known to be available for sale. This can lead to a situation where a share price (or other security or commodity price) is depressed because of an anticipated sale of a large quantity of shares (or other security or commodity).

Overhead The business expenses not chargeable to a particular part of the work or product; a cost that is not directly associated with producing the merchandise.

Overtrading When a business has insufficient finance to sustain its level of trading. Too much cash is tied up on stocks (inventory) and debtors (receivables), and too little is available to pay creditors and meet day-to-day expenses. A business is said to be overtrading when it tries to engage in more business than the investment in working capital will allow. This can happen even in profitable circumstances.

Overweighting When a fund invests in an individual asset, industrial sector or country more than in proportion to the asset's, sector's or country's weighting in the relevant benchmark index.

Owner earnings Earnings plus depreciation, depletion, amortisation and certain other non-cash charges less the amount of expenditure for plant and machinery and working capital, etc. that a business requires to fully maintain its long-term competitive position, its unit volume and its investment in value-generating opportunities.

Pac-Man defence In a hostile merger situation the target makes a counter-bid for the bidder.

Paid-up capital The amount of the authorised share capital that has been paid for or subscribed for by shareholders.

Panel *See* City Panel on Takeovers and Mergers.

Paper A term for some securities, e.g. certificates of deposit, commercial paper.

Paper bid In a merger, the acquirer offers shares in itself to buy shares in the target.

Par value (nominal, principal, stated book or face value) A stated and fixed nominal value of a share or bond. Not related to market value, which fluctuates.

Parent company (holding company) The one that partially or wholly owns other companies.

Participating preference share *See* Preference shares.

Partnership An unincorporated business formed by the association of two or more persons who share the risk and profits.

Passive fund *See* Tracker fund.

Path-dependent resources Firm resources that have been created because of the route that the firm took to get to where it is today.

Pathfinder prospectus In a new issue of shares a detailed report on the company is prepared and made available to potential investors a few days before the issue price is announced.

Payables (accounts payable) Credit received from suppliers.

Payback The period of time it takes to recover the initial cash put into a project.

Payout ratio The percentage of after-tax profit paid to shareholders in dividends.

Payment service institutions Firms providing payment services to customers, e.g. cheques transferring money between accounts. These firms include: banks; building societies; e-money issuers; money remitters; non-bank credit card issuers; and non-bank merchant acquirers.

PEG ratio Price–earnings ratio to growth ratio. The PER is divided by the expected percentage growth in earnings per share. It is used to highlight those companies on a low share price relative to their growth prospects. Problem: estimating future growth.

PEITs *See* Private equity investment trusts.

Penny shares Shares priced at only a few pence. Some investors like these, despite the risk of liquidation, because of their large potential if management turns the company around.

Pension funds/scheme These manage money on behalf of members to provide a pension upon the members' retirement. Most funds invest heavily in shares and bonds.

Pension holiday When a pension fund does not need additional contributions for a time, it may grant the contributors (e.g. companies and/or members) a break from making payments.

PER *See* Price–earnings ratio.

Perfect competition (perfect market) Entry to the industry is free and the existing firms have no bargaining power over suppliers or customers. Rivalry between existing firms is fierce because products are identical. The following assumptions hold: There are a large number of buyers. There are a large number of sellers. The quantity of goods bought by any individual transaction is so small relative to the total quantity traded that individual trades leave the market price unaffected. The units of goods sold by different sellers are the same – the product is homogeneous. There is perfect information – all buyers and all sellers have complete information on the prices being asked and offered in other parts of the market. There is perfect freedom of exit from the market.

Perfect hedge Eliminates risk because the movements in the value of the hedge instrument are exactly contrary to the change in value of the underlying.

Perfect market *See* Perfect competition.

Perfect negative correlation When two variables (e.g. returns on two shares) always move in exactly opposite directions by the same proportional amount.

Perfect positive correlation When two variables (e.g. returns on two shares) always move in the same direction by the same proportional amount.

Performance attribution Identifying the factors that led to a fund's performance (e.g. share selection, asset allocation).

Performance fee A fee paid to some fund managers (especially hedge fund managers, but also some investment trust and other collective fund managers) which depends on the returns achieved.

Perks In addition to paying dividends to investors, some companies provide perks such as a reduced rate in hotels or on ferries owned by the company.

Permanent capital Capital, such as through the purchase of shares in a company that cannot be withdrawn.

Permanent interest-bearing shares (PIBS) Loan stock issued by building societies. The 'shares' pay interest and are irredeemable.

Perpetuity A regular sum of money received at intervals for ever.

Personal guarantee An individual associated with a company, e.g. a director, personally guarantees that debt will be repaid.

Personal membership of CREST Investors hold shares in their own accounts with CREST rather than in a broker's nominee company or in certificated form.

Personal/private pension A pension scheme set up for an individual by that individual but through a financial institution. Contributions to the fund are subject to tax relief in the UK.

Physical delivery/settlement Settlement of a futures contract by delivery of the underlying rather than cash settlement determined by price movement during the holding of an open position.

Physical ETFs (physical replication) An exchange traded fund that buys the underlying security such as a collection of shares, rather than uses derivatives to replicate the price movements.

Piece *See* Lot.

Placing, place or placement A method of selling shares and other financial securities in the primary market. Securities are offered to the sponsors' or brokers' private clients and/or a narrow group of institutions.

Plain vanilla A bond that lacks any special features such as a call or put provision.

Platform (investment platform, fund platform) Online organisations that allow investors to invest in a range of unit trusts, investment trusts, shares, bonds ETFs, OEICs, etc. Investors can select one, two or a dozen funds from different management companies together with other investments. They usually charge either a flat fee or a percentage of funds held on the platform.

plc *See* Public limited company.

Poison pills Actions taken, or which will be taken, which make a firm unpalatable to a hostile acquirer.

Political risk Changes in government or government policies impacting on returns and volatility of returns.

Pooled funds Organisations (e.g. unit trusts) that gather together numerous small quantities of money from investors and then invest in a wide range of financial securities.

Portfolio A collection of investments.

Portfolio theory Formal mathematical model for calculating risk–returns trade-offs as securities are combined in a portfolio.

Pound cost averaging An investing system that, through the commitment of a regular sum of money to a company's shares or the market as a whole leads to the purchasing of a greater number of shares when the market is low and less when it is high. For example, investor A commits to investing £10,000 each year over 10 years. The market sells for £1 in one-half of the years and £2 in the other five years (for a typical share, let's say). Thus, in bad years 10,000 shares are bought, in good years 5,000. The average price paid is £1.33 which is below the average market price of £1.50.

PRA *See* Prudential Regulatory Authority.

Precipice bonds Bonds sold by insurance companies to investors offering high income based on stock market returns. The initial capital is guaranteed up to a point, but if the stock market declines by more than a set percentage (say, 20 per cent) investors lose capital. This loss can be highly geared (e.g. for every 1 per cent drop in the FTSE 100 index the capital value falls by 2 per cent).

Pre-emption rights The strong rights of shareholders of UK companies to subscribe for further issues of shares. *See* Rights issue.

Preference shares These normally entitle the holder to a fixed rate of dividend, but this is not guaranteed. Holders of preference shares precede the holders of ordinary shares, but follow bondholders and other lenders in payment of dividends and return of principal. A **participating preference share** receives a share in residual profits. A **cumulative preference share** carries forward the right to preferential dividends. A **redeemable preference share** is a preference share with a finite life. A **convertible preference share/stock** may be converted into another type of security (e.g. an ordinary share).

Preferred ordinary shares Rank higher than deferred ordinary shares for an agreed rate of dividend or share of profits. Not the same as preference shares.

Preliminary annual results (preliminary profit announcement, prelims) After the year-end and before the full reports and accounts are published, a statement on the profit for the year and other information is provided by companies quoted on the London Stock Exchange.

Premium (investment trusts) The amount by which the share price exceeds the net asset value per share.

Premium (on an option) The amount paid to an option writer to obtain the right to buy or sell the underlying.

Premium Listing The London Stock Exchange's normal quality level for companies on the Main Market. The Premium segment is only open to equity shares issued by trading companies and closed and open-ended investment entities. Issuers with a Premium Listing are required to meet the UK's super-equivalent rules which are higher than the EU minimum requirements. Premium Listed companies comply with the UK's highest standards of regulation and corporate governance, as a consequence they may enjoy a lower cost of capital through greater transparency and through building investor confidence, standards of regulation and corporate governance.

Present value The current worth of future cash flows when discounted to time zero.

Pre-tax margin *See* Pre-tax profit margin.

Pre-tax profit Profit on ordinary activities before deducting taxation.

Pre-tax profit margin (pre-tax margin) Profit after all expenses, including interest, but excluding tax on that profit, expressed as a percentage of sales.

Price discovery (price formation) The process of forming prices through the interaction of numerous buy and sell orders in an exchange.

Price–earnings ratio (PER, price–earnings multiple, PE multiple, PE ratio, P/E ratio) Share price divided by earnings per share. **Historical (or trailing) PER** is share price divided by most recently reported annual earnings per share. **Forward (prospective) PER** is share price divided by anticipated annual earnings per share.

Price–earnings ratio game (bootstrapping) Companies increase earnings per share by acquiring other companies with lower price–earnings ratios than themselves. Share price can rise despite the absence of economic value gain.

Price formation *See* Price discovery.

Price improvement service Brokers are frequently able to obtain for clients (retail investors) better buy and sell prices than those shown on the stock exchanges' screens from market makers or other traders. This could occur because of a change in market price or your broker is particularly diligent in getting a good deal.

Price limit The maximum price an investor is willing to pay to buy, or the minimum a seller is willing to accept.

Price-sensitive information That which may influence the share price or trading in the shares.

Price-to-book ratio (market-to-book ratio) The price of a share as a multiple of per share book (balance sheet) value.

Price-weighted index An index of a collection of financial (e.g. shares) or other assets (e.g. houses) which measures through time the average price of the constituents.

Pricing power An ability to raise prices even when product demand is flat without the danger of losing significant volume or market share.

Primary dealer A firm approved by a government to deal in its debt securities. In the UK they are known as Gilt-edged market makers (GEMMs).

Primary investors The household sector contains the savers in society who are the main providers of funds used for investment in the business sector.

Primary listing A company that makes the London Stock Exchanges its primary listing agrees to abide by its high standards of regulation and disclosure – greater than that under the EU directives. This may lower the rate of return it has to offer on capital raised.

Primary market A market in which securities are initially issued to investors rather than a secondary market in which investors buy and sell to each other.

Prime grade *See* Investment grade debt.

Principal (a) The capital amount of a debt, excluding any interest. (b) A person acting on their own account accepting risk in financial transactions, rather than someone acting as an agent for another. (c) The amount invested.

Principal–agent problem In which an agent (e.g. a manager) does not act in the best interests of the principal (e.g. the shareholder).

Private client brokers Stockbrokers acting for investors in the buying and selling of financial instruments and providing other investment-related services for investors.

Private equity Share capital invested in companies not quoted on an exchange.

Private equity investment trusts (PEITs) Investment vehicles allowing investors to buy into an established private equity fund, investing in unquoted companies, run by an experienced management team. The investor buys PEIT shares which are traded on the London Stock Exchange.

Private investors (private clients) Investors buying and selling small quantities of shares on their own account rather than institutions buying and selling for funds.

Private limited company (Ltd) A company which is unable to offer its shares to the wider public.

Privatisation The sale to private investors of government-owned equity (shares) in nationalised industries or other commercial enterprises.

Profit and loss account (Income statement) Records whether a company's sales revenue was greater than its costs.

Profit margin Profits as a percentage of sales.

Pro-forma earnings (a) Projected or forecast earnings. (b) These may be prepared by the directors so as to exclude those items that they regard as unusual or nonrecurring for a recent past period. These are not audited and may be unreliable.

Project finance Finance assembled for a specific project. The loan and equity returns are tied to the cash flows and fortunes of the project rather than being dependent on the parent company/companies.

Promising company Company with a mediocre/ordinary earnings record which the investor *expects* to do better than the average in the future.

Promissory note A debtor promises to pay at a fixed date or a date to be determined by circumstances. A note is created stating this obligation.

Proprietary transactions (proprietary trading) A financial institution trades on the financial markets with a view to generating profits for itself using its own capital or borrowings (e.g. speculate in foreign exchange).

ProShare An independent not-for-profit company set up to help private investors, promote knowledge about investment and assist investment clubs.

Prospective PER *See* Price–earnings ratio.

Prospectus A document containing information about a company (or unit trust or OEIC), to assist with a new issue (initial public offering) by supplying detail about the company and how it operates.

Provision (1) An allowance for a liability that you are unable to be precise about concerning either the amount or when it will be paid (anticipated loss or expenditure). (2) A clause or stipulation in a legal agreement giving one party a right.

Provisional Allotment Letters (PALs) In a rights issue shareholders receive PALs which are temporary documents of title showing each shareholder the number of shares they can apply for. To accept the shareholder fills in and returns the PAL with a cheque or banker's draft.

Proxy votes Shareholders unable to attend a shareholders' meeting may authorise another person (e.g. a director or the chairman) to vote on their behalf, either as instructed or as that person sees fit.

Prudential Regulatory Authority (PRA) A subsidiary of the Bank of England supervising and regulating financial institutions, banks, insurers, brokers, etc. for micro-prudential risk – seeking to enhance the safety and soundness of individual financial institutions, as opposed to the macroprudential view which focuses on welfare of the financial system as a whole.

Public limited company (plc) A company which may have an unlimited number of shareholders and offer its shares to the wider public (unlike a limited company). Must have a minimum share value of £50,000. Some plcs are listed on the London Stock Exchange.

Public-to-private The management of a company currently quoted on a stock exchange return it to unquoted status. The finance to buy the shares often comes from private equity firms.

Put option This gives the purchaser the right, but not the obligation, to sell a financial instrument, commodity or some other underlying asset at a given price, at or before a specified date.

Qualitative analysis Relying on subjective elements to take a view (e.g. valuing shares by judging the quality of management and strategic position).

Quant (Quantum) analysis Quantitative analysis using complex mathematical models.

Quartile A set of numbers e.g. five-year performances of 200 unit trust funds are arranged from highest to lowest. The top 25 per cent form the first quartile, the next 25 per cent the second quartile, and so on.

Quick asset value (net) Current assets minus inventory minus current liabilities.

Quick ratio (acid test) The ratio of current assets, less inventory (stock), to total current liabilities.

Quoted Those shares with a price quoted on a recognised investment exchange (e.g. the London Stock Exchange).

Quote-driven trading system Market makers post bid and offer prices on a computerised system.

R&D Research and development.

Rally A small rise in a market that is generally falling.

Random walk theory The movements in (share) prices are independent of one another; one day's price change cannot be predicted by looking at the previous day's price change.

Ranking (debt) Order of precedence for payment of obligations. Senior debt receives annual interest and redemption payments ahead of junior (or subordinated) debt. So, if the company has insufficient resources to pay its obligation the junior debt holders may receive little or nothing.

Rate of return The gain or loss on an investment over a specified period (usually one year), expressed as a percentage increase over the initial investment cost.

Rating *See* Credit rating.

Real assets Assets used to carry on a business. These assets can be tangible (e.g. a building) or intangible (e.g. a brand), as opposed to financial assets.

Real cash flows Future cash flows are expressed in terms of constant purchasing power.

Real-estate investment trust (REIT) A closed-end investment company which predominantly buys property. If it pays out a high proportion of annual income in dividends each year it is granted tax concessions.

Real rate of return The rate that would be required (or obtained) in the absence of inflation. The nominal return minus inflation.

Realised gain (loss) A gain (increase in value) made when a deal has been completed and money released.

Real-time dealing An online brokerage service. The investor is directly connected to the market maker system. Retail service providers (RSPs) offer competing price quotes and the investor trades directly with one RSP.

Recapitalisation A change in the financial structure (e.g. in debt–equity ratio).

Receivable (accounts receivable) A sum due from a customer(s) for goods delivered: trade credit.

Receiver A receiver takes control of a business if a creditor successfully files a bankruptcy petition. The receiver may then sell the company's assets and distribute the proceeds among the creditors.

Recognised investment exchange (RIE) A body authorised by the Financial Conduct Authority to regulate securities trading in the UK (e.g. the London Stock Exchange).

Record date When a share out of profits is declared by a company those on the share register on record day will receive dividends.

Recovery stock A share that has performed poorly but is expected to pick up.

Redeemable preference share *See* Preference shares.

Redemption The repayment of the principal amount, or par value, of a security (e.g. bond) at the maturity date resulting in the retirement and cancellation of the bond or other security.

Redemption yield *See* Yield.

Registered bond A bond where the owner's details are kept on a register open to the company and the authorities.

Registrar An organisation that maintains a record of share (and other securities) ownership for a company. It also communicates with shareholders on behalf of the company.

Regular bonus *See* Reversionary bonus.

Regulatory Information Services (RIS) Companies on UK stock exchanges are required to announce quickly any price sensitive information. They do this by making an announcement electronically via one of the Regulatory Information Services approved by the Financial Conduct Authority which disseminates the news very quickly to dozens of financial websites and other places.

Regulatory News Service (RNS) A system for distributing important company announcements and other price-sensitive financial news run by the London Stock Exchange.

Relationship banking A long-term, intimate and relatively open relationship is established between a corporation and its banks. Banks often supply a range of tailor-made services rather than one-off services.

Relative return A return made on an asset relative to the performance of an index.

Rembrandt A foreign bond issued in the Netherlands.

Remuneration committee A group of directors of a company, all of which are independent of management, decide the remuneration of executive directors.

Repayment holiday *See* Grace period.

Reporting accountant A company planning to float on the London Stock Exchange employs a reporting accountant to prepare a detailed report on the firm's financial controls, track record, financing and forecasts.

Repurchase of shares A company which has prospered, or has no good use for its cash, buys back some of its shares.

Rescheduling/restructuring finance Rearranging the payments made by a borrower to a lender – usually as a result of financial distress.

Rescue rights issue A company in dire trouble, in danger of failure, carries out a rights issue to raise capital.

Resistance line A line drawn on a price (e.g. share) chart showing the market participants' reluctance to push the price below (or above) the line over a period of time.

Resolution A proposal put to the vote at a shareholders' meeting.

Restructuring costs The costs associated with a reorganisation of the business (e.g. closing factories, redundancies).

Retail banking Banking for individual customers or small firms, normally for small amounts.

Retail brokers *see* Private client brokers

Retail investor (individual investor, small investor) One who is not considered experienced enough to be regarded as a professional or expert. Under the Financial Conduct Authority rules retail investors receive regulatory protection and rights to compensation.

Retail Price Index (RPI) A measure of general inflation for the economy as a whole.

Retail service providers (RSPs) An automated computer dealing service to brokers and investors. Rather than using the telephone for a broker and market maker to strike a deal a computer system polls a number of retail service providers and the investor can trade quickly and cheaply electronically. *See also* Real-time dealing.

Retained earnings That part of a company's profits after deduction of tax not paid as dividends.

Retention ratio Retained profits for the year as a proportion of profits after tax attributable to ordinary shareholders for the year.

Return on assets (ROA); Return on capital employed (ROCE); return on investment (ROI) Traditional measures of profitability. Profit return divided by the volume of resources devoted to the activity. 'Resources' usually includes shareholders' funds, net debt and provisions. Cumulative goodwill, previously written off, may be added back to the resources total. *See also* Accounting rate of return.

Return on equity (ROE) Profit attributable to shareholders as a percentage of equity shareholders' funds. Calculated by dividing the net profit after tax by equity capital.

Revaluation reserve A balance sheet entry that records accumulated revaluations of fixed assets.

Revenue reserves (retained earnings, profit and loss reserves) Profits retained by the company from previous year's profits plus the gains made when non-current assets are sold (after tax deduction and losses on non-current asset sales). These are available to pay cash dividends.

Reverse floating-rate notes *See* Floating-rate notes.

Reverse takeover The acquiring company is smaller than the target in terms of market capitalisation and offers newly created shares in itself as consideration for the purchase of the shares in the acquirer. So many new shares are created that the former shareholders in the target become the dominant shareholders in the combined entity.

Reverse yield gap *See* Yield gap.

Reversing the trade *See* Closing out a futures position.

Reversion to the mean The behaviour of financial markets is often characterised as reverting to the mean, in which an otherwise random process of price changes or returns tends over the medium- to long-term to move towards the average.

Reversionary bonus The annual bonus given by an insurance company to with-profits policyholders.

Revolving credit An arrangement whereby a borrower can draw down short-term loans as the need arises, to a maximum over a period of years.

Revolving underwriting facility (RUF) A bank(s) underwrites a corporate borrower's access to funds at a specified rate in the short-term financial markets throughout an agreed period. If the notes are not bought in the market the underwriter is obliged to purchase them.

Reward-to-variability ratio *See* Sharpe's ratio.

Reward-to-volatility ratio *See* Treynor's ratio.

Rights issue An invitation to existing shareholders to purchase additional shares in the company in proportion to their existing holdings.

Ring-fencing The separation of assets so that, for example, a customer's cash and investments are not combined with their broker's assets.

Risk A future return has a variety of possible values. Sometimes measured by standard deviation.

Risk arbitrage Taking a position (purchase or sale) in a security, commodity, etc., because it is mispriced relative to other securities with similar characteristics. The comparator securities are not identical (e.g. shares in Unilever and shares in Procter & Gamble) and therefore there is an element of risk that the valuation gap will widen rather than reduce. An extreme form of risk arbitrage is to take a position hoping to make a profit if an event occurs (e.g. a takeover). If the event does not occur there may be a loss. The word 'arbitrage' has been stretched beyond breaking point, as true arbitrage should be risk-free.

Risk averter Someone who prefers a more certain return to an alternative with an equal return but which is more risky.

Risk-free rate of return (RFR) The rate earned on riskless investment. A reasonable proxy is short-term lending to a reputable government.

Risk lover (seeker) Someone who prefers a more uncertain position to an alternative with an equal but less risky outcome.

Risk premium The extra return, above the risk-free rate, for accepting risk.

Risk transformation Intermediaries offer low-risk securities or arrangements to primary investors to attract funds (e.g. bank account deal), which are then used to purchase higher risk securities issued by the ultimate borrowers (e.g. bank buys corporate bond).

Risk warning notice A statement from a UK broker to a private client alerting them to the risks inherent in trading particular financial securities.

Roadshow Companies and their advisers make a series of presentations to potential investors, usually to entice them into buying a new issue of securities.

ROI *See* Return on assets.

Rolled-over overdraft Short-term loan facilities are perpetuated into the medium term and long term by the regular renewal of the facility.

Rolling cash spread betting (Rolling daily bets) A bet with a spread betting company on the cash price of the share. The investor 'rolls' his or her position overnight to the next day.

Rolling settlement Shares and cash are exchanged after a deal had been struck a fixed number of days later (usually two or three days) rather than on a specific account day.

RPI (Retail Price Index) A measure of general inflation.

Running yield *See* Yield.

S&P 500 Standard and Poor's index of 500 leading US shares.

Safe haven A secure investment in time of trouble, such as major financial turmoil. UK or US government bonds and Treasury bills are usually regarded as safe havens.

Sale and leaseback Assets (e.g. land and buildings) are sold to another firm (e.g. bank, insurance company) with a simultaneous agreement for the vendor to lease the asset back for a stated period under specific terms.

Sales charge *See* Initial charge.

Samurai bonds A foreign bond, yen-denominated, issued by a non-Japanese entity in the Japanese domestic market.

Scaledown In a new issue, when a company floats on a stock exchange, if demand is greater than supply at the offer price the applicants receive fewer shares than they applied for, according to a prearranged formula.

Scheme of arrangement A relatively quick and cheap way of combining two companies is a scheme of arrangement, whereby the target managers and the acquiring managers agree to allow the target shareholders to vote on a merger. If three-quarters of them vote in favour, and the arrangement is sanctioned by a court, then the scheme is binding on all shareholders. All the target shareholders are then required to sell to the acquirer. Thus the acquirer can avoid having a rump minority hanging on to their shares.

Scrip dividends Shareholders are offered the alternative of additional shares rather than a cash dividend.

Scrip issue The issue of more shares to existing shareholders in proportion to their current holdings. Shareholders do not pay for these shares. Company reserves are converted into issued capital.

Scuttlebutt Obtaining knowledge about a company by talking to a wide range of people who have had dealings with the corporation: customers, suppliers, employees, ex-employees etc.

SEAQ (Stock Exchange Automated Quotation) System A computer screen-based quotation system for securities where market makers on the London Stock

Exchange report bid–offer prices and trading volumes, and brokers can observe prices and trades.

Seasoned equity offerings (SEOs) Companies that have been on a stock exchange for some time selling new shares (e.g. via a rights issue).

SEATS (Stock Exchange Alternative Trading Service) Plus A former London Stock Exchange system for trading less liquid securities where there was either a single, or no, market maker.

Second-tier markets Financial centres often establish more lightly regulated share markets alongside their main highly regulated markets. This allows companies with say a short trading history or with a low free-float of shares to obtain a quotation for their shares. Also the on-going rules are less strict, e.g. few requirements to inform all investors in writing of a major move.

Secondary buy-out (sale) A company that has been backed by private equity finance is then sold to another private equity firm(s).

Secondary listing Those companies that choose to make the London Stock Exchange their secondary listing – their primary listing will usually be on another stock exchange.

Secondary market Securities already issued are traded between investors.

Secondary purchase A private equity-backed company is sold to another private equity fund.

Securities and Exchange Commission (SEC) The US federal body responsible for the regulation of securities markets (exchanges, brokers, investment advisers, etc.).

Securities house This may mean simply a sponsor. However, the term is sometimes used more broadly for an institution concerned with buying and selling securities or acting as agent in the buying and selling of securities.

Securitisation Financial payments (e.g. a claim to a number of mortgage payments) which are not tradable can be repackaged into other securities (e.g. a bond) and then sold. These are called asset-backed securities (ABSs).

Security (1) A financial asset, e.g. a share or bond. (2) Asset pledged to be surrendered in the event of a loan default.

SEDOL, *Stock Exchange Daily Official List.* A journal published daily giving prices and deals for shares on the London Stock Exchange's Official List.

Seed Enterprise Investment Scheme (SEIS) Tax relief is available to investors in qualifying company shares (unquoted firms not focused on financial investment and property, with under 25 employees and gross assets under £200,000).

Seedcorn capital or money (seed capital or money) The financing of the development of a business concept. High risk; usually provided by venture capitalists, entrepreneurs or business angels.

Self-invested personal pension (SIPP) Similar to a standard personal pension scheme except that the investor can select the shares, etc., that the fund is invested into. There are tax advantages in investing through a SIPP.

Self-regulation Much of the regulation of financial services in the UK is carried out by self-regulatory organisations (i.e. industry participants regulate themselves within a light-touch legislated framework).

Self-select ISA The investor can decide which shares, gilts, etc., should be bought for an individual savings account.

Selling the rights nil paid In a rights issue existing shareholders are entitled to sell the rights to the new shares without the need to purchase the new shares.

Sell-side Organisations in the securities business that help to create and trade securities and also sell their services to buy-side institutions and individuals (examples of sell-side organisations are investment banks, analysts, brokers and securities firms).

Semi-strong efficiency Share prices fully reflect all the relevant, publicly available information.

Senior debt *See* Subordinated debt.

Serious Fraud Office Investigates and prosecutes crimes of serious or complex fraud and corruption exceeding £1 million in the UK.

SETS (Stock Exchange Electronic Trading System) An electronic order book-based trading system for the London Stock Exchange. Brokers, investors, and some market makers input buy and sell orders directly into the system. Buyers and sellers are matched and the trade executed automatically.

SETSqx (Stock Exchange Trading System) A share trading system run by the London Stock Exchange with a focus on lightly traded shares, few trades per day.

Settlement The completion of a transaction, e.g. there is a transfer of ownership of a share from seller to buyer in return for a cash payment.

Settlement price The price calculated by a derivatives exchange at the end of each trading session as the closing price that will be used in determining profits and losses for the marking-to-market process for margin accounts.

Shadow banking Powerful non-banking organisations that move money and risk without involving banks, e.g. hedge funds, money market funds.

Share Companies divide the ownership of the company into ordinary shares. An owner of a share usually has the same rights to vote and receive dividends as another owner of a share. Also called equity. Shares other than ordinary shares may also be created which carry different rights e.g. preference shares.

Share buy-back The company buys back a proportion of its shares from shareholders.

Share certificate A document showing ownership of part of the share capital of a company.

Share exchange scheme Some unit trusts permit investors to purchase units with shares rather than cash.

Share market Institutions which facilitate the regulated sale and purchase of shares; includes the primary and secondary markets.

Share option scheme Employees are offered the right to buy shares in their company at a pre-agreed price some time in the future.

Share perks *See* Perks.

Share premium account A balance sheet entry representing the difference between the price received by a company when it sells shares and the par value of those shares.

Share repurchase The company buys back some of its own shares.

Share split (stock split) Shareholders receive additional shares from the company without payment. The nominal (par) value of each share is reduced in proportion to the increase in the number of shares, so the total book value of shares remains the same.

Shareholders' funds (equity) The net assets of the business (after deduction of all short- and long-term liabilities and minority interests) shown in the balance sheet.

Sharpe's ratio (Reward-to-variability ratio) A measure relating risk and return. The extent to which a portfolio's (or share's) return has been greater than a risk-free asset, divided by its standard deviation.

Shell company A company with a stock market quotation but with very little in the way of real economic activity. It may have cash but no production.

Short position In a derivative contract, the counterparty in a short position is the one that has agreed to deliver the underlying.

Short selling The selling of financial securities (e.g. shares) not yet owned (they are borrowed), in the anticipation of being able to buy at a later date at a lower price.

Short-term selectivity The buying or selling of a financial security based on the analysis of a corporation's or an industry's near-term business prospects.

Short-termism A charge levelled at the financial institutions in their expectations of the companies to which they provide finance. It is argued that long-term benefits are lost because of pressure for short-term performance.

Shorting *See* Short selling.

Shorts Bonds (e.g. gilts) with less than five years to maturity.

Sight bank account (current account, cheque account) One where deposits can be withdrawn without notice.

Sigma A measure of dispersion of returns; same as standard deviation.

Signalling Some financial decisions are interpreted as signals from the managers to the financial markets (e.g. an increase in gearing, or a change in dividend policy).

Simple interest Interest is paid on the original principal: no interest is paid on the accumulated interest payments.

Simple yield *See* Yield.

Single premium bond An insurance plan with a small amount of life cover. The money contributed by the policyholder is invested to provide returns after a number of years.

Small claims court A fast and relatively informal way to deal with complaints and claims e.g. for financial loss.

Small firm effect (Size effect) The tendency of small firms to give abnormally high returns on the stock market as observed in some academic studies, but not in others.

Smoothing A collective investment fund manager, such as a with-profits fund manager, hold back profits from investors in good years so that they can continue with bonuses in poor years.

Social technology Tools of social organisation that allow for the better working of society. Examples include: laws on limited liability, corporate entities and financial market regulations; accepted norms of behaviour; widespread knowledge of the way in which processes work, such as stock market buying and selling.

Society of Lloyds (Lloyds) *see* Lloyd's Insurance Market.

Solvency The ability to pay debts as and when they become due.

South Sea Bubble A financial bubble in which the price of shares in the South Sea Company were pushed to ridiculously high levels on a surge of over-optimism in the early eighteenth century. *See* Bubble.

Sovereign debt Debt (e.g. bond) issued by a government.

Sovereign wealth fund (SWF) Run by governments on behalf of their people for the long term, investing, say oil income, in shares and other assets around the world.

Special dividend An exceptionally large dividend paid on a one-off basis.

Special-purpose vehicle or entity (SPV, SPE) Companies set these up as separate organisations (usually as limited companies) for a particular purpose.

They are designed so that their accounts are not consolidated with the rest of the group.

Special resolution A company's shareholders' vote at a AGM or EGM with a majority of 75 per cent of those voting in favour for it to be carried. Normally special resolutions are reserved for important changes in the constitution of the company. Other matters are normally dealt with by way of ordinary resolution (50 per cent or more of the votes required).

Specific inflation The price changes in an individual good or service.

Speculative grade Bonds with a credit rating below investment grade.

Speculators Those who take a position in financial instruments and other assets with a view to obtaining a profit on changes in their market price.

Split-capital investment trusts These investment trusts simultaneously issue different types of shares. Income shares entitle the holder to receive all (or most) of the income from the portfolio. Capital shares entitle the owner to receive all (or most of) the rise in the capital value of the portfolio. Zero divided preference shares (Zeros) pay no income but do offer a predetermined return at the end of the trust's life.

Sponsor An organisation (usually an investment bank or stockbroker) that lends its reputation to a new issue of securities, advises the client company (along with the issuing broker) and co-ordinates the new issue process. Also called an issuing house.

Sponsored membership of CREST *See* Personal membership of CREST.

Spot market A market for immediate transactions (e.g. spot forex market, spot interest market), as opposed to an agreement to make a transaction at some time in the future (e.g. forward, option, future).

Spread The difference between the price to buy and the price to sell a financial security. Market makers quote a bid–offer spread for shares. The lower price (bid) is the price an investor receives if selling to the market maker. The higher (offer) price is the price if the investor wishes to buy from the market maker.

Spread betting Laying a bet with a spread betting company that a particular outcome will occur in the future (e.g. that a share price will rise). You bet, say, £10 for every 1p rise.

Square mile *See* City of London.

Stagging Buying shares in a new issue and then selling immediately the shares begin trading on the market.

Stakeholder A party with an interest (financial or otherwise) in an organisation, e.g. employees, customers, suppliers, the local community.

Stakeholder pension Similar to a standard personal pension except that there are low management charges, contributions can be small and the investor can move to another provider easily. Even non-taxpayers can claim back assumed tax paid on income.

Stamp duty A tax levied on share purchase on the Main Market of the London Stock Exchange (0.5 per cent of the new purchase value).

Standard & Poor's A leading credit rating agency and financial information provider.

Standard & Poor's 500 (S&P 500) An index of US shares. *See* S&P 500.

Standard deviation A statistical measure of the dispersion around an average (a mean). A measure of volatility. The standard deviation is the square root of the variance. A fund's or a share's return can be expected to fall within one standard deviation of its average two-thirds of the time if the future is like the past.

Standard Listing This is a quality of listing on the Main Market of the London Stock Exchange for the issuance of equity shares, Global Depositary Receipts (GDRs), debt securities and securitised derivatives that are expected merely to comply with EU minimum requirements. A Standard Listing allows issuers to access the Main Market by meeting EU harmonised standards. Most UK Main Market companies subject themselves to higher standards under the Main Market's Premium Listing rules, thus providing greater reassurance to their investors.

Start-up capital Finance for young companies which have not yet sold their product commercially. High risk; usually provided by venture capitalists, entrepreneurs or business angels.

Start-up companies Companies with a limited or non-existent trading history.

Statement of cash flows Alternative title for cash flow statement.

Statement of changes in equity Includes the profit shown in the profit and loss account plus all other gains and losses that are not permitted in the profit and loss account such as surpluses or deficits on revaluation of fixed assets, currency translation gains and losses.

Statement of financial position. The term for balance sheet under International Accounting Standards.

Statutory Established, regulated or imposed by or in conformity with laws passed by a legislative body (e.g. Parliament).

Sterling bonds Corporate bonds which pay interest and principal in pounds sterling.

Stock (1) Inventory of raw materials, work-in-progress and finished items. (2) US term for a share.

Stockbroker (1) A regulated professional who arranges the buying and selling of shares and other securities for investors. (2) (Corporate broker) Assists corporations in representing themselves to the financial markets, advises the company on market conditions and for fund raising. May match buyers and sellers of the client firm's securities.

Stock exchange A market in which securities are bought and sold. In continental Europe the term *bourse* may be used.

Stock Exchange Automated Quotation *See* SEAQ.

Stock Exchange Electronic Trading System *See* SETS.

Stock futures Futures in a particular company's shares. Also called single stock futures.

Stock market *See* Stock exchange.

Stock-market-linked bond *See* Guaranteed equity bonds.

Stock split *See* Share split.

Stock symbols (codes, tickers, EPIC, TIDM) Three or four letter abbreviations given to a company share which are used by stockbrokers and on financial websites as shorthand for the company.

Stock transfer form A form used to transfer ownership of shares without the use of a broker or a stock exchange.

Stocks and shares There is some lack of clarity as to the distinction between stocks and shares. Shares are equities in companies. Stocks are financial instruments that pay interest (e.g. bonds). However, in the USA shares are also called 'common stocks' and the shareholders are sometimes referred to as the stockholders. So when some people use the term 'stocks' they could be referring to either bonds or shares.

Stop-loss orders An order from an investor to a broker to sell if the share price breaches a lower threshold – used to limit possible losses. Stop-loss orders may also be used in derivative markets to prevent losses exceeding set limits with either a long or a short position.

Straight bond One with a regular fixed rate of interest and without the right of conversion (to, say, shares) or any other unusual rights.

Straight-line depreciation A fixed asset is depreciated by the same amount each year over its useful life.

Strategic analysis The analysis of industries served by the firm and the company's competitive position within the industry.

Strategy Selecting which product or market areas to enter/exit and how to ensure a good competitive position in those markets/products.

Strike price (1) In an offer for sale by a tender it is the price which is chosen to sell the required quantity of shares given the offers made. (2) The price paid by the holder of an option when/if the option is exercised.

Strips (Separate Trading of Registered Interest and Principal of Securities) bonds Bonds which can be broken down into their constituent parts, e.g. individual coupons, and these are then traded separately.

Strong form efficiency All relevant information, including that which is privately held, is reflected in the security (e.g. share) price.

Structured investment product Offered by insurance companies and other financial service companies, these collective investment vehicles invest most of the investor's cash in bonds. Some is used to buy derivatives to allow the provider to offer the investor a stock-market-linked return (e.g. 100 per cent return of capital plus 55 per cent of the rise in the FTSE 100 index over five years). Examples include guaranteed equity bonds and precipice bonds.

Style An investment style is an approach or strategy to selecting shares for purchase (e.g. high-dividend yields, small companies).

Subordinated debt (Junior debt) A debt which ranks below another liability in order of priority for payment of interest or principal. Senior debt ranks above junior debt for payment.

Sub-prime mortgage A mortgage designed for people with a low credit score, charged at an interest rate above that for prime borrowers.

Subscription rights A right to subscribe for some shares.

Subsidiary A company is a subsidiary of another company if the parent company holds the majority of the voting rights (more than 50 per cent), or has a minority of the shares but has the right to appoint or remove directors holding a majority of the voting rights at meetings of the board on all, or substantially all, matters or it has the right to exercise a dominant influence.

Substitute Products or services that perform the same function (at least in approximate terms).

Sucker's rally A rise in prices during a period of overall market decline. The temporary rise draws in investors fooled into believing that the downward drift has ended.

Summary financial statement Companies often send small investors a summary of the financial statements rather than the full report and accounts. This suits many investors and saves the company some money. However, an investor is entitled to receive the full annual report and accounts. It may be necessary to make a request for this.

Supernormal returns A rate of return above the normal rate.

Surrender value The amount payable to an insurance policyholder (e.g. with-profits policy) when it is cancelled.

Swap An exchange of cash payment obligations. An interest rate swap is where one company arranges with a counterparty to exchange interest rate payments. In a currency swap the two parties exchange interest obligations (receipts) for an agreed period between two different currencies.

Swaption or swap-option An option to have a swap at a later date.

Sweep facility Automatic transfer of funds from one bank/savings/investment account to another, usually to maximise interest received.

Swinging single price When there are large numbers of buyers or sellers of shares in an open ended investment company the fund may incur high costs to buy/sell the underlying securities. To balance the interests of the old and new shareholders the new/leaving members may be charged an adjusted price for their shares which includes the transaction cost.

Switching cost The cost of changing supplier.

Syndicated loan A loan made by more than one bank to one borrower.

Synergy A combined entity (e.g. two companies merging) will have a value greater than the sum of the parts.

Synthetic replication The use of derivatives to replicate an index of underlying securities, e.g. for shares in the FTSE 100 index or gold, rather than buying the underlying physical security/commodity.

Systematic (undiversifiable or market or residual) risk That element of return variability from an asset which cannot be eliminated through diversification. Measured by beta. It comprises the risk factors common to all firms.

Systemic risk The risk of failure within the financial system causing a domino-type effect bringing down large parts of the system e.g. in 2008 the collapse of Lehman Brothers triggered the failure of many other financial institutions.

T+2, T+3 *See* Two-day (Three-day) rolling settlement.

Take-out Market expression of a bid made to a seller to 'take-out' his position – e.g. venture-capital-backed companies are bought allowing the venture capitalist to exit from the investment.

Takeover (acquisition) Many people use these terms interchangeably with 'merger'. However, some differentiate 'takeover' as meaning a purchase of one firm by another with the concomitant implication of financial and managerial domination. Usually applied to hostile (without target management approval) mergers.

Takeover Panel The committee responsible for supervising compliance with the UK City Code on Takeovers and Mergers.

Tangible assets Those that have a physical presence.

Tariff Taxes imposed on imports.

Tax allowance An amount of income or capital gain that is not taxed.

Tax avoidance Steps taken to reduce tax that are permitted under the law.

Tax evasion Deliberately giving a false statement or omitting a relevant fact to escape legitimate tax. Illegal.

Tax haven A country or place with low rates of tax and less (or more flexible) regulations.

Taxable profit That element of profit subject to taxation. This frequently differs from reported profit.

techMARK The London Stock Exchange launched techMARK in 1999 as a subsection of the shares within the Main Market. It is a grouping of technology companies for which there are different rules on seeking a flotation from those which apply to the other companies on the Main Market (e.g. only one year's accounts is required).

techMARK mediscience A group of London Stock Exchange Main Market companies focused on health care.

Technical analysis *See* Chartism.

Tender offer A public offer to purchase securities.

TER *See* Ongoing charge.

Term assurance Life assurance taken out for less than the whole life – the insured sum is paid only in the event of the insured person dying within the term.

Term loan A loan of a fixed amount for an agreed time and on specified terms, usually with regular periodic payments. Most frequently provided by banks.

Term structure of interest rates The pattern of interest rates on bonds with differing lengths of time to maturity but with the same risk. Strictly it is the zero-coupon implied interest rate for different lengths of time. *See also* Yield curve.

Terminal bonus A bonus paid on a with-profits policy at the end of the policy's life.

Terminal value The forecast future value of sums of money compounded to the end of a common time horizon.

Theoretical ex-rights price (TERP) The theoretical share price after a rights issue on the assumption that the newly issued shares are taken up by the existing shareholders. TERP is lower than the market value of a share prior to the rights issue because shares under rights issue transactions are normally issued at a price below the prevailing market price. It can be calculated as the market value of the company's shares prior to the rights issue plus the cash raised in the issue divided by the total number of shares after the new shares have been sold.

Three-day rolling settlement (T+3) After a share transaction in the stock exchange investors pay for shares three working days later.

Tick The minimum price movement of a security or derivative contract.

TIDM code *See* Stock symbols.

Time loans Loan with a specific maturity (US usage).

Time value That part of an option's value that represents the value of the option expiring in the future rather than now. The longer the period to expiry, the greater the chance that the option will become in-the-money before the expiry date. The amount by which the option premium exceeds the intrinsic value.

Time value of money A pound received in the future is worth less than a pound received today – the value of a sum of money depends on the date of its receipt.

Tipsters People who put forward a view on the wisdom of buying or selling a share – usually based on superficial knowledge.

Top-down Analysis of shares or other securities or the market as a whole, where the first step is to consider macroeconomic influences, leading to sector allocations (e.g. shares rather than bonds, then mining company shares) and finally individual security analysis.

Total expense ratio (TER) *See* Ongoing charge.

Total shareholder return (TSR) or total return The total return earned on a share over a period of time: dividend per share plus capital gain, divided by initial share price.

Touch *See* Yellow strip.

Tracker fund An investment fund which is intended to replicate the return of a market index. Also called an index fund or passive fund.

Tracking difference (performance difference) Measures the actual magnitude of the underperformance or outperformance of a market tracking collective investment fund such as an ETF. It is the annualised difference between a fund's actual return and its benchmark return over a specific period of time.

Tracking error The extent to which the return on an index tracking fund differs from its benchmark over a period of time. This is often measured as the standard deviation of a fund's absolute difference between the fund's performance and that of its benchmark index – a measure of volatility of difference.

Trade credit (payables) Where goods and services are delivered to a firm for use in its production and are currently still outstanding are not paid for immediately.

Trade debtors (receivables) Amounts owing by customers of a firm for goods and services delivered.

Trade execution The actual completion of the buying/selling of securities.

Trade sale A company buys another company in the same line of business.

Traded endowment policy (TEP) market A market in the buying and selling of with-profits endowment policies.

Traded option An option tradable on a market separate from the underlying.

Trading floor A place where traders in a market (or their representatives) can meet to agree transactions face to face. However, the term has been stretched so that investment banks own 'trading floors', which means merely that they have a big office with lots of desks and employees transacting with investors and other financial institutions. They communicate with these other parties through telephones and computers over great distances, without face-to-face dealing.

Trading margin *See* Operating profit margin.

Trading statements (trading updates) *See* Interim management statement.

Trading update *See* Interim management statement.

Traditional option An option available on any security but with an exercise price fixed as the market price on the day the option is bought. They are set up as special deals between option writers and buyers rather than being generally available on a regulated financial market (unlike trade options on **NYSE.liffe**). All such options expire after three months and cannot be sold to a secondary investor.

Trail commission A commission that used to be paid to sales organisations such as independent financial advisers and fund supermarkets by funds, e.g. unit trusts. The amount was set as a percentage of the value held in the units each year.

Trailing PER *See* Price–earnings ratio.

Transactions Monitoring Unit (TMU) The part of the Financial Conduct Authority responsible for surveillance of UK markets, the collection of transaction reports from the industry and for monitoring firms' compliance with the transaction reporting rules.

Treasury UK government department responsible for financial and economic policy.

Treasury bill A short-term money market instrument issued (sold) by the government, mainly in the UK and USA, usually to supply the government's short-term financing needs.

Treasury bond Long-term (maturity greater than 10 years) government bond.

Treynor's ratio or index (reward-to-volatility ratio) A measure relating return to risk. It is the return on a portfolio (or share) minus the risk-free rate of return, divided by beta.

TRRACK system A system to assist the analysis of a company's extraordinary resources under the headings: tangible; relationships; reputation; attitude; capabilities; and knowledge.

Trust deed A document specifying the regulation of the management of assets on behalf of beneficiaries of the trust.

Trustees Those that are charged with the responsibility for ensuring compliance with the trust deed.

Tulipmania A seventeenth-century Dutch bubble in which the price of tulip bulbs was bid up because people expected to be able to sell to someone else at a higher price. *See* Bubble.

Turnarounds Companies that have been going through a bad time and (it is hoped) will soon revive.

Turnover (revenue or sales) (1) Money received or to be received by the company from goods and services sold during the period. (2) In portfolio management, the amount of trading relative to the value of the portfolio.

Two-day rolling settlement (T+2) After a share transaction in the stock exchange investors pay for shares two working days later.

UCITS, Undertaking for Collective Investment in Transferable Securities A series of EU regulations for collective funds regulated under European law. Once the funds are designated as UCITS-compliant they can be marketed freely across EU member states.

UKLA *See* United Kingdom Listing Authority.

UK Shareholders' Association (www.uksa.org.uk) represents small shareholders and lobbies companies, regulators and government on their behalf.

Ultimate borrowers Firms investing in real assets need finance, which ultimately comes from the primary investors.

Umbrella structure for OEICs Open-ended investment companies may be created as a group of sub-funds each with a different investment objective.

Uncertainty Strictly (in economists' terms), uncertainty is when there is more than one possible outcome to a course of action; the form of each possible outcome may or may not be known, but the probability of any one outcome is not known. However, the distinction between risk (the ability to assign probabilities) and uncertainty has largely been ignored for the purposes of this text.

Unconditionality (unconditional offer) In a merger, once unconditionality is declared, the acquirer becomes obliged to buy. Target shareholders who accepted the offer are no longer able to withdraw their acceptance.

Uncovered (naked) call option writing Writing a call option on an underlying when the writer does not own the underlying securities included in the option.

Underlying The asset (e.g. share or commodity) that is the subject of a derivative contract.

Underlying earnings per share *See* Headline earnings per share.

Underweighting Allocating the money in a fund to particular securities, sectors or countries less than in proportion to their representation in the relevant benchmark index.

Underwriters (1) These (usually large financial institutions) guarantee to buy the proportion of a new issue of securities (e.g. shares) not taken up by the market, in return for a fee paid at the time of the underwriting. (2) Assess insurance risk and set the amount and terms of the premium.

Undifferentiated product One that is much the same as that supplied by other companies.

Undiversifiable risk *See* Systematic risk.

Uninformed investors Those who have no/little knowledge about financial securities and the fundamental evaluation of their worth.

Unintelligent speculation Buying and selling shares and other financial securities with a lack of proper knowledge and skill; risking more money than the stock picker can afford to lose; ignoring quantitative material; placing the emphasis on the rewards of speculation rather than on the individual's capacity to speculate successfully.

Unique risk Alternative term for unsystematic risk.

Unit-linked policies These insurance policies incorporate both life insurance and investment on behalf of the policyholder. The investor (policyholder) buys units in a similar way to the purchase of units in a unit trust.

Unit trust An investment organisation that attracts funds from individual investors by issuing units to invest in a range of securities (e.g. shares or bonds). It is open-ended, the number of units expanding to meet demand.

Unit valuation system A way of keeping track of the proportion of an investment club's overall pot of investments belonging to each individual members after allowing for inflows and outflows to the fund over time.

United Kingdom Listing Authority (UKLA) This organisation is part of the Financial Conduct Authority and rigorously enforces a set of demanding rules on companies joining the stock market and in subsequent years. It is mostly concerned with maintaining a list of all companies listed on the London Stock Exchange.

Unitised with-profits policy Similar to a standard with-profits policy, except that premiums paid by investors buy units of a fund and there is no basic sum assured. Bonuses are smoothed.

Universal banks Financial institutions involved in many different aspects of finance, including retail banking and wholesale banking.

Unlisted Shares and other securities not on the Official List approved by the UK Listing Authority. Shares on the Alternative Investment Market of the London Stock Exchange are described as unlisted.

Unquoted firms Those shares with a price not quoted on a recognised investment exchange (e.g. not on the Official List or AIM of the London Stock Exchange).

Unrealised gain (loss) One part of a deal has taken place, but the second has not. There is a 'paper' gain or loss.

Unsecured A financial claim with no collateral or any charge over the assets of the borrower.

Unsystematic (unique or diversifiable or specific) risk That element of an asset's variability in returns that can be eliminated by holding a well-diversified portfolio.

Valuation risk (price risk) The possibility that, when a financial instrument matures or is sold in the market, the amount received is less than anticipated by the owner.

Value-based management A managerial approach in which the primary purpose is long-term shareholder wealth maximisation. The objective of the firm, its systems, strategy, processes, analytical techniques, performance measurements and culture have as their guiding objective long-term shareholder wealth maximisation.

Value chain The interlinking activities that take place within an organisation or between organisations in the process of converting inputs into its outputs. Identifying these activities and finding ways to perform them more efficiently is a way for companies to gain competitive advantage over their rivals.

Value drivers Crucial organisational capabilities, giving the firm competitive advantage.

Value investing The identification and holding of shares which are fundamentally undervalued by the market, given the prospects of the firm.

Vanilla bond *See* Straight bond.

Variable costs Costs that rise or fall with company output and sales.

Variable-rate bond (loan) The interest rate payable varies with short-term rates (e.g. three-month LIBOR).

Variable-rate notes *See* Floating-rate notes.

Variance A measure of volatility around an average value: the square of the standard deviation.

Variation margin The amount of money paid after the payment of the initial margin required to secure an option or futures position, after it has been revalued by the exchange or clearing house on a daily basis by marking to market. Variation margin payments may be required daily to top the account up to the maintenance margin level.

Vendor placing Shares issued to a company to pay for assets, or issued to shareholders to pay for an entire company in a takeover, are placed with investors keen on holding the shares in return for cash. The vendors can then receive the cash.

Venture capital (VC) Finance provided to unquoted firms by specialised financial institutions. This may be backing for an entrepreneur, financing a start-up or developing business, or assisting a management buyout or buy-in. Usually it is provided by a mixture of equity, loans and mezzanine finance. It is used for medium-term to long-term investment in high-risk situations.

Venture capital trusts (VCTs) An investment vehicle introduced to the UK in 1995 to encourage investment in small and fast-growing companies. The VCT invests in a range of small businesses. The providers of finance to the VCT are given important tax breaks.

Vertical merger Where the two merging firms are from different stages of the production chain.

Virtual bid (indicative offer) When a proper merger/acquisition offer of one company for another has not been made but the potential acquirer has raised the possibility of making a bid for the target firm without any commitment.

Virtual portfolio Investors can create an imaginary portfolio on some websites and follow its progress.

Volatility The speed and magnitude of price change over time, measured by standard deviation or variance.

Volume The amount of a company's shares traded on any given day, week or other period. Measured in number of shares or pound amount. It is taken to be an indicator of the level of investor interest in the company.

Volume transformation Intermediaries gather small quantities of money from numerous savers and repackage these sums into larger bundles for investment in the business sector or elsewhere.

Voting by proxy If a shareholder is unable to attend an AGM or EGM to vote on important matters they may indicate their voting wishes on a proxy statement (enclosed with the annual report, say) and thus authorise a representative (usually the chairman) to vote at the meeting on their behalf in the way indicated by the investor on the proxy statement.

Wall Street Originally describing the location of the New York Stock Exchange and some financial institutions it is now a term used to mean securities trading and financial markets/services generally in the USA.

Warrant A financial instrument which gives the holder the right but not the obligation to purchase shares in the company from the company at a fixed price at some time in the future (during or at the end of a specific time period).

Weak-form efficiency Share prices (or other securities) fully reflect all information contained in past price movement. This precludes the possibility of studying past movements to successfully predict future movement sufficiently well to systematically outperform the stock market after adjustment for risk.

Wealth Management Association A trade association for investment managers and stockbrokers.

White knight A friendly company that makes a bid for a company which is welcomed by the directors of that target company. This is usually because the target is the subject of a hostile takeover bid from another company.

Whole-of-life policy Life assurance that pays out to beneficiaries when the insured dies (not limited to, say, the next 10 years).

Wholesale bank One that lends, arranges lending or supplies services on a large scale to corporations, other large organisations and within the interbank market. As opposed to retail banks dealing in relatively small sums for depositors and borrowers.

Wholesale financial markets Markets available only to those dealing in large quantities. Dominated by interbank transactions.

Winding up The process of ending a company, selling its assets, paying its creditors and distributing the remaining cash among shareholders.

Winner's curse In winning a merger battle, the acquirer suffers a loss in value because it overpays.

With-profits bonds A long-term investment via a with-profits fund. *See also* With-profits policy.

With-profits policy A form of life insurance with a large element of saving so that if you survive a payout from the fund is received. The insurance companies use investors' payments to invest in financial securities and guarantee investors a minimum return. They then add bonuses as the fund makes profits.

Withholding tax Taxation deducted from payments made such as interest on bonds before the recipient receives the payment.

Working capital The difference between current assets and current liabilities – net current assets or net current liabilities.

Write-down (Write-off) Companies change the recorded value of assets when they are no longer worth the previously stated value.

Writer of an option The seller of an option contract, granting the right but not the obligation to the purchaser.

Writing down allowance (WDA) (capital allowance) Reductions in taxable profit related to a firm's capital expenditure (e.g. plant, machinery, vehicles). A portion of the value is a tax-deductible expense in the year.

Xetra DAX 30 A stock market index of German shares quoted on the Deutsche Börse.

Yankee A foreign bond US-denominated, issued by a non-US entity in the US market.

Yellow strip The yellow strip is displayed on the London Stock Exchange's SEAQ, SETS or SETSqx security trading system screens. It shows the best offered buy and sell prices for a security – these are collectively called the 'touch' or 'yellow strip' prices.

Yield The income from a security as a proportion of its market price. The flat yield (current yield, interest yield, running yield, simple yield and income yield) on a fixed-interest security is the gross interest amount, divided by the current market price, expressed as a percentage. The redemption yield or **yield to maturity** of a bond is the discount rate such that the present value of all cash inflows from the bond (interest plus principal) is equal to the bond's current market price.

Yield curve A graph showing the relationship between the length of time to the maturity of bonds of the same risk class and the interest rate. *See also* Term structure of interest rates.

Yield gap The difference between average dividend yields on quoted shares and the long-term gilt yield to maturity. It is sometimes used as an indicator of share market over- or under-valuation. In recent years we had a 'reverse yield gap' when the yield on a typical share was around 3–4 per cent and the yield on ten-year UK government bonds was under 2 per cent. This is unusual, because normally the anticipated growth in dividends encourages a higher share price, thus lowering the dividend yield below the gilt yield.

Yield stock *See* High-yield shares.

Yield to maturity *See* Yield.

Zero coupon bond (or zero coupon preference share) A bond (preference share) that does not pay regular interest (dividend) but instead is issued at a discount (i.e. below par value) and is redeemable at par, thus offering a capital gain.

Zero dividend preference shares *See* Split-capital investment trusts.

Zeros *See* Split-capital investment trusts.

Index

Page numbers in **bold** indicate glossary entries.